NATIONAL SECURITY LAW

CANADIAN PRACTICE IN INTERNATIONAL PERSPECTIVE

ESSENTIALS OF CANADIAN LAW

NATIONAL SECURITY LAW

CANADIAN PRACTICE IN
INTERNATIONAL PERSPECTIVE

CRAIG FORCESE

Faculty of Law, Common Law
University of Ottawa

www.nationalsecuritylaw.ca

IRWIN
LAW

National Security Law: Canadian Practice in International Perspective
© Irwin Law Inc., 2008

Published in 2008 by

Irwin Law Inc.
14 Duncan Street
Suite 206
Toronto, ON
M5H 3G8

www.irwinlaw.com

ISBN: 978-1-55221-144-1

Library and Archives Canada Cataloguing in Publication

Forcese, Craig
    National security law : Canadian practice in international perspective / Craig Forcese.

(Essentials of Canadian law)
Includes bibliographical references and index.
ISBN 978-1-55221-144-1

1. National security—Law and legislation—Canada. I. Title. II. Series.

KE4486.F67 2007   344.7105'32   C2007-906338-1
KF4850.F67 2007

The publisher acknowledges the financial support of the Government of Canada through the Book Publishing Industry Development Program (BPIDP) for its publishing activities.

We acknowledge the assistance of the OMDC Book Fund, an initiative of Ontario Media Development Corporation.

Printed and bound in Canada.

1 2 3 4 5   12 11 10 09 08

SUMMARY
TABLE OF CONTENTS

DETAILED
TABLE OF CONTENTS

CHAPTER 4:

THE INSTITUTIONAL FRAMEWORK IN TIMES OF EMERGENCY *114*

CHAPTER 7:

COUNTERING TERRORISM AT THE NATIONAL LEVEL *255*

Part I: Pre-9/11 *Criminal Code* Provisions *256*

Part II: U.N. Act Regulations *257*

A. U.N. Al-Qaida and Taliban Regulations *258*

**B. *Suppression of Terrorism Regulations* *258*

C. Critique *260*

Part III: *Anti-terrorism Act* *261*

A. New Definitions *263*

CHAPTER 8:

LIMITING PROLIFERATION OF WEAPONS OF MASS DESTRUCTION *301*

CHAPTER 11:
SURVEILLANCE   434

FOREWORD

This book on national security law fills a notable vacuum in Canadian legal writing. With no particular partisan agenda, Professor Craig Forcese of the University of Ottawa, Faculty of Law sets out to present an appropriate and comprehensive description of Canada's complex system of laws, institutions, and policies, post-September 11, 2001.

While more than a handbook or a digest, it should nevertheless be at the elbow of every Canadian security intelligence officer, law enforcement official, government policy-maker, elected politician, lawyer, or judge who must deal with national security issues in their professional life.

The author's focus is naturally on anti-terrorism and the actions taken by Canadian government agencies, the courts, and Parliament which, of necessity, may limit individual freedoms. His work has rightly identified the tension that exists as Canadian institutions and policy-makers grapple with the difficult task of striking the right balance.

Not only are the descriptions accurate in terms of Canadian law and practice, but they are usefully informed by international and comparative law, the sign of good scholarship. Where this author on rare occasions veers into a critique of this area of the law, he is careful to identify this — "to graft critical assessment onto description" — as he describes it in his Preface.

Hopefully, this seminal work will give its readers a foretaste of what is yet to come from this up-and-coming Canadian law professor who understands the rule of law and who has so much to contribute by way of critical analysis of serious attempts to promote security while securing liberty.

Ronald G. Atkey, P.C., Q.C.
Toronto
(first chair of the Security Intelligence Review Committee, 1984–89, and *amicus curiae* to the Arar Commission, 2004–2007)

PREFACE AND ACKNOWLEDGMENTS

In 2000, I noticed in the library of the Yale Law School a relatively slim volume on U.S. national security law. This was a topic I have never seriously considered substantial enough in Canada to justify a book-length treatment. I was wrong.

For several years, I have taught a seminar course on international, Canadian and comparative national security law at the University of Ottawa's law school. That course constitutes my effort to grapple with the immensity of the events of September 11, 2001 and its aftermath. Like many others, I have been torn between the need to respond decisively to the horrors of that day—spent in my case, in a Washington law office three blocks from the White House—and a growing discomfort with the actions taken by some governments in the name of counterterrorism. That tension—the need for action without overreaction—drives the perspective I have brought to this book.

This work is part of Irwin Law's "Essentials of Canadian Law" series. It is intended, therefore, as a handbook and a digest of national security law, as practised in Canada and informed by international and comparative law. It is not a theoretical work and it does not try to draw general conclusions about national security law or its utility. Nor does it present a sustained critique of this area of the law.

It is not possible, however, to be entirely clinical about many of the issues addressed in this volume—among them war, terrorism, torture and detention without trial. I have found it necessary, therefore, to graft critical assessment onto description in several places. For the most part, I have distinguished these two objectives with headings and subheadings. I have also judged it proper to flag key dilemmas and challenges that run through national security law, mostly in Chapter 2. I hope readers will find these contextual materials helpful in drawing their own conclusions about whether Canadian national security law has found the soft-spot between promoting security and securing liberty.

This book is the product of much research. It would not have been possible without the assistance of Koren Marriott, a third-year student at the University of Ottawa law school and a dedicated, determined and reliable researcher. I have also benefited enormously from the comments and criticisms of a number of other people. I extend heartfelt thanks to Kirby Abbott, Ron Atkey, Ritu Banerjee, John Currie, Wayne Hanniman, David Paciocco, Jodie van Dieen and Lorne Waldman, each of whom took time from their busy schedules to comment on draft chapters. This book also benefited from the input of an anonymous peer reviewer. My thanks go to that person. A number of my students have contributed time and insight in the finalization of this book. I would like to single out, in particular, the students in my intensive January 2007 national security law course, many of whom reviewed draft chapters. Particular thanks go to Arryn Ketter, Zen Drebot, Anne-Marie Duquette and Heather Fogo for their written comments. I hope I have done justice to the contributions made by these many individuals. I stress that any mistakes made here are my own. The opinions expressed are also, obviously, ones I hold and are not necessarily shared by those who have contributed their expertise in commenting on this book.

As always, thanks go to the team at Irwin Law. Jeff Miller has been an enthusiastic supporter of this and other book projects. As always, Pamela Erlichman was a speedy, thorough and accurate line editor and Alisa Posesorski a meticulous legal editor. Thanks also go to Heather Raven for her work on the book's design and layout

I also owe a debt of gratitude to the Social Science and Humanities Research Council and the Law Foundation of Ontario for their financial support of my research work. Without these grants, it would be impossible to retain the services of research assistants and complete research works of this sort.

Above all, my thanks go to my wife, Sandra Cotton, and to my daughter, Madeleine Forcese. Once again, they have tolerated long hours of research and writing with good grace and understanding. I dedicate this book to Madeleine, in the hope that when she reaches my age it will constitute a quaint relic of more uncertain times.

Research for this book was completed in early 2007, and references in the text to "at the time of this writing" refer to this date. I have, however, done my best to update the material during final production of the book to reflect important developments up until mid-August 2007.

To maintain the timeliness of this work, I have created an online "blog" describing and assessing ongoing developments in the rapidly developing area of national security law. This service is online: www. nationalsecuritylaw.ca.

Craig Forcese
August 2007

The saying "when the cannons roar, the muses are silent" is well known. A similar idea was expressed by Cicero, who said "during war, the laws are silent" (*silent enim legis inter arma*). Those sayings are regrettable. They reflect neither the existing law nor the desirable law.... It is when the cannons roar that we especially need the laws.... Every struggle of the state — against terrorism or any other enemy — is conducted according to rules and law. There is always law which the state must comply with. There are no "black holes."

—President A. Barak, Israeli Supreme Court,
Public Committee against Torture in Israel v. The Government of Israel[1]

---

1   (2006) HCJ 769/02 at para. 61.

PART ONE

SETTING THE STAGE

CHAPTER 1

DEFINING
NATIONAL SECURITY

This is a book about the law governing the Canadian state's response to serious crises; that is, events that jeopardize its "national security." "National security" is a term familiar to most people. A search of Canada Newsstand — an electronic archive of stories drawn from Canadian newspapers — suggests that the words "national security" appeared 23,065 times in articles between September 11, 2001 and January 2007. During an equivalent period of time prior to September 11, 2001, the phrase occurred just 8,313 times. This is not a scientific survey. It does, however, point to the prevalence — and increased prominence — of the concept in popular discourse.

And yet, despite its ubiquity, the expression "national security" does not lend itself to precise definitions. As noted in a 2002 think-tank report, "the term national security is used frequently to refer to matters ranging from domestic or internal security through to international security, but is seldom defined."[1] This paradox obliges a careful attempt in this introduction to define the project of this book, before mapping its content.

---

1   W.D. Macnamara & Ann Fitz-Gerald, "A National Security Framework for Canada" (2002) 3:10 Policy Matters at 7.

A. TOWARDS A DEFINITION OF NATIONAL SECURITY

1) Popular Definitions

Over time, security experts have proposed assorted definitions of national security. For instance, instructors at Canada's National Defence College defined national security in 1980 as: "the preservation of a way of life acceptable to the Canadian people and compatible with the needs and legitimate aspirations of others." National security, these authorities asserted, "includes freedom from military attack or coercion, freedom from internal subversion, and freedom from the erosion of the political, economic, and social values which are essential to the quality of life in Canada."[2] As is immediately evident, this definition wraps much of what governments exist to do within the blanket of national security, a fact acknowledged even by those comfortable with this definition.[3] Its breadth provides no assistance in setting the ambit of a book on Canadian national security law.

More helpful and recent guidance is offered by the Government of Canada's April 2004 national security policy. That document describes national security as dealing "with threats that have the potential to undermine the security of the state or society."[4] The three specific threats the government seeks to address are: first, "protecting Canada and the safety and security of Canadians at home and abroad" (which includes "protecting the physical security of Canadians, our values, and our key institutions"); second, "ensuring that Canada is not a base for threats to our allies"; and third, "contributing to international security."[5]

While this threat-based description of national security is narrower than the Defence College version, it is still extremely general. Note especially the reference to the protection of "Canadian values" as a national security objective in the government's definition. Moreover, the description does little to define exactly when threats of the sort

---

2   *Ibid.* at 8.

3   See, for example, Professor Douglas Bland, Chair, Defence Management Studies Program, School of Policy Studies, Queen's University in evidence before the Standing Senate Committee On Defence and Security (29 October 2001) (indicating that "if a broad definition of 'national security' is taken, there is a danger that there will be no obvious limits to policy," but then citing with a measure of approval the National Defence College definition).

4   Canada, *Securing an Open Society: Canada's National Security Policy* (Ottawa: Privy Council Office, 2004) at 3 [*Securing an Open Society*].

5   *Ibid.* at 5.

listed in the definition constitute national security concerns. As the 2004 policy acknowledges, most criminal offences threaten personal security but do not generally challenge the "security of the state or society." The policy does not answer the question, however, of when exactly a threat to the physical safety of Canadians becomes a legitimate national security concern rather than a regular policing matter, an uncertainty that has important implications when national security is invoked to justify special state powers.

In part to limit ambiguity in the definition of national security, courts have occasionally added their own gloss to the concept. In *Suresh v. Canada (Minister of Citizenship and Immigration)*, the Supreme Court employed the *Canadian Charter of Rights and Freedoms*[6] to signal some constraints on government invocations of national security. At issue was the meaning of the phrase "danger to the security of Canada" in the *Immigration Act*, as it then was. The Court acknowledged that the term "danger to the security of Canada" is difficult to define and "is highly fact-based and political in a general sense." Nevertheless, the Court concluded that a person constitutes a "danger to the security of Canada" where he or she poses a direct or indirect threat to the security of Canada that is "serious" — that is, grounded on an objectively reasonable suspicion based on evidence — and "substantial" — that is, the threatened harm must be significant rather than negligible.[7]

2) This Book's Approach

In circumscribing the meaning of national security, this book draws both on the Supreme Court's approach in *Suresh* and the Government of Canada's 2004 national security policy. Specifically, it focuses on how law and legal instruments grapple with *serious* threats of *substantial* harm; that is, plausible threats with the potential to inflict massive injury on life and property in Canada. In practice, these threats stem from a variety of sources, including those that loom large in the 2004 government policy, namely, terrorism (especially involving weapons of mass destruction), natural disasters and epidemic disease, and foreign attacks and domestic insurrections.

These national security threats are different from the dangers countered by the classic criminal law or remedied by civil causes of action. It is not that national security threats necessarily pose a greater harm

---

6   Part I of the *Constitution Act, 1982*, being Schedule B to the *Canada Act 1982* (U.K.) 1982, c. 11.

7   [2002] 1 S.C.R. 3 at para. 85.

to the physical safety of Canadians. Assaults, murder and traffic fatalities occur in larger numbers than terrorist attacks, epidemics or missile strikes, and as a result injure and kill Canadians in larger numbers. Assaults, murder and traffic fatalities—and the harm they cause—are, however, the backdrop of everyday life, however tragic. What distinguishes these sources of injury from national security threats is their very banality.

By comparison, terrorism, natural disasters, epidemic disease, foreign attacks and domestic insurrection manifest themselves infrequently. They are, in other words, uncommon, low-probability events. However, when they arise, they risk injury to Canadians on a scale that is potentially unbounded and indiscriminate unless checked by the state. As a result, they are shocking to public opinion and potentially destabilizing of the political and social *status quo*. These assaults on the state and the society that underpins it, galvanize strong political responses. September 11, 2001—the horrific, traumatizing and televised loss of almost three thousand lives—produced a tumultuous "war on terror," still underway more than half a decade later. In contrast, the loss of 42,611 lives in traffic fatalities in the United States in 2001[8] generated no equivalent response.

This analysis guides the approach to national security taken in this book. Put simply, in this book, national security threats are those posed by low-probability, high-consequence events that risk producing significant political turmoil.

B. PREVALENCE OF NATIONAL SECURITY LAW

Grappling with these politicized, low-probability/high-consequence dangers is a richly legal pursuit, governed by a vast array of international, federal and provincial laws that determine how governmental power may be exercised in response to actual or feared harm.

One simple means of describing national security law is to outline the prevalence of the national security concept in Canada statutes. The expression "national security," or close equivalents such as "security of Canada," appear in more than thirty Canadian federal Acts, each amenable to categorization of the basis of their effect on the regular law

---

8   U.S. Department of Transportation, *Traffic Safety Facts 2001: State Traffic Data*, online: www-nrd.nhtsa.dot.gov/pdf/nrd-30/NCSA/TSF2001/2001statedata.pdf.

of the land:[9] laws creating special government powers; laws penalizing specific national security threats; and laws that limit regular governmental obligations.

1) Creating Special Government National Security Powers

Some statutes invoke national security to authorize special government action to pre-empt, or respond to, national security concerns. Most prominently, the federal *Emergencies Act*, the successor to the infamous *War Measures Act*,[10] accords extraordinary powers to the government in a "national emergency"; that is, "an urgent and critical situation of a temporary nature that ... seriously threatens the ability of the Government of Canada to preserve the sovereignty, security and territorial integrity of Canada ... and that cannot be effectively dealt with under any other law of Canada."[11]

The *Canadian Security Intelligence Service Act*,[12] meanwhile, establishes an intelligence service whose exact objective is to compile, analyze and retain information and intelligence on "threats to the security of Canada,"[13] a carefully defined term discussed in Chapter 3. Other laws authorizing unusual government powers on national security grounds incorporate by reference this CSIS Act definition. For instance, the *Security Offences Act* "federalizes" prosecution and police investigations of crimes stemming from conduct constituting a "threat to the security of Canada."[14]

2) Penalizing National Security Threats

Several other statutes are punitive in nature, imposing penalties or other special disadvantages on persons on national security grounds. The concept of national security appears in several offences found in the *Criminal Code*[15] and the *Security of Information Act*.[16] These statutes bar certain predicate acts done for a purpose prejudicial to the Can-

---

9   For a fuller treatment of this topic, see Craig Forcese "Through a Glass Darkly: The Role and Review of 'National Security' Concepts in Canadian Law" (2006) 43 Alta. L. Rev. 963.
10   R.S.C. 1970, c. 288.
11   R.S.C. 1985, (4th Supp.), c. 22, s. 3.
12   R.S.C. 1985, c. C-23 [CSIS Act].
13   *Ibid.*, s. 12.
14   R.S.C. 1985, c. S-7, s. 2.
15   R.S.C. 1985, c. C-46.
16   R.S.C. 1985, c. O-5.

adian security. Moreover, the *Criminal Code* includes numerous other offences that, although they do not invoke national security *per se*, are clearly intended to preserve it. Terrorism offences are key examples in point. Also notable are various other statutes punishing violations of Canada's weapons of mass destruction nonproliferation laws.

Meanwhile, the *Citizenship Act*[17] includes a procedure for denying citizenship to individuals where the government believes that the person constitutes a threat to the security of Canada. For its part, the *Immigration and Refugee Protection Act*[18] applies its own penalties in relation to national security threats. Certainly, this law is not intended as a punitive statute, instead fostering the conditional presence of aliens in Canada. Nevertheless, it includes provisions that, in practice, may result in the imposition of special disadvantages on foreign nationals up to and including incarceration where national security concerns are engaged. For instance, the IRPA denies entry to Canada (and potential detention pending removal) by a permanent resident or a foreign national for "being a danger to the security of Canada."[19] "Security certificates" may also be issued by the government, resulting in the detention and possible removal of aliens on national security grounds.[20]

3) Limiting Regular Government Obligations

Finally, a number of statutes also include specific national security exemptions from the constraints otherwise imposed on government action. For instance, there are various national security exemptions under the *Access to Information Act*,[21] negating the public's general right to government information. The flipside to information-limiting invocations of national security are those provisions in the *Privacy Act*[22] and elsewhere allowing select, national security-motivated interception, collection and disclosure of information that would otherwise be protected. More generally, several laws establish a national security exemption from the usual regulatory regime established by the statute.[23]

---

17   R.S.C. 1985, c. C-29.
18   S.C. 2001, c. 27 [IRPA].
19   *Ibid.*, s. 34.
20   Certain procedural aspects of this system were declared unconstitutional by the time of this writing. See Chapter 14.
21   R.S.C. 1985, c. A-1 [*Access Act*].
22   R.S.C. 1985, c. P-21.
23   See, for example, *Canadian Environmental Assessment Act*, S.C. 1992, c. 37, s. 59(c)(i); *Mackenzie Valley Resource Management Act*, S.C. 1998, c. 25, s. 124(1)(b); *Canadian Environmental Protection Act, 1999*, S.C. 1999, c. 33, s. 24(a)(ii); *Species at Risk Act*, S.C. 2002, c. 29, s. 83(1)(a); *Canada National Marine Conservation Areas*

C. OVERVIEW OF NATIONAL SECURITY LAW

While valuable, this simple typology of Canadian statutes invoking national security does not alone provide a sufficiently comprehensive measure of national security law, as it is practised and influenced in Canada. It does not unearth important patterns or connections, or give a sense of the architecture of national security law. It fails to include core international, constitutional or common law doctrines critically important in the area, and fails also to draw on the comparative legal experience of other states.

For all these reasons, I have chosen to examine national security law from a different analytical perspective, focusing on the three themes into which this book is divided: national security structure; national security objectives; and national security techniques.

1) National Security Structure

Most, if not all, states create a special institutional infrastructure to grapple with politically charged, low-probability/high-consequence dangers. Canada is no exception. A veritable alphabet soup of government agencies have important roles in preserving national security, and the mandate, powers and responsibilities of each of these agencies is established by law. A detailed appreciation of national security law must commence, therefore, with a careful review of this government national security structure as it exists in normal times, and also the very different form it may take during states of emergency. Chapters 3 and 4 of this book describe and analyze this institutional infrastructure.

Chapter 3 reviews the basic architecture of both international- and national-level bodies with national security functions. At the international level, its primary focus is on the peace and security functions of the U.N. Security Council. In its discussion of domestic institutions, Chapter 3 outlines the conventional separation of powers among branches of the Canadian government and concentrates on the national security actors in the federal executive.

Chapter 4 then explores the extent to which the executive enjoys enhanced powers during states of emergency, and in doing so provides a detailed substantive overview of the key Canadian federal emergency law, the *Emergencies Act*.

Act, S.C. 2002, c. 18, s. 17(a); *Mutual Legal Assistance in Criminal Matters Act*, R.S.C. 1985 (4th Supp), c. 30, s. 9.4.

2) National Security Objectives

a) A Synergy of Threats

With that institutional backdrop, Part Three of the book then examines selected national security objectives; that is, the law related to several specific threats that the state seeks to curb or forestall. As the preceding discussion suggests, this list of objectives could be very long, and might be packaged in different ways. The Government of Canada's 2004 national security policy lists a number of specific threats to be countered by the state: terrorism and organized crime; foreign espionage; proliferation of weapons of mass destruction; failed and failing states; critical infrastructure vulnerability; natural disasters; and pandemics. The subsequent government international policy statement warned that

> all countries face new and diverse challenges. Terrorists have harnessed the modern tools of globalization and exploited our open societies with devastating effect. Modern transportation allows a deadly disease to spread from one part of the globe to the other in a matter of hours. Environmental degradation spawns unexpected natural disasters. Failed and fragile states displace hundreds of thousands of people, with destabilizing regional and global consequences.[24]

As this passage suggests, and as the 2004 national security policy notes, these threats "do not exist in isolation from one another. For example, the proliferation of weapons of mass destruction is a problem in itself, but when terrorism is involved, the threat increases dramatically. The danger of pandemics is amplified if groups seek to spread disease deliberately."[25] Other patterns are also apparent: terrorism itself may be financed by organized criminal activities in the drug trade or in the smuggling of "blood diamonds" from failed or failing states. Indeed, terrorists may be harboured in these uneasy countries. Foreign espionage revealing special technologies or techniques may undermine the effectiveness of government defence-related actions, and may assist foreign weapons proliferation efforts. Natural disasters may expose and exacerbate critical infrastructure vulnerabilities, and vice versa, and these disasters may themselves stem from the intentional actions of terrorists or other governments.

---

24   Canada, *International Policy at a Crossroads — Overview* (Ottawa: Foreign Affairs and International Trade Canada, 2005), online: http://geo.international.gc.ca/cip-pic/ips/ips-overview3-en.aspx.

25   *Securing an Open Society*, above note 4 at 8.

b) Threat-Oriented National Security Law

The cross-cutting nature of national security threats presents dilemmas of organization for a book like this one. Not every threat implicates its own specialized area of law; instead, some threats are addressed through the application of regular legal principles, including conventional criminal law. It is, however, the case that relatively specialized legal regimes do exist directed specifically at several of the threats enumerated in the 2004 security policy. These unique substantive areas constitute the focus of the book's Part Three.

Chapter 5 discusses reactions to international insecurity and foreign attack. It deals, therefore, with the specialized law on the use of military force, deployed both internationally and domestically. Chapter 6 continues this discussion by examining the specific case of counterterrorism at the international level, assessed first from the optic of the law of armed force. It then describes the international criminal law relating to terrorism. Chapter 7 shifts the counterterrorism focus to the domestic level and Canadian domestic criminal law. Chapter 8 then discusses both international and domestic law designed to guard against proliferation of weapons of mass destruction, including that governing technology transfer. Finally, Chapter 9 examines the special law governing state responses to disasters, particularly in the area of public health.

3) National Security Tools and Techniques

a) Reaction versus Pre-emption

As these chapters show, national security threats—terrorism, insurgency, armed attack and the like—may be opposed after the fact—through prosecution or counterattack, for example. A reactive system guards against the continuation of a security peril by deterring (or making physically impossible) its repetition. For example, a policy of deterrence through the criminal or sanctions law governing terrorism or weapons proliferation hopes to prevent recidivism or copycat crimes by imposing a penalty that gives potential perpetrators pause.

Success in this area depends, however, on actors amenable to deterrence. These laws may prove impotent in dealing with contemporary security threats. The prospect of individual punishment does little to dissuade a suicide bomber intent on his or her own destruction. Prevention, if it is to come, will depend on pre-emption by the state. If the peril we fear is not what Alan Dershowitz has called "retail" crimes—one-off or sequential events of localized effect—but instead "wholesale" events—mass murder through the detonation of a nuclear weapon—insufficient pre-emptive action by the state comes close to a suicide pact.[26] For this reason, much national security activity is geared towards anticipating, analyzing, detecting and preventing threats.

b) Tools of Pre-emption

To perform their pre-emptive role, government agencies employ a number of often quite special tools and techniques. Overarching all of these tools and techniques is the need for secrecy. The precise nature of state national security techniques, tactics and responses must be protected from prying eyes. Judicious secrecy maintains the effectiveness of the government's national security approach.

This national security strategy will likely involve clandestine intelligence gathering, whether through surveillance, inter- or intrastate information exchange or interrogation. Interception and interdiction of the person posing the security threat then follows, denying him or her access to vulnerable information and places. In more extreme circumstances, the state may detain those believed to pose a sufficiently imminent national security threat.

Part Four of the book examines these tools and techniques. Chapter 10 discusses the national security secrecy apparatus employed to limit information disclosure both by the government and before the courts. Chapter 11 focuses on intelligence gathering through surveillance. Chapter 12 then discusses intelligence sharing between and within governments. Chapter 13 focuses on interception and interdiction through security screening of persons posing security risks. Chapter 14 assesses the law of detention and Chapter 15 examines interrogation.

D. A FINE BALANCE

As important as these tools and techniques are, each risks trenching on important rights and freedoms if used indiscriminately. Protecting national security is often a highly emotive and urgent challenge, one that risks driving states to exercise extraordinary power in ways that sit uncomfortably with conventional understandings of the rule of law and the rights and liberties of human beings. Active efforts to pre-empt security threats place the state in the difficult role of prognosticator. It must anticipate events that have not yet unfolded and sometimes take firm steps to halt danger. Here, there is a real risk of what Alan Dershowitz calls "false positives"; that is, circumstances where action seems

---

26   Alan Dershowitz, *Preemption: A Knife that Cuts Both Ways* (New York: W.W. Norton, 2006) at 23.

necessary but that, with hindsight, turn out to be benign.[27] Privacy is invaded where it should not have been. Persons are detained who prove to be innocent. In these circumstances, as Dershowitz argues, "acting preemptively ... comes with a price tag, often measured in lost liberties and other even more subtle and ineffable values."[28]

In national security law, the core challenge is to loosen constraints on state power without precipitating significant collateral damage to other rights and social values. The difficulty in balancing legal regimes — that crafted to preserve national security and that which exists to create a state worth securing — is the matter to which the next chapter turns. In doing so, it describes several national security dilemmas that cross-cut the field, underscoring along the way certain recurring substantive legal themes.

27   *Ibid.*
28   *Ibid.* at 19.

CHAPTER 2

DILEMMAS
IN NATIONAL
SECURITY LAW

Canada's 2004 national security policy notes that there is "no greater role, no more important obligation for a government, than the protection and safety of its citizens."[1] It urges that a "clear and effective approach to security is not just the foundation of our prosperity—it is the best assurance that future generations will continue to enjoy the very best qualities that make this country a place of hope in a troubled world."[2]

There is undeniable truth in these assertions. At core, national security creates the environment in which other values flourish. In a recent national security case before the Supreme Court, the government's lawyer reportedly argued that protecting national security "is not just an option or a policy choice, such as the amount to be invested in health care. It is the *sine qua non* to the very existence of the rule of law and our democratic system of government."[3] Without adequate security, the rights found in instruments such as the *Canadian Charter of Rights and Freedom*[4] would be unattainable.

---

1 Canada, *Securing an Open Society: Canada's National Security Policy* (Ottawa: Privy Council Office, 2004) at vii [*Securing an Open Society*]. See also *Charkaoui v. Canada*, 2007 SCC 9 at para. 1 [*Charkaoui*].
2 *Securing an Open Society*, *ibid.* at 1.
3 Bernard Laprade as cited by Jim Brown, "Canadian Security, Liberty Debated" *Canadian Press*, (14 June 2006). The case was decided as *Charkaoui*, above note 1, and is discussed in several places in this book.
4 Part I of the *Constitution Act, 1982*, being Schedule B to the *Canada Act 1982* (U.K.) 1982, c. 11.

To extrapolate from this, however, that national security should necessarily trump these other democratic values is to overstate the case. In response to the government's Supreme Court argument, Justice Fish reportedly shot back that, absent rights and the rule of law, "we'll be living in North Korea."[5] In other words, lending too much primacy to national security at the expense of rights and liberties creates a state probably not worth securing.

The challenge lies, therefore, in defending national security in a manner that affirms rather than undermines these other values. This difficulty runs through both national security law and this book. This chapter draws out several key themes implicated by the balancing of national security with individual rights and liberties. It begins with a broad discussion of the relationship between rights and security and then highlights a number of specific rights/security dilemmas. In so doing, it also provides an overview of several recurring, core legal doctrines.

PART I: THE RELATIONSHIP BETWEEN NATIONAL SECURITY AND RIGHTS

A. SECURITY AS THE FOUNDATION FOR RIGHTS

The seventeenth-century philosopher Thomas Hobbes famously described the lives of humans in the anarchic "state of nature" as "solitary, poor, nasty, brutish, and short."[6] Where no states exist, only those individuals individually powerful enough to subdue threats enjoy liberties and freedoms, or indeed survive. In contrast, a successful state marshals power and resources, collectivizing responses to hazards and creating a climate of security for its inhabitants. Indeed, Hobbes urged that it is exactly the human need for security that prompts people to form states in the first place.

Hobbes saw little room in his model for inherent rights: to wrest humanity from fatal anarchy, the state must be absolute, and all civil

---

5   Brown, "Canadian Security, Liberty Debated," above note 3. In *Charkaoui*, above note 1 at para. 1, the Court held: "One of the most fundamental responsibilities of a government is to ensure the security of its citizens. This may require it to act on information that it cannot disclose and to detain people who threaten national security. Yet in a constitutional democracy, governments must act accountably and in conformity with the Constitution and the rights and liberties it guarantees."

6   Thomas Hobbes, *The Leviathan* (1651) (Oxford: B. Blackwell, 1957), c. 13.

rights possessed by individuals are subject to the overarching imperative of preserving security. Western states no longer embrace this model of absolutism. However, even those warmly predisposed to rights agree with the emphasis on security. For instance, former Canadian justice minister Irwin Cotler rejects a stark dichotomy between national security and civil liberties. Referring specifically to anti-terrorism, Cotler has argued that "anti-terrorism law and policy is human rights legislation in that we're dealing with the protection of a democracy and the fundamental human rights of its inhabitants."[7] Cotler and the government's 2004 national security policy[8] both see national security as underpinning the right to life, liberty and security of the person, a concept enshrined in section 7 of the *Charter*. These views demand attention. While from a strictly legal perspective, section 7 has generally been interpreted as a *constraint* on state power, not a justification for its exertion,[9] the political point is indisputable: creating an environment of security is a prerequisite to universal rights.

There would be dangers, however, in treading too far in envisaging national security as foundational to rights. Most obviously, this is a perspective that may be abused by governments to forestall, limit or eliminate individual rights and liberties in overreaction to a national security crisis. Substantial international and domestic law exists attempting to guard against the abuse of rights in the name of national security emergencies.

More subtly, security primacy may create human rights winners and losers. In the name (putatively) of securing the life, liberty and security of the person of the majority, the national security policies of the state may sacrifice the rights of a minority, a point explored later in this chapter. Alternatively, there may be a geography of rights observance: rights are violated abroad in the name of preserving them at home. States may accept collateral injuries to foreigners to a much greater extent and in much greater number than they will allow equivalent harm to their own nationals. The record of law in guarding against these patterns is mixed.

---

7   Irwin Cotler, "Terrorism, Security & Rights in the Post-September 11th Universe" (2002) 21 Windsor Y.B. Access Just. 519; Irwin Cotler, "Terrorism, Security and Rights: The Dilemma of Democracies" (2002–03) 14 N.J.C.L. 13 at 15.

8   *Securing an Open Society*, above note 1 at 1.

9   In *Gosselin v. Quebec (Attorney General)*, [2002] 4 S.C.R. 429 at para. 81, the Supreme Court noted that "[n]othing in the jurisprudence thus far suggests that s. 7 places a positive obligation on the state to ensure that each person enjoys life, liberty or security of the person. Rather, s. 7 has been interpreted as restricting the state's ability to deprive people of these."

B. RIGHTS AS THE FOUNDATION FOR SECURITY

One counter to the dangers of security primacy is to reverse the rights/security linkage. The secretary-general of Amnesty International's Canadian section has argued, for instance, that "above all else security must be about human rights. People simply are not secure and will never be secure unless their basic human rights are scrupulously observed."[10] Rights, this passage might be read to imply, are not to be tempered in the name of national security, because without rights, there is no security. Indeed, Hobbes's near-contemporary, John Locke, would urge that without rights, the state itself has no legitimacy.[11]

There is obvious merit to this view, especially when examined over a medium- to long-term time scale. Rights-repressing states may fuel the very insecurity they purportedly seek to forestall.

Still, an unalloyed policy of rights primacy would create its own perils. It is indisputable that unswerving adherence to rights will curtail the national security responses open to governments and may make rights-observing states more vulnerable in the immediate term to security threats. For those who accept this constraint, that is a cost of liberty and brings with it longer-term security. This, the Israeli Supreme Court has concluded,

> is the destiny of democracy, as not all means are acceptable to it, and not all practices employed by its enemies are open before it. Although a democracy must often fight with one hand tied behind its back, it nonetheless has the upper hand. Preserving the rule of law and recognition of an individual's liberty constitutes an important component in its understanding of security. At the end of the day, they strengthen its spirit and its strength and allow it to overcome its difficulties.[12]

Jim Judd, the director of the Canadian Security and Intelligence Service, has made a similar observation: "Democracies have taken a long period to develop and their values, laws and institutions continue to provide inspiration to those without the luxury of living in one. It is

---

10 Amnesty International Canada, *Agenda for Real Security*, online: www.amnesty.ca/realsecurity/.

11 John Locke, *Second Treatise of Civil Government* (1690) (Oxford: B. Blackwell, 1948).

12 *Public Committee against Torture in Israel v. The State of Israel*, HCJ 5100/94 at para. 39.

thus essential that in responding to threats such as terrorism we do so in a fashion that best reflects what democracies stand for."[13]

It is also true, however, that rights must not be the rigid "suicide pact" about which U.S. Supreme Court Justices Jackson[14] and Goldberg[15] both warned in litigation concerning the U.S. Constitution. To envisage rights as always unyielding may empower those who seek to destroy the very social and political structures that permit rights in the first place.[16]

C. THE CHICKEN AND THE EGG

In sum, lending primacy to one or other of rights or security creates a real risk that the other value may not be realized. The more nuanced approach, therefore, is to view security and rights, not as hierarchical concepts, but as mutually synergetic. Irwin Cotler's writings point in this direction, as do those of Stanley Cohen[17] and constitutional schol- ar Errol Mendes.[18] Amnesty International has made this claim as well, urging that rights will "always be precarious if security is not assured, and security will inevitably be tenuous at best if not firmly grounded in human rights."[19]

---

13   Jim Judd, Director of CSIS, Talking Points for 2007 Raoul Wallenberg Inter- national Human Rights Symposium, "How Should a Democracy Respond to Domestic Terrorist Threats" (January 2007), online: www.csis-scrs.gc.ca/en/ newsroom/speeches/speech19012007.asp.

14   *Terminiello v. City of Chicago*, 337 U.S. 1 at 37 (1949), Jackson J. dissenting.

15   *Kennedy v. Mendoza-Martinez*, 372 U.S. 144 at 160 (1963).

16   This is a point made by then U.K. Home Secretary, John Reid, cited in Nigel Morris, "Reid Attacks Judges Who Hamper 'Life and Death' Terrorism Battle" *The Independent* (10 August 2006). ("Sometimes we may have to modify some of our freedoms in the short term in order to prevent their use and abuse by those who oppose our fundamental values and would destroy all of our freedoms in the long term"). It has also been made, colourfully, by Richard Posner, *Not a Suicide Pact: The Constitution in a Time of National Emergency* (Oxford: Oxford University Press, 2006).

17   Stanley A. Cohen, *Privacy, Crime and Terror: Legal Rights and Security in a Time of Peril* (Markham, ON: LexisNexis Butterworths, 2005) at 546.

18   Irwin Cotler, "Terrorism, Security and Rights: The Dilemma of Democracies," above note 7; Errol Mendes, "Between Crime and War: Terrorism, Democracy and the Constitution" (2002–03) 14 N.J.C.L. 72 at 73.

19   Amnesty International Canada, *Submission to the Special Senate Committee on the Anti-Terrorism Act and House of Commons Sub-Committee on Public Safety and National Security as part of the Review of Canada's Anti-Terrorism Act* (16 May 2005), online: www.amnesty.ca/canada/C36_submission.doc.

This approach obviates the need to sacrifice automatically one interest for the other where they clash in the immediacy of the moment. However, in doing so, it complicates decision making, creating new challenges. Those challenges have been made stark in Supreme Court of Canada decisions judging Canada's counterterrorism laws. That Court has described terrorism as a "manifest evil" involving the "random and arbitrary taking of innocent lives, rippling out in an ever-widening spiral of loss and fear." [20] Governments must craft laws to meet and match this peril: "The challenge for democracies in the battle against terrorism is not whether to respond, but rather how to do so. This is because Canadians value the importance of human life and liberty, and the protection of society through respect for the rule of law."[21]

At the same time, this passage implies that the law speaks, even in times of peril. There is a "need to ensure that those legal tools do not undermine values that are fundamental to our democratic society — liberty, the rule of law, and the principles of fundamental justice."[22] A "response to terrorism within the rule of law preserves and enhances the cherished liberties that are essential to democracy."[23] It would, the Court has urged, be "a Pyrrhic victory if terrorism were defeated at the cost of sacrificing our commitment to those values."[24] At core, a democratic state must perform "a balancing of what is required for an effective response to terrorism in a way that appropriately recognizes the fundamental values of the rule of law."[25]

The Israeli Supreme Court — the highest court of the democracy most harried by terrorism — has used a similar image of "balance": "human rights cannot receive their full protection, as if there was no terrorism, and state security cannot receive its full protection, as if there were no human rights. A delicate and sensitive balancing is needed."[26]

How this balancing is conducted may vary depending on the interests in play. Part II outlines several specific dilemmas posed by the security/rights relationship.

---

20 *Suresh v. Canada (Minister of Citizenship and Immigration)*, [2002] 1 S.C.R. 3 at paras. 3 & 4 [*Suresh*].
21 *Application under s. 83.28 of the Criminal Code (Re)*, [2004] 2 S.C.R. 248 at para. 5 *et seq.*, Iacobucci and Arbour JJ. [*Application*].
22 *Suresh*, above note 20 at para. 4.
23 *Application*, above note 21 at para. 7 *et seq.*
24 *Suresh*, above note 20 at para. 4.
25 *Application*, above note 21 at para. 7 *et seq.*
26 *Ajuri v. The Military Commander of the Judea and Samaria Area* (2002), HCJ 7015/02 at para. 41.

PART II: NATIONAL SECURITY DILEMMAS

The core national security dilemmas can be labelled as follows: preserving democracy in combatting tyranny; deploying the rule of law in reacting to chaos; preserving liberty in defending freedom; protecting people while leaving them alone; acting transparently in responding covertly; and acting decisively in a fog of war.

A. PRESERVING DEMOCRACY IN COMBATTING TYRANNY

1) Structural Foundations of Democracy Accountability

Democracy is "that form of government in which the sovereign power resides in the people as a whole, and is exercised either directly by them ... or by officers elected by them."[27] In a representative democracy, the expectation is that the elected representatives of the people will exercise the authority of the state.[28] In a modern democracy, however, not all — or even most — of the people engaged in the business of governing are elected. The contemporary, administrative state depends on a massive bureaucratic apparatus, staffed mostly by unelected officials. The classic response in the liberal democratic tradition is to shape rules ensuring that those who are not selected by the people are somehow accountable to those who are. Elected officials, in other words, have primacy over their unelected counterparts. Together, these rules create the two levels of democratic accountability — direct election and the pre-eminence of the elected over the appointed — and ensure that majorities shape, however indirectly, governance.

Checking the excesses of the majoritarian impulse in order to preserve rights requires a separate, third set of accountability mechanisms less receptive to democratic desires. Elected officials, and the unelected bureaucracy they direct, are creatures and servants of the majority. They are ill equipped to prevail in the face of that majority's opposition. Thus, if there are to be rights that the democratically elected government cannot trump, those rights must be protected by institutions

---

27   *Oxford English Dictionary*, online edition.
28   This section amplifies a discussion found in Craig Forcese & Aaron Freeman, *Laws of Government: The Legal Foundations of Canadian Democracy* (Toronto: Irwin Law, 2005) and also appearing in the discussion paper drafted by Craig Forcese for the Law Commission of Canada, *Crossing Borders: Law in a Globalized World* (Ottawa, Law Commission of Canada, 2006).

other than those controlled by the majority itself. In practice, these bodies are courts protected by a concept resistant to raw democratic accountability: judicial independence.

In the Anglo-Canadian and American liberal democratic tradition, the net result of these systems of accountability are three branches of government—the legislature, mostly or entirely elected; the executive, governed by directly elected chiefs (in republican systems) or somehow subordinated to the elected legislature (in parliamentary systems); and the judiciary.

In much modern Western political thought, the "separation of powers" among these three branches is seen as essentially synonymous with liberty; it ensures that no one institution assumes dictatorial powers.[29] Strongly influenced by this perspective, U.S.-style republican democracies carefully partition powers among executive, legislative and judicial branches, not quite hermetically sealing each off from the other but nevertheless demarcating careful lines of responsibility that each may assume.[30]

For their part, classic Westminster-style parliamentary democracies are less anxious about such delimitations and have less robust institutional separations between executive and legislature. Most notably, in British-style parliamentary systems those who exercise executive power—the "political" executive of cabinet and the prime minister—are drawn from the ranks of the largest party in the legislature or some coalition of parties capable of securing the backing of a majority of legislators. Through a robust system of party discipline in the legislature, the political executive usually controls the legislative branch. Nevertheless, the executive branch is legally *subordinate* to Parliament. In a Westminster system, Parliament is generally the source of all legitimate power, precluding the possibility of permanent, unilateral executive government.

Thus, although quite different in their details, republican and parliamentary systems both include rules circumscribing unilateral exercises of power by one branch or another. Domestic legal systems often maintain this relationship through the interventions of the third branch of government—the judiciary. The latter is generally authorized to police the exercise of power by legislative and executive branches, applying both constitutional and (in relation to the executive) administrative law to ensure that neither strays beyond permissible bounds. In per-

---

29 See, for example, Baron Montesquieu, *Spirit of Laws* (1748), bk. 11 (New York: Hafner Publishing Company, 1966) c. 6.

30 See, for example, U.S. Const. art. I–III.

forming this function, courts are protected from the maneuverings of the other branches by the potent concept of judicial independence.[31]

2) National Security and Democratic Accountability

Perhaps more than any other area, questions of national security shift the balance of power and influence among the three branches. In national security matters, the executive branch has a privileged position. As in many other areas, legislatures are ill equipped to conduct detailed management functions. Instead, they typically delegate substantial discretionary national security authority to the executive branch. In doing so, however, they may create a system that excludes close scrutiny by the legislative branch itself of the powers exercised under national security laws.[32] They also authorize the executive to protect a principle notoriously difficult to define, and reviewable by courts only with difficulty.

a) Discretion and the Failure of Definition

The difficulty in defining national security is discussed in Chapter 1. This uncertainty of meaning spills over to the legal realm. The expression "national security," or close equivalents such as "security of Canada," appear in at least thirty-three Canadian federal statutes.[33] There, it acts as a potent legal concept. National security is obviously the touchstone in many specialized national security statutes, laws that greatly expand the powers of the government either to regulate or penalize. It is also an important feature of more general laws, freeing the government from constraints it would otherwise face under these

---

31 While the judicial check on legislative power has generally been less potent in Westminster systems than in republican democracies, the judicial review function of courts, even in places like the United Kingdom, is now significant by virtue of the *European Convention on Human Rights* as implemented by U.K. law. It is even more so in parliamentary systems—such as that of Canada—with constitutionalized bills of rights.

32 The failure of legislatures to scrutinize closely the actions of executive governments in the post-9/11 era has been the subject of some controversy. In the United States, Congress has only recently moved in a significant way to limit the president's assertion of executive authority in the "war on terror," a move prompted by scandals such as Abu Ghraib and galvanized by several Bush administration losses before the U.S. Supreme Court. For discussion, see Dana Priest, "Rethinking Embattled Tactics in Terror War" *Washington Post* (11 July 2006) A.1.

33 For a fuller treatment of this topic, see Craig Forcese "Through a Glass Darkly: The Role and Review of 'National Security' Concepts in Canadian Law" (2006) 43 Alta. L. Rev. 963.

statutes or expanding the range of powers to which it would otherwise be normally restricted.

Yet, the national security expression is rarely defined. Indeed, in the final analysis, only nine of thirty-three federal statutes — or 27 percent — invoking national security expressions define the concept.[34] This failure of definition produces a Canadian statute-book replete with a concept whose precise content is extremely amorphous. As the Federal Court of Appeal has noted, describing the proliferation of terms describing security risks in immigration law, these concepts constitute "a veritable abstract work of art in which everyone can see or discover what they wish."[35] This ambiguity confers substantial discretion on the executive branch to define national security as it wills.

In part to limit uncertainty in the definition of national security, courts have occasionally added their own gloss to the concept. As noted in Chapter 1, in *Suresh v. Canada (Minister of Citizenship and Immigration)*,[36] the Supreme Court concluded that the phrase "danger to the security of Canada" in the then-*Immigration Act* had to be read as requiring the government to adduce evidence producing an objectively reasonable suspicion of a serious threat of substantial harm.[37]

b) Court Review of Discretionary National Security Decisions

Although a real constraint on the absolute liberty of government to define national security, definitions such as that employed in *Suresh* leave substantial freedom of action in government hands. In *Suresh*, the Court applied its standard administrative law "pragmatic and functional" test to determine the degree of deference to be accorded the government in reviewing its decision on the security issue; in that case, the removal under immigration law of a suspected terrorist. The Court concluded that the minister's decision would be disturbed only in egregious circumstances; that is, when it was patently unreasonable. In partial support of this conclusion, the Court noted that it was the minister — with access to special information and expertise — making the determination.

In so concluding, it cited with approval the U.K. House of Lords decision in *Rehman*.[38] There, the appellant was denied indefinite leave to

---

34   The most notable definition is that found in the *Canadian Security Intelligence Service Act*, R.S.C. 1985, c. C-23, s. 2, defining a "threat to the security of Canada," a concept discussed at length in Chapter 3.

35   *Charkaoui v. Canada*, 2004 FCA 421 at para. 118.

36   *Suresh*, above note 20.

37   *Ibid.* at para. 90.

38   *Secretary of State For The Home Department v. Rehman (AP)*, [2001] 3 W.L.R. 877 (H.L.) [*Rehman*]. United Kingdom courts have traditionally not employed

remain in the United Kingdom by virtue of an affiliation with a group defined by the U.K. government as a terrorist organization. The decision was rendered pursuant to a provision in U.K. law authorizing such a determination, and a subsequent deportation, "in the interests of national security." At issue by the time the matter reached the House of Lords was the meaning of this phrase.

In their speeches, their Lordships were not prepared to grant the government a *carte blanche* in its assessment of national security. Lord Slynn of Hadley wrote, for example, that under the relevant statute, "'the interests of national security' cannot be used to justify any reason the Secretary of State has for wishing to deport an individual from the United Kingdom. There must be some possibility of risk or danger to the security or well-being of the nation which the Secretary of State considers makes it desirable for the public good that the individual should be deported."[39]

However, at least one Law Lord was quick to point out that the question of whether a threat to national security existed or not was best left in the hands of the government. Thus, Lord Hoffman, in his speech, urged that "decisions as to whether something is or is not in the interests of national security are not a matter for judicial decision. They are entrusted to the executive."[40] In a remarkable postscript, Lord Hoffman added:

> I wrote this speech some three months before the recent events in New York and Washington. They are a reminder that in matters of national security, the cost of failure can be high. This seems to me to underline the need for the judicial arm of government to respect the decisions of ministers of the Crown on the question of whether support for terrorist activities in a foreign country constitutes a threat to national security. It is not only that the executive has access to special information and expertise in these matters. It is also that such decisions, with serious potential results for the community, require a legitimacy which can be conferred only by entrusting them to persons responsible to the community through the democratic process.

---

a spectrum of review standards, or a pragmatic and functional test, instead relying on a concept of "reasonableness" in reviewing discretionary administrative decision making. As *Rehman* illustrates, deference has recently become an important consideration in select cases, involving such things as foreign affairs and immigration. See discussion in H.W.R. Wade & C.F. Forsyth, *Administrative Law,* 9th ed. (Oxford: Oxford University Press, 2004) at 351 *et seq.* and 369.

39   *Rehman, ibid.* at para. 15.
40   *Ibid.* at para. 50.

If the people are to accept the consequences of such decisions, they must be made by persons whom the people have elected and whom they can remove.[41]

National security-related judicial deference is also acute outside the immigration context. In *Aleksic*, the Ontario Divisional Court adjudicated a tort claim stemming from the air war in Yugoslavia in 1999. In dismissing the matter, it concluded that such a decision is not justiciable in the law of tort:

> an executive decision to participate in the bombing of Yugoslavia is a matter of "high policy." It is closely analogous to a declaration of war.... It was a pure policy decision made at the highest levels of government, dictated by purely political factors.... By what yardstick could a court determine whether the Crown's decision to bomb was wrongful? How could a judge weigh competing political considerations to determine whether NATO's concern for the plight of the Kosovo Albanians constituted sufficient justification for the actions it took? ... If the court is to ask itself whether the Crown's action was wrongful, it must necessarily "second guess" the government in the political cost/benefit analysis that led to the decision to bomb. A court is simply not equipped to do so.[42]

Moreover, even if it were justiciable, the government would likely enjoy substantial immunity to such a lawsuit. The government's decision to participate in NATO bombing being one of high policy, it would be immunized from tort liability by the operational/policy distinction in Canadian law.[43] Even if it were not, the government owed no duty of care in the law of negligence to avoid injury to private individuals (or other soldiers) during the course of hostilities.[44]

---

41   *Ibid.* at para. 62.
42   *Aleksic v. Canada* (2002), 215 D.L.R. (4th) 720 at para. 31 *et seq.* (Ont. Div. Ct.) [*Aleksic*].
43   See *Just v. British Columbia*, [1989] 2 S.C.R. 1228 for the enunciation of this doctrine. In *Aleksic, ibid.* at para. 39, the court summarized this distinction as follows: "the Crown will be immune from tort liability arising out of true policy decisions, but may well be held liable for losses that flow from 'operational' decisions."
44   *Aleksic, ibid.* at para. 47 *et seq.*, citing, *inter alia*, *Mulcahy v. Ministry of Defence*, [1996] Q.B. 732 (C.A.).

B. DEPLOYING THE RULE OF LAW IN REACTING TO CHAOS

Given these patterns of legislative and judicial deference to the executive, national security imperatives raise evident challenges to the separation of powers and to democratic accountability.

Closely connected to concerns about democratic accountability are dilemmas related to the rule of law. The "rule of law" requires that government officials exercise their powers in accordance with the law of the land. The government, like any individual, is not above the law, but is subordinate to it.

As in any other area, government national security matters must be conducted lawfully. However, exactly *which* rule of law applies (and where) may prove a complicated question in national security matters. In the modern legal system, two different forms of law exist: international and domestic.[45] As this book will suggest from time to time, important questions about the scope and geographic reach of each of these areas of the law recur in the national security area.

1) International Law

a) Sources of International Law

The two most important sources of international law are treaties and "customary international law." Treaties are essentially law-making contracts between states. They are binding on the states that are parties to them, and generally no other state. To become a party, states must sign and, especially in the case of multilateral treaties between multiple states, must "ratify" the treaty. Ratification is simply a supplemental process for approving the treaty undertaken pursuant to each state's own constitutional order. In Canada, ratification is done exclusively by the executive branch, as part of its traditional "royal prerogative," discussed later in this chapter.

Unlike treaty law, customary international law binds all states regardless of express indications of consent, excepting only those states that have been sufficiently persistent in rejecting the customary principle prior to its emergence as a binding norm. The content of a treaty is discerned from its text. Customary international law, in comparison, is much more amorphous. It is created by sufficiently general and universal state practice, undertaken by states with a sense of legal obliga-

---

45   A variant of the discussion in this section was prepared by this author in *Crossing Borders: Law in a Globalized World*, above note 28.

tion (called *opinio juris*). Where these two ingredients—state practice and the *opinio juris*—become sufficiently widespread among the states of the world (a threshold not clearly defined by international law), the practice in question is said to become legally binding as customary international law. For example, the *Universal Declaration of Human Rights* (UDHR), while nonbinding in its own right, is now said to be customary international law (in whole or in part).[46]

Canada may be bound to a treaty or by a norm of customary international law in its relations with other states and the international community. However, that same rule of law may not be part of Canadian domestic law, enforceable by the Canadian legal system. Certainly, customary law is automatically part of the Canadian law—specifically, the common law—so long as not displaced or overturned by a statute that is inconsistent with it.[47] In relation to treaties, however, Canada traditionally envisages domestic law and treaty law as distinct. Thus, an international treaty may oblige Canada, as a matter of international law, to change its domestic law. However, in the "dualist" tradition Canada has traditionally followed, that treaty has no direct effect in domestic law until domestic legislation is passed to "transform" or "implement" it into Canadian law.

This policy creates important paradoxes. For example, Canada is bound by the prohibition on deportations of persons to torture under

---

46 G.A. res. 217A (III), U.N. Doc A/810 at 71 (1948). See Statement 95/1 Notes for an Address by The Honourable Christine Stewart, Secretary of State (Latin America and Africa), at the 10th Annual Consultation Between Non-Governmental Organizations and the Department of Foreign Affairs and International Trade, Ottawa, Ontario, 17 January 1995 ("Canada regards the principles of the Universal Declaration of Human Rights as entrenched in customary international law binding on all governments"); *Alvarez-Machain v. United States*, 331 F.3d 604, at 618 (9th Cir. 2003) ("We have recognized that the Universal Declaration, although not binding on states, constitutes 'a powerful and authoritative statement of the customary international law of human rights'"), citing *Siderman de Blake v. Republic of Argentina*, 965 F.2d 699 (9th Cir. 1992).

47 *R. v. Hape*, 2007 SCC 26 at para. 39 [*Hape*] ("the doctrine of adoption operates in Canada such that prohibitive rules of customary international law should be incorporated into domestic law in the absence of conflicting legislation. The automatic incorporation of such rules is justified on the basis that international custom, as the law of nations, is also the law of Canada unless, in a valid exercise of its sovereignty, Canada declares that its law is to the contrary. Parliamentary sovereignty dictates that a legislature may violate international law, but that it must do so expressly. Absent an express derogation, the courts may look to prohibitive rules of customary international law to aid in the interpretation of Canadian law and the development of the common law").

the U.N. *Convention Against Torture*.[48] It has not, however, implemented this obligation into its domestic immigration law; on the contrary, that law anticipates exceptional, national security-related circumstances in which people can be removed to torture. As discussed in Chapter 14, following that course of action could put Canada in violation of its international obligations.

b)   The Problem of *Lex Specialis*

Even where international rules are clear, the circumstances in which they apply may vary. Not every substantive rule in international law applies always. International law includes *lex speciali*; that is, specialized bodies of law that may trump the application of more general rules.

International humanitarian law (IHL) — the laws of war found in the Geneva Conventions and related instruments and in customary international law — is a case in point. IHL applies only in circumstances of "armed conflict," a concept that is not precisely defined. Moreover, IHL distinguishes between international and noninternational armed conflicts. The Geneva Conventions deal almost exclusively with the former, leaving noninternational armed conflicts (such as civil wars) less closely regulated.

To further complicate matters, it now seems clear that the mere existence of an armed conflict should not be viewed as automatically displacing other rules of international law, including human rights law. The principles found in the latter would continue to apply, albeit often in attenuated form.[49] Which of these human rights laws apply, and how, presents challenges in observing the rule of law.

c)   Geographical Reach of International Law

International obligations may also have geographic limitations. One particularly important question in the post-9/11 context has been the geographic reach of human rights treaties, not least the *International Covenant on Civil and Political Rights* (ICCPR).[50] The ICCPR ranks among the most important human rights treaties in the international system. It obliges state parties to meet a lengthy list of elemental human rights.

---

48   *Convention Against Torture and Other Cruel, Inhuman or Degrading Treatment or Punishment*, Adopted and opened for signature, ratification and accession by General Assembly resolution 39/46 of 10 December 1984; entry into force 26 June 1987, Art. 3.

49   See Chapter 5.

50   999 U.N.T.S. 171.

Whether the ICCPR has any extraterritorial reach—that is, applicability in imposing obligations on a state when acting outside of that state's borders—has sparked animated discussion among states and commentators in national security contexts.[51] Logically, however, a state cannot authorize its personnel to commit human rights abuses abroad that a state cannot inflict within its own territory. This view has prevailed in several international institutions. For instance, the U.N. Human Rights Committee—the treaty-body created by the ICCPR and charged with monitoring its application—has noted that "a State party must respect and ensure the rights laid down in the Covenant to anyone within *the power or effective control* of that State Party, *even if not situated within the territory* of the State Party."[52] Rights are guaranteed "to those *within the power or effective control of the forces of a State Party acting outside its territory*, regardless of the circumstances in which such power or effective control was obtained, such as forces constituting a national contingent of a State Party assigned to an international peace-keeping or peace-enforcement operation."[53] The committee has applied this approach in its case law—for example, by allowing a complaint against Uruguay brought by an individual kidnapped in Argentina by the Uruguayan security forces.[54] In its review of state reports on compliance with the ICCPR, the committee has also suggested that state obligations extend to a state's armed forces stationed abroad.[55]

---

51 See, for example, Report of the U.N. Special Rapporteurs, *Situation of Detainees at Guantánamo Bay* (15 Feb. 2006), U.N. Doc. E/CN.4/2006/120 (concluding that the International Covenant has extraterritorial reach). But see also the discussion in Michael J. Dennis, "ICJ Advisory Opinion On Construction Of A Wall In The Occupied Palestinian Territory: Application Of Human Rights Treaties Extraterritorially In Times Of Armed Conflict And Military Occupation" (2005) 99 A.J.I.L. 119 (rejecting the notion that the International Covenant has extraterritorial reach and canvassing opinion on this matter).

52 U.N. Hum. Rts. Comm., *General Comment 31*, para. 12, U.N. GAOR, 59th Sess., Supp. No. 40, Vol. 1, at 175 and 177, U.N. Doc. A/59/40 (2004) (noting that Article 2(1)'s references to jurisdiction and territory "does not imply that the State party concerned cannot be held accountable for the violations of rights under the Covenant which its agents commit upon the territory of another State, whether with the acquiescence of the Government of that State or in opposition to it").

53 *Ibid.*

54 *Lopez v. Uruguay*, U.N. Hum. Rts. Comm., Communication No. 52/1979, U. N. Doc. CCPR/C/13/D/52/1979 (1981).

55 See, for example, U.N. Hum. Rts. Comm., Concluding Observations of the Human Rights Committee: Netherlands, para. 8, U.N. Doc CCPR/CO/72/NET (2001) (relating to the "alleged involvement of members of the [Netherlands]

Recently, the International Court of Justice referred to this committee jurisprudence in *Legal Consequences of the Construction of a Wall in the Occupied Palestinian Territory*. In that advisory opinion, it concluded that a state's ICCPR obligations had extraterritorial reach: "the Court considers that the *International Covenant on Civil and Political Rights* is applicable in respect of acts done by a State in the exercise of its jurisdiction outside its own territory."[56]

2) Domestic Law

a) Sources of Domestic Law

In Canada, most domestic law stems from legislation enacted by the federal or provincial legislatures or made as regulations by the federal or provincial executives. Domestic law in each province except Quebec also comes in the form of the common law. The common law is a body of jurisprudence developed by common law courts through the application of precedent and persisting, most notably, in the private law areas of torts, contracts and property. The royal prerogative, meanwhile, comprises "the powers and privileges accorded by the common law to the Crown."[57]

State party's peacekeeping forces in the events surrounding the fall of Srebrenica, Bosnia and Herzegovina, in July 1995").

56 (2004), ICJ General List No. 131, 43 I.L.M. 1009 at para. 111. It is notable, however, that at least one other international court applying an analogous instrument—the European Convention of Human Rights—has come to an apparently different conclusion. *Bankovic v. Belgium* (2001), 41 I.L.M. 517 (E.C.H.R.) (concluding that the victims of the bombing of a foreign state were not within the "jurisdiction" of the bombing European countries). The European jurisprudence does, however, include at least one case accepting that the E.C.H.R. has extraterritorial reach where the European state is occupying and controlling the foreign territory. See *Issa v Turkey* (Merits) (2004), 41 E.H.R.R. 567 (applying a state party's European Convention obligations extraterritorially to foreign state territory "found to be under the former state's authority and control through its agents operating—whether lawfully or unlawfully in the latter state"). Notably, however, the U.K. House of Lords rejected the *Issa* interpretation of the European Convention, ultimately construing the reach of the convention narrowly to territories within the Counsel of Europe or activities done by diplomatic or consular officials abroad or, by analogy, by the state's soldiers at a military base operated by them in the foreign state. *Al-Skeini and others (Respondents) v. Secretary of State for Defence*, [2007] UKHL 26.

57 *Ross River Dena Council Band v. Canada*, [2002] 2 S.C.R. 816 at para. 54, citing Peter Hogg, *Constitutional Law*, 4th ed. (looseleaf) (Scarborough, ON: Thomson Carswell, 1997–2006) at 1-14.

Common law may be displaced by legislation enacted by legislatures. Constitutional law, in comparison, lies at the pinnacle of domestic law. In Canada, constitutional law comes in both written and unwritten forms. Written constitutional law is essentially entrenched legislation, incapable of amendment without special procedures and given pre-eminence over conflicting statutory law. Unwritten constitutional law also has this primacy, but is the product of common law-like, judicial decision making (putatively) unearthing inherent constitutional principles. One particular important sort of unwritten constitutional norm, constitutional conventions, are referred to at several junctures in this book. Put simply, a convention is a political practice that has achieved sufficient status to be labelled constitutionally obligatory.

b) Extraterritorial Domestic Law

Domestic law is not necessarily exclusively domestic in geographic reach. More than in many other areas of state action, preserving national security may require the government to act beyond Canada's borders by, for example, dispatching the Canadian Forces or other government personnel. Threats to national security may also originate overseas and cause harm either in Canada or to Canadians or Canadian interests abroad. Domestic law may govern or affect how the government reacts to these situations.

In public international law, there are several justifications for extraterritorial "prescriptive" domestic law; that is, one state's efforts to regulate conduct in another state. Pursuant to the "universal principle" of state jurisdiction, some international wrongs are so offensive that every state should be entitled to criminalize these acts, without regard to where and by whom they are committed. Under the "nationality" principle of jurisdiction, states may regulate the conduct of their own nationals overseas. Alternatively, they may apply the "passive personality" principle: pass laws applicable where the victim of the overseas act is a national. Finally, they may follow the "protective principle": regulate certain overseas conduct that is fundamental to a state's interests.[58]

Although permissible in these enumerated situations, extraterritorial laws applied in an effort to regulate conduct in another state might conflict with the jurisdiction of that other state and complicate international relations. Largely for this reason, Canada has been quite conservative in extending its statute law beyond its borders. Generally

---

58 For an overview of these and other principles of "prescriptive" state jurisdiction, see John Currie, *Public International Law* (Toronto: Irwin Law, 2001) at 297 *et seq.* See also *Hape*, above note 47 at para. 57 *et seq.*

speaking, Canadian statutory law's reach is confined to the territorial extent of Canada.[59] Thus, Canadian criminal offences are almost exclusively territorial in scope. Subsection 6(2) of the *Criminal Code* reads: "subject to this Act or any other Act of Parliament, no person shall be convicted ... of an offence committed outside Canada." [60] At the same time, there are exceptions to this principle of territoriality.

Express statutory exceptions to the territorial limit on Canada's criminal law are found in section 7 of the *Code*. Of particular relevance to this book, they include the terrorism offences discussed in Chapter 7. These rules enable Canadian courts to convict individuals for certain overseas acts of terrorism in a number of circumstances, including where the accused is Canadian, the victim is Canadian or where, simply, the accused is present in Canada after the commission of the offence.

It is also true that law governing the behaviour of government officials may travel with that official, and apply when the official conducts public business abroad. For instance, under statutes governing the Canadian Forces, territorial restrictions are relaxed. For members of Canada's military, the regular territorial limits of Canada's criminal law do not apply,[61] and convictions may be entered for conduct violating Canadian law committed while posted overseas.[62]

Canadian constitutional law also has an extraterritorial reach. In *Hape*,[63] the Supreme Court developed a clear test on the extraterritorial application of the *Charter*. Generally, Canadian state officials conducting business abroad do so pursuant to the law of the foreign jurisdiction, not the *Charter*. If subsequently, an overseas investigation mounted by Canadian officials produces evidence adduced in a Canadian court, the propriety of that evidence is tested against *Charter* fair trial standards and evidence extracted in a manner that taints a fair trial would be excluded. This would preclude, for instance, the deployment of evidence produced via overseas torture.[64] There may be, however, circumstances where the *Charter* would apply in a purely extraterritorial manner to regulate directly the foreign actions of Canadian officials: "Comity means that when one state looks to another for help in crim-

---

59   Indeed, there is a common law presumption against extraterritoriality. See Ruth Sullivan, *Sullivan and Dreidger on the Construction of Statutes*, 4th ed. (Markham ON: Butterworths, 2002) at 592.

60   R.S.C. 1985, C-46, as amended [*Criminal Code*].

61   See *Criminal Code*, ibid., s. 5 ("Nothing in this Act affects any law relating to the government of the Canadian Forces").

62   *National Defence Act*, R.S.C. 1985, c. N-5, ss. 130 and 273.

63   *Hape*, above note 47.

64   *Ibid* at para. 109.

inal matters, it must respect the way in which the other state chooses to provide the assistance within its borders. That deference ends where clear violations of international law and fundamental human rights begin."[65] Thus, Canadian officers are most likely barred from "participating in activities that, though authorized by the laws of another state, would cause Canada to be in violation of its international obligations in respect of human rights."[66]

C. PRESERVING LIBERTY IN DEFENDING FREEDOM

As this discussion suggests, the rules of law applicable in national security cases may be a patchwork quilt. Adhering to this rule of law, therefore, requires careful attention.

The law is, however, sometimes an impediment, or may be perceived as such by those acting under pressure to secure public safety. U.S. Vice President Cheney observed famously in 2001 that his government might have to reach to "the dark side" in handling terrorist suspects, adding, "it's going to be vital for us to use any means at our disposal."[67]

In the national security area, the temptation to stretch the bounds of legal authorization or act extralegally may be enormous, especially where the possible consequences of inaction are dire. Meanwhile, drastic temporary limitations on rights authorized in a time of peril might creep into the mainstream. David Paciocco has urged that "crisis is a dangerous milieu in which to attempt to redefine basic political priorities in a liberal democracy. Insecurity reduces the resistance to the exercise of government power.... In effect, a legislative honeymoon

---

65   *Ibid* at para. 52.

66   *Ibid* at paras. 90 and 101. Given this decision, it is unclear whether the *Charter* would apply to Canadian participation in, for example, the interrogation of a terrorism suspect for prosecution in a foreign country. See, for example, the earlier decision of *Khadr v. Canada* (2005), 257 D.L.R. (4th) 577 at para. 30 (F.C.) (suggesting in an application to enjoin questioning of a Canadian detainee at Guantanamo Bay by Canadian intelligence agents that "there may be a sufficient nexus between the investigation by Canadian agents, the passing of information to the U.S. and subsequent prosecution by the U.S. to engage the *Charter*"). The prospect that the *Charter* applies to this situation may increase if the foreign prosecution violates international human rights standards, although an obvious question is whether a foreign state's violations of its own human rights obligations encumbers Canada with an equivalent obligation not to aid and abet that violation.

67   Jane Mayer, "A Deadly Interrogation," *The New Yorker* (14 November 2005), online: www.newyorker.com/archive/2005/11/14/051114fa_fact.

is created. It enables governments, who trust themselves and are less apt to worry about checks and balances than about security, to say 'trust us.'"[68] Supreme Court Justice Binnie has made similar comments, speaking specifically about counterterrorism: "The danger in the 'war on terrorism' lies not only in the actual damage the terrorists can do to us but what we can do to our own legal and political institutions by way of shock, anger, anticipation, opportunism or overreaction."[69]

On a similar note, David Dyzenhaus warns forcefully that in perceived emergencies, democratic states often create "grey holes"—that is, zones in which the law putatively applies, but in such a limited procedural or substantive manner as to render legal limitations on executive power meaningless. He cautions that in these circumstances, the façade of the rule of law is maintained, but in a manner that creates a simple "rule by law" and not adherence to fundamental moral values.[70]

This risk of overreaction is real. As the Federal Court of Appeal has commented, "a possible danger to international relations or national security is not so easily capable of being recognized and, as a result, may be feared and evoked somewhat too quickly, albeit in perfect, good faith."[71]

Several specific rights that might be affected by national security-motivated actions are summarized in Table 2.1 that follows.

Table 2.1:   Possible National Security-Related Limitations on Rights

Right	Circumstance
Life and security of the person	Confronted with serious threats to national security, a state may eliminate the perceived or actual source of this threat through a policy of extrajudicial executions or other, less drastic measures that impair a person's security of the person right.
Torture and cruel, inhuman and degrading treatment and punishment	In order to extract intelligence deemed necessary to preserve national security, a state may resort to abusive forms of interrogation.

---

68   David Paciocco, "When Open Courts Meet Closed Government" (2005) 29 Sup. Ct. L. Rev. (2d) 385 at 396.

69   *Application*, above note 21 at para. 116, Binnie J. (dissenting).

70   David Dyzenhaus, *The Constitution of Law: Legality in a Time of Emergency* (Cambridge: Cambridge University Press, 2006).

71   *Gougeon v. Gibson* (1984), 10 C.C.C. (3d) 492 at 504 (F.C.A.) (discussing government secrecy motivated by national security and concern for protecting Canadian international relations).

Right	Circumstance
Rights relating to liberty, lawful detention and conditions of imprisonment	In order to neutralize threats to national security, a state may detain secretly or indefinitely persons viewed as security threats.
Nondiscrimination	Where threats are perceived to originate from particular ethnic, religious or national groups, security strategies may be overbroad in targeting these groups indiscriminately.
Fair trial rights, the presumption of innocence and nonretroactivity of criminal law	To preserve national security confidentiality or to ease the state's burden in securing convictions in national security cases, states may relax fair trial rules.
Freedom of movement	To more closely monitor persons believed to be national security threats, states may limit their movement between and within states.
Freedom of opinion and expression	To counter positions viewed as antithetical to national security, states may curb the expression of these views.
Freedom of association and assembly	To disrupt the activities of groups believed to pose threats to national security, a state may make them illegal, or may ban gatherings of larger than a set number of people.

1) The Flexibility of Domestic Constitutional Rights

It is notable, however, that rights instruments can accommodate action in the interest of *bona fide* national security threats. In crises, the legal field of action is more open to governments than in times of normalcy.

In Canadian constitutional law, it seems clear that *Charter* protections may be tempered where national security threats are at issue. Most obviously, the "notwithstanding" clause in section 33 of the *Charter* allows Parliament or the provincial legislatures to remove a statute from (most) *Charter* scrutiny by explicitly indicating it operates "notwithstanding" the *Charter*. A legislature with sufficient time to react to a true crisis with legislation might be sorely tempted to employ section 33, although to date Parliament has not done so, even in the wake of 9/11.[72]

Even if section 33 was not used, and Parliament's enactment violated the *Charter*, the statute could be saved from a *Charter* challenge

---

72   As discussed in Chapter 4, the existing *Emergencies Act*, R.S.C. 1985 (4th Supp.), c. 22 is not enacted using s. 33, and thus is constrained by the *Charter*. This book cannot answer whether Parliament might wish to reenact emergency law to suspend these constitutional constraints in a time of overwhelming crisis.

by section 1. Section 1 circumscribes all *Charter* rights by "such reasonable limits prescribed by law as can be demonstrably justified in a free and democratic society." Drawing from this language, the Court has articulated a complex justification test that may excuse a violation of a substantive *Charter* right, should the test's conditions be met.[73] In other words, rights in the Canadian Constitution are not absolute.

More than that, the content of the rights themselves apparently varies according to the vicissitudes of the moment. Speaking specifically of the right to life, liberty and security of the person in section 7, Wilson J. concluded in *Operation Dismantle v. Canada Inc.* that

> the concept of "right" as used in the *Charter* must take account of the fact that the self-contained political community which comprises the State is faced with at least the possibility, if not the reality, of external threats to both its collective well-being and to the individual well-being of its citizens. In order to protect the community against such threats, it may well be necessary for the State to take steps which incidentally increase the risk to the lives or personal security of some or all of the State's citizens. … [T]here must be a strong presumption that governmental action which concerns the relations of the State with other states, and which is therefore not directed at any member of the immediate political community, was never intended to be caught by s. 7 even … though such action may have the incidental effect of increasing the risk of death or injury that individuals generally have to face.[74]

Drawing on this reasoning, the Ontario Divisional Court concluded in *Aleksic v. Canada* that a government declaration of war, or a decision to participate in a military bombing campaign overseas, "cannot … constitute a violation of the s. 7 rights of those affected. … To hold otherwise would permit any citizen to, in effect, hijack Canadian foreign policy. In any case where Canadian military intervention was contemplated, a citizen could choose to place himself in the target zone, and then complain that the intended actions of the government would vitiate his right to life and security."[75] It stands to reason that a foreign national on the receiving end of that bombing campaign has no section 7 right, although he or she would have important rights under international humanitarian law.

In practice, the precise guarantees in section 7 of the *Charter* are mutable in situations involving national security. In *Suresh* at issue, in

---

73   See, for example, *R. v. Oakes*, [1986] 1 S.C.R. 103 and its progeny.
74   [1985] 1 S.C.R. 441 at 489–90.
75   *Aleksic*, above note 42 at paras. 68–69.

part, was the scope of the due process guarantee associated with section 7 in a case involving the deportation of a suspected terrorist to possible torture. In allowing Suresh's appeal, the court held that, confronted with the prospect of being deported to torture, Suresh "must be informed of the case to be met" and that an "opportunity be provided to respond to the case presented to the Minister," including through the presentation of evidence countering the view that he constituted a national security threat.[76] However, information provided by the government to inform Suresh of the case against him was legitimately "subject to privilege or similar valid reasons for reduced disclosure, such as safeguarding confidential public security documents."[77] Further, the Court emphasized that "the Minister must be allowed considerable discretion in evaluating future risk and security concerns."[78]

The more recent *Charkaoui* case also concerned the legitimacy of secretive national security-related proceedings under Canada's immigration law. In that decision, the Supreme Court demonstrated less willingness to limit section 7 rights outside of a section 1 analysis. It also confirmed, however, that national security might temper the precise procedural guarantees offered up by section 7.[79]

National security, in other words, moderates the sort of procedures courts will insist upon as part of constitutional fundamental justice, even outside any section 1 analysis.[80]

---

76   *Suresh*, above note 20 at paras. 122–23.
77   *Ibid.* at para. 122.
78   *Ibid.* at para. 120.
79   *Charkaoui*, above note 1 at para. 27. ("The procedures required to conform to the principles of fundamental justice must reflect the exigencies of the security context. Yet they cannot be permitted to erode the essence of s. 7. The principles of fundamental justice cannot be reduced to the point where they cease to provide the protection of due process that lies at the heart of s. 7 of the *Charter*. The protection may not be as complete as in a case where national security constraints do not operate. But to satisfy s. 7, meaningful and substantial protection there must be.") It is also notable that in R. v. *Heywood*, [1994] 3 S.C.R. 761 at 802, the Supreme Court suggested that a violation of the s. 7 right to life, liberty and security of the person, though generally difficult to justify on section 1 grounds, could be reasonable "in times of war or national emergencies." See also *Reference re Motor Vehicle Act (British Columbia) S. 94(2)*, [1985] 2 S.C.R. 486 at 518. As discussed in Chapter 11, the Court has also suggested that national security can temper the protections offered by s. 8, in relation to searches and seizures. *Hunter v. Southam Inc.*, [1984] 2 S.C.R. 145 at 186.
80   For a critique of this approach, see David Mullan, "Deference from *Baker* to *Suresh* and Beyond: Interpreting the Conflicting Signals," in David Dyzenhaus, ed., *The Unity of Public Law* (Oxford: Hart, 2004) at 47.

2) The Flexibility of International Human Rights

International human rights law also attempts to grapple with the rights/national security dilemma. Most importantly, the ICCPR and several other human rights treaties include an overarching provision permitting limitations in the gravest national emergencies. Article 4 allows most rights to be limited to the extent strictly necessary "in time of public emergency which threatens the life of the nation," a closely circumscribed circumstance.[81]

The ICCPR also expressly acknowledges that a handful of rights may be tempered in the interests of "national security" or such things as "public order" or "public health or morals." These rights are listed in Table 2.2.

Table 2.2:   Rights with Express National Security Limitations in the ICCPR

Subject	Right	Limitation
Art. 12: Liberty of movement	Everyone lawfully within the territory of a State shall, within that territory, have the right to liberty of movement and freedom to choose his residence. Everyone shall be free to leave any country, including his own.	These rights shall not be subject to any restrictions except those which are provided by law, are necessary to protect national security, public order (*ordre public*), public health or morals or the rights and freedoms of others, and are consistent with the other rights recognized in the Covenant.
Art. 13: Expulsion of aliens	An alien lawfully in the territory of a State Party to the Covenant may be expelled therefrom only in pursuance of a decision reached in accordance with law and shall be allowed to submit the reasons against his/her expulsion and to have his/her case reviewed by, and be represented for the purpose before, the competent authority or a person or persons especially designated by the competent authority.	Compelling reasons of national security may limit the alien being allowed to submit the reasons against his/her expulsion and to have his/her case reviewed by, and be represented for that purpose before, the competent authority or a person or persons especially designated by the competent authority.

---

81   There are, however, certain rights from which no derogation is permissible, even in the most extreme circumstances. See Chapter 4.

Subject	Right	Limitation
Art. 14: Fair trial rights	All persons shall be equal before the courts and tribunals. In the determination of any criminal charge against him/her, or of his/her rights and obligations in a suit at law, every person shall be entitled to a fair and public hearing by a competent, independent and impartial tribunal established by law.	The press and the public may be excluded from all or part of a trial for reasons of morals, public order (*ordre public*) or national security in a democratic society.
Art. 19: Freedom of expression	Everyone shall have the right to freedom of expression; this right shall include freedom to seek, receive and impart information and ideas of all kinds, regardless of frontiers, either orally, in writing or in print, in the form of art, or through any other media of his/her choice.	The exercise of this right carries with it special duties and responsibilities. It may therefore be subject to certain restrictions, but these shall only be such as are provided by law and are necessary, *inter alia*, for the protection of national security or of public order (*ordre public*), or of public health or morals.
Art. 21: Free assembly	The right of peaceful assembly shall be recognized.	No restrictions may be placed on the exercise of this right other than those imposed in conformity with the law and which are necessary in a democratic society in the interests of national security or public safety, public order (*ordre public*), the protection of public health or morals or the protection of the rights and freedoms of others.
Art. 22: Free association	Everyone shall have the right to freedom of association with others, including the right to form and join trade unions for the protection of his interests.	No restrictions may be placed on the exercise of this right other than those which are prescribed by law and which are necessary in a democratic society in the interests of national security or public safety, public order (*ordre public*), the protection of public health or morals or the protection of the rights and freedoms of others. This article shall not prevent the imposition of lawful restrictions on members of the armed forces and of the police in their exercise of this right.

National security, public order or public health or morals are not terms defined in the ICCPR itself, a matter of concern.[82] For this reason, a group of experts convened by the International Commission of Jurists in 1984 proposed the *Siracusa Principles*.[83] Though of no legal force, the principles provide a helpful interpretive tool. Taken together, the *Siracusa Principles* impose sensible constraints, designed to guard against governments invoking these limitations for improper, ulterior motivations.[84] "National security" is given the most comprehensive definition. Under the principles, "national security may be invoked to justify measures limiting certain rights only when they are taken to protect the existence of the nation or its territorial integrity or political independence against force or threat of force." It is not an appropriate response to "merely local or relatively isolated threats to law and order."[85]

In relation to national security, the *Siracusa Principles* have arguably now been superseded by the more detailed—and arguably more authoritative—*Johannesburg Principles: National Security, Freedom of Expression and Access to Information*, at least in the area of limitations on free expression. Formulated in 1995 by a group of legal experts, the *Johannesburg Principles* have since been endorsed by the U.N. Special Rapporteur on Freedom of Opinion and Expression.[86] They were also

---

82   Erica-Irene A. Daes, *A Study on the Individual's Duties to the Community and the Limitations on Human Rights and Freedoms under Article 29 of the Universal Declaration of Human Right* (New York: United Nations, 1990). ("The terms 'public safety' and 'national security' are not sufficiently precise to be used as the basis for limitation or restriction of the exercise of certain rights and freedoms of the individual. On the contrary, they are terms with a very broad meaning and application. Therefore they can be used by certain States to justify unreasonable limitations or restrictions.")

83   *Siracusa Principles on the Limitation and Derogation of Provisions in the International Covenant on Civil and Political Rights*, UNESCOR, 41 Sess., U.N. Doc. E/CN.4/1985/4 (1985) [*Siracusa Principles*].

84   Thus, "public order" is defined "as the sum of rules which ensure the functioning of society or the set of fundamental principles on which society is founded. Respect for human rights is part of public order." *Ibid.* at para. 22. "Public health" should include only "measures dealing with a serious threat to the health of the population or individual members of the population. These measures must be specifically aimed at preventing disease or injury or providing care for the sick and injured." *Ibid.* at para. 25. "Public morals" may only be invoked to limit rights where the "limitation in question is essential to the maintenance of respect for fundamental values of the community." *Ibid.* at para. 27.

85   *Ibid.* at paras. 29–30.

86   See Report of the Special Rapporteur, *Promotion and Protection of the Right to Freedom of Opinion and Expression*, U.N. Doc. E/CN.4/1996/39 (22 March 1996) at para. 145 ("the Special Rapporteur recommends that the Commission on

invoked by the then-U.N. Human Rights Commission in the preamble of many of its resolutions (each time, during years in which Canada was a member).[87] Finally, the Principles have been cited with a measure of approval by the House of Lords in *Rehman*.[88] For these reasons, the *Johannesburg Principles*, although nonbinding, have plausible soft-law status.

In their material part, the *Johannesburg Principles* read:

(a) A restriction sought to be justified on the ground of national security is not legitimate unless its genuine purpose and demonstrable effect is to protect a country's existence or its territorial integrity against the use or threat of force, or its capacity to respond to the use or threat of force, whether from an external source, such as a military threat, or an internal source, such as incitement to violent overthrow of the government.

(b) In particular, a restriction sought to be justified on the ground of national security is not legitimate if its genuine purpose or demonstrable effect is to protect interests unrelated to national security, including, for example, to protect a government from embarrassment or exposure of wrongdoing, or to conceal information about the functioning of its public institutions, or to entrench a particular ideology, or to suppress industrial unrest.

Also notable is a 1990 study published by the U.N. Centre of Human Rights, discussing limitations on human rights permissible under

---

Human Rights endorse the *Johannesburg Principles on National Security, Freedom of Expression and Access to Information*, which are contained in the annex to the present report and which the Special Rapporteur considers give useful guidance for protecting adequately the right to freedom of opinion, expression and information").

87 See U.N. Human Rights Commission, *The Right to Freedom of Opinion and Expression*, Resolution 2003/42 ("Recalling the *Johannesburg Principles on National Security, Freedom of Expression and Access to Information* adopted by a group of experts meeting in South Africa on 1 October 1995 (E/CN.4/1996/39, annex)"); U.N. Human Rights Commission, Resolution 2002/48 (same); U.N. Human Rights Commission, Resolution 2001/47 (same); U.N. Human Rights Commission, Resolution 2000/38 (same); U.N. Human Rights Commission, Resolution 1999/36 (same); U.N. Human Rights Commission, Resolution 1998/42 (same); U.N. Human Rights Commission, Resolution 1997/27 (same).

88 *Rehman*, above note 38 at paras. 14–15, Lord Slynn (referring to the *Johannesburg Principles* and then indicating that "[i]t seems to me that the appellant is entitled to say that 'the interests of national security' cannot be used to justify any reason the Secretary of State has for wishing to deport an individual from the United Kingdom. There must be some possibility of risk or danger to the security or well-being of the nation which the Secretary of State considers makes it desirable for the public good that the individual should be deported").

the *Universal Declaration of Human Rights*.[89] On the issue of national security, that report notes:

> National security means peace and stability in the community. The concept would seem to relate to measures enacted with a view to safeguarding territorial integrity and national independence from any external threat. It covers any activity prejudicial to the very existence of the State. Nevertheless, this requirement should not be used as a pretext for imposing arbitrary limitations or restrictions on the exercise of human rights and freedoms.[90]

D. PROTECTING PEOPLE WHILE LEAVING THEM ALONE

One specific right almost always in play in national security investigations is that of privacy. Privacy has been defined as "the claim of individuals, groups, or institutions to determine for themselves when, how, and to what extent information about them is communicated to others."[91] In modern democracies, privacy rights exist to "impose limits on the extent of control and direction that the state exercises over the day-to-day conduct of individual lives."[92] Sometimes labelled "a right to be left alone," an erosion of privacy potentially results in innocent people being "identified, tagged and monitored by the state."[93] Privacy protection reinforces the concept of limited government: the notion that there are areas of private life in which even a democratic government should not go.

---

89   The *Universal Declaration of Human Rights* A/RES/217 A (III) (1948) is a U.N. General Assembly resolution that now is in whole or in part customary international law. Article 29 of that instrument reads: "In the exercise of his rights and freedoms, everyone shall be subject only to such limitations as are determined by law solely for the purpose of securing due recognition and respect for the rights and freedoms of others and of meeting the just requirements of morality, public order and the general welfare in a democratic society."

90   Erica-Irene A. Daes, *Freedom of the Individual under Law: An Analysis of Article 29 of the Universal Declaration of Human Rights*. Human Rights Study Series No. 3 (Geneva: United Nations Centre for Human Rights, 1990) at para. 1028.

91   Alan Westin, *Privacy and Freedom* (New York: Atheneum, 1967) at 7.

92   Jed Rubenfeld, "The Right of Privacy," (1989) 102 Harv. L. Rev. 737 at 805.

93   Canada, Privacy Commissioner, *Annual Report 2002–03* (Ottawa: Minister of Public Works and Government Services) at 5, online: www.privcom.gc.ca/information/ar/02_04_11_e.pdf.

In *R. v. Dyment*,[94] Justice La Forest vigorously underscored the connection between democracy and privacy: "society has come to realize that privacy is at the heart of liberty in a modern state. ... Grounded in man's physical and moral autonomy, privacy is essential for the well-being of the individual. ... The restraints imposed on government to pry into the lives of the citizen go to the essence of a democratic state."[95]

Subsequently, in *Dagg v. Canada (Minister of Finance)*, La Forest J. held that "the protection of privacy is a fundamental value in modern, democratic states. ... An expression of an individual's unique personality or personhood, privacy is grounded on physical and moral autonomy — the freedom to engage in one's own thoughts, actions and decisions."[96] Indeed, privacy interests have a "privileged, foundational position ... in our social and legal culture."[97] Other Supreme Court justices have since echoed this position. Thus, Justice L'Heureux-Dubé urged in *R. v. O'Connor* that "respect for individual privacy is an essential component of what it means to be 'free.' As a corollary, the infringement of this right undeniably impinges upon an individual's 'liberty' in our free and democratic society."[98]

Yet, defending national security may depend on invading the privacy of those persons intent on doing harm. Nuancing these invasions of privacy, confining them to the limited circumstances where *bona fide* national security interests are legitimately at risk, is — and should be — a key preoccupation of national security law.

---

94   [1988] 2 S.C.R. 417, La Forest J., concurring.

95   *Ibid.* at 427.

96   [1997] 2 S.C.R. 403 at para. 65, La Forest J. dissenting in the result [*Dagg*]. See also *Lavigne v. Canada (Office of the Commissioner of Official Languages)*, [2002] 2 S.C.R. 773 at para. 25 [*Lavigne*], citing this passage with approval and noting that while La Forest J. dissented, "he spoke for the entire Court on this point."

97   *Dagg, ibid.* at para. 69. See also *Lavigne, ibid.* at para. 25, citing this passage with approval.

98   [1995] 4 S.C.R. 411 at para. 113, speaking for herself, La Forest, & Gonthier JJ., with McLachlin J. concurring. See also *R. v. Osolin*, [1993] 4 S.C.R. 595 at 614, L'Heureux-Dubé J., dissenting but not on this point ("[t]he importance of privacy as a fundamental value in our society is underscored by the protection afforded to *everyone* under s. 8 of the *Charter* 'to be secure against unreasonable search or seizure.' This value finds expression in such legislation as the *Privacy Act* ... which restricts the purposes for which information may be used to those for which it was received") [emphasis added], cited with approval in *Lavigne*, above note 96 at para. 25.

E. ACTING TRANSPARENTLY IN RESPONDING COVERTLY

Intrusive national security investigations and policies may be (and often are) secret. "Secrecy," said the French Cardinal Richelieu in 1641, "is the first essential in affairs of the State."[99] Constraints on information may give governments a leg-up over their international rivals, preserve them from their enemies and insulate them from domestic opponents. Protection of the nation and its inhabitants may depend on keeping information about weapons systems, troop strengths, intelligence assets or physical vulnerabilities away from enemies. As the famous World War II–era admonishment warned, "loose lips ... sink ships."[100] For these reasons and more, "it is difficult to think of national security without also thinking about government secrecy."[101]

Of course, what was virtue in Cardinal Richelieu's day may be vice in today's modern democracies. One fierce opponent of government secrecy, Ralph Nader, has called information the "currency of democracy."[102] Only openness and transparency preserve citizens from the malfeasance, incompetence, corruption and expedient behaviour of incumbent governments. Information is, as U.S. Supreme Court Justice Louis Brandeis once quipped, "the best of disinfectants."[103]

Relative latecomers to the open government game, Canadians have shared this suspicion of government secrecy. Former auditor general of Canada Denis Desautels has urged that "information is the current that charges accountability in government."[104] Government accountability, in this view, requires timely and extensive access to government information. Absent a capacity to compel disclosure of information unfavourable to government, citizens—including elected members of

---

99 Duc de Richelieu, "Maxims" in *Testament Politique* (Amsterdam: Henri Desbordes, 1691), Bartleby, online: www.bartleby.com/66/34/46534.html.
100 The phrase was an allusion to the dangers to Atlantic convoys of German foreknowledge of sailing times and routes.
101 Alasdair Roberts, "National Security and Open Government" (2004) 9 Geo. Pub. Pol'y Rev. 69 ["National Security"].
102 See, for example, "Ralph Nader Interview" Academy of Achievement, online: www.achievement.org/autodoc/page/nad0int-4.
103 Louis D. Brandeis, *Other People's Money and How the Bankers Use It* (New York: Frederick A. Stokes, 1914) at 92.
104 Canada, Office of the Information Commissioner of Canada, *Annual Report 2000–2001* (Ottawa: Minister of Public Works and Government Services, 2001) online: www.infocom.gc.ca/reports/pdf/oic00_01e.pdf.

Parliament—remain dependent on the potentially self-serving information the government chooses to release.

Indeed secrecy, even when motivated by an objective as fundamental as national security, may sometimes create more perils than it forestalls. In 2003, the Standing Senate Committee on National Security and Defence released its report *The Myth of Security at Canada's Airports*. The study documented deeply inadequate security at Canadian airports, even in the post-9/11 era, and concluded that "the front door of air security ... [is] now being fairly well secured, with the side and back doors wide open."[105] In the course of preparing its report, the committee was "criticized for calling witnesses that have shared knowledge of these breaches with the Canadian public."[106] It rejected this criticism, observing:

> You can be sure that ships really will sink if they have a lot [sic] holes in them. And those holes aren't likely to get patched unless the public applies pressure to get the job done. They certainly aren't patched yet.
>
> The Committee recognizes the need to balance the public's right to know against the interests of national security. But unreasonable secrecy acts against national security. It shields incompetence and inaction, at a time that competence and action are both badly needed.[107]

---

105 Canada, Standing Senate Committee on National Security and Defence, *The Myth of Security at Canada's Airports* (Ottawa: Standing Senate Committee on National Security and Defence, 2003) at 9, online: www.parl.gc.ca/37/2/parlbus/ commbus/senate/Com-e/defe-e/rep-e/rep05jan03-e.htm [*Myth of Security*]. The issue of reporting on security matters has galvanized controversy in the United States as well, where the Bush administration has been vocal on media disclosure of such programs as the National Security Agency's practice of warrantless intercepts within the United States. See, for example, Mark Sappenfield & Mark Clayton, "How Media Leaks Affect War on Terror" *Christian Science Monitor* (30 June 2006); Geoffrey R. Stone, "The U.S. Can Keep a Secret" *Los Angeles Times* (6 June 2006).

106 *Myth of Security*, ibid. at 11.

107 *Ibid.* at 12–13. Similar comments have been made by academic observers. See Sandra Coliver, "Commentary on The *Johannesburg Principles on National Security, Freedom of Expression and Access to Information*" in Sandra Coliver, Paul Hoffman, Joan Fitzpatrick, & Stephen Brown, eds., *Secrecy and Liberty: National Security, Freedom of Expression and Access to Information* (The Hague: M. Nijhoff, 1999) 11 at 11–12 ("[f]reedom of expression and access to information, by enabling public scrutiny of government action, serve as safeguards against government abuse and thereby from a crucial component of genuine national security"); Paul H. Chevigny, "Information, the Executive and the Politics of Information" in Shimon Shetreet, ed., *Free Speech and National Security* (Boston: M. Nijhoff, 1991) 130 at 138 ("[t]he problem with the 'national security state' is

National security, in other words, is not about insulating governments from embarrassment.

The director of the Canadian Security Intelligence Service has urged that undue secrecy may also undermine the credibility of the government's national security policies. In his words, "there is a risk that, absent adequate public dialogue and a surfeit of secrecy, the justification for action by governments against terrorism will be undermined or misunderstood. This in turn can put in jeopardy the legitimacy of the government response."[108]

The dilemma of any government information regime lies in balancing the strong public interest in disclosure in all areas, including national security, against legitimate refusals to disclose. As the 2003 senate committee acknowledged, seeking assurances that secure doors at airports are actually locked is a proper public concern. Demanding disclosure of the combination codes to those doors would not be.[109]

F. ACTING DECISIVELY IN A FOG OF WAR

Even with the best of intelligence from highly effective, convert intrusions on privacy, the real world of national security has few of what former U.S. defense secretary Donald Rumsfeld famously called "known knowns"—things we know we know. As Rumsfeld noted: "We also know there are known unknowns; that is to say we know there are some things we do not know. But there are also unknown unknowns—the ones we don't know we don't know. And if one looks throughout the history of our country and other free countries, it is the latter category that tend to be the difficult ones."[110]

In making these statements in 2002, Rumsfeld was dismissing the absence of actual evidence linking Saddam's Iraq to terrorist organizations. The resulting Iraq war may be the proof of how a policy of action

---

not so much that it violates [fundamental] rights, although it sometimes does just that, but that it can lead to the repetition of irrational decisions").

108 Judd, "How Should a Democracy Respond to Domestic Terrorist Threats," above note 13. Similar comments were made in 2007 by Peter Clarke, the head of British counterterrorism at Scotland Yard. Jane Perlez and Elaine Sciolino, "Openness Sought in British Terror Trials" *New York Times* (25 May 2007) (discussing secrecy in terrorism prosecutions in the United Kingdom).

109 *Myth of Security*, above note 105 at 12.

110 See U.S. Department of Defense, "DoD News Briefing—Secretary Rumsfeld and Gen. Myers," Tuesday, 12 February 2002—11:30 a.m, online: www.defenselink. mil/transcripts/transcript.aspx?transcriptid=2636.

built on suspicion may precipitate its own crises. Still, it is true that in the fog of war, a lawyerly requirement for evidence prior to action may mean no action at all.

U.S. Vice President Richard Cheney reportedly sought to overcome this problem by pronouncing the so-called one percent solution—a doctrine in which U.S. authorities act as if a threat of terrible attack is confirmed where there is a one percent chance of it occurring.[111] This approach—if actually applied—would quickly drive otherwise even-handed officials to extreme responses.

The Cheney doctrine's emphasis on action even in the face of un-certainty does, however, underscore an important dimension of nation-al security: pre-emptive action may have to be grounded in suspicions, rather than based on the probabilistic standards used to justify action in other areas of the law. Canadian anti-terrorism law, for example, often permits state action—whether in the form of surveillance or detention—on a "reasonable grounds to believe" or even "reasonable grounds to suspect" standard.[112] For instance, under the *Immigration and Refugee Protection Act*, a detention made pursuant to a security cer-tificate on a "reasonable grounds to believe" standard will be upheld by a court where "there is an objective basis ... which is based on compel-ling and credible information."[113]

Rights-impairing actions grounded on suspicion and mere possi-bility present obvious difficulties to a system of law that generally de-mands more substantial proof when the state seeks to strip individuals of liberties.

G. CONCLUSION: THE DANGERS OF UTILITARIANISM

Lurking in all of the above-noted dilemmas is the notion that rigid adherence to conventional values must give way in the face of security threats. Much ink has been spilled since 9/11 about "lesser evils": that

---

111 Ron Suskind, *The One Percent Doctrine* (New York: Simon & Schuster, 2006).

112 "Reasonable grounds to suspect" is "a lesser but included standard in the threshold of reasonable and probable grounds to believe." *R. v. Monney*, [1999] 1 S.C.R. 652 at para. 49.

113 *Charkaoui*, above note 1 at para. 39. Federal Court jurisprudence has described this standard as "a serious possibility that the facts exist based on reliable, cred-ible evidence." *Charkaoui (Re)*, [2004] 3 F.C.R. 32 at para. 128 (F.C.).

sometimes a small evil must be done to avert a larger evil.[114] That may be true. No political leader may responsibly urge *fiat justitia et pereat mundus*—let justice be done, though the world perish. But the lesser evil remains just that, an evil, and it is not always clear when a lesser evil graduates to the more significant wrong.

Underlying this point, and each of the foregoing dilemmas, is a concern with the utilitarian impulse of national security. Securing national security is, by definition, a majoritarian project: it serves the interest of the greatest number, enabling a state's inhabitants to continue their affairs in safety. Serving the interests of the majority may easily become conflated with serving the greater good. In extreme instances, maximizing the good for the greatest number may justify injustices done to a minority. That minority may be large—Japanese interned in World War II—or relatively small—suspected terrorists tortured for intelligence. Nevertheless, the result is the same: the rights of the few are sacrificed in the name of securing the rights of the many. There are two objections to this approach, one principled and the other practical.

First, the concept of individual rights and freedoms and the principles of nondiscrimination are designed to guard against this sacrifice of the individual in the name of the society. They do so from long experience with the consequences of nonobservance of rights: those in today's majority are tomorrow's victims. Left to define the needs of the majority, a state prepared to sacrifice individual and minority rights may find itself on a slippery slope to observance of the rights of none. Caution should be exercised, therefore, in any balancing exercise in which the rights, interests or needs of the many outweigh the rights of the few.

Second and more practically, the utilitarian calculus, applied prospectively in the fog of war, may prompt extreme behaviour that compounds more than it relieves threats. For example, a common image in much of the contemporary debate around interrogation in the post-9/11 environment is the famous "ticking time bomb" scenario or its variants. This scenario imagines a stolen, suitcase-sized thermonuclear device set to detonate imminently somewhere in a large urban area. State agents have in their custody the terrorist who planned this attack and who is aware of the precise location of the weapon. That person refuses to cooperate and indeed is willing to die for his or her cause. The dilemma posed is stark: do the agents engage in interrogational torture—torture

---

114 See, for example, Michael Ignatieff, *The Lesser Evil: Political Ethics in an Age of Terror* (Toronto: Penguin Canada, 2004).

employed strictly to extract the critical information from the terrorist bomber, and designed to save millions of innocent lives?[115]

Faced with this imaginary scenario, some commentators have answered in the affirmative. As Jean Bethke Elshtain observes:

> Far greater moral guilt falls on a person in authority who permits the death of hundreds of innocents rather than choosing to "torture" one guilty or complicit person. ... Were I the parent or grandparent of a child whose life might be spared [in a ticking time-bomb scenario], I would want officials to rank their moral purity far less important in the overall scheme of things than eliciting information that might spare my child or grandchild.[116]

Oren Gross writes that given the ticking time-bomb case, "legal rigidity in the face of severe crises" like the ticking time-bomb scenario "is not merely hypocritical but is, in fact, detrimental to long-term notions of the rule of law. It may also lead to more, rather than less, radical interference with individual rights and liberties."[117]

Civil libertarian Alan Dershowitz points to the ticking time-bomb scenario in his famous argument that because it is already happening *sub rosa*, torture should be a regulated practice, available in extreme circumstances but governed by judicially issued warrants.[118] Judge Richard Posner—although critical of Dershowitz's warrant idea—supports his premises: "only the most doctrinaire civil libertarians ... deny that if the stakes are high enough, torture is permissible. No one who doubts that should be in a position of responsibility."[119]

There are serious dangers, however, in contemplating an exception to the torture prohibition in response to a "ticking time-bomb" scenario. The premises underlying the ticking time-bomb scenario are dubious. It is possible to imagine a scenario in which interrogators *know* (not just suspect) that the detainee is the bomber; in which they *know* the suspect *will* crack under pain and torture *will* save the day, in which they *know* the bomb's detonation is *certain* to happen; in which

---

115 See, for example, Henry Shue, "Torture," in Sanford Levinson, ed., *Torture: A Collection* (Toronto: Oxford University Press, 2004) at 53 [Levinson, *Torture*].

116 Jean Bethke Elshtain, "Reflection of the Problem of 'Dirty Hands,'" in Levinson, *Torture, ibid.* at 87.

117 Oren Gross, "The Prohibition on Torture and the Limits of the Law," in Levinson, *Torture, ibid.* at 237.

118 Alan Dershowitz, *Why Terrorism Works* (New Haven, CT: Yale University Press, 2002); Alan Dershowitz, "Tortured Reasoning," in Levinson, *Torture, ibid.* at 257.

119 Richard Posner, "Torture, Terrorism, and Interrogation," in Levinson, *Torture, ibid.* at 295.

they *know* that other investigative techniques are *certain* to fail. Knowing all this, the utilitarian calculus is impossibly weighted in favour of torture.

But such scenarios are vanishingly rare.[120] It is claimed, for example, that Philippine authorities "tortured a terrorist into disclosing information that may have foiled plots to assassinate the pope and to crash eleven commercial airliners carrying approximately four thousand passengers into the Pacific Ocean."[121] President Bush, meanwhile, urged in 2006 that the use of "alternative" CIA interrogation techniques at CIA "ghost" detention centres foiled multiple terrorist attacks.[122]

What is unknown, however, is how many false positives have been created by extreme interrogation — false confessions made to halt the interrogation which then divert attention from real threats. Inevitably, a body of law permitting torture where interrogators believed themselves confronted with an immediate and extreme threat would permit torture in situations where, after the fact, the inefficacy and the inutility of the torture are clear, or the magnitude of the threat proves nowhere close to that associated with the time-bomb scenario. This is acutely the case given the notorious unreliability of information extracted under torture, a matter discussed in Chapter 15. Elaine Scarry, in her attack on the ticking time-bomb's logic, has made exactly this point:

> [Since 9/11] five thousand foreign nationals suspected of being terrorists have been detained without access to counsel, only three of whom have ever eventually been charged with terrorism-related acts; two of those three have been acquitted. When we imagine the ticking time bomb situation, does our imaginary omniscience enable us to get the information by torturing one person? Or will the numbers more closely resemble the situation of the detainees: we will be certain, and incorrect, 4,999 times that we stand in the presence

---

120 See discussion on this point in Emanuel Gross, *The Struggle of Democracy Against Terrorism* (Charlottesville, VA: University of Virginia Press, 2006) at 66 *et seq.* For an elegant discussion of balancing in the context of, *inter alia*, torture, see Dieter Grimm, "How to Balance Freedom and Security," *Speigel Atlantic Forum* (26 April 2007).

121 Gross, *Struggle of Democracy*, ibid. at 295, citing Dershowitz, *Why Terrorism Works*, above note 118 at 137.

122 See also Jamie Doward, "U.S. Claims Guantanamo 'Saved Lives,'" *[London] Observer* (8 October 2006). For similar claims by former CIA director George Tenet, see Tim Reid, "Tough U.S. Interrogation 'Saved Lives'" *[London] Times* (26 April 2007). It is not certain which attacks were foiled by stress techniques, but for a list of apparently foiled attacks against the United States between 2001 and 2007, see "Foiled Plots in U.S. Since Sept. 11" *Associated Press* (8 May 2007).

of someone with the crucial data, and only get it right with the five thousandth prisoner? Will the ticking time bomb still be ticking?[123]

In light of these observations, national security law should not rush too quickly to embrace lesser evils. If it were to do so, we might well suffer lesser evil without doing anything to forestall the greater wrong.

This book now turns to a specific examination of how Canadian, international and comparative law has responded to the dilemmas outlined in this chapter.

---

123 Elaine Scary, "Five Errors in the Reasoning of Alan Dershowitz," in Levinson, *Torture*, above note 115 at 284.

NATIONAL SECURITY STRUCTURE

CHAPTER 3

THE INSTITUTIONAL FRAMEWORK FOR NATIONAL SECURITY LAW

If preserving the security of the state and the safety of its inhabitants is the classic function of government, then governments must be organized to perform this role. In Canada, both provincial and federal levels of government have important public safety responsibilities, but the principal *national* security function falls to the federal level. National security is mostly a federal executive branch function, with legislative and judicial branches playing distinctly secondary roles.

That said, in the modern era, national executives do not act exclusively at the domestic level. They interact instead with their counterparts from other countries either bilaterally or in international venues, not least international organizations like the United Nations.

This chapter provides a summary of the institutional framework for national security law in Canada by describing both the international and Canadian governmental institutions tasked with preserving national security and discussing how they are overseen and reviewed. It is necessarily a constrained description—detailed analyses of the role and functions of these agencies follow in later chapters.

PART I: UNITED NATIONS FRAMEWORK

A. UNITED NATIONS SYSTEM

The world's most important international organization is the United Nations. Created in 1945 by the United Nations *Charter*[1]—an international treaty concluded by the vast bulk of the planet's then existing states—the United Nations has near-universal state membership: 192 states by 2006.

The United Nations is not a world government capable of legislating *per se*. Instead, it is a venue for resolving international disputes and proposing common policies on matters of international significance. The U.N. comprises six main "organs" and an array of subsidiary and specialized agencies and organizations. The most significant of these bodies for the purposes of this book is the United Nations Security Council, with the General Assembly and the International Court of Justice discussed occasionally in chapters to come.

1) General Assembly

Briefly, the General Assembly is a plenary body of U.N. member states, meeting annually in regular sessions in New York. The General Assembly makes decisions pursuant to a one state–one vote formula,[2] an approach consistent with the notion that in international law all states are equally sovereign regardless of their real power and influence. On its face, the General Assembly resembles a legislature, and is sometimes called a "parliament of nations."[3] Yet, despite its universal membership, the General Assembly has no autonomous law-making powers, being competent only to recommend courses of action.[4] That said, the General Assembly sometimes proposes principles that are subsequently

---

1   U.N. *Charter*, 26 June 1945, 59 Stat. 1031, T.S. 993, 3 Bevans 1153, entered into force 24 October 1945.
2   U.N. *Charter*, Art. 18.
3   United Nations, *The UN in Brief*, online: www.un.org/Overview/uninbrief/index.html.
4   U.N. *Charter*, Art. 10 ("The General Assembly may discuss any questions or any matters within the scope of the present *Charter* or relating to the powers and functions of any organs provided for in the present *Charter*, and, except as provided in Article 12, may make recommendations to the Members of the United Nations or to the Security Council or to both on any such questions or matters.")

adopted by states through a process of negotiation and ratification of international treaties.

Notably, the General Assembly's consideration of matters relating to peace and security can be supplanted by the Security Council, when the latter chooses to seize itself of the question.[5] The Security Council's power to usurp General Assembly consideration of peace and security matters is not as robust as the literal language of the U.N. *Charter* suggests.[6] It does, however, differentiate the U.N. system from the standard democratic model in which a legislative body exerts significant autonomy.

2) International Court of Justice

While the General Assembly resembles—although does not act—as a global legislature, the International Court of Justice (ICJ) approximates a world court, and indeed is sometimes called such. "The Court's role is to settle, in accordance with international law, legal disputes submitted to it by States and to give advisory opinions on legal questions referred to it by authorized United Nations organs and specialized agencies"[7]

While advisory decisions are just that—advisory—rulings in cases contested between states are technically binding on the states who were parties to the dispute. In practice, however, states often resist disputes being brought before the ICJ, contesting its limited jurisdiction vigorously and leaving the ICJ with a very sparse court docket.

Nevertheless, in performing its roles, the ICJ often pronounces on questions of international law in an influential manner, guiding subsequent interpretation of these principles.[8]

---

5   U.N. *Charter*, Art. 12 ("While the Security Council is exercising in respect of any dispute or situation the functions assigned to it in the present *Charter*, the General Assembly shall not make any recommendation with regard to that dispute or situation unless the Security Council so requests.")

6   The International Court of Justice has given a narrow read to the Security Council's power to usurp consideration of peace and security matters by the General Assembly. *Legal Consequences of the Construction of a Wall in the Occupied Palestinian Territory* (2004), ICJ General List No. 131, 43 I.L.M. 1009 at para. 27 ("the Court notes that there has been an increasing tendency over time for the General Assembly and the Security Council to deal in parallel with the same matter concerning the maintenance of international peace and security").

7   ICJ, online: www.icj-cij.org/court/index.php?p1=1.

8   It is true there is no formal concept of *stare decisis* in international law. Nevertheless, the ICJ (and other international jurists) often points to past decisions in justifying current positions.

B. SECURITY COUNCIL POWERS AND AUTHORITY

Despite the sometimes important role played by the ICJ and the General Assembly, their powers and influence are dwarfed by those of the U.N. Security Council in matters of peace and security. The section that follows outlines in details the Council's structure and the scope of its authority.

1) Structural Considerations

Two well-known structural qualities distinguish the Security Council from the General Assembly. First, the Security Council is not a plenary body in which every U.N. state sits. Instead, it has a rotating nonpermanent membership of ten members, selected by their peer states—following usually intense lobbying—to sit on the council for two years. Even more notably, the final five spots on the Security Council are occupied permanently by the United States, Russia, China, the United Kingdom and France (the so-called P5).[9]

Second, there is a decision-making power imbalance between the permanent and nonpermanent members. Pursuant to Article 27 of the U.N. *Charter*, each member of the council—whether permanent or nonpermanent—has one vote and decisions are taken by an affirmative vote of nine members. However, Article 27 generally requires the "concurring votes of the permanent members," at least in relation to nonprocedural matters. In practice, this famous "veto" power means that any nonprocedural resolution of the Security Council may only pass if it does not attract a negative vote from one or more of the P5.[10]

2) Chapter VII and Discretionary Power

a) Nature of Powers

The Security Council is further distinguished from other U.N. organs by the scope of its powers.

---

9   U.N. *Charter*, Art. 23.

10   The language of Art. 27 suggests that a Security Council decision is vetoed where either a P5 member votes against it, or otherwise fails to cast an affirmative vote (for example, abstains). Security Council practice, however, requires an affirmative exercise of the veto through a negative vote. Mere abstention does not constitute a veto. For a discussion (and acceptance) of this practice by the International Court of Justice, see *Legal Consequences for States of the Continued Presence of South Africa in Namibia (South West Africa) notwithstanding Security Council Resolution 276* Advisory Opinion (1970), [1971] I.C.J. Rep. 16 at 22.

By virtue of Chapter VII of the U.N. *Charter*, the U.N. Security Council is easily the most potent of the world's international organizations. First, under Article 39, the Council is empowered to decide the existence of "any threat to the peace, breach of the peace, or act of aggression"—all undefined expressions leaving substantial discretion in the hands of the Security Council.

Second, under Article 40 it may "call upon" states to comply with provisional measures designed to forestall the threat to international peace and security and, under Article 39, may make recommendations on the resolution of the issue.

Third, under Article 41, it may impose measures short of force such as economic or other sanctions.

Fourth, under Article 42, where the Security Council considers measures short of force would be inadequate, it may authorize use of military force. The virtual monopoly exercised by the Security Council in relation to the legal use of force is discussed in Chapters 5 and 6.

The Security Council expresses its views in different ways. It may recommend actions by states—"calling on" all or some states to take a particular action. Alternatively, it may "decide" that actions should be taken, a euphemism for a binding legal dictate.

A binding Security Council resolution issued under Chapter VII—and particularly Articles 41 and 42—is an extremely robust species of international law. In *Prosecutor v. Dusko Tadic*, the International Criminal Tribunal for the Former Yugoslavia (ICTY) noted that Chapter VII decisions are "mandatory vis-à-vis the other Member States, who are under an obligation to cooperate with the Organization."[11] Article 25 of the U.N. *Charter* specifies that "the Members of the United Nations agree to accept and carry out the decisions of the Security Council in accordance with the present *Charter*." Article 48 underscores this requirement: "The action required to carry out the decisions of the Security Council for the maintenance of international peace and security shall be taken by all the Members of the United Nations or by some of them, as the Security Council may determine."

These provisions should be read together with Article 103: "In the event of a conflict between the obligations of the Members of the United Nations under the present *Charter* and their obligations under

---

11   *Prosecutor v. Dusko Tadic*, Decision of the U.N. International Tribunal for the Prosecution of Persons Responsible for Serious Violations of International Humanitarian Law Committed in the Territory of Former Yugoslavia since 1991, Case No. IT-94-1-AR72, reprinted in (1996), 35 I.L.M. 32 at 43 [*Tadic*].

any other international agreement, their obligations under the present *Charter* shall prevail."[12]

b) Scope of Discretion

The Security Council's discretion to impose measures under Chapter VII may not be absolute. It is, however, substantial. In *Tadic*,[13] the ICTY commented on whether the Council had acted properly pursuant to Article 41 of the *Charter* in constituting the ICTY itself. The court acknowledged:

> The Security Council is ... subjected to certain constitutional limitations, however broad its powers under the constitution may be. Those powers cannot, in any case, go beyond the limits of the jurisdiction of the Organization at large, not to mention other specific limitations or those which may derive from the internal division of power within the Organization. In any case, neither the text nor the spirit of the *Charter* conceives of the Security Council as *legibus solutus* (unbound by law).[14]

Thus, in deciding whether a threat to peace and security exists under Article 39, the Security Council is not totally unfettered: "it has to remain, at the very least, within the limits of the Purposes and Principles of the *Charter*."[15] However, ultimately "it is the Security Council that makes the determination that there exists one of the situations justifying the use of the 'exceptional powers' of Chapter VII."[16]

The breadth of this discretion should not be underestimated. Since the end of the Cold War, circumstances viewed by the Security Council as constituting a threat to international peace and security have proliferated. Reviewing this pattern, one observer has written:

> Since 1992, a wide variety of situations has been classified as a "threat to the peace" by both the Security Council and the General Assem-

---

12   The significance of Arts. 25 and 103 was considered by the ICJ in an early phase of the *Aerial Incident over Lockerbie Case*. In that matter, the ICJ indicated that Members of the United Nations "are obliged to accept and carry out the decisions of the Security Council in accordance with Article 25 of the *Charter*; [and] in accordance with Article 103 of the *Charter*, the obligations of the Parties in that respect prevail over their obligations under any other international agreement." [1992] I.C.J. Rep. 3 at para. 39.

13   *Tadic*, above note 11.

14   *Ibid.* at 42.

15   *Ibid.* at para. 29.

16   *Ibid.*

bly. These include the proliferation and development of weapons of mass destruction (as well as their means of delivery), acts of international terrorism, the use of mercenaries, emergency situations, and the violent disintegration of states.[17]

Notably, it is also the Security Council that chooses the remedy to the threat it declares. Thus, as the ICTY observed in *Tadic*, "once the Security Council determines that a particular situation poses a threat to the peace or that there exists a breach of the peace or an act of aggression, it enjoys a wide margin of discretion in choosing the course of action,"[18] albeit one "limited to the measures provided for in Articles 41 and 42."[19] Article 41 in particular has a potentially vast ambit. For instance, the ICTY in *Tadic* held that Article 41 includes more than the sample actions included in the provision itself, extending to the creation of an international judicial body; that is, the ICTY itself.[20]

For these reasons, Security Council observers have been unprepared to pin down the precise scope of council's Chapter VII powers. Some authorities have concluded that the council is not limited by international law (other than the U.N. *Charter*) in tailoring its Chapter VII resolutions. Thus, "when acting under Chapter VII, the SC is not bound to respect international law apart from the *Charter* itself; in particular, it need not delve into lengthy discussions on the position of the parties under general international law."[21] Certainly, if the council were entirely to disregard humanitarian and human rights norms, it might arguably act contrary to the purposes of the United Nations, set out in Article 1 of the *Charter*. However, "it is up to the SC to strike the concrete balance between humanitarian and human rights concerns and the goal of maintaining peace."[22] At best, "humanitarian law and human rights norms, rather than establishing precise limits to Chapter VII powers, form guidelines in the exercise of those powers."[23]

---

17   Stefan Talmon, "The Security Council as World Legislature" (2005) 99 A.J.I.L. 175 at 180–81.

18   *Tadic*, above note 11 at para. 31.

19   *Ibid.* at para. 32.

20   *Ibid.* at para. 34 *et seq.*

21   Bruno Simma, ed., *The Charter of the United Nations: A Commentary* (New York: Oxford University Press, 2002) at 711.

22   *Ibid.*

23   *Ibid.* A possible exception to this conclusion relates to *jus cogens* principles: "Peremptory norms of international law have to a great extent been developed through the organs of the UN, and they must in principle be considered to be binding on the UN as well as on individual States." *Ibid.* See *ad hoc* Judge Lauterpacht, in his separate opinion in *Application of the Convention on the Prevention and Punishment of the Crime of Genocide (Bosnia & Herzegovina v. Yugoslavia*

The scope of Security Council powers is a particularly acute issue in relation to several of its recent terrorism and weapons of mass destruction–related resolutions, a matter discussed in Chapters 6, 7 and 8.

PART II: CANADIAN INSTITUTIONS

The balance of this chapter focuses on Canadian national security bodies. The institutional structure for domestic, Canadian national security law and practice is complex. The discussion that follows provides a brief overview of the constitutional context in which national security law arises. It then focuses particular attention on executive institutions with national security functions.

A. CONSTITUTIONAL CONTEXT FOR NATIONAL SECURITY LAW

The structure of national security law in Canada is governed, in the final analysis, by Canada's constitution. Notable constitutional considerations include the division of powers between federal and provincial levels of organization and the separation of powers among the legislative, executive and judicial branches of government.

1) Division of Powers between Federal and Provincial Levels

The division of powers between the federal and provincial governments is a matter governed by the *Constitution Act, 1867*.[24] The 1867 Act includes a list of powers to be exercised by the provincial legislatures and a list of powers to be exercised by the federal Parliament. At the provincial level, the most relevant provision of the 1867 Act is that giving the province jurisdiction over the "administration of justice in the province." While this language enables provinces to establish their own law enforcement agencies, the 1867 Act clearly assigns the bulk of national security responsibility to the federal level of government.

(*Serbia & Montenegro*)), 1993 I.C.J. 407 at 440, para. 100 *et seq.* (13 September 1993), Lauterpacht J., sep. op.

24   Formerly the *British North America Act* (U.K.), 30 & 31 Victoria, c. 3 [*Constitution Act, 1867*].

Specifically, the most material provisions of the 1867 Act for this book are the federal powers over defence,[25] the criminal law[26] and over "laws for the Peace, Order, and good Government of Canada, in relation to all Matters not coming within the Classes of Subjects by this Act assigned exclusively to the Legislatures of the Provinces."[27] The latter power has been interpreted by the Supreme Court of Canada as permitting Parliament to legislate in areas, for example, of national concern and in response to national emergencies.[28]

2) The Separation of Powers

a) Branches of Government

At least in theory, democratic government in Canada is conducted by several branches: the Crown, as represented by the governor general and his or her provincial equivalent, the lieutenant governor; the legislative body; the executive; and the courts.[29] The Crown and the executive are often categorized together, producing three branches: the executive, the legislature and the judiciary.

Each branch has its own function: "in broad terms, the role of the judiciary is … to interpret and apply the law; the role of the legislature is to decide upon and enunciate policy; the role of the executive is to administer and implement that policy."[30] This theoretical division of labour is a generalization, often tempered with exceptions. Nevertheless, the Supreme Court requires that each branch be cognizant of the mandate of the others: "It is fundamental to the working of government as a whole that all these parts play their proper role. It is equally fundamental that no one of them overstep its bounds, that each show proper deference for the legitimate sphere of activity of the other."[31]

---

25 *Ibid.*, s. 91(7).

26 *Ibid.*, s. 91(27).

27 *Ibid.*, s. 91 (chapeau).

28 See, for example, *Reference Re: Anti-Inflation Act (Canada)*, [1976] 2 S.C.R. 373; *R. v. Crown Zellerbach Canada Ltd.*, [1988] 1 S.C.R. 401.

29 *New Brunswick Broadcasting Co. v. Nova Scotia (Speaker of the House of Assembly)*, [1993] 1 S.C.R. 319 at 389 [*New Brunswick Broadcasting*]. For an amplification of the issues discussed in this part, see Craig Forcese & Aaron Freeman, *The Laws of Government: The Legal Foundations of Canadian Democracy* (Toronto: Irwin Law, 2005) [Forcese & Freeman, *The Laws of Government*].

30 *Fraser v. Canada (Public Service Staff Relations Board)*, [1985] 2 S.C.R. 455 at 469–70.

31 *New Brunswick Broadcasting*, above note 29 at 389.

b) The Political Executive

The executive includes all the agencies and departments of government—that is, the public administration of Canada. Ministers and the prime minister form the apex of the executive branch. Together, these officials comprise the ministry,[32] a body referred to in practice as the Cabinet. The ministry is sometimes also referred to as the "political executive."

In the Canadian system, the prime minister is the so-called first among equals, or *primus inter pares*, in the ministry and Cabinet system. By convention, the governor general appoints the prime minister. Indeed, this power has been described as a personal prerogative of the governor general: the governor general exercises discretion in an effort to appoint a prime minister who can form a government enjoying the support of Parliament, or more exactly the House of Commons.[33] The governor general will usually call upon the leader of the party with the greatest number of seats to form a government,[34] and serve as prime minister. This person is expected to be (or at least soon become) an elected member of Parliament.

Ministers are also appointed by the governor general, but by constitutional convention the latter acts at the direction of the prime minister, appointing as ministers persons named by the prime minister. As with prime ministers, the Canadian constitutional convention is that ministers will be or will soon become elected members of Parliament, although unelected senators hold ministerial posts from time to time.[35]

The collective body of ministers known as Cabinet is not itself expressly anticipated in law. Various departmental and other Acts of Parliament contemplate the existence of "ministers." They do not,

---

32   See Privy Council Office, The Canadian Ministry in Order of Precedence, online: webinfo.parl.gc.ca/MembersOfParliament/MainCabinetCompleteList. aspx?TimePeriod=Current&Language=E.

33   Peter Hogg, *Constitutional Law of Canada*, 4th ed. looseleaf (Scarborough, ON: Thomson Carswell, 1997–2006) at 9-7. See also *Angus v. Canada* (1990), 72 D.L.R. (4th) 672 at 683 (F.C.A.). The governor general "retains reserve or personal powers, such as the choice of a prime minister." See also *Quebec (Attorney General) v. Blaikie*, [1981] 1 S.C.R. 312 at 320, discussing the provincial lieutenant governor and observing that this official "appoints members of the Executive Council and ministers . . . and these, according to constitutional principles of a customary nature referred to in the preamble of the *B.N.A. Act* [above note 24] ... must be or become members of the Legislature and are expected, individually and collectively, to enjoy the confidence of its elected branch."

34   *Reference re Amendment of the Constitution of Canada*, [1981] 1 S.C.R. 753 at 857, Dickson, Estey, & McIntyre JJ., dissenting (although not on this point).

35   A constitutional convention is, in essence, a political practice of sufficient regularity that has become constitutionally obligatory with the passage of time.

however, compel the existence of a community of ministers known as Cabinet. Nevertheless, these statutes often refer to something known as the governor-in-council, and accord it substantial power, including in the national security area. The federal *Interpretation Act* defines this governor-in-council as "the Governor General of Canada acting by and with the advice of, or by and with the advice and consent of, or in conjunction with the Queen's Privy Council for Canada."[36] This "Queen's Privy Council for Canada" is created by the *Constitution Act, 1867*. Its task is to "aid and advise in the Government of Canada."[37]

In modern Canada, the Privy Council is not the same thing as Cabinet: all Cabinet ministers are privy councillors, but not all (or even a majority) of privy councillors are sitting Cabinet ministers. Nevertheless, Cabinet exercises the power of the governor-in-council by constitutional convention: only those privy councillors who are also presently in Cabinet are entitled to perform the role of the Privy Council,[38] and the governor general is expected to heed their advice. The latter, in other words, is reduced to a near figurehead, and executive governance in Canada is conducted by Cabinet.

Cabinet itself may operate on a plenary or committee basis. At the time of this writing, for example, there was a Cabinet committee on "Foreign Affairs and National Security" chaired by the minister of foreign affairs and co-chaired by the minister of public safety and including, among others, the ministers of national defence and justice.

c) Parliament and Parliamentary Supremacy

The federal legislative branch comprises the House of Commons and the senate, known collectively as Parliament.[39] The separation between the executive branch — known colloquially as the "government" — and Parliament is the oldest, most-settled, but in practice most-disregarded relationship. In practice, the same people who control the executive branch usually control the legislative branch (at least in majority Parliaments) — namely, the Cabinet and particularly the prime minister. Recognizing this fact, the Supreme Court has noted that there is "a considerable degree of integration between the Legislature and

---

36 *Interpretation Act*, R.S.C. 1985, c. I-21, s. 35.

37 *Constitution Act, 1867*, above note 24, s. 11.

38 Andrew Heard, *Canadian Constitutional Conventions* (Toronto: Oxford University Press Canada, 1991) at 18.

39 Of course, legally, the "Parliament of Canada" includes not only the Commons and the Senate, but also the Queen (who directly, or through her representative the governor general, accords royal assent to bills at the last stage of the parliamentary law-making process). *Constitution Act, 1867*, above note 24, s. 17.

the Government. ... [I]t is the Government which, through its majority, does in practice control the operations of the elected branch of the Legislature on a day to day basis."[40] For this reason, the separation between the two branches is not rigid and, in adjudicating such matters, the "Court should not be blind to the reality of Canadian governance that, except in certain rare cases, the executive frequently and *de facto* controls the legislature."[41]

Nevertheless, the executive branch is legally *subordinate* to Parliament. The constitutional law of the United Kingdom (incorporated "in principle" into the Canadian Constitution by the preamble to the 1867 Act),[42] has been a history of struggle between Parliament and the Crown. The culmination of this conflict made Parliament supreme over the monarch.

This parliamentary supremacy means that Parliament is the arbiter of all power. Of course, in Canada, this parliamentary supremacy is tempered by other constraints in the Constitution, not least the *Canadian Charter of Rights and Freedoms*.[43] Outside of these constraints, however, Parliament is free to do as it pleases.

d) Limits of Executive Power

Parliamentary supremacy has implications for how the executive operates. Most fundamentally, parliamentary supremacy means that "there is a *hierarchical* relationship between the executive and the legislature, whereby the executive must execute and implement the policies which have been enacted by the legislature in statutory form."[44] For these reasons, official actions undertaken by the executive branch usually must flow from "statutory authority clearly granted and properly exercised."[45]

The executive, in other words, has very few self-standing, autonomous powers. Certain powers are, however, reserved for the executive in the *Constitution Act, 1867*—technically in the person of the Queen or the governor general, practically in the person of the prime minister or in Cabinet. These powers are inviolable, without constitutional

---

40   *Quebec (Attorney General) v. Blaikie*, above note 33 at 320.

41   *Wells v. Newfoundland*, [1999] 3 S.C.R. 199 at para. 54.

42   *Constitution Act, 1867*, above note 24, preamble (invoking "a Constitution similar in Principle to that of the United Kingdom").

43   Part I of the *Constitution Act, 1982*, being Schedule B to the *Canada Act 1982* (U.K.) 1982, c. 11.

44   *Reference re Remuneration of Judges of the Provincial Court of Prince Edward Island*, [1997] 3 S.C.R. 3 at para. 139 [emphasis added] [*Remuneration of Judges*].

45   *Babcock v. Canada (Attorney General)*, [2002] 3 S.C.R. 3 at para. 20.

amendment. As well, Cabinet and the prime minister exercise other powers by unwritten constitutional convention, discussed occasionally later in this chapter.

Other than these very limited powers, parliamentary supremacy means the executive is almost always beholden to Parliament for its legal authority, usually in the form of parliamentary delegation of power in a statute. Most of the executive powers described in this book, for instance, are authorized by parliamentary statute.

Other powers may exist by virtue of the executive's historic "royal prerogative." The prerogative — important in the discussion on the deployment of the military in Chapter 5 — is the residue of discretionary or arbitrary authority possessed by the Crown.[46] It is described, rather obtusely, as "the pre-eminence the Sovereign enjoys over and above all other persons. It comprehends all the special dignities, liberties, privileges, powers and royalties allowed by common law to the Crown of England, and all parts of the Commonwealth."[47] More succinctly, the royal prerogative means "the powers and privileges accorded by the common law to the Crown."[48]

The royal prerogative is not, however, a catch-all for whatever it is that the executive branch wishes to do, and for which it lacks delegated power. In keeping with parliamentary supremacy, the royal prerogative may be supplanted by Parliament. Some courts have implied substantial staying power for the royal prerogative, concluding that it "cannot be limited except by clear and express statutory language."[49] Other courts have implied a less stringent test. As one lower court has observed, "where Parliament, or in the case of a province the legislature, has provided a regime of law to govern the affairs of citizens, the original prerogative of the Crown is excluded."[50] In these circumstances, "[t]he Crown may no longer act under the prerogative, but must act under

---

46   See *Krieger v. Law Society of Alberta*, [2002] 3 S.C.R. 372, at para. 31; *Reference re Effect of Exercise of Royal Prerogative of Mercy Upon Deportation Proceedings*, [1933] S.C.R. 269 at 272–73.

47   *Ontario v. Mar-Dive Corp.* (1996), 141 D.L.R. (4th) 577 at 588 (Ont. Ct. Gen. Div.) [*Mar-Dive*].

48   *Ross River Dena Council Band v. Canada*, [2002] 2 S.C.R. 816 at para. 54 [*Ross River Dena Council Band*], citing Hogg, *Constitutional Law*, above note 33 at 1-14.

49   *Mar-Dive*, above note 47 at 588. See also *Interpretation Act*, above note 36, s. 17 ("No enactment is binding on Her Majesty or affects Her Majesty or Her Majesty's rights or prerogatives in any manner, except as mentioned or referred to in the enactment").

50   *Scarborough (City) v. Ontario (Attorney-General)* (1997), 144 D.L.R. (4th) 130 at 135 (Ont. Ct. Gen. Div.).

and subject to the conditions imposed by the statute."[51] This threshold for abrogation was a live issue in the Supreme Court case of *Ross River Dena Council Band*, where a majority apparently resolved this debate: an Act of Parliament may curtail a prerogative power, both explicitly and by necessary implication.[52]

In practice, courts have held that "legislation has severely curtailed the scope of the Crown prerogative."[53] As the Privy Council Office — effectively, the prime minister's governmental department — has noted, "the history of parliamentary government has been a process of narrowing the exercise of the prerogative authority by subjecting it increasingly to the pre-eminence of the statutory authority, substituting the authority of the Crown in Parliament for the authority of the Crown alone."[54]

e) Review of Executive Actions

As the Supreme Court notes, "in a system of responsible government, once legislatures have made political decisions and embodied those decisions in law, it is the constitutional duty of the executive to implement those choices."[55] Moreover, because the executive's jurisdiction over these matters typically extends only as far as mandated by Parliament, it must be careful not to overstep that authorization.

If the executive branch were to act without regard to its empowering parliamentary statutes (or, in the limited circumstances where it persists, the royal prerogative), it would behave inconsistently with parliamentary supremacy and the rule of law, two unwritten principles of the Constitution. The "rule of law" requires that government officials exercise their powers in accordance with the law of land. As Justice Rand observed in the famous *Roncarelli v. Duplessis* case, for statutory duties imposed by legislatures to be supplanted "by action dictated by and according to the arbitrary likes, dislikes and irrelevant purposes of public officers acting beyond their duty, would signalize the beginning

---

51   *Black v. Canada (Prime Minister)* (2001), 54 O.R. (3d) 215 at para. 27 (C.A.) [*Black*].

52   *Ross River Dena Council Band*, above note 48 at para. 54. See also discussion in *Khadr v. Canada (Attorney General)*, 2006 FC 727 at para. 87 *et seq.*

53   *Black*, above note 51 at para. 27.

54   Privy Council Office, *Responsibility in the Constitution* (1993), online: www.pco-bcp.gc.ca/default.asp?Language=E&Page=InformationResources&Sub=Publicati ons&doc=constitution/toc_e.htm.

55   *Remuneration of Judges*, above note 44 at para. 139.

of disintegration of the rule of law as a fundamental postulate of our constitutional structure."[56]

All three branches of government play a role in ensuring executive compliance with the law.

i)   Executive Role

The ways in which the executive polices itself are manifold, ranging from simple employer–employee disciplinary mechanisms through to full-blown public inquiries.

a. Central Agencies

Central agencies lie at the heart of the Government of Canada. The Privy Council Office (PCO), for example, "serves as the Prime Minister's public service department and secretariat to the Cabinet and its committees."[57] Acting under the guidance of the Clerk of the Privy Council, the PCO plays a key role in coordinating government policy; indeed, it has sometimes been called the "nerve centre of government."[58]

For its part, Treasury Board is a legislatively prescribed Cabinet committee with a bureaucratic secretariat. Its chief responsibilities are review of government spending and overseeing government personnel management.[59] Thus, with the assistance of its secretariat, Treasury Board assesses departmental money requests, as well as setting public service salary and employment policies. Control of these two dimensions of government places Treasury Board and its secretariat in a position of substantial influence in the public administration of Canada.

b.   Independent Tribunals and Inquiries

Influence over the management of executive government is also exercised by independent tribunals and commissions. Examples include the Canadian Human Rights Commission and Tribunal. Persons staffing these bodies tend to enjoy a reasonably robust level of security of tenure, financial independence and administrative independence from the regular departments of government.

Occasionally, the government may also create *ad hoc* independent commissions to probe particular public policy issues or scandalous

---

56   [1959] S.C.R. 121 at 142.

57   Privy Council Office, *Decision-Making Processes and Central Agencies in Canada* (1998), online: www.pco-bcp.gc.ca/default.asp?Language=E&Page=Information Resources&Sub=Publications&doc=Decision/canada_e.htm.

58   Donald Savoie, *Governing from the Centre* (Toronto: University of Toronto Press, 1999) at 109.

59   *Financial Administration Act*, R.S.C. 1985 c. F-11, s. 7.

events, employing its powers to do so under the *Inquiries Act.*[60] Recent examples in the national security area include the 2004 O'Connor inquiry on "the actions of Canadian officials in relation to Maher Arar"[61] (Arar inquiry), the 2006 Major inquiry in the "bombing of Air India Flight 182"[62] (Air India inquiry), and the 2006 Iacobucci internal inquiry concerning the actions of "Canadian officials in relation to Abdullah Almalki, Ahmad Abou-Elmaati and Muayyed Nureddin."[63]

Of less recent vintage are: the 1995 inquiry into "certain matters pertaining to the deployment of Canadian Forces to Somalia,"[64] the 1977 McDonald royal commission into "certain activities of the Royal Canadian Mounted Police," and the 1969 MacKenzie royal commission on security. The impacts of several of these commissions are discussed from time to time in this book.

ii) Parliamentary Role

a. Parliamentarians

Parliament plays an important role in scrutinizing the bounds of executive power and ensuring that the executive remains onside its jurisdiction. Canada's Westminster democracy is built on the concept of "responsible government"; that is, the notion that the executive branch should be rendered accountable to an elected legislature by requiring that those who run the executive also sit in Parliament and answer to it. Responsible government includes both collective and individual ministerial responsibility to Parliament, and particularly to the Commons. The collective responsibility to the Commons is manifested in the constitutional convention that a ministry may persist only so long as it possesses the "confidence" of the House; that is, it is not defeated by a majority of voices in a confidence vote in the Commons.

The Commons control of the government's purse strings, meanwhile, provides a parliamentary check on Cabinet's agenda that is more nuanced than an outright confidence vote. Referring to one aspect of Parliament's financial role, the auditor general has noted that "the House of Commons has the right and the obligation to review and approve all spending from the public purse. It can hold the government to account because the government must retain the confidence of the

---

60   R.S.C. 1985, c. I-11.
61   Order-in-Council, P.C. 2004-0048 (5 February 2004).
62   Order-in-Council, P.C. 2006-0293 (1 May 2006).
63   Order-in-Council, P.C. 2006-1526 (11 December 2006).
64   Order-in-Council, P.C. 1995-0442 (20 March 1995).

House of Commons in order to continue to govern."[65] Parliament's control over the federal fisc comes in two flavours: control over the process of raising revenues (ways and means proceedings) and the power to authorize government expenditures (the business of supply).

For its part, individual ministerial responsibility means that "Ministers are responsible for providing answers to Parliament on questions regarding the government's policies, programs and activities, and for providing as much information as possible about the use of powers assigned to them or delegated by them to others."[66] Questions are posed (and occasionally answered) during Parliament's plenary sessions, including Question Period. More detailed questioning may occur in parliamentary committees. The working of these committees in the national security context is discussed in detail later in this chapter.

b.   Officers of Parliament

Three hundred and eight members of Parliament and 105 senators are in no position, however, to review the actions of the full, sprawling federal bureaucracy. With all the goodwill in the world, a handful of parliamentarians, charged with a busy legislative task, cannot possibly monitor the minutiae of government administration. A partial solution is to empower agents—or officers—of Parliament to do just that: probe the inner secrets of the public administration of Canada.

These officers are essentially executive arms of the legislative branch. A shared and unique attribute of officers is their obligation to report directly to Parliament, rather than to a minister. The roles of the auditor general, the information commissioner and the privacy commissioner are discussed at several points in this book, and are tied to their statutory mandate under the *Auditor General Act*,[67] the *Access to Information Act*[68] and the *Privacy Act*,[69] respectively.

iii) Judicial Role

An even more elemental review role is performed by the courts. The area of law known as "administrative law" is preoccupied with ensuring that the executive complies either with the grant of power dele-

---

65 Auditor General of Canada, *Parliamentary Committee Review of the Estimates Documents* (March 2003), online: www.oag-bvg.gc.ca/domino/other.nsf/html/2003est_e.html.

66 Privy Council Office, *Governing Responsibly: A Guide for Ministers and Ministers of State* (2004), online: www.bcp.gc.ca/default.asp?Language=E&Page=InformationResources&Sub=Publications&doc=guidemin/guidemin_toc_e.htm.

67 R.S.C. 1985, c. A-17.

68 R.S.C. 1985, c. A-1.

69 R.S.C. 1985, c. P-21.

gated by Parliament, or with another source of authority, usually the royal prerogative.

Applying this body of law, courts defend parliamentary supremacy, and the hierarchical relationship between the legislative and executive branches. They also preserve the rule of law: members of the executive branch must "justify their actions by pointing to specific legislative authority in the same way that any citizen would have to be prepared to show that his or her acts were lawful."[70]

At the federal level, the function of administrative judicial review is undertaken by the Federal Courts of Canada — comprising the Federal Court and the Federal Court of Appeal — and on appeal, the Supreme Court of Canada.

Courts also examine the constitutionality of executive action, measuring compliance with constitutional instruments such as the *Canadian Charter of Rights and Freedoms*. The Federal Courts perform this role, as do the provincial "superior courts"; that is, the courts established under section 96 of the *Constitution Act, 1867*. The latter usually examine federal actions in the course of performing their functions as the general courts of criminal law and/or in response to a pure constitutional challenge to government action.

B. FEDERAL AGENCIES AND BODIES

Accountable to the political executive, Parliament and ultimately to the electorate are the specific departments and agencies of the executive branch. The section that follows provides a more detailed assessment of the roles of specific executive agencies involved in national security. Many of these bodies play an operational role, performing the national security functions of the state. Others are more involved in *oversight* — that is, the command and control over operational decisions. Canada also has a number of special, independent executive bodies charged with *review* of national security agencies — that is, the scrutiny of past performance. These agencies are discussed in a separate section near the end of this chapter.

---

70 *National Corn Growers Association v. Canada (Import Tribunal)*, [1990] 2 S.C.R. 1324 at 1333, Dickson, Lamer, & Wilson JJ.

Readers are referred to the 2006 Policy Report of the Arar inquiry for a more detailed description of the government national security structure than is possible in a general work like this one.[71]

1) Privy Council Office

As noted above, PCO plays a key role in coordinating government policy. In the national security area, PCO houses the prime minister's National Security Advisor, the Security and Intelligence Secretariat and the International Assessment Staff.

As the title suggests, the National Security Advisor provides advice to the prime minister on national security matters. He or she also serves a coordinating role among Canadian security and intelligence agencies and acts as an important liaison with foreign governments on national security matters. Administratively, the National Security Advisor is the deputy minister for the Communications Security Establishment (CSE), discussed later in this chapter, and has responsibilities in relation to the Integrated Threat Assessment Centre.[72]

PCO's Security and Intelligence Secretariat also provides advice to the prime minister and Cabinet and plays a coordinating role with other agencies. The International Assessment Staff, meanwhile, assess developments in foreign countries affecting Canadian foreign policy, security and economic interests.[73]

2) Department of National Defence and the Canadian Forces

A state's military has a clearly elemental role in national security. The Department of National Defence (DND) is a federal government department presided over by the minister of national defence (MND) and established by the *National Defence Act*.[74] That same act creates the Canadian Forces (CF), Canada's armed forces.[75]

The DND includes some twenty thousand civilian employees charged with supporting the operations of these Canadian Forces. The

---

71 Commission of Inquiry into the Actions of Canadian Officials in Relation to Maher Arar, *A New Review Mechanism for the RCMP's National Security Activities* (2006), online: www.ararcommission.ca/eng/EnglishReportDec122006.pdf [Arar inquiry, Policy Report].

72 *Ibid.* at 196–97.

73 *Ibid.* at 197–98.

74 R.S.C. 1985, c. N-5, s. 3 [NDA].

75 *Ibid.*, s. 15.

latter comprises a regular and reserve force and potentially special forces.[76] At the time of this writing, the regular forces numbered sixty-two thousand, with twenty-five thousand serving in the reserves,[77] although the military was in the process of expanding its ranks.

a) Canadian Forces Structure

The CF's unit organization is undertaken at the instruction of the MND,[78] as formalized by the military chain of command in a Canadian Forces Organization Order. The latter instrument establishes the responsibilities of a unit's commanding officers and confirms the allocation of the unit within the CF's structure.[79]

"Units" are the basic building blocks of the Canadian Forces, and may consist of "a ship, battalion, regiment, company, squadron, station, base or any other appropriate designation in accordance with its role and the custom of the service, but in each case it is designated a unit by the authority responsible for its original organization."[80] Units may be grouped into "formations." Units and formations are assigned to "commands." Until recently, the CF comprised three "functional" commands corresponding to the classic division between navy, army and air force: Maritime Command, Land Forces Command and Air Command.[81] Layered onto this functional division was a geographic portioning of Canada, producing regional commands.

At the time of this writing, however, the CF was in the process of implementing a supplemental "operational" command structure. Thus, Canada Command, in place in early 2006, now provides "a unified and integrated chain of command at the national and regional levels that will have the immediate authority to deploy maritime, land and air assets in support of domestic operations."[82]

---

76   *Ibid.*, s. 16 (a "special force" may be established by the GIC in reaction to an emergency or pursuant a multilateral defence agreement).

77   National Defence, "National Defence and the Canadian Forces," online: www. forces.gc.ca/site/about/index_e.asp.

78   NDA, s. 17.

79   See discussion in National Defence, A-AE-219-001/AG-001 (CFP 219-1), Canadian Forces Organization and Establishment Policy and Procedures (2003) at 28 *et seq.*, online: www.vcds.forces.gc.ca/dgsp/pubs/rep-pub/dfppc/CFP219v12_e.doc.

80   *Ibid.* at 18.

81   *Ibid.* at 19.

82   National Defence, News Release, NR-05.052, "Canadian Forces Begin Transformation" (28 June 2005), online: www.forces.gc.ca/site/newsroom/view_news_e.asp?id=1691.

For its part, the Canadian Expeditionary Forces Command "is the unified command that is responsible for all … CF … international operations, with the exception of operations conducted solely by Special Operations Group (SOG) elements."[83] The latter is "composed of Joint Task Force 2 (JTF2), the Canadian Forces' special operations and counterterrorism unit; a special operations aviation capability centred on helicopters; a Joint Nuclear, Biological and Chemical Defence Company; and supporting land and maritime forces."[84] These units are now situated in Canadian Special Operations Forces Command.

Finally, the recent restructuring created a Canadian Operational Support Command, tasked with providing "combat support and combat service support functions such as logistics, military engineering, health services and military police."[85]

b) Security Intelligence Function

In performing its military role, the Canadian Forces/DND has developed a significant intelligence capacity. Defence Intelligence performs a number of functions, including collecting and analyzing intelligence in support of the CF's deployments. It also cooperates with other government agencies such as Canadian Security Intelligence Service (CSIS) and the Royal Canadian Mounted Police (RCMP) in the area of domestic intelligence.[86]

DND also hosts the Communications Security Establishment (CSE), Canada's national cryptologic and signals intelligence agency. The functions of CSE are described in detail in Chapter 11 and include acquiring and using "information from the global information infrastructure for the purpose of providing foreign intelligence, in accordance with Government of Canada intelligence priorities."[87]

---

83 National Defence, Backgrounder, BG 05.024, "Canadian Expeditionary Forces Command (CEFCOM)" (13 September 2005), online: www.forces.gc.ca/site/newsroom/view_news_e.asp?id=1751.

84 National Defence, Backgrounder, BG–05.025, "Special Operations Group (SOG)" (13 September 2005), online: www.forces.gc.ca/site/newsroom/view_news_e.asp?id=1752.

85 National Defence, CANOSCOM Webpage (2006), online: www.canoscom.forces.gc.ca/en/index_e.asp.

86 Arar inquiry, Policy Report, above note 71 at 148.

87 NDA, above note 74, s. 273.64.

c) Oversight

Command of the Canadian Forces is constitutionally vested in the governor general.[88] In practice, this power is exercised by the governor-in-council (GIC) — that is, the federal Cabinet acting under the leadership of the prime minister.[89] The key minister in that Cabinet is obviously the minister of national defence. This individual is statutorily charged with the "management and direction of the Canadian Forces and of all matters relating to national defence."[90]

Except as directed otherwise by the GIC, the government issues orders to the Canadian Forces by or through an officer in those Forces known as the Chief of Defence Staff (CDS). The latter is appointed by the GIC and controls and administers the Canadian Forces, under the direction of the MND.[91] The CDS lies, therefore, at the apex of the CF's command structure, and unit commanders are responsible to this officer for their activities.[92] He or she is also the senior military advisor to the MND, and ultimately to the political executive as a whole.

For its part, CSE is managed and controlled by the Chief of the CSE under "the direction of the Minister" of national defence. The latter "may issue written directions to the Chief respecting the carrying out of the Chief's duties and functions."[93] The Chief reports to the minister through the National Security Advisor on policy and operational matters, and through the deputy minister of national defence on financial and administrative issues.

3) Public Safety Canada and Its Specialized Agencies

a) Department

Public Safety Canada is a new department on the Canadian bureaucratic landscape. In a report issued in March 2004, the auditor general of Canada examined Canadian anti-terrorism spending since 9/11 through to

---

88 *Constitution Act, 1867*, above note 24, s. 15 (assigning the role of Commander in Chief to the Queen). By Letters Patent issued by George VI in 1947, C. Gaz. (1947) I.3104, vol. 81, the governor general is empowered "to exercise all powers and authorities lawfully belonging to Us in respect of Canada."

89 Library of Parliament, *International Deployment of Canadian Forces: Parliament's Role*, PRB 00-06E (18 May 2006) at 1, online: www.parl.gc.ca/information/library/PRBpubs/prb0006-e.htm.

90 NDA, above note 74, s. 4.

91 *Ibid.*, s. 18.

92 Above note 79 at 13.

93 NDA, above note 74, s. 273.62.

2003.[94] That study noted a lack of coordination and information sharing on public security issues between government departments as they then existed, with various security-related agencies reporting to an array of different ministers.

In December 2003, the Martin government responded to the diffuse quality of Canada's civilian security apparatus. At that time, the GIC created a new "Public Safety and Emergency Preparedness" portfolio by using the *Public Service Rearrangement and Transfer of Duties Act*[95] to peel the then Office of Critical Infrastructure Protection and Emergency Preparedness away from the Department of National Defence, and place it into the Department of the Solicitor General.[96] Likewise, it transferred supervision over the Canada Border Services Agency from the minister of citizenship and immigration to the solicitor general, now styled the minister of public safety,[97] and then transferred assorted other security and border organizations into the Canada Border Services Agency.[98]

Subsequently, the Department of Public Safety and Emergency Preparedness was formally created by statute in 2005, and as of February 2006 goes by the name Public Safety Canada. Under the *Department of Public Safety and Emergency Preparedness Act*, the "powers, duties and functions" of the minister of public safety "extend to and include all matters over which Parliament has jurisdiction—and that have not been assigned by law to another department, board or agency of the Government of Canada—relating to public safety and emergency preparedness."[99] Specifically, the minister is charged with exercising "leadership relating to public safety and emergency preparedness"[100] and coordinating the "activities of the entities for which the Minister is responsible, including the Royal Canadian Mounted Police, the Canadian Security Intelligence Service, the Canada Border Services Agency, the Canadian Firearms Centre, the Correctional Service of Canada and the National Parole Board."[101]

The breadth of the minister's responsibilities makes him or her the key player in terms of the civilian national security apparatus. In

---

94 Auditor General of Canada, "National Security in Canada: The 2001 Anti-Terrorism Initiative" (March 2004), online: www.oag-bvg.gc.ca/domino/reports. nsf/html/20040303ce.html/$file/20040303ce.pdf.

95 R.S.C. 1985, c. P-34.

96 Order-in-Council, P.C. 2003-2086 (12 December 2003).

97 Order-in-Council, P.C. 2003-2061 (12 December 2003).

98 See, for example, Order-in-Council, P.C. 2003-2063 to 2065 (12 December 2003).

99 S.C. 2005, c. 10, s. 4(1).

100 *Ibid.*, s. 4(2).

101 *Ibid.*, s. 5.

consultation with the portfolio agencies, the eight hundred employees in the core department support the minister in performing his or her functions, providing policy advice and delivering public safety and emergency preparedness–related programs and services. For instance, the department hosts the Government Operations Centre, an interdepartmental and interagency body tasked with coordinating responses to "anything — real or perceived, imminent or actual, natural disaster or terrorist activity — that threatens the safety and security of Canadians or the integrity of Canada's critical infrastructure."[102] The department is also involved in the issuance of security certificates under the *Charities Registration (Security Information) Act* and the *Immigration and Refugee Protection Act* and in the terrorist listing process under the *Criminal Code*.[103]

b)   Canadian Security Intelligence Service

The Canadian Security Intelligence Service (CSIS) is one of the key agencies lying within the minister of public safety's portfolio.

i)   Security Intelligence Function

The Service is constituted by the *Canadian Security Intelligence Service Act*[104] and is charged with several functions, the most important of which are listed in section 12: collecting, analyzing and retaining information and intelligence on "threats to the security of Canada."[105] CSIS is principally a security intelligence agency, in other words. It is tasked with intelligence gathering and analysis. It is not a law enforcement body, performing peace officer functions.

a.   Threat to the Security of Canada

The scope of CSIS's proper functions depends in large measure on the meaning of "threat to the security of Canada." It should also be noted that this threat definition has implications that extend beyond CSIS's activities. Several statutes cross-reference this definition for the purpose of describing the powers of other government bodies, including the RCMP under the *Security Offences Act*.

This expression "threat to the security of Canada" is carefully defined in section 2 of the statute, as set out in Table 3.1. Probably by necessity, each of the categories of threat found in section 2 is broad

---

102 Public Safety Canada, "Government Operations Centre," online: www.securite-publique.gc.ca/prg/em/goc/index-en.asp.
103 Arar inquiry, Policy Report, above note 71 at 201.
104 *Canadian Security Intelligence Service Act*, R.S.C. 1985, c. C-23, s. 3 [CSIS Act].
105 *Ibid.*, s. 12.

and vague, and thus capable of expansive definition. The formulation and inclusion of this definition was the subject of sustained discussion at the time Parliament enacted the CSIS Act in 1984. It has also drawn the attention of the review agency empowered to scrutinize CSIS activities, the Security Intelligence Review Committee (SIRC). The precise composition and mandate of SIRC are discussed later in this chapter. Suffice it to note here that in one of its early reports of CSIS, the SIRC questioned several aspects of the threat definition in the Act. These concerns are summarized in Table 3.1.

The section 2 definition includes a caveat that expressly excludes "lawful advocacy, protest or dissent, *unless carried on in conjunction* with any of the activities referred to" in the table.[106] The obvious intent of this exclusion is to limit CSIS's role in investigating actions viewed as legitimate in democracy. It is an effort, in other words, to distinguish dissent from subversion. It is not clear, however, whether this exemption has much significance. First, "lawful" advocacy, protest or dissent may be a narrow term, excluding, for example a demonstration undertaken without proper permits.

Second, the exemption only applies to the extent the lawful advocacy, protest or dissent activities are not "carried on in conjunction" with espionage, sabotage, foreign-influenced activities, political violence or terrorism or subversion. "Carried on in conjunction" is an ambiguous phrase. At some point, advocacy, protest or dissent could become so tied to security threats that it would amount to aiding, abetting or facilitating crimes associated with those security threats. Such advocacy, protest or dissent would, in other words, no longer be lawful, and would be excluded from the exemption anyway. To be read sensibly, therefore, the exemption for "lawful" advocacy, protest or dissent must reach activities that fall short of aiding, abetting or facilitating; that is, actions having more tenuous connections to the security threats. The expression "carried on in conjunction" may, therefore, exclude a broad swath of otherwise legitimate behaviour from the exemption, and thereby authorize CSIS investigations of these activities.

This approach to lawful actions somehow linked to *bona fide* threats may be necessary and desirable; insurrectional political movements should not be excluded from CSIS's mandate simply because elements of those bodies (also) engage in lawful protests. At the same time, investigations of behaviours deemed acceptable, and even essential, in a democracy raise obvious concerns.

---

106 CSIS Act, above note 104, s. 2 [emphasis added].

Table 3.1: Definition of "Threats to the Security of Canada"

Type of Threat	CSIS Act	Critique[1]	CSIS Interpretation [2]
Espionage and sabotage	(a) espionage or sabotage that is against Canada or is detrimental to the interests of Canada or activities directed toward or in support of such espionage or sabotage	*Detrimental to the Interests of Canada:* The phrase is "wholly subjective" as "no criteria are provided to offer any standard for determining what is 'detrimental.'" It should, therefore, be defined in the Act.	*Espionage:* "Activities conducted for the purpose of acquiring by unlawful or unauthorized means information or assets relating to sensitive political, economic, scientific or military matters, or for the purpose of their unauthorized communication to a foreign state or foreign political organization." *Sabotage:* "Activities conducted for the purpose of endangering the safety, security or defence of vital public or private property, such as installations, structures, equipment or systems."
Foreign-influenced activities	(b) foreign-influenced activities within or relating to Canada that are detrimental to the interests of Canada and are clandestine or deceptive or involve a threat to any person	*Foreign influenced:* The phrase "foreign influenced" is broad, covering "foreign interest groups, political organizations, individuals, associations and corporations," while the concept of "influenced" is ambiguous and should be replaced with "directed." *Within or Relating to Canada:* "There are no criteria set out in the *Act* to help determine how much any particular activity must 'relate' to Canada before CSIS can take jurisdiction, creating a requirement that may be too easily met."	"Activities detrimental to the interests of Canada, and which are directed, controlled, financed or otherwise significantly affected by a foreign state or organization, their agents or others working on their behalf."

Type of Threat	CSIS Act	Critique[1]	CSIS Interpretation [2]
Foreign-influenced activities (cont'd)		*Clandestine or Deceptive:* "The precise meaning of the term 'clandestine' is uncertain. It may connote an element of underhandedness or *male fides*, but some dictionary definitions would support an interpretation that merely 'secret' activities may be 'clandestine.' The term should be replaced with a word like 'surreptitious,' which more clearly connotes some element of underhanded behaviour." *Detrimental to the Interests of Canada:* The phrase is "wholly subjective" as "no criteria are provided to offer any standard for determining what is 'detrimental.'" It should, therefore, be defined in the *Act*. *Involve a Threat to Any Person:* The term "threat" should be modified by an adjective like "serious."	
Political violence and terrorism	(c) activities within or relating to Canada directed towards or in support of the threat or use of acts of serious violence against persons or property for the purpose of achieving a political, religious or ideological objective	*Political, Religious or Ideological Objectives:* The reference to "political, religious or ideological objective" was added to the CSIS Act by the 2001 *Anti-terrorism Act*.[3] As discussed in Chapter 7, the phrase "political, religious or ideological objective" when used in the context of the *Criminal Code*'s definition of "terrorist activity" was declared unconstitutional	"Threat or acts of serious violence may constitute attempts at compelling the Canadian government to respond in a certain way. Acts of serious violence cause grave bodily harm or death to persons, or serious damage to or the destruction of public or private property, and are contrary to Canadian law or would be if committed in Canada."

Type of Threat	CSIS Act	Critique[1]	CSIS Interpretation[2]
Political violence and terrorism (cont'd)	within Canada or a foreign state	by a lower court in 2006. In the wake of that decision, jurists speculated that the equivalent phrase in the CSIS Act might render information collected by CSIS constitutionally suspect, if employed in a subsequent criminal prosecution.[4] To minimize the prospect of ethnic profiling, the special senate committee on anti-terrorism law recommended its repeal in its 2007 report.[5]	
Subversion	(d) activities directed towards undermining by covert unlawful acts, or directed towards or intended ultimately to lead to the destruction or overthrow by violence of the constitutionally established system of government in Canada.	SIRC recommended repeal of this provision, urging that it presented the greatest risk in a democracy and that its core content—avoiding political violence—is already covered in the other paragraphs.	"Activities intended to undermine or overthrow Canada's constitutionally established system of government by violence. Subversive activities seek to interfere with or ultimately destroy the electoral, legislative, executive, administrative or judicial processes or institutions of Canada."

[1] Unless otherwise noted, critiques drawn from SIRC, *Annual Report 1988–1989* at 55 *et seq.*, online, www.sirc-csars.gc.ca/pdfs/88-89_e.pdf.

[2] Extracts cited in this column drawn from CSIS, Backgrounder #1: *CSIS Mandate* (2005), online: www.csis-scrs.gc.ca/en/newsroom/backgrounders/backgrounder01.asp.

[3] S.C. 2001, c. 41.

[4] See discussion in Ian MacLeod, "Ruling Threatens Law That Lets CSIS Probe Terrorism" *Ottawa Citizen* (27 November 2006).

[5] Special Senate Committee on the *Anti-terrorism Act, Fundamental Justice in Extraordinary Times* (February 2007) at 20, online: www.parl.gc.ca/39/1/parlbus/commbus/senate/Com-e/anti-e/rep-e/rep02feb07-e.htm [Senate, *Fundamental Justice in Extraordinary Times*].

CSIS is apparently alive to these issues, reporting that it "is especially sensitive in distinguishing lawful protest and advocacy from potentially subversive actions. Even when an investigation is warranted, it is carried out with careful regard for the civil rights of those whose actions are being investigated."[107]

b.   Limiters in Section 12

CSIS's security intelligence function is also limited by certain criteria imposed by section 12 of the Act. It may collect information only to the extent "that it is strictly necessary," and it must have "reasonable grounds" to suspect the threat to the security of Canada.

These considerations are amplified by several ministerial directions. As described by CSIS's inspector general in 1996, "CSIS is expected to employ an objective standard, namely demonstrable grounds for suspicion and to ensure that it documents its grounds." Further, that documentation must indicate that the investigation has been focused to a scope "strictly necessary" and that "techniques of investigation that penetrate areas of privacy [were] used only when justified by the severity and imminence of the threat to national security." Further, "where the proposed targeting and investigation may involve activities relating to lawful advocacy, protest or dissent, or sensitive institutions," CSIS documentation must include "indications that these interests have been appropriately considered and protected."[108]

c.   CSIS Security Intelligence Cycle

CSIS describes a five-phase "security intelligence cycle" that governs its security intelligence operations.[109] First, in designing its own policy guidelines covering investigative techniques and intelligence priorities, CSIS responds to policy direction from the government, communicated by the minister of public safety. CSIS currently has six security intelligence priorities: terrorism; proliferation of weapons of mass destruction; espionage and foreign interference; transnational criminal activity; information security threats; and, security screening.[110]

Second, CSIS plans its investigations, striving to strike a balance between intrusiveness and respect for rights and freedoms. Third, CSIS investigators employ assorted methods to collect relevant information

---

107 CSIS, Backgrounder #1, above, Table 3.1, note [2].

108 CSIS Inspector General, 1996 Certificate Made Public (June 1998) Pursuant to a Request under Canada's *Access to Information Act*, online: ww2.ps-sp.gc.ca/publications/igcsis/1996_e.asp.

109 CSIS, *Security Intelligence Cycle* (2006), online: www.csis-scrs.gc.ca/en/about_us/cycle.asp.

110 CSIS, *Priorities* (2005), online: www.csis-scrs.gc.ca/en/priorities/priorities.asp.

on individuals or groups suspected of posing a threat to the security of Canada. Information sources include "open sources" — that is, data in the public domain — as well as more private sources — such as informants and communication intercepts. Fourth, CSIS investigators assess the quality of information obtained via the investigation, a review process repeated by CSIS analysts at CSIS headquarters. The information is then combined with other sources to provide intelligence reports and threat assessments, tailored to the needs of specific government departments who consume CSIS intelligence products. Fifth, these analyses are disseminated to government and law enforcement agencies, including the RCMP.

ii) Foreign Intelligence

CSIS's section 12 security intelligence function is not geographically limited. It may and does operate abroad in performing this function. Indeed, CSIS "now has more people deployed abroad on a full-time basis than ever before, as well as more people operating from offices in Canada but assigned overseas on a part-time basis for a particular case or investigation."[111]

However, unlike some allied agencies, CSIS is not principally concerned with extracting foreign intelligence; that is, intelligence relating to something *other* than threats to the security of Canada. The CSIS Act is quite careful on this point. Certainly, CSIS is empowered under the Act to "assist the Minister of National Defence or the Minister of Foreign Affairs, within Canada, in the collection of information or intelligence relating to the capabilities, intentions or activities of" foreign states and persons, "in relation to the defence of Canada or the conduct of the international affairs of Canada." In practice, this means collection of "non-threat related intelligence" relating, for example, "to Canada's international competitiveness."[112] The Act, however, carefully circumscribes CSIS's role: CSIS's foreign intelligence role must be performed "within Canada."[113]

The practical significance of this geographic constraint is unclear. In the past, CSIS's inspector general has expressed concern that the geographic limiter on CSIS's foreign intelligence role may be impossible to

---

111 Arar inquiry, Policy Report, above note 71 at 140 (summarizing Jim Judd, CSIS Director General).

112 Talking Points for W.P.D. Elcock, Director of the Canadian Security Intelligence Service at the Canadian Centre for Intelligence and Security Studies Carleton University (2002), online: www.csis-scrs.gc.ca/en/newsroom/speeches/speech06122002.asp.

113 CSIS Act, above note 104, s. 16.

enforce in practice. In the course of performing a *bona fide* security intelligence function outside of Canada, CSIS presumably comes across incidental foreign intelligence, which it then shares within government.[114]

Nevertheless, the official geographic constraint on CSIS foreign intelligence functions has fuelled discussion of whether Canada should create a new foreign intelligence service capable of working everywhere.[115] This proposal attracted the support of at least the Conservative Party[116] and was raised again by the minister of public safety in 2006.[117] By the time of this writing, the Conservative government had backed away from its original proposal and suggested that it would modify the CSIS Act to expand the Service's foreign intelligence role.[118]

The value-added of an overseas foreign intelligence service or function is, however, questionable. Since CSIS is already tasked with a geographically unbounded security intelligence mandate, a pure foreign intelligence agency would presumably collect other information; most likely that supporting Canadian economic or political (as opposed to security) interests. Since the Department of Foreign Affairs and International Trade probably already collects at least some of this information through its network of diplomats and public source information (see below) and the CSE intercepts foreign signals communication, the gap filled by a new foreign intelligence service or function would presumably be that of covert intelligence gathering; that is, spying by human assets.[119] In performing this new role, the new agency (or expanded CSIS) might be steered to spy on Canada's economic competitors, who tend also to be Canada's allies and on whom we often depend

114 CSIS Inspector General, *2004 Certificate*, online: ww2.ps-sp.gc.ca/publications/igcsis/2004_e.asp. See also CSIS Act, *ibid.*, s. 19 (permitting information sharing of incidentally collected information). See discussion in Chapter 12.

115 For an assessment of Canada's foreign intelligence needs, and the merits of a specialized agency, see Jerome Mellon, *Missing Agency*, 2d ed. (2003), online: http://cv.jmellon.com/cfis_2.pdf.

116 Conservative Party Election Platform, *Standing Up for Canada* (2006) at 26 (pledging to "create a Canadian Foreign Intelligence Agency to effectively gather intelligence overseas, independently counter threats before they reach Canada, and increase allied intelligence operations"), online: www.conservative.ca/media/20060113-Platform.pdf.

117 Jim Bronskill, "More Foreign Spy Muscle Needed to Combat Islamic Extremists, Day Says" *Canadian Press* (10 May 2006).

118 Tonda MacCharles, "Anti-Terror Measures Would Restore 'Preventive Arrests' and Help CSIS Spies Overseas" *Toronto Star* (16 May 2007).

119 See discussion in Jim Judd, director of CSIS, Standing Senate Committee on National Security and Defence, *Evidence* (30 April 2007).

for crucial security intelligence.[120] Spying on these allies, if revealed, might jeopardize these close relationships in a manner that runs counter to Canada's security interests.

iii) Security Clearance Function

CSIS has several other functions, in addition to its core section 12 security intelligence role and its more incidental foreign intelligence task. Not least, it serves as the government's security auditor, performing security assessments for government agencies and in relation to government personnel.[121] The Service also provides advice to ministers on security and criminal matters related to ministerial duties under either the *Citizenship Act* or the *Immigration and Refugee Protection Act*.[122] In performing these functions, CSIS conducts whatever investigations are necessary to meet its mandate.[123] These functions are discussed in detail in Chapter 12.

iv) Integrated Threat Assessment Centre

Finally, CSIS hosts the Integrated Threat Assessment Centre (ITAC), a body created in 2004. ITAC's primary function "is to produce comprehensive threat assessments, which are distributed within the intelligence community and to relevant first-line responders, such as law enforcement, on a timely basis."[124] It is staffed with personnel from assorted government security-related agencies.

v) Oversight

CSIS is headed by a director, charged with the "control and management of the Service" under the direction of the minister of public safety.[125] The latter is specifically empowered to "issue to the Director written directions with respect to the Service."[126] The director, meanwhile, is obliged to consult the deputy minister of public safety on "the general operational policies of the Service" and on any other matter that the minister directs.[127]

---

120 See discussion in Andrew Mayeda, "Ottawa May Still Boost Canada's Foreign Intelligence" *National Post* (1 May 2007).
121 CSIS Act, above note 104, s. 13.
122 *Ibid.*, s. 14.
123 *Ibid.*, s. 15.
124 CSIS, Backgrounder No. 13: The Integrated Threat Assessment Centre (ITAC) (July 2006), online: www.csis-scrs.gc.ca/en/newsroom/backgrounders/backgrounder13.asp.
125 CSIS Act, above note 104, s. 6(1).
126 *Ibid.*, s. 6(2).
127 *Ibid.*, s. 7.

These and other provisions in the Act create a more aggressive level of political oversight than exists for the RCMP, discussed below. Indeed, oversight extends into CSIS investigations. A CSIS warrant application can only be made (or renewed) before a Federal Court with ministerial authorization.[128]

CSIS is also subject to several layers of review by specialized review agencies. These entities are discussed later in this chapter.

c)   The Royal Canadian Mounted Police

A second key agency within the public safety minister's portfolio is the Royal Canadian Mounted Police. Constituted by the *Royal Canadian Mounted Police Act*,[129] the RCMP is Canada's national police force and is charged with enforcing most federal laws nationwide. Thus, the RCMP performs policing functions in relation to drugs and organized crime, financial crimes and border integrity. The *Criminal Code* is enforced by provincial and municipal police forces where these exist, and otherwise by the RCMP, usually under provincial or municipal contract arrangements. In practice, *Criminal Code* enforcement falls to the RCMP in the territories, Nunavut, all the provinces (except Ontario and Quebec) and 197 municipalities.[130]

i)   *National Security Function*

While primarily a law enforcement body, the RCMP has historically also played an important national security function.

Most obviously, the RCMP performs a protective policing role, providing security for federal political leaders, judges and internationally protected persons, such as diplomats, and acting as aircraft protective officers on select flights.[131] The RCMP inherited both the protective function and a broader national security role from the Dominion Police in 1920.[132]

By the Second World War, the RCMP was also performing intelligence functions, mostly directed at communist and fascist elements in Canada. In the postwar period, the emphasis shifted to Soviet espionage

---

128 *Ibid.*, ss. 21 & 22.
129 *Royal Canadian Mounted Police Act*, R.S.C. 1985, c. R-10, s. 3 [RCMP Act].
130 RCMP, *Organization of the RCMP*, online: www.rcmp-grc.gc.ca/about/organi_ e.htm.
131 RCMP, *Protective Policing*, online: www.rcmp-grc.gc.ca/prot_ops/index_e.htm.
132 Except as otherwise noted, this brief history summarizes Commission of Inquiry into the Actions of Canadian Officials in Relation to Maher Arar (Arar Inquiry), *The RCMP and National Security: Background Paper* (2004) at 5 *et seq.*, online: www.ararcommission.ca/eng/RCMP%20and%20National%20Security.pdf.

and counterintelligence efforts, government personnel security screening and countersupervision activities, including an eventual focus on Quebec separatist groups and supporters, antiwar groups and terrorists.

Controversy over the RCMP's activities in these areas sparked two separate royal commissions—the Royal Commission on Security (the Mackenzie Commission) in 1966 and the McDonald Commission in 1977. Both bodies proposed the establishment of a separate civilian security intelligence agency, noting the incompatibility of security intelligence with traditional policing.[133] Though slow in the making, the ultimate product of these deliberations was the Canadian Security Intelligence Service, discussed above, tasked with performing Canada's security intelligence functions.

The enactment of the CSIS Act in 1984 did not, however, eliminate entirely the RCMP's national security functions. For one thing, its protective policing role continued. For another, at the same time CSIS was created, Parliament enacted the *Security Offences Act*.[134]

a.   *Security Offences Act*

The *Security Offences Act* federalizes the prosecution and police role in relation to crimes implicating national security—more concretely, those offences against internationally protected persons, defined in the *Criminal Code*, and those that fall within the ambit of a "threat to the security of Canada," as that term is used in the CSIS Act.[135] Put another way, the RCMP is the law enforcement agency charged with investigating criminal acts of sufficient gravity to be a national security threat. More than that, the Act charges the RCMP with "apprehension of the commission" of these offences, tasking the police force with a preemptive function and not simply a reactive role.

The range of criminal offences that are potentially encompassed by "threats to the security of Canada" is unbounded. Any criminal act, undertaken in the right circumstances, might fall within the definition of "threat to security of Canada." There are, however, a number of criminal offences that are almost certainly captured by this concept. On top of the terrorist offences discussed in Chapter 7 and the information and espionage offences described in Chapter 10, this list of crimes would likely also include many of the actions listed as "public

---

133   Mackenzie Commission, *Report of the Royal Commission on Security* (Ottawa: Queen's Printer, 1969); McDonald Commission, Report of the Commission of Inquiry Concerning Certain Activities of the Royal Canadian Mounted Police, *Freedom and Security under the Law: Second Report* (Ottawa: The Commission, 1981) [McDonald Commission].

134   R.S.C. 1985, c. S-7.

135   *Ibid.*, s. 6.

order offences" in the *Criminal Code*, sometimes also called "crimes against the state."[136]

The quintessential public order offence is treason. In Canada, treason comes in two flavours: "high treason" and "treason." The treason offence is bolstered by a loosely related series of other *Criminal Code* crimes, some of which employ antiquated concepts and most of which involve elements of disloyalty and political violence, and by the *Foreign Enlistment Act* (Canada's neutrality law).[137] The *Security of Information Act* includes its own crime of political violence; namely, foreign-influenced acts or threats of violence. These offences are summarized in broad terms in Table 3.2.[138]

Table 3.2: Key Public Order Offences

Offence	Criminalized Acts
High treason[1]	While in Canada (or in the case of a Canadian citizen, while in or outside Canada): • seriously harms, imprisons or restrains the monarch; • levies or prepares to levy war on Canada; or • assists an enemy at war with Canada or an armed force against whom Canadian Forces are engaged in hostilities.
Treason[2]	While in Canada (or in the case of a Canadian citizen, while in or outside Canada): • uses force or violence for the purpose of overthrowing the government; • discloses without authorization to a foreign agent military or scientific evidence that may be used for a purpose prejudicial to the safety or defence of Canada; • conspires to commit high treason or to use violence to overthrow the government; • forms an intention to commit high treason and completes an overt act; or • conspires to disclose military or scientific evidence or forms an intention to do so and completes an overt act.

---

136 Canada, Law Reform Commission, *Crimes Against the State* (Ottawa: The Commission, 1986).

137 R.S.C. 1985, c. F-28.

138 Note that the offences themselves include intent and sometimes savings provisions not reproduced in the table.

Offence	Criminalized Acts
Foreign-influenced acts or threats of violence[3]	At the direction of, for the benefit of or in association with a foreign entity, induces or attempts to induce, by threat, accusation, menace or violence, any person to do anything or to cause anything to be done • that is for the purpose of increasing the capacity of a foreign entity to harm Canadian interests; or • that is reasonably likely to harm Canadian interests.[4]
Assisting an enemy alien to leave Canada or omitting to prevent treason[5]	Assists a subject of a state that is at war with Canada, or a state against whose forces Canadian Forces are engaged in hostilities to leave Canada without the consent of the Crown, unless the accused proves he or she did not intend to assist; or Knowing that a person is about to commit high treason or treason does not, with all reasonable dispatch, inform a justice of the peace or other peace officer.
Sabotage[6]	Impairs the efficiency or impedes the working of any vessel, vehicle, aircraft, machinery, apparatus or other thing or causes property to be lost, damaged or destroyed for a purpose prejudicial to: • the safety, security or defence of Canada; or • the safety or security of the naval, army or air forces of any state other than Canada that are lawfully present in Canada.
Inciting mutiny[7]	Attempts, for a traitorous or mutinous purpose, to seduce a member of the Canadian Forces from his duty and allegiance to Her Majesty; or Attempts to incite or to induce a member of the Canadian Forces to commit a traitorous or mutinous act.
Assisting deserter[8]	Aids, assists, harbours or conceals a person who is a deserter or absentee without leave from the Canadian Forces.
Offences in relation to military forces[9]	Interferes with, impairs or influences the loyalty or discipline of a member of a force; Publishes, edits, issues, circulates or distributes a writing that advises, counsels or urges insubordination, disloyalty, mutiny or refusal of duty by a member of a force; or Advises, counsels, urges or in any manner causes insubordination, disloyalty, mutiny or refusal of duty by a member of a force.
Foreign enlistment[10]	In the case of a Canadian national, within or outside Canada enlists (or boards a conveyance to leave Canada in order to enlist) in the armed forces of any foreign state at war with any friendly foreign state; In the case of anyone within Canada, induces any such enlistment or attempt to leave Canada to enlist; Within Canada, recruits any person to enlist in the armed forces of another state;

Offence	Criminalized Acts
Foreign enlistment (cont'd)	Within Canada, fits out any military expedition against a friendly foreign state or arms or equips a ship for the armed forces of a foreign state at war with a friendly foreign state.
Sedition[11]	Speaks seditious words, publishes a seditious libel, or is a party to a seditious conspiracy;
	Seditious intention—required for each of these acts—exists, *inter alia*, where a person (a) teaches or advocates, or (b) publishes or circulates any writing that advocates, the use, without the authority of law, of force as a means of accomplishing a governmental change within Canada.
Alarming Her Majesty or breaking the public peace[12]	In the presence of the monarch: • does an act with the intent of alarming the monarch or breaking the public peace; or • does an act that is intended or likely to cause bodily harm to the monarch.
Intimidating Parliament or a legislature[13]	An act of violence in order to intimidate Parliament or the legislature of a province.
Unlawful assembly[14]	Groups of three or more persons with a common purpose that act in such a manner as to cause persons in the neighbourhood of the assembly to fear, on reasonable grounds, that they: • will disturb the peace tumultuously; or • will by that assembly needlessly and without reasonable cause provoke other persons to disturb the peace tumultuously.
Riot[15]	An unlawful assembly that has begun to disturb the peace tumultuously.

[1] *Criminal Code*, R.S.C. 1985, c. C-46, s. 46.
[2] *Ibid*.
[3] *Security of Information Act*, R.S.C. 1985, c. O-5, s. 20.
[4] Canadian interests are defined in the manner set out in Chapter 10, Table 10.4.
[5] *Criminal Code*, above note [1], s. 50.
[6] *Ibid.*, s. 52.
[7] *Ibid.*, s. 53.
[8] *Ibid.*, s. 54.
[9] *Ibid.*, s. 62.
[10] *Foreign Enlistment Act*, R.S.C. 1985, c. F-28.
[11] *Criminal Code*, above note [1], s. 59.
[12] *Ibid.*, s. 49.
[13] *Ibid.*, s. 51.
[14] *Ibid.*, s. 63.
[15] *Ibid.*, s. 64.

The Law Reform Commission of Canada noted in 1986 many deficiencies in Canada's crimes against the state provisions. Not least, many of these offences are duplicative and overlap.[139] Treason, for instance, covers espionage, but in a manner different than the *Security of Information Act*. Moreover, the language and concepts are antiquated and often uncertain, hinging on inherently ambiguous phrases (for example, "levies war," "alarm Her Majesty," or "intimidate Parliament") or terms of undefined breadth like "assists the enemy."

Prosecutions under these provisions are rare. It is conceivable that several of these offences would run afoul of the *Canadian Charter of Rights and Freedoms* if ever tested in court. Not least, they might be vulnerable to criticism under the doctrine of unconstitutional vagueness. This concept, springing from section 7 of the *Charter*, may render a statutory provision unconstitutional either "(1) because it fails to give those who might come within the ambit of the provision fair notice of the consequences of their conduct; or (2) because it fails to adequately limit law enforcement discretion."[140] Sedition offences, moreover, may be unsustainable under the free expression provisions found in section 2 the *Charter*. Likewise, the assistance to the enemy provision includes a reverse onus of proof of dubious validity under section 11(d) of the *Charter*.[141]

Nevertheless, these offences remain on the statute books, and thus provide justifications for RCMP investigations and investigative tactics, like search warrants.

b.   Intelligence-Led Policing

The RCMP's pre-emptive mandate under the *Security Offences Act* dovetails with new approaches to policing adopted in the 1990s, not least "intelligence-led" policing. As defined by the RCMP,

> intelligence-led policing involves the collection and analysis of information to produce an intelligence end product designed to inform police decision-making at both the tactical and strategic levels. It is a model of policing in which intelligence serves as a guide to operations, rather than the reverse. It is innovative and, by some standards, even radical, but it is predicated on the notion that a principal task of the police is to prevent and detect crime rather than simply to react to it.[142]

---

139 Canada, Law Reform Commission, *Crimes Against the State*, above note 136 at 26.

140 *Suresh v. Canada (Minister of Citizenship and Immigration)*, [2002] 1 S.C.R. 3 at para. 81.

141 For discussion, see Canada, Law Reform Commission, *Crimes Against the State*, above note 136 at 39.

142 RCMP, *Intelligence-Led Policing: A Definition*, online: www.rcmp-grc.gc.ca/crimint/intelligence_e.htm.

Intelligence-led policing is a now a widely invoked concept, and not confined to the national security field. Nevertheless, the emphasis on prevention in intelligence-led policing means that information collected by the police may be identical in nature and scope to security intelligence information sought by intelligence agencies.[143]

ii) Current National Security Structure

The RCMP's national security functions are coordinated through the RCMP's National Headquarters and implicate a number of different branches and divisions within the RCMP hierarchy.[144] National security investigations fall within the purview of the Deputy Commissioner, Operations, and more specifically within the National Security Criminal Investigations Directorate (NSCI) headed by an Assistant Commissioner NSCI. As of September 2006, the NSCI was composed of the National Security Criminal Operations Branch (NSCOB), National Security Criminal Operations Support Branch (NSCOSB), National Security Legislative Affairs Branch and National Security Intelligence Requirements and Strategic Integration Branch.

Each of these branches performs a number of roles. For instance, the NSCOB monitors, assesses and coordinates RCMP national security investigations and projects, supports field operations and counter-terrorism strategies and coordinates reporting on national security matters to RCMP senior management and government. Thus, it approves national security investigations undertaken by the INSET and NSIS units, described later.

NSCOSB, for its part, coordinates the collection of national security criminal intelligence and supports the RCMP protective function. It contains the Threat Assessment unit that manages a national threat assessment program, relating to the RCMP's protective responsibilities for diplomatic personnel and other sensitive persons or facilities.

Actual national security criminal investigations are conducted by National Security Investigations Sections (NSISs) and Integrated National Security Enforcement Teams (INSETs). NSISs are staffed entirely by RCMP members while INSETs include personnel from other police and nonpolice entities, including municipal and provincial police forces, CSIS, the Canada Border Services Agency, Citizenship and Immigration Canada and the Canada Revenue Agency.

---

143 See discussion in Arar inquiry, *The RCMP and National Security*, above note 132 at 27.

144 Unless otherwise noted, the description contained in this section summarizes the findings of the Arar inquiry, Policy Report, above note 71, Chapter IV, as updated by author via personal communication with the RCMP (March 2007).

The RCMP also participates in Integrated Border Enforcement Teams (IBETs). As their name suggests, IBETs focus on border security, among other things interdicting persons and organizations posing a threat to national security. IBETs are staffed by personnel from both Canadian and U.S. law enforcement agencies.

iii) Oversight

The Force is headed by a commissioner who, "under the direction of the Minister [of public safety], has the control and management of the Force."[145] In reality, however, the level of ministerial direction is constrained by the concept of police independence.

a. Police Independence

Police independence is a common law construct,[146] now with a constitutional imprimatur.[147] At core, it means that the police (in performing at least their criminal investigation role) are not agents of the Crown or under the direction of the political executive. This doctrine attempts to remove political influence from ordinary police decision making. In the Arar inquiry's words, "if the Government could order the police to investigate, or not to investigate, particular individuals, Canada would move towards becoming a police state in which the Government could use the police to hurt its enemies and protect its friends, rather than a free and democratic society that respects the rule of law."[148]

The precise reach of police independence is, however, contested. Commentators have repeatedly resisted the notion that the police are truly independent. The 1999 Patten inquiry into policing in Northern Ireland, for example, concluded that

> all public officials must be fully accountable to the institutions of that society for the due performance of their functions, and a chief of police cannot be an exception. No public official, including a chief of

---

145 RCMP Act, above note 129, s. 5.

146 See, most famously, *Ex Parte Blackburn*, [1968] 1 All E.R. 763 at 769 (Eng. C.A.) ("every constable in the land ... should be, and is, independent of the executive. ... [H]e is not the servant of anyone, save of the law itself. No Minister of the Crown can tell him that he must, or must not, keep observation on this place or that; or that he must, or must not, prosecute this man or that one. Nor can any police authority tell him so. The responsibility for law enforcement lies on him. He is answerable to the law and to the law alone").

147 *R. v. Campbell*, [1999] 1 S.C.R. 565 at para. 29 (in criminal investigations, "police are independent of the control of the executive government" and noting that this principle "underpins the rule of law," a constitutional concept).

148 Arar inquiry, Policy Report, above note 71 at 458.

police, can be said to be "independent." Indeed, given the extraordinary powers conferred on the police, it is essential that their exercise is subject to the closest and most effective scrutiny possible.[149]

While the need to minimize political influence on police decision-making is a real one, the better approach is to invoke police "responsibility": police may have autonomy in making operational decisions, but they are not immunized from subsequent inquiry or review into their behaviour.[150]

For their part, Canadian inquiries have emphasized the limited functional reach of any independence concept. The McDonald Commission, for example, concluded that the doctrine extended only so far as to preclude ministerial direction "with respect to the exercise by the RCMP of the powers of investigation, arrest and prosecution."[151] Moreover, even in these cases, the minister should be informed of operational matters raising important questions of public policy and should be able to apprise the RCMP commissioner of the government's views on the issue.[152]

The Hughes inquiry into the RCMP's actions during the 1997 APEC summit in Vancouver made similar observations. Commissioner Hughes agreed that when "the RCMP are performing law enforcement functions (investigation, arrest and prosecution) they are entirely independent of the federal government and answerable only to the law." However, while performing other functions, the RCMP is "accountable to the federal government through the Solicitor General of Canada [now the minister of public safety] or such other branch of government as Parliament may authorize," subject to the important caveat that an RCMP member "acts inappropriately if he or she submits to government direction that is contrary to law."[153]

These views attracted the support of the Arar inquiry in its 2006 policy report. That body concurred with the Patten inquiry's views on *ex post* review of police decision making and with the McDonald Com-

---

149 Independent Commission on Policing for Northern Ireland, *A New Beginning: Policing in Northern Ireland* (London: H.M.S.O., 1999) at para. 6.20.
150 *Ibid.* at para. 6.21.
151 McDonald Commission, above note 133 at 1013.
152 *Ibid.*
153 Commission Interim Report into the Complaints regarding the events that took place in connection with demonstrations during the Asia Pacific Economic Cooperation Conference in Vancouver, B.C., in November 1997 at the UBC Campus and at the UBC and Richmond detachments of the RCMP (2001) at 10.4, online: www.cpc-cpp.gc.ca/DefaultSite/Reppub/index_e.aspx?CategoryID=74.

mission's conclusions on the need for the minister to be apprised of sensitive investigations. The Arar inquiry also urged that the minister be empowered to provide broad policy guidance, preferably of a public nature.[154]

b.   Police Independence in National Security Investigations

Although some authorities have seen no reason to distinguish between types of police activities,[155] the commission conclusions cited above suggest strongly that police independence should be restricted to police criminal investigation functions, a distinction that limits its reach in the national security arena.

Police independence is acceptable in criminal investigations for one reason: that task is a reasonably transparent one, amenable to scrutiny in the courts either as a collateral issue in a criminal trial once charges are laid or in abuse of process or power proceedings. National security investigations—even if nominally directed at bringing criminal charges in order to comply with the RCMP's core policing mandate—are conducted more clandestinely and do not always or even often lead to prosecutions before courts.[156] For this reason, full-blooded police independence in the national security context might convert independence into a species of impunity, producing a police force unaccountable to anyone.

In fact, since 2001, the legislature and political executive has grafted modest new oversight requirements onto RCMP national security functions. For example, no "proceedings" in respect to terrorism offences under the *Criminal Code*[157] and no "prosecution" under the *Security of Information Act*[158] may be commenced without the consent of the federal attorney general. Crossing the threshold from plain investigation to court proceedings, in other words, requires political sign-off.

On the other hand, the regular police *investigation* that precedes the actual commencement of prosecutions is presumably not subject to any political blessing. At best, these investigations would be informed by special "ministerial directives" issued by the minister of public safety, pursuant to the RCMP Act and its reference to the commissioner acting "under the direction of the minister." No doubt conscious of the police

---

154   Arar inquiry, Policy Report, above note 71 at 463.
155   See, for example, then Prime Minister Pierre Trudeau urging police independence in both the criminal and national security area. Cited in Arar inquiry, *Police Independence from Governmental/Executive Direction*. Background Paper (2004) at 9, online: www.commissionarar.ca/eng/Police%20Independence.pdf.
156   Arar inquiry, Policy Report, above note 71 at 460.
157   *Criminal Code*, above, Table 3.2, note [1], s. 83.24.
158   *Security of Information Act*, above, Table 3.2, note 3, s. 24.

Table 3.3:   2003 Ministerial Directives on RCMP National Security Investigations

Ministerial Direction	Application	RCMP Obligation	Ministerial Role
National security responsibility and accountability	RCMP investigations under the *Security Offences Act* or related to terrorist offences or activities under the *Criminal Code* ("national security investigations")	Commissioner must ensure that operational policies are in place to guide members and that national security investigations be centrally coordinated at RCMP national headquarters.	• Minister is accountable to Parliament for the RCMP • Minister is to be advised or informed regarding high profile or potentially controversial national security investigations
National security–related arrangements and cooperation	Entry by the RCMP into arrangements with foreign security or intelligence organizations in order to perform national security investigation functions	• RCMP may enter into these arrangements and the commissioner is to manage them; • Several guidelines are imposed (some discussed in Chapter 12), including the requirement that the RCMP maintain records relating to these arrangements and their terms; • Commissioner should advise minister of any potentially controversial issues arising from an arrangement; • Commissioner must report annually to the minister on the status of these arrangements.	Minister is to approve in advance any arrangement and may impose conditions
National security investigations in sensitive sectors	National security investigations that relate to sensitive sectors of Canadian society, including academia, politics, religion, the media and trade unions.	• Investigations undertaken on university campuses must not interfere with the free flow and exchange of ideas associated with an academic milieu or adversely affect the rights or freedoms of persons associated with academic institutions; • Assistant commissioner, CID, must approve all RCMP investigations involving sensitive sectors	

independence concept, the three ministerial directives on national security investigations issued in 2003 are limited in scope. Their content is distilled in Table 3.3.

In sum, the level of oversight exercised by the political executive over the RCMP is relatively modest, certainly as compared to that applied to CSIS. Control of the RCMP's national security functions was a matter squarely before the Arar inquiry. In 2006, that commission effectively endorsed the present level of oversight, while recommending a substantial redesign in the *ex post* review of RCMP national security activities. Review of national security functions is discussed separately later in this chapter.

d) Canada Border Services Agency

The Canada Border Services Agency (CBSA) is of more recent vintage than the other key Public Safety Canada agencies. Formally established as a body corporate by the *Canada Border Services Agency Act*[159] in 2005, the CBSA is charged with providing "integrated border services that support national security and public safety priorities and facilitate the free flow of persons and goods."[160] It unifies in a single agency the customs function of the former Canada Customs and Revenue Agency, the intelligence, interdiction and enforcement tasks of Citizenship and Immigration Canada, and the border import inspection program of the Canadian Food Inspection Agency.[161]

The CBSA is Canada's frontier protection agency, in other words. For instance, "among the issues addressed by the CBSA are terrorism, illegal migration, illegal trade of weaponry, drugs and unsafe goods and foodstuffs, and the attempted introduction of contaminants and threats to public health."[162] It is also responsible for "preventing the admission into Canada of persons involved in war crimes or crimes against humanity, for assistance in combating money laundering, and for the detention and removal from Canada of inadmissible persons."[163]

In performing its functions, the CBSA administers provisions found in more than ninety statutes, regulations and international agreements.[164]

---

159 S.C. 2005, c. 38, s. 3 [CBSA Act].

160 *Ibid.*, s. 5.

161 See Robin MacKay, Law and Government Division, Library of Parliament, *Bill C-26: The Canada Border Services Agency* (1 December 2004), online: www.parl.gc.ca/legisinfo/index.asp?Language=E&query=4355&Session=13&List=ls.

162 *Ibid.*

163 *Ibid.*

164 CBSA, *About Us*, online: www.cbsa-asfc.gc.ca/agency-agence/menu-eng.html.

For instance, the CBSA shares responsibility with Citizenship and Immigration Canada in administering the *Immigration and Refugee Protection Act*, including in interdicting and removing persons judged inadmissible to Canada on national security grounds. Under various customs laws and the *Proceeds of Crime (Money Laundering) and Terrorist Financing Act*, CBSA has search and seizure powers and responsibility for enforcing export control laws. When acting pursuant to these laws, CBSA perform law enforcement functions and has peace officer powers.[165]

The CBSA is headed by a president who has the control and management of the agency under the direction of the minister of public safety.[166] The agency exercises its powers "subject to any direction given by the Minister."[167] However, the CBSA often acts as a law enforcement body, suggesting that, as with the RCMP, the level of ministerial oversight should be limited to policy and not operational matters to preserve police independence.

4) Other Federal Departments and Agencies

A large number of other federal departments and agencies play assorted roles in securing Canadian national security, broadly defined. Other bodies mentioned from time to time in this book are listed in Table 3.4.

Table 3.4:   Other Departments and Agencies

Agency	Key National Security Functions
Canada Revenue Agency	Performs functions under the *Charities Registration (Security Information) Act* related to de-registration of charities involved in the financing of terrorist activities.
Canadian Air Transport Security Authority	Mandated with "the effective and efficient screening of persons who access aircraft or restricted areas through screening points, the property in their possession or control and the belongings or baggage that they give to an air carrier for transport."[1]
Citizenship and Immigration Canada	With the assistance of CSIS and in cooperation with the CBSA, performs security screening of non-Canadians arriving in Canada and makes immigration admissibility determinations.[2]
	Conducts "pre-removal risk assessments" under the *Immigration and Refugee Protection Act* of, *inter alia*, persons deemed a security risk seeking protection from removal on grounds that deportation would put them at risk of serious harm.[3]

---

165 See, for example, *Immigration and Refugee Protection Act*, S.C. 2001, c. 27, ss. 4, 6, and 138 [IRPA].
166 CBSA Act, above note 159, s. 8.
167 *Ibid.*, s. 12.

Agency	Key National Security Functions
Financial Transactions and Reports Analysis Centre	Tasked with reviewing financial data disclosed to it by financial institutions, among other entities, for evidence of money laundering and terrorist financing.[4]
Foreign Affairs and International Trade Canada	Houses a foreign intelligence division—Foreign Intelligence Division (ISI)—which prepares intelligence assessments in order to protect Canadian citizens and government facilities in foreign countries, and to assist government decision making.
	Manages expulsion of diplomats on security grounds and responses to foreign terrorist activities involving Canadian citizens.[5]
	Plays the key role in the listing of terrorist entities under the *United Nations Suppression of Terrorism Regulations* and the *United Nations Al-Qaida and Taliban Regulations*.[6]
Public Health Agency of Canada	Performs key coordinating role in responding to public health threats, such as epidemic diseases.[7]
Transport Canada	In cooperation with other agencies, performs an intelligence role in relation to transportation security. Determines whether to accord persons security clearance at airports, ports and other transportation facilities.
	Implements Passenger Protect, a no-fly list.[8]

[1]   *Canadian Air Transport Security Authority Act*, S.C. 2002, c. 9, s. 6.
[2]   See discussion in Arar inquiry, Policy Report, above note 71 at 170.
[3]   IRPA, above note 168, s. 112 *et seq.*
[4]   *Proceeds of Crime (Money Laundering) and Terrorist Financing Act*, S.C. 2000, c. 17.
[5]   Arar inquiry, Policy Report, above note 71 at 194.
[6]   See Chapter 7.
[7]   See Chapter 9.
[8]   Arar inquiry, Policy Report, above note 71 at 177 *et seq.*

C. NATIONAL SECURITY REVIEW

1) Basic Principles

a) Justifications for Review

Examining review mechanisms for national security agencies was the key preoccupation of the Arar inquiry's policy phase, and that commission's analysis represents the most comprehensive treatment of this issue in Canadian history.

i)   Defining "Review"

It its 2006 report, the Arar inquiry defined "review" as a means to as-sess "an organization's activities against standards like lawfulness and/or propriety," and to deliver a report of "that assessment, with recom-mendations, to those in government politically responsible for the organ-ization." Security agency actions "are usually examined after they have occurred." Further, "a review mechanism is not responsible for carrying out recommendations. It remains at arm's length from both the manage-ment of the organization being reviewed and from the government."[168]

ii)   Rationale for Review

The Arar report enunciated several key considerations favouring a ro-bust review mechanism for security and intelligence bodies. National security activities

> involve the most intrusive powers of the state: electronic surveillance; search, seizure and forfeiture of property; information collection and exchange with domestic and foreign security intelligence and law en-forcement agencies; and, potentially, the detention and prosecution of individuals. The use of such powers may adversely affect individ-ual rights and freedoms.[169]

Unlike regular criminal investigations, however, national security matters are more deeply surreptitious and secret. The writ of Canada's information access laws stops short of national security matters.[170] Those who have been investigated may be eternally oblivious to this fact, and in no position to complain about misconduct. Indeed, if no charge is laid and no decision is made to commence a prosecution, none of the investigation undertaken by the authorities will ever be tested before an impartial decision maker.

Even where courts are implicated, that review may be attenuated, curtailed by special secrecy or other rules that constrain the full ex-pression of the adversarial system on which Canadian justice is predi-cated.[171] Parliament, meanwhile, has a traditionally limited role in security and intelligence review, a point explored more fully below.

For all these reasons and more, the national security structure lacks many of the checks and balances deemed essential in other aspects of Canadian political and legal life. Absent these constraints, the proper functioning of national security agencies depends heavily on the integ-

---

168 Arar inquiry, Policy Report, above note 71 at 456–57.
169 *Ibid.* at 425–26.
170 See Chapter 10.
171 *Ibid.*

rity of those who populate it. There is no reason to doubt that integrity on an individual level. Every bureaucracy suffers, however, from its own shortcomings, some serious. A bureaucracy immune to external scrutiny may find it difficult to resist the temptation to stretch uncertain boundaries. It may also stray into patterns, policies or group-think impairing its effectiveness.

These considerations all counsel effective review mechanisms—audits and complaint systems able to measure agency compliance with legal or other standards and query problematic behaviour. National security law expert and government lawyer Stanley Cohen aptly captures the standard to be applied in national security review: trust, but verify.[172]

b)   Elements of Effective Review

Designing a review mechanism to accomplish these goals presents important challenges. Academic experts view effective review as resting on several design elements. First, review must be conducted by a body that is independent of the government and the agencies that it reviews. The body is not, in other words, both the watcher and the watched. Second, this body must be mandated to audit, review and assess the legitimacy of security intelligence actions. Third, it must have real powers to review and investigate at its discretion, compel and examine even secret information, respond (and propose resolutions) to public complaints, make public reports of its findings and conclusions and have in place a means to protect and secure confidential information.[173]

The Arar inquiry proposed its own, similar list of design criteria. First, review should ensure compliance with national and international law and "standards of propriety that are expected in Canadian society."[174] Second, it should enhance accountability of security and intelligence agencies to the government, and ultimately Parliament and the public. Third, by enhancing accountability, a review system should encourage public trust and public credibility of the agency. To achieve this goal, it should be independent and staffed in a transparent manner by qualified individuals. It should also disclose, as much as possible, details of its actions and findings.[175]

---

172 Stanley A. Cohen, *Privacy, Crime and Terror: Legal Rights and Security in a Time of Peril* (Markham, ON: LexisNexis Butterworths, 2005) at 561.
173 See Ottawa Principles on Anti-terrorism and Human Rights (2006), Principle 9.3, online: http://aix1.uottawa.ca/~cforcese/hrat.princples.pdf.
174 Arar inquiry, Policy Report, above note 71 at 502.
175 *Ibid.*

. At the time of this writing, Canada's security intelligence review mechanisms were variable in their structure and performance and uneven in their distribution. The Arar inquiry recommended reforms that would radically change this landscape. The current structure and the Arar inquiry reforms are discussed in the sections that follow.

2) Executive Branch Review

Specialized security intelligence review bodies exist within the government of Canada for both CSIS and the CSE. The more generic RCMP commission of public complaints plays a more incidental role in reviewing the national security functions of that police force. Other government agencies, meanwhile, are currently subject to no form of specialized national security review.

a) Review of CSIS

The *Canadian Security Intelligence Service Act* sets out a multitiered CSIS review mechanism.

i) Inspector General

First, the CSIS director is obliged to prepare reports on the operational activities of CSIS on an annual basis or more frequently on demand of the minister of public safety, and to submit these documents to the minister and the CSIS inspector general.[176] This latter official is appointed by the governor-in-council and is responsible to the deputy minister of public safety. Described as the minister's "eyes and ears" in the Service,[177] the inspector general monitors compliance by the Service with its operational policies and examines its operational activities.[178] To this end, the inspector general is given full access to the Service's information, except Cabinet confidences.[179]

The inspector general certifies whether the reports provided by the director are adequate and whether they reveal any action of the Service

---

176 CSIS Act, above note 104, s. 33.
177 Arar inquiry, Policy Report, above note 71 at 280.
178 CSIS Act, above note 104, s. 30.
179 *Ibid.*, s. 31. Cabinet confidences are, in essence, the papers supporting or describing Cabinet deliberations. For a definition of these papers, see *Canada Evidence Act*, R.S.C. 1985, c. C-5, s. 37; *Access to Information Act*, R.S.C. 1985, c. A-1, s. 69. For discussion, see Forcese & Freeman, *The Laws of Government*, above note 29 at 507 *et seq.*

that the inspector general views as an unauthorized, unreasonable or unnecessary exercise of its powers.[180]

ii)   Security Intelligence Review Committee

The minister transmits the inspector general's report and certificate to the Security Intelligence Review Committee (SIRC).[181] The members of SIRC are appointed by the governor-in-council (after consultation with the leaders of official parties in the Commons) for five-year terms, and sworn into the Queen's Privy Council for Canada.

Like the inspector general, SIRC has broad rights to CSIS information.[182] It may not see Cabinet confidences, but it does regularly see data supplied to CSIS by foreign governments and agencies.[183] Members of SIRC and its employees must comply with all security requirements under the CSIS Act and take an oath of secrecy.[184] They are also "persons permanently bound to secrecy" under the *Security of Information Act*, and are therefore subject to that statute's penalties for wrongful disclosure of sensitive information.[185]

a.   Auditing

SIRC is tasked with, among other things, reviewing the performance by the Service of its duties and functions, including reviewing reports of the director and certificates of the inspector general.[186] SIRC may order the inspector general to complete a review, or may conduct its own review, where deemed more appropriate than a review by CSIS or the inspector general, in order to ensure that the Service has not exercised any of its powers unreasonably or for unnecessary reasons.[187]

b.   Complaints

SIRC also has a complaints function. The most generic complaint concerns "any act or thing done by the Service."[188] Examples include allegations of unreasonable delays in CSIS security screening and of improper investigation of lawful activities.[189] Any person may make such a complaint concerning CSIS, directed first to the CSIS director. SIRC may

---

180 CSIS Act, above note 104, s. 33.
181 *Ibid.*
182 CSIS Act, above note 104, s. 39(2).
183 Arar inquiry, Policy Report, above note 71 at 278.
184 CSIS Act, above note 104, s. 37.
185 See Chapter 10.
186 CSIS Act, above note 104, s. 38.
187 *Ibid.*, s. 40.
188 *Ibid.*, s. 41.
189 Arar inquiry, Policy Report, above note 71 at 274.

investigate nonfrivolous, good faith complaints if the director fails to respond in a period of time the committee views as reasonable, or provides an inadequate response.[190] These investigations are held in private, subject to a right by the parties to make representations on at least an *ex parte* basis.[191] In balancing national security and fairness, SIRC may disclose summaries of evidence produced on an *ex parte* basis to the other parties.[192] In *ex parte* proceedings, a senior SIRC counsel "will cross-examine witnesses on [the complainant's] behalf and may provide [the complainant] with a summary of the information presented in [the complainant's] absence."[193] In performing its investigative functions, the committee has broad powers to subpoena persons and documents.[194]

The outcome of the SIRC investigation is conveyed to the minister and the CSIS director, along with SIRC's recommendations. SIRC recommendations are not binding on the government.[195] The complainant is also notified of the committee's finding,[196] subject to security requirements on disclosure of information.[197]

c.   Special and Annual Reports
SIRC also has more general reporting functions. It prepares special reports where requested by the minister or at any other time[198] and an annual report, tabled by the minister in Parliament,[199] which in practice contains summaries of the committee's investigations.

b)   Review of CSE
The *National Defence Act* establishes a commissioner of the Communications Security Establishment—a supernumerary or a retired judge of a superior court appointed by the governor-in-council.[200] Like SIRC, the persons employed in the office of the CSE commissioner are "per-

---

190 CSIS Act, above note 104, s. 41.
191 *Ibid.*, s. 48.
192 Rules of Procedure of the Security Intelligence Review Committee in Relation to its Function under Paragraph 38(C) of the *Canadian Security Intelligence Service Act* (1985), s. 48, online: www.sirc-csars.gc.ca/complaints_rules_e.html.
193 SIRC, "Complaints," online: www.sirc-csars.gc.ca/complaints_e.html.
194 CSIS Act, above note 104, s. 50. Several of SIRC's more specific review and complaint resolution roles are discussed in other chapters of this book.
195 *Thomson v. Canada (Deputy Minister of Agriculture)*, [1992] 1 S.C.R. 385.
196 CSIS Act, above note 104, s. 52.
197 *Ibid.*, s. 55.
198 *Ibid.*, s. 54.
199 *Ibid.*, s. 53.
200 NDA, above note 74, s. 273.63.

sons permanently bound to secrecy" under the *Security of Information Act*.[201]

The commissioner is tasked with reviewing the activities of the CSE to ensure that they are in compliance with the law and informs the minister of national defence and the attorney general of Canada of any activity of the CSE that the commissioner believes may not be in compliance with the law.[202]

Further, the commissioner is required to review CSE's activities undertaken in response to a ministerial authorization to intercept "private communications," and report annually to the minister of national defence.[203] These intercepts are discussed in Chapter 11. The commissioner reports on his or her activities in an annual report tabled in Parliament.[204]

The commissioner may also undertake any investigation that the commissioner considers necessary in response to a complaint.[205] Nonfrivolous, good faith, timely complaints are investigated by the commissioner. Upon conclusion of the investigation, the commissioner makes findings and recommendations.[206]

In performing all of his or her functions, the commissioner possesses the powers of a person appointed under Part II of the *Inquiries Act*. This authority includes the ability to summon witnesses, compel production of documents and administer oaths.[207]

c) Review of the RCMP

Unlike CSIS or the CSE, the RCMP had no specialized national security review mechanism at the time of this writing. At best, review was conducted through the Commission of Public Complaints (CPC) against the RCMP, a body whose members are appointed by the governor-in-council.[208] The CPC does not perform the sort of auditing function undertaken by SIRC and the CSE. Instead, it addresses complaints concerning RCMP conduct.

---

201 See Chapter 10.
202 NDA, above note 74, s. 273.63.
203 *Ibid.*, s. 273.66. See Chapter 11 for a discussion.
204 *Ibid.*, s. 273.63(3).
205 *Ibid.*, s. 273.63(2)(b).
206 Commissioner of the CSE, *Complaints Procedure* (2006), online: http://csec-ccst. gc.ca/functions/complaints-proced_e.php.
207 *Inquiries Act*, above note 60, ss. 7–8.
208 RCMP Act, above note 129, s. 45.29.

Nonfrivolous, good faith public complaints properly subject to the RCMP procedure are investigated first by the RCMP itself.[209] A complainant dissatisfied by this internal process may refer their complaint to the CPC for review.[210] That body may confirm the RCMP internal review or take a number of other steps, including investigating the complaint itself.[211] A CPC investigation may include a hearing,[212] generally held in public.[213] Upon completion of its investigation, the CPC sends a report on its findings and recommendations to the RCMP commissioner and the minister of public safety.[214] The commissioner then responds to the CPC and the minister with the Force's reply to the recommendations.[215]

The CPC itself may initiate its own complaints process, if satisfied that there are reasonable grounds to investigate conduct in the performance of any duty or function under the RCMP Act.[216] This power is used rarely, but was employed in relation to the Arar matter.

The CPC does not have the same powers as do SIRC or the CSE commissioner to view secret information. The RCMP Act does require the commissioner to furnish the CPC "materials under the control of the Force as are relevant to the complaint."[217] Moreover, where a hearing is held, the CPC has powers to summon persons and papers and receive evidence under oath.[218] Despite these powers, inability to access information is among the CPC's greatest weakness.[219] The CPC's failings as an effective review body in the national security area were repeatedly underscored by its former chair, Shirley Heafey, an active proponent of an enhanced and consolidated review process in the national security area.[220]

The Arar inquiry echoed Heafey's conclusion, urging that a complaints-based system with inadequate access to information could not

---

209 *Ibid.*, ss. 45.36(4) and 45.38.
210 *Ibid.*, s. 45.41.
211 *Ibid.*, s. 45.42.
212 *Ibid.*, s. 45.43.
213 *Ibid.*, s. 45.45.
214 *Ibid.*, s. 45.43.
215 *Ibid.*, s. 45.46.
216 *Ibid.*, s. 45.37.
217 *Ibid.*, s. 45.41(2).
218 *Ibid.*, s. 45.45.
219 See discussion in Arar inquiry, Policy Report, above note 71 at 251.
220 See, for example, Shirley Heafey, Chair, Commission for Public Complaints Against the RCMP, *Civilian Review of the RCMP's National Security Activities*, CACOLE Confrerence 2005, Montreal, Quebec (3 October 2005), online: www.cpc-cpp.gc.ca/DefaultSite/Archive/index_e.aspx?articleid=874.

perform the essential review function in relation to RCMP national security activities.[221] It recommended instead the creation of a restructured CPC, styled the Independent Complaints and National Security Review Agency (ICRA) for the RCMP. This entity would have powers and functions in relation to RCMP national security functions largely analogous to those exercised by SIRC *vis-à-vis* CSIS, including a reviewing and complaints mandate, and with a much enhanced ability to extract information from the RCMP.[222]

This approach was endorsed in principle by the special senate committee on anti-terrorism law in 2007.[223] By the time of this writing, the government had not responded to either the Arar inquiry or senate recommendation.

d)   Towards a Consolidated Review Process

The Arar inquiry did not confine its recommendations to a reformed RCMP review mechanism. As well, it addressed concerns about the uneven nature of review in Canada's security and intelligence community. In appreciation of their important national security functions, the inquiry recommended that several other government agencies be subjected to review. The CBSA, as a law enforcement-oriented entity, would be incorporated into the new RCMP ICRA's mandate. Meanwhile, SIRC's functions would be expanded to include the national security activities of CIC, Transport Canada, FINTRAC and DFAIT.[224]

Further, it recommended close integration of CSE commissioner, SIRC and ICRA functions through "statutory gateways" facilitating the exchange of information, referrals of investigations, joint investigations and coordination of reporting. Cooperation would be enhanced by an umbrella committee, the Integrated National Security Review Coordinating Committee (INSRCC), comprising the head officials from the ICRA, SIRC and the CSE commissioner. This body would ensure the effective operation of the tripartite Canadian review mechanism.[225]

By the time of this writing, the government had not responded to the inquiry's recommendations, although it had promised that legislative changes to the governance mechanisms for security and intelligence were being developed.[226]

---

221 Arar inquiry, Policy Report, above note 71 at 491 *et seq.*
222 *Ibid.* at 603–6.
223 Senate, *Fundamental Justice in Extraordinary Times*, above Table 3.1, note 5 at 118.
224 Arar inquiry, Policy Report, above note 71 at 606.
225 *Ibid.*
226 MacCharles, "Anti-Terror Measures," above note 118.

3) Parliamentary Review

Another reform effort percolating, but incomplete, by the time of this writing was the formation of a new parliamentary committee on national security.

a) Conventional Role of Parliamentary Committees

In many areas of government, parliamentary committees play a key role in holding ministers (and, *de facto*, their officials) to account. Parliament has powers to summon and even compel the appearance of officials,[227] including ministers.[228] Likewise, under the Common's Standing Orders, Standing Committees may "send for persons, papers and records."[229] Parliament and its committees may administer oaths requiring truthful responses,[230] a rarely utilized power. Parliament (and by extension, its committees) also possess contempt powers. Thus, "any act or omission that obstructs or impedes either House of Parliament in the performance of its functions, or that obstructs or impedes any Member or officer of such House in the discharge of his duty, or that has a tendency, directly or indirectly, to produce such results may be treated as contempt even though there is no precedent of the offence."[231]

All of this suggests that parliamentary committees are potentially potent review bodies in the area of national security. To date, however, parliamentary review in national security matters has been largely perfunctory. Both the senate and the House of Commons have national security and defence committees.[232] The senate defence and national security committees, in particular, have been active in holding hearings and producing reports on various aspects of Canada's national security and defence policy. Most recently, the Commons national security committee held hearings examining the role of the then commissioner

---

227 See discussion in Derek Lee, *The Power of Parliamentary Houses to Send for Persons, Papers and Records* (Toronto: University of Toronto Press, 1999); *Telezone Inc. v. Canada (Attorney General)* (2004), 235 D.L.R. (4th) 719 at 726 (Ont. C.A.); *Canada (Attorney General) v. Prince Edward Island (Legislative Assembly)* (2003), 46 Admin. L.R. (3d) 171 (P.E.I.S.C.).

228 Lee, *The Power of Parliamentary Houses, ibid.* at 129 ("[u]nder the law, Ministers of the Crown enjoy no special status or privilege before the House or a committee").

229 Commons *Standing Orders*, Order 108(1).

230 See *Parliament of Canada Act*, R.S.C. 1985 c. P-1, ss. 10–13.

231 Joseph Maingot, *Parliamentary Privilege in Canada*, 2d ed. (Montreal: McGill-Queen's University Press, 1997) at 193.

232 Standing Senate Committee on National Security and Defence; Special Senate Committee on the *Anti-terrorism Act*; House of Commons Standing Committee on Public Safety and National Security; House of Commons Standing Committee on Defence.

of the RCMP in the Arar matter, a focus precipitated by the findings of the Arar inquiry and then fuelled by apparent contradictions in the commissioner's testimony. Controversy sparked by these hearings culminated in the resignation of the commissioner in late 2006.

Parliamentary committees—and Parliament as a whole—have not, however, played a systemic or concentrated role in reviewing the activities of Canada's security agencies. Indeed, some critics describe their performance in this area as utterly inadequate.[233]

b) National Security Committee of Parliamentarians
The Canadian Parliament's record in national security matters compares unfavourably with that of other Westminster democracies. The United Kingdom, Australia and New Zealand have relatively potent national security parliamentary committees, bodies whose attributes are summarized in Table 3.5.

In 2004, the Canadian government tabled a discussion paper noting this comparative experience and identifying means of enhancing the parliamentary role in national security matters.[234] That more prominent role was endorsed in the subsequent national security policy, which proposed the creation of a "National Security Committee of Parliamentarians."[235] An interim committee of parliamentarians on national security also provided their views in October 2004, recommending a statutorily created committee of Parliament.[236]

Subsequently, in 2005, the then Martin government tabled Bill C-81 in the House of Commons to establish such a "National Security Committee of Parliamentarians."[237] The bill went no further than first

---

233   See, for example, Douglas L. Bland & Roy Rempel, "A Vigilant Parliament: Building Competence for Effective Parliamentary Oversight of National Defence and the Canadian Armed Forces" (2004) 5 Policy Matters 1, online: www.irpp.org/pm/archive/pmvol5no1.pdf.

234   Canada, *A National Security Committee of Parliamentarians: A Consultation Paper to Help Inform the Creation of a Committee of Parliamentarians to Review National Security* (2004), online: http://ww2.ps-sp.gc.ca/publications/national_security/nat_sec_cmte_e.asp.

235   Government of Canada, *Securing an Open Society: Canada's National Security Policy* (2004) at 19, online: www.pco-bcp.gc.ca/docs/InformationResources/Publications/NatSecurnat/natsecurnat_e.pdf.

236   Interim Committee of Parliamentarians on National Security, *Report* (October 2004), online: www.pco-bcp.gc.ca/docs/InformationResources/Publications/cpns/01-cov-e.htm.

237   Bill C-81, *An Act to establish the National Security Committee of Parliamentarians*, 1st Sess., 38th Parl., 2005.

reading in the Commons before it died on the order paper at the time of the 2006 election.

Had it been passed, the new law would have established something unusual in the Canadian context: a legislatively created committee comprising members from both the senate and Commons. The committee's members were to be appointed by the governor-in-council and to hold office during pleasure until the dissolution of Parliament. Given these terms, the committee was to be a *de facto* executive body, staffed by parliamentarians. Indeed, the bill explicitly specified that the committee was not a committee of Parliament and carved out exceptions to the general rules that parliamentarians cannot be employed by the executive branch. These provisions meant that the committee would enjoy none of Parliament's powers and privileges, including its inherent power to compel evidence and summon persons and hold persons in contempt. More than that, individual members' parliamentary privileges concerning immunity for the communication of information were emphatically abrogated.[238]

The committee was to have a broad mandate focused on reviewing

(a) the legislative, regulatory, policy and administrative framework for national security in Canada, and activities of federal departments and agencies in relation to national security; and

(b) any matter relating to national security that the Minister refers to the Committee.

Committee members were to be sworn to secrecy and named "persons permanently bound by secrecy" under the *Security of Information Act*. The committee would be empowered to request information from ministers. The latter could provide any such information so long as compliant with the *Privacy Act*, not including Cabinet confidences. However, there was no requirement that the government supply the requested data, and information requests were to be judged by ministers with an eye to solicitor–client privilege, the extent to which the information concerned an actual investigation or operation, the provenance of the information from a foreign source and the need to protect confidential sources and methods.

Reports prepared by the committee in the course of its functions were to be filed annually with the prime minister, who would then

---

238 Parliamentarians possess freedom of speech, meaning that a parliamentarian cannot be held liable for what is said in Parliament, at least on the floor of the House. *Re Ouellet* (1976), 67 D.L.R. (3d) 73 at 86 (Que. S.C.) (agreeing that "communications by a Member to another person outside the walls of the House are not covered by the privilege,") aff'd (1976), 72 D.L.R. (3d) 95 (Que. C.A.).

table a version in Parliament, redacted for information that would be injurious to national security, defence or international relations.

By the time of this writing, the bill and the committee proposal had not been formally resuscitated by the Harper government, although it seemed likely that some system would be proposed.[239] In 2007, the Commons committee reviewing anti-terrorism law recommended that the bill be re-introduced.[240] For its part, the special senate committee on anti-terrorism law urged the creation of a standing senate committee to monitor, examine and report on national security law and policy on an ongoing basis.[241]

---

239 MacCharles, "Anti-Terror Measures," above note 118.
240 House of Commons Subcommittee on the Review of the *Anti-terrorism Act*, *Rights, Limits, Security: A Comprehensive Review of the Anti-terrorism Act and Related Issues* (March 2007) at 85, online: http://cmte.parl.gc.ca/Content/HOC/committee/391/secu/reports/rp2798914/sterrp07/sterrp07-e.pdf.
241 Senate, *Fundamental Justice in Extraordinary Times*, above Table 3.1, note 5 at 122.

Table 3.5:   Parliamentary Review in Commonwealth Countries

Attribute	Canada (as proposed in Bill C-81)	Australia	New Zealand	U.K.
Name	National Security Committee of Parliamentarians	Joint Committee on Intelligence and Security	Intelligence and Security Committee	Intelligence and Security Committee
Statutory basis	✓	✓ [1]	✓ [2]	✓ [3]
Bicameral representation	✓	✓	N/A	✓
Multiparty membership	✓ [4]	✓	✓	✓
Review authority				
• Administration and expenditures of security and intelligence agencies	✓	✓	✓	✓
• Review any matter referred by minister	✓	✓	✓	
• Review any matter referred by Parliament		✓		
• Review operation and effectiveness of security law		✓	✓	
• Named operational areas excluded from review	✓ [5]	✓	✓	
Report directly to Parliament	✓	✓	✓	
Report indirectly to Parliament through minister/Prime Minister	✓			✓
Rules on receipt and disclosure of secret information	✓	✓	✓	✓
Rules on secrecy obligations of members	✓	✓	✓	✓ [6]

[1]   Intelligence Services Act 2001 (Cth.), Act No. 152, Part 4.
[2]   Intelligence and Security Committee Act 1996 (N.Z.), 1996/46.
[3]   Intelligence Services Act 1994 (U.K.), c. 13, s. 10.
[4]   This aspect was not explicit in C-81, although clearly possible.
[5]   This exclusion was implicit. It was listed among the considerations that the minister was to take into account in deciding whether to provide information.
[6]   Members of the committee are "notified" under the Official Secrets Act, 1989 (U.K.), 1989, c. 6, s. 1, and are therefore bound by that statute's strictures on security intelligence.

CHAPTER 4

THE INSTITUTIONAL FRAMEWORK IN TIMES OF EMERGENCY

National security threats should not be confused with states of emergency. In Canada, very few threats reach the magnitude of an emergency, and as a consequence national security law is generally the regular law of the land and not a special corpus of rules applicable only in extraordinary circumstances. The 2001 *Anti-terrorism Act*[1] is a case in point: legislation promulgated precipitously after the events of 9/11, but enacted pursuant to the regular powers and procedures of Parliament and intended to be mostly permanent.[2]

There will, however, be threats so far in excess of the normal state of affairs and so immediate that the state will treat them as emergencies. Such a state of emergency may change the institutional structure within which national security law operates. As noted in prior chapters, democracies are built on a system of checks and balances that *constrain* the exercise of power. Yet, emergencies often, if not usually, require the *exercise* of power. Moreover, this power must be implemented swiftly and with resolution. While law applicable in normal situations diffuses power, emergencies concentrate it.

In the 1970 October Crisis, for example, the federal Cabinet debated whether to rely on executive powers under the *War Measures Act*[3] to au-

---

1 S.C. 2001, c. 41.
2 For a discussion on this point, see *Application under s. 83.28 of the Criminal Code (Re)*, [2004] 2 S.C.R. 248 at para. 39, Iacobucci & Arbour JJ.
3 R.S.C. 1970, c. 288 (now repealed).

thorize the detention of suspects in Quebec or to enact special legislation.[4] Then Justice Minister John Turner urged recourse to Parliament, but noted that with letters from the political and police authorities in Quebec, the government could proclaim the *War Measures Act*, rendering unusual police raids and detentions legal. The government could then go to Parliament asking it to approve further, more specialized legislation.[5] In other words, the executive branch could exercise powers immediately, leaving the potential delays associated with the parliamentary process to another day.[6] In the end, Cabinet chose to rely on the *War Measures Act*, authorizing extraordinary police powers.

Canada learned from the October Crisis that during political emergencies, the executive branch is typically strengthened at the expense of the legislative and judicial branches. Urgency tends to trump sober second thought, and the rule of law may be suspended for a perceived greater good. "Society," argued Prime Minister Pierre Trudeau three days before the *War Measures Act* was invoked, "must take every means at its disposal to defend itself against the emergence of a parallel power which defies the elected power in this country."[7]

This chapter takes up the issue of emergencies and their impact on the democratic institutional structure and regular law of Canada. It examines, first, the concept of emergencies and the challenges they present to the rule of law and conventional democratic order. Second, it looks at emergencies as a constraint on democracy and civil and human rights in international law. It then examines the extent to which Canadian constitutional and statutory law permit similar abrogations.

---

4   "The FLQ Situation," RG2, Privy Council Office, Series A-5-a, vol. 6359 (15 October 1970; afternoon session) at 5.

5   See discussion *ibid.* at 6. For an historical review of emergency law in Canada and its use, see Martin Robert, "Notes on Emergency Powers in Canada" (2005) 54 U.N.B.L.J. 161.

6   In fact, these fears of delays in part explain the government's ultimate decision to invoke the *War Measures Act*. See "The FLQ Situation,"*ibid.* at 6 for Prime Minister Trudeau explaining that there was no way legislation could be put through all its stages to authorize action before the next morning.

7   Pierre Elliott Trudeau, interview by CBC-TV reporter Tim Ralfe, 13 October 1970, reprinted in J.R. Colombo, *Famous Lasting Words* (Vancouver: Douglas & McIntyre, 2000) at 376.

PART I: STATES OF EMERGENCY AND THE RULE OF LAW IN A DEMOCRACY

Any emergency presents three questions, the answer to which determines the emergency's impact on democracy and the rule of law. First, how does one determine when and where an emergency exists? Second, how should the state respond to the emergency? Third, when does the emergency end? Answering these questions may not always be straightforward. On one end of the spectrum are "clear" emergencies. In recent Canadian history, these are usually natural disasters, such as the Manitoba flood of 1997 or the Central Canadian ice storm of 1998. Other such clear emergencies are unexpected, but noncatastrophic systems failures, like the blackout of 2003 in Central Canada and the Eastern United States.

The course of action to be followed in responding to natural or accidental disaster emergencies is usually uncomplicated. If a sizeable portion of a region is flooded, flood interdiction, search and rescue, and financial, medical and material assistance are the order of the day. If power supplies are disrupted, restoring electricity and accommodating essential services pending the return of power are the priorities. Further, with these sorts of crises, the duration of the emergency is reasonably certain: floodwaters recede, electrical supplies return. Emergencies like these may require the assistance of the military or the deployment of extra policing resources to deter civil unrest. Nevertheless, although a truly catastrophic natural or artificial disaster could undermine Canadian democracy, calamities like these historically have not disrupted democratic practices or institutions. Whether this pattern will remain true in the face of global threats of climate change or infectious diseases remained unknowable at the time of this writing.

More problematic to any democracy, historically, are political emergencies: a state of war, an insurrection, a terrorist threat or strike, or the like. Citizens can turn on their televisions or even glance out their windows to have a clear sense of the gravity and immediacy of a flood or ice storm. The scope of political emergencies is more difficult to assess. In this respect, political crises are less "empirical" than natural or artificial disasters. As Prime Minister Trudeau observed in the course of Cabinet discussions prior to the invocation of the *War Measures Act*, one only knows *after* the fact whether one is facing an insurrection or not.[8] Perhaps most troubling, the uncertainty prompted by this "fog of war" may be motivated by other concerns. Thus, emergencies are most corrosive of democracy where, as Michael Ignatieff puts it, they are pro-

---

8   "The FLQ Situation," above note 4 (15 October 1970; morning session) at 8.

claimed "on grounds that involve bad faith, manipulation of evidence, exaggeration of risk, or the prospect of political advantage."[9]

Ultimately, a government's assessment of the scope of a political emergency, and the propriety of the government response to it, are difficult to second-guess. This uncertainty is particularly problematic where, as is usually the case, political emergencies require that those constituting the threat be interdicted quickly, before they compound the danger. Moreover, deciding whether political emergencies have abated is also tremendously difficult. As Ignatieff has noted, the problem with these sorts of emergencies is that

> only the executive has sufficient information to know whether they remain justified. Hence the speedy termination of emergencies remains a recurrent problem. Electorates and legislators are invariably told by their leaders, "If you only knew what we know ...," in justification of the continued suspension of civil liberties."[10]

The result may be a prolonged state of emergency, and measures designed to give the executive branch extraordinary and temporary powers may persist.

All told, therefore, emergencies—particularly political emergencies—may constitute a serious threat to democracy. Discussing the current "war on terror," Ignatieff proposes that "in a long twilight war, largely fought by secret means, the key issue is maintaining as much legal and legislative oversight as is compatible with the necessity for decisive action."[11] To this end, any assessment of emergency action obliges three questions, echoing those listed at the outset of this section: first, is the action authorized by law; second, are the extraordinary measures authorized by this law proportional and adequately linked to reasonable assessments of the threat; and, third, does the law contain provisions for the review and termination of these extraordinary powers.

PART II: EMERGENCY POWERS AND INTERNATIONAL LAW

International human rights law provides important guidance on how states may legitimately respond to emergencies. The *U.N. Internation-*

---

9   Michael Ignatieff, *The Lesser Evil: Political Ethics in an Age of Terror* (Toronto: Penguin Canada, 2004) at 37.

10   *Ibid.* at 51.

11   *Ibid.* at 39.

al Covenant on Civil and Political Rights (ICCPR)[12]—a cornerstone of international human rights law—contemplates derogation from some of the rights it guarantees in times of emergency. Pursuant to Article 4(1), states may take measures abridging most rights in the time of a public emergency that "threatens the life of the nation."

There are safeguards. The derogation may only be what is strictly required by the exigencies of the situation. A state making use of the right of derogation must immediately inform the other states that are parties to the ICCPR and justify the measure. Further, the rights limitations introduced must not be inconsistent with a state's other obligations under international law and must not involve discrimination solely on the ground of race, colour, sex, language, religion or social origin. Finally, not all rights are trumped. Article 4(2) asserts that *no* derogation is permissible from the rights to life, to recognition as a person, and to freedom of thought, conscience and religion. Likewise, an Article 4 emergency may not negate the bans on torture or cruel, inhuman or degrading treatment or punishment, and the prohibition on slavery and servitude, imprisonment for contractual breach and retroactive criminal law.

Still, Article 4 accords substantial authority to states to negate rights unilaterally. It applies to many of the Covenant's most important provisions, including most of the legal rights, the freedom of expression and association provisions, the right to privacy and the democratic rights. Concern with the reach of this Article has prompted the U.N. Human Rights Committee—the treaty body established by the ICCPR—to offer narrow interpretations of the provision. In 1981, the committee urged that "measures taken under article 4 are of an exceptional and temporary nature and may only last as long as the life of the nation concerned is threatened and that in times of emergency, the protection of human rights becomes all the more important, particularly those rights from which no derogations can be made."[13]

In a more expansive commentary adopted in 2001, the committee echoed this view, concluding that "measures derogating from the provisions of the Covenant must be of an exceptional and temporary nature."[14] Moreover, because states must abide by their other international law obligations, Article 4 cannot, in fact, authorize derogations from international humanitarian law applicable in armed conflicts and

---

12   19 December 1966, 999 U.N.T.S. 171 (entered into force 23 March 1976).
13   U.N. Human Rights Committee, *General Comment 5*, A/36/40 (1981) Annex VII at 110; CCPR/C/21/Rev.1 at para 3.
14   U.N. Human Rights Committee, *General Comment 29*, CCPR/C/21/Rev.1/Add.11 (2001) at para 2.

so-called peremptory (or *jus cogens*) norms of international law. These include the bars on taking hostages, the imposition of collective punishments, arbitrary deprivations of liberty or deviations from fundamental principles of a fair trial. Further, with the coming into force of the *Rome Statute of the International Criminal Court* (of which Canada is a party), emergency situations clearly do not relieve perpetrators of culpability for crimes against humanity.[15]

At the end of the day, therefore, international law accommodates legitimate public emergencies. However, it would be wrong to view it as extending states a *carte blanche* to respond to these calamities as they will.

PART III: EMERGENCY POWERS AND THE CONSTITUTION

Unlike the *International Covenant on Political and Civil Rights*, Canadian constitutional and quasi-constitutional law generally does not expressly anticipate abridgment of rights in the event of emergencies. With the exception of section 4(2) of the *Charter*, discussed later in this chapter, both the *Canadian Charter of Rights and Freedoms*[16] and the 1960 *Canadian Bill of Rights*[17] are silent on emergencies. However, both of these instruments allow Parliament to circumscribe at least some of the rights they protect, pursuant to "notwithstanding" provisions.

A. *CANADIAN BILL OF RIGHTS*

An Act of Parliament may expressly limit the reach of the *Canadian Bill of Rights*.[18] For example, the *War Measures Act*, prior to its repeal by the *Emergencies Act*[19] in 1988, provided that "any act or thing done or authorized or any order or regulation made under the authority of this Act, shall be deemed not to be an abrogation, abridgement or in-

---

15   *Ibid.* at para. 12 *et seq.*
16   Part I of the *Constitution Act, 1982*, being Schedule B to the *Canada Act 1982* (U.K.) 1982, c. 11.
17   S.C. 1960, c. 44.
18   *Ibid.*, s. 2. noting that the rights described in that section may be negated if it is "expressly declared by an Act of the Parliament of Canada that [a statute] shall operate notwithstanding the *Canadian Bill of Rights*."
19   R.S.C. 1985 (4th Supp.), c. 22.

fringement of any right or freedom recognized by the *Canadian Bill of Rights*."[20]

B. *CHARTER OF RIGHTS AND FREEDOMS*

1) Section 33

Likewise, the "notwithstanding" clause in section 33 of the *Charter* allows Parliament or the provincial legislatures to remove a statute from *Charter* scrutiny by explicitly indicating it operates "notwithstanding" the *Charter*. This immunity persists for five years, subject to any renewal.

Critically, this section applies to most, but not all, rights in the *Charter*. It extends to the fundamental freedoms provisions in section 2, the legal rights in sections 7 to 14, and the equality provisions in section 15. It does not, however, authorize Parliament to negate many other *Charter* rights, including the mobility right in section 6 or, notably, the democratic rights in sections 3 to 5. These democratic rights affirm the right to vote (section 3), limit the duration of a House of Commons to five years (section 4(1)) and require annual sittings of Parliament (section 5).

As a result, subject to the following discussion of section 4(2) of the *Charter*, were Parliament to rely on section 33 to negate the *Charter's* civil rights sections in response to an emergency, it could *not* also rely on section 33 to deny voting rights to citizens, or prolong its existence past the five years anticipated by section 4(1).[21] Also section 5, requiring an annual sitting of Parliament, restricts Parliament's capacity to delegate governance to the executive and retire pending the conclusion of a state of emergency. In any event, a Parliament tempted to delegate indefinitely its full plenary powers, perhaps in response to an emergency, would also run afoul of a long-established, pre-*Charter* constitutional restriction barring complete abdication of Parliament's responsibilities in favour of the executive.[22]

---

20   *War Measures Act*, s. 6.

21   The importance of s. 4's immunity from s. 33 has been noted by the Supreme Court. See *Reference re Secession of Quebec*, [1998] 2 S.C.R. 217 at para. 65, holding that the democratic principle said to reside in the Canadian Constitution "is affirmed with particular clarity in that s. 4 is not subject to the notwithstanding power contained in s. 33."

22   See *Re Gray* (1918), 57 S.C.R. 150 at 157, holding that the broad delegation of powers under the *War Measures Act, 1914* was *intra vires* Parliament, but also noting "Parliament cannot, indeed, abdicate its functions, but within reasonable limits at any rate it can delegate its powers to the executive government. Such

2) Section 1

Even if section 33 were not used, and Parliament's enactment violated the *Charter*, the statute could be saved from a *Charter* challenge by section 1. Section 1 circumscribes all *Charter* rights by "such reasonable limits prescribed by law as can be demonstrably justified in a free and democratic society." What those reasonable limits might be in an emergency would depend on the nature of the crisis. It seems likely, however, that courts would be prepared to endorse some abridgment of rights in a good faith emergency. For instance, in *R. v. Heywood*,[23] the Supreme Court suggested that a violation of the section 7 right to life, liberty and security of the person, though generally difficult to justify on section 1 grounds, could be reasonable "in times of war or national emergencies."

3) Section 4(2)

The discussion thus far suggests that the Canadian Constitution is a flexible instrument, able to accommodate legitimate emergencies. At the same time, it does not extend a *carte blanche* to the government. The section 33 override could insulate a law from court scrutiny in relation to civil rights, but the House of Commons that chose to invoke section 33 could not use that same provision to prolong its existence in violation of section 4(1) and stave off the judgment of the electorate. Generally, a failure to comply with the democratic rights in sections 3 to 5 of the *Charter* could only be justified under section 1, again putting courts in the position as ultimate arbiter of whether the constitutional infraction is justified. All told, this system of checks and balances would make it very difficult for a government to remain onside the Constitution while maintaining an unwarranted, permanent state of emergency.

That said, there is an evident Achilles heel in this effort to preserve constitutional probity in a time of emergency: section 4(2) of the *Charter*. Section 4(2) provides that "in time of real or apprehended war, invasion or insurrection, a House of Commons may be continued by Parliament … beyond five years if such continuation is not opposed

---

powers must necessarily be subject to determination at any time by Parliament, and needless to say the acts of the executive, under its delegated authority, must fall within the ambit of the legislative pronouncement by which its authority is measured."

23   [1994] 3 S.C.R. 761 at 802. See also *Reference re Motor Vehicle Act (British Columbia) s. 94(2)*, [1985] 2 S.C.R. 486 at 518. In another context, see *also Newfoundland (Treasury Board) v. Newfoundland and Labrador Association of Public and Private Employees (N.A.P.E.)*, 2004 SCC 66 for court citing a putative fiscal crisis in upholding a discriminatory law under s. 1.

by the votes of more than one-third of the members of the House of Commons." Since constitutionally "Parliament" consists of the Queen (usually in the person of the governor general), the senate and the Commons,[24] section 4(2) should be read as authorizing the continuance of the Commons by two-thirds vote of the Commons, a majority vote of the senate, and assent by the governor general. Once this continuance is obtained, the same House of Commons that employs section 33 to curb civil rights could also insulate itself from electoral pressure for the duration of a "real or apprehended war, invasion or insurrection."

Exactly how parliamentary reliance on section 4(2) could be policed is unclear. Presumably, the courts could review the existence of a "real or apprehended war, invasion or insurrection." How aggressively a court would query the judgment of the political branches of government on this issue is an open question, especially where the emergency justifying the invocation of section 4(2) is "apprehended" rather than real.[25]

There is a real possibility, in other words, that section 4(2) could inhibit efforts to hold the government accountable in times of emergency by rendering the Commons immune to electoral displeasure.

---

24   *Constitution Act, 1867* (U.K.), 30 & 31 Vict., c. 3, reprinted in R.S.C. 1985, App. II, No. 5, s. 17.

25   Another, perhaps only academic uncertainty is the relationship between s. 4(2) and s. 50 of the *Constitution Act, 1867, ibid.* The latter provides that "[e]very House of Commons shall continue for Five Years from the Day of the Return of the Writs for choosing the House (subject to be sooner dissolved by the Governor General), and no longer." While the *British North America Act* (as the *Constitution Act, 1867* was called prior to 1982) contained a provision equivalent to s. 4(2) of the *Charter*, this section was repealed by the *Constitution Act, 1982*, being Schedule B to the *Canada Act 1982* (U.K.), 1982, c. 11. See *British North America (No. 2) Act, 1949*, 13 Geo. VI, c. 81 (U.K.), s. 91(1) reading, in part, "a House of Commons may in time of real or apprehended war, invasion or insurrection be continued by the Parliament of Canada if such continuation is not opposed by the votes of more than one-third of the members of such House."

The Constitution now contains, therefore, a limit on the duration of the House of Commons in both the *Charter* and the *Constitution Act, 1867*, but an exception to that limit in only the *Charter*. There is an apparent inconsistency, in other words, between two instruments, each of which constitutes equal parts of the Constitution of Canada. See s. 52 of the *Constitution Act, 1982*. The Supreme Court has declared that the Constitution is to be read as a whole, and not as a set of hermetically sealed obligations. *Reference re Secession of Quebec*, above note 21 at para. 50 ("Our Constitution has an internal architecture, or ... a 'basic constitutional structure.' The individual elements of the Constitution are linked to the others, and must be interpreted by reference to the structure of the Constitution as a whole.") The most sensible interpretation of these two provisions is to view s. 4(2) as authorizing derogation from s. 50 of the *Constitution Act, 1867* as much as from s. 4(1) of the *Charter*. Any other reading would render s. 4(2) a nullity.

PART IV: *EMERGENCIES ACT*

The constitutional discussion set out above is entirely hypothetical. No emergency attracting the application of section 33 or section 4(2) of the *Charter* has ever been declared. Perhaps of more immediate relevance are those statutes designed to deal with anticipated emergencies. In this regard, the *Emergencies Act* lies at the heart of Canada's emergency powers law. Other statutes are also important. These include the *Emergency Management Act*,[26] the *National Defence Act*[27] and the omnibus *Public Safety Act, 2002*.[28] The latter three instruments are discussed elsewhere in this book.

Canada's emergency laws are on balance consistent with the criteria set out in the introduction to this chapter for evaluating such measures. First, the key statute—the *Emergencies Act*—contemplates that actions taken by the government in the event of an emergency will be authorized by law, not arbitrary or *ad hoc*.

Second, this statute is not so open-ended as to permit the invocation of an emergency in every circumstance. The threshold for the declaration of an emergency is spelled out in the Act, albeit in broad terms likely to attract only the most deferential of judicial review. Further, the measures authorized by this declaration are limited to those believed necessary on reasonable grounds to deal with the situation. Some effort is made, in other words, to ensure that the measures authorized by this Act are proportional and adequately linked to reasonable assessments of the threat.

Third, the *Emergencies Act* contemplates fairly substantial review and involvement by Parliament, requires a proactive continuance of an emergency declaration to circumvent automatic sunsetting provisions, and preserves the administrative and constitutional law judicial review powers of the courts.

Each of these propositions is discussed below.

A. CORE CONTENT

The *Emergencies Act*[29] has never been used since its enactment in 1988. In fact, although the statute was passed to replace the *War Measures*

---

26   S.C. 2007, c. 15 (not in force at time of this writing).
27   R.S.C. 1985, c. N-5.
28   S.C. 2004, c. 15.
29   Above note 19.

Act,[30] it is arguable whether the new law could ever be employed the way the *War Measures Act* was in October 1970, to abridge fundamental civil rights. A post-*Charter* instrument, the *Emergencies Act* rebalances the separation of powers between Parliament and the executive in times of emergency, subject to a series of important safeguards, but leaves intact *Charter* and *Canadian Bill of Rights* provisions and, implicitly, the judicial review authority of the courts.

Indeed, the Act notes in its preamble that "the preservation of the sovereignty, security and territorial integrity" of Canada may be seriously threatened by national emergencies, and thus the governor-in-council "should be authorized, subject to the supervision of Parliament, to take special temporary measures that may not be appropriate in normal times." It goes on to say, however, that these "special temporary measures" are subject to the *Charter*, the *Canadian Bill of Rights* and "must have regard to the International Covenant on Civil and Political Rights, particularly with respect to those fundamental rights that are not to be limited or abridged even in a national emergency."

1) Definition of Emergency

The Act defines a "national emergency" as "an urgent and critical situation of a temporary nature that ... seriously endangers the lives, health or safety of Canadians and is of such proportions or nature as to exceed the capacity or authority of a province to deal with it, or ... seriously threatens the ability of the Government of Canada to preserve the sovereignty, security and territorial integrity of Canada" and that cannot be dealt with effectively under any other law of Canada.[31]

2) Nondiscrimination

The statute states emphatically that it does not confer on the government the power to make orders or regulations "providing for the detention, imprisonment or internment" of Canadian citizens or permanent residents "on the basis of race, national or ethnic origin, colour, religion, sex, age or mental or physical disability."[32]

This provision is more definitive than the equivalent concept in Article 4 of the *International Covenant on Civil and Political Rights*, which bars discrimination "solely" on one of the enumerated grounds.

---

30   *Ibid.,* s. 80.
31   *Ibid.,* s. 3.
32   *Ibid.,* s. 4.

By the Covenant's logic, discrimination motivated by considerations *in addition to* (for example) religion, could conceivably satisfy its nondiscrimination requirements. A controversial example might be religious profiling of Muslims, based not on religion *per se*, but on a perceived correlation of Islamic religious beliefs and terrorism. This result could be allowed, in fact, by the interpretation of the Article adopted by the United States in its ratification of the ICCPR.[33] On its face, the *Emergencies Act* is not so forgiving, barring detention on the basis of enumerated grounds outright.

3) Power to Amend the Act

The *Emergencies Act* also bars the government from employing its emergency powers under the statute to amend the Act itself.[34] The government cannot, in other words, use the *Emergencies Act* to broaden the powers available to it under the *Emergencies Act*.

4) Types of Emergency

The Act anticipates four categories of emergencies: public welfare emergency, public order emergency, international emergency and war emergency. Table 4.1 describes how the Act defines each of these concepts, the circumstances in which the emergency can be triggered, the extraordinary government powers it extends and how these states of emergency may be terminated.

---

33   See U.N. Treaty Database, *International Covenant on Civil and Political Rights*, Declarations and Reservations ("The United States understands distinctions based upon race, colour, sex, language, religion, political or other opinion, national or social origin, property, birth or any other status—as those terms are used in article 2, para. 1 and article 26—to be permitted when such distinctions are, at minimum, rationally related to a legitimate governmental objective. The United States further understands the prohibition in para. 1 of article 4 upon discrimination, in time of public emergency, based 'solely' on the status of race, colour, sex, language, religion or social origin, not to bar distinctions that may have a disproportionate effect upon persons of a particular status"), online: www.unhchr.ch/tbs/doc.nsf/73c66f02499582e7c1256ab7002e2533/ 39c8aba1188dd494c1256aa10049d802?OpenDocument.

34   *Emergencies Act*, above note 19, s. 4.

Table 4.1: Four Categories of Emergencies in the *Emergencies Act*

Type	Definition	Trigger	Powers	Termination
Public welfare emergency	Section 5—An emergency caused by a real or imminent fire, flood, drought, storm, earthquake or other natural phenomenon; disease in human beings, animals or plants; or accident or pollution that results or may result in danger to life or property, social disruption or breakdown in the flow of essential goods, services or resources so serious as to be a national emergency.	Section 6—Upon consultation with the provincial cabinet in the affected provinces, the governor-in-council (GIC) may, if it believes on reasonable grounds that a public welfare emergency exists and necessitates special temporary measures, declare by proclamation such an emergency. This declaration must identify the state of affairs constituting the emergency, the special temporary measures anticipated and the area affected by the emergency. This sort of emergency may not be declared unless, where the emergency is confined to one province, the provincial cabinet indicates that the emergency exceeds the capacity of the province to deal with it.	Section 8—The GIC may issue orders or regulations to the extent it believes (on reasonable grounds) necessary for dealing with the emergency in the declared area, covering the following: (a) travel restrictions where necessary for the protection of the health or safety of individuals; (b) evacuation of persons and the removal of personal property from any specified area and the making of arrangements for the adequate care and protection of the persons and property; (c) requisition, use or disposition of property; (d) authorization of or direction to any person to render essential services of a type that that person is competent to provide (with compensation provided for the services); (e) regulating distribution of essential goods, services and resources; (f) authorization and making of emergency payments; (g) establishment of emergency shelters and hospitals; (h) assessment of damage to any works or	Subsection 7(2)—At the end of ninety days unless continued by the GIC, after consultation with the implicated provincial cabinet. This, and any subsequent continuation, also expires after ninety days. Under section 10, Parliament may revoke the declaration of a public welfare emergency.

Type	Definition	Trigger	Powers	Termination
Public welfare emergency (cont'd)			undertakings and the repair, replacement or restoration thereof; (i) assessment of damage to the environment and the elimination or alleviation of the damage; and (j) imposition of a fine or imprisonment or both, for contravention of any order or regulation made under the section. These powers may not be exercised to impose a settlement in a labour dispute.	
Public order emergency	Section 16—An emergency that arises from threats to the security of Canada that are so serious as to be a national emergency. Threats to the security of Canada are defined in keeping with the *Canadian Security Intelligence Service Act*.[1]	Section 17—On consultation with the provincial cabinet in the affected provinces, the GIC may, if it believes on reasonable grounds that a public order emergency exists and necessitates special temporary measures, declare by proclamation such an emergency. This declaration must identify the state of affairs constituting the emergency, the special temporary measures anticipated and	Section 19—The GIC may issue orders or regulations to the extent it believes (on reasonable grounds) necessary for dealing with the emergency in the declared area, covering the following: (a) regulation or prohibition of (i) any public assembly that may reasonably be expected to lead to a breach of the peace, (ii) travel to, from or within any specified area, or (iii) the use of specified property; (b) designation and securing of protected places; (c) assumption of the control, and the restoration and maintenance, of public utilities and services;	Subsection 18(2)—At the end of thirty days unless continued by the GIC, after consultation with the implicated provincial cabinet. This, and any subsequent continuation, also expires after thirty days. Under section 21, Parliament may revoke the declaration of a public order emergency.

1   See R.S.C. 1985, c. C-23, s. 2.

Type	Definition	Trigger	Powers	Termination
Public order emergency (cont'd)		the area affected by the emergency. This sort of emergency may not be declared unless, where the emergency is confined to one province, the provincial cabinet indicates that emergency exceeds the capacity of the province to deal with it. However, where the effects of the emergency extend beyond one province, the GIC need not consult with provincial cabinets prior to issuance of the declaration where consultation would unduly jeopardize the effectives of the proposed action.	(d) authorization of or direction to any person to render essential services of a type that that person is competent to provide (with compensation provided for the services); and (e) imposition of a fine or imprisonment or both for contravention of any order or regulation made under the section.	
International emergency	Section 27 — An emergency involving Canada and one or more other countries that arises from acts of intimidation or coercion or the real or imminent use of serious force or violence and	Section 28 — After whatever consultation with provincial Cabinets that is practicable, the GIC may declare by proclamation such an emergency. This declaration must identify the state of affairs constituting the emergency, and	Section 30 — The GIC may issue orders or regulations to the extent it believes (on reasonable grounds) necessary for dealing with the emergency, including: (a) control or regulation of any industry or service; (b) appropriation, control, forfeiture, use and disposition of property or services;	Subsection 29(2) — At the end of sixty days unless continued by the GIC, after any practicable consultation with provincial cabinets. Under section 32, Parliament may revoke the

Type	Definition	Trigger	Powers	Termination
International emergency (cont'd)	that is so serious as to be a national emergency.	the special temporary measures anticipated.	(c) authorization and conduct of inquiries in relation to defence contracts or defence supplies or to hoarding, overcharging, black marketing or fraudulent operations in respect of scarce commodities; (d) search and seizure authorization for any thing that may be evidence relevant to any matter that is the subject of an inquiry referred to in paragraph (c); (e) authorization of or direction to any person to render essential services of a type that that person is competent to provide (with compensation provided for the services); (f) designation and securing of protected places; (g) travel restrictions outside Canada by Canadian citizens or permanent residents; (h) deportation of persons, other than citizens, permanent residents or otherwise admissible protected persons; (i) control or regulation of international financial activities within Canada; (j) authorization of expenditures for dealing with an international emergency in excess	declaration of an international emergency.

Type	Definition	Trigger	Powers	Termination
International emergency (cont'd)			of any limit set by an Act of Parliament; (k) authorization of any Cabinet minister to discharge specified responsibilities of a political, diplomatic or economic nature; and (l) imposition of a fine or imprisonment or both for contravention of any order or regulation made under the section. However, these powers must not be exercised for the purpose of censoring, suppressing or controlling the publication or communication of any information.	
War emergency	Section 37—A war or other armed conflict, real or imminent, involving Canada or any of its allies that is so serious as to be a national emergency.	Section 38—After whatever consultation with provincial cabinets that is practicable, the GIC may, if it believes on reasonable grounds that a war emergency exists and necessitates special temporary measures, declare by proclamation such an emergency. The declaration must specify the state of affairs constituting the emergency to the extent that the GIC believes is possible without jeopardizing any special temporary measures proposed.	Section 40—The GIC may issue orders or regulations to the extent it believes (on reasonable grounds) necessary for dealing with the emergency. These orders may not include conscription into the Canadian Forces. Cabinet may make regulations governing the imposition of a fine or imprisonment or both for contravention of any order or regulation made under the section.	Subsection 39(2)—At the end of 120 days unless continued by the GIC, after any practicable consultation with provincial cabinets. Under section 41, Parliament may revoke the declaration of a war emergency.

B. PARLIAMENTARY REVIEW

As Table 4.1 suggests, the *Emergencies Act* bestows substantial power to the governor-in-council to declare public emergencies, and then to employ extraordinary powers. The effect is to rebalance the relative powers of the executive branch and Parliament. Nevertheless, the Act clearly recognizes its impact on the separation of powers and incorporates certain checks and balances designed to subordinate executive action to parliamentary review.

First, a motion for confirmation of any declaration of emergency, complete with reasons and a report on any consultation with the provinces, must be tabled in Parliament within seven sitting days after the governor-in-council issues the declaration. If Parliament is not sitting, it must be summoned to sit within seven days of the declaration, and if dissolved, it must be summoned to sit at the earliest opportunity. In either case, the motion is to be laid before Parliament on the first sitting day after Parliament is summoned.

The motion must be taken up the day after it is tabled, and is to be debated without interruption and voted on in each chamber of Parliament when it is ready for the question. If either House votes down the motion, the declaration of emergency is revoked.[35] The Act sets out similar provisions for the continuance or amendment of a declaration of emergency, although without the requirement that Parliament be summoned if the continuance or amendment occurs when Parliament is not sitting.[36]

Even when a declaration of emergency is affirmed, Parliament may act subsequently to revoke it. If ten senators or twenty MPs file a motion with the Speaker seeking revocation, this motion is taken up within three sitting days after it is filed. Debate may continue for no more than ten hours, at which point the vote is called. If adopted by the relevant chamber of Parliament, the declaration of emergency is revoked.[37]

Meanwhile, except as discussed later, every order or regulation made by the governor-in-council pursuant to its powers under the Act must be tabled in Parliament within two sitting days. A motion may then be brought by no fewer than ten senators or twenty MPs calling for the revocation or amendment of a given order or regulation. This motion must be considered within three sitting days, and debated without interruption until the House is ready for the question. If one House

---

35   *Emergencies Act*, above note 19, s. 58.
36   *Ibid.*, s. 60.
37   *Ibid.*, s. 59.

adopts the motion, and if the other House concurs, the order or regulation is revoked or amended.[38]

The Act also provides for a Parliamentary Review Committee, comprising members from each official party in the Commons and at least one counterpart senator. An order or regulation is referred to this committee within two days.[39] The committee may then adopt a motion revoking or amending the order within thirty days.[40] The committee is also charged with reviewing "the exercise of powers and the performance of duties and functions pursuant to a declaration of emergency." It is required to report to Parliament on the results of this review at least once every sixty days, and more frequently in specified cases.[41]

As a final accountability mechanism, the governor-in-council must call an inquiry into the circumstances resulting in the declaration of emergency with sixty days of its termination. The report of this inquiry must be tabled in Parliament within 360 days after the end of the declaration.[42]

All told, these rules ensure Parliament may intervene and quickly annul an emergency declaration it judges inappropriate.

C. JUDICIAL REVIEW OF ORDERS AND REGULATIONS UNDER THE *EMERGENCIES ACT*

The *Emergencies Act* is silent on the role of the courts in relation to an emergency declaration and any subsequent orders or regulations issued by the government. This failure to formally identify a role for the courts was cited as a shortcoming in Parliamentary debate on the Act.[43] However, silence on this issue likely leaves intact conventional court review powers under administrative law and the *Charter*, even during a declared emergency. Indeed, when the law was enacted, the government clearly contemplated judicial review of emergency measures.[44]

---

38   *Ibid.*, s. 61.
39   *Ibid.*, s. 61(2).
40   *Ibid.*, s. 62.
41   *Ibid.*
42   *Ibid.*, s. 63.
43   See, for example, *House of Commons Debates*, 33d Parl., 2d Sess., vol. 9 (1987) at 10890 (John Parry (Kenora–Rainy River)).
44   See *House of Commons Debates*, *ibid.* at 14765 (Bud Bradley, parliamentary secretary to minister of national defence).

1) Administrative Law

a) Jurisdiction

The Federal Courts conduct judicial review of federal executive authority pursuant to the *Federal Courts Act*.[45] One of the key roles of the Federal Courts is to ensure that the executive branch operates within the parameters of the powers delegated to it by Parliament. The *Emergencies Act* does not purport to change this Federal Court role; it does not explicitly authorize the executive to curb access to the courts as part of its extraordinary powers. Thus, under conventional administrative law doctrine, the executive would be acting outside the jurisdiction conferred by the statute were it to issue an order precluding judicial review of its actions.

The one arguable exception to this observation is in relation to war emergencies. The war emergencies provisions bear the closest resemblance to the old *War Measures Act*, extending to the executive virtually unfettered powers once an emergency is declared. Even here, however, it seems unlikely that the government could issue a regulation under its emergency powers precluding judicial review of whether its action comported with the *Emergencies Act*. Even an express *statutory* privative clause attempting to supplant the jurisdiction of the courts to review executive decisions likely cannot bar court review on jurisdictional grounds; namely, judicial review scrutinizing whether the executive has the power it purports to exercise.[46] As the Supreme Court noted in *Babcock*, even "draconian" statutory language meant to usurp a review power by the court "cannot oust the principle that official actions must flow from statutory authority clearly granted and properly exercised."[47] It follows that a mere regulation, even one issued in emergency circumstances, cannot bar court review by, for instance, purporting to limit Federal Court jurisdiction under the *Federal Courts Act*.[48]

For these reasons, standard judicial review of executive regulation making under the *Emergencies Act* would persist. This view is support-

---

45 R.S.C. 1985, c. F-7.

46 See *Crevier v. Québec*, [1981] 2 S.C.R. 220. See also *Blanchard v. Control Data Canada Ltd.*, [1984] 2 S.C.R. 476 at 488, Lamer J., concurring in the result, and interpreting *Crevier* as teaching that a privative clause "can in no way impede judicial review regarding questions of jurisdiction."

47 *Babcock v. Canada (Attorney General)*, [2002] 3 S.C.R. 3 at para. 39 [*Babcock*].

48 See *Friends of the Oldman River Society v. Canada (Minister of Transport)*, [1992] 1 S.C.R. 3 at 38 ("[j]ust as subordinate legislation cannot conflict with its parent legislation ... so too it cannot conflict with other Acts of Parliament ... unless a statute so authorizes ... Ordinarily, then, an Act of Parliament must prevail over inconsistent or conflicting subordinate legislation").

ed by parliamentary debates on the Act. In the Commons, opposition members expressed concern that courts would not probe rigorously a government declaration of emergency. This fear was sparked by language in the original bill authorizing declaration of an emergency where Cabinet was "of the opinion" the necessary trigger circumstances existed.[49] In response, the government amended the original bill to indicate that government action would require "reasonable grounds." This amendment was made, in the words of the parliamentary secretary to the minister of national defence, to ensure that "all important decisions by the Governor in Council relating to the invocation and use of emergency powers will be challengeable in the courts."[50]

b)   Standard of Review

Nevertheless, any administrative law judicial review likely would be conducted on a highly deferential basis, in keeping with the Supreme Court's jurisprudence on the standard of review to be applied where the executive has a high measure of expertise or disproportionate access to relevant information.

The closest analogy to judicial review of emergency powers is jurisprudence on the review of national security provisions in immigration law. In *Suresh*,[51] the Supreme Court of Canada was asked, among other things, to review the minister of citizenship and immigration's "discretionary" determination that a refugee, Mr. Suresh, constituted a "danger to the security of Canada," as that phrase was used in the then *Immigration Act*. Applying its standard "pragmatic and functional" test to determine the measure of deference to be accorded the minister, the Court pointed to the fact that the minister "has access to special information and expertise in" matters of national security.[52] This fact—read together with the limited appeal mechanism in the Act, the difficult balancing of the competing humanitarian purposes of the Act and the extremely fact-intensive and contextual nature of the national security determination—prompted the Court to extend a large measure of judicial deference to the minister. The minister's decision would only be disturbed if "patently unreasonable" which, in the Court's mind, meant a decision "made arbitrarily or in bad faith, [un]supported on

---

49   See *House of Commons Debates*, above note 44 at 10900 (Dan Heap (Spadina)).
50   *House of Commons Debates*, *ibid.* at 14765 (Bud Bradley (parliamentary secretary to minister of national defence)).
51   *Suresh v. Canada (Minister of Citizenship and Immigration)*, [2002] 1 S.C.R. 3 [*Suresh*].
52   *Ibid.* at paras. 31 and 33.

the evidence, or [where] the Minister failed to consider the appropriate factors."[53]

All told, a government order or regulation under the *Emergencies Act* would also reflect these same considerations invoked in *Suresh*. Normal, statutory appeal rights do not exist in the *Emergencies Act*. The Act will likely be viewed as requiring the balancing of competing, legitimate objectives. Any emergency declaration or resulting decision to issue regulations will be fact-intensive and highly contextual. Finally, the government will likely have access to special information and expertise in rendering its decisions. On this basis, it seems improbable a court would review a government decision connected to the *Emergencies Act* on anything other than a highly deferential standard of review, the reference to "reasonable grounds" in the Act's provisions notwithstanding.

Judicial review is likely to be undemanding even in an area where courts have traditionally extended little deference to governments—procedural fairness.[54] Common law due process standard requires that notice of a pending decision be given to affected persons, that these persons be given an opportunity to comment and that decisions be rendered by an unbiased decision-maker. The precise content of these obligations—how much notice, how much opportunity to comment and how unbiased a decision-maker—is decided by the courts on a contextual basis, and is often affected by the gravity of the decision to the affected persons.

Yet, courts have carved out an exception to procedural fairness in circumstances where the decision taken by the executive is characterized as "legislative" rather than "administrative."[55] The distinction between these concepts is opaque in Supreme Court jurisprudence. Suffice it to say that a legislative decision is one that is general, rather than directed at a single person or class of persons, and is based on broad policy considerations. Delegated law making by the executive—the making of regulations or orders pursuant to a power set out in an Act of

---

53 *Ibid.* at para. 29.

54 *Moreau-Bérubé v. New Brunswick (Judicial Council)*, [2002] 1 S.C.R. 249 at para. 74 (procedural fairness requires "no assessment of the appropriate standard of judicial review. Evaluating whether procedural fairness, or the duty of fairness, has been adhered to by a tribunal requires an assessment of the procedures and safeguards required in a particular situation").

55 *Cardinal v. Director of Kent Institution*, [1985] 2 S.C.R. 643 at 653 (there is a "duty of procedural fairness lying on every public authority making an administrative decision which is not of a legislative nature and which affects the rights, privileges or interests of an individual").

Parliament—is almost invariably viewed as a legislative decision, and a court would likely place the orders and regulations issued under the *Emergencies Act* in this category. Where the executive exercises these "legislative" powers, the courts will not impose procedural fairness requirements.

Moreover, even if courts did conclude procedural fairness obligations attached to such regulations or orders, the very context in which these instruments are introduced—in response to an emergency—likely limits the due process requirements courts would impose. Procedural fairness requirements where executive decisions are made in the face of an emergency are minimal.[56]

2) Constitutional Review

Judicial review of measures introduced under the *Emergencies Act* on constitutional grounds may be more demanding than review on administrative law bases. As its own preamble indicates, the *Emergencies Act* and any orders or regulations issued under its authority are subordinate to the *Charter* and the *Canadian Bill of Rights*. As noted earlier in this chapter, an Act of Parliament may abridge, in part, these two instruments, should certain requirements be met. However, the key trigger here is "an Act of Parliament," certainly not an executive regulation or order, issued under the *Emergencies Act* or any other statute. For these reasons, executive orders or regulations made pursuant to the *Emergencies Act* cannot trump constitutional rights, including the fundamental freedoms and legal rights found in sections 2 and 7 to 14 of the *Charter* and the equivalent provisions of the *Canadian Bill of Rights*.

In fact, if the government were to exercise its full powers under the Act, it is difficult to imagine it would remain fully onside in relation to *Charter* rights, not least the free association rights in section 2(c) and (d), the section 6 mobility right and the section 8 search and seizure right. As a consequence, a government relying on the full range of authority issued to it under the *Emergencies Act* would either have to

---

56 See, for example, *Walpole Island First Nation v. Ontario* (1996), 31 O.R. (3d) 607 at 617 (Gen. Div.) (holding that emergency character of an order authorizing discharge of waste water from an industrial holding pond after heavy precipitation "clearly takes it out of the reach of the doctrine" of procedural fairness). But see *Ross v. Mohawk of Kanesatake*, 2003 FCT 531 at para. 79 ("the right to procedural fairness may be suspended in an emergency situation. It is not eliminated. It is respected by the provision of an opportunity to be heard, after the emergency situation has been relieved").

seek an additional parliamentary statute authorizing its action under section 33 (assuming it was applicable to the right in question), or rely instead on a section 1 justification in any litigation over the government measures.[57]

For all these reasons, the *Emergencies Act* can be read as leaving intact constitutional civil liberties and the role of the courts in protecting these rights.

---

57 As noted previously, the Supreme Court has implied that s. 1 may well justify otherwise impermissible infringements in times of war or national emergencies.

PART THREE

KEY NATIONAL
SECURITY
OBJECTIVES

CHAPTER 5

PROTECTING AGAINST INTERNATIONAL INSECURITY AND ARMED ATTACK

In classic terms, a state's most pressing national security objective is to protect its territory from foreign invasion or attack. To counter exactly these threats, military response is a key plank in the national security strategies of some nations. For instance, the 2002 National Security Strategy of the United States famously pledged to use force to pre-empt threats from states developing weapons of mass destruction.[1]

With a substantially smaller military and a different place in the hierarchy of international power, Canada has not historically projected military power as readily as the United States. Nevertheless, its 2004 national security policy noted that Canadian military assets may be deployed "to protect against direct threats to international peace and security."[2] Likewise, the 2005 Canadian International Policy Statement (IPS) concluded that "in making a distinctive contribution to a safer world, we will rely heavily on the Canadian Forces."[3]

---

1   White House, *National Security Strategy of the United States* (2002) at 15, online: www.whitehouse.gov/nsc/nss.pdf [U.S. National Security Strategy 2002].

2   Canada, *Securing an Open Society: Canada's National Security Policy* (2004) at 6, online: www.pco-bcp.gc.ca/docs/InformationResources/Publications/NatSecur-nat/natsecurnat_e.pdf [*Securing an Open Society*].

3   Canada, *International Policy Statement—Overview* (2005), online: http://geo.international.gc.ca/cip-pic/ips/overview-en.aspx.

The defence paper that accompanied the IPS[4] highlighted "the importance of meeting threats to our security as far away from our borders as possible, wherever they may arise. Security in Canada ultimately begins with stability abroad," especially in the world's failed or failing states. The defence statement listed these weak states, anti-terrorism, countering weapons proliferation and regional "hot spots" as issues implicating the Canadian Forces (CF).

These defence priorities continued by the time of this writing. Planning records employed in developing the Department of National Defence's anticipated 2007 Defence Capability Plan predict that "no large-scale conventional military threat to Canada currently exits" but that "the Canadian Forces will continue to deploy overseas in an environment marked by failed states, global terrorism and proliferation of weapons of mass destruction."[5]

International instability has ramifications for domestic use of military force as well. Violence originating abroad may spill over to Canada, for example, in the form of a terrorist attack. Indeed, the 2005 defence paper placed great emphasis on defending Canada itself as the CF's first priority, while the 2004 national security strategy emphasized the CF's key role "in protecting Canadians from internal threats to their security, both accidental and intentional."[6] Canada's Special Forces, for instance, may be called upon to counter terrorism both internationally and domestically,[7] and its airforce might be called upon to down a hijacked aircraft en route to a 9/11-type attack.

Exactly how military force may be deployed internationally and domestically is a richly legal topic. This chapter discusses both international and domestic deployments of the CF, examining the international and domestic law that governs when and how military force may be used.

---

4   Canada, *A Role of Pride and Influence in the World: Defence* (2005), online: www.dnd.ca/site/reports/dps/index_e.asp [*Defence Policy Statement*].

5   See David Pugliese, "Military Gears Up for 20 Years of Overseas Anti-Terror Efforts" *Ottawa Citizen* (4 December 2006) A.1.

6   *Defence Policy Statement*, above note 4 at 47.

7   *Ibid.* at 48.

PART I: INTERNATIONAL USE OF FORCE

A. DEPLOYING FORCE

1) Basic Principles of International Law

Jus ad bellum is the body of international rules determining when recourse to military force is permissible. Article 2(4) of the U.N. *Charter* lies at the core of the modern international law on use of force. It specifies that "all Members shall refrain in their international relations from the threat or use of force against the territorial integrity or political independence of any state, or in any other manner inconsistent with the Purposes of the United Nations." The rule exists also as part of customary international law[8] and is widely regarded as a *jus cogens* norm.[9]

There is occasional debate as to the reach of Article 2(4) and its customary equivalent. Certain jurists urge, for example, that a use of force might fall short of impairing the "territorial integrity or political independence of any state" and therefore would not be prohibited.[10] In practice, however, it is difficult to imagine any nonconsensual use of force involving states that does not in some way impair a state's territorial integrity or political independence. For instance, the very act of using the force is an assault on a state's sovereign control over affairs within its borders.[11]

---

8   *Nicaragua v. United States of America*, [1986] I.C.J. Rep. 14 at para. 187 *et seq.*

9   A *jus cogens*, or peremptory, norm "is a norm accepted and recognized by the international community of States as a whole as a norm from which no derogation is permitted and which can be modified only by a subsequent norm of general international law having the same character." *Vienna Convention on the Law of Treaties*, 23 May 1969, 1155 UNTS 331, Art. 53. See discussion in Helen Duffy, *The "War on Terror" and the Framework of International Law* (Cambridge: Cambridge University Press, 2005) at 147 [*War on Terror*].

10 The narrow interpretation of Art. 2(4) is sometimes raised to justify "humanitarian intervention." See discussion, for example, in Celeste Poltak, "Humanitarian Intervention: A Contemporary Interpretation of the *Charter* of the United Nations" (2002), 60 U.T. Fac. L. Rev. 1. Humanitarian intervention is discussed further below.

11 See Malcolm Shaw, *International Law*, 5th ed. (Cambridge: Cambridge University Press, 2003) at 1021 (noting that the "weight of opinion probably" supports a demanding reading of Art. 2(4)). Support for this strict reading of the prohibition on the use of force is found in the U.N. General Assembly's influential *Declaration on Principles of International Law concerning Friendly Relations and Co-operation*. G.A. Res. 2625, Annex, 25 U.N. GAOR, Supp. (No. 28), U.N. Doc. A/5217 at 121 (1970). The Declaration denounces "armed intervention and all other forms of interference or attempted threats against the personality of the

There are, however, limited exceptions to the prohibition on use of force. For one thing, use of force by one state within the territory of another is permissible where the territorial state gives its permission.[12] Beyond this situation, military force directed by one state against another state or its territory is acceptable in international law in only two circumstances, both expressly anticipated by the U.N. *Charter.*[13] First,

---

State or against its political, economic and cultural elements, are in violation of international law." While not binding in its own right, the Declaration "elaborates the major principles of international law in the U.N. *Charter*, particularly on use of force, dispute settlement, nonintervention in domestic affairs, self-determination, duties of cooperation and observance of obligations, and 'sovereign equality.' [I]t has become the international lawyer's favorite example of an authoritative U.N. resolution." Oscar Schachter, "United Nations Law" (1994) 88 A.J.I.L. 1. Referring in part to this Declaration, Schachter has strongly urged a strict reading of the Art. 2(4) prohibition. See Oscar Schachter, "The Right of States to Use Armed Force" (1984) 82 Mich. L. Rev. 1620 ["Right of States"]. This approach is consistent with the International Court of Justice's recent ruling in *Case Concerning Armed Activities on the Territory of the Congo*, (2005) ICJ General List No. 116 at para. 163 *et seq.* [*Case Concerning Armed Activities*] ("The Court further affirms that acts which breach the principle of non-intervention "will also, if they directly or indirectly involve the use of force, constitute a breach of the principle of non-use of force in international relations").

12   See discussion in Davis Brown, "Use of Force against Terrorism After September 11th: State Responsibility, Self-Defense And Other Responses" (2003) 11 Cardozo J. Int'l & Comp. L. 1 at 30. NATO's current deployment in Afghanistan, for example, is done with the agreement of the Afghan government. See, for example, *Afghanistan Compact*, London Conference on Afghanistan (2006) at 3, online: www.fco.gov.uk/Files/kfile/20060130%20Afghanistan%20Compact%20Final%20Final,0.doc (in which Afghanistan and the "international community" agreed to the presence of the "NATO-led International Security Assistance Force (ISAF) and the U.S.-led Operation Enduring Freedom (OEF)"); *Declaration by the North Atlantic Treaty Organisation and the Islamic Republic of Afghanistan* (September 2006), online: www.nato.int/docu/basictxt/b060906e.htm ("Afghanistan recognises that at present it is unable to fully meet its own security needs and highly appreciates NATO's contribution to providing security and stability in Afghanistan").

13   This book does not discuss circumstances in which force is used, not by one state against another, but by U.N. peacekeepers deployed pursuant to Security Council resolutions in the territory of a state. The legal bases for these deployments varies. Classic peacekeeping missions are those in which belligerents consent to the presence of the peacekeepers on their territories and in which force is used by peacekeepers only in self-defence (a concept that is sometimes broadly defined). Authorization for these missions is provided by Security Council resolution, an instrument that in turn is implicitly authorized by Chapter VI of the U.N. *Charter*. For a discussion of the legal architecture of U.N. peacekeeping, see Joseph P. "Dutch" Bialke, "United Nations Peace Operations: Applicable Norms and the Application of the Law of Armed Conflict" (2001) 50 A.F.L. Rev. 1.

pursuant to Chapter VII of the U.N. *Charter*, the U.N. Security Council may legitimize and authorize this use of force. Second, an inherent right to self-defence is also recognized by the U.N. *Charter*.

a) Security Council Authorization

As noted in Chapter 3, under Article 39 of the U.N. *Charter*, the council is empowered to decide the existence of "any threat to the peace, breach of the peace, or act of aggression"—all undefined expressions. Under Article 42, where the Security Council considers measures short of force would be inadequate in grappling with these crises, it may authorize the use of military force. Article 42 of the U.N. *Charter* reads:

> Should the Security Council consider that measures provided for in Article 41 would be inadequate or have proved to be inadequate, it may take such action by air, sea, or land forces as may be necessary to maintain or restore international peace and security. Such action may include demonstrations, blockade, and other operations by air, sea, or land forces of Members of the United Nations.

Article 42 "authorizations" are uncommon. Indeed, Article 42 has never been expressly invoked by the council. The most famous example of a resolution precipitating the use of force is Resolution 678 (1990), authorizing member states to "use all necessary means" to enforce other resolutions calling on Iraq's withdrawal from Kuwait and to restore international peace and security to the region. The use of military force by the U.S.-led coalition of allied state in the 1991 Gulf War was largely predicated on this resolution, and indeed, participants in the 2003 Iraq war invoked (unpersuasively, in the opinion of most of the international community) Resolution 678 as a sort of standing authorization justifying that conflict.[14]

The formula "all necessary means" used in Resolution 678 is widely viewed as a coded invocation of Article 42,[15] although that view is occa-

---

14 See, for example, United Kingdom Government, *Memorandum from the Attorney General to the Prime Minister of the United Kingdom* (7 March 2003), online: www.number-10.gov.uk/output/Page7445.asp.

15 Duffy, *War on Terror*, above note 9 at 175 ("The 'all necessary means' language, while a euphemism, is universally understood in the diplomatic context as synonymous with the authorization of necessary force"); Jochen Abr. Forwein, "Article 42," in Bruno Simma, ed., *The Charter of the United Nations* (New York: Oxford University Press, 2002) (examining the Gulf War as an example of Article 42 authorization).

sionally contested.[16] Since 1990, it has been used several times.[17] However, it was not employed in relation to the two most famous situations in which the CF have been engaged in armed conflict in the last decade: the 1999 Kosovo air war and the 2001 Operation Enduring Freedom operation in Afghanistan.

The Kosovo conflict constituted a species of "humanitarian intervention," a justification for use of armed force that is not anticipated by the U.N. *Charter* and the validity of which is dubious.[18] The Afghan operation in its initial phases in 2001 constituted an exercise of self-defence, an issue discussed in Chapter 6 and more generally in the section that follows.

b) Self-Defence

Article 51 of the U.N. *Charter* preserves "the inherent right of individual or collective self-defence if an armed attack occurs against a Member of the United Nations, until the Security Council has taken measures necessary to maintain international peace and security." As the invocation of an "inherent right" suggests, the self-defence concept exists also as part of customary international law.[19] The precise relationship between the customary norm and Article 51 is a point of some debate. Certainly in all cases, the act of self-defence must be both proportional

---

16   See, for example, Yoram Dinstein, *War, Aggression and Self-Defence*, 4th ed. (Cambridge: Cambridge University Press, 2005) at 296. See also discussion in Oscar Schachter, "United Nations Law in the Gulf Conflict" (1991) 85 A.J.I.L. 452.

17   S/RES/794 (1992) (regarding Somalia); S/RES/816 (1993) (regarding airspace over Bosnia); S/RES/929 (1994) (regarding Rwanda); S/RES/940 (1994) (regarding Haiti); S/RES/1264 (1999) (regarding East Timor); S/RES/1386 (2001) (regarding Afghanistan, and issued after the overthrow of the Taliban); S/RES/1484 (2003) (regarding Congo). Close variants on the expression were used in S/RES/787 (1992) (regarding the arms embargo on the former Yugoslavia) and S/RES/1464 (2003) (regarding Ivory Coast). See discussion in Dinstein, *War, Aggression and Self-Defence*, *ibid.* at 303–4.

18   See, for example, the diversity of views canvassed in U.K. House of Commons, *Fourth Report*—Select Committee on Foreign Affairs (U.K.) (May 2000), online: www.publications.parliament.uk/pa/cm199900/cmselect/cmfaff/28/2802.htm. See also Duffy, *War on Terror*, above note 9 at 179 *et seq.* (reviewing the positions on the existence of a right to use force in humanitarian intervention and concluding that "it is doubtful that the heavy burden of establishing a customary right of humanitarian intervention has been satisfied at the present time, particularly given the scarcity with which such a right has been invoked by states").

19   See *Nicaragua v. United States of America*, above note 8. For a discussion of Art. 51 and the persistence of a parallel customary source of the right to self-defence, see Leo Van Den Hole, "Anticipatory Self-Defence under International Law" (2003) 19 Am. U. Int'l L. Rev. 69.

and necessary.[20] More contentious is the question of imminence; that is, whether the defending state must actually have suffered the blow of the "armed attack" invoked in Article 51 before responding. This section discusses the issues of armed attack, imminence, proportionality and necessity.

i) Imminence of Armed Attack

a. Armed Attack

Article 51 of the U.N. *Charter* specifies that the right to self-defence arises in response to "an armed attack." There is no bright line as to the degree of violence that must be exerted before an armed attack exists. Even a minor state military assault could be considered an armed attack for self-defence purposes.[21] Moreover, while an armed attack was once commonly associated with purely state conduct, that understanding has shifted in the post-9/11 era. The international community appears now to accept that nonstate actors may also commit an armed attack, a matter discussed in Chapter 6.

b. Imminence

Article 51 anticipates the existence of the right to self-defence only where an armed attack *occurs*, up until such time as the Security Council has taken measures necessary to maintain international peace and security. The language of the U.N. *Charter* envisages, therefore, self-defence as reactive and not preventive.

More complicated is the question of whether an attack that is imminent but has not yet arisen may trigger a right to self-defence in customary international law. The issue of imminence was addressed most famously in the *Caroline* incident, a dispute between the United States and Great Britain involving an American ship. The British believed that this vessel—the *Caroline*—would be employed by American sympathizers to support the 1837 uprising in Upper Canada. It was destroyed by British forces, on the American side of the border. In a series of let-

---

20 *Nicaragua v. United States of America*, ibid. at para. 176. See also *Case Concerning Oil Platforms (Islamic Republic of Iran v. United States of America)* (2003), ICJ General List No. 90 at para. 76 [*Oil Platforms Case*].

21 In the *Oil Platforms Case*, ibid., for instance, the United States characterized occasional exchanges of missile and gunfire with U.S. forces and mining of sea lanes in which American and international shipping travelled over multiple years, allegedly by Iran, as acts of violence constituting an "armed attack." For commentary on how the level of violence associated with an "armed attack" should be defined, see Emmanuel Gross, *The Struggle of Democracy Against Terrorism* (Charlottesville, VA: University of Virginia Press, 2006) at 32 *et seq.* See also Dinstein, *War, Aggression and Self-Defence*, above note 16 at 195.

ters between the U.S. and U.K. governments designed to resolve the resulting diplomatic dispute, the U.S. Secretary of State expressed the view, apparently shared by both sides, that self-defence was only warranted where there existed "no moment for deliberation."[22]

What this language means in practice is a point of disagreement among international lawyers. It seems plausible (although far from universally accepted) that customary international law allows "anticipatory self-defence": "where there is convincing evidence not merely of threats and potential danger but of *an attack being actually mounted*, then an armed attack may be said to have begun to occur, though it has not passed the frontier."[23] Put another way, the state need not suffer the blow it sees approaching, before responding in self-defence.

More contentious is whether "anticipatory self-defence" should be expanded to incorporate a concept of "pre-emptive self-defence," sometimes referred to as the "Bush Doctrine." In the 2002 National Security Strategy of the United States, the Bush administration asserted the right to act in self-defence against nascent, embryonic threats (such as the development of a weapon of mass destruction by a hostile regime), and not just against attacks that are imminent in a more conventional sense.[24]

This doctrine of "pre-emptive" self-defence has not been welcomed readily by the international community,[25] in part because of its close association with the (initial and ultimately ill-grounded) weapons of mass destruction justifications offered for the Iraq war. Not least among its flaws, pre-emptive self-defence is particularly vulnerable to abuse. It is an easily contorted justification for military force capable of accommodating most acts of aggression. Unlike conventional self-defence, where the existence of an attack is readily and objectively ascertained,

---

22   Letter from Daniel Webster to Lord Ashburton (6 August 1842), online: www. yale.edu/lawweb/avalon/diplomacy/britain/br-1842d.htm#web2.

23   C.H.M. Waldock, "The Regulation of the Use of Force by Individual States in International Law" (1952) 81 Hague Recueil 451 at 498 [emphasis added]. See also, for example, Schachter, "Right of States," above note 11 at 1633–35. It should also be noted that the terminology in this area is confused. Anticipatory self-defence is sometimes distinguished from the Bush doctrine of pre-emptive self-defence, discussed also in this section on the basis of the immediacy of the threat. This book follows this pattern.

24   U.S. National Security Strategy 2002, above note 1 at 15.

25   For a careful review on this point, see W. Michael Reisman & Andrea Armstrong, "The Past and Future of the Claim of Preemptive Self-Defence" (2006) 100 A.J.I.L. 525. For an analysis rejecting any claim that pre-emptive self-defence has emerged as a customary norm, see James Thuo Gathii, "Assessing Claims of a New Doctrine of Pre-emptive War under the Doctrine of Sources" (2005) 43 Osgoode Hall L.J. 67.

pre-emptive self-defence is built on intelligence and inferences of prospective enemy intentions, a notoriously difficult basis for decision
making. Ready acceptance of the doctrine would gravely undermine
the historic restraints on use of force imposed by the U.N. *Charter*, with
serious consequences for human rights and global stability. The U.N.
Secretary-General's High-Level Panel addressed this issue persuasively
in its 2004 report: "in a world full of perceived potential threats, the
risk to the global order and the norm of non-intervention on which it
continues to be based is simply too great for the legality of unilateral
preventive action, as distinct from collectively endorsed action, to be
accepted. Allowing one to so act is to allow all."[26]

ii) Necessity

The other elements of self-defence are less contentious, although their
application can sometimes produce complications. To be legal, force
used in self-defence must be necessary to respond to (and repel) the
armed attack. In practice, this means that force must be the only available means of staving off the armed attack.[27] In the words of the U.S.
Secretary of State in the *Caroline* dispute: the necessity of self-defence
must be "instant, overwhelming, and leaving no choice of means."[28]
Necessity depends, therefore, on the facts. In the *Nicaragua* case, there
was no necessity where the use of force in alleged self-defence took
place months after the putative armed attack had been repulsed.[29] In
the *Oil Platforms Case* the International Court of Justice viewed force as
unnecessary where, on the facts, it was directed at targets considered
targets of opportunity by the allegedly defending state.[30]

iii) Proportionality

Proportionality is usually taken to mean use of force in self-defence no
greater than is required to halt and repel the armed attack; that is, pro-

---

26   *A More Secure World: Our Shared Responsibility*, Report of the U.N. Secretary-
     General's High-level Panel on Threats, Challenges and Change (2004), online:
     www.un.org/secureworld/.
27   Schachter, "Right of States," above note 11 at 1635 ("force should not be consid-
     ered necessary until peaceful measures have been found wanting or when they
     clearly would be futile"); Dinstein, *War, Aggression and Self-Defence*, above note
     16 at 237 ("Necessity comes to the fore when war is begun following an isolated
     armed attack. Before the defending State opens the floodgates to full-scale hos-
     tilities, it is obligated to verify that a reasonable settlement of the conflict in an
     amicable way is not attainable.").
28   Letter from Daniel Webster to Lord Ashburton, above note 22.
29   *Nicaragua v. United States of America*, above note 8 at para. 237.
30   *Oil Platforms Case*, above note 20 at para. 76.

portional to the military objective of countering the threat.[31] Assessed against this standard, armed force is proportional if properly directed at forestalling the recurrence of attack. Proportionality would persist even if the exercise of force for this purpose produced civilian casualities in excess of those injured in the initial armed attack. The legitimacy of these civilian, "collateral" consequences of resort to force in self-defence would fall to be measured by international humanitarian law, the *jus in bello* that applies when armed conflicts are in progress.[32] Modest support for this view may be extracted from the ICJ's reasoning in *Legality of the Threat or Use of Nuclear Weapons*. There, the Court suggested that at the very least "a use of force that is proportionate under the law of self-defence, must, in order to be lawful, also meet the requirements of the law applicable in armed conflict which comprise in particular the principles and rules of humanitarian law."[33] The rules of international humanitarian law in relation to civilian casualties are discussed later in this chapter.

For some jurists, however, the proportionality of the response is to be assessed with reference to the scale of the armed attack defended against, at least in circumstances where the armed attack is isolated.[34]

---

31 See discussion in Shaw, *International Law*, above note 11 at 1031, n88; Duffy, *War on Terror*, above note 9 at 162 ("the proportionately test should be applied *vis-à-vis* the requirements of averting the threat, as opposed to in respect of the scale of that threat or of any prior armed attack. Arguments as to numbers of persons killed in the original attack outweighing numbers killed in subsequent counter-measures are of political relevance only"); Dinstein, *War, Aggression and Self-Defence*, above note 16 at 237–38 (noting that notion that proportionality should be assessed in relation to the initial armed attack "throughout the hostilities in the course of war" enjoys no state support).

32 For a discussion on this issue, see Judith Gardam, "Proportionality and Force in International Law" (1993) 87 A.J.I.L. 391. For instance, *Protocol Additional to the Geneva Conventions of 12 August 1949, and relating to the Protection of Victims of International Armed Conflicts* [AP I], online: www.unhchr.ch/html/menu3/b/93.htm, regards as indiscriminate "[a]n attack which may be expected to cause incidental loss of civilian life, injury to civilians, damage to civilian objects, or a combination thereof, which would be excessive in relation to the concrete and direct military advantage anticipated." AP I, Art. 51(5)(b).

33 *Legality of the Threats or Use of Nuclear Weapons*, General List No. 95 (8 July 1996) at para. 42.

34 For a discussion of the different methods of computing proportionality, applied in the specific case of terrorism, see Robert J. Beck & Anthony Clark Arend, "'Don't Tread On Us': International Law and Forcible State Responses to Terrorism" (1994) 12 Wis. Int'l L.J. 153 at 206. See also Dinstein, *War, Aggression and Self-Defence*, above note 16 at 238 ("it would be irrational to permit an all-out war whenever a State absorbs an isolated armed attack, however marginal. . . . Some sort of proportionality has to be a major consideration in pondering the

Measured against this standard, an armed response could become disproportionate if the consequences of the response—measured in civilian casualties, perhaps—outstrip those of the initial armed attack.[35]

c)   Collective Self-Defence

The U.N. *Charter*'s self-defence provision explicitly acknowledges the propriety of "collective" self-defence; that is, self-defence exercised by nations allied to the state actually attacked. The *Charter* also endorses the existence of regional organizations, including those dealing with the maintenance of international peace of security.[36]

Canada participates in collective self-defence organizations through its membership in the North Atlantic Treaty Organization (NATO), constituted under the *North Atlantic Treaty*. It also works in close alliance with the United States pursuant to the North American Aerospace Defence Command (NORAD) agreement.

The 1949 *North Atlantic Treaty* is a true collective self-defence instrument. It provides that an armed attack against one NATO state

> shall be considered an attack against them all and consequently they agree that, if such an armed attack occurs, each of them, in exercise of the right of individual or collective self-defence recognised by Article 51 of the *Charter* of the United Nations, will assist the Party or Parties so attacked by taking forthwith, individually and in concert

---

legitimacy of a defensive war"). Notably, in several cases, the ICJ has apparently contrasted the harm caused by armed attack against the scale of the act of self-defence in assessing the existence of proportionality. In *Nicaragua v. United States of America*, above note 8 at para. 176, the ICJ described proportionality as "proportional to the armed attack," without further discussing this point. In the *Oil Platforms Case*, above note 20 at para. 76, the court concluded that the destruction by the United States of two Iranian oil platforms, "two Iranian frigates and a number of other naval vessels and aircraft," was not proportionate to the mining, by an unidentified agency, of a single United States warship, which was severely damaged but not sunk, and without loss of life." *Ibid.* at para. 77. See also *Case Concerning Armed Activities*, above note 11 at para. 147 (noting, without deciding, "that the taking of airports and towns many hundreds of kilometres from Uganda's border would not seem proportionate to the series of transborder attacks it claimed had given rise to the right of self-defence").

35   See discussion in Schachter, "Right of States," above note 11 at 1637 ("when defensive action is greatly in excess of the provocation, as measured by relative casualties or scale of weaponry, international opinion will more readily condemn such defense as illegally disproportionate. Some of the Security Council decisions that declared the use of force to be illegal reprisal rather than legitimate defense noted the much higher number of casualties resulting from the defense in relation to those caused by the earlier attack").

36   U.N. *Charter*, Art. 52.

with the other Parties, such action as it deems necessary, including the use of armed force, to restore and maintain the security of the North Atlantic area.[37]

This provision has been invoked only once in NATO's history: after the 9/11 attacks on the United States.[38]

The NORAD agreement, in place since the 1950s, was renewed in 2006 and tasks NORAD with aerospace warning and control over the skies of North America, and maritime warning for North American waters. "Warning" involves scrutiny over the air and maritime approaches to the continent to detect attacks (and, in the case of maritime warning) threats. "Aerospace control" includes operational control over Canadian and U.S. airspace; that is, "the authority to direct, coordinate, and control the operational activities of forces assigned, attached, or otherwise made available to NORAD."[39]

A recent controversy concerns Canada's participation via NORAD or otherwise in the United States' missile defence project. While Canada has declined to participate in this initiative, the revised NORAD agreement now clarifies that "NORAD's aerospace warning mission for North America shall include aerospace warning … in support of United States national commands responsible for missile defense."[40]

It should be noted that collective self-defence treaties do not embellish or somehow counter the limitations on use of force found in the U.N. *Charter*. The mere existence of NATO, for example, does not change the terms of self-defence, and the circumstances in which it may be triggered.[41]

---

37   *North Atlantic Treaty*, 4 April 1949, Art. 5.

38   NATO, Press Release, "Invocation of Article 5 Confirmed" (2 Oct. 2001), online: www.nato.int/docu/update/2001/1001/e1002a.htm.

39   *Agreement Between The Government Of Canada And The Government Of The United States Of America On The North American Aerospace Defense Command* (28 April 2006), Art. 1, online: www.treaty-accord.gc.ca/ViewTreaty.asp?Treaty_ID=105060.

40   *Ibid.*

41   See Duffy, *War on Terror*, above note 9 at 167 ("No autonomous right to use of force is, or could be, contained in the NATO treaty or any other agreement. Indeed the *Charter* would prevail over any other agreement inconsistent with its terms"). Indeed, the *North Atlantic Treaty*, Art. 5, expressly invokes Art. 51 of the U.N. *Charter* in its discussions of self-defence. The Treaty will be triggered by an armed attack against the territory and/or forces of its members, including while the latter are deployed in the Mediterranean or North Atlantic seas.

2) International Deployment of Military Force in Domestic Law

a) Executive Discretion

Under Canada's Constitution, the federal Parliament has exclusive authority over defence.[42] In keeping with this power, Parliament has enacted the *National Defence Act* constituting the CF.[43] Constitutionally, command of this military vests in the governor general.[44] In this latter capacity, the governor general "encourages excellence and dedication in military personnel, visits Canadian Forces bases in all regions of the country, often welcomes troops on their return from overseas missions and performs other ceremonial duties."[45]

The governor general does not, however, decide when and where to deploy the CF. In practice, this power is exercised by the governor-in-council; for all practical purposes, the federal Cabinet acting under the leadership of the prime minister.[46]

By long-standing tradition, a decision to deploy the CF is made exclusively by the executive branch as an exercise of the royal prerogative. There is no obligation that its use be authorized by Parliament or even preceded by a debate in that body. "The federal Cabinet," a 2006 Library of Parliament study concluded, "can, without parliamentary approval or consultation, commit Canadian Forces to action abroad, whether in the form of a specific current operation or future contingencies resulting from international treaty obligations."[47] This passage echoes the view expressed by the Standing Senate Committee on Foreign Affairs in 2000.[48]

---

42 *Constitution Act, 1867* (U.K.), 30 & 31 Victoria, c. 3, s. 91(7), reprinted in R.S.C. 1985, App. II, No. 5.

43 R.S.C., 1985, c. N-5 [NDA].

44 *Constitution Act, 1867*, above note 42, s. 15 (assigning the role of Commander in Chief to the Queen). By Letters Patent issued by George VI in 1947, C. Gaz. (1947) I.3104, vol. 81, the governor general is empowered "to exercise all powers and authorities lawfully belonging to Us in respect of Canada."

45 Commons Standing Committee on Government Operations and Estimates, *Second Report: The Governor General of Canada: Role, Duties and Funding for Activities* (37th Parl., 3d Sess., 2004), online: http://cmte.parl.gc.ca/cmte/Com-mitteePublication.aspx?COM=8799&Lang=1&SourceId=76177.

46 Library of Parliament, *International Deployment of Canadian Forces: Parliament's Role*, PRB 00-06E (18 May 2006) at 1, online: www.parl.gc.ca/information/library/PRBpubs/prb0006-e.htm [*International Deployment*].

47 *Ibid.* at 1.

48 Standing Senate Committee on Foreign Affairs, *The New NATO and the Evolution of Peacekeeping: Implications for Canada* (April 2000) c. VIII, online: www.

b) Parliamentary Role

An Act of Parliament may curtail a prerogative power, both explicitly and (according to one recent Supreme Court decision) by necessary implication.[49] There is no compelling argument, however, that Parliament has so acted in relation to the prerogative to deploy the Canadian Forces abroad. Certainly, Canadian statute law does anticipate a parliamentary role in relation to some CF functions. The dispatch of the CF pursuant to an order under the *Emergencies Act* would be subject to scrutiny in Parliament, *per* that statute's system of Parliamentary review.[50] Further, the *National Defence Act* does anticipate a parliamentary role when the CF are placed on "active service." The government may place the CF on active service in an emergency, for the defence of Canada, as part of Canadian actions undertaken under the U.N. *Charter*, the North Atlantic Treaty, the NORAD Agreement or any like instrument.[51] The Act requires that Parliament then be called back to session, if adjourned or prorogued, within ten days.[52] Parliament will be in session, in other words, presumptively to scrutinize the active service order.

Although there are different views on the issue,[53] the active service provision has not been treated as a statutory rule on when the CF may be deployed. In practice, active service has no other implication than to affect some pension benefits, the application of the *Code of Service Discipline*, discussed later in this chapter, and provisions for release of personnel from the CF.[54] Notably, the CF have been in a standing state of active service for generations.[55]

Parliament's real control over deployment comes through the confidence convention — its ability to bring down a government in a vote of nonconfidence — and its control of the business of supply, provisioning

---

parl.gc.ca/36/2/parlbus/commbus/senate/com-e/fore-e/REP-E/rep07apr00-e.htm [*The New NATO*].

49   *Ross River Dena Council Band*, [2002] 2 S.C.R. 816 at para. 54. As discussed elsewhere, whether a prerogative may be displaced by implication is a point of contention.

50   See Chapter 4.

51   NDA, above note 43, s. 31.

52   *Ibid.*, s. 32.

53   But see *Aleksic v. Canada (Attorney General)* (2002), 215 D.L.R. (4th) 720 at para. 7 (Ont. Div. Ct.), Wright J., dissenting in the result (suggesting that the executive may not use the royal prerogative to commit the CF to active service because the active service provision displaces the common law prerogative). The majority did not come to a conclusion on this point. See *ibid.* at para. 26.

54   Library of Parliament, *International Deployment*, above note 46 at 2, n6.

55   *Ibid.* at 3. See, in particular, the order placing the CF on active service for the purpose of fulfilling Canada's NATO obligations. S.I./89-103. Since NATO is a standing obligation, this active service order has a permanent application.

the Forces with funds. Both of these controls are largely theoretical instruments, applicable only when a critical mass of members of Parliament is prepared to vote out a government, or vote down money for deployed troops. Such circumstances arise rarely, although in late 2006 the Bloc Québécois threatened to topple the minority Harper government over the Afghan mission.

There is also now a (soft) tradition of debating at least some aspects of deployments through a take-note debate in the Commons; that is, a debate on a motion asking the house to take note of an issue, but not requiring a vote and in no way binding on the government. It is conceivable that this practice will someday crystallize into a "constitutional convention" — essentially regularized political practices that in time are regarded as mandatory. That time has almost certainly not yet arrived, given the infrequency of these debates in practice.[56] Parliamentarians may also probe deployments in committee hearings and query ministers in Question Period, a way to raise questions about deployments but not a means of approving them.

In sum, Parliament has a perfunctory role in influencing the deployment of the CF on foreign missions. This situation has not sat easily with some parliamentarians. "Both Houses of Parliament," recommended the Senate foreign affairs committee in 2000, should "have the opportunity to debate and approve at the earliest possible moment Canadian participation in any military intervention or external conflict situation, including peacekeeping and peacemaking missions, with the Government clearly spelling out Canada's interest in the situation and the scope of Canadian involvement."[57] Private members' bills have occasionally been tabled that, if enacted, would limit the executive's prerogative powers.[58] Similar constraints have been proposed in the United Kingdom.[59] By the time of this writing none had been enacted.

---

56   See Library of Parliament, *International Deployment*, above note 46 for a careful review of the (in)frequency with which Parliament has debated deployments.

57   Standing Senate Committee on Foreign Affairs, *The New NATO*, above note 48.

58   Library of Parliament, *International Deployment*, above note 46 at 7.

59   U.K. MPs voted on the deployment of U.K. forces in Iraq in 2003, breaking with U.K. precedent. Subsequently, the Public Administration Select Committee's Fourth Report of the 2003–04 Session, *Taming the Prerogative: Strengthening Ministerial Accountability*, HC 422, online: www.publications.parliament.uk/pa/cm200304/cmselect/cmpubadm/422/422.pdf, recommended full parliamentary scrutiny of the prerogative decisions on armed conflict. The U.K. government response was noncommittal. However, now-Prime Minister Gordon Brown has endorsed a role of Parliament in approving deployments. BBC, Brown calls for MPs to decide war (30 April 2005), online: http://news.bbc.co.uk/2/hi/uk_news/politics/vote_2005/frontpage/4500295.stm. See also *Prime Minister's*

c) Judicial Review

It should also be observed that the government's prerogative power to deploy the CF is also not easily reviewed in court. In the several instances in which CF deployments were challenged on judicial review in Federal Court, the matters were dismissed as nonjusticiable questions of "high policy" beyond the purview of the courts.[60]

The exact scope of this high policy immunized from judicial scrutiny is not clear. It seems, however, that not all exercises of the prerogative of defence are insulated from court scrutiny, at least where the government decision also raises *Canadian Charter of Rights and Freedoms* issues.[61]

B. PROPER USE OF DEPLOYED MILITARY FORCE

1) Basic Principles of International Law

A legitimate justification for use of force, measured by the *jus ad bellum*, does not authorize any and all forms of violence. The actual manner in which violence is used must comply with the *jus in bello*. The exact content of this *jus in bello* is usually assumed to be international humanitarian law (IHL). IHL is best known in its treaty form. Key among these instruments are the four Geneva Conventions of 1949 and their two 1977 Additional Protocols. These treaties are discussed repeatedly in this book. A basic sense of their coverage is set out in Table 5.1. Most

---

Constitutional Reform statement (3 July 2007), online: www.number-10.gov.
uk/output/Page12274.asp. See also U.K. House of Commons, Bill 31 (2004–05)
(Armed Forces [Parliamentary Approval for Participation in Armed Conflict]
Bill), a U.K. private members' law-project, online: www.publications.parliament.
uk/pa/cm200405/cmbills/031/2005031.pdf.

60   *Turp v. Canada (Prime Minister)*, 2003 FCT 301 at para. 14 (describing the
prerogative power to deploy the CF as one of high policy therefore as nonjusticiable); *Aleksic v. Canada*, above note 53 at para. 31 *et seq.* (similar holding);
Blanco v. Canada, 2003 FCT 263 (similar holding). For United Kingdom equivalents, see *R. v. Ministry of Defence, ex parte Smith*, [1995] 4 All E.R. 427 (Q.B.)
(exercise of prerogative of defence not justiciable where it concerns issues of
national security and where court had insufficient expertise to form judgment).
See also *Campaign for Nuclear Disarmament v. The Prime Minister of the United
Kingdom and others*, [2002] EWHC 2777 (Q.B.) (court refusing to the issue declaration on the international legality of the U.K. deployment to Iraq).

61   *Operation Dismantle Inc. v. Canada*, [1985] 1 S.C.R. 441 (prerogative defence
powers subject to review under the *Charter*).

of the rules contained in these instruments exist also as customary international law.[62]

Table 5.1:   Scope of the Geneva Conventions and Additional Protocols

Instrument	Scope
Geneva Convention I[1]	Wounded soldiers on the battlefield
Geneva Convention II[2]	Wounded and shipwrecked sailors
Geneva Convention III[3]	Prisoners of War
Geneva Convention IV[4]	Civilians under control of an occupying power
Additional Protocol I[5]	Amplification of the rules applicable in international armed conflicts
Additional Protocol II[6]	Amplification of the rules applicable in noninternational armed conflicts

[1] *Convention for the Amelioration of the Condition of the Wounded and Sick in Armed Forces in the Field*, 12 August 1949 [Geneva Convention I].

[2] *Convention for the Amelioration of the Condition of Wounded, Sick and Shipwrecked Members of Armed Forces at Sea*, 12 August 1949 [Geneva Convention II].

[3] *Convention relative to the Treatment of Prisoners of War*, 12 August 1949 [Geneva Convention III].

[4] *Convention relative to the Protection of Civilian Persons in Time of War*, 12 August 1949 [Geneva Convention IV].

[5] AP I, above note 32, 8 June 1977.

[6] *Protocol Additional to the Geneva Conventions of 12 August 1949, and relating to the Protection of Victims of Non-International Armed Conflicts*, 8 June 1977 [AP II].

a)   Application of IHL

i)   Concept of Armed Conflict

IHL applies in circumstances of armed conflict, a term that is not precisely defined.[63] The existence of an armed conflict does not require a declared war.[64] Instead, armed conflict usually requires the use of mil-

---

62   See Yoram Dinstein, *The Conduct of Hostilities under the Law of International Armed Conflict* (Cambridge: Cambridge University Press, 2004) at 5. This is especially true of the 1949 Geneva Conventions. The customary status of the 1977 Additional Protocols is less certain, although a recent and comprehensive review by the International Committee of the Red Cross presents strong evidence of the customary status of many of the rules found in the latter instruments. Jean-Marie Henckaerts & Louise Doswald-Beck, *Customary International Humanitarian Law* (Cambridge: Cambridge University Press, 2005).

63   See Gross, *Struggle of Democracy Against Terrorism*, above note 21 at 53.

64   Christopher Greenwood, "Scope of the Application of Humanitarian Law," in Dieter Fleck, ed., *The Handbook of Law in Armed Conflicts* (Oxford: Oxford University Press, 1995) at 41 [*Handbook*]. The Geneva Conventions provide, in Common Article 2, that the Conventions "shall apply to all cases of declared war *or of any other armed conflict* which may arise between two or more of the

itary force reaching a certain threshold of intensity. The International Committee of the Red Cross sets this threshold very low: "Any difference arising between two States and leading to the intervention of armed forces is an armed conflict ..., even if one of the Parties denies the existence of a state of war. It makes no difference how long the conflict lasts, or how much slaughter takes place."[65] In *Tadic*, the International Criminal Tribunal for the Former Yugoslavia (ICTY) concluded that

> an armed conflict exists whenever there is a resort to armed force between States or protracted armed violence between governmental authorities and organized armed groups or between such groups within a State. International humanitarian law applies from the initiation of such armed conflicts and extends beyond the cessation of hostilities until a general conclusion of peace is reached; or, in the case of internal conflicts, a peaceful settlement is achieved. Until that moment, international humanitarian law continues to apply in the whole territory of the warring States or, in the case of internal conflicts, the whole territory under the control of a party, whether or not actual combat takes place there.[66]

Note that the ICTY approach bifurcates the armed conflict threshold between international (as in interstate) conflicts and noninternational conflicts — that is, conflicts between states and nonstate actors. In the latter case, the existence of an armed conflict requires "protracted" armed violence.[67] In the former instance, mere "resort" to armed force suffices.

State practice may suggest, however, a more demanding threshold than mere "resort" to armed force in relation to even interstate conflicts. It is sometimes urged, for instance, that to constitute an international armed conflict, the use of military force must involve more than isolated incidents; that is, more than occasional border skirmish-

---

High Contracting Parties, *even if the state of war is not recognized by one of them*" [emphasis added]. A declared war may trigger the application of the Geneva Conventions, as will a situation of military occupation, even when not met by armed resistance. *Ibid*. at 41.

65   ICRC *Commentary* to Art. 2, *Convention (I) for the Amelioration of the Condition of the Wounded and Sick in Armed Forces in the Field. Geneva, 12 August 1949*, online: www.icrc.org/ihl.nsf/COM/370-580005?OpenDocument.

66   *Prosecutor v. Dusko Tadic*, Decision of the U.N. International Tribunal for the Prosecution of Persons Responsible for Serious Violations of International Humanitarian Law Committed in the Territory of Former Yugoslavia since 1991, Case No. IT-94-1-AR72, reprinted in (1996), 35 I.L.M. 32 at para. 70.

67   For a more detailed discussion of the armed conflict concept in state-nonstate conflicts, see Chapter 6.

es or naval exchanges.[68] On the other hand, even an isolated incident of great magnitude can cross the threshold of armed conflict. Further, a situation of armed conflict can exist even if only one side has used armed force.[69] As one jurist has noted, "[I]f Iraq had used a special weapon and killed 3000 people in New York, one would not doubt that such an attack constituted an armed conflict, although it might have been isolated and sporadic."[70]

ii)   International and Noninternational Armed Conflicts

As the discussion to this point suggests, IHL distinguishes between international (or interstate) and noninternational (or state–nonstate) armed conflicts. The Geneva Conventions deal almost exclusively with the former; that is, conflicts between two state parties to the Conventions. Noninternational conflicts—conflicts between a state and a nonstate actor, usually in a civil war context—are governed only by "Common Article 3"—the common provision found as Article 3 in the four Geneva Conventions and also in customary international law—and Additional Protocol II and its customary equivalents. Additional Protocol II amplifies the fundamental guarantees found in Common Article 3; namely, the right of persons taking no active part in hostilities to humane treatment. Common Article 3 bars the following conduct in relation to these protected persons:

(a)   Violence to life and person, in particular murder of all kinds, mutilation, cruel treatment and torture;

(b)   Taking of hostages;

(c)   Outrages upon personal dignity, in particular, humiliating and degrading treatment;

(d)   The passing of sentences and the carrying out of executions without previous judgment pronounced by a regularly consti-

---

68   Greenwood, *Handbook*, above note 64 at 42; U.K. Ministry of Defence, *The Manual of the Law of Armed Conflict* (Oxford: Oxford University Press, 2004) at 29. See also discussion in Duffy, *War on Terror*, above note 9 at 219, n11 and the views canvassed in International Committee of the Red Cross, *XXVIIth Round Table on Current Problems of International Humanitarian Law: "International Humanitarian Law and Other Legal Regimes: Interplay in Situations of Violence"* (2003) at 3, online: www.icrc.org/Web/eng/siteeng0.nsf/htmlall/5UBCVX/$File/Interplay_other_regimes_Nov_2003.pdf.

69   Silja Vöeky, "The Fight Against Terrorism and the Rules of the Law of Warfare," in Christian Walter *et al.*, *Terrorism as a Challenge for National and International Law: Security Versus Liberty* (Berlin: Springer, 2004) at 903 *et seq.*

70   *Ibid.* at 931.

tuted court affording all the judicial guarantees which are recognized as indispensable by civilized peoples.

Paragraph (d) figured prominently in the U.S. Supreme Court's 2006 condemnation of the then existing U.S. military tribunals used to try "enemy combatants" in the "war on terror,"[71] a matter discussed in Chapter 14.

The existence of a noninternational armed conflict requires more than sporadic violence between a state and a nonstate actor. First, the violence must reach a sufficient level of intensity. The *Tadic* standard of "protracted" armed violence is noted above. On its own terms, meanwhile, Additional Protocol II considers "situations of internal disturbances and tensions, such as riots, isolated and sporadic acts of violence and other acts of a similar nature, as not being armed conflicts."[72]

Second, the nonstate actor that is a party to the conflict must be sufficiently organized. Additional Protocol II applies to "armed conflicts … which take place in the territory of a [state party] … between its armed forces and *dissident armed forces or other organized armed groups which, under responsible command, exercise such control over a part of its territory as to enable them to carry out sustained and concerted military operations.*"[73] While not express in the Geneva Conventions, a similar standard of organization may apply as a prerequisite to the application of Common Article 3.[74]

b)   Key Principles of International Humanitarian Law

International humanitarian law is built on the concept that not all means and methods of warfare are legitimate and that distinctions must be drawn between combatants and noncombatants.

i)   *Protected Persons*

The core thrust of international humanitarian law is to protect persons who do not take part in the fighting. These people include civilians and medical and religious military personnel and also those who have stopped participating in hostilities, such as wounded, shipwrecked and

---

71   *Hamdan v. Rumsfeld*, 126 S. Ct. 2749 (2006).
72   AP II, above Table 5.1, note 6, Art. 1.
73   *Ibid.* [emphasis added].
74   International Committee of the Red Cross, *XXVIIth Round Table on Current Problems of International Humanitarian Law: "International Humanitarian Law and Other Legal Regimes: Interplay in Situations of Violence"* (2003) at 5–6, online: www.icrc.org/Web/eng/siteeng0.nsf/htmlall/5UBCVX/$File/Interplay_other_regimes_Nov_2003.pdf.

sick combatants, and prisoners of war. These "protected" persons are entitled to important rights, including the requirement that they be treated humanely in all circumstances. IHL bars, for instance, the killing or wounding of a surrendered enemy. Prisoners of war are to be treated in keeping with a series of detailed rules, and the Conventions and Protocols also spell out important standards for civilians under the authority of an enemy power.

To enhance protection of civilians, IHL limits attacks to combatants and military objectives and outlaws methods of warfare that do not discriminate between combatants and civilians. IHL does accept what are colloquially termed "collateral" casualties—civilians injured unintentionally in a legitimate attack on military objectives. However, this harm must be proportional to the *bona fide* military advantage. An attack is prohibited "which may be expected to cause incidental loss of civilian life, injury to civilians, damage to civilian objects, or a combination thereof, which would be excessive in relation to the concrete and direct military advantage anticipated."[75] "Concrete and direct military advantage" is an important limiter. It means an "advantage that is identifiable and quantifiable and one that flows directly from the attack, and not some pious hope that it might improve the military situation in the long term."[76]

Proportionality in IHL is an inherently fact-intensive concept, one that attempts to "balance the conflicting military and humanitarian interests."[77] It requires what the Israeli Supreme Court has called a "values-based test" to be conducted on a case-by-case basis.[78] That court has suggested that returning the fire of a sniper shooting at soldiers or civilians from his or her porch is proportionate, "even if as a result, an innocent civilian neighbor or passerby is harmed. That is not the case

---

75   AP I, above note 32, Art. 51. See also AP I, Art. 57.

76   U.K. Ministry of Defence, *Manual*, above note 68 at 86.

77   A.P.V. Rogers, *Law on the Battlefield* (Manchester: Manchester University Press, 2004) at 17. See also Canada, Judge Advocate General, *Law of Armed Conflict Manual*, B-GJ-005-104/FP-021 (2001) at 2-2 ("In deciding whether the principle of proportionality is being respected, the standard of measurement is the anticipated contribution to the military purpose of an attack or operation considered as a whole. The anticipated military advantage must be balanced against other consequences of the action, such as the adverse effect upon civilians or civilian objects. It involves weighing the interests arising from the success of the operation on the one hand, against the possible harmful effects upon protected persons and objects on the other").

78   *The Public Committee against Torture in Israel v. The Government of Israel*, (2006) HCJ 769/02 at paras. 45 and 46.

if the building is bombed from the air and scores of its residents and passersby are harmed."[79]

Committing a "grave" breach of the Geneva Conventions or certain other violations of customary IHL rules is a "war crime" amenable to prosecution before the International Criminal Court,[80] assuming that body has jurisdiction over the offender.[81] For their part, state parties to the Conventions are obliged to exercise their own criminal jurisdiction over these crimes.[82]

ii) Combatant's Privilege

IHL accepts that violence can be intentionally directed at persons other than protected persons; that is, at other combatants.[83] As the Israeli Supreme Court noted in 2006: "in general, combatants and military objectives are legitimate targets for military attack. Their lives and bodies are endangered by the combat. They can be killed and wounded. However, not every act of combat against them is permissible, and not every military means is permissible. Thus, for example, they can be shot and killed. However, 'treacherous killing' and 'perfidy' are forbidden. Use of certain weapons is also forbidden."[84]

---

79   *Ibid.* at para. 46.

80   A grave breach includes: wilful killing; torture or inhuman treatment, including biological experiments; wilfully causing great suffering, or serious injury to body or health; extensive destruction and appropriation of property, not justified by military necessity and carried out unlawfully and wantonly; compelling a prisoner of war or other protected person to serve in the forces of a hostile Power; wilfully depriving a prisoner of war or other protected person of the rights of fair and regular trial; unlawful deportation or transfer or unlawful confinement; and taking of hostages. Other acts considered war crimes in customary international law and prosecutable before the International Criminal Court include: intentionally directing attacks against the civilian population as such or against individual civilians not taking direct part in hostilities; attacking or bombarding, by whatever means, towns, villages, dwellings or buildings which are undefended and which are not military objectives; and, killing or wounding a combatant who, having laid down his arms or having no longer means of defence, has surrendered at discretion. *Rome Statute of the International Criminal Court*, U.N. Doc. A/CONF.183/9, Art. 8 [*Rome Statute*].

81   The court has jurisdiction where the accused is a national of a party to the treaty, or the crime took place on the territory of such a party. The U.N. Security Council is also empowered to refer a matter to the Court. *Rome Statute, ibid.*, Arts. 12 and 13.

82   See, for example, Geneva Convention III, above Table 5.1, note 3, Art. 129.

83   AP I, above note 32, Art. 43 (noting that "armed forces" "have the right to participate directly in hostilities").

84   Above note 78 at para. 23. See, for example, AP I, *ibid.*, Art. 37 (dealing with perfidy).

If captured, a lawful combatant in an international conflict cannot be prosecuted by the detaining state for bearing arms in the conflict and conducting hostilities, if done in a manner otherwise lawful under international humanitarian law.[85] This notion creates what is called "combatant's privilege."[86] Who is entitled to combatant's privilege is a pressing issue in the post-9/11 era. There is no express concept of "unlawful" or "illegal" combatant in the Geneva Conventions or the Additional Protocols, notwithstanding the use of these terms in the post-9/11 era.[87] It is clear, however, that in international conflicts, prisoner of war status and treatment (and the accompanying privilege from prosecution) are denied to spies, mercenaries and, by default, to any sort of combatant not listed as entitled to them in the Geneva Conventions, a matter discussed in Chapter 14. It is also true that civilians who "take a direct part in hostilities" may be the object of attack.[88] For these reasons, the civilian combatant loses protected states, and at the same time enjoys

---

85   Geneva Convention III, above Table 5.1, note 3, Art. 99, for example, provides: "No prisoner of war may be tried or sentenced for an act which is not forbidden by the law of the Detaining Power or by international law." Combatant's privilege also has customary international law status.

86   For a discussion of combatant's privilege, see Robert Goldman & Brian Tittemore, "Unprivileged Combatants and the Hostilities in Afghanistan: Their Status and Rights Under International Human Rights and Humanitarian Law," in Am. Soc. Intl. L.: Task Force Papers (Dec. 2002), online: www.asil.org/taskforce/goldman.pdf; Knutt Dormann, "The Legal Situation of "Unlawful/Unprivileged Combatants" (2003) 85 Int'l Rev. Red Cross 45 at 45 ("(lawful) combatants cannot be prosecuted for lawful acts of war in the course of military operations even if their behaviour would constitute a serious crime in peacetime. They can be prosecuted only for violations of international humanitarian law, in particular for war crimes"); Joseph Bialke, "Al-Qaeda and Taliban Unlawful Combatant Detainees, Unlawful Belligerency, And The International Laws Of Armed Conflict" (2004) 55 A.F.L. Rev. 1 at 9; Kenneth Watkin, *Warriors without Rights? Combatants, Unprivileged Belligerents, and Struggle over Legitimacy*, Harvard Program on Humanitarian Policy and Conflict Research (Cambridge, MA: Program on Humanitarian Policy and Conflict Research, 2005) at 12.

87   There is a debate as to whether the concept exists *per se* anywhere in IHL. See, for example, *The Public Committee against Torture in Israel v. The Government of Israel*, above note 78 at paras. 27 *et seq.* (rejecting the notion that IHL currently creates a special *sui generis* class of "unlawful combatants," but agreeing that civilians who engage in hostilities are not entitled to the protections otherwise accorded to them by IHL). Note that under AP I, above note 32, "national liberation movements" may declare their adherence to IHL, and thereby agree to its strictures and benefit from its privileges. As discussed in Chapter 6, none has apparently done so.

88   AP I, *ibid.*, Art. 51. For further discussion on this issue, see Chapter 6.

no combatant's privilege.[89] They may, therefore, be prosecuted for their acts of violence. This book uses the term "unprivileged belligerent" to describe combatants who do not enjoy combatant's privilege.

c) Continued Application of Human Rights Law

In a situation of armed conflict, international humanitarian law is without question the *lex specialis*; that is, a specialized body of law that applies in lieu of conflicting, general rules.[90] However, it now seems clear that the mere existence of an armed conflict should not be viewed as automatically displacing other rules of international law. For instance, international humanitarian law does not totally replace the more comprehensive rights guarantees of international human rights law.[91] In its 1996 Advisory Opinion on the *Legality of the Threat or Use of Nuclear Weapons*,[92] the International Court of Justice rejected arguments that the *International Covenant of Civil and Political Rights* (ICCPR) was "directed to the protection of human rights in peacetime, and that all questions relating to unlawful loss of life in hostilities were governed by the law applicable in armed conflict." It held instead that "the protection of the *International Covenant of Civil and Political Rights* does not cease in times of war, except by operation of Article 4 of the Covenant whereby certain provisions may be derogated from in a time of national emergency."[93] Under Article 4, key human rights are nonderogable even in the most extreme circumstances.[94]

---

89   Dinstein, *Conduct of Hostilities*, above note 62 at 29 ("A person who engages in military raids by night, while purporting to be an innocent civilian by day, is neither a civilian nor a lawful combatant. He is an unlawful combatant. He is a combatant in the sense that he can be lawfully targeted by the enemy, but he cannot claim the privileges appertaining to lawful combatancy"). Note, however, that there are certain classes of persons who, while not members of armed forces, may be entitled to lawful combatancy status. These include members of a *levée en masse*. See discussion in Chapter 14. The concept of combatant's privilege only really applies to international conflicts. In non-international conflicts, those who take up arms against the government enjoy no privileges from prosecution and no PW status. Goldman & Tittemore, "Unprivileged Combatants and the Hostilities in Afghanistan," above note 86 at 6.

90   See discussion of *lex specialis* in Chapter 2.

91   Greenwood, *Handbook*, above note 64 at 40; Theodor Meron, "The Humanization of Humanitarian Law" (2000) 94 A.J.I.L. 239. See also Kenneth Watkin, "Controlling the Use of Force: A Role for Human Rights Norms in Contemporary Armed Conflict" (2004) 98 A.J.I.L. 1.

92   [1996] I.C.J. Rep. 226 at para. 24 [*Legality of Nuclear Weapons*].

93   *Ibid.* at para. 25.

94   *International Covenant on Civil and Political Rights*, 19 December 1966, 999 U.N.T.S. 171, Art. 4 [ICCPR]. See discussion in Chapter 2.

The International Court of Justice (ICJ) amplified this position *in Legal Consequences of the Construction of a Wall in the Occupied Palestinian Territory*:

> the Court considers that the protection offered by human rights conventions does not cease in case of armed conflict, save through the effect of provisions for derogation of the kind to be found in Article 4 of the *International Covenant on Civil and Political Rights*. As regards the relationship between international humanitarian law and human rights law, there are thus three possible situations: some rights may be exclusively matters of international humanitarian law; others may be exclusively matters of human rights law; yet others may be matters of both these branches of international law.[95]

In both of these decisions, the ICJ interpreted human rights and international humanitarian law harmoniously. It suggested that the ICCPR's "right not arbitrarily to be deprived of one's life applies also in hostilities. The test of what is an arbitrary deprivation of life, however, then falls to be determined by the applicable *lex specialis*, namely, the law applicable in armed conflict which is designed to regulate the conduct of hostilities."[96] The content of the right to life is mutable, in other words.

Under this reasoning, a violation of international humanitarian law may also constitute a violation of the ICCPR, but the ICCPR does not vitiate a combatant's privilege to use deadly force against another combatant.

2) Domestic Legal Standards on the Proper Use of Deployed Military Force

Canada is a party to the Geneva Conventions and their Additional Protocols. CF members deployed internationally apply a CF Code of Conduct, operationalizing international humanitarian law rules.[97]

The Geneva Conventions and the Additional Protocols are made part of the law of Canada by the *Geneva Conventions Act*. That statute makes grave breaches—such as willful killing or torture—of the Conventions and Additional Protocol I a crime prosecutable in Canada.[98]

---

95   ICJ General List No. 131, (2004), 43 I.L.M. 1009 at para. 106 [*Israeli Wall Case*].

96   *Legality of Nuclear Weapons*, above note 92, cited in *Israeli Wall Case, ibid.* at para. 105.

97   Canada, Judge Advocate General, *Code of Conduct for CF Personnel*, B-GG-005-027/AF-023.

98   For a list of grave breaches, see above note 80. See also Canada, Judge Advocate General, *Law of Armed Conflict Manual*, above note 77 at 16-2 *et seq.*

Canada has also enacted a *War Crimes and Crimes Against Humanity Act*,[99] anticipating prosecutions for war crimes occurring both within and outside Canada.

It should also be noted that for CF members, the regular territorial limits of Canada's criminal law do not apply.[100] This means that convictions may be entered against CF members violating Canada's criminal law while abroad.[101] For this reason, a CF member committing a war crime while deployed internationally is most likely to be charged with a conventional *Criminal Code* offence—such as murder—and court-martialed under the *Code of Service Discipline*.[102] This code is enacted in the *National Defence Act* and among other things imposes regular Canadian criminal law on CF members, prosecutable before civilian or military courts.[103]

PART II: DOMESTIC USE OF FORCE

A. DEPLOYING FORCE

On top of any international mission, the CF have varied and significant domestic roles. The CF, reported the 2005 Defence Policy Statement,

> have conducted thousands of sovereignty and search and rescue missions. They have assisted other government departments in deterring

---

99 S.C. 2000, c. 24.

100 See *Criminal Code*, R.S.C. 1985, c. C-46, s. 5 ("Nothing in this Act affects any law relating to the government of the Canadian Forces").

101 NDA, above note 43, s. 130(1) (specifying that an act or omission "that takes place outside Canada and would, if it had taken place in Canada" have constituted an offence under the *Criminal Code* or any other Act of Parliament is liable to conviction). See also NDA, *ibid.*, s. 273 ("Where a person subject to the Code of Service Discipline does any act or omits to do anything while outside Canada which, if done or omitted in Canada by that person, would be an offence punishable by a civil court, that offence is within the competence of . . . a civil court having jurisdiction in respect of such an offence in the place in Canada where that person is found in the same manner as if the offence had been committed in that place"). Note that the question of which court may try such an offence may be complicated where the CF member committed the act in a jurisdiction with a "Status of Force Agreement" (SOFA) with Canada. See, for example, *R. v. Saunders*, 2005 NSPC 13 (where the provincial court declined jurisdiction in relation to criminal charges brought against a Canadian Forces member for acts that took place in Germany by reason of the SOFA with the latter).

102 Canada, *Law of Armed Conflict Manual*, above note 77 at 16-8.

103 See NDA, above note 43, s. 60 *et seq.*

illegal fishing, countering drug smuggling, intercepting ships carrying illegal migrants and protecting our environment. In addition, the Forces have helped civilian authorities respond to natural disasters and other incidents, including floods, ice storms, forest fires, hurricanes, plane crashes and the Year 2000 transition.[104]

However, as Canada's national security policy observes, "the primary obligation of the Canadian Forces is to defend Canada and Canadians, particularly from external military threats."[105] In this capacity, the CF might be called upon to use military force on the territory of Canada.

Coercive military force would likely only be used in Canada in two circumstances: first, to repel an insurrection or foreign attack or, second, to assist the civil authorities in grappling with a crisis exceeding their capacities.

While there is no modern precedent, a foreign attack would almost certainly prompt the government to apply the *Emergencies Act* and declare a "war emergency."[106] In those circumstances, some significant proportion of the actions taken by the Canadian Forces would likely be authorized under this statute, in addition to the royal prerogative of defence or the *National Defence Act* (NDA).

However, anything short of a foreign attack (or an abrupt and massive insurrection) would probably initially be dealt with using other measures. For example, Quebec premier Robert Bourassa requested deployment of the CF during the 1970 October Crisis pursuant to the "aid of the civil power" provision of the NDA, immediately prior to the ultimate invocation by the Trudeau government of the *War Measures Act* (the predecessor statute to the *Emergencies Act*). The same premier requested aid of the civil power during the 1990 Oka cisis.[107]

---

104 Canada, *Defence Policy Statement*, above note 4 at 10.

105 Canada, *Securing an Open Society*, above note 2 at 47.

106 See Chapter 4 for a discussion of the *Emergencies Act*, R.S.C. 1985 (4th Supp.), c. 22.

107 See discussion in Eric Lerhe (Ret'd), *Civil Military Relations and Aid of the Civil Power in Canada: Implications for the War on Terror*, CDAI-CDFAI 7th Annual Graduate Student Symposium, RMC, October 29–30, 2004, online: www.cdacdai.ca/symposia/2004/Lerhe,%20Eric-%20Paper.pdf; Sean Maloney, "Domestic Operations: The Canadian Approach" (1997) 27 Parameters: U.S. Army War College Quarterly 135, online: www.carlisle.army.mil/usawc/Parameters/97autumn/maloney.htm.

1) NDA Provisions

As these examples suggest, the NDA's long-standing aid of the civil power provision may be triggered by a provincial government (and specifically, its attorney general) "in any case in which a riot or disturbance of the peace, beyond the powers of the civil authorities to suppress, prevent or deal with and requiring that [calling out of the Canadian Forces for] service, occurs or is, in the opinion of an attorney general, considered as likely to occur."[108] The procedure for calling out the CF in aid of the civil power is set out in Table 5.2. The CF does not replace the civil authorities when called out in aid, instead assisting them in the maintenance of law and order.[109]

Recent amendments to the NDA establish powers for the federal government itself to order a domestic deployment of the CF to assist civil authorities. Thus, the governor-in-council (GIC) or the minister of national defence may authorize the Canadian Forces to perform any duty involving "public service."[110] This may include assistance to law enforcement. Aid to law enforcement under the new public service provision is available when such aid is authorized by the GIC or minister of national defence on request from a federal minister and when it is both in the national interest and the matter could not be dealt with effectively without CF assistance.[111]

2) Prerogative Orders-in-Council

Analogous call-out powers are found in two federal orders-in-council,[112] issued by the GIC in the 1990s pursuant to the royal prerogative. First, the *Canadian Forces Assistance to Provincial Police Forces Directions* (CFAPPFD) establishes a federal system of approving CF assistance to provincial law enforcement agencies.[113]

Second, the CF may provide law enforcement assistance to the RCMP under the *Canadian Forces Armed Assistance Directions* (CFAAD).[114] In fact, the CFAAD serves as the means by which the aid of the CF's elite

---

108 NDA, above note 43, s. 275.
109 *Queen's Regulations and Orders*, Art. 23.03 [QR&O], online: www.admfincs. forces.gc.ca/qr_o/intro_e.asp.
110 NDA, above note 43, s. 273.6.
111 *Ibid*.
112 A third, older OIC is the *Assistance to Federal Penitentiaries Order*, P.C. 1975-131, authorizing CF assistance to suppress unrest at federal prisons.
113 P.C. 1996-833.
114 P.C. 1993-624.

Special Forces and anti-terrorism unit, JTF2, would be sought by the commissioner of the RCMP or the minister of public safety.[115]

The mechanics of all of these domestic deployment powers are set out in Table 5.2.

Table 5.2: Domestic Deployment Powers

Instrument	Trigger	Requirements
NDA Aid of the Civil Power[1]	Request of provincial attorney general	Anticipated riot or disturbance of the peace is beyond the powers of the civil authorities to suppress, prevent or deal with. Chief of Defence Staff (CDS), subject to any directions from the minister of national defence and in consultation with the affected provinces, shall call out those parts of the CF necessary to suppress or prevent any riot or disturbance.
NDA Public Service[2]	Authorization from the GIC or the minister of national defence	CF to perform a duty related to public service, an undefined term.
NDA Public Service—Law Enforcement[3]	Authorization from the GIC or the minister of national defence, on request from the minister of public safety or any other minister	CF to provide assistance in respect of any law enforcement matter where authorizing minister or GIC considers that the assistance is in the national interest; and the matter cannot be effectively dealt with except with the assistance of the CF and the assistance is more than of a minor nature or limited to logistical, technical or administrative support.
CFAPPFD	Request of provincial minister responsible for policing, communicated to the federal minister of public safety	Provincial police force is unable to deal effectively with a disturbance of the peace that is occurring or may occur, and the ministers of public safety and defence agree that the disturbance affects or is likely to affect the national interest and cannot be effectively prevented, suppressed or otherwise resolved except with CF assistance.

---

115 Canada, Department of National Defence, *Joint Task Force Two: The National Counter-terrorism Plan* (2003), online: www.jtf2.forces.gc.ca/en/plan_e.asp.

Instrument	Trigger	Requirements
CFAAD	Request from the commissioner of the RCMP	RCMP is unable to deal effectively with a disturbance of the peace affecting the national interest that is occurring or may occur. Upon request of the RCMP commissioner, the CDS may pre-position a military force to the site of the disturbance. Meanwhile, if persuaded that the RCMP is or may be unable to deal effectively with a disturbance of the peace affecting the national interest, the minister of public safety may request the provision of armed assistance from the minister of national defence. The latter may then direct the military commander on-site to take whatever lawful action deemed appropriate, upon request of the police commander.

[1]   NDA, above note 43, s. 275.
[2]   *Ibid*, s. 273.6.
[3]   *Ibid*.

As Table 5.2 suggests, there is substantial duplication between these legal sources for CF deployment. The NDA "public service" powers are obviously broad enough to encompass the more specific deployments anticipated in the CFAPPFD and the CFAAD. The latter two royal pre-rogative–based instruments predate the introduction of the NDA public service powers in 1998. The enactment of an NDA public service power encompassing a procedure for federally authorized assistance to law enforcement suggests that Parliament has now occupied that terrain, at least implicitly. There is controversy in the jurisprudence as to whether the royal prerogative may be displaced in legislation by implication.[116] However, if displacement by implication suffices, there is a *bona fide* question as to whether the two orders-in-councils persist pursuant to an extant royal prerogative power. Only adjudication of this question could resolve this question. Out an abundance of caution, however, the preferable approach might be to treat the order-in-council provisions as procedures governing the application of the NDA public service powers to the particular circumstances to which they relate.

---

116 See Chapter 3.

B. PROPER USE OF DEPLOYED MILITARY FORCE

1) Basic Principles of International Human Rights Law

As a matter of international law, domestic use of military force in situations short of armed conflict would be governed by international human rights law and not the Geneva Conventions and their protocols. As discussed in Chapter 2, a limited number of those rights are subject to internal limitations for reasons of national security. A broader series of rights are derogable; that is, under Article 4 of the ICCPR they may be suspended to the extent strictly necessary "in time of public emergency which threatens the life of the nation." Nevertheless, there are other rights—including the right to life—from which no derogation is permissible, even in the most extreme circumstances. Use of force impinging these nonderogable rights would constitute a violation of Canada's international human rights obligations.

If the domestic conflict reached the level of an armed conflict—a concept defined above—the application of human rights law would be tempered by the *lex specialis*, international humanitarian law. As noted earlier, this body of principle accepts the existence of a "combatant's privilege" to use deadly force, significantly tempered by an obligation to meet IHL's standards on treatment of noncombatants.

2) Domestic Legal Standards on the Proper Use of Deployed Military Force

a) Constitutional Considerations

As this discussion suggests, the Geneva Conventions and their Additional Protocols and/or their customary equivalents would apply to the CF in any use of force on Canadian territory during an "armed conflict" as a matter of both international and domestic law.[117] However, Canadian law is not suspended in a time of crisis up to and including a foreign attack. There is no emphatic Canadian doctrine of *lex specialis* giving IHL primacy in event of an armed conflict.[118] Nor is there any such thing as true "martial law" anticipated in the Canadian statute book.

---

117 *Geneva Conventions Act*, R.S.C. 1985, c. G-3, s. 2 ("approving" the Geneva Conventions and their Protocols and thus arguably receiving them into Canadian domestic law); s. 3 (making a grave breach of these instruments a crime when committed "within or outside of Canada").

118 As noted below, the *Geneva Conventions Act* comes closest to creating this rule, but probably does not have a *lex specialis* effect.

As noted, the federal government might trigger application of the *Emergencies Act*.[119] That statute limits civil liability for persons exercising powers pursuant to an emergency order.[120] However, *Emergencies Act* powers do not suspend the *Canadian Charter of Rights and Freedoms*[121] or the *Canadian Bill of Rights*.[122] An override of these instruments would require enactment on a separate parliamentary emergency law, invoking the "notwithstanding clause" of the *Charter* and limiting operation of the *Bill of Rights*.

Absent this extraordinary measure, the CF's domestic use of force would be assessed against conventional constitutional standards. These standards likely have some flexibility. Thus, section 1 of the *Charter* might forgive action in an emergency that would otherwise be adjudged improper.[123] Section 1 is best viewed, however, as a justification for a constitutional violation, not an *ex ante* authorization. Its applicability would be assessed in adjudication after a crisis has passed, if ever. Notably, much that appears necessary at the time of an emergency may be deemed excessive in the cool after-gaze of constitutional adjudication. The constitutionality of a CF action in a time of crisis could not, therefore, be predicted with certainty in advance.

b)   Existing Legal Protections for Use of Force

i)   *Peace Officer Status*
It is true, however, that CF members deployed to respond to domestic crises currently enjoy some protections from liability and criminal culpability. Most fundamentally, the *Criminal Code* forgives force where exercised reasonably (that is, not excessively)[124] by anyone in defence of persons or property.[125] Any person also has a limited right to use force to prevent the commission of an offence.[126]

Lawful authority to use force is expanded for peace officers. A "peace officer" includes a "constable,"[127] which in turn includes an officer or noncommissioned member of the CF called out under the

---

119 Above note 106.
120 *Ibid.*, s. 47.
121 Part I of the *Constitution Act, 1982, being* Schedule B to the *Canada Act 1982* (U.K.) 1982, c. 11.
122 S.C. 1960, c. 44.
123 See discussion in Chapter 4.
124 *Criminal Code*, above note 100, s. 26.
125 *Ibid.*, ss. 34–42.
126 *Ibid.*, s. 27.
127 *Ibid.*, s. 2.

National Defence Act's aid of the civil power provisions.[128] "Constable" status does not remove these members from the regular rules governing CF members. While acting as a "constable," members have all the "powers and duties" of that office, but they "shall act only as a military body and are individually liable to obey the orders of their superior officers."[129] More specifically, they continue to be "governed as such by the ordinary norms of service discipline."[130]

More generally, peace officer status also extends to "officers and non-commissioned members of the Canadian Forces" duly appointed as such under the NDA or employed on duties that necessitate these persons having this status, set out in regulations under the NDA.[131] Officers and noncommissioned CF members appointed as military police are "peace officers."[132] So too are officers and noncommissioned CF members engaged in "lawful duties performed as a result of a specific order or established military custom or practice" related to: "(a) the maintenance or restoration of law and order; (b) the protection of property; (c) the protection of persons; (d) the arrest or custody of persons; or (e) the apprehension of persons who have escaped from lawful custody or confinement."[133]

Notably, military assistance provided in response to a request made by the minister of public safety or the commissioner of the RCMP is deemed a duty related to the enforcement of law, whether that assistance is requested under an Act, regulation, statutory instrument or memorandum of understanding.[134] Thus, officers and noncommissioned members are peace officers when turned out under the NDA public service provision governing assistance to law enforcement or the *Canadian Forces Assistance to Provincial Police Forces Directions* and *Canadian Forces Armed Assistance Directions*.[135]

Under the *Criminal Code*, peace officers (and those acting in aid of them) enjoy substantial authority to use force to secure lawful objectives. These powers are outlined in Table 5.3. Generally, a peace officer may not use force that "is intended or is likely to cause death or griev-

---

128 NDA, above note 43, s. 282.

129 *Ibid.*

130 *QR&O*, above note 109, Art. 23.11, Note B, interpreting NDA, *ibid.*, s. 282.

131 *Criminal Code*, above note 100, s. 2; NDA, *ibid.*, s. 156; *QR&O*, *ibid.*, Arts. 22.01 & 22.02.

132 NDA, *ibid.*, s. 156; *QR&O*, *ibid.*, Art. 22.02.

133 *QR&O*, *ibid.*, Art. 22.01.

134 *Ibid.*

135 They are not, however, standing peace officers. For example, they do not enjoy that status when, outside of a military operation or duty, they assist a police officer in arresting a suspect. *QR&O*, *ibid.*, Art. 22.01, Note (D).

ous bodily harm" outside of the regular self-defence or defence of third persons exceptions.[136] Such force may, however, be used in limited circumstances to prevent the flight of a dangerous person. Further, peace officers, and those assisting them, may use force to suppress riots. Where the authorities "read the riot act,"[137] peace officers and those assisting them have a duty to disperse or arrest the rioters. They are civilly and criminally immune for "any death or injury that by reason of resistance" that is caused in the performance of this duty.[138]

If CF personnel were to act outside of these lawful justifications for the use of force, or if the use of force was authorized but excessive in the circumstances, members would be civilly and criminally liable and subject to discipline under the *Code of Service Discipline*.

ii)   Other Situations

Exactly what rules would apply if the CF was engaged in a *bona fide* armed conflict or otherwise obliged to deploy force in significant quantities within Canada is less clear. The *Criminal Code* peace officer use of force justifications and the concept of self-defence or defence of protected persons likely are not expansive enough to capture true military operations directed, for example, at repelling an enemy army. Some of these defensive operations would have offensive elements (that is, involve a calculated counterattack) and thus might fit poorly with the *Criminal Code*'s obvious focus on staving off immediate perils.

Canadian law does not include any emphatic combatant's privilege analogous to the principle applied in international humanitarian law. It stretches plausibility to suggest that the mere reference in the *Geneva Conventions Act* to the Geneva Conventions and their Additional Protocols being "approved" vitiates application of the regular Canadian criminal law in times of armed conflict. That said, it is conceivable that the regular application of the *Criminal Code* could be suspended by an order declared under the *Emergencies Act*. That statute delegates virtually unfettered power to the executive during a "war emergency."[139] In addition, it seems unlikely a prosecutor would exercise his or her discretion to bring charges against a soldier acting in a manner consistent with international humanitarian law.

Even if such charges were brought, moreover, certain defences would likely be available. First, the *Criminal Code* preserves common law defences—that is, "every rule and principle of the common law that ren-

---

136 *Criminal Code*, above note 100, s. 25(3).
137 *Ibid.*, s. 67.
138 *Ibid.*, s. 33.
139 See Chapter 4.

Table 5.3: Lawful Use of Force

Right to Use Force	Application	Amount of Force	Trigger Elements
Self-defence short of use of deadly force[1]	Any person	No more force than is necessary to enable the person to defend themselves	Person using force is unlawfully assaulted without provocation
Self-defence up to deadly force[2]	Any person	Up to deadly force if person under reasonable apprehension of death or grievous bodily harm from the assault	Person using force is unlawfully assaulted without provocation and believes, on reasonable grounds that this force is necessary to preserve themselves from death or grievous bodily harm
Defence of person under protection[3]	Any person	No more force than is necessary to prevent the assault or its repetition	Person being defended must be under protection of person using force in defence
Defence of personal property[4]	Any person	Force short of bodily harm or striking	Person in peaceable possession of personal property acting to prevent a trespasser from taking it or acts to retrieve it from the trespasser
Defence of dwelling-house or real property[5]	Any person	No more force than is necessary to prevent forcible entry into a dwelling-house or trespassing on the dwelling-house or real property or the removal of the trespassor from them	Person in peaceable possession of a dwelling-house or real property acting to prevent a trespasser from trespassing
Preventing breach of peace[6]	Any person witnessing a breach of the peace	No more force than is reasonably necessary to prevent the continuance or renewal of the breach of the peace or is proportional to the danger from the continued breach	Force is used to detain any person who commits or is about to join in or to renew the breach of the peace, for the purpose of giving him into the custody of a peace officer
Suppression of riots[7]	Peace officer	No more force than is necessary to suppress the riot and that is not excessive in light of the danger from a continued riot	Good faith and reasonable grounds for believing that this force is necessary

Right to Use Force	Application	Amount of Force	Trigger Elements
Suppression of riots (cont'd)	Those bound by military law acting in response to an order from superior officer	As ordered by superior officer	Order must not be manifestly unlawful
	Any person	As ordered by a peace officer	Acting in good faith and the order must not be manifestly unlawful
	Any person	No more force than is necessary to suppress the riot and is not excessive in light of the danger from a continued riot	Good faith and reasonable grounds for believing that this force is necessary and that serious mischief will result from the riot before the arrival of a peace officer
Making lawful arrest[8]	Peace officers, and those lawfully assisting them	Up to deadly force	Lawful arrest is underway with or without warrant, the offence is one for which a person may be arrested without warrant, the person takes flight, reasonable grounds exist to believe that force is needed to protect any person from death or grievous harm and the flight cannot reasonably be prevented by less violent means
Preventing escape from penitentiary[9]	Peace officer	Up to deadly force	Escaping inmate and reasonable grounds exist to believe that person poses threat of death or grievous bodily harm to any person and the escape cannot reasonably be prevented by less violent means

[1] Criminal Code, s. 34.
[2] Ibid.
[3] Ibid., s. 37.
[4] Ibid., s. 38.
[5] Ibid., ss. 40–41.
[6] Ibid., s. 30.
[7] Ibid., s. 32.
[8] Ibid., s. 25(4).
[9] Ibid., s. 25(5).

ders any circumstance a justification or excuse for an act or a defence to a charge."[140] Since combatant's privilege exists as part of customary international humanitarian law, and since the customary international law is part of the common law of Canada,[141] a common law defence to otherwise criminal conduct undertaken in a time of armed conflict may exist.

Second, Canadian law includes a defence (although not an *ex ante* justification) of "necessity"; that is, an excuse for noncompliance with the criminal law "in emergency situations where normal human instincts, whether of self-preservation or of altruism, overwhelmingly impel disobedience."[142] The defence is available "in urgent situations of clear and imminent peril,"[143] and not as part of a premeditated policy outside of this context.[144] Compliance with the law must also be "demonstrably impossible."[145] Finally, there must be proportionality "between the harm inflicted and the harm avoided."[146]

Force used to repel a foreign invasion or deploy force in a civil conflict seems a likely candidate for the necessity defence. The force would be impelled by a clear and imminent peril. Compliance with the ordinary law would be impossible, as the invasion or violent insurrection could not be forestalled using legal processes. Proportionality might be satisfied by actions taken in compliance with international humanitarian law, largely restricting violence to combatants.

c)   Controlled Access Zones

As this Part II suggests, CF operations are generally subject to the full panoply of statutory and constitutional civil and political rights, and the mere presence of the military acting pursuant to the *National Defence Act* does not authorize the imposition of martial law.

This situation would have been changed somewhat had Parliament enacted the original *Public Safety Act*, introduced as Bill C-42 in November 2001. In Bill C-42, and several successive bills, the government proposed amendments to the *National Defence Act* permitting the creation of something called, ominously, "Military Security Zones."[147] These

---

140 *Criminal Code*, above note 100, s. 8(3).
141 See discussion in Chapter 2.
142 *R. v. Perka*, [1984] 2 S.C.R. 232 at 248 [*Perka*].
143 *Ibid.* at 244 and 251.
144 *R. v. Campbell*, [1999] 1 S.C.R. 565 at para. 41.
145 *Perka*, above note 142 at 251.
146 *R. v. Latimer*, [2001] 1 S.C.R. 3 at para. 28.
147 See Bill C-42, *An Act to amend certain Acts of Canada, and to enact measures for implementing the Biological and Toxin Weapons Convention, in order to enhance public safety*, 1st Sess., 37th Parl., 2001, cl. 84 (House of Commons).

zones were to be created at the discretion of the minister of national defence if, in the opinion of the minister, necessary for the protection of international relations or national defence or security, all terms left undefined by the bill. Among other things, the zone could be declared over material or property under control of the government, or, even more ambiguously, any other place that the CF were directed to protect in order to fulfill a duty required by law. The CF would then control entry into this zone, with unauthorized persons subject to forcible removal.[148] In fact, persons violating regulations respecting the access to, or exclusion from, military security zones, faced criminal prosecution, and possibly twelve months in prison.[149] While the bill proposed compensating any person who suffered loss, damage or injury by reason of the zone, government liability for harm suffered by reason of the designation or implementation of the zone would have been precluded.[150]

Civil society groups reacted fiercely to the proposal, and similar provisions in later iterations of the bill. The Canadian Bar Association, for instance, worried that the zone provisions would be used to subdue and control democratic dissent. Indeed, media reports suggested that military security zones would be declared around international meeting places, in an effort to control regular civil society protests at such events.[151]

When passed in 2004, the Public Safety Act no longer included provisions relating to a military security zone. However, in December 2002, the federal Cabinet issued an order-in-council creating "controlled access zones" in Halifax, Esquimalt and Nanoose Harbours, all key naval facilities.[152] These measures were issued, not pursuant to statutory authority, but under royal prerogative.[153] It seems unlikely that any equivalent royal prerogative authority exists that could be employed to create controlled access zones in other, nonmilitary facilities.[154]

---

148 Ibid., cl. 84.
149 Ibid., cl. 90.
150 Ibid., cl. 84.
151 Canadian Bar Association, Submissions on Bill C-42 (Feb. 2002) at 11, online: www.cba.org/pdf/2002-03-22_safetyE.pdf.
152 P.C. 2002-2190, S.I./2003-0002.
153 See Library of Parliament, Bill C-7: The Public Safety Act, 2002, LSE-463-E, online: www.parl.gc.ca/common/bills_ls.asp?Parl=37&Ses=3&ls=c7.
154 Such a use of the prerogative power would likely exceed the purposes to which prerogative power can be put. See, for example, Reference Re: Anti- Inflation Act (Canada), [1976] 2 S.C.R. 373 at 433 ("There is no principle in this country, as there is not in Great Britain, that the Crown may legislate by proclamation or order in council to bind citizens where it so acts without the support of a statute of the Legislature").

COUNTERING TERRORISM AT THE INTERNATIONAL LEVEL

Whatever else it may be, an act of terrorism is almost certainly a crime. Indeed, as discussed in detail later in this chapter, the common response to terrorism has come in the form of international and domestic criminal law. Terrorism is, however, an unusual crime. It is overtly political, and often intended to destabilize the political, social and/or economic status quo. As such, terrorism is a crime with potential geopolitical repercussions.

Two events, separated by almost a century, underscore this point. In 1914, Archduke Franz Ferdinand of the Austro-Hungarian Empire was assassinated by a Serb terrorist in Sarajevo, ultimately precipitating the First World War. On September 11, 2001, Islamist terrorists brought down the twin towers of the World Trade Center in New York, damaged the Pentagon in Washington and hijacked and crashed another flight in Pennsylvania, prompting the subsequent invasion of Afghanistan and creating a climate for the Bush administration's "war on terror" and its doctrine of "pre-emptive self-defence." Since that day, the threat from terrorism has predominated national security policy in much of the world, and indeed has had significant impacts on everything from law enforcement to foreign policy.

This chapter begins by briefly describing the nature of the terrorist threat. It then examines the response to terrorism from the optic of international law, specifically, the international law on the use of force and international criminal law.

PART I: TERRORISM AND NATIONAL SECURITY

The word "terrorism" stems from the French equivalent "terrorisme," an expression devised during the French revolution's tumultuous "reign of terror." In colloquial English, "terrorism" is defined as a "policy intended to strike with terror those against whom it is adopted; the employment of methods of intimidation; the fact of terrorizing or condition of being terrorized."[1]

Much hinges on definition. As this chapter outlines, the difficulty in devising a precise legal definition of terrorism has stymied efforts to criminalize terrorism *per se* in international law. For the purposes of this initial, nonlegal discussion, however, this chapter accepts the understanding of terrorism employed by the U.S.-based Memorial Institute for the Prevention of Terrorism (MIPT), an agency that collects the terrorist statistics discussed below. This entity defines terrorism as

> violence, or the threat of violence, calculated to create an atmosphere of fear and alarm. These acts are designed to coerce others into actions they would not otherwise undertake, or refrain from actions they desired to take. All terrorist acts are crimes. Many would also be violation of the rules of war if a state of war existed. This violence or threat of violence is generally directed against civilian targets. The motives of all terrorists are political, and terrorist actions are generally carried out in a way that will achieve maximum publicity. Unlike other criminal acts, terrorists often claim credit for their acts. Finally, terrorist acts are intended to produce effects beyond the immediate physical damage of the cause, having long-term psychological repercussions on a particular target audience. The fear created by terrorists may be intended to cause people to exaggerate the strengths of the terrorist and the importance of the cause, to provoke governmental overreaction, to discourage dissent, or simply to intimidate and thereby enforce compliance with their demands.[2]

For reasons discussed at length later in this chapter, terrorism is usually a term reserved for nonstate actors, although there is a popular discourse on so-called state terrorism; that is, violence directed at civilians by governments themselves.[3]

---

1 *Oxford English Dictionary*, online.
2 MIPT Terrorism Knowledge Database, online: www.tkb.org.
3 As discussed below, this form of state misfeasance is captured by international human rights and humanitarian law and while the latter does include a prohibi-

A. PAST PATTERNS OF TERRORISM

Terrorism has both a lengthy historical pedigree and a stubborn persistence in contemporary times. David Rapoport has written of several modern "waves" of terrorism: the anarchist wave at the end of the nineteenth century; the anticolonial wave, beginning in the 1920s but concentrated in the post-WWII period; the leftist wave of the 1970s, and today's religious wave.[4] To this list, other scholars add the fascist, paramilitary wave in Europe in the interwar years, and insurgencies with terrorist trappings (and inspiring terrorist imitators) in postwar China and post-Soviet invasion Afghanistan.[5] Sectarian and insurgency violence in contemporary Iraq may fuel yet another wave (or augment the existing religious wave) in a manner that will have ripple effects outside of that country, including in the form of newly radicalized, so-called home-grown terrorists.[6]

Various institutions, including the U.S. State Department, the RAND Institute and more recently the MIPT, have tried to monitor the empirical scope of terrorist violence. These figures should be treated with caution, given political disputes over the meaning of terrorism. The State Department figures in particular have been adjusted (upwards) in response to changing methodologies.[7] Nevertheless, these numbers are revealing.

The MIPT database of terrorist acts between 1968 and January 2007 lists almost 40,000 terrorist incidents, producing 105,000 injuries and

---

tion on terrorist acts by state armed forces in armed conflict, the concept of state terrorism *per se* is alien to international law.

4   David C. Rapoport, "The Four Waves of Modern Terrorism," in Audrey Cronin & James Ludes, eds., *Attacking Terrorism: Elements of a Grand Strategy* (Washington: Georgetown University Press, 2004) at 46–73.

5   Mark Sedgwick, "Inspiration and the Origins of Global Waves of Terrorism" (2007) 30 Studies in Conflict and Terrorism 97.

6   See "Declassified Key Judgments of the U.S. National Intelligence Estimate," *Trends in Global Terrorism: Implications for the United States* (April 2006) ("We assess that the Iraq jihad is shaping a new generation of terrorist leaders and operatives; perceived jihadist success there would inspire more fighters to continue the struggle elsewhere"), online: http://hosted.ap.org/specials/interactives/wdc/documents/terrorism/keyjudgments_092606.pdf. See also discussion in James Gordon, "Iraq War Breeds More Terrorists" *The Ottawa Citizen* (22 June 2005) A1; Greg Miller, "Spy Agencies Say Iraq War Fuels Terror" *Los Angeles Times* (24 September 2006).

7   See, for example, the critique in Center for Defense Information, *Terrorism Statistics Flawed* (April 2006), online: www.cdi.org/program/document.cfm?DocumentID=3391. See also Susan Glasser, "U.S. Figures Show Sharp Global Rise in Terrorism" *Washington Post* (27 April 2005) A.01.

almost 45,000 fatalities. Most of those events, injuries and casualities have occurred since September 11, 2001 — 32,000 fatalities are listed for the period September 11, 2001 to January 2007. Table 6.1 reproduces data from the MIPT database showing terrorism by tactic.[8]

Table 6.1:   Terrorist Statistics by Tactic, 1968–2007

Tactic	Incidents	Injuries	Fatalities
Armed Attack	6,906	14,002	11,865
Arson	1,010	327	382
Assassination	2,343	1,241	3,000
Barricade/Hostage	209	2,209	903
Bombing	17,538	83,754	23,274
Hijacking	228	376	482
Kidnapping	2,116	172	1,364
Other	164	426	151
Unconventional Attack	56	2,440	3,004
Unknown	388	284	511
TOTAL	30,958	105,231	44,936

Care is warranted in reading too much into these data. For one thing, these MIPT figures include 18,000 casualties in the Middle East for the period after March 2003 — the date of the U.S.-led invasion of Iraq. Sectarian violence and insurgencies in that country have precipitated an obvious upswing in the data. In 2005, for example, the U.S. State Department noted that Iraq accounted for 55 percent of all fatalities in terrorist attacks that year, a figure totalling 8,300 in 2005 alone.[9] The figures for 2006 demonstrate an even more dramatic skewing of terrorist attacks, with two-thirds of fatalities in worldwide terrorist attacks occurring in Iraq.[10] Meanwhile, the State Department terrorist incident database lists a total of over 16,000 casualties attributable to terrorist violence in Iraq from the period 2004 to January 2007.[11] Put another way, the situation in Iraq greatly distorts the overall pattern of terrorist violence.

---

8   MIPT Terrorism Knowledge Database. Terrorist Incident Reports, Terrorism by Tactics, online: www.tkb.org/IncidentTacticModule.jsp.

9   U.S. Department of State, *Country Reports on Terrorism 2005* (April 2006), online: www.state.gov/documents/organization/65462.pdf.

10   U.S. Department of State, *Country Reports on Terrorism 2006* (April 2007), online: www.state.gov/s/ct/rls/crt/2006/. See analysis in Scott Shane, "Terrorist Attacks in Iraq and Afghanistan Rose Sharply Last Year, State Department Says" *New York Times* (1 May 2007) A12.

11   U.S. Department of State, Worldwide Incidents Tracking System, online: http://wits.nctc.gov/.

Without this concentrated and unique regional distortion, the statistics may be more revealing of global patterns. The 2005 State Department report fixed the number of global terrorist incidents that year at 11,111. Removing Iraqi incidents from this figure, there were still over 7,600 such attacks, producing over 6,000 fatalities. These are sobering numbers. Nevertheless, in absolute terms, this is a modest figure. The world population was 6.5 billion in 2005. The rate of fatalities to population was 1 fatality per 1,000,000 persons.[12] By way of comparison, the rate of fatalities in motor vehicle accidents in Canada in 2003 was 90/1,000,000.[13]

B. FUTURE THREAT

These statistics prompt obvious questions about the magnitude of the terrorist threat, and whether the manifold resources deployed in the campaign against terrorism carry with them an opportunity cost; that is, whether they divert attention and resources from potentially graver security threats posed, for example, by novel pandemic diseases or climate change. On the other hand, one should be wary of attributing too much significance to past patterns of terrorism. Historically, terrorism has constituted a tragedy, but one that has never amounted to an existential threat to the state. Even 9/11, with its unprecedented death toll and tremendous economic cost, did not put at risk the very existence of the United States.

The terrorism of the twenty-first century may take different forms. First, the nature of terrorism has shifted. The recent social science literature on terrorism points to the emergence of a so-called new terrorism; that is, terrorism focused on mass casualties, motivated by religious ideologies and geographically unbounded. Describing the causes of this new terrorism, one scholar points to the emergence of the information age (and the prominence given dramatic acts in attracting world media attention), the increased vulnerability of highly integrated, technologically advanced societies to acts of violence and the segmentation of societies into winners and others acutely aware (and embittered) that they have been left behind.[14]

---

12   Calculated on the basis of the 2005 world population of 6.5 billion.

13   Computed from Statistics Canada, *Age-standardized mortality rates by selected causes, by sex*, Statistics Canada, CANSIM, Table 102-0552, online: www40. statcan.ca/l01/cst01/health30a.htm.

14   Frank Schorkopf, "Behavioural and Social Science Perspectives on Political Violence," in Christian Walter *et al.*, eds., *Terrorism as a Challenge for National*

Notably, this new terrorism produces protagonists much more prone to suicide attacks than were earlier practitioners of political violence. In the period from 1968 to 10 September 2001, approximately 11 percent of terrorist-caused deaths and 0.84 percent of terrorist incidents were caused by suicide bombers. The equivalent figures for the post-9/11 era are 34 percent of deaths and 4.4 percent of incidents.[15]

The counterterrorism implications of this trend are grave. Countering a suicide bomber is much more difficult than interdicting a conventional attacker.[16] Not least, the former need not have an exit plan, and thus may attack in circumstances that would discourage a conventional assailant. The prospect of death, in other words, is no deterrent.

Moreover, suicide bombings are more deadly, perhaps because suicide bombers are present to detonate their weapon with greater effect than is possible using remote or timed bombings. Between the period 1968 to 2007, deaths and injuries per nonsuicide bombings were 0.87 and 3.5 persons respectively. For the same period, deaths and injuries per suicide bombings were 9.7 and 28.5 persons.[17]

Second, the technologies available to this terrorism of mass casualties are also evolving. The U.S. government's National Intelligence Council predicted in a 2004 report on future security risks:

> Most terrorist attacks will continue to employ primarily conventional weapons, incorporating new twists to keep counterterrorist planners off balance. Terrorists probably will be most original not in the technologies or weapons they employ but rather in their operational concepts—i.e., the scope, design, or support arrangements for attacks.[18]

However, it also warns of "an intensified search by some terrorist groups to obtain weapons of mass destruction. Our greatest concern is that these groups might acquire biological agents or less likely, a nuclear device, either of which could cause mass casualties."[19] On the nuclear question, it comes to this conclusion:

---

and International Law: Security versus Liberty? (Berlin: Springer, 2004) at 17 et seq. [Terrorism as a Challenge].

15   Figures calculated by the author from the MIPT Terrorism Knowledge Database.

16   See discussion in U.S. Congressional Research Service, Terrorists and Suicide Attacks (2003), RL32058, online: www.fas.org/irp/crs/RL32058.pdf.

17   Figures calculated by the author from the MIPT Terrorism Knowledge Database.

18   National Intelligence Council, Mapping the Global Future, Report of the National Intelligence Council's 2020 Project (Dec. 2004) at 95, online: www.foia.cia.gov/2020/2020.pdf.

19   Ibid.

With advances in the design of simplified nuclear weapons, terrorists will continue to seek to acquire fissile material in order to construct a nuclear weapon. Concurrently, they can be expected to continue attempting to purchase or steal a weapon, particularly in Russia or Pakistan. Given the possibility that terrorists could acquire nuclear weapons, the use of such weapons by extremists before 2020 cannot be ruled out.[20]

A 1999 CSIS report reached similar conclusions: "although it is impossible to estimate the precise likelihood of a mass-casualty terrorist attack using CBRN [chemical, biological, radiological, nuclear] materials, the technical obstacles to such an attack are by no means insuperable. It appears to be a case not of 'if,' but rather of 'when,' the next such event will occur."[21]

A more recent, 2005 Harvard study reported several instances of terrorist groups seeking nuclear or radiological material, and carefully documented the extent to which WMD material is poorly secured in the former Soviet Union.[22] Pointing to these trends, analysts have also expressed fear that terrorists will use a conventional explosive device salted with radiological material—a so-called dirty bomb that disperses radioactive material over an extended region.[23]

Without question, it is this fear of WMD-armed terrorists that drives the counterterrorism policies of key states. U.K. Prime Minister Tony Blair, for instance, conflated terrorism and the WMD threat, seeing the two as inextricably linked.[24] The invasion of Iraq was very

---

20   *Ibid.*

21   CSIS, *Report No. 2000/02: Chemical, Biological, Radiological and Nuclear (CBRN) Terrorism* (December 18, 1999), online: www.csis-scrs.gc.ca/en/publications/perspectives/200002.asp.

22   Matthew Bunn & Anthony Wier, *Securing the Bomb 2005* (Harvard University, May 2005), online: http://bcsia.ksg.harvard.edu/BCSIA_content/documents/thebomb2005.pdf.

23   See Lewis Smith, "Seizures of Radioactive Materials Fuel Dirty Bomb Fears" [*London*] *Times* (6 October 2006). See also Jim Bronskill & Sue Bailey, "Dirty bomb's economic fallout: $23 billion" *Globe and Mail* (3 July 2007) A7 (reporting a government study that estimates the cost of a modest dirty bomb explosion in the vicinity of the CN Tower in Toronto at $23.5 billion).

24   See, in particular, "Speech Given by the Prime Minister in Sedgefield [March 2004], Justifying Military Action in Iraq and Warning of the Continued Threat of Global Terrorism," reproduced by *The Guardian*, online: www.guardian.co.uk/Iraq/Story/0,,1162993,00.html. His ministers took a similar line. See John Reid, then U.K. home secretary, interviewed in Nigel Morris, "Reid Attacks Judges Who Hamper 'Life and Death' Terrorism Battle" *Independent* (10 August 2006), online: http://news.independent.co.uk/uk/politics/article1218053.ece.

publicly motivated by (ultimately misplaced or exaggerated) WMD proliferation concerns and the risk of collaboration between Saddam Hussein and terrorists. More recently, in a 2007 speech, U.S. Homeland Security Secretary Michael Chertoff described runaway weapons of mass destruction proliferation in the hands of nonstate actors as a "genie" that must be kept "in the bottle." Otherwise, we risk "a type of destruction and a magnitude of destruction that would have been unthinkable a century ago."[25]

C. IMPLICATIONS FOR LAW

Suicidal terrorists attracted to mass casualty events and actively in search of WMDs create real dilemmas for national security law.

1) Hardening Society

First, a terrorism of mass destruction may compel a redirection of counterterrorism efforts away from simply neutralizing terrorists themselves. In an era of portable WMD, a counterterrorism strategy dependent on identifying and intercepting individual terrorists or destroying terrorist groups is an invitation for disaster. Missing even one nuclear-armed terrorist would constitute a failure of epic proportions.

Instead (or additionally), counterterrorism must be directed at renewed efforts to keep WMD out of the hands of terrorists, at protecting critical infrastructure against such an attack, at ensuring that this infrastructure itself is not converted into the WMD (for example, a nuclear power plant) and at developing a response capacity sufficient to meet the challenges of an WMD attack.[26] The U.S. State Department proposes, for instance, that

---

25   Paul Haven, "Chertoff: 21st Century More Dangerous" *Associated Press* (25 January 2007).

26   See, for example Canada, PSEPC, *The Chemical, Biological, Radiological and Nuclear Strategy of the Government of Canada* (2005) at 4, online: http://public-safety.gc.ca/pol/em/cbrnstr-en.asp (describing the four strategic objectives of counterterrorism in relation to CBRN weapons as "prevention and mitigation; preparedness; response and recovery"). See also Kent Roach, "Must We Trade Rights for Security? The Choice between Smart, Harsh or Proportionate Security Strategies in Canada and the United Kingdom" (2006) 27 Cardozo L. Rev. 2151 (discussing access controls to sensitive material and sites as preferable to mere criminalization of terrorism).

a comprehensive and systematic approach to reducing the risk of a WMD terrorism attack involves (1) reducing the probability that terrorists will attack a given target in a given manner during a given time period (threat), (2) reducing the probability that a given attack with result in damage to a given target (vulnerability), and (3) reducing the expected damage of a successful terrorist attack on a given target (consequence).[27]

Canada also has responded to this threat by enhancing its emergency preparedness, a matter discussed in Chapter 9.

2) Implications for Criminal Law Primacy

Second, these developments in terrorist strategy and objectives may challenge conventional international legal responses to terrorism; namely, the codification of international criminal law instruments designed to proscribe various acts of terrorism and provide for the prosecution of terrorists. It is notable that despite the rich body of international law criminalizing various forms of terrorism discussed below, terrorist prosecutions have been astonishingly rare since 9/11. By one count, there had, for example, been 114 terrorist criminal cases brought in the United States between 2001 and 2007, of which 93 had resulted in convictions or guilty pleas. Only 14 of these 114 cases involved members of the most notorious Islamic terrorist organizations, the key terrorist protagonists in the campaign against terrorism.[28] Other estimates cite a higher number of U.S. prosecutions, but also suggest that criminal cases are in decline[29] or concerned minor infractions unrelated to actual terrorism.[30] In the United Kingdom, 1,116 people were arrested on terrorism-related suspicions between September 11, 2001, and the end of 2006. Of these, only 221 were actually charged with a terrorism offence and only 40 were convicted. Another 186 persons were charged with other offences, and 74 were transferred to immigration

---

27   U.S. Department of State, *WMD Terrorism Risk*, online: www.state.gov/t/isn/c16585.htm.

28   Statistics computed from MIPT Terrorism Knowledge Database, above note 2. The fourteen cases included in this figure were brought against members of al-Qaeda, Hamas, Hezbollah, the Taliban, and persons that the MIPT database describes as "Linked to September 11 Hijackers" and "World Trade Center bombing (WTC)/ Jihad Organization."

29   Eric Lichtblau, "Study Finds Sharp Drop in the Number of Terrorism Cases Prosecuted" *New York Times* (4 September 2006).

30   Dan Eggen, "Officials Tout U.S. Anti-Terrorism Record" *Washington Post* (25 May 2006) A.08.

proceedings. Meanwhile, 652 persons were eventually released without charge.[31] In Canada, 19 individuals had been charged with terrorism offences under Canada's 2001 anti-terrorism law by early 2007, but none had completed the trial process.[32]

There are a number of reasons for these modest figures. First, evidence supporting prosecutions is difficult for states to supply in an area shrouded in covert intelligence gathering.[33] In addition, that evidence may be procured by means that would not withstand scrutiny in court.[34] For these and other reasons, the cases are long, complicated and expensive.[35] It is also true that effective pre-emption may require states to act against terrorism suspects even before they have secured evi-

---

31   David Byers, "Only One Fifth of Terror Arrests Charged" [*London*] *Times* (5 March 2007). By the time of this writing, it was estimated that 100 people were awaiting terror trials in the United Kingdom. Jane Perlez & Elaine Sciolino, "Openness Sought In British Terror Trials" *New York Times* (25 May 2007).

32   Michelle Shephard, "Huge Terror Cell Case Begins Its Costly Course" *Toronto Star* (20 December 2006) C1.

33   See discussion of secrecy and judicial processes in Chapter 10. The difficulty of prosecuting international terrorism cases in courts applying strict due process standards have resulted in some cases being dismissed. See, for example, *R. v. Thomas*, 2006 VSCA 165 (Australia) (dismissing a terrorism case on the basis of the inadmissibility of evidence obtained by interrogators while the suspect was incarcerated in Pakistan). The matter has also arisen in the United Kingdom and the United States. See Jenny Booth, "Goldsmith's Change of Heart of Phone Tap Evidence" [*London*] *Times* (21 September 2006); Curt Anderson, "Suspect Padilla Gets Access to Secrets" *Associated Press* (13 July 2006). In Germany, prosecutions of 9/11 conspirators have been complicated by the U.S. government's reluctance to authorize the use of intelligence information in court. See discussion in David Byers, "Maximum Sentence for September 11 Helper" [*London*] *Times* (9 January 2007). In Canada, the Commission of Inquiry into the Investigation of the Bombing of Air India Flight 182 has been charged, among other things, with examining "the manner in which the Canadian government should address the challenge, as revealed by the investigation and prosecutions in the Air India matter, of establishing a reliable and workable relationship between security intelligence and evidence that can be used in a criminal trial." P.C. 2006-293 (1 May 2006).

34   See Warren Richey, "U.S. Antiterror Tactics Crimp New Terror Case" *Christian Science Monitor* (16 April 2007), online: www.csmonitor.com/2007/0416/p01s03-usju.html (discussing how coercive interrogation techniques were used to extract information in the Padilla case in the United States that is not, as a result, admissible in court, prompting prosecutors to pursue different legal theories).

35   See, for example, Sean O'Neill & Nicola Woolcock, "Legal System Creaks under Weight of Terror Cases" [*London*] *Times* (30 April 2007) (discussing the U.K. experience and, particularly, the prosecution of the conspirators in Operation Crevice, the longest and most expensive criminal trial in U.K. history).

dence of a calibre and quantity likely to support a conviction in court.[36] Second, perhaps for exactly this reason, the international community, and the United States in particular, has militarized its counterterrorism strategies.[37] As discussed below, post 9/11, the United States certainly has resisted a full-scale criminal justice model as the appropriate response to modern terrorism, even when that terrorism is conducted with conventional arms.

In fact, there may be good reason to resort to military force in some instances. Discussing Israel's conflict with Palestinian terrorist organizations, the Israeli Supreme Court commented in 2006 that the modern "terrorist organization is likely to have considerable military capabilities. At times they have military capabilities that exceed those of states. Confrontation with those dangers cannot be restricted within the state and its penal law. Confronting the dangers of terrorism constitutes a part of the international law dealing with armed conflicts of international character."[38]

However, this militarization of anti-terrorism responses raises serious concerns. Ready and excessive resort to military force as a counterterrorism strategy could prove corrosive of important values, not least due process and the human right to life.[39] Consider the following implications of choosing armed conflict over law enforcement, some of which are discussed further later in this chapter: The laws of war accept use of lethal force as a proper instrument of policy, at least when directed at those labeled combatants; criminal law rules are more demanding, requiring self-defence or other justifications that narrow the circumstances in which lethal force may be used. The laws of war accept that enemies may and indeed should be killed without due process; criminal law rules are geared towards due process. The laws of war accept that there will be collateral casualties and that innocents

---

36   See, for example, Dan Bilefsky, "Danish Investigators Fear Evidence is Insufficient to Hold 5 Suspects in Possible Bombing Plot" *New York Times* (8 September 2006); Eric Lipton, "Recent Arrests in Terror Plots Yield Debate on Pre-emptive Action by Government" *New York Times* (10 July 2006).

37   For a discussion of the paucity of criminal prosecutions and the reasons for that phenomenon, see Helen Duffy, *The "War on Terror" and the Framework of International Law* (Cambridge: Cambridge University Press, 2005) at 122 *et seq.* [*War on Terror*].

38   *Public Committee against Torture in Israel v. The Government of Israel*, (2006) HCJ 769/02 at para. 21 [*Public Committee*].

39   For exactly this reason, senior officials of even those governments inclined to employ war rhetoric have sometimes queried the propriety of this language. See, for example, Sir Ken Macdonald, head of the U.K. Crown Prosecution Service, cited in Clare Dyer, "There Is No War on Terror" *The Guardian* (24 January 2007).

will be injured; criminal law rules generally do not. The laws of war accept that the object of war is the defeat and submission of an enemy; criminal law is about punishment, but also about rehabilitation.

In sum, the urgency of countering mass casualty terrorism may drive a controversial (and potentially counterproductive) redesign of international or national laws. The rest of this chapter turns first to the difficult legal issues surrounding the use of force in counterterrorism. It then discusses in detail existing and prospective international criminal law instruments. Subsequent chapters discuss developments in domestic anti-terrorism criminal law, weapons proliferation law and public safety law.

PART II: TERRORISM AND MILITARY FORCE

As noted in Chapter 5, the international law on the use of military force is principally oriented towards state–state conflicts. It does not include special, *sui generis* rules for terrorism cases; that is, rules on when force may be used in response to violence directed at states or their populations by nonstate actors. With the arguable exception of circumstances where these nonstate actors are found on the high seas, these persons and entities will always be found in the territory of a state. For this reason, the general rules on use of military force directed by one state against the territory of another state remain applicable. Specifically, other than in circumstances of consent, it is permissible in international law to use force against another state or its territory in only two circumstances, both anticipated by the U.N. *Charter*. First, the U.N. Security Council may legitimize and authorize this use of force. Second, an inherent right to deploy force in self-defence is recognized by Article 51 of the *Charter*.

A. U.N. SECURITY COUNCIL PRACTICE

As discussed in Chapter 5, the U.N. Security Council has responsibility in the United Nations system for declaring a threat to, or breach of, international peace and security and for authorizing responses, including the possible use of force.[40] The council has repeatedly recognized

---

40   U.N. *Charter*, Art. 42 ("Should the Security Council consider that measures provided for in Article 41 [for example, economic sanctions] would be inadequate or have proved to be inadequate, it may take such action by air, sea, or land for-

that terrorism may constitute a threat to international peace and security. In Resolution 1566 (2004), for instance, the council condemned "in the strongest terms all acts of terrorism irrespective of their motivation, whenever and by whomsoever committed, as one of the most serious threats to peace and security."[41]

In practice, the council has issued resolutions requiring states to enhance anti-terrorism cooperation,[42] respond to terrorism with criminal law measures[43] and sanctioning specific terrorist or terrorist-supporting entities[44] or terrorist-harbouring or -supporting states.[45] The council has not, however, expressly authorized the use of force in response to a terrorist act, even those of 9/11.[46]

B. USE OF FORCE IN SELF-DEFENCE

Because no Security Council authorization has been issued, military action in response to terrorism has usually been justified — where legal justifications are in fact offered up — as self-defence. Article 51 of the U.N. *Charter* preserves "the inherent right of individual or collective

---

ces as may be necessary to maintain or restore international peace and security. Such action may include demonstrations, blockade, and other operations by air, sea, or land forces of Members of the United Nations").

41   See also S/RES/1526 (2004) (labelling terrorism a threat to international peace and security).

42   See, for example, S/RES/1373 (2001).

43   See *ibid*. (requiring the criminalization of terrorism and particularly terrorist financing).

44   See, for example, S/RES/1267 (1999) (against the Taliban).

45   See, for example, S/RES/1054 (1996) (sanctions against Sudan for failing to extradite alleged terrorists); S/RES/748 (1992) (sanctions against Libya in relation to the Lockerbie bombings).

46   That said, there is a literature suggesting that the language in S/RES/1373 reaffirming "the need to combat by all means, in accordance with the *Charter* of the United Nations, threats to international peace and security caused by terrorist acts," and calling upon all states to "cooperate ... to prevent and suppress terrorist attacks and take action against perpetrators of such acts" constitutes authorization to use force against al-Qaeda, even if the language used is different from past instances where the council has clearly authorized force (that is, resolutions authorizing "all necessary means," discussed in Chapter 5). See, for example, discussion in Sean D. Murphy, "Terrorism and the Concept of 'Armed Attack' in Article 51 of the U.N. *Charter*" (2002) 43 Harv. Int'l L.J. 41 at 44; Michael Byers, "Terrorism, the Use of Force and International Law after 11 September" (2002) 51 Int'l & Comp. L.Q. 401 at 401–2; Jordan Paust, "Use of Armed Force against Terrorists in Iraq, Afghanistan and Beyond" (2002) 35 Cornell Int'l L.J. 533 at 545.

self-defence if an armed attack occurs against a Member of the United Nations, until the Security Council has taken measures necessary to maintain international peace and security."

As a doctrinal matter, the right to self-defence is a narrow one, a matter discussed in Chapter 5. By the express terms of Article 51, self-defence is authorized only when an "armed attack" occurs, although customary international law may permit a limited anticipatory self-defence in response to an armed attack about to occur. As a matter of customary international law, self-defence must also be proportional and necessary. These elements are discussed below.

1) Terrorism as an Armed Attack

a) Past Practice

i) Nonstate Actors and Armed Attacks

In many, pre-9/11 understandings of international law, an act of terrorism (that is, an act of violence by a nonstate actor) would not be an "armed attack" justifying self-defence. In some measure, this may reflect differences in scale: pre-9/11 terrorism caused limited injury, as compared to the typical assault by a state military in a war. Still, even a minor state military assault would likely be considered an "armed attack" for self-defence purposes.[47] In conventional analyses, what distinguished "terrorism" from an armed attack justifying self-defence, therefore, is not necessarily the scope of the violent act, but rather the identity of its perpetrator: terrorism is an act undertaken by nonstate actors while an armed attack is a violent act mounted by a state (directly or through a nonstate proxy). Pearl Harbour in 1941, for instance, would constitute an armed attack within the meaning of Article 51 and customary international law. The Madrid bombing of 2004 was an act of terrorism, but certainly not an armed attack. In fact, the International Court of Justice has concluded that acts of violence directed against a state by nonstate actors from *within* that state or from a territory occupied by that state cannot generally trigger a right to self-defence under Article 51.[48]

ii) State Nexus to Nonstate Actor

Nevertheless, it was widely accepted even before 9/11 that an act of terrorism would give rise to self-defence if the nexus between the terrorist

---

47   See Chapter 5.
48   *Legal Consequences of the Construction of a Wall in the Occupied Palestinian Territory* (2004), ICJ General List No. 131, 43 I.L.M. 1009 at para. 139 [*Israeli Wall Case*].

act and *another state* was sufficiently close. The peril lies in determining the scope of that connection. This issue was engaged by the 1986 response of the United States to the bombing of a Berlin discotheque in Germany. The latter event killed two U.S. military personnel and a Turkish civilian. It was greeted enthusiastically by Libya's leader, Colonel Qaddafi. The United States claimed, in addition, conclusive evidence of direct Libyan involvement in the bombing. The net result was U.S. air strikes against Libya.

In justifying this course of action, the U.S. ambassador to the United Nations maintained that the United States had acted in self-defence against Libya's "continued policy of terrorist threats and the use of force, in violation of ... Article 2(4) of the *Charter*."[49] This explanation failed to sway most of the world's states, a fact illustrated most starkly by a condemnation of the U.S. attacks in a resolution of the General Assembly.[50] A disapproval of the U.S. actions was also proposed in the Security Council, but vetoed by the United States, the United Kingdom and France.[51] One scholar explains the poor reception given to the U.S. self-defence claim as follows:

> While a significant part of the reaction of the United Nations to America's raid on Libya can be explained by Cold War politics, serious legal questions were also raised. A perceived lack of evidence tying the West Berlin discotheque bombing and other terrorist activities to Libya, questions regarding the propriety under Article 51 of an armed response against a state for the actions of terrorists, the suggestion of retaliatory motives, related arguments against the necessity and proportionality of U.S. actions, and the absence of an "armed attack" owing in part to an isolated murder of American servicemen abroad, all contributed to criticism by states and scholars of the raid on Libya as an illegitimate act of self-defense.[52]

More recently, U.S. armed responses in Sudan and Afghanistan to the 1998 U.S. embassy bombings in Kenya and Tanzania—again explained by the United States as an act of self-defence[53]—provoked less sweep-

---

49   Letter from the Acting Permanent Representative of the United States of America to the United Nations, Addressed to the President of the Security Council (14 April 1986), U.N. SCOR, 41st Sess., U.N. Doc. S/17990.

50   A/RES/41/38.

51   U.N. SCOR, 41st Sess., 2682d mtg. at 43, U.N. Doc. S/PV.2682 (1986).

52   Jack M. Beard, "America's New War on Terror: The Case for Self-Defense under International Law" (2002) 25 Harv. J.L. & Pub. Pol'y 559 at 564–65.

53   See "Letter to Congressional Leaders Reporting on Military Action Against Terrorist Sites in Afghanistan and Sudan," 34 Weekly Comp. Pres. Doc. 1650

ing criticism. Those states critical of the United States tended to hang their objections on the proportionality and necessity of the U.S. armed response (to the extent they raised legal issues at all).[54]

b) Modern Trends

i)   Al-Qaeda and 9/11

These more muted reactions in the 1990s to force deployed in response to terrorism suggest an international warming to (although far from enthusiasm for) the notion that the actions of nonstate actors could constitute an "armed attack" under Article 51. Certainly, the actual text of Article 51 does not close the door to violence by non-state actors against a state being viewed as an armed attack. [55]

The international response to 9/11 seems to have removed most doubt on this point. Given the shocking scale of the terrorist strike, and the fact that it was so evidently directed against the territory of the United States, it is not surprising that the international community embraced the view that self-defence against the terrorist perpetrators was warranted, despite their nonstate nature. The U.N. Security Council, for instance, invoked the right to self-defence in condemning the terrorist acts.[56] For its part, the North Atlantic Treaty Organization declared that the 9/11 acts satisfied the requirements of an armed attack under Article 5 of the North Atlantic Treaty, triggering a collective response from NATO.[57] The Organization of American States arrived at a similar conclusion, invoking Article 3 of the Inter-American Treaty of Reciprocal Assistance.[58]

(21 August 1998), reported in Sean D. Murphy, "Contemporary Practice of the United States Relating to International Law" (1999) 93 A.J.I.L. 161 at 162–63.

54   See discussion in Tal Becker, *Terrorism and the State: Rethinking the Rules of State Responsibility* (Oxford: Hart Monographs, 2006) at 203–4 [*Terrorism and the State*].

55   See, for example, Darren C. Huskisson, "The Air Bridge Denial Program and the Shootdown of Civil Aircraft Under International Law" (2005) 56 A.F.L. Rev. 109 at 144 ("The concept of an armed attack was left deliberately open to the interpretation of Member States and U.N. Organs, and the wording is broad enough to include the acts of non-State actors as 'armed attacks.'"); see also Carsten Stahn, "'Nicaragua is Dead, Long Live Nicaragua'—The Right to Self-defence under Art. 51" in Walter *et al.*, *Terrorism as a Challenge*, above note 14 at 830.

56   S/RES/1368 (2001); S/RES/1373 (2001).

57   NATO, Press Release, "Invocation of Article 5 Confirmed" (2 October 2001), online: www.nato.int/docu/update/2001/1001/e1002a.htm.

58   See Twenty-fourth Meeting of Consultation of Ministers of Foreign Affairs, Terrorist Threat to the Americas, OAS Doc. RC.24/Res.1/01 (21 September 2001). Article 3 reads: "an armed attack by any State against an American State shall be considered as an attack against all the American States and, consequently, each

These responses, and the widespread reaction of individual states offering assistance to the United States, support the conclusion that al-Qaeda's terrorist act on 9/11 reached the level of an armed attack. Under these circumstances, a common (although not unanimous view) is that the armed response to al-Qaeda was permissible under international law (as it is now understood), so long as other elements of self-defence law such as proportionality and necessity were observed.[59]

ii)   The Problem of Attribution

A particularly complex issue, however, is whether armed force was properly used in 2001 against al-Qaeda's hosts, the Taliban *de facto* government of Afghanistan. Al-Qaeda found shelter in the Taliban's Afghanistan, but it was reportedly never the Taliban's proxy; as one scholar summarizes, "the United States and its allies never expressly advanced the argument that the Taliban regime directed or controlled the actions of al-Qaeda or adopted al-Qaeda conduct as its own."[60] If true, these facts suggest force used against Afghanistan and its government (as opposed to al-Qaeda itself) may not have been warranted under standard self-defence rules.

For the International Court of Justice (ICJ), the existence of a right to self-defence against a state for the actions of a nonstate actor depends on an armed attack being attributable to the state against whom the act of self-defence is directed.[61] The question of attribution was addressed most clearly by the ICJ in the *Military and Paramilitary Activities in and against Nicaragua Case*. There, the ICJ concluded that "an armed attack must be understood as including not merely action by regular armed forces across an international border, but also the *sending by or on behalf of a State* of armed bands, groups, irregulars or mercenaries, which

---

one of the said Contracting Parties undertakes to assist in meeting the attack in the exercise of the inherent right of individual or collective self-defense recognized by Article 51 of the *Charter* of the United Nations."

59   See, for example, Paust, "Use of Armed Force," above note 46 at 533. See also discussion in Duffy, *War on Terror*, above note 37 at 158 *et seq.*

60   Becker, *Terrorism and the State*, above note 54 at 217. See also Duffy, *War on Terror, ibid.* at 189 (making a similar point).

61   *Case Concerning Oil Platforms (Islamic Republic Of Iran v. United States Of America)* (2003), ICJ General List No. 90 at para. 51 ("in order to establish that it was legally justified in attacking the Iranian platforms in exercise of the right of individual self-defence, the United States has to show that attacks had been made upon it for which Iran was responsible; and that those attacks were of such a nature as to be qualified as 'armed attacks' within the meaning of that expression in Article 51 of the United Nations *Charter*, and as understood in customary law on the use of force").

carry out acts of armed force against another State of such gravity as to amount to (*inter alia*) an actual armed attack conducted by regular forces, or its substantial involvement therein."[62] The ICJ expressly ruled out "assistance to rebels in the form of the provision of weapons or logistical or other support" as an "armed attack."[63]

More recently, in *Armed activities on the territory of the Congo (Democratic Republic of the Congo v. Uganda)*, the ICJ invoked Article 3(g) of General Assembly Resolution 3314 as the standard for attribution of private violent action to the state. This resolution specifies in Article 3(g) that aggression includes "the sending by or on behalf of a State of armed bands, groups, irregulars or mercenaries, which carry out acts of armed force against another State of such gravity as to amount to the acts listed above, or its substantial involvement therein." [64] The "acts listed above" include such things as attacks on the territory of a state, or its occupation or annexation, bombardment or use of weapons against the territory of a state, attacks on a state's armed forces and a blockade of state's ports or coast.

In the 2007 *Crime of Genocide Case*, the Court underscored that attribution rules require "effective control" over a nonstate actor by the state; that is, a situation "where an organ of the State gave the instructions or provided the direction pursuant to which the perpetrators of the wrongful act acted or where it exercised effective control over the action during which the wrong was committed."[65]

---

62   *Case Concerning Military and Paramilitary Activities In and Against Nicaragua (Nicaragua v. United States of America)*, [1986] I.C.J. Rep. 14 at para. 195 [*Nicaragua Case*] [citations omitted, emphasis added].

63   *Ibid.*

64   A/RES/3314 (XXIX) (14 December 1974). See *Armed Activities on the Territory of the Congo (Democratic Republic of the Congo v. Uganda)* (2005), ICJ General List No. 116 at para. 146 [*Armed Activities*] (holding that there was "no satisfactory proof of the involvement in these attacks [on Uganda], direct or indirect, of the Government of the DRC. The attacks did not emanate from armed bands or irregulars sent by the DRC or on behalf of the DRC, within the sense of Article 3 (g) of General Assembly resolution 3314 (XXIX) on the definition of aggression, adopted on 14 December 1974.")

65   *Application of the Convention on the Prevention and Punishment of the Crime of Genocide (Bosnia and Herzegovina v. Serbia and Montenegro)* (2007), ICJ General List 91 at para. 406 [*Crime of Genocide Case*]. The International Criminal Tribunal for the Former Yugoslavia (ICTY) has proposed a caveat to these rules where the group in question is a military or paramilitary group:

> In order to attribute the acts of a military or paramilitary group to a State, it must be proved that the State wields overall control over the group, not only by equipping and financing the group, but also by coordinating or helping in the general planning of its military activity. Only then can the State be held

Read together, therefore, the ICJ appears to take the view that an armed attack may be attributable to a state where a state dispatches the attackers, or gives sufficient direction to, or is in a role of sufficient agency with, the nonstate perpetrator of the assault. This emphasis on agency is reflected also in the current understanding of the law of state responsibility. The International Law Commission's draft articles on that topic contain a number of circumstances in which internationally wrongful acts may be attributed to a state. Thus, "the conduct of a person or group of persons shall be considered an act of a State under international law if the person or group of persons is in fact acting on the instructions of, or under the direction or control of that State in carrying out the conduct."[66] Similarly, attribution may exist where the state acknowledges and adopts the conduct of these nonstate actors as its own.[67]

Where attribution rules are not satisfied, it seems unlikely force in self-defence may be directed at targets beyond the terrorist group itself.[68]

---

internationally accountable for any misconduct of the group. However, it is not necessary that, in addition, the State should also issue, either to the head or to members of the group, instructions for the commission of specific acts contrary to international law.

Prosecutor v. Dusko Tadic, Decision of the U.N. International Tribunal for the Prosecution of Persons Responsible for Serious Violations of International Humanitarian Law Committed in the Territory of Former Yugoslavia since 1991, reprinted in (1999), 38 I.L.M. 1518 at para. 131. This position was rejected by the International Court of Justice in the *Crime of Genocide Case*, at para. 404 *et seq.*, which reaffirmed its position in the *Nicaragua Case*, above note 62. It remains to be seen which approach other bodies, such as the International Criminal Court, will adopt.

66 International Law Commission, *Responsibility of States for Internationally Wrongful Acts*, Official Records of the General Assembly, Fifty-sixth Session, Supplement No. 10 (A/56/10), Art. 8 [*State Responsibility Articles*].

67 *Ibid.*, Art. 11.

68 Indeed, without attribution, it may be that force should not be applied even against the territory of the state on which the terrorists are found, at least without the consent of the territorial state. Nonconsensual use of force could properly be viewed as a violation of Art. 2(4) of the U.N. *Charter*. This view has been criticized as impermissibly constraining the capacity of an attacked state to respond. Some jurists urge that the use of force against terrorists on the territory of a state should be permitted if certain criteria are met. See, for example, Emmanuel Gross, *The Struggle of Democracy Against Terrorism* (Charlottesville, VA: University of Virginia Press, 2006) at 42 (arguing that the presence of the terrorist threat must be supported by sufficient evidence that force is limited to the removal of the terrorist threat; that the force is proportional to the size of the threat; that the threat is likely to be realized without action; and, last, all nonviolent means of addressing the threat have been addressed).

This was a commonly held view prior to 9/11,[69] and continues to be held by at least some scholars today:

> Harboring terrorists, providing formal or effective amnesty for terrorists ..., otherwise tolerating, acquiescing, encouraging, or inciting terrorists within one's borders, or providing certain other forms of assistance to terrorists can implicate state responsibility and justify various political, diplomatic, economic, and juridic sanctions in response ... Yet, unless the state is organizing, fomenting, directing, or otherwise directly participating in armed attacks by non-state terrorists, the use of military force against the state, as opposed to only the non-state terrorists, would be impermissible.[70]

Yet, the international community moved swiftly in supporting massive military action against Afghanistan, culminating in the displacement of the Taliban from government. This fact has led some scholars to conclude that attribution rules for states harbouring terrorists have shifted, and that the threshold is (or at least should) be much lower than the agency-type requirements invoked by the International Court of Justice in the *Nicaragua Case*. Indeed, some jurists have proposed something approximating a negligence-like theory; that is, attribution of responsibility to a state where the terrorist armed attack would not have occurred "but for" the state's action or inaction.[71]

There is an evident risk to lowering that threshold for use of force against states that, while perhaps not complying with their anti-terrorism obligations to suppress terrorism, do not themselves direct or participate in a terrorist act. More aggressive rules on attribution may serve as a wedge in the unraveling of vital constraints on the exercise of state violence, legalizing wider interstate wars in response to terrorism.

2) Terrorism, Proportionality and Necessity

This last observation raises questions about self-defence, proportionality and necessity. As discussed in Chapter 5, "proportionality" in response to an isolated armed attack might be construed as proportional

---

69   See discussion in Becker, *Terrorism and the State*, above note 54 at 163 *et seq.*

70   Paust, "Use of Armed Force," above note 46 at 540; Duffy, *War on Terror*, above note 37 at 161 ("While support for terrorists falling short of effective control may be prohibited in international law, it does not necessarily render the state constructively responsible for an armed attack, or entitle other states to use force against it").

71   Becker, *Terrorism and the State*, above note 54. See also the discussion of this topic in Carsten Stahn, "'Nicaragua is dead, long live Nicaragua' — the Right to Self-Defence under Art. 51 UN-Charter and International Terrorism," in *Terrorism as a Challenge*, above note 14 at 838 *et seq.* [Stahn, "Nicaragua"].

to the armed attack itself; that is, proportional to the initial injury. Another (and probably dominant) view assesses whether the use of force is proportional to the military objective of countering the threat. These standards produce very different measures for evaluating an act of self-defence in response to a terrorist armed attack.

Assessed against the first standard, the armed response to 9/11 in Afghanistan—Operation Enduring Freedom—was disproportionate if the consequences of the response—measured in civilian casualties, perhaps—outstripped those caused by the terrorist attack.[72] Assessed against the second standard, armed force remained proportional if properly directed at dislodging the terrorists (and their Taliban hosts, assuming that attribution rules were met), and thus forestalling the recurrence of the 9/11 attack.[73]

As well as proportional, force used in self-defence must be necessary to respond to and repel the armed attack. Military responses to terrorism in particular have often precipitated debate among states and scholars as to whether they are truly "necessary" to repel the attack or rather simply retaliatory. International criticism describing military action as reprisals rather than self-defence was acute, for instance, after the 1986 U.S. bombing of Libya, and in response to at least some Israeli reactions to terrorism.[74] The 9/11 reaction differed. After 9/11, Operation Enduring Freedom against Afghanistan was specifically justified by the United States (plausibly, given the uncertainty of the period) as a response to an "ongoing threat" and "designed to prevent and deter further attacks on the United States."[75]

---

72 9/11 produced roughly 3,000 casualties, and substantial property damage. Estimates of civilian deaths in the initial conflict in Afghanistan are unofficial and suspect because of methodological difficulties, but in some studies range from just over 1,000 (during the period 7 October to 1 January 2002) to 3,600 (7 October 2001 to March 2003). See, respectively, Carl Conetta, Project on Defense Alternatives *Briefing Report #11, Operation Enduring Freedom: Why a Higher Rate of Civilian Bombing Casualties* (18 January 2002), online: www.comw.org/pda/0201oef.html, and the database maintained by Professor Marc Herold at http://pubpages.unh.edu/~mwherold/AfghanDailyCount.pdf.

73 See Chapter 5 for a more detailed discussion of proportionality.

74 See discussion in William V. O'Brien, "Reprisals, Deterrence and Self-Defense in Counterterror Operations" (1990) 30 Va. J. Int'l L. 421; Christine Gray, *International Law and the Use of Force* (Oxford: Oxford University Press, 2000) at 118.

75 Letter from Ambassador John Negroponte, Permanent Representative of the U.S.A to the U.N. in New York, to the President of the Security Council, S/2001/946, 7 October 2001. See also the British statement, noting that the war in Afghanistan was designed to "avert the continuing threat of attacks." Letter from Stewart Eldon, Chargé d'Affaires, U.K. Mission to the U.N. in New York, to the President of the Security Council, S/2001/947, 7 October 2001.

C. TARGETED KILLINGS

In the post-9/11 campaign against terrorism, military force has also been deployed selectively in theatres other than Afghanistan (and Iraq). Press reports suggest, for instance, that the United States has a global targeted killing program, employing missiles from drone aircraft to strike at suspected terrorist leaders.[76]

Reports from 2006[77] suggest that approximately nineteen strikes have been made, with at least nine conducted outside Iraq. The actual locations of these attacks are closely guarded secrets. However, journalistic reports suggest that missile strikes have occurred in Pakistan, Yemen and Somalia. In January 2006, for instance, a missile strike failed to kill al-Qaeda second-in-command Ayman Zawahiri in Pakistan. It did, however, reportedly kill as many as eighteen civilians.[78] In 2005, Haitham Yemeni and Abu Hamza Rabia, both al-Qaeda leaders, were killed in Pakistan. Several others, including possible civilians, were injured or killed in these attacks.[79] Earlier, in 2002, another al-Qaeda leader, Qaed Sinan Harithi, and several associates were killed by a U.S. military drone aircraft in a missile strike in Yemen. More recently, in 2007, the United States bombed al-Qaeda members suspected of participating in the 1998 U.S. Kenyan and Tanzanian embassy attacks in Somalia. This strike took place at about the same time as that country's *de jure* government and its Ethiopian allies displaced the Islamic movement that had consolidated control over much of the nation.[80]

1) Self-Defence

There was no credible claim that any of these missile strikes were precipitated by an imminent attack against the United States. They were, therefore, unlikely candidates for a self-defence justification. As one scholar observes, discussing the Yemeni case:

---

76 See, in particular, Josh Meyer, "CIA Expands Use of Drones in Terror War" *Los Angeles Times* (29 January 2006) A1.

77 *Ibid.*

78 Amnesty International, *Pakistan: U.S. involvement in civilian deaths*, (31 January 2006), online: http://web.amnesty.org/library/Index/ENGASA330022006.

79 See Amnesty International, *Pakistan: Human Rights Ignored in the "War on Terror"* (29 Sept. 2006), online: www.amnestyusa.org/document.php?lang=e&id=E NGASA330352006.

80 David Cloud, "U.S. Airstrike Aims at Qaeda Cell in Somalia" *New York Times* (9 January 2007) A3.

Can the mere fact that six men in the car were at a place vulnerable to attack and, eventually, planning future strikes against the U.S. justify their killing on the basis of anticipatory self-defence? Obviously not, even if this was the only way to eliminate them effectively. The threat lacked specificity. The mere likelihood of future attacks does not even meet the broadest understanding of "imminence."[81]

Difficulty reconciling militarized anti-terrorism with conventional *jus ad bellum* rules is not, however, the only challenge to international law presented by the post-9/11 strategy. Perhaps even more troubling are the implications the war metaphor has for the *jus in bello*—the rules of law that should apply once a conflict is engaged.

2) Standards Applicable to the Killings

In this last respect, targeted killings in the campaign against terrorism (and in the Israeli–Palestinian conflict) are enormously controversial. Human rights organizations[82] and the U.N. Special Rapporteur on extrajudicial executions[83] have condemned these targeted assassinations as illicit extrajudicial executions, inconsistent with human rights principles. There is support for this view. Article 6 of the *International Covenant on Civil and Political Rights* provides that "every human being has the inherent right to life. This right shall be protected by law. No one shall be arbitrarily deprived of his life." This right is nonderogable, even in times of emergency that threaten the life of the nation.[84]

American authorities, however, reportedly described the missile attacks listed above as conducted in a situation of continuing armed conflict against al-Qaeda,[85] and presumably governed by international humanitarian law (IHL) rather than human rights law in its full form.[86]

81   Stahn, "Nicaragua," in *Terrorism as a Challenge*, above note 14 at 875.

82   See, for example, Amnesty International, *United States of America: An Extrajudicial Execution by the CIA?* (18 May 2005), online: http://web.amnesty.org/library/Index/ENGAMR510792005?open&of=ENG-2AM.

83   U.N. Special Rapporteur on Extrajudicial, Summary or Arbitrary Executions, *Report of the Special Rapporteur, Asma Jahangir, submitted pursuant to Commission on Human Rights resolution 2002/36*, U.N. Doc. E/CN.4/2003/3 (13 January 2003) (noting that the "attack in Yemen constitutes a clear case of extrajudicial killing"), online: www.unhchr.ch/huridocda/huridoca.nsf/(Symbol)/E.CN.4.200 3.3.Add.4.En?Opendocument.

84   *International Covenant on Civil and Political Rights*, 999 U.N.T.S. 171, Art. 4 [ICCPR].

85   Duffy, War *on Terror*, above note 37 at 340.

86   See Chapters 2 and 5 for a discussion of IHL as *lex specialis* in a situation of armed conflict.

The legality of this policy of targeted killing may hinge, therefore, on whether it occurs in a situation of armed conflict or not.

a) Targeted Killings outside Theatres of Armed Conflict

In fact, there was no armed conflict in Yemen or Pakistan at the time of the strikes noted above, and it stretches all credulity to argue that the indisputable conflict in Afghanistan against al-Qaeda and/or elements of the Taliban created a geographically attenuated armed conflict existing everywhere al-Qaeda might be found.[87] If it did, then IHL—with its receptivity to the use of lethal force against combatants—would permit targeted and proportional missile strikes within even North American and European states in which al-Qaeda agents operate.[88]

Nor could the missile strikes *themselves* constitute a use of military force triggering IHL as *lex specialis*. Selective anti-terrorism strikes on terrorist targets within states that are not themselves targeted probably do not give rise to an "armed conflict" within the meaning of IHL. In deciding the application of IHL, the international criminal tribunals for the former Yugoslavia and Rwanda have suggested that acts of vio-

---

87   See, for example, Avril McDonald, "Defining the War on Terror and the Status of Detainees" (2002) 4 Humanitäres Völkerrecht 207, online: www. icrc.org/Web/Eng/siteeng0.nsf/htmlall/5P8AVK/$FILE/Avril+McDonald-final. pdf?OpenElement.

> In fact, the "war on terror" is clearly not an armed conflict at all. It con-
> sists of a multi-faceted counter-terrorism campaign, some aspects of which
> involve the use of military force, most of it carried out in States where there
> is no armed conflict, although aspects of the counter-terrorism campaign
> assume the characteristics of armed conflict where the U.S. attacks a State
> considered to be harbouring or assisting Al Qaeda, as it did in Afghanistan.
> … Otherwise, the so-called "war on terror" which the U.S. is waging against
> Al Qaeda does not satisfy the conditions of the Geneva Conventions to be
> considered as an armed conflict.

See also Duffy, *War on Terror*, above note 37 at 341 *et seq.* The *Tadic* definition of armed conflict speaks of a "protracted armed violence between govern-mental authorities and organized armed groups or between such groups within a State." *Prosecutor v. Dusko Tadic, Decision of the U.N. International Tribunal for the Prosecution of Persons Responsible for Serious Violations of International Humanitarian Law Committed in the Territory of Former Yugoslavia since 1991,* Case No. IT-94-1-AR72, reprinted in (1996), 35 I.L.M. 32 at para. 70 [*Tadic*]. The "war on terror" may involve protracted violence, but it is certainly not "within a State" (except in Afghanistan and Iraq).

88   Of course, such attacks, if undertaken without the consent of the territorial state, would violate the latter's sovereignty and likely constitute a violation of Art. 2(4) of the U.N. *Charter*, subject to the discussion on self-defence and at-tribution above.

lence between states and nonstate actors must be "protracted" for a situation of "armed conflict" to arise.[89]

Moreover, it is not clear that principles like Common Article 3 that apply to truly noninternational conflicts—that is, between states and nonstate armed groups—extend also to actions against terrorists acting clandestinely as part of a shadowy, geographically disparate network that do not act as dissident armed forces controlling territory.[90] Similar comments can be made about Additional Protocol II, dealing squarely with noninternational armed conflicts.[91]

The 2002 missile strike in Yemen and the more recent strikes in Pakistan against terrorist targets do not fit these criteria for the initiation of an armed conflict. They were incidental uses of armed force of insufficient intensity to truly constitute an armed conflict and were directed against a nonstate actor who controlled no portion of the territory of the state and who, arguably, lacked the proto-armed forces qualities Common Article 3 and Additional Protocol II seem to require. IHL was likely not triggered, therefore, to serve as the *lex specialis* applicable to

---

89   *Tadic*, above note 87 at para. 70; *The Prosecutor v. Zejnil Delalic*, Judgment, IT-96-21 at para. 184 (ICTY (Trial Chamber) 1998), online: www.un.org/icty/celeb-ici/trialc2/judgement/index.htm (in internal conflicts, "in order to distinguish from cases of civil unrest or terrorist activities, the emphasis is on the protracted extent of the armed violence and the extent of organisation of the parties involved"); *The Prosecutor v. Jean Paul Akayesu*, ICTR-96-4-T at para. 619 (ICTR (Trial Chamber) 1998), online: http://69.94.11.53/default.htm (citing *Tadic*).

90   ICRC *Commentary* to Art. 3, Convention (I) for the Amelioration of the Condition of the Wounded and Sick in Armed Forces in the Field. Geneva, 12 August 1949, online: www.icrc.org/ihl.nsf/COM/365-570045?OpenDocument (noting that Common Article 3 of the Geneva Conventions is not intended to deal with banditry or unorganized and short-lived insurrections. Although clearly not meant as exhaustive, the criteria proposed by the Red Cross to distinguish the latter situation from a genuine non-international armed conflict tend to imagine insurgents formed as militaries and potentially controlling portions of state territory). See the debate on this issue in International Committee of the Red Cross, *XXVIIth Round Table on Current Problems of International Humanitarian Law: "International Humanitarian Law and Other Legal Regimes: Interplay in Situations of Violence"* (2003) at 5–8, online: www.icrc.org/Web/eng/siteeng0.nsf/htmlall/5UBCVX/$File/Interplay_other_regimes_Nov_2003.pdf.

91   *Protocol Additional to the Geneva Conventions of 12 August 1949, and Relating to the Protection of Victims of Non-International Armed Conflicts*, 8 June 1977, Art. 1 [AP II] (applying to "armed conflicts … which take place in the territory of a [state party] … between its armed forces and *dissident armed forces or other organized armed groups which, under responsible command, exercise such control over a part of its territory as to enable them to carry out sustained and concerted military operations*") [emphasis added].

the strikes. As a result, basic human rights principles applied in full form, including the ICCPR's Article 6 right to life obligations.

b) Targeted Killings during Armed Conflict

The analysis is different where targeted killings occur in a situation of armed conflict. The 2007 U.S. strike on al-Qaeda targets during the armed conflict in Somalia, as well as sorties launched in Afghanistan, likely fit the definition, as do (arguably) the Israeli targeted killings in the occupied territories.

International humanitarian law allows lethal force to be directed by combatants against other combatants.[92] Combatants are (usually) members of the armed forces of a party to a conflict and may be targeted, unless otherwise viewed as protected persons.[93] Civilians are generally noncombatants, and may not be attacked. However, the strict prohibition on attacks directed against civilians is relaxed where the latter "take a direct part in hostilities,"[94] an ambiguous phrase in international humanitarian law.[95] Summarizing the applicable principles, the Israeli Supreme Court has concluded:

> a civilian—that is, a person who does not fall into the category of combatant—must refrain from directly participating in hostilities. A civilian who violates that law and commits acts of combat does not lose his status as a civilian, but as long as he is taking a direct part in hostilities he does not enjoy—during that time—the protection granted to a civilian. He is subject to the risks of attack like those to which a combatant is subject, without enjoying the rights of a combatant, e.g., those granted to a prisoner of war.[96]

For this reason, the Israeli court concluded that targeted killings of terrorists—civilians who have taken up arms—in Israel's ongoing armed conflict in the occupied territories may be legal:

> Harming such civilians, even if the result is death, is permitted, on the condition that there is no other less harmful means, and on the

---

92 See discussion in Chapter 5.

93 *Protocol Additional to the Geneva Conventions of 12 August 1949, and relating to the Protection of Victims of International Armed Conflicts*, 8 June 1977, Art. 43 [AP I]. See discussion in Chapters 5 and 14.

94 *Ibid.*, Art. 51.

95 See the review of this concept in *Public Committee*, above note 38 at para. 33 *et seq.* See also Duffy, *War on Terror*, above note 37 at 230 (urging that "direct participation should be narrowly construed, and does not include for example support for, or affiliation to, the adversary").

96 *Public Committee, ibid.* at para. 31.

condition that innocent civilians nearby are not harmed. Harm to the latter must be proportionate. That proportionality is determined according to a values based test, intended to balance between the military advantage and the civilian damage. As we have seen, we cannot determine that a preventative strike is always legal, just as we cannot determine that it is always illegal. All depends upon the question whether the standards of customary international law regarding international armed conflict allow that preventative strike or not.[97]

In sum, targeted killings of combatants, including terrorists, may be legal, but that legality will hinge on the particulars of the situation, viewed through the optic of IHL rules on proportionality.[98]

PART III: TERRORISM AND INTERNATIONAL CRIMINAL LAW

If international law is the guide, it should be the case that military use of force in response to terrorism will be the exception, not the norm. The Security Council should only authorize use of force where the terrorist act rises to the level of a threat to international peace and security. The latter concept is notoriously fluid and, as noted, the council has characterized "all acts of terrorism irrespective of their motivation, whenever and by whomsoever committed, as one of the most serious threats to peace and security." However, this statement may be overbroad; not every act of political violence by nonstate actors truly threatens the international order in the same manner as the massive attack of 9/11, or feared use of weapons of mass destruction.[99] Meanwhile, the right to self-defence depends on the existence of an armed attack. Once again, not every, discrete terrorist act will meet this threshold requirements.

If the military tool is only narrowly applicable, then international criminal law should have a default primacy. This Part traces the content of counterterrorism international criminal law. Chapter 7 focuses on Canada's domestic criminal law response.

---

97   *Ibid.* at para. 60.
98   See Chapter 5 for a discussion of proportionality in IHL.
99   See also the point made by Duffy, *War on Terror*, above note 37 at 171 (doubting that any and all acts of terrorism are threats to international peace and security, "particularly given the absence of international accord around the substance and scope of the definition of terrorism").

A. THE CHALLENGE OF DEFINITION

In international criminal law, one issue above any other has complicated efforts to grapple with terrorism, especially at the international level: controversy over the definition of terrorism. The adage "one person's terrorist is another person's freedom fighter" is more than cliché; it appears also to be an empirical reality. Terrorism is a tactic, monopolized by no single political, religious or ideological cause. As such, it has attracted derision or support according to the sympathies generated by the cause of those who practise or espouse it. Acts of politically motivated violence undertaken as part of an anticolonial struggle for self-determination, for instance, have been evaluated very differently from similar acts of violence committed in different contexts.

The problem of definition persists post-9/11. As one scholar has noted, "terrorism is a loaded term that is often used as a politically convenient label by which to deny legitimacy to an adversary while claiming it for oneself."[100] In these circumstances, not everyone is prepared to condemn unequivocally every act of political violence, although the world community now emphatically denounces terrorism writ large. Key international legal instruments like U.N. Security Council Resolution 1373 abet this apparent contradiction. Resolution 1373 requires that "terrorist acts are established as serious criminal offences in domestic laws and regulations and that the punishment duly reflects the seriousness of such terrorist acts." It fails, however, to define terrorism or terrorist acts. While the council has provided more guidance since 2001, terrorism may continue to exist in the eye of the beholder. By the time of this writing, it was unclear whether this failure of definition would be cured in the proposed comprehensive international anti-terrorism treaty, a matter discussed again below.

B. THE INTERNATIONAL LAW OF ANTI-TERRORISM IN HISTORICAL CONTEXT

Not surprisingly, politically inspired violence has sparked efforts at international condemnation and regulation for decades. The most notable early effort to grapple with terrorism in international law dates from the interwar period. In October 1934, King Alexander of Yugoslavia and French Foreign Minister Louis Barthou were assassinated in Mar-

---

100 Becker, *Terrorism and the State*, above note 54 at 85.

seilles by a Croatian nationalist. The assassin escaped to Italy, prompting the French government to seek his extradition under an 1870 extradition treaty. The Italians refused to extradite the killer, citing a provision in the 1870 convention barring surrender of those accused of politically motivated crimes. In response, France called for a convention on terrorism that would include an international court competent to try accused terrorists. This court was to have jurisdiction where the state on whose territory the accused was found did not wish to extradite or prosecute.[101]

Facing intense pressure to respond to the 1934 assassination, and earlier such attacks and attempts, the Council of the League of Nations appointed a Committee for the International Repression of Terrorism to examine the issue and devise a draft convention. The committee ultimately drafted two separate conventions—one on the prevention and punishment of terrorism and the other on the creation of an international criminal court.[102] The terrorism convention required parties to criminalize "acts of terrorism," defined as "criminal acts directed against a state and intended or calculated to create a state of terror in the minds of particular persons, or groups of persons or the general public."[103] It included rules on the extradition (or, in the absence of extradition, trial) of accused and grappled with several other notable conundrums in terrorism criminal law. Indeed, its subject-matter resonates to this day. As one scholar notes, the League's work "anticipated most of the legal issues which would plague the international community's response to terrorism in the following seven decades: the political and technical difficulties of definition; the problem of 'freedom fighters' and self-determination; 'state terrorism' and the duty of non-intervention; state criminality and applicability to armed forces; the scope of the political offence exception to extradition; the impact on freedom of expression; and the relationship between terrorism and asylum."[104]

Ultimately, the international community received both the terrorism and the accompanying 1937 international court conventions coolly. When the conventions were eventually opened for signature and rati-

---

101 M. Lippman, "Towards an International Criminal Court" (1995) 3 San Diego Jus. J. 1 at 38.

102 Committee for the International Repression of Terrorism, *Draft Convention for Prevention and Punishment of Terrorism and Draft Convention for the Creation of an International Criminal Court*, in Report to the Council Adopted by the Committee on 15 January 1936. C.36(I).1936.V.

103 See discussion in J. Starke, "The Convention for the Prevention and Punishment of Terrorism" (1938) 19 Brit. Y.B. Int'l L. 214.

104 Ben Saul, "The Legal Response of the League of Nations to Terrorism" (2006) 4 J. Int'l Crim. Jus. 78 at 79.

fication, only one state ratified the Convention on Terrorism. No state ratified the Convention for the Creation of an International Criminal Court.

C. PIECEMEAL ANTI-TERRORISM CONVENTIONS

The failure to agree to a comprehensive, multilateral anti-terrorism treaty persisted to the time of this writing. International law, however, is rich with less ambitious anti-terrorism treaties. The pre-9/11 solution to the conundrum of developing a universal anti-terrorism convention — and particularly to the controversy over defining terrorism — was to adopt a piecemeal approach; that is, to condemn individual activities and actions without trying to define the entire universe of possible terrorist acts. The net result is thirteen multilateral antiterrorist treaties, only two of which attempt a generic definition of terrorist act. All but two of the thirteen multilateral conventions create international criminal offences and oblige state parties to the treaties to criminalize these acts in their domestic penal codes.

The names of these treaties and their subject-matter are outlined in Table 6.2. Many of these instruments reflect the historical circumstances in which they were negotiated. For instance, the aircraft and hostage-related terrorism conventions date to the 1960s and 1970s, and reflected the terrorist tactics of the Palestinian and left-wing radical groups of the era. The *Convention on the Marking of Plastic Explosives for the Purpose of Identification* was a response to the Lockerbie bombing, conducted with the use of plastic explosive. The recent *International Convention for the Suppression of Acts of Nuclear Terrorism* reflects contemporary concerns that weapons of mass destruction may find their way into the hands of nonstate actors.

Despite their different subject matters, the treaties follow a roughly similar template, dealing with several common issues. The sections that follow outline these features.

Table 6.2:   Existing Anti-terrorism Conventions

Convention	Subject-Matter
A. Conventions Banning Certain Terrorist Techniques and Practices	
1. Terrorism Against Transportation and Infrastructure	
Convention on Offences and Certain Other Acts Committed on Board Aircraft (Tokyo Convention, 1963)	Authorizes aircraft commanders to take steps to protect an in-flight aircraft from acts which are penal offences or may or do jeopardize the safety of the aircraft or of persons or property in it or which jeopardize good order and discipline on board. Requires state parties to take into custody a person performing these acts upon disembarkation and to restore control of the aircraft to its commander.
Convention for the Suppression of Unlawful Seizure of Aircraft (Hague Convention, 1970)	Requires state parties to criminalize the offence of unlawfully, by force or threat thereof, or by any other form of intimidation, seizing, or exercising control of an in-flight aircraft, or attempting to perform or being an accomplice to any such act.
Convention for the Suppression of Unlawful Acts Against the Safety of Civil Aviation (Montreal Convention, 1971)	Requires state parties to criminalize the following offences (and attempts and being an accomplice to such offences): • performing an act of violence against a person on board an aircraft in flight if that act is likely to endanger the safety of that aircraft; or • destroying an aircraft in service or causing damage to such an aircraft which renders it incapable of flight or which is likely to endanger its safety in flight; • placing or causing to be placed on an aircraft in service, by any means whatsoever, a device or substance which is likely to destroy that aircraft, or to cause damage to it which renders it incapable of flight, or to cause damage to it which is likely to endanger its safety in flight; • destroying or damaging air navigation facilities or interfering with their operation, if any such act is likely to endanger the safety of aircraft in flight; or • communicating information which the perpetrator knows to be false, thereby endangering the safety of an aircraft in flight.

Convention	Subject-Matter
Protocol for the Suppression of Unlawful Acts of Violence at Airports Serving International Aviation (Montreal Convention Protocol, 1988)	Extends the scope of the Montreal Convention to require state parties to criminalize: • performance of an act of violence against a person at an airport serving international civil aviation which causes or is likely to cause serious injury or death; or • destruction or serious damage to the facilities of an airport serving international civil aviation or an aircraft not in service located there or disrupting the services of the airport, if such an act endangers or is likely to endanger safety at that airport.
Convention for the Suppression of Unlawful Acts Against the Safety of Maritime Navigation (Maritime Convention, 1988), as amended by 2005 Protocol (not in force at time of writing)	Requires state parties to criminalize the following offences: • seizing or exercising control over a ship by force or threat thereof or any other form of intimidation; • performing an act of violence against a person on board a ship if that act is likely to endanger the safe navigation of that ship; • destroying a ship or causing damage to a ship or to its cargo which is likely to endanger the safe navigation of that ship; • placing or causing to be placed on a ship, by any means whatsoever, a device or substance that is likely to destroy that ship, or causing damage to that ship or its cargo which endangers or is likely to endanger the safe navigation of that ship; • destroying or seriously damaging maritime navigational facilities or seriously interfering with their operation, if any such act is likely to endanger the safe navigation of a ship; • communicating information which that person knows to be false, thereby endangering the safe navigation of a ship; • making threats aimed at compelling a physical or juridical person to do or refrain from doing any act, or committing any of the offences in the second, third and fifth bullets above, if that threat is likely to endanger the ship's safe navigation; • using on or from a ship or transporting on a ship various radioactive or nuclear materials or nuclear or chemical or biological weapons to intimidate a population, or to compel a government or an international organization to do or to abstain from doing any act.

Convention	Subject-Matter
Maritime Convention, 1988 (cont'd)	State parties are also to criminalize attempts, participating as an accomplice or organizing or directing others to commit an above-listed offence or in any other way intentionally contributing to the commission of one or more offences by a group of persons acting with a common purpose with the aim of furthering the general criminal activity or purpose of the group or made in the knowledge of the intention of the group to commit the offence or offences concerned.
Protocol for the Suppression of Unlawful Acts Against the Safety of Fixed Platforms Located on the Continental Shelf (Maritime Convention Protocol, 1988), as amended by 2005 Protocol (not in force at time of writing)	Requires state parties to criminalize the following offences (and attempts, aiding and being an accomplice to such offences): • seizing or exercising control over a fixed platform by force or threat thereof or any other form of intimidation; • performing an act of violence against a person on board a fixed platform if that act is likely to endanger its safety; • destroying a fixed platform or causing damage to it which is likely to endanger its safety; • placing or causing to be placed on a fixed platform, by any means whatsoever, a device or substance which is likely to destroy that fixed platform or likely to endanger its safety; • making threats aimed at compelling a physical or juridical person to do or refrain from doing any act, or committing any of the offences in the second and third bullets above, if that threat is likely to endanger the safety of the fixed platform; • using on or from a fixed platform (or threatening to do so) various radioactive or nuclear materials or nuclear or chemical or biological weapons to intimidate a population, or to compel a government or an international organization to do or to abstain from doing any act. State parties are also to criminalize attempts, participating as an accomplice or organizing or directing others to commit an above-listed offence or in any other way intentionally contributing to the commission of one or more offences by a group of persons acting with a common purpose with the aim of furthering the general criminal activity or purpose of the group or made in the knowledge of the intention of the group to commit the offence or offences concerned.

Convention	Subject-Matter
2. Terrorism Against Protected Persons	
Convention on the prevention and punishment of crimes against internationally protected persons, including diplomatic agents (Protected Person Convention, 1973)	Requires state parties to criminalize the intentional commission of (and an attempt or a threat to or acting as an accomplice in) a murder, kidnapping or other attack upon the person or liberty of an internationally protected person or a violent attack upon the official premises, the private accommodation or the means of transport of an internationally protected person likely to endanger his or her person or liberty. "Internationally protected person" is defined as: • a Head of State, including any member of a collegial body performing the functions of a Head of State under the constitution of the State concerned, a Head of Government or a Minister for Foreign Affairs, whenever any such person is in a foreign State, as well as members of his or her family who accompany him or her; • any representative or official of a State or any official or other agent of an international organization of an intergovernmental character who, at the time when and in the place where a crime against him or her, his or her official premises, his or her private accommodation or his or her means of transport is committed, is entitled pursuant to international law to special protection from any attack on his or her person, freedom or dignity, as well as members of his or her family forming part of his or her household.
3. Nuclear Terrorism	
International Convention for the Suppression of Acts of Nuclear Terrorism (Nuclear Terrorism Convention, 2005) (not in force at time of writing)	Requires state parties to criminalize: • possession of radioactive material or making or possessing a nuclear or radiological explosive device with the intent to cause death or serious bodily injury; or with the intent to cause substantial damage to property or to the environment; • using in any way radioactive material or a device, or using or damaging a nuclear facility in a manner which releases or risks the release of radioactive material with the intent to cause death or serious bodily injury; or with the intent to cause substantial damage to property or to the environment; or with the intent to compel a natural or legal person, an international organization or a State to do or refrain from doing an act.

Convention	Subject-Matter
Nuclear Terrorism Convention, 2005 (cont'd)	The above noted offences include attempts. State parties are also to criminalize: • threats, under circumstances which indicate the credibility of the threat, to commit an offence listed in the second bullet point above; • demanding, unlawfully and intentionally, radioactive material, a nuclear or radiological device or a nuclear facility by threat, under circumstances which indicate the credibility of the threat, or by use of force. State parties are also to criminalize participating as an accomplice or organizing or directing others to commit an above-listed offence or in any other way intentionally contributing to the commission of one or more offences by a group of persons acting with a common purpose with the aim of furthering the general criminal activity or purpose of the group or made in the knowledge of the intention of the group to commit the offence or offences concerned.

4. Certain Other Forms of Terrorist Violence

Convention	Subject-Matter
International Convention Against the Taking of Hostages (Hostage Convention, 1979)	Requires state parties to criminalize the seizing or detention and threat to kill, to injure or to continue to detain a person ("hostage") in order to compel a third party, namely, a State, an international intergovernmental organization, a natural or juridical person, or a group of persons, to do or abstain from doing any act as an explicit or implicit condition for the release of the hostage.
International Convention for the Suppression of Terrorist Bombings (Bombing Convention, 1997)	Requires state parties to criminalize the unlawful and intentional delivery, placement, discharge or detonation of an explosive or other lethal device in, into or against a place of public use, a State or government facility, a public transportation system or an infrastructure facility with the intent to cause death or serious bodily injury; or with the intent to cause extensive destruction of such a place, facility or system, where such destruction results in or is likely to result in major economic loss. State parties are also to criminalize attempts, participating as an accomplice or organizing or directing others to commit an above-listed offence or in any other way intentionally contributing to the commission of one or more offences by a group of persons acting with a common purpose with the aim of furthering the general criminal activity or purpose of the group or made in the knowledge of the intention of the group to commit the offence or offences concerned.

Convention	Subject-Matter
B. Conventions Relating to Terrorist Materiel	
Convention on the Physical Protection of Nuclear Material (Nuclear Material Convention, 1980)	Requires state parties to criminalize the intentional commission (and attempted commission) of: • an act without lawful authority which constitutes the receipt, possession, use, transfer, alteration, disposal or dispersal of nuclear material and which causes or is likely to cause death or serious injury to any person or substantial damage to property; • a theft or robbery of nuclear material; • an embezzlement or fraudulent obtaining of nuclear material; • an act constituting a demand for nuclear material by threat or use of force or by any other form of intimidation; or • a threat to use nuclear material to cause death or serious injury to any person or substantial property damage, or to steal nuclear material in order to compel a natural or legal person, international organization or State to do or to refrain from doing any act.
Convention on the Marking of Plastic Explosives for the Purpose of Identification (Plastic Explosive Convention, 1991)	Each state party shall take the necessary and effective measures to prohibit and prevent the manufacture in its territory of unmarked explosives. Each state party shall take the necessary and effective measures to prohibit and prevent the movement into or out of its territory of unmarked explosives. "Marking" means introducing into an explosive a detection agent.
International Convention for the Suppression of the Financing of Terrorism (Financing Convention, 1999)	Requires state parties to criminalize the following offence: directly or indirectly, unlawfully and wilfully, providing or collecting funds with the intention that they should be used or in the knowledge that they are to be used, in full or in part, in order to carry out: (a) an act which constitutes an offence within the scope of and as defined in most of the treaties listed in this table; or (b) any other act intended to cause death or serious bodily injury to a civilian, or to any other person not taking an active part in the hostilities in a situation of armed conflict, when the purpose of such act, by its nature or context, is to intimidate a population, or to compel a Government or an international organization to do or to abstain from doing any act. State parties are also to criminalize attempts, participating as an accomplice or organizing or directing others to commit this offence or intentionally contributing to the commission of one or more offences by a group of persons acting with a common purpose with the aim of furthering the general criminal activity or purpose of the group or made in the knowledge of the intention of the group to commit the offence or offences concerned.

1) Limitations on Scope

The scope of many of the anti-terrorism conventions is limited both geographically and substantively. Geographic rules in the treaties limit the reach of treaty rules to acts that are truly international in character, excluding those that take place strictly within national boundaries. In some treaties, these geographic limiters are nuanced by rules of state jurisdiction over the offences proscribed by the treaty, a matter discussed below.

For their part, substantive limiters come in several flavours. Table 6.3 outlines each of these. Two are worthy of particular discussion: the exclusions for armed forces and state militaries and the exclusions, in some treaties, for nonstate actors in a national liberation struggle.

a)   State Terrorism

Several treaties exempt (at least certain) state actors. A common critique is that because of these exclusions, so-called state terrorism is unregulated by international law. To the extent this view suggests that states may use violence indiscriminately, this is an exaggerated claim, although it rightfully suggests that state violence is licit in international law to an extent nonstate violence is not.

i)   Exemption for Armed Forces during Armed Conflict

In now standard language drawn from the bombing convention, the "activities of armed forces during an armed conflict, as those terms are understood under international humanitarian law, which are governed by that law, are not governed by this Convention."[105] The financing convention also includes a limitation incorporating the law of armed conflict. It qualifies its generic description of terrorism by confining it to acts intended to cause "death or serious bodily injury to a civilian, or to any other person *not taking an active part in the hostilities in a situation of armed conflict.*"[106] It does not apply, therefore, to actions directed at combatants in armed conflicts.

These provisions do not provide a *carte blanche* for state terrorism. They are instead a choice of law provision, confirming that the laws of war, and in particular IHL, rather than the terrorism conventions, govern armed forces in armed conflicts. IHL greatly restricts the nature and targets of armed forces violence in armed conflict situations. Not least, the Geneva Conventions and their protocols preclude armed forces in an armed conflict targeting civilians, and they emphatically

---

105 Bombing Convention, 1997, Art. 19.
106 Financing Convention, 1999, Art. 2.

Table 6.3:   Limiters in Multilateral Terrorist Conventions

Convention	Geographic Limiters	Substantive Limiters
A. Conventions Banning Certain Terrorist Techniques and Practices		
1. Terrorism Against Transportation and Infrastructure		
Convention on Offences and Certain Other Acts Committed on Board Aircraft (Tokyo Convention, 1963)	Applies only where aircraft is in flight or on the surface of the high seas or in any other area outside the territory of any state.	Does not apply to aircraft used in military, customs or police services.
Convention for the Suppression of Unlawful Seizure of Aircraft (Hague Convention, 1970)	Applies only where aircraft is in flight and the place of take-off or the place of actual landing of the aircraft on board which the offence is committed is situated outside the territory of the State of registration of that aircraft; however, the prosecution/extradition obligation discussed below applies regardless of place of take-off or landing if the offender or the alleged offender is found in the territory of a state other than the state of registration of that aircraft.	Does not apply to aircraft used in military, customs or police services.
Convention for the Suppression of Unlawful Acts Against the Safety of Civil Aviation (Montreal Convention, 1971)	Applies where the aircraft is in flight or in service (that is, from the beginning of the pre-flight preparation of the aircraft by ground personnel or by the crew for a specific flight until twenty-four hours after any landing) and (for most of the proscribed acts) only if the place of take-off or landing, actual or intended, of the aircraft is situated outside the territory of the state of registration of that aircraft or the offence is committed in the territory of a State other than the state of registration of the aircraft.	Does not apply to aircraft used in military, customs or police services.

Convention	Geographic Limiters	Substantive Limiters
Protocol for the Suppression of Unlawful Acts of Violence at Airports Serving International Aviation (Montreal Convention Protocol, 1988)	Applies to airports serving international civil aviation.	N/A
Convention for the Suppression of Unlawful Acts Against the Safety of Maritime Navigation (Maritime Convention, 1988), as amended by 2005 Protocol	Applies if the ship is navigating or is scheduled to navigate into, through or from waters beyond the outer limit of the territorial sea of a single state, or the lateral limits of its territorial sea with adjacent states; however, also applies when the offender or the alleged offender is found in the territory of a state party other than the single state referred to above.	Does not apply to: a warship; or a ship owned or operated by a state when being used as a naval auxiliary or for customs or police purposes; or a ship which has been withdrawn from navigation or laid up; or to the activities of armed forces during an armed conflict, as those terms are understood under IHL.
Protocol for the Suppression of Unlawful Acts Against the Safety of Fixed Platforms Located on the Continental Shelf (Maritime Convention Protocol, 1988)	Applies if offences are committed on board or against fixed platforms located on the continental shelf; however, also applies when the offender or the alleged offender is found in the territory of a state party other than the state in whose international waters or territorial sea the fixed platform is located.	N/A
2. Terrorism Against Protected Persons		
Convention on the Prevention and Punishment of Crimes Against Internationally Protected Persons, Including Diplomatic Agents (Protected Person Convention, 1973)	N/A	N/A

Convention	Geographic Limiters	Substantive Limiters
3. Nuclear Terrorism		
International Convention for the Suppression of Acts of Nuclear Terrorism (Nuclear Terrorism Convention, 2005)	Subject to a number of exceptions, does not apply where the offence is committed within a single state, the alleged offender and the victims are nationals of that state, and the alleged offender is found in the territory of that state.	The activities of armed forces during an armed conflict, as those terms are understood under international humanitarian law, are not governed by the treaty, and the activities undertaken by military forces of a state in the exercise of their official duties, inasmuch as they are governed by other rules of international law, are not governed by the treaty.
4. Certain Other Forms of Terrorist Violence		
International Convention Against the Taking of Hostages (Hostage Convention, 1979)	Does not apply where the offence is committed within a single state, the hostage and the alleged offender are both nationals of that state and the alleged offender is found in the territory of that state.	The treaty does not apply to an act of hostage-taking committed in the course of armed conflicts as defined in international humanitarian law, including armed conflicts in which peoples are fighting against colonial domination and alien occupation and against racist regimes in the exercise of their right of self-determination.
International Convention for the Suppression of Terrorist Bombings (Bombing Convention, 1997)	Generally does not apply where the offence is committed within a single state, the alleged offender and the victims are nationals of that state, the alleged offender is found in the territory of that state and no other state can assert jurisdiction under certain provision of the treaty.	The activities of armed forces during an armed conflict, as those terms are understood under international humanitarian law, are not governed by the treaty, and the activities undertaken by military forces of a state in the exercise of their official duties, inasmuch as they are governed by other rules of international law, are not governed by the treaty.

Convention	Geographic Limiters	Substantive Limiters
B. Conventions Relating to Terrorist Materiel		
Convention on the Physical Protection of Nuclear Material (Nuclear Material Convention, 1980)	Applies to nuclear material used for peaceful purposes while in international nuclear transport and in most cases to nuclear material used for peaceful purposes while in domestic use, storage and transport.	N/A
Convention on the Marking of Plastic Explosives for the Purpose of Identification (Plastic Explosive Convention, 1991)	N/A	N/A
International Convention for the Suppression of the Financing of Terrorism (Financing Convention, 1999)	Generally does not apply where the offence is committed within a single state, the alleged offender and the victims are nationals of that state, the alleged offender is found in the territory of that state and no other state can assert jurisdiction under certain provision of the treaty.	N/A

outlaw acts of "terror" and "terrorism."[107] Many of the acts of violence against civilians that comprise terrorism also constitute grave breaches of the Geneva Conventions,[108] attracting penal sanction.[109]

Still, it is true that IHL more readily accepts injury to combatants and even incidental (although not targeted) injury among civilians than does, for instance, the bombing convention. Put another way, an aerial bombing of a military headquarters in an armed conflict by an armed force likely would not be illegal under the laws of war. In comparison, a car bomb detonated with identical effect against an identical target by an actor not considered an armed force in an armed conflict would be a violation of the bombing convention. The net effect of the international legal regime, therefore, is to privilege (although not give a free hand) to violence by states (as opposed to nonstate actors).

ii)   Exemption for Military Forces Exercising Their Official Duties
The bombing, nuclear and maritime conventions single out state "military forces" for an even more emphatic, second exception: the conventions do not apply to "military forces of a State in the exercise of their official duties, inasmuch as they are governed by other rules of international law." Military forces of a state are defined in these treaties as "the armed forces of a State which are organized, trained and equipped under its internal law for the primary purpose of national defence or security and persons acting in support of those armed forces who are under their formal command, control and responsibility." Notably, this

---

107   See, for example, *Geneva Convention Relative to the Protection of Civilians in Times of War* [Geneva Convention IV], Art. 33 ("all measures of intimidation or of terrorism are prohibited"); AP I, above note 93, Art. 51 ("acts or threats of violence the primary purpose of which is to spread terror among the civilian population are prohibited"); AP II, above note 91, Art. 4(2) ("the following acts … are and shall remain prohibited at any time and in any place whatsoever … (d) acts of terrorism"). See also discussion at Becker, *Terrorism and the State,* above note 54 at 104 *et seq.*

108   See, for example, Geneva Convention IV, *ibid.*, Art. 147 ("Grave breaches to which the preceding Article relates shall be those involving any of the following acts, if committed against persons or property protected by the present Convention: wilful killing, torture or inhuman treatment, including biological experiments, wilfully causing great suffering or serious injury to body or health, unlawful deportation or transfer or unlawful confinement of a protected person, compelling a protected person to serve in the forces of a hostile Power, or wilfully depriving a protected person of the rights of fair and regular trial prescribed in the present Convention, taking of hostages and extensive destruction and appropriation of property, not justified by military necessity and carried out unlawfully and wantonly").

109   Geneva Convention IV, *ibid.*, Art. 148.

definition does not apply to other agencies of the state that might engage in violence (such as police or civilian security services).

This second exception is not confined to armed conflicts and thus reaches beyond the situations in which international humanitarian law applies. For instance, it could exempt the drone aircraft missile strikes in Pakistan and Yemen described above from the scope of the 1997 terrorist bombing convention, at least if these attacks had been conducted by a military force.[110]

As a consequence, this exclusion leaves the actions of military forces operating outside of armed conflicts only weakly "governed by other rules of international law." As Bruce Broomhall has noted:

> The "other rules of international law" that "govern" here would include a wide range of norms, from the prohibitions of genocide and crimes against humanity to the regional and international instruments of human rights law (as applicable), as well as the fundamental human rights norms protected under customary law. The results flowing from such norms vary widely. … [O]nly with torture does a clear conventional obligation to extradite in the event of a failure to prosecute arise, while with genocide and crimes against humanity the view of the majority of commentators is that only a permissive universal jurisdiction exists at customary international law, without any "extradite or prosecute" obligation to serve as a bulwark against impunity. … As for human rights norms, their rules may "govern" a situation at a considerable level of generality, with potential enforcement often through only the sporadic and relatively weak supervision of international oversight bodies with their reporting requirements, special rapporteurs and sometimes visiting rights.[111]

Put another way, the exclusion of military forces from the conventions is more than simply a choice of law provision. Rather, it displaces scrutiny of violence perpetrated by the military to a body of law potentially much less robust than the criminal law provisions in the bombing, nuclear and (amended) maritime conventions.

---

110 In fact, the U.S. targeted killing program involving Predator drone aircraft reportedly is run by the CIA, an agency that probably does not satisfy the requirements of "military forces" in the treaty. See Josh Meyer, "CIA Expands Use of Drones in Terror War," above note 76.
111 Bruce Broomhall, "Terrorism on Trial: State Actors in an International Definition of Terrorism from a Human Rights Perspective" (2004) 36 Case W. Res. J. Int'l L. 421 at 435–36.

b)   Terrorism by Insurgencies or National Liberation Movements

This asymmetrical law of violence raises issues in asymmetrical warfare—conflict between state militaries and insurgent forces.

i)   Insurgencies and the Armed Forces Exception

In Additional Protocol I of the Geneva Conventions, armed forces are defined as "all organized armed forces, groups and units which are under a command responsible to that Party for the conduct of its subordinates, even if that Party is represented by a government or an authority not recognized by an adverse Party. Such armed forces shall be subject to an internal disciplinary system which, *inter alia*, shall enforce compliance with the rules of international law applicable in armed conflict."[112] Measured against this standard, insurgencies in Iraq and Afghanistan are not "armed forces," even if commanded by authorities who claim to represent these states (a doubtful claim). They may be organized in a command structure, but in systematically targeting civilians in many of their attacks, they cannot seriously be viewed as possessing an internal disciplinary system enforcing "compliance with the rules of international law applicable in armed conflict."

These insurgencies are not, therefore, entitled to the exception carved out for armed forces in situations of armed conflict under, for instance, the bombing convention. An improvised explosive device deployed against a NATO force in Afghanistan, therefore, is a terrorist bombing and a criminal act.[113] In comparison, a shelling of a Taliban position by the NATO force is not criminal under the bombing convention. Instead, it is an appropriate exercise of force under the law applicable to that state military, namely, international humanitarian law.

ii)   National Liberation Movements

A related issue that has historically muddied discussions of terrorism at the international level has been the treatment of national liberation (and particularly, anticolonial) conflicts—the classic manifestation of asymmetrical conflict. Additional Protocol I of the Geneva Conventions includes as among the circumstances governed by that instrument "armed conflicts in which peoples are fighting against colonial domination and alien occupation and against racist regimes in the exercise of their right of self-determination."[114]

---

112 AP I, above note 93, Art. 43.
113 Afghanistan acceded to the Bombing Convention, 1997 in 2003.
114 AP I, above note 93, Art. 1(4).

a.   Hostage Convention

In keeping with this approach, the hostage convention does "not apply to an act of hostage-taking committed in the course of armed conflicts as defined in the Geneva Conventions of 1949 and the Protocols thereto, including armed conflicts mentioned in article 1, paragraph 4, of Additional Protocol I of 1977, in which peoples are fighting against colonial domination and alien occupation and against racist regimes in the exercise of their right of self- determination."[115]

This is not to say that national liberation movements are therefore free to take hostages. First, the Geneva Conventions and their protocols themselves preclude hostage taking in armed conflicts.[116] Indeed, hostage taking is a grave breach of Geneva Convention IV,[117] requiring penal sanction.[118]

Second, the hostage convention's exception only applies "in so far as the Geneva Conventions of 1949 for the protection of war victims or the Additional Protocols to those Conventions *are applicable to a particular act of hostage-taking*, and in so far as States Parties to this Convention are bound under those conventions to prosecute or hand over the hostage-taker."[119] Put another way, a national liberation movement is exempted from the hostage convention only when it is bound by the strictures on hostage taking in the Geneva Conventions and their protocols.

It seems unlikely that any liberation movement has ever met this latter requirement. Additional Protocol I of the Geneva Conventions permits national liberation movements to declare their adherence to international humanitarian law, thereby according that movement the same rights, and imposing on it the same obligations, as an actual state party to the Geneva Conventions and the Protocol.[120] Where a national liberation movement fails to make this declaration, the Conventions

---

115 Hostage Convention, 1979, Art. 12.
116 See, for example, Geneva Convention IV, above note 107, Art. 34 (prohibiting hostage-taking); Common Art. 3 of the Geneva Conventions relating to non-international armed conflicts ("the following acts are and shall remain prohibited at any time and in any place whatsoever with respect to the above-mentioned persons [i.e., non-combatants]: ... (b) Taking of hostages"); AP I, above note 93, Art. 75(2) ("The following acts are and shall remain prohibited at any time and in any place whatsoever, whether committed by civilian or by military agents ... (c) The taking of hostages"); AP II, above note 91, Art. 4 (similar to AP I).
117 Geneva Convention IV, *ibid.*, Art. 147 (declaring hostage taking to be a "grave breach").
118 *Ibid.*, Art. 146.
119 Hostage Convention, 1979, Art. 12 [emphasis added].
120 AP I, above note 93, Art. 96.

and their protocols do not apply to it.[121] No liberation movement, and no contemporary insurgency, has ever squarely made such a declaration.[122] Put another way, in practice, the hostages convention applies in full force to national liberation movements as much as to any other nonstate actor.

b.   More Recent Conventions

As noted above, the more recent bombing, nuclear terrorism and post-2005 protocol on maritime navigation conventions confine the IHL exception to instances where "armed forces" are engaged in armed conflict, without further qualification concerning national liberation movements. The bombing and the nuclear terrorism conventions also exclude the possibility of ideological justifications for the offences they proscribe by asserting:

> Each State Party shall adopt such measures as may be necessary, including, where appropriate, domestic legislation, to ensure that criminal acts within the scope of this Convention, in particular where they are intended or calculated to provoke a state of terror in the general public or in a group of persons or particular persons, are under no circumstances justifiable by considerations of a political, philosophical, ideological, racial, ethnic, religious or other similar nature and are punished by penalties consistent with their grave nature.[123]

The tide seems, therefore, to have shifted against special treatment for liberation movements in anti-terrorism law. In 2005, the U.N. secretary-general urged that this issue now be set aside in discussions of anti-terrorism law: "the right to resist occupation must be understood in its true meaning. It cannot include the right to deliberately kill or maim civilians."[124]

---

121 George Aldrich, "Prospects for United States Ratification of Additional Protocol I to the 1949 Geneva Conventions" (1991) 85 A.J.I.L. 1 at 6 ("As a result of this provision [Article 96], in the absence of such a declaration, the Conventions and Protocol have by their terms no application to wars of national liberation. Members of the armed forces of a national liberation movement do not therefore enjoy the protections of those treaties unless the movement formally accepts all the obligations of the Conventions and the Protocol in the same way as the state parties").

122 See Becker, *Terrorism and the State*, above note 54 at 104, n86; Shabatai Rosenne, *The Perplexities of Modern International Law* (Leiden: Martinus Nijhoff, 2004) at 172, n59.

123 Bombing Convention, 1997, Art. 5; Nuclear Terrorism Convention, 2005, Art. 6. The Financing Convention, 1999 contains a similar provision in Art. 6.

124 U.N. Secretary-General, *In Larger Freedom* (2005) at para. 91, online: www. globalpolicy.org/eu/en/publ/inlargerfreedom.pdf.

2) Scope of Jurisdiction

As noted earlier, many of the piecemeal conventions create international-al offences and oblige states to criminalize these acts in their domestic laws. In so doing, they raise the question of jurisdiction; that is, in what circumstance may the criminal law of a state party apply to a given proscribed act, including one that might have taken place outside of that state's territory.

To resolve this question, the treaties generally include provisions on the "prescriptive jurisdiction" of state parties.[125] Thus, they acknowledge that a state will have jurisdiction over a proscribed act where it is undertaken on the territory of that state. A state may, however, also have extraterritorial jurisdiction where, for instance, an offence is committed on board a vessel flying the flag of that state or an aircraft which is registered under the laws of that state or the offence is committed by a national of that state.

A distinction is made in several of the conventions between circumstances in which jurisdiction is mandatory and others in which states may choose to exercise jurisdiction. Generally speaking, state parties are obliged to establish jurisdiction over offences that take place in their territory or are committed by their nationals. They are also obliged to establish jurisdiction in circumstances where the alleged offender is present within their territory and they fail to extradite him or her, per the discussion that follows. Table 6.4 outlines the basis of state jurisdiction required or permitted by each treaty.

3) State Obligations to Enforce Prohibitions

The multilateral anti-terrorism conventions require states to do more than simply criminalize proscribed acts and establish prescriptive jurisdiction over those who perpetrate them. They generally also include obligations actually to respond to the presence of an alleged offender or terrorist plot on their territory. Table 6.5 outlines the key obligations found in the treaties.

---

125 Prescriptive jurisdiction is a concept discussed in Chapter 2. In general terms, it concerns a state's capacity to regulate a given person or activity under its domestic law.

Table 6.4: Basis for State Jurisdiction over Terrorism Offences

Basis for Jurisdiction	Terrorist Financing Convention	Nuclear Material Convention	Bombing Convention	Hostage Convention	Nuclear Terrorism Convention	Protected Person Convention	Maritime Convention Protocol	Maritime Convention	Montreal Convention Protocol	Montreal Convention	Hague Convention	Tokyo Convention
Offence committed on state territory	M	M*	M	M	M	M	M	M	M	M		×
Offence committed on aircraft or ship registered to state	M‡	M	M‡	M	M‡	M		M	M†	M†	M†	M**
The aircraft on board which the offence is committed lands in state territory with the alleged offender still on board										M	M	
Offence committed against national of state	×		×	×	×	M‡*	×	×				×
Offence committed against permanent resident of state												×
Offence committed by national of state	M	M	M	M	M	M	M	M				×
Offence committed by permanent resident of state												×
Offence committed by stateless person habitually resident in state	×		×	×	×		×	×				
Offence against security of state				M								×
Offence committed in an attempt to compel that State to do or abstain from doing any act			×		×		×	×				

Basis for Jurisdiction	Tokyo Convention	Hague Convention	Montreal Convention	Montreal Convention Protocol	Maritime Convention	Maritime Convention Protocol	Protected Person Convention	Nuclear Terrorism Convention	Hostage Convention	Bombing Convention	Nuclear Material Convention	Terrorist Financing Convention
Offence committed against state or government facility of that state abroad, including an embassy or other diplomatic or consular premises of that state								×		×		×
Alleged offender is present in state's territory and state does not extradite	M	M	M	M	M	M	M	M	M	M	M	M

M = State must take such measures as to establish jurisdiction. × = State may establish its jurisdiction.

* Note also that "each State Party may, consistent with international law, establish its jurisdiction over the offences ... when it is involved in international nuclear transport as the exporting or importing State."

** Jurisdiction also exists if the offence consists of a "breach of any rules or regulations relating to the flight or manoeuvre of aircraft in force" in the state or the "exercise of jurisdiction is necessary to ensure the observance of any obligation of such state under a multilateral international agreement."

† Jurisdiction also exists if "the offence is committed on board an aircraft leased without crew to a lessee who has his [or her] principal place of business or, if the lessee has no such place of business, his [or her] permanent residence, in that State."

‡ Jurisdiction also exists where the "offence is committed on board an aircraft which is operated by the Government of that State."

‡* More exactly, jurisdiction exists where the protected person has that status because of functions he performs for the state. In most instances, the protected person performing these functions will be a national of that state.

Table 6.5: State Obligations under Anti-terrorism Conventions

Nature of Obligation	Obligation to cooperate to prevent the commission of the offence	Obligation to take alleged offender into custody if within territory	Obligation to investigate alleged crime	Obligation to either extradite or submit offence to state's competent authorities for prosecution	Obligation to provide assistance to other states for the purpose of prosecuting the offence
Tokyo Convention	×	×			
Hague Convention		×	×	×	×
Montreal Convention	×	×	×	×	×
Montreal Convention Protocol	×		×	×	×
Maritime Convention	×	×	×	×	×
Maritime Convention Protocol	×	×	×	×	×
Protected Person Convention	×	×*	×	×	×
Nuclear Terrorism Convention	×	×*	×	×	×
Hostage Convention	×	×	×	×	×
Bombing Convention	×	×*	×	×	×
Nuclear Material Convention	×	×	×	×	×
Terrorist Financing Convention	×	×*	×	×	×

* Custody is not emphatically mentioned, but the convention requires state parties to take the appropriate measures under its internal law to ensure the alleged offender's presence for the purpose of prosecution or extradition.

The most notable obligations include the requirement that state parties cooperate to prevent the commission of the proscribed offence and, when an alleged perpetrator is in their jurisdiction, that they extradite that person to face trial or submit the case to domestic prosecution.

a) Obligation to Cooperate in Prevention

The obligation to cooperate in the treaties generally specifies that state parties will "co-operate to prevent" the proscribed offences, particularly by:

> taking all practicable measures to prevent preparations in their respective territories for the commission of those offences within or outside their territories, including measures to prohibit in their territories illegal activities of persons, groups and organizations that encourage, instigate, organize or engage in the perpetration of [proscribed] acts ...; [and] exchanging information and co-ordinating the taking of administrative and other measures as appropriate to prevent the commission of those offences.[126]

In recent treaties, the obligation to cooperate is extremely detailed. Thus, in the financing convention, "States Parties shall cooperate in the prevention of the offences set forth in [the treaty] by taking all practicable measures, *inter alia*, by adapting their domestic legislation, if necessary, to prevent and counter preparations in their respective territories for the commission of those offences within or outside their territories."[127] The treaty then lists a series of extensive steps state parties must take to regulate financial institutions and transactions.[128]

b) Obligation to Extradite or Prosecute

A second common feature of all but one of the multilateral treaties creating international terrorism offences is the obligation to extradite or prosecute an offender found within the territory of the state. Representative language containing this obligation is as follows:

> The State Party in the territory of which the alleged offender is present shall, in cases to which [the state has prescriptive jurisdiction under the treaty] ..., if it does not extradite that person, be obliged, without exception whatsoever and whether or not the offence was committed in its territory, to submit the case without undue delay to its competent authorities for the purpose of prosecution, through

---

126 See, for example, Hostage Convention, 1979, Art. 4.
127 Financing Convention, 1999, Art. 18.
128 *Ibid.*

proceedings in accordance with the laws of that State. Those authorities shall take their decision in the same manner as in the case of any
other offence of a grave nature under the law of that State.[129]

i)   *Extradition*

The extradite or prosecute obligation encourages extradition, failing
which a state must submit a matter to prosecution. The treaties therefore typically include several provisions governing extradition. Most
notably, the treaties often specify that the offences they proscribe

> shall be deemed to be included as extraditable offences in any extra-
> dition treaty existing between any of the States Parties before the
> entry into force of this Convention. States Parties undertake to in-
> clude such offences as extraditable offences in every extradition
> treaty to be subsequently concluded between them.[130]

The conventions are more uneven on whether extradition may be
resisted on the basis that the offences in question are political in nature. The latter concept is found in international extradition law as a
standard ground for states to reject extradition requests. The model
U.N. extradition treaty, for instance, specifies that "extradition shall
not be granted …If the offence for which extradition is requested is
regarded by the requested State as an offence of a political nature."[131]
A serious flaw in the 1937 terrorism convention was its failure to limit
state recourse to the political offences concept to deny extradition—a
particularly acute problem for the inherently political crime of terrorism. The recent multilateral terrorism conventions—the bombing,
financing and nuclear terrorism treaties—expressly overrule the political offences concept:

> None of the offences [in the treaty] shall be regarded, for the pur-
> poses of extradition or mutual legal assistance, as a political offence
> or as an offence connected with a political offence or as an offence
> inspired by political motives. Accordingly, a request for extradition
> or for mutual legal assistance based on such an offence may not be
> refused on the sole ground that it concerns a political offence or an
> offence connected with a political offence or an offence inspired by
> political motives.[132]

---

129 Financing Convention, 1999, Art. 10(1).
130 See, for example, Bombing Convention, 1997, Art. 9.
131 A/RES/45/116 (1990), Art. 3.
132 Bombing Convention, 1997, Art. 11; Financing Convention, 1999, Art. 14;
     Nuclear Terrorism Convention, 2005, Art. 15.

Other conventions, however, preserve a political offences exclusion[133] or are silent on the matter.

Removing the political offences exclusion potentially opens the door to extradition in response to ill-motivated requests. The bombing, financing and nuclear terrorism conventions limit this prospect by specifying that the treaties do not impose

> an obligation to extradite or to afford mutual legal assistance, if the requested State Party has substantial grounds for believing that the request for extradition for offences set forth in [the treaty] or for mutual legal assistance with respect to such offences has been made for the purpose of prosecuting or punishing a person on account of that person's race, religion, nationality, ethnic origin or political opinion or that compliance with the request would cause prejudice to that person's position for any of these reasons.[134]

These conventions therefore define in detail (and limit) the political circumstances that might justify refusal to extradite, albeit using broad language that could mask failures to extradite premised on sympathy with the terrorist's cause. Note, in particular, that extradition may be refused if the state believes the anticipated prosecution is on account of the accused's "political opinion."

ii) Prosecution

As observed above, where a state does not extradite, it is obliged to submit the matter for prosecution. The extradite-or-try language of the conventions creates, therefore, a form of universal jurisdiction.[135]

Ultimately, there will be a state with both the jurisdiction and the obligation to try the perpetrator. Note, however, that there is some nuance in the standard treaty requirement to "submit the case without undue delay to its competent authorities for the purpose of prosecution, through proceedings in accordance with the laws of that State." Submission of a case for prosecution is not the same thing as actual prosecution. The treaty language accommodates prosecutorial discre-

---

133 Tokyo Convention, 1963, Art. 2.
134 Bombing Convention, 1997, Art. 12; Financing Convention, 1999, Art. 15; Nuclear Terrorism Convention, 2005, Art. 16. The hostages convention, while it does not exclude the political offences concept of regular extradition law, contains similar language. Hostage Convention, 1979, Art. 9.
135 For a discussion of this point, see *Arrest Warrant of 11 April 2000 (Democratic Republic of the Congo v. Belgium)*, Judgment, online: www.icj-cij.org/docket/files/121/8126.pdf; Separate Opinion of President Guilluime at para. 7 *et seq.*, online: www.icj-cij.org/docket/files/121/8128.pdf.

tion, including, presumably, on the question of whether the evidence is sufficient to submit a matter to trial.[136] It also opens the door to possible impunity for terrorist actions. As one scholar notes, "if the criminal justice system lacks integrity, the risk of political intervention in the prosecution or at the trial exists. Such intervention may prevent the trial, a conviction, or the appropriate punishment of the accused."[137]

From this discussion, it is clear that prosecution for international terrorism crimes depends on the criminal courts of individual states; there is no international tribunal charged with trying terrorism offences *per se*. An early proposal would have extended jurisdiction to try terrorism offences (as they existed under the piecemeal conventions) to the International Criminal Court. That suggestion was dropped, however, leaving the court without competence in the anti-terrorism area. That said, terrorist acts of the magnitude of 9/11 are also crimes against humanity, as that term is defined in the *Statute of Rome*, establishing the International Criminal Court. That instrument defines "crimes against humanity" as, *inter alia*,

> any of the following acts when committed as part of a widespread or systematic attack directed against any civilian population, with knowledge of the attack:
> (a) Murder; ...
> (e) Imprisonment or other severe deprivation of physical liberty in violation of fundamental rules of international law; ...
> (k) Other inhumane acts of a similar character intentionally causing great suffering, or serious injury to body or to mental or physical health.[138]

In a legal opinion to the Government of Canada, the Legal Bureau of the Department of Foreign Affairs and International Trade concluded that the 9/11 attacks met the definitional requirements of crimes against humanity. That day's events obviously constituted murder and

---

136 See, for example, Christopher C. Joyner, "International Extradition and Global Terrorism: Bringing International Criminals to Justice" (2003) 25 Loy. L.A. Int'l & Comp. L.J. 493 at 512–13 ("this language preserves for the alleged offender the rights of due process, a fair trial, and guarantees the concept of innocent until proven guilty. Presumably, an investigation into the facts of the allegation against an accused offender determines whether to proceed to the trial phase. If the investigation produces sufficient evidence, the offender may be prosecuted").

137 John Murphy, "The Control of International Terrorism," in John Norton Moore & Robert Turner, eds., *National Security Law* (Durham, NC: Carolina Academic Press, 2005) at 466.

138 *Rome Statute of the International Criminal Court*, U.N. Doc. A/CONF.183/9, Art. 7 [*Rome Statute*].

the causing of great suffering. Moreover, they likely were also "widespread and systematic":

> The September 11 attack involved four virtually simultaneous hijackings from different airports by different teams, all designed to bring the planes to specifically targeted buildings within a one-half to one hour period. At least some of the hijackers had undergone pilot training in the months prior to the attack. In addition, if other attacks are also considered, such as those on the U.S. embassies in 1998, then the September 11 acts may be seen as part of a larger systematic plan to target U.S. citizens, interests and buildings. ... There is a strong argument that the September 11 attack was numerically widespread, as thousands of people died.[139]

Terrorist acts of this gravity are, therefore, amenable to prosecution before the International Criminal Court, assuming that entity's other jurisdictional requirements are met.[140]

4) Safeguards

As the discussion above suggests, states have been acutely sensitive to how politically motivated violence is criminalized in international law. An evident fear, reflected in limitations on extradition tied to political offences and more recent language on discriminatory purpose, is of politicized prosecutions of dissidents. International anti-terrorism instruments increasingly include, therefore, certain safeguards against their manipulation for dubious ends. Several also include language denying that the treaty authorizes an erosion of a party's territorial integrity or a usurpation of its territorial jurisdiction. Put another way, the treaties do not authorize one state to exercise enforcement jurisdiction—for example, the detention and removal of an accused—on the territory of another.

The most important of these safeguards are set out in Table 6.6.

---

139 Legal Bureau, Department of Foreign Affairs and International Trade, from "Canadian Practice of International Law" (2002) 40 Can. Y.B. Int'l Law at 470–71.

140 For example, the accused must be a national of a state party or the crime would have to take place on the territory of a state party. Alternatively, the prosecution could be authorized by the Security Council. *Rome Statute*, above note 138, Arts. 12 and 13.

Table 6.6:   Safeguards

Safeguards	Guarantee of fair treatment of accused. Some treaties emphatically guarantee the application of international human rights law.	An accused taken into custody has the right to (a) communicate without delay with the nearest appropriate representative of the state of which that person is a national or which is otherwise entitled to protect that person's rights or, if that person is a stateless person, the state in the territory of which that person habitually resides; (b) to be visited by a representative of that state. More recent treaties also specify a right: (c) to be informed of that person's rights under subparagraphs (a) and (b). Older treaties simply specify that an accused is to be assisted in communicating with a state representative.	When a state party has taken a person into custody, it shall immediately notify the states parties that have also established jurisdiction under the treaty that such person is in custody and of the circumstances which warrant that person's detention. Some treaties also specify that, if it considers it advisable, it shall notify any other interested states parties. The hostages convention include a comprehensive list of interested states to be notified.
Terrorist Financing Convention	×	×	×
Nuclear Material Convention	×		×
Bombing Convention	×	×	×
Hostage Convention	×	×	×
Nuclear Terrorism Convention	×	×	×
Protected Person Convention	×		
Maritime Convention Protocol		×	×
Maritime Convention		×	×
Montreal Convention Protocol			×
Montreal Convention		×	×
Hague Convention		×	×
Tokyo Convention			

Safeguards	Where the accused is prosecuted (or in some treaties, extradited), states must communicate the final outcome of the proceedings to the relevant depository or the secretary-general (of the U.N. or the International Maritime Organization, depending on the treaty), who shall transmit the information to the other states parties.	Nothing in the convention is to affect other rights, obligations and responsibilities of states and individuals under international law, in particular the purposes of the *Charter* of the United Nations, IHL and other relevant conventions.	Nothing in the convention entitles a state party to undertake in the territory of another state party the exercise of jurisdiction or performance of functions which are exclusively reserved for the authorities of that other state party by its domestic law.	The states parties are to carry out their obligations under the convention in a manner consistent with the principles of sovereign equality and territorial integrity of states and that of nonintervention in the domestic affairs of other states.
Terrorist Financing Convention	×	×	×	×
Nuclear Material Convention	×			
Bombing Convention	×	×	×	×
Hostage Convention	×			×
Nuclear Terrorism Convention	×	×	×	×
Protected Person Convention	×			
Maritime Convention Protocol	×			
Maritime Convention	×			
Montreal Convention Protocol	×			
Montreal Convention	×			
Hague Convention	×			
Tokyo Convention				

D. GENERAL ANTI-TERRORISM TREATY OBLIGATIONS

The piecemeal, multilateral treaties are extensive in their coverage, both in terms of subject-matter and in terms of acceptance by the international community. Table 6.7 notes the ratification status of each of these instruments, as well as whether Canada is a party.

Table 6.7:   Ratifications of Anti-terrorism Conventions

Ratifications	Tokyo Convention	Hague Convention	Montreal Convention	Montreal Convention Protocol	Maritime Convention	Maritime Convention Protocol	Protected Person Convention	Nuclear Terrorism Convention	Hostage Convention	Bombing Convention	Nuclear Material Convention	Plastic Explosive Convention	Terrorist Financing Convention
Number of ratifications (2006)	182	182	185	159	136	126	163	5	154	148	120	128	155
Canada party	×	×	×	×	×	×	×		×	×	×	×	×

With the exception of the new nuclear terrorism convention, all of the anti-terrorism conventions have attracted majority—and in some cases, near-universal—ratification by states. Even so, however, there are obvious gaps. The most obvious gap is geographic—there are significant minorities of states that have not ratified conventions on terrorist bombings, hostage-takings, nuclear material and plastic explosive marking. Likewise, the maritime terrorism conventions remain unratified by a significant number of states (although these states account for little of the world's shipping tonnage).[141]

The second gap is substantive. The piecemeal conventions are just that: piecemeal. The terrorist bombing convention provides a case in point. That treaty deals with the use of an "explosive or other lethal device." The latter is "an explosive or incendiary weapon or device that is

---

141   The IMO reports that states that have ratified the two maritime conventions account for roughly 90 percent of the world's tonnage. See www.imo.org/Conventions/mainframe.asp?topic_id=247.

designed, or has the capability, to cause death, serious bodily injury or substantial material damage; or ... a weapon or device that is designed, or has the capability, to cause death, serious bodily injury or substantial material damage through the release, dissemination or impact of toxic chemicals, biological agents or toxins or similar substances or radiation or radioactive material." It would not, therefore, include a firearm. A terrorist attack on a public place using a bomb would be captured by the treaty. An attack identical in its consequences, but conducted using a machine gun, would not be. Indeed, so long as the latter attack did not involve airplanes, airports, ships or fixed maritime platforms and assuming it was not directed at internationally protected persons, it would not fall within the ambit of any of the anti-terrorism treaties.

The incongruity created by the piecemeal outlawing of some forms of terrorism but not others has prompted work on a comprehensive anti-terrorism treaty. While efforts to finalize such an instrument at the multilateral level have thus far failed, there are now several regional comprehensive treaties. Meanwhile, both substantive and geographic gaps in the piecemeal treaty system have been rendered less significant in the post-9/11 era because of binding U.N. Security Council resolutions. The section that follows discusses these developments, and the efforts to generalize comprehensive anti-terrorism obligations.

1) Comprehensive Anti-terrorism Conventions

As discussed above, the central impetus for a piecemeal approach to anti-terrorism law was the problem of definition. The financing convention includes a now oft-repeated generic description of terrorist acts: an "act intended to cause death or serious bodily injury to a civilian, or to any other person not taking an active part in the hostilities in a situation of armed conflict, when the purpose of such act, by its nature or context, is to intimidate a population, or to compel a Government or an international organization to do or to abstain from doing any act."

This theme of violence done to compel a person, organization or state to do something is also echoed in the nuclear terrorism convention and in the 2005 protocols to the maritime conventions. It also resonated with the U.N. Secretary-General's 2004 High Level Panel on Threats, Challenges and Change and with the secretary-general himself. The High Level Panel noted the extent to which disputes over definition had stymied efforts to develop a comprehensive anti-terrorism strategy. It then proposed:

[the] definition of terrorism should include the following elements:

(a) recognition, in the preamble, that State use of force against civilians is regulated by the Geneva Conventions and other instruments, and, if of sufficient scale, constitutes a war crime by the persons concerned or a crime against humanity;

(b) restatement that acts under the 12 [now 13] preceding anti-terrorism conventions are terrorism, and a declaration that they are a crime under international law; and restatement that terrorism in time of armed conflict is prohibited by the Geneva Conventions and Protocols;

(c) reference to the definitions contained in the 1999 International Convention for the Suppression of the Financing of Terrorism [cited above] and Security Council resolution 1566 (2004) [discussed below];

(d) description of terrorism as "any action, in addition to actions already specified by the existing conventions on aspects of terrorism, the Geneva Conventions and Security Council resolution 1566 (2004), that is intended to cause death or serious bodily harm to civilians or non-combatants, when the purpose of such act, by its nature or context, is to intimidate a population, or to compel a Government or an international organization to do or to abstain from doing any act."[142]

In his own statement on terrorism, the U.N. secretary-general called for a "definition of terrorism, which would make it clear that, in addition to actions already proscribed by existing conventions, any action constitutes terrorism if it is intended to cause death or serious bodily harm to civilians or non-combatants with the purpose of intimidating a population or compelling a Government or an international organization to do or abstain from doing any act."[143]

a)   Draft Comprehensive Anti-terrorism Treaty

Despite the emergence of a definition that, in the financing convention, has been accepted by 155 ratifying states, definition and exemptions from it have remained a stumbling block in work on a comprehensive multilateral anti-terrorism convention.

i)   Core Content

The 2005 consolidation of the draft comprehensive convention follows the pattern of the more recent anti-terrorism treaties in its basic

---

142 U.N. High Level Panel, *A More Secure World* (2004) at para. 164, online: www. un.org/secureworld/.

143 U.N. Secretary-General, *In Larger Freedom*, above note 124 at para. 91.

architecture.[144] Thus, it defines the circumstances in which states may assume jurisdiction over an accused, renders the terrorism crime extraditable (and precludes the application of the political offences doctrine) and includes the omnipresent extradite-or-try obligation.

Its provisions on prevention are quite robust, barring state harbouring and support and mandating detailed interstate cooperation and information sharing. Provisions on information-sharing, for instance, require states to:

(a) Establish and maintain channels of communication between their competent agencies and services to facilitate the secure and rapid exchange of information concerning all aspects of offences set forth in article 2;

(b) Cooperat[e] with one another in conducting inquiries, with respect to the offences set forth in article 2, concerning:

   (i) The identity, whereabouts and activities of persons in respect of whom reasonable suspicion exists that they are involved in such offences;

   (ii) The movement of funds, property, equipment or other instrumentalities relating to the commission of such offences.[145]

ii) *Scope*

The draft convention is distinguished from the piecemeal approach by its scope. Thus, under the draft Article 2,

1. Any person commits an offence within the meaning of the present Convention if that person, by any means, unlawfully and intentionally, causes:

(a) Death or serious bodily injury to any person; or

(b) Serious damage to public or private property, including a place of public use, a State or government facility, a public transportation system, an infrastructure facility or to the environment; or

(c) Damage to property, places, facilities or systems referred to in paragraph 1 (b) of the present article resulting or likely to result in major economic loss;

when the purpose of the conduct, by its nature or context, is to intimidate a population, or to compel a Government or an international organization to do or to abstain from doing any act.

---

144 U.N. Doc. A/59/894 (2005).
145 *Ibid.*, Art. 9 of the consolidated draft.

Note that this definition, while it includes the standard reference to coercion of a population, government or international organization, extends terrorism beyond the death or serious bodily harm found in the financing convention definition and its successors and variants.

iii) The Problem of State Terrorism

At the time of this writing, debate on the draft treaty seemed to hinge in large measure on how this definition would apply to state militaries and during times of armed conflict.[146] Draft Article 18 (which appeared as Article 20 in the 2005 consolidated draft) includes the standard exemption for armed and military forces that appeared, initially, in the bombing convention. This provision reads, in part:

> 2. The activities of armed forces during an armed conflict, as those terms are understood under international humanitarian law, which are governed by that law, are not governed by this Convention.
>
> 3. The activities undertaken by the military forces of a State in the exercise of their official duties, inasmuch as they are governed by other rules of international law, are not governed by this Convention.

This proposal has been countered by one from the Organization of the Islamic Conference (OIC), which reads, in part:

> 2. The activities of the parties during an armed conflict, including in situations of foreign occupation, as those terms are understood under international humanitarian law, which are governed by that law, are not governed by this Convention.
>
> 3. The activities undertaken by the military forces of a State in the exercise of their official duties, inasmuch as they are in conformity with international law, are not governed by this Convention.[147]

The OIC proposal includes notable differences from the original draft. First, paragraph 2 emphatically abandons the reference to "armed forces" (in favour of "parties") and includes situations of foreign occupation as an "armed conflict," at least as these terms are understood in IHL. The obvious intent is to extend the reach of the exemption to nonstate actors not otherwise meeting the definition of "armed forces"

---

146 See U.N. Doc. A/61/37 (2006) at Annex 1, para. 2 (describing draft Art. 18 as the central focus of discussions).

147 See Annex IV, U.N. Doc. A/57/37 (2002).

(that is, groups using violence in response to the Israeli presence on the West Bank).

It would be wrong, however, to view the OIC language as authorizing indiscriminate violence by "parties," including in situations of foreign occupation. "Parties" in international humanitarian law was a term once assumed to refer to the armed forces of the state parties to the relevant conventions. Recall that the "armed forces" concept requires an organized hierarchical structure and "an internal disciplinary system which, *inter alia*, shall enforce compliance with the rules of international law applicable in armed conflict."[148] This latter requirement probably excludes most, if not all, insurgency, guerrilla or similar groups.[149]

As noted previously, however, under Additional Protocol I, armed conflicts were expanded to include "armed conflicts in which peoples are fighting against colonial domination and alien occupation and against racist regimes in the exercise of their right of self-determination." Further, as discussed in Chapters 5 and 14, other nonstate actor combatants may be recognized as lawful belligerents by IHL. Put another way, parties to conflicts now include nonstate actors.[150]

However, the OIC draft also acknowledges that armed conflicts are exempted from the convention only if "governed" by IHL. As noted above, national liberation movements engaged in a legitimate self-determination struggle would not be "governed" by IHL absent a declaration that they accept the application of this law.[151] Without this declaration, these groups would presumably not meet the strictures of the OIC exemption and would continue to be subject to the comprehensive anti-terrorism treaty: they would act illegally if they committed an act of terrorism.

Meanwhile, any putative national liberation movement actually issuing the requisite declaration (or any nonstate actors otherwise considered lawful belligerents) would be subject to the rules of international humanitarian law.[152] As discussed above, the latter outlaws targeted violence against civilians, and emphatically proscribes terror-

---

148 AP I, above note 93, Art. 43.

149 See discussion earlier in this chapter.

150 For discussion, see Nathaniel Berman, "Privileging Combat? Contemporary Conflict and the Legal Construction of War" (2004) 43 Colum. J. Transnat'l L. 1 at 47.

151 See discussion earlier in this chapter.

152 See AP I, above note 93, Art. 96(3) (specifying that, after the declaration, the nonstate actor "assumes the same rights and obligations as those which have been assumed by a High Contracting Party to the Conventions and this Protocol").

ism.[153] Either way, therefore, nonstate actors would commit a crime by attacking civilians, whether in IHL or under the terrorism convention.

Still, it is also the case that these nonstate actors would no longer have criminal responsibility under the convention for violence directed at other combatants, and proportionate injury inflicted on civilians in the course of attacking militarily necessary objectives — that is, violence undertaken in compliance with IHL.[154] In the right circumstances, for instance, a suicide bombing at a military checkpoint that causes collateral injury to civilians would be excluded from the terrorism convention's reach. Limiting the reach of the treaty in this manner is likely unacceptable to many states.

An even more sweeping substantive difference between the OIC and the original draft lies in paragraph 3: an exemption to the treaty applies to military forces of a state, but only when they act in conformity with international law (as opposed to the less demanding "governed by international law" in the original draft). As discussed above, the language in the original draft draws on the bombing convention, and can be criticized as replacing penal sanction under international criminal law for state military violence undertaken outside of an armed conflict with the much more amorphous remedies of regular international law.

The OIC provision, however, would exempt these military acts from the treaty only if they actually *conformed* to this broader body of international law. If they did not, then presumably, these acts would remain criminalized under the treaty, assuming they met its definition of terrorism. The effect of the OIC language, therefore, is to level on state military personnel (when functioning outside of armed conflicts) criminal responsibility under the convention for acts that meet a double-illegality threshold; that is, acts that violate general international law and also constitute the sort of terrorism penalized by the comprehensive treaty. This seems a sensible outcome.

b) Regional Comprehensive Anti-terrorism Conventions

While efforts at the United Nations to conclude a comprehensive anti-terrorism convention have not yet been successful, there are at least eight regional anti-terrorism treaties. These are, by date:

- OAS Convention to Prevent and Punish the Acts of Terrorism Taking the Form of Crimes Against Persons and Related Extortion that are of International Significance (1971);

---

153 See Becker, *Terrorism and the State* above note 54 at 106 *et seq.* for a further discussion on this point.
154 See discussion on international humanitarian law in Chapter 5.

- European Convention on the Suppression of Terrorism (1977);
- SAARC Regional Convention on Suppression of Terrorism (1977);
- Arab Convention on the Suppression of Terrorism (1998);
- Treaty on Cooperation among the States Members of the Commonwealth of Independent States in Combating Terrorism (1999);
- Convention of the Organization of the Islamic Conference on Combating International Terrorism (1999);
- OAU Convention on the Prevention and Combating of Terrorism (1999); and
- Inter-American Convention Against Terrorism (2002).

Canada ratified the last of these instruments in 2002. The Inter-American Convention pledges state parties to ratify the core U.N. piecemeal anti-terrorism treaties, and then implement these in their internal laws. Among other things, it pledges parties to "prevent, combat, and eradicate the financing of terrorism,"[155] as well as "promote cooperation and the exchange of information in order to improve border and customs control measures to detect and prevent the international movement of terrorists and trafficking in arms or other materials intended to support terrorist activities."[156] The convention also includes a provision on mutual legal assistance and makes the political offences exception of extradition agreements nonapplicable where one of the piecemeal terrorist crimes occurs.[157]

2) Obligations under Chapter VII of the U.N. *Charter*

The regional treaties have an obvious limitation: they are regional, not universal. Meanwhile, even if a comprehensive anti-terrorism treaty were to be adopted, its geographic reach would depend on state ratification of that instrument. Since a sizable minority of states has yet to ratify even some of the piecemeal instruments, the expectation must be that a comprehensive treaty would not have universal adherence. Such a phenomena is commonplace in international law, a body of principle predicated (at least in theory) on individual sovereign states agreeing and subscribing to the rules.

That standard *modus operandi* of international law has undergone a sea change in the wake of 9/11, certainly in the anti-terrorism area. Specifically, the existing international law of anti-terrorism cannot be understood without careful consideration of U.N. Security Coun-

---

155 AG/Res. 1840 (XXXII-O/02), Art. 4.
156 *Ibid.*, Art. 7.
157 *Ibid.*, Arts. 9 and 11.

cil action, taken under Chapter VII of the U.N. *Charter*. As discussed in Chapter 3, resolutions issued by the council employing the powers bestowed on it by Chapter VII, and intended to be binding, have mandatory effect, irrespective of some additional requirement of state consent. The Security Council may legislate for the world, in other words.

a) Anti-terrorism Sanctions

The classic Security Council resolution imposes sanctions of various forms on a designated target state, particularly in relation to the shipment of arms. However, even prior to 9/11, the Security Council had directed particularly aggressive sanctions at the Taliban regime in Afghanistan, because of its connection to terrorism. This pattern is discussed below, prior to an overview of post-9/11 practice.

i) *Listing*

Resolution 1267 (1999) creates a subcommittee of the Council (1267 Committee) charged with listing individuals affiliated with the Taliban, then the *de facto* government in Afghanistan. It then obliges governments to bar financial transactions by their nationals or those within their territories with the listed persons. Listed persons are, in otherwords, blacklisted. Resolution 1333 extended these provisions to Osama Bin Laden and his associates (including al-Qaeda) in 2000.[158] The basic architecture of these resolutions remains intact, as modified and enhanced by several additional resolutions.[159] Several hundred persons and entities are now listed.[160]

The 1267 process represents an unusually detailed and intrusive sanctioning regime, one that implicates a subset of the Security Council in the almost quasi-judicial function of identifying individual suspected terrorists and terrorist entities. The due process implications of this approach are obvious, and indeed, the 1267 Committee process as a whole may be extremely vulnerable to abuse by states with ulterior

---

158 S/RES/1333 (2000).
159 S/RES/1364 (2001); S/RES/1388(2002); S/RES/1390 (2002); S/RES/1452(2002); S/RES/1455 (2003); S/RES/1456 (2003); S/RES/1526 (2004); S/RES/1617 (2005); S/RES/1730 (2006); S/RES/1735 (2006).
160 See United Nations, *The New Consolidated List of Individuals and Entities Belonging to or Associated with the Taliban and Al-Qaida Organisation as Established and Maintained by the 1267 Committee*, online: www.un.org/sc/committees/1267/consolist.shtml.

motives for terrorist listing.[161] The International Helsinki Federation for Human Rights critiqued the listing system in 2003, noting that

> the [listing] criteria and evidence are not publicly available, leaving it unclear which criteria are used and whether they are applied consistently. This lack of clarity contravenes international due process standards and is likely to make it extremely difficult effectively to challenge a decision to list either an individual or an entity. ... Since the names of entities are made public as soon as they are listed, there remains no opportunity to ameliorate the potential damage to an individual or organization's reputation or livelihood that results solely from being wrongly identified in public as a terrorist financier.[162]

The 1267 process was also criticized by the U.N. Secretary-General's 2004 High Level Panel on U.N. Reform.[163] European states have also expressed strong concerns.[164]

In late 2006, the Security Council bolstered the listing rules, deciding that states proposing names for inclusion on the list should provide "as much detail as possible" justifying the listing, including "(i) specific information supporting a determination that the individual or entity" meets listing criteria; "(ii) the nature of the information and (iii) supporting information or documents that can be provided."[165]

---

161   See Eric Rosand, "The Security Council's Efforts to Monitor the Implementation of Al Qaeda/Taliban Sanctions" (2004) 98 A.J.I.L. 745 at 752 ("some [observers] have worried that the committee, in the interest of satisfying the domestic political concerns of certain members, has added persons or entities to the list whose links to Al Qaeda are questionable").

162   International Helsinki Federation for Human Rights, *Anti-terrorism Measures, Security and Human Rights: Developments in Europe, Central Asia and North America in the Aftermath of September 11* (April 2003) at 130, online: www.ihf-hr.org/documents/doc_summary.php?sec_id=3&d_id=4082 [*Anti-terrorism Measures*].

163   U.N. High Level Panel, *A More Secure World*, above note 142 at para. 152 ("The way entities or individuals are added to the terrorist list maintained by the Council and the absence of review or appeal for those listed raise serious accountability issues and possibly violate fundamental human rights norms and conventions").

164   See, for example, Richard Ryan, permanent representative of Ireland to the United Nations, Statement on Behalf of European Union, U.N. Doc. S/PV. 4892 at 23 (12 January 2004) (urging the inclusion in an amended process of the following steps: "individuals entered into the consolidated sanctions list should, to the extent possible, be informed about the listing as well as its reasons and consequences; and the right of listed individuals to be heard should be further developed").

165   S/RES/1735 (2006).

The 1267 Committee rules by the time of this writing[166] call on states to "provide a statement of case in support of the proposing listing." This statement should include as much detail as possible including:

> (1) specific findings demonstrating the association or activities alleged; (2) the nature of the supporting evidence (e.g., intelligence, law enforcement, judicial, media, admissions by subject, etc.) and (3) supporting evidence or documents that can be supplied. States should include details of any connection with a currently listed individual or entity. States should indicate what portion(s) of the statement of case the Committee may publicly release or release to Member States upon request.[167]

The committee considered requests "expeditiously"[168] and decided whether to list the individual on a consensus basis.[169] A listing is released promptly, and communicated to states where the person is believed to be located. The latter country is asked to give notice to the individual concerned, to the extent possible. There is, however, no formal adjudication by the 1267 Committee and no opportunity for the person so designated to make representations prior to listing. Indeed, the committee generally meets in closed sessions.[170]

ii) De-listing

Subsequently, a person who wishes to be removed from the list must petition their government of residence or citizenship (the "petitioned" state) or alternatively a new "focal point," providing justifications for the de-listing request. If the person approaches their state, that petitioned state may then approach the governments that originally proposed the listing ("designating" states), holding bilateral consultations and collecting additional information. The rules specify that the petitioned government "should seek to persuade the designating government(s) to submit jointly or separately a request for de-listing to the Committee." Alternatively, the petitioned government may act unilaterally, with the de-listing request circulated in writing to Committee members and deemed approved where no objections are voiced.[171]

---

166 1267 Committee, *Guidelines of the Committee for the Conduct of its Work* (Adopted on 7 November 2002, as amended on 10 April 2003, 21 December 2005, 29 November 2006 and 12 February 2007), online: www.un.org/sc/committees/1267/pdf/1267_guidelines.pdf [*Guidelines*].

167 *Ibid.* at 4.

168 *Ibid.*

169 *Ibid.* at 2 ("The Committee shall make decisions by consensus of its members").

170 *Ibid.*

171 *Ibid.* at 7.

If the person instead approaches the "focal point"—an entity housed in the U.N. secretariat[172]—this body forwards the request to the designating state and the state(s) of citizenship and residence. These states then consult and if any agree to the de-listing, this recommendation is forwarded to the 1267 Committee. Likewise, if any state opposes de-listing, this information is also sent to the Committee. States on the 1267 Committee may themselves recommend de-listing. Where no state recommends de-listing, the application is deemed rejected.[173]

The Security Council has provided guidelines that the committee must follow in deciding whether to de-list. The committee, for instance, may consider whether the listee was listed due to mistake of identity or whether they no longer meet the criteria for listing. In respect to the latter possibility, "the Committee may consider, among other things, whether the individual is deceased, or whether it has been affirmatively shown that the individual or entity has severed all association" with al-Qaeda or the Taliban.[174]

Ultimately, the 1267 Committee renders a de-listing decision on a consensus basis. If no consensus exists on the committee, the matter is returned to the full-fledged Security Council.[175] Presumably, at the Security Council, to be de-listed, at least nine members would have to agree and every single permanent member would have to decline a veto.

The consensus approach to 1267 Committee decision making places each member of the Security Council in a spoiler position. For instance, three Swedish citizens of Somali origin were designated by the 1267 Committee in 2001, at the urging of the United States. The listing proved controversial in Sweden, especially after Swedish authorities concluded that the activities of these men did not warrant criminal charges. When Sweden sought the de-listing of these individuals, the United States, the United Kingdom and Russia objected, precipitating an intense bilateral negotiation between Sweden and the United States. The individuals were ultimately removed from the 1267 Committee list in August 2002.[176]

The similar Canadian case of Liban Hussein is discussed in Chapter 7. As in the Swedish case, the de-listing of Mr. Hussein on the 1267 Committee appears to have depended in large measure on the cooper-

---

172   S/RES/1730 (2006).
173   *Ibid.*; *Guidelines*, above note 166 at 6–7.
174   S/RES/1735 (2006).
175   *Ibid.* at 7.
176   Rosand, "Security Council's Efforts," above note 161 at 749–50.

ation of the United States.[177] Absent that agreement, Mr. Hussein would not have been de-listed. The Hussein case also demonstrates how the listing process can act as more than a blacklist and come close to an act of attainder; that is a determination of guilt by decree rather than adjudication. By placing Hussein and his company on its own domestic list (albeit even before the 1267 Committee acted), the Canadian government made Hussein both a person with whom it was impossible to have any transactions *and* a person in violation of that prohibition: Hussein's dealing with his company were considered a transaction with a prohibited entity, and thus a criminal offence.

b) Universal Obligation to Criminalize and Punish Terrorist Acts

Chief among the post-9/11 Security Council measures is Resolution 1373 (2001). In some large measure, Resolution 1373 imposes via Chapter VII the substantive obligations of the 1999 terrorist financing convention. Its writ is, however, even broader, and in some respects it constitutes a universal, comprehensive anti-terrorism instrument. It requires states to "ensure that any person who participates in the *financing, planning, preparation or perpetration of terrorist acts* or in supporting terrorist acts is brought to justice and ensure that, in addition to any other measures against them, such terrorist acts are established as serious criminal offences in domestic laws and regulations and that the punishment duly reflects the seriousness of such terrorist acts."[178]

Resolution 1373 differs from the piecemeal conventions in several ways. First, it targets "terrorist acts," not a subset of terrorist behaviours. "Terrorist acts" is not a defined term in Resolution 1373, a not surprising failing given difficulties of definition discussed above. In Resolution 1566 (2004), the council partially corrected its omission by offering up its understanding of terrorism: "criminal acts, including against civilians, committed with the intent to cause death or serious bodily injury, or taking of hostages, with the purpose to provoke a state of terror in the general public or in a group of persons or particular persons, intimidate a population or compel a government or an international organization to do or to abstain from doing any act,

---

177 Colum Lynch, "U.S. Seeks to Take 6 Names Off U.N. Sanctions List; Administration Was Criticized for Offering Little Proof That Individuals, Groups Aided Al Qaeda" *Washington Post* (22 August 2002) A13 ("U.S. officials said they agreed to remove the individual, Liban Hussein, after he persuaded them that he had severed his ties to al-Barakaat").

178 [Emphasis added.]

which constitute offences within the scope of and as defined in the international conventions and protocols relating to terrorism."[179]

Second, it is notable that Resolution 1373 requires states to "ensure that any person who participates in the financing, planning, preparation or perpetration of terrorist acts or in supporting terrorist acts *is brought to justice*." This reference to "justice" is more categorical than the careful language found in the piecemeal conventions of submitting a case to prosecution: it demands an outcome, not just a process. This language would appear, therefore, to preclude *pro forma* investigations and dilatory prosecutions by state authorities.

c)   Universal Obligation to Prevent Terrorist Acts

Beyond listing suspected al-Qaeda and Taliban affiliated and creating a *de facto* universal obligation to criminalize terrorist acts (and punish those implicated in them), Security Council resolutions have compounded state obligations to cooperate in anti-terrorism efforts. Pre-9/11 resolutions, such as resolution 1269 (1999), "called upon" states to "cooperate with each other, particularly through bilateral and multilateral agreements and arrangements, to prevent and suppress terrorist acts, protect their nationals and other persons against terrorist attacks and bring to justice the perpetrators of such acts" and to "exchange information in accordance with international and domestic law, and cooperate on administrative and judicial matters in order to prevent the commission of terrorist acts." After 9/11, this hortatory language gave way to binding legal dictates. Thus, in Resolution 1373, the council decided that all states must, *inter alia*, "take the necessary steps to prevent the commission of terrorist acts, including by provision of early warning to other States by exchange of information ... [and] afford one another the greatest measure of assistance in connection with criminal investigations or criminal proceedings relating to the financing or support of terrorist acts, including assistance in obtaining evidence in their possession necessary for the proceedings."

The resolution also includes language barring state-sponsorship or harbouring of terrorists. States are to

> refrain from providing any form of support, active or passive, to entities or persons involved in terrorist acts, including by suppressing recruitment of members of terrorist groups and eliminating the supply of weapons to terrorists; ... deny safe haven to those who finance, plan, support, or commit terrorist acts, or provide safe havens; ... prevent those who finance, plan, facilitate or commit terrorist acts

---

179   S/RES/1566 (2004).

from using their respective territories for those purposes against other States or their citizens; [and] prevent the movement of terrorists or terrorist groups by effective border controls and controls on issuance of identity papers and travel documents, and through measures for preventing counterfeiting, forgery or fraudulent use of identity papers and travel documents.

In the specific area of nuclear terrorism, Security Council Resolution 1540 (2004) also imposes important prevention and cooperation obligations. Under this instrument, for instance, states "shall refrain from providing any form of support to non-State actors that attempt to develop, acquire, manufacture, possess, transport, transfer or use nuclear, chemical or biological weapons and their means of delivery."

d) Obligation to Report on Progress

Resolution 1373 also created a "Counter Terrorism Committee" (CTC), comprising all of its members, "to monitor implementation of this resolution, with the assistance of appropriate expertise." The resolution called upon "all States to report to the Committee, no later than 90 days from the date of adoption of this resolution and thereafter according to a timetable to be proposed by the Committee, on the steps they have taken to implement this resolution." Since 2001, the CTC has received state reports on adherence to resolution 1373. Now supported by a CTC Executive Directorate,[180] it has also been instructed by the Security Council to develop "best practices" in the counterterrorism area and, recently, to "as a matter of priority and, when appropriate, in close cooperation with relevant international, regional and subregional organizations to start visits to States, with the consent of the States concerned, in order to enhance the monitoring of the implementation of resolution 1373 (2001) and facilitate the provision of technical and other assistance for such implementation."[181]

e) Human Rights and Security Council Measures

The impact of the Security Council's post-9/11 counterterrorism activities on human rights has attracted particular attention. As noted, Resolution 1373 mandated significant state actions to suppress terrorism, but failed to define the concept. In the wake of this failure, human rights groups noted that some states cited their U.N. anti-terrorism obligations to justify abusive policies and practices. Human Rights Watch, for instance, canvassed in 2002 what it characterized as state

---

180 S/RES/1535 (2004).
181 S/RES/1566 (2004).

"opportunism in the face of tragedy"; that is, repression in the name of anti-terrorism.[182] That organization, like others, has also documented the extent to which counterterrorism strategies have run counter to state human rights obligations.[183]

In 2003, U.N. special rapporteurs and independent experts issued a joint statement[184] expressing

> alarm at the growing threats against human rights, threats that necessitate a renewed resolve to defend and promote these rights. ... Although they share in the unequivocal condemnation of terrorism, they voice profound concern at the multiplication of policies, legislation and practices increasingly being adopted by many countries in the name of the fight against terrorism which affect negatively the enjoyment of virtually all human rights—civil, cultural, economic, political and social. They draw attention to the dangers inherent in the indiscriminate use of the term "terrorism," and the resulting new categories of discrimination.

The statement deplored

> the fact that, under the pretext of combating terrorism, human rights defenders are threatened and vulnerable groups are targeted and discriminated against on the basis of origin and socio-economic status, in particular migrants, refugees and asylum-seekers, indigenous peoples and people fighting for their land rights or against the negative effects of economic globalization policies.

In Resolution 1456 (2003), and in other instruments since then, the Security Council has been careful to acknowledge that anti-terrorism is to be conducted in a manner compliant with human rights obligations.[185] Moreover, both the General Assembly[186] and the now-superseded Commission on Human Rights[187] have tasked the U.N. Office of the High Commissioner for Human Rights with examining and mak-

---

182 Human Rights Watch, *Opportunism in the Face of Tragedy* (2002), online: http://hrw.org/campaigns/september11/opportunismwatch.htm.

183 See, for example, Human Rights Watch, *In the Name of Counter-Terrorism: Human Rights Abuses Worldwide* (25 March 2003), online: http://hrw.org/un/chr59/counter-terrorism-bck.htm.

184 E/CN.4/2004/4, annex 1.

185 Specifying that "States must ensure that any measure taken to combat terrorism comply with all their obligations under international law, and should adopt such measures in accordance with international law, in particular international human rights, refugee, and humanitarian law."

186 A/RES/58/187 (2003).

187 Commission on Human Rights, Res. 2003/68.

ing recommendations on the issue of human rights and terrorism. The U.N. human rights machinery also includes a special rapporteur on human rights and terrorism, reporting on this issue on a periodic basis.

3) Obligations under Customary International Law

The Security Council resolutions requiring states to prevent terrorism directed from their territory embellish generic customary international law obligations binding on states. The U.N. General Assembly's influential *Declaration on Principles of International Law concerning Friendly Relations and Co-operation*, quite likely an expression of customary international law, [188] declares:

> Every State has the duty to refrain from organizing, instigating, assisting or participating in acts of civil strife or terrorist acts in another State or acquiescing in organized activities within its territory directed towards the commission of such acts, when the acts referred to in the present paragraph involve a threat or use of force. ... Also, no State shall organize, assist, foment, finance, incite or tolerate subversive, terrorist or armed activities directed towards the violent overthrow of the regime of another State, or interfere in civil strife in another State.

This and similar assertions have been repeated in subsequent General Assembly resolutions. While early resolutions contain an evident focus on acts of "colonial, racist and alien regimes,"[189] by the late 1970s, the General Assembly's pronouncements also included a general condemnation of terrorism and a call on states to prevent terrorism and cooperate in its suppression.[190] Beginning in 1985, these assertions were supplemented by a declaration that "all acts, methods and practices of terrorism wherever and by whomever committed, including those which jeopardize friendly relations among States and their security" were criminal.[191]

---

188 A/RES/2625, Annex, 25 U.N. GAOR, Supp. (No. 28), U.N. Doc. A/5217 at 121 (1970). While not binding in its own right, the Declaration "elaborates the major principles of international law in the U.N. *Charter*, particularly on use of force, dispute settlement, nonintervention in domestic affairs, self-determination, duties of cooperation and observance of obligations, and 'sovereign equality.' [I]t has become the international lawyer's favorite example of an authoritative U.N. resolution." Oscar Schachter, "United Nations Law" (1994) 88 A.J.I.L. 1 at 3.

189 See, for example, A/RES/31/102 (1976) and 32/157 (1976).

190 A/RES/34/145 (1979); 38/130 (1983).

191 A/RES/40/61 (1985); 42/159 (1987); 46/51 (1991).

The General Assembly's 1994 *Declaration on Measures to Elimin-ate International Terrorism* repeats this assertion and calls on states to introduce comprehensive anti-terrorism measures, including: refrain-ing "from organizing, instigating, assisting or participating in terrorist acts in territories of other States, or from acquiescing in or encouraging activities within their territories directed towards the commission of such acts"; taking "appropriate practical measures to ensure that their respective territories are not used for terrorist installations or training camps, or for the preparation or organization of terrorist acts intended to be committed against other States or their citizens"; ensuring "the apprehension and prosecution or extradition of perpetrators of terrorist acts, in accordance with the relevant provisions of their national law"; and cooperating "with one another in exchanging relevant information concerning the prevention and combating of terrorism."[192]

Most recently, the resolution stemming from the 2005 World Sum-mit provided as follows:

> We reiterate our call upon States to refrain from organizing, finan-cing, encouraging, providing training for or otherwise supporting terrorist activities and to take appropriate measures to ensure that their territories are not used for such activities.[193]

Read together, these instruments may reflect the *opinio juris* re-quired to support the emergence of customary norms,[194] independent of the binding legal force of the Security Council's Chapter VII resolu-tions. With the recent expansion of anti-terrorism activity by states, and thus clear expressions of state practice in the area, a customary obligation to suppress terrorism may now exist.

At minimum, this would mean all states must exercise due diligence in forestalling the use of their territory by terrorists. [195] The precise scope of customary anti-terrorism obligations may be more uncertain, however, when it comes to prosecuting terrorist acts. For instance, at least one U.S. federal court of appeal has expressed doubt that the

---

192 A/RES/49/60 (1994).

193 A/RES/60/1 (2005) at para. 86.

194 For discussion, see Ross E. Schreiber, "Ascertaining *Opinio Juris* of States Con-cerning Norms Involving the Prevention of International Terrorism: A Focus on the U.N. Process" (1998) 16 B.U. Int'l L.J. 309.

195 See Becker, *Terrorism and the State*, above note 54 at 130 for an expansive series of state anti-terrorism obligations, at least in part based on customary inter-national law. For an early discussion of the due diligence obligation to prevent terrorist acts, see Richard B. Lillich & John M. Paxman, "State Responsibility for Injuries to Aliens Occasioned by Terrorist Activities" (1977) 26 Am. U. L. Rev. 217 at 245–46.

extradite-or-try obligations in anti-terrorism treaties create a customary "universal" criminal jurisdiction for states not party to the treaties.[196] This conclusion may be unsustainable. The scope of ratification of these treaties, coupled with whatever new anti-terrorism laws have been introduced even in nonratifying states after resolution 1373, strongly supports the customary nature of extradite-or-try obligations. There may now be a sufficiently universal practice undertaken with a sense of legal obligation to give rise to a customary extradite-or-try norm.

---

196 *United States v. Yousef*, 327 F.3d 56 at 96 (2d Cir. 2003) ("The jurisdiction ... created [in the Montreal Convention] is not a species of universal jurisdiction, but a jurisdictional agreement among contracting States to extradite or prosecute offenders who commit the acts proscribed by the treaty—that is, the agreements between contracting States create *aut dedere aut punire* ("extradite or prosecute") jurisdiction").

CHAPTER 7

COUNTERING
TERRORISM AT
THE NATIONAL LEVEL

As discussed in Chapter 6, terrorist acts are international crimes. Whether by treaty or by virtue of U.N. Security Council Resolution 1373, all states are obliged to criminalize terrorist acts. The existing multilateral piecemeal conventions on terrorism define the sorts of acts constituting crimes. The more generic reference to "terrorist acts" in Resolution 1373 does not, although the international community's understanding of the content of such acts arguably has been refined by subsequent resolutions. States have substantial latitude, therefore, to introduce anti-terrorism terrorist measures *per* their particular inclinations. As noted in Chapter 6, this has sparked concern about opportunistic anti-terrorism; that is, the tarring by some regimes of dissident, separatist or other politically undesirable groups as "terrorist." Even in countries with firm democratic traditions and strong adherence to the rule of law, the exact content of antiterrorist criminal law has proven controversial.

Canada's anti-terrorism criminal laws predate 9/11. As Kent Roach has forcefully argued, conventional criminal law in the area of murder, sabotage, bodily harm and (more recently) criminal organization were, and remain, of direct relevance in outlawing the acts constituting terrorism. So too, the "inchoate" offences of attempting, conspiring, counselling, aiding and abetting, and being an accessory are broad concepts in Canadian law, capable of outlawing most of the actions on the periphery of an actual terrorist act.[1]

Nevertheless, in the immediate aftermath of 9/11, the government moved rapidly to create a significant new anti-terrorism criminal law architecture. Its initial response to U.N. Security Council Resolution 1373 was the making of regulations under Canada's *United Nations Act* creating terrorism financing crimes. A more comprehensive response followed in the form of Bill C-36 (2001),[2] Canada's *Anti-terrorism Act*.[3] All of these sources of anti-terrorism criminal laws remain in force, and thus merit discussion.

PART I: PRE-9/11 *CRIMINAL CODE* PROVISIONS

As noted, many conventional criminal offences — not least, murder and/ or assault — could be committed in the course of terrorist violence. In addition, prior to the 2001 *Anti-terrorism Act* (ATA), the *Criminal Code* included a number of provisions implementing Canada's international anti-terrorism obligations; specifically, those found in the piecemeal international anti-terrorism obligations discussed in Chapter 6. The specifics of these criminal offences are outlined in Table 7.3, and govern crimes involving nuclear material and against aircraft and airports, maritime navigation and internationally protected persons, as well as criminalizing hostage taking.

---

1   See discussion in Kent Roach, "The New Terrorism Offences and Criminal Law," in Ronald Daniels, Patick Macklem & Kent Roach, eds., *The Security of Freedom* (Toronto: University of Toronto Press, 2002) at 152 *et seq.* [Roach, "New Terrorism Offences"]. See also Kent Roach, *September 11: Consequences for Canada* (Montreal: McGill-Queen's University Press, 2003) [Roach, *September 11*]. For these and related reasons, critics like Don Stuart have characterized the post-2001 anti-terrorism criminal law amendments as unnecessary and undesirable "quick fix" legislation. Don Stuart, "The Dangers of Quick Fix Legislation in the Criminal Law: The Anti-terrorism Bill C-36 should be Withdrawn," in Daniels et al., *The Security of Freedom, ibid.*; Don Stuart, "Avoiding Myths and Challenging Minister of Justice Cotler to Undo the Injustices of Our Anti-terrorism Laws" (2006) 51 Crim. L.Q. 11.

2   Bill C-36, *An Act to amend the Criminal Code, the Official Secrets Act, the Canada Evidence Act, the Proceeds of Crime (Money Laundering) Act and other Acts, and to enact measures respecting the registration of charities, in order to combat terrorism,* 1st Sess., 37th Parl., 2001.

3   S.C. 2001, c. 41.

PART II: U.N. ACT REGULATIONS

By 9/11, however, Canada had not ratified the international terrorism financing convention, and lacked a *Criminal Code* provision governing terrorism financing. This omission became an acute problem after the U.N. Security Council issued Resolution 1373, obliging terrorism financing crimes.

For exactly this reason, the federal government's first criminal law response to the events of 9/11 was not new statute law introduced in and promulgated by Parliament, but rather regulations quickly issued under the *United Nations Act*.[4] This statute exists to expedite Canadian compliance with U.N. Security Council resolutions imposing economic or other sanctions under Chapter VII of the U.N. *Charter*. Thus, it empowers the governor-in-council (GIC) to make orders and regulations that appear to it "to be necessary or expedient" as means to implement a measure called for by the U.N. Security Council under Article 41 of the United Nations *Charter*. Put another way, it delegates authority to the federal executive to legislate via regulations, a commonplace and entirely constitutional practice in Canadian law. Under the *Act* itself, a violation of these regulations is a crime, attracting a substantial penalty of up to ten years' imprisonment.[5]

With one exception discussed below, the existing *United Nations Act* regulations all involve classic sanctions measures, often relating to arms sales to geographically defined, sanctioned regimes, groups or persons.[6] These provisions bar persons in Canada and Canadians outside Canada from engaging in the prohibited transactions with the sanctioned entity. However, the regulations motivated by terrorism concerns have morphed considerably in their scope since 9/11. In doing so, they have tracked the evolution of Security Council Resolutions 1267 and 1373. In responding to the events of 9/11, the government embellished its approach to implementing the sanctions regime for persons listed by the Security Council's 1267 Committee because of their affiliation with the Taliban or al-Qaeda (discussed in Chapter 6).

---

4   R.S.C. 1985, c. U-2.
5   *Ibid.*, s. 3.
6   *United Nations Iraq Regulations* (SOR/90-531 and SOR/2004-221); *United Nations Liberia Regulations* (SOR/2001-261); *United Nations Rwanda Regulations* (SOR/94-582); *United Nations Sierra Leone Regulations* (SOR/98-400); *United Nations Sudan Regulations* (SOR/2004-197); *United Nations Democratic Republic of the Congo Regulations* (SOR/2004-222); and *United Nations Côte d'Ivoire Regulations* (SOR/2005-127).

A. U.N. AL-QAIDA AND TALIBAN REGULATIONS

Soon after Security Council resolution 1267 was issued in 1999, barring financial transactions with Taliban affiliates listed by the Security Council, the Canadian government issued the *United Nations Afghanistan Regulations*,[7] made pursuant to the *United Nations Act*. This instrument was amended in early 2001 to reflect the inclusion of al-Qaeda by Resolution 1333,[8] and has since been renamed the *United Nations Al-Qaida and Taliban Regulations*. The regulations incorporate the 1267 Committee listing process into their fabric by defining Taliban and al-Qaeda affiliates as those listed by the committee. Canadians and those in Canada are barred from dealing in the property of these entities, or from providing financial services to them. In the present version of the regulations, an appeal mechanism exists allowing a person "claiming not to be Usama bin Laden or his associates or a person associated with the Taliban" to petition the minister of public safety "in writing to be delisted from the list of the Committee of the Security Council in accordance with the Guidelines of the Committee of the Security Council." A negative determination may be challenged before a court according to a procedure broadly similar to that discussed below in relation to the *Criminal Code* listing process.[9] If the judge agrees the minister's determination was not reasonable, he or she may order the minister to "seek a review of the case."[10] This language suggests that the government can be compelled by court order to commence the delisting process before the 1267 Committee discussed in Chapter 6.

B. *SUPPRESSION OF TERRORISM REGULATIONS*

While these regulations remain on the books, the government responded to the 9/11 events and Security Council Resolution 1373 with a related, but supplemental measure, one creating new offences for financing named terrorists. In October 2001, it issued the *United Na-*

---

7   SOR/99-444.

8   SOR/2001-86. It was amended again in 2004 by SOR/2004-160 to reflect the nuance in the Afghan sanctions regime introduced by Security Council resolutions 1390 (2002) and 1526 (2004).

9   SOR/99-444, ss. 5.3–5.4.

10   *Ibid.*, para. 5.4(2)(d).

tions Suppression of Terrorism Regulations,[11] again made pursuant to the *United Nations Act*.

These *Suppression of Terrorism Regulations* easily constitute the most sweeping use of the *United Nations Act* to date. First, the exact reach of these provisions is mutable, depending on the periodic "listing" of individuals and entities as banned persons. Up until 2006, a person was incorporated in the Canadian list because they had been identified as a Taliban or al-Qaeda member by the Security Council's 1267 Committee, producing a double-listing under both the *Afghanistan* and *Suppression of Terrorism Regulations*. The current version of the instrument simply preserves an ability by the government to unilaterally list someone; that is, to list persons not on the actual 1267 list.[12] Thus, a person may be "listed" by the GIC under the regulations where there are reasonable grounds to believe that person has carried out, participated in or facilitated a terrorist activity, or is controlled by or acting for someone who has.[13] Up until June 2006, there was no formal appeal from this listing. This situation has now changed, with the introduction of a listing appeal mechanism analogous to that described below for terrorist group listing under the *Criminal Code*.[14]

Second, the conduct criminalized by the regulations reaches well past prior precedents, regulating a broad swath of economic actors and extending beyond the narrow geographic focus of typical U.N. resolution implementation provisions. Thus, the Canadian regulations criminalize a number of different sorts of transactions with listed persons. For instance, it is illegal to provide or collect funds with the intention that the funds be used by a listed person or to deal in any property of a listed person, or provide any financial service in respect of that prop-

---

11 *Regulations Implementing the United Nations Resolutions on the Suppression of Terrorism*, SOR/2001-360 [*Suppression of Terrorism Regulations*].

12 See *Regulations Amending the United Nations Suppression of Terrorism Regulations*, SOR/2006-165 (23 June 2006).

13 *Suppression of Terrorism Regulations*, above note 11, s. 2. These requirements were narrower than the equivalent U.S. rules. Under the original U.S. rules, the secretary of the treasury was authorized, among other things, to designate anyone who assists, sponsors or provides "services to" or is "otherwise associated with" a designated terrorist group. Exec. Order No. 13224. The "otherwise associated with" phrase was challenged on constitutional grounds. See *Humanitarian Law Project v. United States Dep't of the Treasury*, 463 F.Supp. 2d 1049 (C.D. Cal., 2006). There, the court concluded that the phrase "otherwise associated with" was unconstitutionally overbroad, impairing free association rights. *Ibid.* at 57. The government has since clarified the nature of the prohibited association and the new measure has since been upheld in a subsequent proceeding in the same case. 484 F.Supp. 2d 1099 (C.D. Cal., 2007).

14 Below, Table 7.1, note 1.

erty. Further, it is a crime for a financial institution to fail to report monthly to its regulator that it is not in possession of property owned by a listed person. It is also an offence for anyone to fail to disclose to the security services any property in their possession or control that they believe is owned by a listed person.[15] The full reach of these provisions are outlined in Table 7.3.

C. CRITIQUE

The shortcomings of the *Suppression of Terrorism Regulations* became apparent soon after their introduction. In November 2001, Liban Hussein, a resident of Ottawa, Canada, was indicted in Massachusetts for the operation of an unlicensed money transfer business, said to have moved US$3 million to the United Arab Emirates during the first nine months of 2001.[16] The charges stemmed from the unlicensed nature of the money transfer business undertaken by Mr. Hussein's U.S.-based firm, but were part of larger efforts of U.S. officials to shut down the operations of suspected terrorist financiers. Hussein was listed by Canada under the unilateral listing provision in the *Suppression of Terrorism Regulations*,[17] soon after the U.S. charges were laid. Mr. Hussein's assets were immediately frozen, reportedly ruining him.[18]

The United States then sought Hussein's extradition from Canada to face trial in the United States. Canada had no equivalent crime to the licensing misdemeanour with which Hussein was charged in the United States. Federal Justice Department officials, however, apparently treated the *Suppression of Terrorism Regulations* listing as meeting the standard dual criminality requirement of extradition law. The government's theory was reportedly that Mr. Hussein had committed the crime of having financial dealings with a listed person—namely, himself and his companies—thus justifying his removal to the United

---

15   *Suppression of Terrorism Regulations*, above note 11, ss. 3–8.

16   See discussion in *Hearing on "The Financial War on Terrorism and the Administration's Implementation of the Anti-Money Laundering Provisions of the U.S.A. Patriot Act,"* Prepared Statement of the Honorable Michael Chertoff, Assistant Attorney General, Criminal Division, U.S. Department of Justice (29 January 2002), online: http://banking.senate.gov/02_01hrg/012902/chertoff.htm.

17   Above note 11.

18   See Jake Rupert, "Government Pays Off Victim of Terror Smear: Ottawa Man Was Arrested, His Business Ruined" *The Ottawa Citizen* (2 October 2003) A.1.

States to serve trial for unlicensed money transfers.[19] Hussein's counsel mounted a constitutional challenge to the *Suppression of Terrorism Regulations*, arguing among other things that the creation of comprehensive criminal offences of the sort found in the regulations went beyond what the executive may properly do via delegated legislation never vetted in Parliament.[20]

The merits of this case were never contested, as the dubious extradition effort collapsed in June 2002 when the Canadian government concluded that "based on a full and thorough investigation of the information collected in relation to the extradition proceedings, the Government of Canada has concluded that there are no reasonable grounds to believe Mr. Hussein is connected to any terrorist activities."[21] The government then removed him from its list under the *Suppression of Terrorism Regulations* and *Afghanistan Regulations*. The government also ultimately paid Mr. Hussein an undisclosed amount in compensation for financial and emotional hardship.[22]

However, by November 2001, the 1267 Committee had also listed Mr. Hussein.[23] He was, therefore, still subject to international censure, and indeed Canada's unilateral de-listing placed it in noncompliance with its U.N. obligations. In June 2002, Canada promised to seek his de-listing at the United Nations and, in fact, Mr. Hussein was deleted from the 1267 Committee list in July 2002.[24] The 1267 Committee subsequently introduced the formal process for de-listing described in Chapter 6.[25]

PART III: *ANTI-TERRORISM ACT*

The *Suppression of Terrorism Regulations* remain in force. They have, however, largely been duplicated by new *Criminal Code* provisions en-

---

19 Applicant's Factum, *U.S.A. v. Liban M. Hussein* [on file with author]. See also discussion in E. Alexandra Dosman, "For the Record: Designating 'Listed Entities' for the Purposes of Terrorist Financing Offences at Canadian Law" (2004) 62 U.T. Fac. L. Rev. 1 at 17.
20 Applicant's Factum, *U.S.A. v. Liban M. Hussein*, above note 19.
21 Justice Canada, Press Release, *Canada Halts Extradition Process, Liban Hussein De-Listed* (3 June 2002), online: www.justice.gc.ca/en/news/nr/2002/doc_30513. html. See SOR/2002-210 and SOR/2002-211.
22 Rupert, "Government Pays Off Victim," above note 18.
23 U.N. Press Release SC/7206 (9 November 2001).
24 U.N. Press Release SC/7447 (11 July 2002).
25 U.N. Press Release AFG/203-SC/7487 (16 August 2002).

acted via the ATA.[26] A massive omnibus statute, the ATA was promulgated at dizzying speed in just over two months. The law is sweeping, creating a new definition of terrorist activity in Canada's *Criminal Code* and barring multiple terrorism-related financial activities and assorted inchoate offences. More than this, the law includes significant new government secrecy laws, discussed in Chapter 10.

In its reporting to the U.N. Security Council's Counter-Terrorism Committee on anti-terrorism measures, Canada has characterized the ATA as responsive to resolution 1373.[27] As described by the then deputy prime minister to a parliamentary committee in 2002, "the *Anti-terrorism Act* is an unprecedented piece of legislation and brings Canada into full compliance with United Nations Security Council Resolution 1373."[28] Likewise, Canada's then justice minister told a parliamentary committee in 2005 that specific offences in the ATA were enacted to comply with the Security Council's dictates.[29]

It is arguable whether the general language of resolution 1373 obliged all the minutiae of the ATA, especially given the absence of a definition of "terrorist act" in the Security Council instrument. Nevertheless, the ATA represents an extraordinary law: one motivated and designed at least in part to comply with the specific instructions of the U.N. Security Council. This author is aware of no other Canadian statu-

---

26   Indeed, up until the regulations were amended in June 2006 to avoid double (and potentially triple) listing of persons under the *Criminal Code*, R.S.C. 1985, c. C-46, the *Suppression of Terrorism Regulations* and the *Afghanistan Regulations*, the persons listed were sometimes the same. See Regulatory Impact Statement, *Canada Gazette*, vol. 140, No. 20 (20 May 2006).

27   See, for example, *Report of the Government of Canada to the Counter-Terrorism Committee of the United Nations Security Council on Measures Taken to Implement Resolution 1373* (2001), online: www.dfait-maeci.gc.ca/trade/resolution_1373_dec14-en.asp. See also Justice Canada, *The Anti-terrorism Act* ("The ATA allows Canada to meet its international counter-terrorism obligations through the ratification of the two most recent U.N. Conventions on terrorism, as well as U.N. Security Council Resolution 1373, which requires states to take measures against terrorist financing, amongst other things"), online: www.justice.gc.ca/en/anti_terr/faq.html.

28   The Hon. John Manley (Deputy Prime Minister, Lib.), Evidence, 37th Parl., 1st Sess., Sub-Committee on National Security of the Standing Committee of Justice and Human Rights (10 April 2002).

29   The Hon. Irwin Cotler, P.C., M.P., Minister of Justice and Attorney General of Canada, Department of Justice Canada, Proceedings of the Special Senate Committee on the *Anti-terrorism Act*, Issue 2—Evidence —Meeting of 21 February 2005, Morning meeting ("There are specific mandates that we were asked by the U.N. Security Council to incorporate and enact by way of Bill C-36.... Therefore, in response to this U.N. Security Council mandate ... you then have specific offences").

tory provision enacted specifically to comply with Security Council instructions, a fact that reflects the unusual scope of resolution 1373.[30]

Despite its evident provenance in the horror of 9/11, the *Anti-terrorism Act* is quite emphatically not emergency legislation. It is a regular statute of Parliament, not an extraordinary executive branch regulation issued under the *Emergencies Act*.[31] Nor does the ATA invoke the *Canadian Charter of Rights and Freedoms*[32] section 33, the notwithstanding clause. It is, therefore, subject to exactly the same constitutional discipline as any other piece of legislation. This point was underscored by the Supreme Court of Canada in *Application under s. 83.28 of the Criminal Code*, a 2004 constitutional challenge to certain provisions in the ATA.[33] Writing for a majority on this point, Justices Iacobucci and Arbour observed that the *Anti-terrorism Act* was not an instrument aimed at national security in general, but had a narrower anti-terrorism objective. Moreover, they cautioned that courts applying the new law "must not fall prey to the rhetorical urgency of a perceived emergency or an altered security paradigm."[34]

The sections that follow outline the key substantive components of the ATA's changes to the *Criminal Code*, found mostly in Part II.1 of the latter instrument. By the time of this writing, a total of nineteen individuals had been charged under the new terrorism offence provisions, eighteen of them in 2006 in relation to an alleged conspiracy to attack Canadian public buildings.

A. NEW DEFINITIONS

It is essential in reviewing the ATA to begin with an analysis of the new terrorism-related definitions now incorporated into the *Criminal Code*.

1) Terrorist Activity

Subsection 83.01(1) includes, for the first time in Canadian criminal law, a definition of "terrorist activity." Terrorist activity comes in two forms. First, it is a terrorist activity to engage in any of the acts out-

---

30   See discussion in Chapter 6.
31   R.S.C. 1985 (4th Supp.), c. 22.
32   Part I of the *Constitution Act, 1982*, being Schedule B to the *Canada Act 1982* (U.K.) 1982, c. 11.
33   2004 SCC 42. The challenge was to the investigative hearings provision discussed in Chapter 15.
34   *Ibid.* at para. 39.

lawed in international law by ten of the piecemeal international anti-terrorism conventions to which Canada is a party.[35]

Second, and more controversially, section 83.01 includes a generic definition of terrorist activity. There are several components to this latter definition. To be a terrorist activity, the impugned act or omission is one that, inside or outside Canada, intentionally

(A) causes death or serious bodily harm to a person by the use of violence;

(B) endangers a person's life;

(C) causes a serious risk to the health or safety of the public or any segment of the public;

(D) causes substantial property damage, whether to public or private property, if causing such damage is likely to result in the conduct or harm referred to in any of clauses (A) to (C); or

(E) causes serious interference with or serious disruption of an essential service, facility or system, whether public or private, other than as a result of advocacy, protest, dissent or stoppage of work that is not intended to result in the conduct or harm referred to in any of clauses (A) to (C).

Moreover, this act or omission must be committed

(A) in whole or in part for a political, religious or ideological purpose, objective or cause; and

(B) in whole or in part with the intention of intimidating the public, or a segment of the public, with regard to its security, including its economic security, or compelling a person, a government or a domestic or an international organization to do or to refrain from doing any act, whether the public or the person, government or organization is inside or outside Canada.

---

35   Namely, *Convention for the Suppression of Unlawful Seizure of Aircraft* (1971), 860 U.N.T.S. 105; *Convention for the Suppression of Unlawful Acts against the Safety of Civil Aviation* (1973), 974 U.N.T.S. 178; *Convention on the Prevention and Punishment of Crimes against Internationally Protected Persons, including Diplomatic Agents* (1973), 1035 U.N.T.S. 167; *International Convention against the Taking of Hostages* (1979), 1316 U.N.T.S. 205; *Convention on the Physical Protection of Nuclear Material* (1980), 1456 U.N.T.S. 124; *Protocol for the Suppression of Unlawful Acts of Violence at Airports Serving International Civil Aviation* (1988); *Convention for the Suppression of Unlawful Acts against the Safety of Maritime Navigation* (1988), 1678 U.N.T.S. 221; *Protocol for the Suppression of Unlawful Acts against the Safety of Fixed Platforms Located on the Continental Shelf* (1988); *International Convention for the Suppression of Terrorist Bombings* (1997), 2149 U.N.T.S. 256; and *International Convention for the Suppression of the Financing of Terrorism*, U.N. Doc. A/RES/54/109 (1999).

This generic definition of terrorist activity "includes a conspiracy, attempt or threat to commit any such act or omission, or being an accessory after the fact or counselling in relation to any such act or omission," so-called inchoate offences.

It also includes an exemption for situations of armed conflict. Thus, it "does not include an act or omission that is committed during an armed conflict and that, at the time and in the place of its commission, is in accordance with customary international law or conventional international law applicable to the conflict, or the activities undertaken by military forces of a state in the exercise of their official duties, to the extent that those activities are governed by other rules of international law."

As Table 7.1 portrays, the generic definition of "terrorist activity" in the *Criminal Code* is broader than international definitions and those employed by key allied nations. It raises five issues warranting further discussion: the scope of penalized action; the criminalization of motive; the duplication of inchoate crimes; the significance of the armed conflict/military forces exemption; and the presence of a dual terrorism definition in the *Criminal Code*.

a)   Scope of Penalized Action

The violent acts or omissions now listed in paragraphs (A) through (E) of the generic definition of terrorist activity are considerably broader than those found in existing terrorism conventions. The piecemeal conventions are focused on specific violent acts on, for instance, aircraft or ships, or specific terrorist techniques, such as bombing and hostage-taking. The more general definitions of terrorist act found in the *International Convention for the Suppression of the Financing of Terrorism* are restricted to acts "intended to cause death or serious bodily injury," a focus reflected also in U.N. Security Council Resolution 1566[36] and in definitions proposed by the U.N. Secretary-General's 2004 High Level Panel on Threats, Challenges and Change[37] and by the secretary-general himself.[38]

The Canadian definition, in comparison, is broader, referring also to a risk to public health or safety. And it, like the proposed comprehensive

---

36   S/RES/1566 (2004) (describing terrorism as "criminal acts, including against civilians, committed with the intent to cause death or serious bodily injury, or taking of hostages").

37   U.N. High Level Panel, *A More Secure World*, U.N. Doc. A/59/565 at para. 164 (2004), online: www.un.org/secureworld/.

38   U.N. Secretary-General, *In Larger Freedom*, U.N. Doc. A/59/2005 at para. 91 (2005), online: www.un.org/largerfreedom/.

Table 7.1: Comparative Definitions of Terrorism

Source	Physical Act — Death or bodily harm	Violent acts	Hostage taking	Endangering life	Risk to health or safety	Substantial property damage	Disruption of infrastructure	Mental Element — Intended to intimidate or compel: Person	Population/Public	Government	International Organization	Political, religious or ideological motive
Domestic Definitions												
General Criminal Code (Canada) definition[1]	✓			✓	✓	✓	✓		✓	✓	✓	✓
Criminal Code (Canada) definition for terrorism financing[2]	✓								✓	✓	✓	
U.K. definition[3]		✓		✓	✓	✓	✓ [4]		✓	✓		✓
Australian definition[5]	✓			✓	✓	✓	✓ [6]		✓	✓		✓
New Zealand definition[7]	✓				✓ [8]	✓	✓		✓	✓	✓	✓
U.S. federal definition (international terrorism)[9]		✓		✓					✓	✓		
U.S. federal definition (domestic terrorism)[10]				✓				✓	✓	✓		
International Definitions												
International Convention for the Suppression of the Financing of Terrorism[11]	✓		✓					✓	✓	✓	✓	
Draft comprehensive anti-terrorism convention	✓					✓	✓		✓	✓	✓	
U.N. Security Council Resolution 1566	✓		✓						✓	✓	✓	

[1] Criminal Code, R.S.C. 1985, c. C-46, s. 83.01(1).
[2] Ibid., s. 83.02(b).
[3] Terrorism Act 2000 (U.K.), 2000, c. 11, s. 2.
[4] "Designed seriously to interfere with or seriously disrupt an electronic system."
[5] Criminal Code Act 1995, No. 12, 1995 (as amended), s. 101.1.
[6] "Seriously interferes with, seriously disrupts, or destroys, an electronic system."
[7] Terrorism Suppression Act 2002, No. 34, 2002, s. 5.
[8] Includes also "introduction or release of a disease-bearing organism, if likely to devastate the national economy of a country."
[9] 18 U.S.C ¶ 2331(1).
[10] 18 U.S.C ¶ 2331(5).
[11] For a discussion of these instruments, see Chapter 6.

international convention on terrorism,[39] extends to substantial property damage. In paragraph (D) of the Canadian definition, this property damage must be *likely* to result in death, serious bodily harm or endangerment to life or constitute a serious risk to public health or safety.[40]

Paragraph (D) possibly reaches as far as now commonplace anti-globalization protests; that is, it may apply to vandalism that, depending on its scope, could likely constitute a serious risk to the health or safety of the public or a segment of the public. The prospect that these sorts of acts might be tarred with the terrorist activity designation has excited controversy among civil liberties groups.[41]

A fourth, self-standing act or omission said to constitute a terrorist activity is serious interference with or serious disruption to an essential service, facility or system. The latter is qualified to exclude "advocacy, protest, dissent or stoppage of work" that is not intended to result in death, serious bodily harm or endangerment to life or constitute a serious risk to public health or safety. In its original iteration, this provision, paragraph (E), qualified these protest activities with the word "lawful," a caveat that provoked concern that actions that were nominally unlawful (for example, a wild-cat strike) might be drawn within the ambit of the paragraph. The word was deleted, but some critics continue to voice concern about overbreadth, not least because of uncertainty concerning the meaning of an essential service, facility or system.[42]

b) Criminalizing Motive

i) Scope

The scope of the predicate acts included in the Canadian definition necessitated a subsequent effort to limit its reach. The Canadian def-

---

39   See Chapter 6.

40   The accused need not actually intend these consequences for their actions to be captured by the provision. Roach, "The New Terrorism Offences," above note 1 at 157. However, these consequences must be objectively (and almost certainly, given the stigma associated with the terrorist label, subjectively) foreseeable to satisfy constitutional requirements. For a discussion of stigma and *mens rea*, see *R. v. DeSousa*, [1992] 2 S.C.R. 944; *R. v. Creighton*, [1993] 3 S.C.R. 3.

41   For a discussion of "terrorist activity" and its application to these sorts of protest movements, see, for example, British Columbia Civil Liberties Association, Brief Prepared for the House of Commons Subcommittee on Public Safety and National Security and the Senate Special Committee on the *Anti-Terrorism Act*, *National Security: Curbing the Excess To Protect Freedom and Democracy* (October 2005), online: www.bccla.org/othercontent/curbing%20excess.pdf; Canadian Civil Liberties Association, Brief Prepared for the Special Senate Committee on the *Anti-terrorism Act* (May 2005), online: www.ccla.org/pos/briefs/C-36%20Brief%20As%20Submitted.pdf.

42   Roach, "The New Terrorism Offences," above note 1 at 158.

inition does this by grafting both intent and motive elements onto the predicate acts.

The intent requirement in the generic definition of "terrorist activity" is broader, but similar in thrust, to the generic definitions of terrorist act found in the terrorism financing convention, U.N. Security Council Resolution 1566[43] and in definitions proposed by the U.N. Secretary-General's 2004 High Level Panel on Threats, Challenges and Change[44] and by the secretary-general himself.[45] Specifically, the intent element found in the *Criminal Code* is the intention to intimidate "the public, or a segment of the public, with regard to its security, including its economic security, or compelling a person, a government or a domestic or an international organization to do or to refrain from doing any act, whether the public or the person, government or organization is inside or outside Canada." Note the reference to compelling a single "person," an inclusion that greatly broadens the reach of the intent provision relative to international analogues.

More controversially, the 2001 Canadian definition followed the 2000 U.K. model by including a motive element. This motive provision—to an act undertaken for a "political, religious or ideological purpose, objective or cause"—was added to distinguish terrorist activity from regular criminal offences. As described by Stanley Cohen, "these words were inserted in order to distinguish terrorist activity from other criminal behaviours that also are intended to intimidate people by use of violence."[46]

ii)   Criticism

Nevertheless, the motive clause has provoked animated discussion, and a recent constitutional challenge.

Even before the promulgation of the ATA, Kent Roach urged that this element broke with a strong Canadian tradition of being indifferent to the motive underlying a crime. He queried whether "criminalization of certain political, religious or ideological motives violates fundamental freedoms in the *Charter* such as freedom of expression and conscience or equality rights."[47] As Roach also observed, freedom

---

43   S/RES/1566 (2004) (describing terrorism as "criminal acts, including against civilians, committed with the intent to cause death or serious bodily injury, or taking of hostages").

44   U.N. High Level Panel, *A More Secure World*, above note 37 at para. 164.

45   U.N. Secretary-General, *In Larger Freedom*, above note 38 at para. 91.

46   Stanley A. Cohen, *Privacy, Crime and Terror: Legal Rights and Security in a Time of Peril* (Markham, ON: LexisNexis Canada, 2005) at 242, n145.

47   Roach, "The New Terrorism Offences," above note 1 at 136.

of expression excludes acts of violence, and even if it did not, criminalization of violent expression would be easily justified under section 1 of the *Charter*. Still, "the implications of prohibiting certain political or religious motives in our criminal law could be far-reaching."[48] Since Professor Roach wrote those words, the inclusion of motive in the definition of terrorist activity has generated further criticism in both the academic literature and among civil and human rights organizations.[49]

Strictly speaking, the motive element increases the burden on the Crown. Where the latter invokes "terrorist activity" in the course of prosecuting an offence, it will have to prove beyond a reasonable doubt the motive as much as the other elements of the definition. Proving motive is notoriously difficult.[50] That fact has two implications. First, it may make the definition of terrorist activity unusable, and thus of little relevance. Second (and alternatively), it may induce law enforcement and prosecutors to focus resources on investigative techniques likely to unearth motive. Subsequently, the express statutory emphasis on motive will have a bearing on the admissibility of any resulting evidence. Evidence of the motive element—such as the presence of *jihadi* literature in the possession of the accused—might be highly prejudicial, and potentially inadmissible. However, in balancing prejudice against probative value, the court would likely be swayed by the fact that the very definition of terrorist activity obliges evidence of motive. Put another way, the probative value of this evidence is enhanced by the motive clause.

The bluntest of the investigative techniques the government might employ to unearth this critical evidence of motive, and the one that civil libertarian organizations warn about most vociferously, is ethnic profiling—that is, the singling out of entire classes of individuals on the basis of shared social qualities that may have little to do with an actual propensity to commit crimes.[51] In response to complaints from

---

48   *Ibid.*

49   See, for example, Maureen Webb, "Essential Liberty or a Little Temporary Safety? The Review of the Canadian *Anti-terrorism Act*" (2005) 51 Crim. L.Q. 53 at 62.

50   For a discussion on this point, see Don Stuart, *Canadian Criminal Law: A Treatise*, 3d ed. (Toronto: Carswell, 1995) at 199. On the conventional role of motive in criminal prosecutions, see *R. v. Lewis*, [1979] 2 S.C.R. 821.

51   See critique by Canadian Association of University Teachers (CAUT), Submission To The House Of Commons, Subcommittee On Public Safety And National Security Regarding The Review Of The *Anti-Terrorism Act* (February 2005), online: www.caut.ca/en/publications/briefs/2005anti_terrorism_brief.pdf. For an academic discussion of ethnic profiling in the national security context, see Reem Bahdi, "No Exit: Racial Profiling and Canada's War Against Terrorism" (2003) 41 Osgoode Hall L.J. 293; Sujit Choudhry & Kent Roach, "Racial and

the Muslim community, Canada's security and intelligence community has repeatedly denied that it engages in ethnic profiling. Indeed, raw ethnic profiling is almost certainly an ineffective investigative technique, diverting scare resources towards a focus on social qualities and away from narrower indicators of risk. The issue continues to percolate, however, in public discourse.[52]

Section 83.01(1.1) constitutes a modest response to these concerns. It reads "for greater certainty, the expression of a political, religious or ideological thought, belief or opinion does not come within ... the definition 'terrorist activity' ... unless it constitutes an act or omission that satisfies the criteria of that paragraph." This section, simply reasserting what should be obvious from a careful reading of the rest of the section, does not preclude ethnic profiling. It simply underscores that ethnic profiling alone does not suffice.

It also falls short of the clearer antidiscrimination provision found in Canada's *Emergencies Act*. The latter statute states emphatically that it does not confer on the government the power to make orders or regulations "providing for the detention, imprisonment or internment" of Canadian citizens or permanent residents "on the basis of race, national or ethnic origin, colour, religion, sex, age or mental or physical disability."[53] No such section (tied to terrorism investigations) was added to the ATA in 2001, despite calls by civil libertarians and some parliamentarians that Parliament do so.[54]

iii) Constitutionality

These objections to the motive clause have attracted parliamentary and court attention. In 2007, the special senate committee reviewing

---

Ethnic Profiling: Statutory Discretion, Constitutional Remedies, and Democratic Accountability," (2003) 41 Osgoode Hall L.J. 1; Kent Roach, "Three Year Review of Canada's *Anti-Terrorism Act*: The Need for Greater Restraint and Fairness, Non-Discrimination, and Special Advocates" (2005) 54 U.N.B.L.J. 308 at 322 [Roach, "Three Year Review"].

52 See discussion in Janice Tibbetts, "Racial Profiling 'Fundamentally Stupid'" *National Post* (16 August 2006) A.5. See also Commission of Inquiry into the Actions of Canadian Officials in Relation to Maher Arar, *A New Review Mechanism for the RCMP's National Security Activities* (2006) at 436, online: www.ararcommission.ca/eng/EnglishReportDec122006.pdf [Arar inquiry, Policy Report].

53 *Emergencies Act*, above note 31, s. 4.

54 In 2007, the senate addressed concerns about ethnic profiling in its report on anti-terrorism law by calling for enhanced training of security and intelligence services and the implementation of clear antidiscrimination policies. Special Senate Committee on the *Anti-terrorism Act, Fundamental Justice in Extraordinary Times* (February 2007) at 24, online: www.parl.gc.ca/39/1/parlbus/commbus/senate/Com-e/anti-e/rep-e/rep02feb07-e.htm.

the anti-terrorism law recommended that the clause be removed.[55] Its Commons counterpart recommended that it be retained, a position subsequently endorsed by the government.[56] Of more immediate legal effect, in 2006, the motive clause was found unconstitutional by the Ontario Superior Court of Justice. In that decision, *R. v. Khawaja*, the court concluded that the effect of the motive clause "will be to focus investigative and prosecutorial scrutiny on the political, religious and ideological beliefs, opinions and expressions of persons and groups both in Canada and abroad." Because of the chilling effect this will have on the expression of such views, the motive clause transgressed *Charter* guarantees of "freedoms of conscience, religion, thought, belief, expression and association."[57] As the court could find no plausible reason why a definition of terrorist activity necessitated the presence of a motive clause, it was not saved under section 1.

In the result, the motive clause was struck out, while the rest of the definition of terrorist activity was left intact. That result technically reduced the evidentiary burden on the Crown: the prosecutor had one fewer thing to prove. More broadly, the residual definition of terrorist activity swelled with the removal of the motive clause. Now acts creating a risk of death or serious bodily harm or to health or safety or which cause serious interference to an essential service are terrorist activities, if done (for instance) to compel a *single* person to do or refrain from doing something, irrespective of their motive. A vast array of criminal activity could now fall within this definition, to the point that the exceptional concept of "terrorist activity" has almost swallowed the *Criminal Code*.

For exactly this reason, if the *Khawaja* decision is upheld or becomes the preferred position of other courts or parliamentarians, the definition of terrorist activity will have to be scaled back, and ideally harmonized with the international definition found in the terrorism financing convention: an act "intended to cause death or serious bodily harm to a civilian or to any other person not taking an active part in the hostilities in a situation of armed conflict, if the purpose of that act

55   *Ibid.* at 13.

56   House of Commons Subcommittee on the Review of the *Anti-terrorism Act, Rights, Limits, Security: A Comprehensive Review of the* Anti-terrorism Act *and Related Issues* (March 2007) at 9, online: http://cmte.parl.gc.ca/cmte/CommitteePublication.aspx?COM=10804&Lang=1&SourceId=199086. Canada, *Government Response: Seventh Report of the Standing Committee on Public Safety and National Security, "Rights, Limits, Security: A Comprehensive Review of the* Anti-terrorism Act *and Related Issues"* (Presented to the House on 18 July 2007) at 3, online: www.justice.gc.ca/en/anti_terr/rep_res/cc_hc/index.html.

57   [2006] O.J. No. 4245 at para. 58 (S.C.J.).

or omission, by its nature or context, is to intimidate the public, or to compel a government or an international organization to do or refrain from doing any act."

This definition restricts the predicate acts to ones of significant violence—that is, those causing death or serious injury—and requires that the purpose be the intimidation or compulsion of a "public" or "government," and not merely a single person. It is, in other words, not as dizzying in its scope as the post-*Khawaja* Canadian "terrorist activity" concept.

c)   Inchoate Crimes Squared

A third concern about the definition of "terrorist activity" relates to its interface with the new terrorist offences linked to this concept. As noted, the definition of "terrorist activity" includes "inchoate" offences—conspiracies, attempts, threats, accessory or counselling—tied to the predicate acts of violence comprising the terrorist activity. When considered alongside the specific new criminal offences created by the ATA—many of them inchoate offences themselves—it layers inchoate offence upon an inchoate activity. What Roach calls the "piling of inchoate liability on top of inchoate crimes"[58] has been criticized as alien to Canadian criminal law.[59] As Roach observes, Canadian courts

> have rejected attempted prosecutions of far-removed crimes such as counseling someone to counsel an offence or attempting to conspire to commit an offence. ... Nevertheless, it is doubtful that the courts can refuse to do so under the *Anti-terrorism Act* because Parliament has clearly provided for such expansions of criminal liability. The net of criminal liability has been widened in complex and undesirable ways.[60]

Widening the net is exactly what the ATA intended. Criminalizing actions that are mere preparation may be unusual in the Canadian criminal law tradition, with its focus on reaction rather than pre-emption. Still, as proponents of the new model urged, "the nature of terrorism requires a different approach to disrupt and disable the terrorist network before it can carry out its design."[61]

---

58   Roach, "The New Terrorism Offences," above note 1 at 159 *et seq.*

59   See also critique by Canadian Association of University Teachers (CAUT), above note 51.

60   Roach, *September 11*, above note 1 at 36. See, for example, *R. v. Déry*, 2006 SCC 53 for a recent case in which the Supreme Court rejected piling an inchoate upon an inchoate—in this case, attemping a conspiracy.

61   Richard Mosley, "Preventing Terrorism—Bill C-36: the *Anti-terrorism Act 2001*," in D. Daubney *et al.*, eds., *Terrorism, Law and Democracy* (Montreal: Éditions Thémis, 2002) at 152.

d) Armed Conflict Exemption

A fourth issue raised by the terrorist activity concept relates to the exception under that definition for an "act or omission that is committed during an armed conflict and that, at the time and in the place of its commission, is in accordance with customary international law or conventional international law applicable to the conflict." This language is different from analogous exceptions found in international treaties, discussed in Chapter 6.

These treaties include an armed conflict exception, but generally restrict it to "armed forces." Armed forces is a term understood in international humanitarian law to mean "all organized armed forces, groups and units which are under a command responsible to that Party for the conduct of its subordinates" and subject to an internal disciplinary system which, *inter alia*, "shall enforce compliance with the rules of international law applicable in armed conflict."[62] Armed forces are not, however, the only "lawful" combatants in an armed conflict—that is, combatants who may use force against at least military objectives and still act in accordance with the international law applicable to the conflict. Other lawful combatants include certain resistance movements or a so-called *levée en masse* (basically, a spontaneous civilian uprising) that meet the requirements of the Geneva Conventions and comport themselves in accordance with international humanitarian law. These entities would be exempted under the Canadian definition of "terrorist activity," but not by international terrorism treaties.

It is also notable that the armed conflict exemption in the terrorism treaties applies where the actions of the armed forces in question are "governed" by international humanitarian law. This language leaves violations of international humanitarian law to be penalized under that law's own regime, if at all. In comparison, the *Criminal Code* exception applies only to actions that are "in accordance" with applicable international law. It does not exclude, therefore, a war crime. The latter may, therefore, be a "terrorist activity" in addition to a violation of war crimes provisions found elsewhere in Canadian law.

e) Multiple Definitions

A last issue raised by the Canadian definition of "terrorist activity" is the inclusion of a different definition for those *Criminal Code* provisions

---

62   *Protocol Additional to the Geneva Conventions of 12 August 1949, and relating to the Protection of Victims of International Armed Conflicts*, Art. 43 [AP I].

relating to terrorism financing.[63] The latter provisions implement the *International Convention for the Suppression of the Financing of Terrorism.* Since this international treaty defines terrorism more narrowly than does the "terrorist activity" concept, the *Criminal Code* has one definition for some of the financing crimes, and another for everything else.[64]

2) Terrorist Group

a) *Criminal Code* Listing

i) Definition of Terrorist Group
Subsection 83.01(1) also includes an unprecedented definition of "terrorist group." A terrorist group is "*a*) an entity that has as one of its purposes or activities facilitating or carrying out any terrorist activity, or *b*) a listed entity, and includes an association of such entities." "Entity" means "a person, group, trust, partnership or fund or an unincorporated association or organization" while a "listed entity" means "an entity on a list established by the Governor in Council under section 83.05."

Paragraph (a) means that a terrorist group is a person, group or organization[65] that has as one (and not necessarily all) of its purposes or activities facilitating or carrying out one of the acts or omissions found in the piecemeal international conventions or in the generic definition of terrorist activity discussed above. As Roach has noted, under this

---

63 The multiplication of definitions also drew comments from the Special Senate Committee on the *Anti-terrorism Act.* This body recommended harmonization around a single definition. See Senate, *Fundamental Justice in Extraordinary Times*, above note 54 at 17.

64 Thus, to be guilty of some of the terrorism financing offences described below, a person must commit the act or omission proscribed by one of the multilateral piecemeal international conventions or one that is "intended to cause death or serious bodily harm to a civilian or to any other person not taking an active part in the hostilities in a situation of armed conflict, if the purpose of that act or omission, by its nature or context, is to intimidate the public, or to compel a government or an international organization to do or refrain from doing any act." (*Criminal Code*, above, Table 7.1, note 1, s. 83.02.) As already noted, this definition is much narrower than the generic definition in the Canadian concept of "terrorist activity." However, as Table 7.2 portrays, the narrower terrorist financing definition is associated with a much broader extraterritorial jurisdiction under the *Criminal Code* than is the broader generic Canadian definition.

65 Organization, in turn, includes "a public body, body corporate, society, company, firm, partnership, trade union or municipality, or (b) an association of persons that (i) is created for a common purpose, (ii) has an operational structure, and (iii) holds itself out to the public as an association of persons." *Criminal Code, ibid.*, s. 2.

definition, a "terrorist group need not have engaged in acts of terrorism; it may only be associated with others that have committed terrorism or that may facilitate the commission of terrorism in the future."[66]

Alternatively, under paragraph (b), a terrorist group is a "listed entity"; that is, one listed by the GIC—effectively, the federal Cabinet.

ii) Listing Process

This listing process—another subject of controversy in the ATA—is governed by section 83.05. That provision, in subsection (1), empowers Cabinet to list an entity by regulation if "on the recommendation of the Minister of Public Safety and Emergency Preparedness, the Governor in Council is satisfied that there are reasonable grounds to believe that (*a*) the entity has knowingly carried out, attempted to carry out, participated in or facilitated a terrorist activity; or (*b*) the entity is knowingly acting on behalf of, at the direction of or in association with an entity referred to in paragraph (*a*)."

Notably, regulatory listing is available only where Cabinet has reasonable grounds to believe that the entity has actually undertaken (or attempted, participated in or facilitated) the terrorist activity, or is working for or with an entity that has. Listing is impermissible where an entity simply has a terrorist activity as one of its "purposes." An entity that clamours for terrorist acts but that has not actually done (or attempted, participated or facilitated) terrorist activity can presumably not be listed, although it may ultimately be considered a terrorist group on "purpose" grounds under the first definition of a terrorist group; that is, that found in paragraph (a) of the definition in subsection 83.01(1).

Section 83.05 includes procedural rules on regulatory listing. As noted, Cabinet may only list on "reasonable grounds to believe." Further, the minister of public safety may only propose to Cabinet an entity for listing on "reasonable grounds to believe" that that entity meets the criteria for that listing. "Reasonable grounds to believe" is a standard employed often in Canadian law to justify warrants and searches.[67] In another context, it has been said to exist where "there is an objective basis ... which is based on compelling and credible information."[68]

---

66   Roach, *September 11*, above note 1 at 36.

67   See discussion in Chapter 14.

68   *Charkaoui v. Canada (Citizenship and Immigration)*, [2007] SCC 9 at para. 39 [*Charkaoui*] (discussing the standard in relation to detentions under *Immigration and Refugee Protection Act* security certificates). Federal Court jurisprudence in the same case has described this standard as "a serious possibility that

iii) De-listing Process

a.   Ministerial Recommendation

Section 83.05 anticipates a listed entity applying to the minister for a decision on "whether there are reasonable grounds to recommend to the Governor in Council that the applicant no longer be a listed entity."[69] Symmetry with the "reasonable grounds" standard for the original listing suggests that the minister's decision might be made where an "objective basis ... based on compelling and credible information" for de-listing exists. Such a standard represents a relatively undemanding threshold, but it is not one that will necessarily produce an actual de-listing. At best, the minister will make a *recommendation* for de-listing on this gentle standard.

The section is far from clear on this point, but Cabinet is presumably free to reject this recommendation; that is, after all, the nature of a recommendation. No grounds for rejecting a de-listing recommendation are provided in the section, leading to a natural supposition that a de-listing may be refused if the original "reasonable grounds to believe" the entity qualifies for listing persist.

The minister's response to the application for a de-listing recommendation is subject to constraints. First, a failure by the minister to respond within sixty days will result in a deemed recommendation against de-listing. Second, the minister must give notice "without delay" of any deemed or actual recommendation.

b.   Judicial Review

Subsequently, the entity has a right to initiate judicial review before a designated judge of the Federal Court for the next sixty days. The latter is to "examine in private, any security or criminal intelligence reports considered in listing the applicant and hear any other evidence or information that may be presented by or on behalf of the Minister and may, at his or her request, hear all or part of that evidence or information in the absence of the applicant and any counsel representing the applicant, if the judge is of the opinion that the disclosure of the information would injure national security or endanger the safety of any person."[70] The section is clear that the judge "may receive into evidence anything that, in the opinion of the judge, is reliable and appropriate, even if it would not otherwise be admissible under Canadian law, and

---

the facts exist based on reliable, credible evidence." *Charkaoui (Re)*, [2004] 3 F.C.R. 32 (F.C.).

69   *Criminal Code*, above, Table 7.1, note 1, s. 83.05(2).

70   *Ibid.*, s. 83.05(6).

may base his or her decision on that evidence."[71] The implications of this language are discussed in Chapter 15.

For its part, the applicant has a right to be heard, and is to be provided by the court with "a statement summarizing the information available to the judge so as to enable the applicant to be reasonably informed of the reasons for the decision, without disclosing any information the disclosure of which would, in the judge's opinion, injure national security or endanger the safety of any person."[72] The statute includes supplemental provisions on information obtained in confidence from a foreign state or international organization.[73] As noted in Chapter 12, Canada is a ready consumer of foreign intelligence. The government is, therefore, acutely sensitive to the implications that disclosure of this information would have on the willingness of foreign agencies to share intelligence. The minister may seek to use this information in the listing process, but if the judge concludes that the information is capable of summarized and sanitized disclosure to the applicant, the judge is to return the information to the government and not to consider it in his or her deliberations.[74]

Ultimately, the judge determines whether the minister's decision is "reasonable on the basis of the information available to the judge" and if not, he or she must "order that the applicant no longer be a listed entity."[75] The qualification of reasonableness "on the basis of the information available to the judge" presumably means that a judge may rely on information not considered by the government in the listing decision. Further, the judge need not have access to all the information available to the minister (or Cabinet) before issuing a decision, nor must his or her decision be based strictly on the sanitized version of the information disclosed to the applicant themselves.[76]

c. Response to Listing Complaints

If the applicant is successful, the minister is to publish notice of the de-listing in the *Canada Gazette*.[77] If unsuccessful, the applicant may not reapply absent a material change of circumstances or until completion of a mandatory two-year review of the entire list. The latter is to be completed by the minister "to determine whether there are still reasonable grounds ... for an entity to be a listed entity." Following the review,

---

71 *Ibid.*, s. 83.05(6.1).
72 *Ibid.*, s. 83.05(6).
73 *Ibid.*, s. 83.06.
74 *Ibid.*
75 *Ibid.*, s. 85.05(6).
76 See discussion in Roach, *September 11*, above note 1 at 37.
77 *Criminal Code*, above, Table 7.1, note 1, s. 85.05(7).

which should be completed within 120 days, the minister is to "make a recommendation to the Governor in Council as to whether the entity should remain a listed entity."[78]

The statute also includes a process for clarifying "mistaken identities." Thus, an entity that claims not to be listed may apply for a certificate to this effect from the government. The latter is to issue this certificate within fifteen days if the entity is not, in fact, listed.[79]

iv) Criticisms

a. Procedural

An obvious omission in the listing scheme is an opportunity for the entity to have notice or opportunity to comment *prior* to listing. Commenting on this absence, Roach has urged that "after-the-fact judicial review … may be too late for a group that has been erroneously placed on the official list of terrorist organizations. They will have been stigmatized as a terrorist group and people will be afraid that they may be charged with terrorism offences if they participate or give money to the organization."[80] Even if successful in its de-listing application, this stigma will not be easily expunged.[81]

The absence of notice and comment also runs counter to a line of constitutional jurisprudence under section 7 of the *Charter* entitling persons to "fundamental justice"—including, especially, notice and comment—where life, liberty or security of the person are jeopardized. As discussed later in this chapter, a terrorist group listing obviously imperils liberty for those who interact with it and the stigma of being tarred a member of a terrorist group is likely so great as to trench on security of the person.[82]

The Supreme Court of Canada has held that notice and comment obligations under section 7 persist even in national security cases, albeit

---

78   *Ibid.*, ss. 85.05(8)–(10).
79   *Ibid.*, s. 83.07.
80   Roach, *September 11*, above note 1 at 37.
81   See discussion in Irwin Cotler, "Terrorism, Security and Rights: The Dilemma of Democracies" (2002–03) 14 N.J.C.L. 13 at 47.
82   Reputational injury almost never violates section 7. Nevertheless, rare circumstances exist where a psychological harm inflicted by government proceedings could attract section 7 protections. *Blencoe v. British Columbia (Human Rights Commission)*, [2000] 2 S.C.R. 307 at para. 81 ("In order for security of the person to be triggered in [cases involving alleged psychological harm], the impugned state action must have had a serious and profound effect on the respondent's psychological integrity …. There must be state interference with an individual interest of fundamental importance").

in attenuated form. Specifically, in *Suresh*, the Court considered whether, among other things, a refugee claimant earmarked for deportation on the ground of being a suspected terrorist had any constitutional notice or comment protections. The Court concluded that, confronted with the prospect of being deported to torture, the applicant "must be informed of the case to be met" and that an "opportunity be provided to respond to the case presented to the Minister," including through the presentation of evidence countering the view that he constituted a national security threat.[83] Information provided by the government to inform Suresh of the case against him was legitimately "subject to privilege or similar valid reasons for reduced disclosure, such as safeguarding confidential public security documents."[84] Further, the Court emphasized that "the Minister must be allowed considerable discretion in evaluating future risk and security concerns. This factor also suggests a degree of deference to the Minister's choice of procedures since Parliament has signaled the difficulty of the decision by leaving to the Minister the choice of how best to make it."[85] Nevertheless, notice and comment—however rudimentary—was available to an actual suspected terrorist.

There is reason to believe, therefore, that the listing process in section 83.05 is constitutionally suspect. If so, then there will be some obligation on government to give notice—and open the door to comment—prior to listing, even if these procedural opportunities are rudimentary. As a practical matter, of course, it is not certain how the government would give notice to sometimes clandestine organizations. Notice via newspaper and in the *Canada Gazette* may be the best that can be expected.

In may also be the case, in the wake of the Supreme Court's holding in *Charkaoui*,[86] that the listing process must include the participation of a security-cleared special advocate, able to probe all the secret evidence relied upon by the government in the listing and restoring an element of full answer and defence guaranteed by section 7 of the *Charter*.

b.   Interface with Terrorism Offences Connected to Terrorist Groups

Another criticism relates to the link between the listing process and the terrorist offences associated with terrorist groups. As discussed later, the *Criminal Code* creates a number of new crimes that arise when a person has a particular relationship with a terrorist group. A key issue

---

83   *Suresh v. Canada (Minister of Citizenship and Immigration)*, [2002] 1 S.C.R. 3 at paras. 122–23 [*Suresh*].
84   *Ibid.* at para. 122.
85   *Ibid.* at para. 120.
86   Above note 68.

is whether the mere listing by the government of an entity as a terrorist group suffices to satisfy what would otherwise be a key element of these offences; namely, that the entity in question was a terrorist group. Typically, the Crown would be obliged to prove this element beyond a reasonable doubt. The administrative act of listing might, however, be interpreted as creating an irrefutable presumption that the entity in question was, in fact, a terrorist group, easing the Crown's burden in securing a conviction.

In his pointed critique, David Paciocco urges that because of the way "terrorist group" listing operates, "persons stand the risk of being convicted of" the offences linked to terrorist groups "without proof ever being offered of the actual activities of the group and without anyone ever having established beyond a reasonable doubt that the group really is a terrorist group";[87] after all, the entity can be listed by the government simply on "reasonable grounds" to believe a connection to terrorist activity. Paciocco concludes that through "indirection and complicated drafting, the government has attempted to lower its standard of proof, and to save itself from discharging its full burden of proof with respect to each of the 'terrorist group' offences."[88]

b)   Terrorist-Financing Charities

The ATA also introduced the *Charities Registration (Security Information) Act*.[89] This statute marks "Canada's commitment to participating in concerted international efforts to deny support to those who engage in terrorist activities, to protect the integrity of the registration system for charities under the *Income Tax Act* and to maintain the confidence of Canadian taxpayers that the benefits of charitable registration are made available only to organizations that operate exclusively for charitable purposes."[90] Under the Act, the government may issue a "certificate stating that it is their opinion, based on information, that there are reasonable grounds to believe that an applicant for charitable status or registered charity"

- "has made, makes or will make available any resources, directly or indirectly, to an entity that is a listed entity" within the meaning of subsection 83.01(1) of the *Criminal Code* (that is, a terrorist group);

---

87   David Paciocco, "Constitutional Casualties of September 11: Limiting the Legacy of the *Anti-terrorism Act*" (2002) 16 Sup. Ct. L. Rev. (2d) 185 at 196.
88   On this issue, see also discussion in Roach, "Three Year Review," above note 51 at 321.
89   *Charities Registration (Security Information) Act*, S.C. 2001, c. 41, s. 113.
90   *Ibid.*, s. 2.

- "made available any resources, directly or indirectly, to an entity as defined in subsection 83.01(1) of the *Criminal Code* and the entity was at that time, and continues to be, engaged in terrorist activities ... or activities in support of them"; or
- "makes or will make available any resources, directly or indirectly, to an entity as defined in subsection 83.01(1) of the *Criminal Code* and the entity engages or will engage in terrorist activities ... or activities in support of them."[91]

If the certificate is subsequently adjudged reasonable by a Federal Court judge, "the applicant will be ineligible to become a registered charity or the registration of the registered charity will be revoked."[92] Proceedings before this judge are governed by confidentiality rules identical in all material respects to those available in *Criminal Code* listing proceedings.[93]

The Federal Court determination on the reasonableness of the certificate is final,[94] subject to a ministerial review in the event of material changes in circumstance.[95]

3) Terrorism Offence

A final definition of importance in the ATA is "terrorism offence." A terrorism offence is broader than a terrorist activity. It is defined in section 2 of the *Criminal Code* as

(*a*) an offence under any of sections 83.02 to 83.04 [terrorism financing] or 83.18 to 83.23 [participating, facilitating, instructing and harbouring];

(*b*) an indictable offence under this or any other Act of Parliament committed for the benefit of, at the direction of or in association with a terrorist group;

(*c*) an indictable offence under this or any other Act of Parliament where the act or omission constituting the offence also constitutes a terrorist activity [for example, the *Criminal Code* provisions implementing the piecemeal international anti-terrorism conventions];[96] or

---

91 *Ibid.*, s. 4.
92 *Ibid.*, s. 5.
93 *Ibid.*, s. 6.
94 *Ibid.*, s. 8.
95 *Ibid.*, s. 10.
96 The Commons committee reviewing the *Anti-terrorism Act* recommended in 2007 that the language in this paragraph be replaced, simply, with "a terrorist

(d) a conspiracy or an attempt to commit, or being an accessory after the fact in relation to, or any counselling in relation to, an offence referred to in paragraph (a), (b) or (c).

Particular attention should be focused in paragraph (d), listing as terrorism offences conspiracies, attempts, accessories and counselling. The net effect of this provision is to create a triple inchoate upon an inchoate upon an inchoate activity.[97] For example, a terrorism offence includes: counselling a person to instruct a "person to carry out any activity for the benefit of ... a terrorist group, for the purpose of enhancing the ability of any terrorist group to facilitate or carry out a *terrorist activity*."[98] Notably, the generic definition of "terrorist activity" itself includes inchoate offences, such as counselling a person to undertake the acts of violence in the definition of terrorist activity. The net result of this layering of inchoate actions could be something like: counselling a person to instruct another person to enhance a terrorist group's ability to counsel yet another person to engage in one of the acts listed in the definition of terrorist activity. The orbit of persons wrapped into the definition of terrorism offences is, in other words, a very wide one, extending far beyond the actual perpetrators of an act of violence.

Because of the way "terrorism offences" are employed in the ATA, the "cubing" of inchoate offences extends the reach of the special provisions found in the *Criminal Code*—most notably, peace bond provision found in section 810.01 and discussed in Chapter 14 and the lawful access powers discussed in Chapter 11.

B. NEW OFFENCES

The ATA does not create a crime of "terrorist activity."[99] Nor does it criminalize mere membership in a "terrorist group." Rather, it grafts onto the *Criminal Code* "terrorist activity" as an aggravating factor in sentencing for regular crimes. Thus, under the ATA, a person convicted

---

activity." House of Commons Subcommittee on the Review of the *Anti-terrorism Act, Rights, Limits, Security: A Comprehensive Review of the Anti-terrorism Act and Related Issues*, above note 56 at 15.

97　For discussion, see Webb, "Essential Liberty," above note 49 at 67.

98　*Criminal Code*, above, Table 7.1, note 1, s. 83.21 [emphasis added].

99　The Commons committee studying the *Anti-terrorism Act* recommended in 2007 making it a specific crime to participate in terrorist activity. House of Commons Subcommittee on the Review of the *Anti-terrorism Act, Rights, Limits, Security: A Comprehensive Review of the Anti-terrorism Act and Related Issues*, above note 56 at 19.

of an indictable offence, other than one for which life imprisonment is the minimum sentence, is liable to imprisonment for life where that indictable offence is also a "terrorist activity."[100] A hostage taking undertaken for a political purpose, for example, will attract this penalty provision, while a hostage taking otherwise identical, but undertaken in a personal dispute, or in a botched getaway, will not.[101]

Further, "terrorist activity" and "terrorist group" are predicate concepts underlying a raft of new terrorist financing and inchoate offences. As noted by Roach, "the new offences in the *Anti-terrorism Act* were defended by the government as a means to disable and dismantle terrorist organizations before they could commit terrible acts of violence such as those seen on September 11. The act accomplishes this goal by criminalizing a broad range of involvement with terrorist groups."[102]

These offences are reproduced in Table 7.3. Broadly speaking, the new offences can be divided between those that are "terrorism offences," as defined above, and those that, while clearly terrorism-related, are not formal "terrorism offences."

1) Terrorism-Related Offences That Are Not Formal "Terrorism Offences"

The ATA includes several property offences that do not fall within the definition of "terrorism offence." These offences—largely duplicative of those found in the *Suppression of Terrorism Regulations* for entities listed there—are built around the concept of "terrorist group" and concern the transacting in property for or providing financial services to a terrorist group.[103] The *Criminal Code* also criminalizes a failure to disclose to the RCMP or CSIS the existence of terrorist group property in a person's possession or control,[104] and imposes reporting obligations in relation to terrorist group property on financial institutions.[105] A more recent addition to the *Criminal Code* is a provision criminalizing

---

100 *Criminal Code*, above, Table 7.1, note 1, s. 83.27.
101 By the time of this writing, this distinction had potentially evaporated because of the constitutional ruling on the "motive" clause in the definition of terrorist activity, discussed above. Under the post-*Khawaja* definition, both sorts of hostage-taking could be regarded as terrorist activity.
102 Roach, *September 11*, above note 1 at 38.
103 *Criminal Code*, above, Table 7.1, note 1, ss. 83.08 and 83.12.
104 *Ibid.*, ss. 83.1 and 83.12.
105 *Ibid.*, ss. 83.11 & 83.12.

a hoax regarding "terrorist activity," designed to penalize particularly disruptive or dangerous false claims of terrorist activity.[106]

2) Formal "Terrorism Offences"

Most of the new crimes created by the ATA fall, however, within the definition of "terrorism offences." These offences may be subdivided in financing and property offences, inchoate offences tied to "terrorist activity" and inchoate offences tied to "terrorist groups."

a) Financing and Property Offences

The core terrorism financing offence in section 83.02 makes it a crime for anyone to "directly or indirectly, wilfully and without lawful justification or excuse" provide or collect property "intending that it be used or knowing that it will be used, in whole or in part, in order to carry out" one of the acts barred by the piecemeal international terrorism conventions, as listed in the definition of "terrorist activity," or "any other act or omission intended to cause death or serious bodily harm to a civilian or to any other person not taking an active part in the hostilities in a situation of armed conflict, if the purpose of that act or omission, by its nature or context, is to intimidate the public, or to compel a government or an international organization to do or refrain from doing any act." As noted, the latter, comprehensive terrorism definition differs from that found in the ATA's concept of "terrorist activity," and is instead drawn directly from the international terrorism financing convention. Other provisions of property and financing offences actually tied to the full definition of "terrorist activity" or "terrorist group" are reproduced in Table 7.3.

The terrorist property and financing provisions have elicited criticism for their breadth. Designed to disrupt the bankrolling of terrorist groups and activities, the provisions apply to bankers, landlords or virtually any other person providing property, financial or analogous services who knows that the client they serve is a terrorist group.[107] Their drafting has created unease among ATA critics. Of particular concern is section 83.03(b). This provision makes it an offence for a person to "directly or indirectly, collect[] property, provide[] or invite[] a person to provide, or make[] available property or financial or other related services ... (b) knowing that, in whole or part, they will be used by or will benefit a terrorist group." Exactly what must be proved by the

---

106 *Ibid.*, s. 83.231.
107 Roach, *September 11*, above note 1 at 41.

Crown to secure a conviction under this section is unclear. May a conviction be entered where the accused provides financial services to an entity he or she knows is listed by the government as a terrorist group? If so, as seems likely, must the government justify the original listing, or (as discussed earlier) is the government's administrative act of listing an entity accepted as a *fait accompli*, satisfying by decree a predicate element to the section 83.03 offence?

The ATA also introduced provisions for the seizure and forfeiture of property "owned or controlled by or on behalf of a terrorist group" or "that has been or will be used, in whole or in part, to facilitate or carry out a terrorist activity."[108] The breadth of the first justification for forfeiture means that seizure is available for property that has not actually been employed in a terrorist activity.[109] Moreover, there need not be an actual conviction — entered on a beyond-a-reasonable-doubt standard — under girding the forfeiture.[110] In fact, forfeiture is available by order of a Federal Court judge on a balance of probabilities standard, and proceeds from the disposition of the forfeited property may be used to "compensate victims of terrorist activities and to fund anti-terrorist initiatives," pursuant to regulations not yet made by the time of this writing.

b) New Inchoate Offences Connected to "Terrorist Activity"

The ATA's new inchoate offences that are connected to "terrorist activity" criminalize facilitating a terrorist activity, instructing to carry out a terrorist activity and harbouring or concealing a person who has or will likely carry out a terrorist activity (at least when done to facilitate the commission of this terrorist activity).

i) Facilitation

Facilitation is a particularly important concept, one that runs through many of the inchoate offences. Particularly notable is section 83.19, making it a crime for a person to knowingly facilitate a terrorist activity, but adding the caveat "whether or not ... the facilitator knows that a particular terrorist activity is facilitated."

It is not immediately clear how one can knowingly facilitate something when one does not know that it is facilitated. The most plausible reading of the provision is that it makes it a crime to facilitate intentionally terrorist activity *writ* large, regardless of whether the accused

---

108 *Criminal Code*, above, Table 7.1, note 1, ss. 83.13 & 83.14.
109 See discussion in Roach, *September 11*, above note 1 at 40.
110 *Ibid.*

knows of the specific, individual terrorist activity that is thereby facilitated.[111] For instance, a member of a terrorist cell may not be apprised of the details surrounding a planned terrorist operation that is nevertheless facilitated by that member's acts. The section reaches beyond this scenario by adding an additional caveat: a facilitation conviction may be secured regardless of whether "any particular terrorist activity was foreseen or planned at the time it was facilitated." A person may be convicted, in other words, of knowingly facilitating a particular terrorist activity that he or she did not know about and which, at the time he or she acted, was not even foreseen.[112]

ii) Instructing

The instructing provision is also broad. Section 83.22 makes it an offence to knowingly instruct,

> directly or indirectly, any person to carry out a terrorist activity, whether or not (a) the terrorist activity is actually carried out; (b) the accused instructs a particular person to carry out the terrorist activity; (c) the accused knows the identity of the person whom the accused instructs to carry out the terrorist activity; or (d) the person whom the accused instructs to carry out the terrorist activity knows that it is a terrorist activity.

Again, this provision would capture the remote leader of a terrorist group issuing a directive through a chain of terrorist cells to the ultimate perpetrator of a terrorist activity. Roach urges, however, that "general instructions to political or religious groups or the public at large to commit a terrorist activity could fall under this new offence."[113]

---

111 *Ibid.* at 43–44.

112 For a critical discussion, see Kent Roach, "New Terrorism Offences in Canadian Criminal Law, in D. Daubney *et al.*, eds., *Terrorism, Law and Democracy*, above note 61 at 136 ("is difficult to knowingly facilitate a terrorist activity when you do not know that 'any particular terrorist activity was foreseen or planned at the time it was facilitated.' There would seem to be little or no *mens rea* at the time that the *actus reus* of facilitation was committed.") But see also Errol Mendes, "Between Crime and War: Terrorism, Democracy and the Constitution" (2002) 14 N.J.C.L. 71 at 81. In *Khawaja*, above note 57 at para. 39, the Ontario Superior Court of Justice commented on these positions and held that it "is unnecessary that an accused be shown to have knowledge of the specific nature of terrorist activity he intends to aid, support, enhance or facilitate, as long as he knows it is terrorist activity in a general way. It doesn't have to be shown that an accused actually facilitated terrorist activity as long as it can be shown that he intended to do so."

113 Roach, *September 11*, above note 1 at 44.

If so, it comes close to a Canadian crime of incitement, one with broad reach.[114] A person calling for insurgency attacks — like roadside bombings — against U.S. forces in Iraq could run afoul of the provision.[115] It is also conceivable that a person promoting the notion of violent *jihad*, one that includes attacks against civilians, could be viewed as knowingly instructing a terrorist activity.

Calling for either of these actions would be grossly reprehensible, but criminalizing such expressions when voiced as a public statement (rather than as an actual directive in circumstances where it is likely to be carried out) may trench on a zone typically protected by free expression guarantees in section 2(b) of the *Charter*. As the Supreme Court of Canada has noted, "the term 'expression' as used in s. 2(b) of the *Charter* embraces all content of expression irrespective of the particular meaning or message sought to be conveyed."[116] While expression manifested in the form of acts of violence lies outside the parameters of the *Charter*, "threats of violence can only be so classified by reference to the content of their meaning. As such, ... their suppression must be justified under s. 1" as a justifiable limitation in a free and democratic society.[117] Since section 83.22 might capture a generalized call for terrorist violence (as much as a specific directive likely to be carried out), the question of overbreadth would likely be an important one for any court considering its legitimacy under section 1.

---

114 The criminalization of incitement (including "glorification") of terrorism has been particularly controversial in the United Kingdom, where such crimes were enacted in the *Terrorism Act, 2006* (U.K.), 2006, c. 11, s. 1. In March 2007, the House of Commons Subcommittee on the Review of the *Anti-terrorism Act* recommended the introduction of a glorification offence in Canada, urging that the existing instructing terrorist activity provision did not reach far enough. See House of Commons Subcommittee on the Review of the *Anti-terrorism Act*, *Rights, Limits, Security: A Comprehensive Review of the* Anti-terrorism Act *and Related Issues*, above note 56 at 12. The government would not commit to proposing such an offence by the time of this writing. Canada, *Government Response*, above note 56 at 5.

115 Per the discussion in Chapter 6, Iraqi insurgents likely do not fall within the ambit of the armed conflict exemption under the terrorist bombing treaty (or the analogous exemption to definition of "terrorist activity" discussed above, despite its broader scope) because they do not meet the criteria for national liberation movements anticipated in AP I, above note 62. Insurgency attacks would be, therefore, terrorist bombings under the international terrorist bombing convention and would fall within the "terrorist activity" instructed by the accused in Canada.

116 *R. v. Keegstra*, [1990] 3 S.C.R. 697 at 729.

117 *Ibid.* at 733.

c)   New Inchoate Offences Connected to "Terrorist Groups"

i)   Criminal Code *Provisions*

The inchoate offences that are tied to "terrorist groups" criminalize participation in, or contributing to, the activity of a terrorist group where the purpose of this participation is to enhance the latter's ability to facilitate or carry out a terrorist activity.[118] The *Criminal Code* lists behaviour viewed as participation and contribution, including recruitment of trainees and crossing an international border for the benefit of, at the direction of or in association with a terrorist group. The latter provision seems a likely supplement (or alternative) to the government's active and controversial use of immigration proceedings to detain and remove suspected terrorists who emigrate or travel to Canada for nefarious purposes. Immigration law and anti-terrorism is discussed in Chapter 14.

The *Criminal Code* specifies that "in determining whether an accused participates in or contributes to any activity of a terrorist group, the court may consider, among other factors, whether the accused (*a*) uses a name, word, symbol or other representation that identifies, or is associated with, the terrorist group; (*b*) frequently associates with any of the persons who constitute the terrorist group; (*c*) receives any benefit from the terrorist group; or (*d*) repeatedly engages in activities at the instruction of any of the persons who constitute the terrorist group."[119]

It is also a crime to instruct a person to do something for a terrorist group, again in order to enhance its capability to facilitate or carry out a terrorist activity.[120] Finally, it is an offence to commit an indictable offence under a federal law for this terrorist group.[121]

---

118   The *mens rea* requirement for this offence has attracted court commentary. See *Khawaja*, above note 57 at para. 38 ("moral blameworthiness of such an offence requires that it be shown that an accused both knowingly participated in or contributed to a terrorist group, but also knew that it was such a group and intend[ed] to aid or facilitate it's terrorist activity").

119   *Criminal Code*, above, Table 7.1, note 1, s. 83.18(4).

120   *Ibid.*, s. 83.21. This anti-terrorism provision is similar to the organized crime amendments added to the *Criminal Code*. The latter have been scrutinized by the lower courts on constitutional overbreadth grounds, and have survived a challenge in Ontario. See *R. v. Lindsay* (2004), 70 O.R. (3d) 131 (S.C.J.). The B.C. Supreme Court concluded that one of these provisions—criminalizing "instructing, directly or indirectly, any person to commit an offence under this or any other Act of Parliament for the benefit of, at the direction of, or in association with, the criminal organization"—was unconstitutionally overbroad and vague. *R. v. Accused No. 1*, 2005 BCSC 1727. This decision was overturned. *R. v. Terezakis*, 2007 BCCA 384. In any event, this criminal organization provision obliges that the accused be "one of the persons who constitute a criminal organization." This problematic language, which grounded the constitutional objection, is not replicated in s. 83.21.

121   *Criminal Code, ibid.*, s. 83.2.

ii) Security of Information Act *Provisions*

It should be noted that the *Security of Information Act* (SOIA) includes its own criminal offences roughly akin to the *Criminal Code* terrorist group inchoate provisions. Thus, it is an offence if anyone, "for the benefit of or in association with … a terrorist group, induces or attempts to induce, by threat, accusation, menace or violence, any person to do anything or to cause anything to be done (a) that is for the purpose of increasing the capacity of a … terrorist group to harm Canadian interests; or (b) that is reasonably likely to harm Canadian interests."[122] Harbouring a person who has committed or is likely to commit this offence is also a crime.[123] Indeed, it is a crime to do anything specifically directed towards preparation of the commission of this offence, including entering Canada at the behest of a terrorist group or asking a person to commit the offence.[124]

The SOIA also creates an offence where a person does reconnaissance for a terrorist group. A person commits a crime if they, "for any purpose prejudicial to the safety or interests of the State, approaches, inspects, passes over, is in the neighbourhood of or enters a prohibited place at the direction of, for the benefit of or in association with … a terrorist group."[125]

"Terrorist group" is defined in the same manner as in the *Criminal Code*.[126] A harm to a "Canadian interest" includes a number of enumerated acts that are also defined as "prejudicial to the safety or interests of the State." [127] These harms are distilled in Table 10.4.

PART IV: EXTRATERRITORIAL JURISDICTION

Notably, the ATA's breadth is geographic as much as substantive. Generally speaking, Canadian statutory law's reach is confined to the territory of Canada.[128] Thus, Canadian criminal offences are almost exclusively territorial in scope. As Cory J. noted in *R. v. Finta*, "the jurisdiction of Canadian courts is, in part, limited by the principle of

---

122 *Security of Information Act*, R.S.C. 1985, c. O-5, s. 20 [SOIA].
123 *Ibid.*, s. 21.
124 *Ibid.*, s. 22.
125 *Ibid.*, s. 6.
126 *Ibid.*, s. 2.
127 *Ibid.*, s. 3.
128 Indeed, there is a common law presumption against extraterritoriality. See Ruth Sullivan, *Sullivan and Dreidger on the Construction of Statutes*, 4th ed. (Markham, ON: Butterworths, 2002) at 592.

territoriality. That is, Canadian courts, as a rule, may only prosecute those crimes which have been committed within Canadian territory."[129] In fact, subsection 6(2) of the *Criminal Code* reads "subject to this Act or any other Act of Parliament, no person shall be convicted ... of an offence committed outside Canada." In *Finta*, Cory J. observed that this section "reflects the principle of sovereign integrity, which dictates that a state has exclusive sovereignty over all persons, citizens or aliens, and all property, real or personal, within its own territory."[130] At the same time, "there are exceptions to the principle of territoriality."[131]

Offences criminalizing acts of terrorism are key among these exceptions, and each has an extraterritorial reach. In the case of the piecemeal international conventions, this extraterritorial scope is expressly anticipated by the treaties themselves. For other terrorism-related criminal provisions, the Canadian assertion of extraterritorial jurisdiction is predicated, plausibly, on the nationality, passive personality or protective principles in public international law. Under the "nationality" principle of jurisdiction, states may regulate the conduct of their own nationals overseas. The "passive personality" principle permits states to pass laws applicable where the victim of the overseas act has a state's nationality. Finally, the "protective principle" allows states to prescribe certain overseas conduct so fundamental to a state's interests that they attract such regulations.[132]

Table 7.2 sets out the basis for extraterritorial jurisdiction asserted in Canadian law for each of Canada's terrorism-related crimes.

---

129 [1994] 1 S.C.R. 701 at 805–6.

130 *Ibid.*

131 *Ibid.* One quasi-exception is an offence that takes place in part overseas, but is sufficiently connected to Canada to have a real and substantial connection there (for example, one of the elements of the offence takes place in Canada). See *R. v. Libman*, [1985] 2 S.C.R. 178.

132 For an overview of these and other principles of "prescriptive" state jurisdiction, see John Currie, *Public International Law* (Toronto: Irwin Law, 2001) at 297 *et seq.*

Table 7.2:   Extraterritorial Jurisdiction over Terrorism Crimes

Offence	Accused is Canadian permanent resident	Accused not a citizen of any state but ordinarily resides in Canada	Accused is corporation incorporated in Canada	Accused Canadian citizen	Crime committed against Canadian or target in Canada	Crime committed on aircraft registered in Canada	Crime committed on ship registered in Canada	Presence of accused in Canada
"Terrorism offence," other than an offence under section 83.02 (terrorist financing) or an offence referred to in the piecemeal international conventions listed below[1]	x[2]	x		x				
Offences that would also be a "terrorist activity," under the generic definition found in s. 83.01(1) (but not proscribed by the piecemeal international conventions listed below)[3]					x[4]			
Freezing property offences[5]	x[6]		x	x				x
Disclosure of terrorist property offences[7]	x[8]		x	x				x
Offences in *Convention for the Suppression of Unlawful Seizure of Aircraft, the Convention for the Suppression of Unlawful Acts Against the Safety of Civil Aviation and the Protocol for the Suppression of Unlawful Acts of Violence at Airports Serving International Civil Aviation*[9]						x	x	x
Offences in *Convention on the Prevention and Punishment of Crimes against Internationally Protected Persons, including Diplomatic Agents*[10]				x	x[11]			x
Offences in *International Convention against the Taking of Hostages*[12]				x	x[13]	x	x	x
Offences in *Convention on the Physical Protection of Nuclear Material*[14]		x		x		x	x	x

Offence	Offences in *Convention for the Suppression of Unlawful Acts against the Safety of Maritime Navigation* and the *Protocol for the Suppression of Unlawful Acts against the Safety of Fixed Platforms Located on the Continental Shelf*[19]	Offences in *International Convention for the Suppression of Terrorist Bombings*[20]	Offences in *International Convention for the Suppression of the Financing of Terrorism* (i.e., section 83.02)[22]	*Security of Information Act* terrorist-group related offence[24]
Accused is Canadian permanent resident				
Accused not a citizen of any state but ordinarily resides in Canada	×		×	×
Accused is corporation incorporated in Canada				
Accused Canadian citizen	×		×	×
Crime committed against Canadian or target in Canada	×[18]		×[21]	×[23]
Crime committed on aircraft registered in Canada		×	×	
Crime committed on ship registered in Canada	×[17]	×	×	
Presence of accused in Canada	×[16]	×	×	

Security of Information Act column: No limitation on extraterritorial application included.

[1] *Criminal Code*, above, Table 7.1, note 1, s. 7(3.74).

[2] Permanent residents must be present in Canada after the commission of the offence.

[3] *Criminal Code*, above, Table 7.1, note 1, s. 7(3.75).

[4] Crime is committed against a Canadian citizen, against a Canadian government or public facility located outside Canada, or with intent to compel the Government of Canada or of a province to do or refrain from doing any act

[5] *Criminal Code*, above, Table 7.1, note 1, s. 83.08 and *Suppression of Terrorism Regulations*, above note 12, ss. 4 and 6 (the latter relating to causing, assisting or promoting a violation of s. 4).

[6] *Suppression of Terrorism Regulations*, *ibid.*, do not include reference to a Canadian permanent resident.

[7] *Criminal Code*, above, Table 7.1, note 1, s. 83.1 and *Suppression of Terrorism Regulations*, *ibid.*, s. 8.

[8] *Suppression of Terrorism Regulations*, *ibid.* do not include reference to a Canadian permanent resident.

[9] *Criminal Code*, above, Table 7.1, note 1, s. 7(2).

[10] *Ibid.*, s. 7(3).

[11] A crime committed against a person who is an internationally protected person because of functions performed in Canada.

[12] *Criminal Code*, above, Table 7.1, note 1, s. 7(3.1).

[13] The victim is a Canadian citizen or the crime is committed to induce the Canadian government to do an act or omission.

[14] *Criminal Code*, above, Table 7.1, note 1, ss. 7(3.4)–(3.6).

[15] *Ibid.*, ss. 7(2.1) & (2.2).

[16] Alternatively, the presence of the accused within the territory of another party to the convention (or protocol, as the case may be) suffices, so long as it is not the territory of the state where the offence actually took place.

[17] Includes crimes committed against or on-board a fixed platform registered in Canada.

[18] A crime was committed in such a way as to seize, injure or kill, or threaten to injure or kill, a Canadian citizen or in an attempt to compel the Government of Canada to do or refrain from doing any act.

[19] *Criminal Code*, above, Table 7.1, note 1, s. 7(3.72).

[20] Includes crimes committed against a Canadian citizen; or with an intent to compel the Government of Canada or of a province to do or refrain from doing any act; or against a Canadian government or public facility located outside Canada.

[21] *Criminal Code*, above, Table 7.1, note 1, s. 7(3.73). The analogous offence in s. 3 of the *Suppression of Terrorism Regulations*, above note 12, applies to Canadians outside of Canada (i.e., both citizens and corporations).

[22] Includes circumstances in which the crime is committed for the purpose of committing an act or omission proscribed in the *Criminal Code*, *ibid.*, ss. 83.02(a) or (b) (see below) in order to compel the Government of Canada; or of an act or omission proscribed in ss. 83.02(a) or (b) against a Canadian government or public facility located outside Canada; or for the purpose of committing an act or omission prescribed in ss. 83.02(a) or (b) in Canada or against a Canadian citizen.

[23] SOIA, above note 122, s. 20

Table 7.3:   Terrorism Criminal Law

"Terrorism Offences" in the Criminal Code	
Terrorist Offences Implementing Piecemeal International Anti-terrorism Conventions	
Offences referred to in s. 7(2) (i.e., ss. 76 and 77(a)–(f)) that implement the *Convention for the Suppression of Unlawful Seizure of Aircraft*, the *Convention for the Suppression of Unlawful Acts Against the Safety of Civil Aviation* and the *Protocol for the Suppression of Unlawful Acts of Violence at Airports Serving International Civil Aviation*	Section 76. Unlawfully, by force or threat thereof, or by any other form of intimidation, seizes or exercises control of an aircraft with intent to (a) cause any person on board the aircraft to be confined or imprisoned against his will, (b) cause any person on board the aircraft to be transported against his will to any place other than the next scheduled place of landing of the aircraft, (c) hold any person on board the aircraft for ransom or to service against his will, or (d) cause the aircraft to deviate in a material respect from its flight plan.

Section 77. (a) On board an aircraft in flight, committing an act of violence against a person that is likely to endanger the safety of the aircraft, (b) using a weapon, committing an act of violence against a person at an airport serving international civil aviation that causes or is likely to cause serious injury or death and that endangers or is likely to endanger safety at the airport, (c) causing damage to an aircraft in service that renders the aircraft incapable of flight or that is likely to endanger the safety of the aircraft in flight, (d) placing or causing to be placed on board an aircraft in service anything that is likely to cause damage to the aircraft, that will render it incapable of flight or that is likely to endanger the safety of the aircraft in flight, (e) causing damage to or interfering with the operation of any air navigation facility where the damage or interference is likely to endanger the safety of an aircraft in flight, (f) using a weapon, substance or device, destroying or causing serious damage to the facilities of an airport serving international civil aviation or to any aircraft not in service located there, or causing disruption of services of the airport, that endangers or is likely to endanger safety at the airport. |
| Offences referred to in s. 7(3) that implement the *Convention on the Prevention and Punishment of Crimes against Internationally Protected Persons, including Diplomatic Agents* | Various criminal acts (i.e., ss. 235, 236, 266, 267, 268, 269, 269.1, 271, 272, 273, 279, 279.1, 280–83, 424 and 431), as directed against an "internationally protected person," defined in s. 2 as: (a) a head of state, including any member of a collegial body that performs the functions of a head of state under the constitution of the state concerned, a head of a government or a minister of foreign affairs, whenever that person is in a state other than the state in which he holds that position or |

"Terrorism Offences" in the *Criminal Code*	
Offences referred to in s. 7(3) (cont'd)	office, (b) a member of the family of a person described in paragraph (a) who accompanies that person in a state other than the state in which that person holds that position or office, (c) a representative or an official of a state or an official or agent of an international organization of an intergovernmental character who, at the time when and at the place where an offence referred to in s. 7(3) is committed against his or her person or any property referred to in section 431 that is used by him, is entitled, pursuant to international law, to special protection from any attack on his person, freedom or dignity, or (d) a member of the family of a representative, official or agent described in paragraph (c) who forms part of his household, if the representative, official or agent, at the time when and at the place where any offence referred to in s. 7(3) is committed against the member of his or her family or any property referred to in s. 431 that is used by that member, is entitled, pursuant to international law, to special protection from any attack on his or her person, freedom or dignity.
Offences referred to in s. 7(3.1) (i.e., s. 279.1) that implement the *International Convention against the Taking of Hostages*	Kidnapping a person with intent (a) to cause the person to be confined or imprisoned against the person's will; (b) to cause the person to be unlawfully sent or transported out of Canada against the person's will; or (c) to hold the person for ransom or to service against the person's will. Also, without lawful authority, confining, imprisoning or forcibly seizing another person.
Offences referred to in s. 7(3.4) or (3.6) that implement the *Convention on the Physical Protection of Nuclear Material*	Various criminal offences (i.e., s. 334, 341, 344 or 380 or para. 62(1)(a) in relation to nuclear material, s. 346 in respect of a threat to commit an offence against section 334 or 344 in relation to nuclear material, s. 423 in relation to a demand for nuclear material, or para. 264.1(1)(a) or (b) in respect of a threat to use nuclear material), including: theft; fraudulent concealment; robbery; fraud; interfering with, impairing or influencing the loyalty or discipline of a member of the Canadian or allied military forces; extortion; intimidation; and uttering threats.
Offences referred to in s. 7(2.1) or (2.2) (i.e., s. 78.1) that implement the *Convention for the Suppression of Unlawful Acts against the Safety of Maritime Navigation* and the *Protocol for the Suppression of Unlawful Acts against the Safety of Fixed Platforms Located on the Continental Shelf*	(2)(a) Committing an act of violence against a person on board a ship or fixed platform, (b) destroying or causing damage to a ship or its cargo or to a fixed platform, (c) destroying or causing serious damage to or interference with the operation of any maritime navigational facility, or (d) placing or causing to be placed on board a ship or fixed platform anything that is likely to cause damage to the ship or its cargo or to the fixed platform, where that act is likely to endanger the safe navigation of a ship or the safety of a fixed platform. (3) Communicating information that endangers

"Terrorism Offences" in the *Criminal Code*

Offences referred to in s. 7(2.1) or (2.2) (cont'd)	the safe navigation of a ship, knowing the information to be false. (4) Threatening to commit an offence under para. (2)(*a*), (*b*) or (*c*) in order to compel a person to do or refrain from doing any act, where the threat is likely to endanger the safe navigation of a ship or the safety of a fixed platform.
Offences referred to in s. 7(3.72) (i.e., s. 431.2) that implement the *International Convention for the Suppression of Terrorist Bombings*	(1) Delivering, placing, discharging or detonating an explosive or other lethal device to, into, in or against a place of public use, a government or public facility, a public transportation system or an infrastructure facility, either with intent to cause death or serious bodily injury or with intent to cause extensive destruction of such a place, system or facility that results in or is likely to result in major economic loss. (2) Paragraph (1) does not apply to an act or omission that is committed during an armed conflict and that, at the time and in the place of its commission, is in accordance with customary international law or conventional international law applicable to the conflict, or to activities undertaken by military forces of a state in the exercise of their official duties, to the extent that those activities are governed by other rules of international law.

Financing and Property Offences

Section 83.02. Providing or collecting property for certain purposes	Directly or indirectly, wilfully and without lawful justification or excuse, providing or collecting property intending that it be used or knowing that it will be used, in whole or in part, in order to carry out (*a*) an act or omission that constitutes an offence referred to in subparagraphs (*a*)(i) to (ix) of the definition of "terrorist activity" in s. 83.01(1) [the piecemeal international conventions], or (*b*) any other act or omission intended to cause death or serious bodily harm to a civilian or to any other person not taking an active part in the hostilities in a situation of armed conflict, if the purpose of that act or omission, by its nature or context, is to intimidate the public, or to compel a government or an international organization to do or refrain from doing any act.
Section 83.03. Providing, making available, etc., property or services for terrorist purposes	Directly or indirectly, collecting property, providing or inviting a person to provide, or making available property or financial or other related services (*a*) intending that they be used, or knowing that they will be used, in whole or in part, for the purpose of facilitating or carrying out any terrorist activity, or for the purpose of benefiting any person who is facilitating or carrying out such an activity, or (*b*) knowing that, in whole or part, they will be used by or will benefit a terrorist group.

"Terrorism Offences" in the Criminal Code	
Section 83.04. Using or possessing property for terrorist purposes	(a) Using property, directly or indirectly, in whole or in part, for the purpose of facilitating or carrying out a terrorist activity, or (b) possessing property intending that it be used or knowing that it will be used, directly or indirectly, in whole or in part, for the purpose of facilitating or carrying out a terrorist activity.
Inchoate Offences Connected to "Terrorist Activity" in the Criminal Code	
Section 83.19. Facilitating a terrorist activity	Knowingly facilitating a terrorist activity, whether or not (a) the facilitator knows that a particular terrorist activity is facilitated; (b) any particular terrorist activity was foreseen or planned at the time it was facilitated; or (c) any terrorist activity was actually carried out.
Section 83.22. Instructing to carry out a terrorist activity	Knowingly instructing, directly or indirectly, any person to carry out a terrorist activity, whether or not (a) the terrorist activity is actually carried out; (b) the accused instructs a particular person to carry out the terrorist activity; (c) the accused knows the identity of the person whom the accused instructs to carry out the terrorist activity; or (d) the person whom the accused instructs to carry out the terrorist activity knows that it is a terrorist activity.
Section 83.23. Harbouring or concealing	Knowingly harbouring or concealing any person whom the accused knows to be a person who has carried out or is likely to carry out a terrorist activity, for the purpose of enabling the person to facilitate or carry out any terrorist activity.
Inchoate Offences Connected to "Terrorist Group" in the Criminal Code	
Section 83.18. Participation in activity of terrorist group	Knowingly participating in or contributing to, directly or indirectly, any activity of a terrorist group for the purpose of enhancing the ability of any terrorist group to facilitate or carry out a terrorist activity, whether or not (a) a terrorist group actually facilitates or carries out a terrorist activity; (b) the participation or contribution of the accused actually enhances the ability of a terrorist group to facilitate or carry out a terrorist activity; or (c) the accused knows the specific nature of any terrorist activity that may be facilitated or carried out by a terrorist group. Participating in or contributing to an activity of a terrorist group includes (a) providing, receiving or recruiting a person to receive training; (b) providing or offering to provide a skill or an expertise for the benefit of, at the direction of or in association with a terrorist group: (c) recruiting

"Terrorism Offences" in the *Criminal Code*	
Section 83.18 (cont'd)	a person in order to facilitate or commit (i) a terrorism offence, or (ii) an act or omission outside Canada that, if committed in Canada, would be a terrorism offence; (d) entering or remaining in any country for the benefit of, at the direction of or in association with a terrorist group; and (e) making oneself, in response to instructions from any of the persons who constitute a terrorist group, available to facilitate or commit (i) a terrorism offence, or (ii) an act or omission outside Canada that, if committed in Canada, would be a terrorism offence.
Section 83.2. Commission of offence for terrorist group	Committing an indictable offence under the *Criminal Code* or any other Act of Parliament for the benefit of, at the direction of or in association with a terrorist group.
Section 83.21. Instructing to carry out activity for terrorist group	Knowingly instructing, directly or indirectly, any person to carry out any activity for the benefit of, at the direction of or in association with a terrorist group, for the purpose of enhancing the ability of any terrorist group to facilitate or carry out a terrorist activity, whether or not (a) the activity that the accused instructs to be carried out is actually carried out; (b) the accused instructs a particular person to carry out the activity referred to in paragraph (a); (c) the accused knows the identity of the person whom the accused instructs to carry out the activity referred to in paragraph (a); (d) the person whom the accused instructs to carry out the activity referred to in paragraph (a) knows that it is to be carried out for the benefit of, at the direction of or in association with a terrorist group; (e) a terrorist group actually facilitates or carries out a terrorist activity; (f) the activity referred to in paragraph (a) actually enhances the ability of a terrorist group to facilitate or carry out a terrorist activity; or (g) the accused knows the specific nature of any terrorist activity that may be facilitated or carried out by a terrorist group.

Terrorism-Related Offences that are not "Terrorism Offences" in the *Criminal Code*

Financing and Property Offences in Suppression of Terrorism Regulations

Section 3. Providing or Collecting Funds	Knowingly providing or collecting by any means, directly or indirectly, funds with the intention that the funds be used, or in the knowledge that the funds are to be used, by a listed person [i.e., a person listed under the regulations].

Terrorism-Related Offences that are not "Terrorism Offences" in the *Criminal Code*

Section 4. Freezing Property	Knowingly (a) dealing directly or indirectly in any property of a listed person, including funds derived or generated from property owned or controlled directly or indirectly by that person; (b) entering into or facilitating, directly or indirectly, any transaction related to a dealing referred to in paragraph (a); (c) providing any financial or other related service in respect of the property referred to in paragraph (a); or (d) making any property or any financial or other related service available, directly or indirectly, for the benefit of a listed person
Section 6. Causing, Assisting or Promoting	Knowingly doing anything that causes, assists or promotes, or is intended to cause, assist or promote, any activity prohibited by section 3 or 4, unless the person has a certificate issued by the Minister under section 11. (Section 11 allows the government to issue a certificate relieving criminal liability under the regulations where the government concludes that Security Council resolution 1373 "does not intend that the act or thing be prohibited," "the act or thing has been approved by the Security Council of the United Nations" or by the 1267 Committee, or the "person named in the certificate is not a listed person.")
Section 7. Duty to Determine	Every entity referred to in paragraphs 83.11(1)(a) to (g) of the *Criminal Code* (essentially, financial institutions) must determine on a continuing basis if it is in possession or control of property owned or controlled by or on behalf of a listed person and must report within the applicable period determined under subsection 83.11(2) of the *Criminal Code* (that is, at least monthly) to the principal agency or body that supervises or regulates it under federal or provincial law either (a) that it is not in possession or control of any property owned or controlled by or on behalf of a listed person; or (b) that it is in possession or control of such property, in which case it must also report the number of persons, contracts or accounts involved and the total value of the property.
Section 8. Disclosure	Failure by a person to disclose forthwith to the Commissioner of the Royal Canadian Mounted Police and to the Director of the Canadian Security Intelligence Service (a) the existence of property in their possession or control that they have reason to believe is owned or controlled by or on behalf of a listed person; and (b) information about a transaction or proposed transaction in respect of property referred to in paragraph (a).

Terrorism-Related Property Offences that are not "Terrorism Offences" in the *Criminal Code*

Sections 83.08 and 83.12. Freezing property	[Unless authorized by the minister of public safety,] knowingly (a) dealing directly or indirectly in any property that is owned or controlled by or on behalf of a terrorist group; (b) entering into or facilitating, directly or indirectly, any transaction in respect of property referred to in paragraph (a); or (c) providing any financial or other related services in respect of property referred to in paragraph (a) to, for the benefit of or at the direction of a terrorist group.
Sections 83.1 and 83.12. Disclosure	Failure by a person to disclose forthwith to the Commissioner of the Royal Canadian Mounted Police and to the Director of the Canadian Security Intelligence Service (a) the existence of property in their possession or control that they know is owned or controlled by or on behalf of a terrorist group; and (b) information about a transaction or proposed transaction in respect of property referred to in paragraph (a).
Sections 83.11 and 83.12. Audit	A [listed financial entities] must report, within the period specified by regulation or, if no period is specified, monthly, to the principal agency or body that supervises or regulates it under federal or provincial law either (a) that it is not in possession or control of any terrorist property, or (b) that it is in possession or control of such property, in which case it must also report the number of persons, contracts or accounts involved and the total value of the property.

Other Terrorism-Related Offences that are not "Terrorism Offences" in *Criminal Code*

Section 83.231. Hoax Regarding Terrorist Activity	Without lawful excuse and with intent to cause any person to fear death, bodily harm, substantial damage to property or serious interference with the lawful use or operation of property, (a) conveying or causing or procuring to be conveyed information that, in all the circumstances, is likely to cause a reasonable apprehension that terrorist activity is occurring or will occur, without believing the information to be true; or (b) committing an act that, in all the circumstances, is likely to cause a reasonable apprehension that terrorist activity is occurring or will occur, without believing that such activity is occurring or will occur.

CHAPTER 8

LIMITING PROLIFERATION OF WEAPONS OF MASS DESTRUCTION

This chapter discusses another key national security objective: limiting the proliferation of weapons that states (or, in the era of catastrophic-scale terrorism, nonstate actors) might employ against Canada or Canadians. It does not, however, discuss all weapons, instead mostly focusing on what are commonly called "weapons of mass destruction" (WMDs); that is, weapons capable of inflicting mass casualties or economic damage via a single use. WMDs comprise nuclear, radiological, chemical and biological weapons.

States have rarely used these destructive instruments, mostly because of the political and military consequences of deploying such heinous devices but probably in part also because of the restrictive laws that govern them. Indeed, to this point in time, conventional weapons — and in particular small arms and land mines — have killed and maimed more people than have WMDs. Even so, this book does not focus on these arms and their control. The decision to concentrate on WMD proliferation and not conventional arms control is not completely arbitrary. Small arms are not capable of reaching across continents and sowing instantaneous mass casualties. WMDs, on the other hand, are. They therefore fit comfortably within this book's vision of national security law: law countering threats posed by low-probability, high-consequence events that risk producing significant political turmoil.

The first part of this chapter examines the international and Canadian law governing both nonstate and state possession and use of nuclear, chemical and biological weapons. The law of nonproliferation for all

WMDs grapples with similar concerns. First, it seeks to limit—and in the case of biological and chemical weapons outlaw—possession of the WMD. Second, it struggles with the problem of dual use; that is, the fact that the technology in question may be deployed for both legitimate civilian purposes and illegitimate weapons purposes. To meet both objectives, it depends on "safeguards"—systems of observation and verification.

In part to meet nonproliferation objectives, international and Canadian law also impose important constraints on technology transfer, often in the form of international physical movement of tools, machines and raw materials, but now also in Canada between authorized and unauthorized persons. A discussion of these technology transfer rules forms the second part of this chapter.

PART I: WEAPONS PROLIFERATION AND NATIONAL SECURITY

Deterring the proliferation of weapons of mass destruction is a national security preoccupation of venerable standing. The department of foreign affairs urges:

> The illicit possession and proliferation of nuclear, chemical and biological weapons …, as well as their means of delivery, presents a grave threat to Canadian national security…. This threat can come from both state and non-state actors. It challenges us at home. And it places our national interests overseas in jeopardy. Given rapid advances in and the spread of scientific and technical knowledge (especially in the life sciences, and missile technology), the threat is likely to grow. Failing to act decisively now risks allowing the problems to fester and multiply.[1]

Similar concerns were expressed in Canada's 2005 international policy statement:

> The international community continues to face the prospect that weapons of mass destruction (WMD)—chemical, nuclear, radiological or biological—might be used by a state or terrorist organization. The desire to acquire these weapons is often driven by regional tensions—in the Middle East, India-Pakistan and the Korean peninsula—and misguided attempts to gain international prestige. Terrorists, who until now have focused on tactics involving car bombs and suicide bombers,

---

1   Canada, DFAIT, *Against the Proliferation of Weapons of Mass Destruction* (2006), online: www.dfait-maeci.gc.ca/foreign_policy/arms_clf1/menu-en.asp.

are seeking new ways to inflict the maximum amount of damage on their victims. An attack with such weapons could have an immense impact on Canada, no matter where in the world it might occur. [2]

As these passages suggests, and as noted in Chapter 6, the events of 9/11 have renewed concerns about the spread of weapons of mass destruction, and their possible use by terrorists. Pre-empting chemical, biological, radiological and nuclear (CBRN) terrorism is the subtext in much contemporary anti-terrorism strategy. For instance, the Canadian government's 2005 CBRN strategy is heavily influenced by fears of WMD terrorism.[3] To prevent such attacks, the government promises, among other things, to:

- continue to be a world leader in the support of non-proliferation, arms control and disarmament; ...
- work with the provinces, territories and the private sector to keep CBRN-related materials out of the hands of terrorists; ...
- support, in collaboration with our allies, international efforts to deter and prevent states with CBRN weapons and CBRN weapons-capable materials from using them and/or transferring them to others;
- work with the international community to improve the security for the storage and movement of CBRN weapons-capable materials as well as the safe destruction of CBRN weapons;
- support the principle that all states adopt and enforce appropriate, effective laws to prohibit the unauthorized manufacture, acquisition, possession, development, transportation, transfer or use of nuclear, chemical or biological weapons.[4]

PART II: REGULATION OF NONSTATE USE AND POSSESSION OF WMD

In response to concerns about WMD terrorism, the international community has unequivocally condemned possession and use of WMDs by nonstate actors.

---

2   Canada, *International Policy Statement—Overview* (2005), online: http://geo. international.gc.ca/cip-pic/ips/ips-overview5-en.aspx.

3   Canada, PSEPC, *The Chemical, Biological, Radiological and Nuclear Strategy of the Government of Canada* (2005) at 4, online: www.publicsafety.gc.ca/pol/ em/cbrnstr-en.asp (describing the four strategic objectives of counterterrorism in relation to CBRN weapons as "prevention and mitigation; preparedness; response and recovery").

4   *Ibid.* at 5.

A. INTERNATIONAL TREATIES

As discussed in Chapter 6, two international treaties oblige parties to criminalize certain acts associated with nuclear or radiological materials. First, the 1980 *Convention on the Physical Protection of Nuclear Material* requires state parties to criminalize any act involving "the receipt, possession, use, transfer, alteration, disposal or dispersal of nuclear material and which causes or is likely to cause death or serious injury to any person or substantial damage to property."[5]

Second, the more recent, 2005 *International Convention for the Suppression of Acts of Nuclear Terrorism*[6] requires state parties to criminalize, among other things:

- possession of radioactive material or making or possessing a nuclear or radiological explosive device with the intent to cause death or serious bodily injury; or with the intent to cause substantial damage to property or to the environment; and
- using in any way radioactive material or a device, or using or damaging a nuclear facility in a manner that releases or risks the release of radioactive material with the intent to cause death or serious bodily injury; or with the intent to cause substantial damage to property or to the environment; or with the intent to compel a natural or legal person, an international organization or a state to do or refrain from doing an act.

B. U.N. SECURITY COUNCIL ACTION

The U.N. Security Council has recently issued is own dictate, pursuant to its potent U.N. *Charter* Chapter VII powers. Resolution 1540 (2004) has the effect of imposing on all states obligations similar to those applicable to parties of the two treaties discussed above, extended also to chemical and biological weapons.

Resolution 1540 requires all states to "refrain from providing any form of support to non-State actors that attempt to develop, acquire, manufacture, possess, transport, transfer or use nuclear, chemical or biological weapons and their means of delivery." Indeed, all states must "adopt and enforce appropriate effective laws which prohibit any non-State actor to manufacture, acquire, possess, develop, transport, trans-

---

5   1456 U.N.T.S. 101, Art. 7.
6   12 April 2005. Not in force at the time of this writing.

fer or use nuclear, chemical or biological weapons and their means of delivery, in particular for terrorist purposes, as well as attempts to engage in any of the foregoing activities, participate in them as an accomplice, assist or finance them."

The council also requires states to "take and enforce effective measures to establish domestic controls to prevent the proliferation of nuclear, chemical, or biological weapons and their means of delivery, including by establishing appropriate controls over related materials." The resolution lists a number of specific obligations in terms of production, use, storage and transport.

C. GLOBAL INITIATIVE TO COMBAT NUCLEAR TERRORISM

At a more political level, in 2006, the United States and Russia launched the "Global Initiative to Combat Nuclear Terrorism" during a meeting at which Canada participated. State participants at the initiative's inaugural meeting pledged to bolster domestic nuclear control measures by, among other things: enhancing "accounting, control and physical protection systems for nuclear and other radioactive materials and substances" and the "security of civilian nuclear facilities." They also committed to improving nuclear and radioactive detection technology and capacity; denying safe haven to terrorists seeking to acquire these materials; criminalizing nuclear terrorism; augmenting the nuclear terrorism response, mitigation and investigation capacity of states and promoting information sharing in the area.[7]

D. CANADIAN IMPLEMENTATION

Canada has implemented these international obligations and commitments largely through the nonproliferation statutes described in Part III that follows,[8] as well as through its anti-terrorism criminal laws. In this last regard, use of a WMD would fall within the ambit of any

---

7   United States, State Department, *Statement of Principles by Participants in the Global Initiative to Combat Nuclear Terrorism* (2006), online: www.state.gov/r/pa/prs/ps/2006/75405.htm.

8   These include the *Nuclear Safety and Control Act*, S.C. 1997, c. 9 [NSCA], the *Chemical Weapons Convention Implementation Act*, S.C. 1995, c. 25 [CWCIA] and the *Biological and Toxin Weapons Convention Implementation Act*, S.C. 2004,

number of *Criminal Code* offences, including various prohibitions on bombings and use of explosives.[9] For example, in implementing the 1997 *International Convention for the Suppression of Terrorist Bombings*, Canada made it a crime to deliver, place, discharge or detonate "an explosive or other lethal device to, into, in or against a place of public use, a government or public facility, a public transportation system or an infrastructure facility" in order to cause death, serious injury or such destruction as to result in major economic loss. "Explosive or other lethal device" includes "a weapon or device that is designed to cause, or is capable of causing, death, serious bodily injury or substantial material damage through the release, dissemination or impact of toxic chemicals, biological agents or toxins or similar substances, or radiation or radioactive material"; for example, a WMD.[10]

PART III: REGULATION OF USE AND POSSESSION OF WMD BY STATES

As the discussion above underscores, international law is unequivocal in banning the possession and use of WMDs by nonstate actors. International law is, however, more accommodating of state possession (and potentially use) of at least nuclear weapons.

A. NUCLEAR WEAPONS

Nuclear weapons have the greatest destructive potential of any weapon yet developed. In 1996, the International Court of Justice described nuclear weapons as

> explosive devices whose energy results from the fusion or fission of the atom. By its very nature, that process, in nuclear weapons as they exist today, releases not only immense quantities of heat and energy, but also powerful and prolonged radiation. According to the material before the Court, the first two causes of damage are vastly more powerful than the damage caused by other weapons, while the

---

c. 15, s. 106 [BTWCIA], as well as export control rules under the *Export and Import Permits Act*, R.S.C. 1985, c. E-19 [EIPA].

9   See Canada's report to the U.N. Security Council's 1540 Committee on compliance with the resolution. U.N. Doc S/AC.44/2004/(02)/98 (2004); U.N. Doc. S/AC.44/2004/(02)/98/Add.1 (2006).

10   *Criminal Code*, R.S.C. 1985, c. C-46, s. 431.2.

phenomenon of radiation is said to be peculiar to nuclear weapons. These characteristics render the nuclear weapon potentially catastrophic. The destructive power of nuclear weapons cannot be contained in either space or time. They have the potential to destroy all civilization and the entire ecosystem of the planet.[11]

Because of the very destructiveness of nuclear weapons, their development and possible use has provoked a substantial body of international law. This law is notable, however, in partitioning the world into states that may legitimately possess nuclear weapons, and those that may not. It is different, in other words, from the rules governing other WMDs in acknowledging the propriety of possessing the regulated weapon, at least by some states.

The discussion in this section examines, first, the rules relating to nuclear weapons states; specifically, restrictions on the use of these weapons, and limits on such things as nuclear weapons testing and the development and stockpiling of weapons by existing nuclear weapon states. Second, it turns to a more detailed examination of nuclear-weapons proliferation in the hands of those states that do not, at present, legally possess such weapons.

1) Use and Development of Nuclear Weapons by Nuclear Weapons States

As discussed below, under the nuclear Non-proliferation Treaty (NPT),[12] five states are legally entitled to possess nuclear weapons, albeit subject to an obligation that they pursue negotiations "in good faith on effective measures relating to cessation of the nuclear arms race at an early date and to nuclear disarmament," and with an eye to an as-of-yet unrealized "treaty on general and complete disarmament under strict and effective international control."[13] These countries are: the United States; the United Kingdom; France; China; and Russia (as the successor to the Soviet Union).

Several other states, not party to the NPT, are now known to possess nuclear weapons. These *de facto* nuclear weapon states are India, Pakistan, Israel and almost certainly now North Korea. Presently, Iran (a NPT party) is believed by much of the international community to

---

11 *Legality of the Threats or Use of Nuclear Weapons* (1996), ICJ General List No. 95 at para. 35.
12 *Treaty on the Non-Proliferation of Nuclear Weapons* (1970), 729 U.N.T.S. 161 [NPT].
13 *Ibid.*, Art. VI.

harbour an active nuclear weapons development program, a matter discussed further below.[14]

a)   Use of Nuclear Weapons

In this environment, an obvious question is whether use of nuclear weapons by any of these states would comply with international law. There is a striking dearth of clear law on this issue. Perhaps for exactly this reason, in 1994, the World Health Organization asked the International Court of Justice (ICJ) for an "advisory opinion" on whether "the threat or use of nuclear weapons [is] in any circumstance permitted under international law." In its 1996 response, the ICJ concluded that there was no treaty or customary international law rule "specifically proscribing the threat or use of nuclear weapons *per se*."[15] However, a closely divided Court also concluded that "the threat or use of nuclear weapons would generally be contrary to the rules of international law applicable in armed conflict, and in particular the principles and rules of humanitarian law." The ICJ was unprepared to rule out the legal use of nuclear weapons, but constrained that possibility to "an extreme circumstance of self-defence, in which the very survival of a State would be at stake."[16] This caveat is greatly limiting. It should deny the legality of a "first strike," or in a more contemporary context, the use of nuclear weapons as part of a policy of "preemptive self-defence" against a threat that has not fully materialized.

b)   Development of Nuclear Weapons

The ICJ's 1996 opinion leaves open, however, the further development of nuclear weapons by nuclear weapons states. The nature of that development falls to be regulated, if at all, by nuclear weapons testing treaties. Such instruments date to the early 1960s and are largely a product of Cold War tensions (and attempts to defuse them). More recent attention has focused on a Comprehensive Nuclear Test-Ban Treaty (CTBT). That convention, opened for signature in 1996, has not yet come into force. By 2006, it had been ratified by 135 states (including Canada),[17] but had not attracted the ratification of some key states necessary to

---

14   Arms Control Association, *Nuclear Weapons: Who Has What at a Glance* (April 2005), online: www.armscontrol.org/pdf/NuclearWeaponsWhoHasWhat.pdf.

15   Above note 11 at para. 74.

16   *Ibid.* at para. 105.

17   Canada will implement the treaty with the *Comprehensive Nuclear-Test-Ban Treaty Implementation Act*, S.C. 1998, c. 32, an instrument that was not in force at the time of this writing.

bring the treaty into force. These included the United States, China, India, Pakistan and Israel, all states possessing nuclear weapons.[18]

The CTBT's core obligation is succinct: every state party undertakes to "not carry out any nuclear weapon test explosion or any other nuclear explosion, and to prohibit and prevent any such nuclear explosion at any place under its jurisdiction or control" and to "refrain from causing, encouraging, or in any way participating in the carrying out of any nuclear weapon test explosion or any other nuclear explosion."[19]

Further, each party is to prohibit "natural and legal persons anywhere on its territory or in any other place under its jurisdiction as recognized by international law" from undertaking any activity prohibited to the party, "to prohibit natural and legal persons from undertaking any such activity anywhere under its control"; and "to prohibit, in conformity with international law, natural persons possessing its nationality from undertaking any such activity anywhere."[20] Put another way, a state party must proscribe nuclear explosions territorially (and extraterritorially where it exercises sufficient control) and regulate its own nationals.

The balance of the treaty deals with: compliance and verification and includes detailed provisions concerning an International Monitoring System; consultation and clarification between parties; on-site inspections; and confidence-building measures. To assist implementation and provide a venue for consultations, a Comprehensive Nuclear Test Ban Treaty Organization is anticipated.[21]

A "conference" of all the state parties is empowered to respond to violations of the treaty by recommending to state parties "collective measures which are in conformity with international law" and/or bringing the issue to the attention of the United Nations.[22] An "executive council" of fifty-one state parties elected regularly on the basis of geographical representation is also empowered to communicate compliance issues to the United Nations. Thus, the CTBT does not create its own *sui generis* remedies system. It does not constitute, for instance, an alternative justification for use of armed force (an area that continues to be monopolized by the U.N. *Charter*) or even trade sanctions (a topic that, barring U.N. Security Council action, would fall to be regulated

---

18   To enter into force, the treaty must be ratified by all "Annex 2" states. The nations listed in the text are among these. CTBT, Art. XIV.

19   *Ibid.*, Art. I.

20   *Ibid.*, Art. III.

21   *Ibid.*, Art. II.

22   *Ibid.*, Art. V.

by the World Trade Organization, at least for states party to it, or other weapons control treaties).

As noted, however, the CTBT has not entered into force, and its prospects are uncertain. The lack of progress a decade after the treaty's conclusion jeopardizes several important objectives of a comprehensive test ban system. The executive director of the U.S.-based nonprofit Arms Control Association urged in August 2006 that an effective CTBT is necessary for four reasons: "to impede the development of new types of nuclear warheads and reduce dangerous nuclear arms competition; to obstruct the emergence of new nuclear powers; to ensure completion of the international monitoring system and availability of on-site inspections to detect and deter cheating; and to restore confidence in the nuclear Non-proliferation Treaty (NPT)."[23] The elimination of environmental damage (and potential negative human health impacts) associated with nuclear testing are other reasons supporting a test ban.

c)   Nuclear Arms Control

i)   Disarmament

Other, less ambitious nuclear arms control and disarmament treaties have been a feature of United States/Soviet Union (and now Russia) relations since the early 1970s. Key U.S./Russian agreements include the various "Strategic Arms Limitation Treaties" (SALT), not all of which have entered into force, an Intermediate-range Nuclear Forces (INF) treaty and the more recent 2002 Treaty on Strategic Offensive Reductions. These instruments include various nuclear weapons and weapon delivery system limitations, albeit often of a modest sort. A full description of the content of these treaties lies beyond the purview of this book.[24]

Also of note was the 1972 Anti-Ballistic Missile (ABM) Treaty between the United States and Russia. This treaty barred the United States and the U.S.S.R. from deploying a defensive ABM system, except in a handful of places. In June 2002, the Bush administration withdrew from the ABM treaty, removing a legal impediment to its missile defence system plans.

---

23   Daryl G. Kimball, *Accelerating the Entry Into Force of the Comprehensive Test Ban Treaty and Securing a Fissile Material Cut Off Agreement*, 18th U.N. Conference on Disarmament Issues in Yokohama (Aug. 2006), online: www.armscontrol. org/pdf/20060821_Kimball_CTBT-FMCT.pdf.

24   For a comprehensive overview of these treaties, see Jozef Goldblat, *Arms Control* (Thousand Oaks, CA: Sage Publications, 2002) [Goldblat, *Arms Control*].

ii) Denuclearized Zones

A variant on arms limitations instruments are treaties defining particular regions of the world as nuclear weapons free zones. The nuclear Non-proliferation Treaty anticipates these regions, specifying that "nothing in this Treaty affects the right of any group of States to conclude regional treaties in order to assure the total absence of nuclear weapons in their respective territories."[25] In 1967, even prior to the NPT, a number of Latin American states negotiated and concluded the Treaty for the Prohibition of Nuclear Weapons in Latin America (the "Treaty of Tlatelolco").[26] By that convention, the state parties commit

> to use exclusively for peaceful purposes the nuclear material and facilities which are under their jurisdiction, and to prohibit and prevent in their respective territories:
>
> (a) The testing, use, manufacture, production or acquisition by any means whatsoever of any nuclear weapons, by the Parties themselves, directly or indirectly, on behalf of anyone else or in any other way, and
>
> (b) The receipt, storage, installation, deployment and any form of possession of any nuclear weapons, directly or indirectly, by the Parties themselves, by anyone on their behalf or in any other way.

They also agree "to refrain from engaging in, encouraging or authorizing, directly or indirectly, or in any way participating in the testing, use, manufacture, production, possession or control of any nuclear weapon."[27] The treaty obliges state parties to enter into "safeguard" agreements with the Atomic Energy Agency (IAEA), a concept discussed below.[28]

Geographically, the almost comprehensive membership of Latin American and Caribbean states in the treaty makes virtually all of Latin America and the Caribbean a "denuclearized zone," including the territorial seas, air space and "any other space over which the State exercises sovereignty in accordance with its own legislation."[29] In fact, the treaty purports to extend to an expansive swath of the Pacific and Atlantic Oceans.

---

25 NPT, above note 12, Art. VII.

26 (1968), 634 U.N.T.S. 9068.

27 Treaty of Tlatelolco (1967), 634 U.N.T.S. 326 (entered into force 22 April 1968), Art. 1.

28 *Ibid.*, Art. 13.

29 *Ibid.*, Art. 3.

By protocols to the treaty, the official nuclear weapons states—the United States, United Kingdom, France, China and Russia—agree not to "contribute in any way to the performance of acts involving a violation" of the regional denuclearization obligation under the treaty or "to use or threaten to use nuclear weapons against" the treaty's parties.[30] There is disagreement, however, among these nuclear powers on whether their adherence to the treaty protocol prohibits transit of nuclear weapons through the denuclearized territory.[31] Moreover, the nuclear weapons states included interpretive declarations in signing and ratifying the protocol reserving the right to reconsider their nonuse commitments if a state in the denuclearized zone mounted an attack supported by another nuclear-weapon state.

Since the Treaty of Tlatelolco, a number of other regional nuclear-free zones have been created by treaty. Notable among these is the 1985 Treaty of Rarotonga, an instrument to which South Pacific and Australasian states are parties. Like its Latin American equivalent, this treaty bars states parties from the manufacture, acquisition, possession or control of any "nuclear explosive device by any means anywhere inside or outside the South Pacific Nuclear Free Zone." Nor are state parties to seek or receive any "assistance in the manufacture or acquisition of any nuclear explosive device" or "assist or encourage the manufacture or acquisition of any nuclear explosive device by any State." The stationing of nuclear explosive devices in state parties is prohibited, although each state is permitted to decide whether to allow visits and transits. Other prohibitions include a ban on testing of nuclear explosive devices, ocean dumping of radioactive material and exports of nuclear material to states without nonproliferation safeguards.[32]

Like the Treaty of Tlatelolco, the South Pacific convention anticipates parties entering into International Atomic Energy Agency safeguard agreements. Also like the Latin American treaty, it includes protocols which all official nuclear weapons states, other than the United States, have ratified in which these states undertake "not to use or threaten to use any nuclear explosive device against parties to the treaty."[33] As with the Americas treaty, these ratifications often contain provisos to the affect that the nonuse obligation is limited or vitiated by an attack by a treaty party supported by another nuclear weapons

---

30   *Ibid.*, Protocol II, Arts. 2 & 3.

31   See discussion in Goldblat, *Arms Control*, above note 24 at 200.

32   *South Pacific Nuclear Free Zone Treaty* (1986), 1445 U.N.T.S. 177, Art. 3-7 [Treaty of Rarotonga].

33   *Ibid.*, Protocol II.

state, and/or a gross violation of the treaty's terms by the latter.[34] In addition, a separate protocol commits nuclear weapons state "not to test any nuclear explosive device anywhere within the South Pacific Nuclear Free Zone."[35] All official nuclear weapons states have ratified this instrument, again with the exception of the United States.

While the particulars differ somewhat, the other nuclear weapons free zones—that created in South East Asia as of 1997 by the Treaty of Bangkok, for Africa, when the Treaty of Pelindaba enters into force, and for Central Asia when a newly concluded treaty for that region comes into effect—have broadly similar qualities to their earlier American and South Pacific counterparts. Meanwhile, three states—Mongolia, Austria and New Zealand—have created internal nuclear weapons free zones and other nations impose restrictions on the presence of nuclear weapons on naval vessels visiting their ports.[36]

Several uninhabited regions of the Earth and its surroundings are also denuclearized zones. Under the 1959 *Antarctic Treaty*, for example, the Antarctic continent is to be demilitarized: "Antarctica shall be used for peaceful purposes only. There shall be prohibited, *inter alia*, any measures of a military nature, such as the establishment of military bases and fortifications, the carrying out of military maneuvers, as well as the testing of any types of weapons."[37] Moreover, "any nuclear explosions in Antarctica and the disposal there of radioactive waste material shall be prohibited."[38]

Under the Outer Space Treaty, meanwhile, state parties are not to

> place in orbit around the Earth any objects carrying nuclear weapons or any other kinds of weapons of mass destruction, install such weapons on celestial bodies, or station such weapons in outer space in any other manner. The Moon and other celestial bodies shall be used by all States Parties to the Treaty exclusively for peaceful purposes. The establishment of military bases, installations and fortifications, the testing of any type of weapons and the conduct of military maneuvers on celestial bodies shall be forbidden.[39]

---

34 See discussion in Goldblat, *Arms Control*, above note 24 at 204.
35 Treaty of Rarotonga, above note 32, Protocol III.
36 Goldblat, *Arms Control*, above note 24 at 217 *et seq.*
37 *Antarctic Treaty* (1961), 402 U.N.T.S. 71, Art. I.
38 *Ibid.*, Art. V.
39 *Treaty on Principles Governing the Activities of States in the Exploration and Use of Outer Space, including the Moon and Other Celestial Bodies* (1967), 610 U.N.T.S. 205, Art. IV [Outer Space Treaty].

Notably, the language employed in this treaty—the stationing of nuclear weapons or any other kinds of weapons of mass destruction—does not preclude placement of nonnuclear missile defence systems in orbit, or the *transiting* of intercontinental ballistic missiles *through* outer space.

2) Development of Nuclear Weapons by Nonnuclear Weapons States

Nuclear nonproliferation efforts date at least to U.S. President Eisenhower's 1953 "Atoms for Peace" speech, before the U.N. General Assembly. In that address, Eisenhower voiced fear of a nuclear weapons era, and the catastrophe it might bring, and proposed the creation of an international atomic energy agency, tasked with promoting the peaceful use of nuclear technology. In 1957, the International Atomic Energy Agency was established by treaty as a specialized agency of the United Nations. Its functions and mandate, expanded with time, are described below.

Subsequently, in 1961, the U.N. General Assembly adopted a resolution calling on all states, and in particular those with nuclear weapons, to conclude an international agreement

> under which the nuclear States would undertake to refrain from relinquishing control of nuclear weapons and from transmitting the information necessary for their manufacture to States not possessing such weapons, and provisions under which States not possessing nuclear weapons would undertake not to manufacture or otherwise acquire control of such weapons.[40]

Ultimately, in 1968, the NPT was opened for signature and entered in force in 1970. That treaty partitions the international community into nuclear weapon state (NWS) parties and nonnuclear weapon state (NNWS) parties. A NWS is defined as "one which has manufactured and exploded a nuclear weapon or other nuclear explosive device prior to 1 January 1967."[41] It is a class occupied exclusively, therefore, by the United States, Russia (as successor to the U.S.S.R.), the United Kingdom, France and China. Under the NPT, each NWS

> undertakes not to transfer to any recipient whatsoever nuclear weapons or other nuclear explosive devices or control over such weapons or explosive devices directly, or indirectly; and not in any way to assist, encourage, or induce any non-nuclear-weapon State to manufacture or

---

40   GA Res. 1665 (XVI) (1961).
41   NPT, Art. IX.

> otherwise acquire nuclear weapons or other nuclear explosive devices, or control over such weapons or explosive devices.[42]

Further, the NWS, like all parties to the treaty, are to "pursue negotiations in good faith on effective measures relating to cessation of the nuclear arms race at an early date and to nuclear disarmament, and on a treaty on general and complete disarmament under strict and effective international control."[43]

All other state parties—the NNWS—are prohibited from possessing nuclear weapons:

> Each non-nuclear-weapon State Party to the Treaty undertakes not to receive the transfer from any transferor whatsoever of nuclear weapons or other nuclear explosive devices or of control over such weapons or explosive devices directly, or indirectly; not to manufacture or otherwise acquire nuclear weapons or other nuclear explosive devices; and not to seek or receive any assistance in the manufacture of nuclear weapons or other nuclear explosive devices.[44]

Moreover, each NNWS agrees to implement "safeguards, as set forth in an agreement to be negotiated and concluded with the International Atomic Energy Agency in accordance with the Statute of the International Atomic Energy Agency and the Agency's safeguards system, for the exclusive purpose of verification of the fulfilment of its obligations assumed under this Treaty with a view to preventing diversion of nuclear energy from peaceful uses to nuclear weapons or other nuclear explosive devices."[45] Where safeguards are not in place, all parties to the treaty agree not to supply to a state, even for a peaceful purpose, "(a) source or special fissionable material, or (b) equipment or material especially designed or prepared for the processing, use or production of special fissionable material."[46]

As these passages suggest, peaceful use of nuclear technology by NNWS is permitted, and even codified as a right in the NPT:

> 1. Nothing in this Treaty shall be interpreted as affecting the inalienable right of all the Parties to the Treaty to develop research, production and use of nuclear energy for peaceful purposes without discrimination and in conformity with Articles I and II [barring transfer or receipt of nuclear weapons by NNWS] ...

---

42   *Ibid.*, Art. I.
43   *Ibid.*, Art. VI.
44   *Ibid.*, Art. II.
45   *Ibid.*, Art. III.
46   *Ibid.*

2. All the Parties to the Treaty undertake to facilitate, and have the right to participate in, the fullest possible exchange of equipment, materials and scientific and technological information for the peaceful uses of nuclear energy. Parties to the Treaty in a position to do so shall also co-operate in contributing alone or together with other States or international organizations to the further development of the applications of nuclear energy for peaceful purposes, especially in the territories of non-nuclear-weapon States Party to the Treaty, with due consideration for the needs of the developing areas of the world.[47]

As this discussion suggests, uniquely among weapons of mass destruction nonproliferation treaties, the NPT permits the possession of the regulated weapon, albeit by a select cadre of states and subject to an obligation to negotiate disarmament. Like other WMD treaties, the NPT also struggles with the problem of dual use: legitimate civilian uses of a technology that may be diverted to weapons production. As discussed in the sections that follow, both of these attributes of the NPT have created important challenges.

a)   *De Facto* Proliferation

The vast majority of states are parties to the NPT. Not every state has accepted, however, the NPT's monopolization of nuclear weapons in the hands of five states. Thus, the *de facto* nuclear states of India, Pakistan and Israel have not ratified the NPT and therefore have remained outside its requirements. North Korea, while once a party, renounced the NPT in 2003, after violating its safeguards obligations by, *inter alia*, expelling IAEA inspectors. It did so under the treaty's generous renunciation provision. Specifically, with sufficient notice to other parties and the U.N. Security Council, the NPT provides that "each Party shall in exercising its national sovereignty have the right to withdraw from the Treaty if it decides that extraordinary events, related to the subject matter of this Treaty, have jeopardized the supreme interests of its country."[48] In justifying its decision to withdraw, North Korea complained, among other things, of President Bush's identification of the country as part of an "axis of evil" and the United States policy of pre-emptive self-defence, described by North Korea one of "pre-emptive nuclear attack, openly declaring a nuclear war."[49] By 2007, internation-

---

47   *Ibid.*, Art. IV.
48   *Ibid.*, Art. X.
49   North Korean government statement (10 January 2003), online: www.korea-dpr. com/library/203.pdf.

al diplomatic efforts designed to curb North Korea's nuclear weapons program, and draw the country back into the NPT and the safeguards regime, continued. In October 2006, in the wake of an apparent nuclear weapon test by North Korea, the U.N. Security Council imposed supplemental economic sanctions on the state.[50]

The North Korea case illustrates the limitations of the NPT as a firm international legal regime. That instrument's reach depends on the consent of states. Where states fail to join, or renounce, the treaty, further legal restraints on proliferation depend on U.N. Security Council action under Chapter VII of the U.N. *Charter.*

b) Safeguards

Unlike other states of proliferation concern, Iran remained a party to the NPT by 2007, denied it had nuclear weapons ambitions and regularly asserted its rights under the NPT to peaceful use of the atom. An international community anxious about the destabilizing impact of nuclear weapons in the hands of terrorist-sponsoring regime viewed these claims with increased disbelief. At the heart of the dispute lay Iran's compliance with IAEA "safeguards."

Several international legal instruments require these "safeguards." As noted above, the nuclear free zone treaties—such as the Treaty of Tlatelolco—anticipate an IAEA safeguard regime. More universally, both the international treaty creating the IAEA and the NPT treaty anticipate safeguards obligations on state parties. Thus, the IAEA Statute lists as an Agency function the establishment and administering of safeguards "designed to ensure that special fissionable and other materials, services, equipment, facilities, and information made available by the Agency or at its request or under its supervision or control are not used in such a way as to further any military purpose; and to apply safeguards, at the request of the parties, to any bilateral or multilateral arrangement, or at the request of a State, to any of that State's activities in the field of atomic energy."[51]

The NPT, for its part, identifies the IAEA as the body tasked with implementing safeguards "with a view to preventing diversion of nuclear energy from peaceful uses to nuclear weapons or other nuclear explosive devices."[52] This mandate is narrower than that under the IAEA Statute. As one scholar notes, "the IAEA safeguards adopted before the conclusion of the NPT were intended to ensure that nuclear items

---

50   S/Res/1718 (2006).
51   Statute of the IAEA (1956), 276 U.N.T.S. 3, Art. III.
52   NPT, above note 12, Art. III.

obtained by non-nuclear-weapon states, with the help of the IAEA or under its supervision, were not used for *any* military purpose. The safeguards adopted for the NPT made allowance for the withdrawal from international control of nuclear material destined for non-explosive military purposes."[53] This distinction in safeguards regimes is most important in relation to nuclear submarines, a device in which the nuclear material used for propulsion is often the same as that used in weapons. The NPT safeguard agreement nonexplosive military use exception proved controversial during Canada's (ultimately aborted) proposal to acquire nuclear submarines in the late 1980s.[54]

In fact, most of the safeguard agreements concluded by the IAEA and states have been made pursuant to the NPT. The standard safeguard model agreement—designated INFCIRC/153 (Corrected)—

> requires a State to accept Agency safeguards on all source or special fissionable material in all peaceful nuclear activities within the territory of the State, under its jurisdiction, or carried out under its control anywhere. It requires that the State establish and maintain a system to account for and control all nuclear material subject to safeguards. Many States with comprehensive safeguards agreements have little or no declared nuclear material and/or nuclear activities. Such States have usually concluded a "Small Quantities Protocol" (SQP), which holds in abeyance most of the detailed provisions of Part II of a comprehensive safeguards agreement.[55]

The safeguard system focuses on auditing state declarations; that is, states are supposed to disclose information on their material and activities, which is then verified by the IAEA. Verification takes the form of IAEA monitoring at declared nuclear facilities and sites. The obvious shortcoming in the system relates to undisclosed nuclear material and activities, which the auditing approach to verification is not likely to reveal.

Since the 1990s, and the discovery at that time of an Iraqi weapons program after the 1990 Gulf War, the IAEA has sought to strengthen its safeguard regime, placing a new focus on unearthing undeclared activities and material. To this end, the IAEA has developed a model Additional Protocol (styled INFCIRC/540 (Corrected)) to its standard NPT safeguard agreement. Most states have now entered into this agreement with the IAEA. However, some key states of concern—such

---

53   Goldblatt, *Arms Control*, above note 24 at 103.
54   *Ibid.*
55   IAEA, *The Safeguards System of the International Atomic Energy Agency* at para. 11, online: www.iaea.org/OurWork/SV/Safeguards/safeg_system.pdf [IAEA, *The Safeguards System*].

as Iran—have not implemented such an understanding. The director-general of the IAEA has noted that "all the nuclear material declared by Iran to the Agency has been accounted for—and, apart from the small quantities previously reported to the Board, there have been no further findings of undeclared nuclear material in Iran."[56] However, by September 2006,

> due to the absence of the implementation of the additional protocol, the Agency is not able to assess fully Iran's enrichment related research and development activities, including the possible production of centrifuges and related equipment. ... Because of this, and the lack of readiness of Iran to resolve these issues, the Agency is unable to make further progress in its efforts to provide assurances about the absence of undeclared nuclear material and activities in Iran. This continues to be a matter of serious concern.

As this discussion suggests, under the Additional Protocol, states provide more information about their nuclear cycle—from uranium mines to waste disposal—and their production or trade in certain nuclear-related technologies. The Agency may request "complementary access" from the state to ensure, among other things, the absence of undeclared nuclear material and activities. Complementary access activities "may include examination of records, visual observation, environmental sampling, utilization of radiation detection and measurement devices, and the application of seal and other identifying and tamper-indicating devices."[57]

The Statute of the IAEA establishes the course of action where the Agency concludes a state is violating its safeguards obligations. IAEA inspectors are charged with reporting noncompliance to the Agency's

> Director General who shall thereupon transmit the report to the [Agency's] Board of Governors. The Board shall call upon the recipient State or States to remedy forthwith any non-compliance which it finds to have occurred. The Board shall report the non-compliance to all members and to the Security Council and General Assembly of the United Nations. In the event of failure of the recipient State or States to take fully corrective action within a reasonable time, the Board may take one or both of the following measures: direct curtailment or suspension of assistance being provided by the Agency or by

---

56 *Introductory Statement to the Board of Governors by IAEA Director General Dr. Mohamed ElBaradei* (11 September 2006), online: www.iaea.org/NewsCenter/ Statements/2003/ebsp2003n019.html.

57 IAEA, *The Safeguards System*, above note 55 at para. 38.

a member, and call for the return of materials and equipment made available to the recipient member or group of members. The Agency may also ... suspend any non-complying member from the exercise of the privileges and rights of membership.[58]

A supplemental provision in the statute specifies that if "in connection with the activities of the Agency there should arise questions that are within the competence of the Security Council, the Agency shall notify the Security Council, as the organ bearing the main responsibility for the maintenance of international peace and security."[59] With or without this referral, the U.N. Security Council possesses the authority to respond to instances of proliferation constituting breaches or threats to international peace and security under Chapter VII of the U.N. *Charter.*

By 2006, the IAEA had referred several reports on to the Security Council on Iran's activities. In July 2006, the Security Council issued resolution 1696, employing its Chapter VII powers to demand that Iran "suspend all enrichment-related and reprocessing activities, including research and development, to be verified by the IAEA." Noncompliance with that instrument sparked Resolution 1737 in December 2006. The latter instrument imposed assorted economic sanctions on Iran.

3) Canadian Implementation of the NPT

Canada is a member of the NPT and a NNWS keenly interested in nonproliferation issues. It has responded to its obligations under the NPT and attempted to guard against misuse of nuclear technology via federal law, most notably the *Nuclear Safety and Control Act.*[60] This statute aims to limit "the risks to national security, the health and safety of persons and the environment that are associated with the development, production and use of nuclear energy and the production, possession and use of nuclear substances, prescribed equipment and prescribed information" and to implement Canada's international obligations in relation to nuclear power and weapons nonproliferation.[61]

The Act creates the Canadian Nuclear Safety Commission, charged with regulating the "development, production and use of nuclear energy and the production, possession and use of nuclear substances, prescribed equipment and prescribed information" to prevent un-

---

58   Statute of the IAEA, above note 51, Art. XII.
59   *Ibid.*, Art. III.
60   NSCA, above note 8.
61   *Ibid.*, s. 3.

reasonable national security, environmental or health and safety risks, to meet Canadian international obligations and to disseminate object-ive information on the risks associated with nuclear technology to the public.[62]

The commission serves as the industry regulator, possessing potent powers to licence, inspect and impose obligations on nuclear and nu-clear-related facilities and activities. The Act creates a series of criminal offences for improper use of nuclear materials or noncompliance with commission rules.[63] For instance, it is a crime to alter without permis-sion any thing designed to "maintain national security or implement international obligations to which Canada has agreed, at a nuclear fa-cility or at a place where, or vehicle in which, a nuclear substance is located."[64] It is also an offence to possess a nuclear substance, or cer-tain equipment or information that may be used to produce a nuclear weapon or explosive device.[65]

B. CHEMICAL WEAPONS

As the preceding discussion indicates, the nuclear nonproliferation regime is encumbered by the ready recognition it gives to nuclear weapons possession by a handful of countries. Moreover, the ICJ's *Legality of Nuclear Weapons* advisory opinion and the various regional nuclear free zones notwithstanding, the international community has not unequivocally banned the use of these weapons. This situation differs from that of chemical weapons. The condemnation of the lat-ter weapons is robust and intended as universal. However, like with nuclear technology, the challenge in deterring chemical weapons pro-liferation is distinguishing between peaceful and permissible use of chemicals and their employment for military ends.

1) 1925 Protocol

The starting point for the international regulation of chemical weapons lies in the 1925 *Protocol for the Prohibition of the Use in War of Asphyxiat-ing, Poisonous or Other Gases, and of Bacteriological Methods of Warfare*, in force in 1928. That brief instrument underscores that the "the use in

---

62   *Ibid.*, s. 9.
63   *Ibid.*, s. 48 *et seq.*
64   *Ibid.*, s. 48.
65   *Ibid.*, s. 50.

war of asphyxiating, poisonous or other gases, and of all analogous liquids, materials or devices" is illegal in international law and reaffirms the parties' commitment to this principle. This ban is widely regarded as customary international law, a view affirmed by the U.N. General Assembly in resolution 2603.[66]

In the latter instrument, the General Assembly expressed its view that "the Geneva Protocol embodies the generally recognized rules of international law prohibiting the use in international armed conflicts of all biological and chemical methods of warfare, regardless of technical developments." It defined the use in an international armed conflict of "any chemical agents of warfare—chemical substances, whether gaseous, liquid or solid—which might be employed because of their direct toxic effects on man, animals or plants" as contrary to the Geneva Protocol.

2) Chemical Weapons Convention

The strong principles barring use of chemical weapons notwithstanding, the development of a robust nonproliferation regime awaited the end of the Cold War. The ultimate result of negotiations on such a system was the 1993 *Convention on the Prohibition of the Development, Production, Stockpiling and Use of Chemical Weapons and on their Destruction* (the Chemical Weapons Convention or CWC), in force in April 1997.[67]

a) Core Obligations
Unlike the NPT or the Biological and Toxin Weapons Convention (discussed later in this chapter), the CWC is a massive treaty, in large part because of detailed annexes on implementation and verification. In its core provisions, the convention commits each party to not use riot control agents as a method of warfare and "never under any circumstances:

(a) To develop, produce, otherwise acquire, stockpile or retain chemical weapons, or transfer, directly or indirectly, chemical weapons to anyone;

(b) To use chemical weapons;

(c) To engage in any military preparations to use chemical weapons;

(d) To assist, encourage or induce, in any way, anyone to engage in any activity prohibited to a State Party under this Convention."[68]

---

66   GA Res. 2603 (1969).
67   (1993), 32 I.L.M. 800 [CWC].
68   *Ibid.*, Art. I.

Moreover, each state party pledges "to destroy chemical weapons it owns or possesses, or that are located in any place under its jurisdiction or control, in accordance with the provisions of this Convention" and "to destroy all chemical weapons it abandoned on the territory of another State Party, in accordance with the provisions of this Convention."[69]

"Chemical weapons" are defined in the treaty as:

(a) Toxic chemicals and their precursors, except where intended for purposes not prohibited under this Convention, as long as the types and quantities are consistent with such purposes;

(b) Munitions and devices, specifically designed to cause death or other harm through the toxic properties of those toxic chemicals specified in subparagraph (a), which would be released as a result of the employment of such munitions and devices;

(c) Any equipment specifically designed for use directly in connection with the employment of munitions and devices specified in subparagraph (b).[70]

The CWC commits parties also to take off-line those industrial facilities marshaled to make chemical weapons. First, "each State Party shall cease immediately all activity at chemical weapons production facilities."[71] Further, every state party must "close, not later than 90 days after [the] Convention enters into force for it, all chemical weapons production facilities."[72] In the longer term,

Each State Party undertakes to destroy any chemical weapons production facilities it owns or possesses, or that are located in any place under its jurisdiction or control, in accordance with the provisions of this Convention.[73]

State compliance with the CWC obligations begins with a declaration issued within thirty days of the entry into force of the treaty for the party of all chemical weapons and chemical weapons production facilities.[74] These weapons and facilities are then subject to verification, and each must be destroyed according to an established timetable. For chemical weapons, destruction must begin within two years of entry into force of the treaty for the state and must be completed no later than ten years after the entry into force of the CWC (that is, by 2007,

---

69   *Ibid.*
70   *Ibid.*, Art. II.
71   *Ibid.*, Art. V.
72   *Ibid.*
73   *Ibid.*, Art. I.
74   *Ibid.*, Art. III.

or where a state accedes to the treaty after this point, as soon as possible thereafter).[75] The order of destruction depends on a classification scheme for chemical weapons, as distilled in Table 8.1. By the time of this writing,

> 100% of the declared chemical weapons production facilities have been inactivated. ... 30% of the 8.6 million chemical munitions and containers covered by the Convention have been verifiably destroyed. 23% of the world's declared stockpile of approximately 71,000 metric tonnes of chemical agent have been verifiably destroyed.[76]

The CWC obliges state parties to "adopt the necessary measures to implement its obligations" under the treaty. In particular, state parties must:

(a) Prohibit natural and legal persons anywhere on its territory or in any other place under its jurisdiction as recognized by international law from undertaking any activity prohibited to a State Party under this Convention, including enacting penal legislation with respect to such activity;

(b) Not permit in any place under its control any activity prohibited to a State Party under this Convention; and

(c) Extend its penal legislation enacted under subparagraph (a) to any activity prohibited to a State Party under this Convention undertaken anywhere by natural persons, possessing its nationality, in conformity with international law.[77]

b) Verification

The CWC also creates its own organization — the Organization for the Prohibition of Chemical Weapons (OPCW) — an expert entity tasked with verification of treaty compliance. Three sorts of inspection regimes lie at the core of CWC, as follows:

- *Routine inspections* of chemical weapons-related facilities and industrial facilities using "dual use" chemicals.[78] These inspections are described as "cooperative events"; that is, "the inspection teams are concerned with verifying the contents of declarations and do not

---

75   *Ibid.*, Arts. IV & V.
76   OPCW, *The OPCW Success Story* (February 2007), online: www.opcw.org/factsandfigures/index.html#successStory.
77   *Ibid.*, Art. VII.
78   *Ibid.*, Arts. IV & V.

Table 8.1:   CWC Destruction Timetable

	Category 1	Category 2	Category 3
Definition	Category 1 chemical weapons are those created with schedule 1 chemicals. The latter are listed in an annex, based on several criteria: the chemical is "developed, produced, stockpiled or used as a chemical weapon"; or it "poses otherwise a high risk to the object and purpose of this Convention by virtue of its high potential for use in activities prohibited under this Convention" because of its similarity to other schedule 1 chemicals, its toxicity or its possible use as "a precursor in the final single technological stage of production of a toxic chemical listed in Schedule 1"; or it has "little or no use for purposes not prohibited under this Convention."[1]	Category 2 chemical weapons are those made from "all other chemicals and their parts and components." Thus, this would include weapons created from schedule II or III chemicals. A schedule II chemical, is listed in an annex on the basis that it poses "a significant risk to the object and purpose of this Convention because it possesses such lethal or incapacitating toxicity as well as other properties that could enable it to be used as a chemical weapon; ... It may be used as a precursor in one of the chemical reactions at the final stage of formation of a chemical listed in Schedule 1 or [the toxic chemicals listed in] Schedule 2 ...; (c) It poses a significant risk to the object and purpose of this Convention by virtue of its importance in the production of a chemical listed in Schedule 1 or Schedule 2, part A; (d) It is not produced in large commercial quantities for purposes not prohibited under this Convention."[2] A schedule III chemical is listed	Category 3 chemical weapons are "[u]nfilled munitions and devices, and equipment specifically designed for use directly in connection with employment of chemical weapons."[3]

	Category 1	Category 2	Category 3
Definition (cont'd)		in the annex because (a) It has been produced, stockpiled or used as a chemical weapon; (b) It poses otherwise a risk to the object and purpose of this Convention because it possesses such lethal or incapacitating toxicity as well as other properties that might enable it to be used as a chemical weapon; (c) It poses a risk to the object and purpose of this Convention by virtue of its importance in the production of one or more chemicals listed in Schedule 1 or [the toxic chemicals listed in] Schedule 2 ...; (d) It may be produced in large commercial quantities for purposes not prohibited under the Convention.[4]	
Destruction Schedule	Destruction to begin not later than two years after the Convention enters into force for the state party, and shall be completed not later than 10 years after entry into force of the Convention. A State Party shall destroy chemical weapons in accordance with the following destruction deadlines (with years counted from date of entry into force of the CWC): (i) Phase 1: Not less than 1 per cent of	Destruction to begin not later than one year after the Convention enters into force for it and shall be completed not later than five years after the entry into force of the Convention. Category 2 and 3 chemical weapons shall be destroyed in equal annual increments throughout the destruction period.[5]	

	Category 1	Category 2	Category 3
Destruction Schedule (cont'd)	destroyed within three years; (ii) Phase 2: Not less than 20 per cent destroyed within five years; (iii) Phase 3: Not less than 45 per cent destroyed within seven years; (iv) Phase 4: All Category 1 chemical weapons shall be destroyed not later than 10 years after the entry into force of this Convention.[6]		
Chemical Weapons Production Facilities	Destruction of facilities that manufacture schedule 1 chemicals facilities must begin not later than one year after the Convention enters into force for the state party, and shall be completed not later than 10 years after entry into force of the Convention.[7]	Destruction of facilities other than those that manufacture schedule 1 chemicals must begin not later than one year after the Convention enters into force for the state party, and be completed not later than five years after entry into force of the Convention.[8]	

[1] CWC, above note 67, Annex on Chemicals, A. Guidelines for Schedules of Chemicals.
[2] Ibid.
[3] Ibid., Annex on Implementation and Verification, Part IV(A). Destruction of Chemical Weapons and Its Verification Pursuant to Article IV.
[4] Ibid.
[5] Ibid.
[6] Ibid.
[7] Ibid., Annex on Implementation and Verification, Part V.
[8] Ibid.

adopt an investigative approach."[79] Inspections of chemical weapons-related facilities are the most intrusive. They are conducted on fairly short notice and inspectors are permitted unimpeded access to these facilities. Inspections of industrial facilities vary in their invasiveness depending on the class of chemical manufactured at the facility.[80]

- *Challenge inspections* designed to "clarify and resolve any questions concerning possible non-compliance with the CWC."[81] Challenge inspections may be requested by any state party.[82] State parties may not resist these challenge inspections, regardless of the place in which they occur. Such inspections are launched on very short notice and "can be directed at declared or undeclared facilities and locations."[83]

- *Use of chemical weapons investigations* designed to respond to alleged use of these weapons. These situations may arise either because a state party requests a challenge inspection in circumstances where another state party is believed to have used chemical weapons or where a state party that believes itself to have been targeted requests assistance from the OPCW.[84] The OPCW would also be involved in investigating uses of weapons by non-state parties, in close cooperation with the United Nations.[85]

3) Canadian Implementation of the CWC

Canada implements its international obligations in relation to chemical weapons via the *Chemical Weapons Convention Implementation Act*.[86] Pursuant to this statute, no person shall use a riot control agent as a method of warfare[87] or

    (a) develop, produce, otherwise acquire, stockpile or retain a chemical weapon, or transfer, directly or indirectly, a chemical weapon to anyone;

    (b) use a chemical weapon;

    (c) engage in any military preparations to use a chemical weapon; or

---

79 OPCW, *Fact Sheet 5: Three Types of Inspection* (2000) at 1, online: www.opcw.org/docs/fs5.pdf.

80 *Ibid.* at 2.

81 *Ibid.* at 3.

82 CWC, above note 67, Art. IX.

83 OPCW, *Fact Sheet 5*, above note 79 at 3.

84 CWC, above note 67, Art. X.

85 OPCW, *Fact Sheet 5*, above note 79 at 4.

86 CWCIA, above note 8.

87 *Ibid.*, s. 7.

(d) assist, encourage or induce, in any way, anyone to engage in any activity prohibited to a State Party under the [CW] Convention.[88]

Production, use, acquisition or possession of certain toxic chemicals or precursors is banned unless done in compliance with regulations under the Act. Likewise, any export or import of these chemicals must comply with the *Export and Import Permits Act*,[89] discussed below.

Those who do have access to these chemicals have strict record-keeping obligations. Further, the government may authorize inspections by the OPCW. These inspectors have broad powers to compel production of information and enter any place in Canada to perform their functions,[90] including pursuant to a special warrant power where access is refused by the occupant.[91] Failure to comply with obligations under the Act is a criminal offence.[92]

C. BIOLOGICAL WEAPONS

Although among the oldest of WMD nonproliferation regimes, the limitations on biological and toxicological weapons are among the most underdeveloped. Most critically, while international law categorically bans these weapons, there is no safeguard regime equivalent to those under the NPT or the CWC to ascertain compliance.

1) 1925 Protocol

As with chemical weapons, the starting point for the international regulation of biological weapons lies in the 1925 *Protocol for the Prohibition of the Use in War of Asphyxiating, Poisonous or Other Gases, and of Bacteriological Methods of Warfare*, in force in 1928. That instrument underscores that the "the use in war of asphyxiating, poisonous or other gases, and of all analogous liquids, materials or devices" is illegal in international law, and extended this prohibition to "the use of bacteriological methods of warfare." As noted above, this ban is widely regarded as customary international law, and was acknowledged as such by the U.N. General Assembly in resolution 2603.[93]

---

88   *Ibid.*, s. 6.
89   *Ibid.*, ss. 8–10.
90   *Ibid.*, ss. 12–13.
91   *Ibid.*, s. 15.
92   *Ibid.*, s. 20.
93   GA Res. 2603 (1969).

In that instrument, the General Assembly expressed its view that "the Geneva Protocol embodies the generally recognized rules of international law prohibiting the use in international armed conflicts of all biological and chemical methods of warfare, regardless of technical developments." It therefore viewed the Protocol as banning the use in international conflicts of "any biological agents of warfare — living organisms, whatever their nature, or infective material derived from them — which are intended to cause disease or death in man, animals or plants, and which depend for their effects on their ability to multiply in the person, animal or plant attacked."

2) Biological and Toxin Weapons Convention

A more detailed legal regime for biological and toxicological weapons followed in 1972, entering into force in 1975: the *Convention on the Prohibition of the Development, Production and Stockpiling of Bacteriological (Biological) and Toxin Weapons and on Their Destruction* (the Biological and Toxin Weapons Convention or BTWC).

a) Core Obligations
As compared to the CWC, the BTWC is a succinct treaty. It performs two key roles. First, it includes a prohibition on the possession of biological and toxicological weapons. Second, it commits states to the nonproliferation of these weapons.

In the convention's Article I, state parties undertake

> never in any circumstances to develop, produce, stockpile or otherwise acquire or retain:
> (1) Microbial or other biological agents, or toxins whatever their origin or method of production, of types and in quantities that have no justification for prophylactic, protective or other peaceful purposes;
> (2) Weapons, equipment or means of delivery designed to use such agents or toxins for hostile purposes or in armed conflict.[94]

Note that this prohibition applies to biological agents "that have no justification for prophylactic, protective or other peaceful purposes." By implication, therefore, the convention is regarded as authorizing defensive possession and research.

Under the treaty, each party also agrees to "destroy, or to divert to peaceful purposes, as soon as possible but not later than nine months

---

94   BTWC (1993), 1015 U.N.T.S. 163 (entered into force 25 March 1975), Art. I.

after entry into force of the Convention, all agents, toxins, weapons, equipment and means of delivery specified [above], which are in its possession or under its jurisdiction or control."[95] The treaty does not replicate the 1925 Protocol's bar on use of these weapons, but it does underscore that "Nothing in this Convention shall be interpreted as in any way limiting or detracting from the obligations assumed by any State" under that instrument.[96]

Nonproliferation guarantees in the convention include an obligation on state parties "not to transfer to any recipient whatsoever, directly or indirectly, and not in any way to assist, encourage, or induce any State, group of States or international organizations to manufacture or otherwise acquire any of the agents, toxins, weapons, equipment or means of delivery specified in article I" above.[97] State parties are also to "prohibit and prevent the development, production, stockpiling, acquisition, or retention of the agents, toxins, weapons, equipment and means of delivery specified in article I of the Convention, within the territory of such State, under its jurisdiction or under its control anywhere."[98]

b) Verification

The treaty includes some modest enforcement language. In particular, parties promise "to consult one another and to cooperate in solving any problems which may arise in relation to the objective of, or in the application of the provisions of, the Convention."[99] Further, "any State Party to this convention which finds that any other State Party is acting in breach of obligations deriving from the provisions of the Convention may lodge a complaint with the Security Council of the United Nations," and state parties agree to cooperate in any subsequent U.N. investigation. State parties also pledge "to provide or support assistance, in accordance with the United Nations *Charter*, to any Party to the Convention which so requests, if the Security Council decides that such Party has been exposed to danger as a result of violation of the Convention."[100]

However, the Biological and Toxin Weapons Convention contains no safeguard regime, the key ingredient in the nuclear and chemical weapons nonproliferation regimes. Since the conclusion of the treaty, repeated efforts have been made to strengthen the verification com-

---

95 *Ibid.*, Art. II.
96 *Ibid.*, Art. VIII.
97 *Ibid.*, Art. III.
98 *Ibid.*, Art. IV.
99 *Ibid.*, Art. V.
100 *Ibid.*, Arts. VI & VII.

ponent of the convention. Thus, beginning in 1986 and with revisions in 1991, the treaty parties have implemented "confidence building measures"; specifically, the disclosure between parties of data on their activities, including on defensive biological and toxin research and development (an activity unregulated by the treaty). State compliance with these nonlegally binding measures has been poor.[101] Further, to date efforts of the state parties to conclude a binding safeguard regime have failed, despite lengthy and repeated discussions.

3) Canadian Implementation of the BTWC

A number of federal statutes currently control access to some biological agents.[102] However, increased fears relating to bioterrorism[103] prompted Parliament to enact the *Biological and Toxin Weapons Convention Implementation Act* as part of the *Public Safety Act* in 2004. By the time of this writing, the former statute was not yet in force.

The biological weapons statute represents a belated attempt to centralize control of dangerous biological and toxic substances and implement Canada's obligations under the biological weapons treaty. It bars any person from developing, producing, retaining, stockpiling, otherwise acquiring or possessing, using or transferring "(a) any microbial or other biological agent, or any toxin, for any purpose other than prophylactic, protective or other peaceful purposes; or (b) any weapon, equipment or means of delivery designed to use such an agent or toxin for hostile purposes or in armed conflict."[104] Exempted from this requirement are authorized biological weapons defense programs.

The Act precludes unauthorized access to, or export or import of, certain biological agents or toxins to be identified in the regulations.[105] Persons who deal in these substances have significant record-keeping obligations.[106]

---

101 Arms Control Association, *The Biological Weapons Convention at a Glance* (February 2004), online: www.armscontrol.org/pdf/bwc.pdf.

102 These include the *Food and Drugs Act*, R.S.C. 1985, c. F-27, the *Health of Animals Act*, S.C. 1990, c. 21, the *Plant Protection Act*, S.C. 1990, c. 22, the *Feeds Act*, R.S.C. 1985, c. F-9, the *Fertilizers Act*, R.S.C. 1985, c. F-10, the *Seeds Act*, R.S.C. 1985, c. S-8, the *Meat Inspection Act*, R.S.C. 1985 (1st Supp.), c. 25, the *Fisheries Act*, R.S.C. 1985, c. F-14, and the *Pest Control Products Act*, S.C. 2002, c. 28.

103 See discussion in Library of Parliament, *Bill C-7: The Public Safety Act, 2002*, LS-463E (2004) at 39, online: www.parl.gc.ca/common/bills_ls.asp?Parl=37&Sess=3&ls=c7.

104 BTWCIA, above note 8, s. 6.

105 *Ibid.*, s. 7.

106 *Ibid.*, s. 17.

The statute anticipates international inspections, and grants substantial powers to both domestic and international inspectors to enter premises and compel production of information. As in the chemical weapons statute, a special warrant process is anticipated for entry into dwelling-houses.[107] Failure to comply with the core prohibitions in the Act is a criminal offence.[108]

PART IV: CONTROLS ON TECHNOLOGY TRANSFER

Limits on the movement of goods and technology to proliferating states are key to restricting weapons proliferation. This part focuses on international export control initiatives and Canadian export control law.

A. INTERNATIONAL EXPORT CONTROLS

1) Trade Law

The regulation of international technology transfers is, at core, the regulation of the movement of goods (and services) between states. The multilateral trading regime—in particular, the agreements constituting the World Trade Organization—governs the international trade in goods (and to a much lesser extent, services). At the heart of international trade law is the General Agreement on Tariffs and Trade (GATT) of 1947. Although since amended and embellished by other agreements, the GATT establishes the core principles of international trade law, one of which is found in Article XXI:

> No prohibitions or restrictions other than duties, taxes or other charges, whether made effective through quotas, import or export licences or other measures, shall be instituted or maintained by any contracting party on the importation of any product of the territory of any other contracting party or on the exportation or sale for export of any product destined for the territory of any other contracting party.

At first blush, this provision appears to constrain state parties' abilities to limit exports. As might be expected, however, the GATT

---

107 *Ibid.*, s. 8 *et seq.*
108 *Ibid.*, s. 14.

regime—like other trade law instruments—includes a number of exemptions. Thus, Article XXI of the GATT provides that:

> Nothing in this Agreement shall be construed ... (b) to prevent any contracting party from taking any action which it considers necessary for the protection of its essential security interests (i) relating to fissionable materials or the materials from which they are derived; (ii) relating to the traffic in arms, ammunition and implements of war and to such traffic in other goods and materials as is carried on directly or indirectly for the purpose of supplying a military establishment; (iii) taken in time of war or other emergency in international relations

The term "essential security interests" is not a legal term of art and is therefore fraught with ambiguity. Indeed, this exception has proven fairly elastic in the past. Countries have regularly argued that determining security interests is a matter for their sole discretion.[109] Whatever the proper outer limits of its scope, however, it seems clear that Article XXI accommodates export constraints designed to restrict the proliferation of weapons of mass destruction.

2) Soft Law Measures

As noted above, the nuclear, chemical and biological weapons conventions usually include language designed to curb the transfer (for nonpeaceful purposes) of relevant technology. There is not, however, a more detailed binding international treaty on technology transfers in the WMD context. Instead, several soft law initiatives have evolved at the international level, essentially coordinating the export controls activity of like-minded industrial countries. The key WMD nonproliferation export control regimes are the Missile Technology Control Regime, the Australia Group, and the Nuclear Suppliers Group. Canada is a participant in each of these initiatives. The mandates of these voluntary regimes are outlined in Table 8.2.

---

109 For a discussion of relevant cases, see discussion in David Shapiro, "Be Careful What You Wish For: U.S. Politics and the Future of the National Security Exception to the GATT" (1997) 31 Geo. Wash. J. Int'l L. & Econ. 97; Hannes L. Schloemann & Stefan Ohlhoff, "Constitutionalization and Dispute Settlement in the WTO: National Security As An Issue Of Competence" (1999) 93 A.J.I.L. 424.

Table 8.2: Soft Law Export Control Regimes

Initiative	Focus	Activities	Undertakings of State Participants
Missile Technology Control Regime	Missile delivery systems capable of deploying WMDs	Maintains common export policy guidelines applied to a common list of missile and missile-related technologies.	Where a transfer could "contribute to a delivery system for weapons of mass destruction, the [exporting] Government will authorize transfers of items in the [control list] only on receipt of appropriate assurances from the government of the recipient state that: A. The items will be used only for the purpose stated and that such use will not be modified nor the items modified or replicated without the prior consent of the Government; B. Neither the items nor replicas nor derivatives thereof will be re transferred without the consent of the Government."[1]
Australia Group	Proliferation of biological and chemical weapons	Maintains a common control list applied under each state's national export controls law relating to 63 chemical weapons precursors and specific: dual-use chemical manufacturing facilities, equipment and related technology; plant pathogens; animal pathogens; biological agents; and dual-use biological equipment.[2]	States agree, *inter alia*, that export will be denied if the exporting state government "judges, on the basis of all available, persuasive information, ... that the controlled items are intended to be used in a chemical weapons or biological weapons program, or for CBW terrorism, or that a significant risk of diversion exists."[3]
Nuclear Suppliers Group	Proliferation of nuclear weapons	Maintains standardizing guidelines on the supply of nuclear technology of two sorts: a nuclear technology "trigger list" listing technology to be supplied only where the recipient has in place IAEA safeguards (INFCIRC/254, Part 1); and a list of dual use technology that may be	States, *inter alia*, "should authorize transfer of items or related technology identified in the trigger list only upon formal governmental assurances from recipients explicitly excluding uses which would result in any nuclear explosive device."[4] For dual use technology, states "should not authorize transfers of [dual use technology]

Initiative	Focus	Activities	Undertakings of State Participants
Nuclear Suppliers Group (cont'd)		employed for both peaceful and weapons purposes (INFCIRC/254, Part 2).	… for use in a non-nuclear-weapon state in a nuclear explosive activity or an unsafeguarded nuclear fuel-cycle activity, or in general, when there is an unacceptable risk of diversion to such an activity, or when the transfers are contrary to the objective of averting the proliferation of nuclear weapons, or when there is an unacceptable risk of diversion to acts of nuclear terrorism.[5]

[1] MTCR Guidelines, Art. 5, online: www.mtcr.info/english/guidetext.htm.
[2] See Australia Group website at www.australiagroup.net/en/agact.htm.
[3] Australia Group Guidelines, Art. 2, online: www.australiagroup.net/en/guidelines.html.
[4] Guidelines for Nuclear Transfers, INFCIRC/254/Rev.8/Part 1 at para. 2.
[5] Guidelines for Nuclear Transfers, INFCIRC/254/Rev.7/Part 2 at para. 2.

3) Interdiction of Maritime Transfers

a) Background

A counterproliferation strategy that has attracted particular attention post-9/11 has involved impeding the movement of WMD material by sea. International shipping is a notoriously underregulated practice. Outside of a narrow strips of coastal waters subject to varying amounts of coastal state jurisdiction—most notably, internal waters, the territorial seas and the contiguous zone—regulatory authority over ships lies almost exclusively with the flagging state; that is, the state of registry. Absent "hot pursuit" of a foreign-flagged vessel suspected of an infraction while within these coastal waters or the intercept of a vessel without flag and/or suspected of piracy, nonflagging states cannot interfere with ships on the high seas. Regulation of shipping on the high seas depends, therefore, on adequate oversight by flagging nations.

Article 91 of the U.N. Law of the Sea (LOS) Convention[110] specifies that there "must exist a genuine link between the State and the ship" for that state to extend nationality to the ship. This provision has fallen on largely deaf ears, and so-called open registry states exist, extending their nationality or "flag" to virtually anyone. These jurisdictions are sometimes called "flag of convenience" states. The Institute of Shipping Economics reports that "[a]s of January 1st, 2004, 13,840 merchant ships ... equal to 64.0 per cent of the total tonnage were not registered in the country of domicile of the owner but flagged-out" to open registry states.[111] These nations, like Panama or Liberia, provide tax regimes advantageous to shipping companies and notoriously underwhelming regulatory schemes. They tend also to be undemanding in relation to disclosure, permitting ships to be registered by true owners through a shadowy (and obscuring) chain of holding companies. Indeed, media reports warn of the threat presented by the so-called al-Qaeda navy, a fleet of freighters owned, ultimately, by bin Laden that reportedly ply the seas carrying mostly legitimate cargoes but also capable (and perhaps guilty in the past) of carrying weapons or explosives.[112]

---

110 (1982), 1833 U.N.T.S. 397.

111 ISL, *Total Merchant Fleet by Country of Domicile*, online: www.isl.org/products_services/publications/samples/COMMENT_4-2004-short.shtml.en.

112 See, for example, untitled news item, *The Washington Post* (5 January 2003) ("U.S. intelligence officials have identified approximately 15 cargo freighters around the world that they believe are controlled by al Qaeda or could be used by the terrorist network to ferry operatives, bombs, money or commodities over the high seas"); John Mintz, "U.S. Tracking 15 Mystery Ships" *Toronto Star* (2 January 2003) A.12.

The terrorism implications of maritime insecurity were under-scored by the 2005 U.S. National Strategy for Maritime Security:

> Terrorists can ... develop effective attack capabilities relatively quickly using a variety of platforms, including explosives-laden suicide boats and light aircraft; merchant and cruise ships as kinetic weapons to ram another vessel, warship, port facility, or offshore platform; com-mercial vessels as launch platforms for missile attacks; underwater swimmers to infiltrate ports; and unmanned underwater explosive delivery vehicles. ... Terrorists can also take advantage of a vessel's legitimate cargo, such as chemicals, petroleum, or liquefied natural gas, as the explosive component of an attack. Vessels can be used to transport powerful conventional explosives or WMD for detonation in a port or alongside an offshore facility.[113]

The National Strategy also underscored the link between terrorism and WMD. In fact, maritime-based proliferation concerns were height-ened by the 2002 shipment by North Korea to Yemen of Scud missiles. Initially intercepted by a U.S.-led naval patrol because it flew no flag and its markings were obscured, the vessel in question was ultimately al-lowed to proceed to its destination (a U.S. ally in the "war on terror").[114]

b) Proliferation Security Initiative

One response to this threat of maritime-based WMDs has been the Proliferation Security Initiative (PSI). Pursuant to the PSI, participat-ing states agree to use their own laws and coordinate their activities to interdict shipments (via sea or air) of dangerous technology to sus-pect states and nonstate actors. Thus, pursuant to the PSI's *Statement of Interdiction Principles*, states agree to:

> Undertake effective measures, either alone or in concert with other states, for interdicting the transfer or transport of WMD, their deliv-ery systems, and related materials to and from states and non-state actors of proliferation concern. "States or non-state actors of prolifera-tion concern" generally refers to those countries or entities that the PSI participants involved establish should be subject to interdiction activities because they are engaged in proliferation through: (a) efforts to develop or acquire chemical, biological, or nuclear weapons and as-

---

113 U.S. Government, *National Strategy for Maritime Security* (2005), online: www.whitehouse.gov/homeland/maritime-security.html.

114 Thom Shanker, "If the Scuds Were Going to Iraq" *New York Times* (15 December 2002) at 4.6.

sociated delivery systems; or (b) transfers (either selling, receiving, or facilitating) of WMD, their delivery systems, or related materials.[115]

The PSI does not change the rules of international law. But states agree to exert existing authority rigorously.[116] Thus, under the *Statement of Interdiction Principles*, state participants promise to police their own internal waters, territorial seas and contiguous zones carefully. Each participating state is also asked to "seriously consider providing consent under the appropriate circumstances to the boarding and searching of its own flag vessels by other states and to the seizure of such WMD-related cargoes in such vessels that may be identified by such states."[117]

In keeping with this last request, at the heart of the PSI are reciprocal, bilateral "ship boarding" agreements between the United States and key ship registry nations, including the world's most important flagging states, Panama and Liberia. These agreements anticipate (but do not require automatic) reciprocal authorization from each state to board the other's commercial ships on the high seas in order to interdict movement of dangerous material and weapons.[118] Put another way, participants signal preparedness in the agreements to delegate their jurisdiction under international law to regulate ships flying their flag. Since the United States is one of the few states with a true "blue water" navy able to conduct interdictions on the high seas, the PSI "ship boarding" agreements provide it with the means to seek (and receive) from flagging states "proxy" authority to regulate the latter's shipping in international waters.

Canada is one of about seventy states that participated in the PSI by 2006, but is not among the several countries that have concluded a bilateral ship boarding agreement with the United States.

B. CANADIAN EXPORT CONTROLS

In its most recent comprehensive statement on nuclear nonproliferation, the Canadian government noted that

> legal obligations, even when reinforced by verification measures, can be evaded. There are also, of course, countries which have yet to ac-

---

115 *Statement of Interdiction Principles*, Principle 1 (4 September 2003), online: www.state.gov/t/isn/rls/fs/23764.htm.

116 Arms Control Association, *The Proliferation Security Initiative at a Glance* (June 2004), online: www.armscontrol.org/pdf/psi%20at%20a%20glance.pdf.

117 *Statement of Interdiction Principles*, above note 115, Principle 4(c).

118 For the text of these agreements, see the U.S. Department of State, at www.state. gov/t/np/c12386.htm.

cept these legal obligations by adhering to the NPT. This is why Canada, along with other like-minded States, has taken measures not to contribute, willingly or unwillingly, to another country's nuclear weapons program. As a legal instrument, the NPT has made this policy an obligation. Canada fulfills these obligations, in part, through its system of national export controls.[119]

1) Core Requirements of the EIPA

Canada's core export control law is the *Export and Import Permits Act* (EIPA).[13] EIPA is a complex statute regulating various aspects of Canada's trade relations and serving as an important tool of trade policy. The Act includes an "Export Control List," an "Import Control List" and an "Area Control List," all of which are capable of restricting trade for certain enumerated reasons.

a) Control Lists

The grounds for placing goods on an Export Control List (ECL) include instances where exported goods might be used in a fashion detrimental to national security. The Act provides that an ECL may be established to "ensure that arms, ammunition, implements or munitions of war, naval, army or air stores or any articles deemed capable of being converted thereinto or made useful in the production thereof or otherwise having a strategic nature or value will not be made available to any destination where their use might be detrimental to the security of Canada."[120] Similarly, many of the bases for placing goods on the Import Control list are arguably grounded in national security justifications.[121] Further, goods may also be placed on both lists "to implement an intergovernmental arrangement or commitment."[122]

For its part, the Area Control list allows Cabinet to "establish a list of countries" where it deems "it necessary to control the export of any goods."[123] This is a discretionary power unconnected with the Export or Import Control lists, and thus unfettered by any conditions. As one observer has stated, the Area Control List mechanism "assumes that the destination of the good is *per se* a reason for the restriction of its export,

---

119 Government of Canada (DFAIT), *Nuclear Disarmament And Non-Proliferation: Advancing Canadian Objectives* (Ottawa: Department of Foreign Affairs and International Trade, 1999).
120 *Ibid.*, s. 3.
121 *Ibid.*, s. 5.
122 *Ibid.*, s. 3(d) and 5(e).
123 *Ibid.*, s. 4.

regardless of the nature of the good and its potential applications under any circumstance."[124] The List has been used to impose sanctions for political reasons. As of 2007, the Area Control List included two states: Belarus and Myanmar (Burma).[125] Belarus was placed on the list in 2006, while Burma was named in the 1990s. In both cases, the government was responding to deteriorating human rights conditions in the countries.

b) Permitting Requirements

Where goods are placed on either the Export or Import Control lists or are destined for a country on the Area Control List, international trade from Canada in these goods is illicit in the absence of ministerial permits.[126] The Act also bars knowing diversion of goods, via transshipment or otherwise, on the Export Control List to a country on the Area Control List.[127] Permits themselves may also not be transferred.[128] Violation of the Act or its regulations is a criminal offence.[129]

c) Expanded Scope to Technologies

In 2004, the *Public Safety Act* amended the EIPA, expanding its reach beyond goods to include the "transfer" of "technology."[130] "Transfer" means "in relation to technology, to dispose of it or disclose its content in any manner from a place in Canada to a place outside Canada." "Technology" includes "technical data, technical assistance and information necessary for the development, production or use of an article included in an Export Control List." It includes, in other words, intangible information, and not just material objects.

These provisions empower the government to regulate technology transfer via the Export or Area Control Lists. Export or transfer permits may be issued by the government, at its discretion. The amendments clarify, however, that in deciding the question of a permit, the government may consider whether the goods and technology subject to the permit may be used in a fashion prejudicial to:

(a) the safety or interests of the State by being used to do anything referred to in paragraphs 3(1)(a) to (n) of the *Security of Information Act*; or

---

124 Selma M. Lussenburg, "The Collision of Canadian and U.S. Sovereignty in the Area of Export Controls" (1994) 20 Can.-U.S.L.J. 145.
125 S.O.R./81-543.
126 EIPA, above note 8, ss. 7, 8, 13, & 14.
127 *Ibid.*, s. 15.
128 *Ibid.*, s. 16.
129 *Ibid.*, s. 19.
130 *Public Safety Act, 2002*, S.C. 2004, c.15, s. 52 *et seq.*

(b) peace, security or stability in any region of the world or within any country.[131]

As discussed in chapter 10, actions prejudicial to Canadian safety and interests enumerated in the *Security of Information Act* include: commission of certain criminal offences designed, for instance, to benefit a foreign entity or terrorist group; terrorist activity; causing an urgent or critical situation in Canada endangering the safety of Canadians or undermining the government's ability to preserve its sovereignty; interruption of essential services; and assorted other threats to what can broadly be labelled national security.

2) Scope of the Export Control List

The Export Control List,[132] established by regulation under the EIPA, classifies restricted items into several categories or "groups." Several of these groups focus specifically on WMD proliferation. These are set out in Table 8.3.

Table 8.3: Export Control Group Categories

WMD	Content
Group 3 (Nuclear Nonproliferation)	Goods the export of which Canada has agreed to control under the Nuclear Nonproliferation Treaty.
	Goods "the export of which Canada is committed to control in accordance with the procedures contained in Information Circular 254/Rev. 2/Part 1 of the International Atomic Energy Agency of October 1995" (that is, the guidelines associated with the Nuclear Suppliers Group, discussed above).
	Goods "the export of which Canada has agreed to control under the *Exchange of Letters between the European Atomic Energy Community (Euratom) and the Government of Canada amending the Agreement between the European Atomic Energy Community (Euratom) and the Government of Canada for cooperation in the peaceful uses of atomic energy of 6 October 1959*, concluded on July 15, 1991."
	Goods "the export of which Canada has agreed to control under bilateral Nuclear Co-operation Agreements concluded with" the countries or organizations listed in the regulations.
Group 4 (Nuclear Dual-Use)	Goods the export of which Canada has agreed to control under the Nuclear Non-Proliferation Treaty.

---

131 *Ibid.*, s. 56, amending s. 7 of the EIPA, above note 8.
132 S.O.R./89-202.

WMD	Content
Group 4 (cont'd)	Goods "the export of which Canada is committed to control in accordance with the procedures contained in Information Circular 254/Rev. 2/Part 2 of the International Atomic Energy Agency of October 1995" (that is, the guidelines associated with the Nuclear Suppliers Group, discussed above).
Group 5 (Miscellaneous Goods)	The list of miscellaneous goods includes nuclear fusion reactors and certain "strategic goods," such as nuclear weapons design and test equipment, and goods intended for use (or where there are reasonable grounds to suspect the goods are intended for use) in "(i) the development, production, handling, operation, maintenance, storage, detection, identification or dissemination of chemical, biological or nuclear weapons, or of materials or equipment that could be used in such weapons, (ii) the development, production, handling, operation, maintenance or storage of missiles capable of delivering chemical, biological or nuclear weapons, or of materials or equipment that could be used in such missiles, or (iii) any chemical, biological or nuclear weapons facility or missile facility."
Group 6 (Missile Technology Control Regime)	Goods "the export of which Canada has agreed to control under bilateral arrangements concluded on April 7, 1987, in accordance with the *Guidelines for Sensitive Missile-Relevant Transfers*, issued by the Missile Technology Control Regime to control the export of missile equipment and technology that could be used in the development of missile systems capable of delivering nuclear weapons."
Group 7 (Chemical and Biological Weapons Nonproliferation)	Goods "the export of which Canada has agreed to control under a bilateral arrangement concluded December 24, 1992, between Canada and the United States, this arrangement having been made in accordance with the guidelines established by the Australia Group for the purpose of considering ways to limit the proliferation of chemical and biological weapons.
	Goods "the export of which Canada has agreed to control under the *Convention on the Prohibition of the Development, Production, Stockpiling and Use of Chemical Weapons and on their Destruction*, as amended from time to time pursuant to Article XV of that Convention."

3) Impact of U.S. Export Control Law on the EIPA

The EIPA cannot be read in isolation, requiring also a clear appreciation of U.S. export control law. The U.S. export control regime is a very strict one, imposing significant constraints on both exports and also re-exports of goods and technology. Because of its extraterritorial reach, it has had an important impact on Canadian law and policy and must, therefore, be discussed in this book.[133]

a)   Overview of U.S. Export Control Laws

i)   ITAR

Commercial arms exports from the United States are governed by the *International Traffic in Arms Regulations* (ITAR),[134] an instrument introduced pursuant to the *Arms Export Control Act* (AECA).[135] Administered by the U.S. Department of State, the ITAR establishes a "U.S. Munitions List" covering military items. Export of these items from the United States requires a licence from the State Department. The AECA provides that:

> Decisions on issuing export licenses under this section shall take into account whether the export of an article would contribute to an arms race, aid in the development of weapons of mass destruction, support international terrorism, increase the possibility of outbreak or escalation of conflict, or prejudice the development of bilateral or multilateral arms control or nonproliferation agreements or other arrangements.[136]

"Export" is defined broadly in the ITAR to include not simply physical transfer, but also "disclosing (including oral or visual disclosure) or transferring technical data to a foreign person, whether in the United States or abroad."[137] Export licences typically include end-use and re-transfer restrictions.[138]

ii)   Export Administration Regulations

A second major U.S. export control regime is that established by the Export Administration Regulations (EAR),[139] made under the authority of the *Export Administration Act*[140] and, from time to time, the *Inter-*

---

133   This discussion is drawn, *inter alia*, from Todd Buchwald & Michael Matheson, "U.S. Security Assistance and Related Programs," in John Norton Moore & Robert Turner, *National Security Law* (Durham, NC: Carolina Academic Press, 2005) and Larry Christensen, "Dual Use Export Controls," in Moore & Turner, *ibid.*
134   22 C.F.R. § 120 *et seq.*
135   22 U.S.C. § 2778.
136   22 U.S.C. § 2778(a).
137   22 C.F.R. § 120.17.
138   See 22 C.F.R. § 123.10.
139   15 C.F.R. § 730 *et seq.*
140   50 U.S.C. § 2401 *et seq.*

national Emergency Economic Powers Act[141] and administered by the U.S. Department of Commerce. The EAR governs dual-use goods and technologies. The term dual-use "serves to distinguish EAR-controlled items that can be used both in military and other strategic uses and in civil applications from those that are weapons and military related use or design and subject to the controls" exercised under the ITAR and other U.S. export control regimes.[142] Some of the EAR controls "are designed to restrict access to dual use items by countries or persons that might apply such items to uses inimical to U.S. interests. These include controls designed to stem the proliferation of weapons of mass destruction and controls designed to limit the military and terrorism support capability of certain countries."[143]

As under the ITAR, "export" is broadly defined to mean "an actual shipment or transmission of items subject to the EAR out of the United States, or release of technology or software subject to the EAR to a foreign national in the United States."[144] "Re-export," for its part, "means an actual shipment or transmission of items subject to the EAR from one foreign country to another foreign country; or release of technology or software subject to the EAR to a foreign national outside the United States."[145]

The EAR include a series of prohibitions on export and re-export. These include the export or re-export of items on the "Commerce Control List" to designated countries. Items on this control list are so classified for a number of national security reasons, including proliferation concerns. These bans may be negated where the export or re-export is properly licenced by the Department of Commerce.

b) Implications for Canada

The close integration of the Canadian and U.S. economies presents particular difficulties for export controls, especially given the long reach of the American laws. The Department of Foreign Affairs and International Trade offers the following warning in its official guide to export controls:

> The Government of the United States has traditionally controlled the export from other countries of goods and technology that had their origins in the United States and as such, imposes re-export controls.

---

141 50 U.S.C. § 1702 *et seq.*
142 15 C.F.R. § 730.3.
143 15 C.F.R. § 730.6.
144 15 C.F.R. § 734.2.
145 *Ibid.*

Exporters are cautioned that some U.S. origin goods and technology, including U.S. origin parts and components incorporated into a finished product, may be subject to U.S. re-export controls.[146]

Traditionally, Canada has enjoyed a privileged status under U.S. export control law, in large measure because of the highly integrated defence relationship between the two countries. Up until the late 1990s, most defence-related goods and technology could be exchanged between Canada and the United States without export licences under the ITAR. Although Canadian firms were still subject to re-export rules, this special export status permitted Canadian defence firms—most of whom depend on U.S. technology in whole or in part—to avoid the transaction costs and delay associated with acquiring U.S. licences, thereby enhancing their competitiveness.

However, the special Canadian status under the ITAR was revoked in the late 1990s, when the "U.S. Department of State *de facto* and unilaterally rescinded many of the Canada-U.S. defence economic agreements and arrangements that lay at the basis of the North American defence and industrial-technological base. The United States increased the number and types of equipment and technologies subject to the ITARs, while revoking substantial quantity of Canada's export licensing exemptions."[147] Among other things, the United States complained that U.S. munitions had been diverted from Canada to third countries without authorization. A 2001 State Department memorandum reported:

> Past inconsistencies between U.S. and Canadian defense export laws and regulations and enforcement practices had made Canada an increasingly attractive location for parties seeking to abuse the original Canadian exemption by illegally retransferring from Canada defense articles and technology subject to ITAR controls to ineligible parties or proscribed destinations.[148]

Most of the Canadian exemptions were restored within two years, but only after significant changes in Canada's own export control regime in relation to U.S. origin defence goods and technology.

---

146 Canada, DFAIT, *A Guide to Canada's Export Controls* (September 2003) at v, online: www.dfait-maeci.gc.ca/eicb/military/documents/exportcontrols2006-en.pdf.

147 Alex Moens & Rafal Domisiewicz, *European and North American Trends in Defence Industry: Problems and Prospects of a Cross-Atlantic Defence Market* (April 2001), online: www.dfait-maeci.gc.ca/arms/isrop/research/moens&domisiewicz_2001/cross-en.asp.

148 See U.S. Department of State, Action Memorandum (19 January 2001), available at www.fas.org/asmp/campaigns/control/Canadianexemptionsfoia/P6BK.pdf.

i)   General Rules on Re-export of U.S.-Origin Goods

First, strict new Canadian rules were introduced for the re-export of U.S. origin goods. Most sweepingly, item 5400 of the Export Control List now lists "all goods that originate in the United States," not covered by other categories. In practice, since military and strategic items are encompassed by other classes (see below), item 5400 is for nonmilitary and nonstrategic items.

Foreign Affairs describes this listing as "designed to ensure Canada is not used as a diversionary route to circumvent U.S. embargoes."[149] All U.S.-origin goods are now subject to Canadian licensing requirements for subsequent export from Canada. Because the key focus is on honouring U.S. embargoes, exporters may avail themselves of "general export permits" in relation to most goods and destinations, and need not obtain permits for individual export transactions. However, these general export permits are unavailable for exports to countries on the Area Control List or to Cuba, North Korea, Iran or Syria.[150] The latter are the proscribed states under the U.S. ITAR, and the Canadian regulations are adjusted from time to time to reflect changes on the U.S. embargo list.[151] For these countries, individual permits are available,[152] but are presumably granted in limited circumstances.

ii)   Special Rules on U.S.-Origin Military or Strategic Goods

The rules for U.S.-origin military or strategic goods are much stricter. Here, Canada expressly harmonized its export control list with the ITAR (U.S.-origin strategic goods with substantial military applicability, in item 5404).[153]

This item, and several more specific arms-related classes in the ECL, are defined as "controlled goods" under the *Defence Production Act*.[154] Regulations under the *Export and Import Permits Act* require that licence applications for the export of such "controlled goods" from Canada include "United States export authorization."[155] Put another way, demonstrated compliance with U.S. licencing requirements for re-export of U.S.-origin strategic goods and technology from Canada is now a precondition to observance of the Canadian licencing require-

---

149 DFAIT, *A Guide to Canada's Export Controls*, above note 146 at v.
150 S.O.R./97-107.
151 See, for example, S.O.R./2005-223 (adding Syria to the list of countries for which General Export Permits are not available and removing Libya).
152 DFAIT, *A Guide to Canada's Export Controls*, above note 146 at vii.
153 S.O.R./89-202, Group 5 at 5504.
154 R.S.C. 1985, c. D-1, Sch. [DPA[.
155 S.O.R./97-204, s. 3(2)(c).

ments. In this manner, Canada acts as a proxy enforcer of U.S. laws, barring diversion of U.S. goods and technology.

iii) *Technology Transfer within Canada*

Another important step taken by Canada to restore the special U.S. export relationship was to institute a U.S.-origin technology control regime applicable *within* Canada.

The *Defence Production Act* (DPA) delegates powers to the minister of national defence "to buy or otherwise acquire defence supplies and construct defence projects" and to undertake defence-related procurement.[156] In 2000, however, the DPA was substantially amended to regulate access to "controlled goods." These changes were enacted as part of the Canadian-U.S. agreement restoring most of Canada's privileged status under the ITAR.[157] As noted above, "controlled goods" includes U.S.-origin strategic goods with substantial military applicability as well as several other munitions and arms related items on the Export Control List.

Federal and provincial officials are exempted from the new rules. However, unless otherwise exempted, everyone else is barred from knowingly examining or possessing a controlled good or transferring a controlled good to another person. "Transfer" means "in respect of a controlled good, to dispose of it or disclose its content in any manner."[158] Violation of these requirements is punishable with serious criminal penalties.[159]

Certain classes of person, such as those already registered under the U.S. ITAR, are exempted.[160] In other circumstances, access to controlled goods may be permitted following registration. In this respect, Canadian citizens or permanent residents or Canadian incorporated or licensed companies may apply for registration under a system administered by Public Works and Government Services Canada. In deciding whether to allow this registration, the government must consider, for example, "based on a security assessment, the extent to which the applicant poses a risk of transferring controlled goods to a person who is not registered or exempt from registration."[161] The requisite security

---

156 DPA, above note 154, ss. 10 and 16.
157 See discussion in Library of Parliament, *Bill S-25: An Act to Amend the Defence Production Act*, LS-370E (6 September 2000), online: www.parl.gc.ca/common/bills_ls.asp?lang=E&ls=S25&Parl=36&Ses=2.
158 DPA, above note 154, s. 37.
159 *Ibid.*, s. 45.
160 S.O.R./2001-32, s. 16.
161 *Ibid.*, s. 4.

assessment is to consider such things as personal references and criminal records.[162]

The DPA controlled goods list essentially imposes a Canadian domestic system of end-user restrictions, one that is expressly designed to forestall the imposition of U.S. ITAR regulations accomplishing the same end. As a partial concession for this remarkable system, the restored U.S. ITAR Canadian exemptions extend to not only Canadian government personnel, nationals and companies, but also dual nationals and permanent residents, so long as these persons are registered under the DPA.[163]

The ITAR licensing exemptions to DPA-registered dual nationals and permanent residents is, however, subject to an important limit: it *does not* apply to dual nationals of states subject to comprehensive U.S. sanctions or arms embargoes.[164]

Differentiating between dual nationals of different nationalities or between dual nations and single nationality Canadians constitutes discrimination. Canadian human rights instruments, for instance, bar discrimination on the basis of "national or ethnic origin."[165] For this reason, a Canadian company that resists hiring a dual national to avoid running afoul of the ITAR might be subjected to a human rights complaint.[166]

For its part, section 15 of the *Canadian Charter of Rights and Freedoms* also precludes discrimination on the basis of "national and ethnic origin." The *Charter* applies, however, only to government, not to the private sector. It is not clear that the ITAR claw-back of exemptions for certain dual nationals applies to Canadian government officials, as opposed simply to dual nationals in the private sector.[167] Nevertheless, by

---

162 *Ibid.*, s. 15.

163 22 C.F.R. § 126.5. The ITAR generally regulates exports on a strict nationality basis, and the sharing of technology with a dual national or permanent resident is typically regarded as an export to that person's state of nationality or nationalities. See U.S. Department of State, Action Memorandum (19 January 2001).

164 22 C.F.R. §§ 126.1 and 126.5. In 2007, these states were Belarus, Cuba, Iran, North Korea, Syria, Venezuela, Burma, China, Liberia, Somalia, and Sudan.

165 See, for example, *Canadian Human Rights Act*, R.S.C., 1985, c. H-6, s. 3.

166 At the time of this writing, a case against General Motors concerning its dual-nationals ITAR policy was pending before the Ontario Human Rights Commission. See, for example, *Sinclair et al. v. General Motors*, 2006 HRTO 30.

167 22 C.F.R. § 126.5 states that U.S. authorities will "permit, when for end-use in Canada by Canadian Federal or Provincial governmental authorities acting in an official capacity or by a Canadian-registered person or return to the United States, the permanent and temporary export to Canada without a license of defense articles and related technical data identified in 22 CFR § 121.1." It then defines "Canadian-registered person" as including dual nationals, subject to the

2006, the State Department was apparently applying the dual national rules to the Canadian government, impeding Canadian efforts to procure military technology from the United States as part of then-active reinvestment in the Canadian Forces.

If the Canadian Department of National Defence were to exclude dual nationals from U.S. embargoed states from access to the U.S.-origin goods, *Charter* equality right would almost certainly be engaged. Pointing to this fact, the Department of National Defence has reportedly taken the view that public officials with dual nationality cannot be treated differently from those without such status.[168] Whether this approach would affect Canadian military procurement policies remained unresolved by the time of this writing.

---

rule on embargoed states. It does not, however, appear to impose the same embargoed state caveat on "Canadian Federal or Provincial governmental authorities acting in an official capacity."

168 Dan Leblanc, "U.S. Regulations Skirt *Charter*, Slow Arms Deals" *The Globe and Mail* (26 September 2006) A4.

CHAPTER 9

PROTECTING PUBLIC SAFETY AND HEALTH

The focus of this book has been almost exclusively on artificial threats to national security—that is, threats intentionally caused by human beings. This emphasis obviously draws on recent history, not least the events of 9/11. A longer-range (and less Canadian-centric) review of threats would, however, conclude that the events of 9/11 pale in comparison to the potential harms to national security posed by extreme natural occurrences or accidents. Moreover, technologies now exist capable of converting acts of violence into *bona fide* natural or public health disasters, tracing their own trajectory in regions far beyond those in which they originally arise. Radioactive fallout from nuclear weapons or diseases spread by bioweapons are obvious cases in point.

Responding to these calamities may require the suspension of normal rules of law, and the imposition of emergency measures. This book has already discussed in chapter 4 the federal *Emergencies Act*,[1] its scope and its impact on the conventional structures of government. The present chapter discusses other laws that might govern responses to natural or human-induced disasters and large-scale accidents, with a focus on public health issues. It begins with a brief overview of disasters as national security threats and then turns to an overview of Canadian emergency law. Finally, it probes more specifically international and national rules designed to grapple with (and forestall) epidemics.

---

1   R.S.C. 1985 (4th Supp.), c. 22.

PART I: DISASTERS AND NATIONAL SECURITY

As the 2004 Canadian government national security policy observes, "many regions of Canada have been subject to severe natural disasters in recent years which have taken lives and caused extensive property damage."[2] The department of public safety disaster database includes 265 entries for the period 1990 to 2006,[3] an average of almost seventeen disasters a year. The Insurance Bureau of Canada—representing an industry acutely sensitive to disaster trends—notes that "the frequency and impact of natural disasters is on the rise worldwide. Earthquakes, hurricanes, tsunamis, forest fires, tornados, ice storms and severe rain storms are happening more often than ever before, and costing us more dearly."[4]

A. EXTREME WEATHER EVENTS

Extreme weather events and flooding, in particular, cause millions of dollars of damage annually.[5] In the worst cases, they also take human lives, and may cause national crises, as events in New Orleans in 2005 demonstrated.

Climate change may precipitate even more radical extreme weather events. The climate of any given region on the Earth is a function of an endless list of factors. However, the planet's climate system, as a whole, exists largely because of the Earth's atmosphere, a soup of gases that slows the dissipation of solar energy striking the Earth and thereby facilitates the existence of a reasonable range of temperatures on the planet's surface. Changing the relative composition of these so-called greenhouse gases alters the rapidity with which this energy dissipates, prompting changes in normal climatic temperatures. All else held equal, where the concentration of greenhouse gases increases, temperatures rise.[6]

---

2 Canada, *Securing an Open Society: Canada's National Security Policy* (2004) at 7, online: www.army.dnd.ca/lf/Downloads/natsecurnat_e.pdf.

3 On-line: www.psepc-sppcc.gc.ca/res/em/cdd/search-en.asp.

4 Insurance Bureau of Canada, *Natural Disasters*, online: www.ibc.ca/en/Natural_Disasters/.

5 See Insurance Bureau of Canada data, online: www.ibc.ca/en/Natural_Disasters/documents/Major-Multiple-payment-Occurences-NatDisast.pdf.

6 For a more detailed discussion of climate change science, see Environment Canada, *Science of Climate Change* (2005), online: www.ec.gc.ca/climate/overview_science-e.html.

At present, there simply is no scientific debate on the role greenhouse gases play in creating Earth's climate. The overwhelming and resounding view of climatic scientists now is that human emissions of greenhouse gases will have (and are having) an impact on the Earth's climate system.[7] Where there remains more uncertainty is in measuring the precise effect changes in the amount of these gases in the atmosphere will have on changes in temperature in given locales. There are, however, sobering predictions.

Discussing the anticipated effects of climate change on Canada, Environment Canada reports:

> We are likely to see changes in our ability to grow food and potential costly changes to the methods we use to do it. Warmer temperatures could create conditions for more severe weather events, including thunderstorms and an increased frequency of tornadoes, with attendant risk to life and property. Drier conditions and warmer temperatures could also cause more frequent forest fires.[8]

Climate change in Canada will also have an impact—often deleterious—on human health, water resources, fisheries, forests, wildlife and ecosystems.[9]

Globally, climate change will also likely have geopolitical implications.[10] Shifting rainfall patterns and changes in the prevalence and location of extreme storms will have obvious impacts on human activity, potentially destabilizing societies already facing resource stress. A new and frightening scientific scholarship warns of substantial glacial melting in Greenland. The disappearance of that island's ice cap (or equivalent melting in the Antarctic) could produce sea-level rises in the range of seven metres, albeit over the span of a millennium.[11] A substantial number of the world's most populated regions would be inundated by a

---

7 *See* Intergovernmental Panel on Climate Change, *Climate Change 2007: The Physical Science Basis: Summary for Policymakers* (February 2007), online: www.ipcc.ch/SPM2feb07.pdf.

8 Environment Canada, *Science of Climate Change*, above note 6.

9 *Ibid.*

10 See, for example, Robert McLeman & Barry Smit, *Climate Change, Migration and Security*, CSIS Commentary No. 86 (March 2004), online: www.csis-scrs.gc.ca/en/publications/commentary/com86.asp; Peter Gizewski, *Environmental Scarcity and Conflict*, CSIS Commentary No. 71 (Spring 1997), online: www.csis-scrs.gc.ca/en/publications/commentary/com71.asp.

11 See, for example, Lowe *et al.*, "The Role of Sea-Level Rise and the Greenland Ice Sheet in Dangerous Climate Change: Implications for the Stabilisation of Climate," in Hans Joachim Schellnhuber *et al.*, eds., *Avoiding Dangerous Climate Change* (Cambridge: Cambridge University Press, 2006).

sea rise of this magnitude, producing refugee crises numbering in the tens and perhaps hundreds of millions. Indeed, some 5 percent of the world's population could be located within regions that may be below sea level within a few centuries.[12]

The extent to which climate change will precipitate national security crises may depend on the speed at which it arrives. A 2003 report commissioned by the U.S. Department of Defense examined the impact for U.S. national security of abrupt climate change; that is, the precipitous alteration of the Earth's climate change some scientists believe plausible once a particular tipping point is reached. That report warned that an "abrupt climate change scenario could potentially de-stabilize the geo-political environment, leading to skirmishes, battles, and even war due to resource constraints." Further,

> As global and local carrying capacities are reduced, tensions could mount around the world, leading to two fundamental strategies: defensive and offensive. Nations with the resources to do so may build virtual fortresses around their countries, preserving resources for themselves. Less fortunate nations especially those with ancient enmities with their neighbors, may initiate in struggles for access to food, clean water, or energy. Unlikely alliances could be formed as defense priorities shift and the goal is resources for survival rather than religion, ideology, or national honor.[13]

A 2007 report endorsed by a military advisory board comprising almost a dozen senior retired U.S. military officers warn of similar national security threats from climate change, even if it does not arise in an abrupt fashion.[14]

B. SEISMIC EVENTS

Earthquakes are relatively common in Canada, occurring at a rate of approximately 1,400 per year. Most of these are undetectable without specialized instruments, but occasional larger quakes do produce substantial damage. The St. Lawrence Valley and the West Coast are par-

---

12   Ibid.

13   Peter Schwartz & Doug Randall, *An Abrupt Climate Change Scenario and Its Implications for United States National Security* (2003) at 2, online: www.gbn.com/GBNDocumentDisplayServlet.srv?aid=26231&url=%2FUploadDocumentDisplayServlet.srv%3Fid%3D28566.

14   CNA Corporation, *National Security and the Threat of Climate Change* (2007), online: http://securityandclimate.cna.org/.

ticularly vulnerable to seismic activity. The department of public safety warns that "structurally-damaging earthquakes can be expected to strike somewhere in southwestern British Columbia each decade."[15] As the 2004 tsunami in Southeast Asia suggests, distant maritime earthquakes may also generate sea surges that cause substantial damage onshore.

C. EPIDEMIC DISEASE

Historically, pandemic diseases have precipitated massive human suffering. For example, the Spanish Influenza — a pandemic that followed the First World War — killed an approximated 50 million people worldwide.

In the worst cases, epidemic disease may constitute serious threats to national security, not least by destabilizing the political *status quo* and degrading social structures of highly affected countries. A 2005 U.S. Council on Foreign Relations report on HIV as a national security issue observed that

> the stability of states with high rates of HIV infection may well be threatened, but more likely through a process of erosion of its elite populations, its political leadership, its college-trained professionals, and its skilled labor forces. There is evidence that HIV is claiming the lives of parliamentarians and political leaders in countries that already experienced acute shortages of highly skilled personnel, such as lawyers, doctors, nurses, teachers, financial planners, managers, engineers, and technicians. ... [T]his depletion of elite workers, professionals, political leaders, and managers is expected to reach crisis proportions in many countries by 2010, challenging the ability of the state to perform even rudimentary aspects of governance.[16]

The staggering consequences of HIV will produce states with demographic profiles heavily weighted to youths, most of whom will be disadvantaged by the deterioration of educational and economic institutions. A large cadre of young people will enhance the prospect of instability: "There is strong evidence that societies with such dramatic

---

15 Canada, PSEPC, *Earthquakes* (2005), online: www.publicsafety.gc.ca/res/em/nh/eq/index-en.asp.

16 Laurie Garrett, *HIV and National Security: Where Are the Links?* (New York: Council on Foreign Relations, 2005) at 10.

youth-bulge demographics are at greater risk of civil disturbance, conflict, and disorder."[17]

This disorder may not be confined to afflicted states themselves. "There is increasing concern," the Council on Foreign Relations reports

> that the nexus of poverty, HIV/AIDS, and alienation from the West could provide fertile ground for anti-Western violence, possibly terrorism. ... [I]t is not inconceivable that AIDS-ravaged societies might spawn movements of strong anti-Western discontent, possibly leading to acts of violence. This would particularly be the case if the wealthy nations are perceived to have abandoned poor, HIV-afflicted states.[18]

Other diseases could provoke more precipitous crises. Substantial attention, for example, has been directed at the risk of an avian flu pandemic. Canadian government predictions of deaths from a moderate modern influenza pandemic range from 11,000 to 58,000 persons in Canada alone.[19] The global impacts could be overwhelming

> some countries might impose useless but highly disruptive quarantines or close borders and airports, perhaps for months. Such closures would disrupt trade, travel, and productivity. No doubt the world's stock markets would teeter and perhaps fall precipitously. Aside from economics, the disease would likely directly affect global security, reducing troop strength and capacity for all armed forces, U.N. peacekeeping operations, and police worldwide.[20]

D. INDUSTRIAL DISASTERS AND FAILURES OF CRITICAL INFRASTRUCTURE

Industrial accidents can have enormous regional and even global impacts. Calamities at places such as Bhopal, India, have paralyzed communities and killed and injured many thousands. In places like Chernobyl, nuclear disasters have semi-permanently irradiated substantial swaths of territory.

---

17   *Ibid.* at 11.
18   *Ibid.* at 12.
19   Public Health Agency of Canada, *Frequently Asked Questions — Pandemic Influenza,* online: www.phac-aspc.gc.ca/influenza/pikf_e.html.
20   Laurie Garrett, "The Next Pandemic" (July/August 2005) Foreign Affairs, online: www.foreignaffairs.org/20050701faessay84401/laurie-garrett/the-next-pandemic.html.

The collapse of key public infrastructure, whether through accident or attack, may also cause injury, even to persons distant from the breakdown. A recent focus of attention in Canada is protection of critical infrastructure. CSIS defines critical infrastructure as "physical and information technology facilities, networks and assets (e.g., energy distribution networks, communications grids, health services, essential utilities, transportation and government services), which, if disrupted or destroyed, could have a serious impact on the health, safety, security and economic well-being of Canadians."[21] In 1999, the Special Senate Committee on Security and Intelligence noted Canada's vulnerability to critical infrastructure attacks, not least because of its dependence on networked computer systems.[22] More recently, the central Canadian blackout of 2003 demonstrated the vulnerability of contemporary power systems on a fragile and highly integrated distribution grid.

PART II: CANADIAN DISASTER LAW

A. FEDERAL EMERGENCY LAWS

1) *Emergency Management Act*

A significant disaster—whether in the form of an industrial accident, critical infrastructure failure, epidemic, weather or seismic event—might trigger application of Canada's emergency laws. The *Emergencies Act* and constitutional issues related to emergencies are described in detail in chapter 4. This chapter includes a more detailed overview of the *Emergency Management Act*,[23] the new, core instrument used to deal with natural disasters. The *Emergency Management Act* was promulgated in 2007 to replace the 1988 *Emergency Preparedness Act*.[24]

a) Prior Statute
The *Emergency Preparedness Act* was the most banal, and yet the most frequently employed, of Canada's federal emergency laws. This statute

21   CSIS, *Information Security Threats* (2005), online: www.csis-scrs.gc.ca/en/priorities/information.asp.
22   Special Senate Committee on Security and Intelligence, *Report* (January 1999), online: www.parl.gc.ca/36/1/parlbus/commbus/senate/com-e/secu-e/rep-e/rep-secintjan99-e.htm.
23   S.C. 2007, c. 15.
24   R.S.C. 1985 (4th Supp.), c. 6 [EPA].

instructed a minister—designated the minister of public safety[25]—to advance "civil preparedness in Canada for emergencies of all types, including war and other armed conflict" by coordinating the development and implementation of civil emergency plans.[26] In relation to these plans, the minister was tasked with, among other things, establishing arrangements for "the continuity of constitutional government during an emergency."[27]

Other ministers were charged with developing plans within their own department for civil emergencies or for war or other armed conflicts.[28] The Act also allowed the governor-in-council to make orders or regulations pertaining, among other things, to the use of federal civil resources in response to civil emergencies and the provision of assistance to a province where a civil emergency had been declared a concern to the federal government, and the province has requested assistance.[29]

Between 1992 and 2005, the federal government issued approximately forty-five orders under the Act declaring floods to be a concern to the federal government and authorizing federal financial assistance. Another eight such orders concerned hurricanes, tornadoes or other severe storms; three involved forest fires; three involved the 1998 ice storm—and in fact authorized "other" assistance beyond financial aid—and one involved a disease outbreak.[30]

b) New Law

Despite its frequent use, the *Emergency Preparedness Act* was perceived by the government as outdated.[31] To enhance the minister of public safety's coordinating role, and to augment harmonization of responses with the provinces, the Martin government introduced a bill modernizing the instrument.[32] That law project died on the order paper, but was resuscitated by the Harper government and received royal assent in 2007. The new law includes a longer list of responsibilities assigned to the minister of public safety in performing his or her emergency management plan development and coordinating rule.

---

25 *Order Designating the Deputy Prime Minister and Minister of Public Safety and Emergency Preparedness as Minister for Purposes of the Act*, S.I./2004-106.

26 EPA, above note 24, s. 4.

27 *Ibid.*, s. 5(1)(f).

28 *Ibid.*, s. 7.

29 *Ibid.*, s. 9.

30 Data collected from the orders-in-council database, available at www.pco-bcp. gc.ca/oic-ddc/oic-ddc.asp?lang=EN.

31 See PSEPC, *FAQs - Tabling of the Emergency Management Act* (2005), online: www.securitepublique.gc.ca/media/bk/2005/bk20051117-1-en.asp.

32 Bill C-78, 1st Sess., 38th Parl., 2005, re-introduced as Bill C-12, 1st Sess., 39th Parl., 2006 (*EMA*).

The *Emergency Management Act* charges the minister of public safety with coordinating emergency management activities, in cooperation with the provinces.[33] To this end, he or she is to perform a number of tasks, including overseeing the preparation of government emergency management plans, coordinating both domestic and international emergency assistance, and developing plans for the continuity of constitutional government in Canada.[34] The minister is also charged with developing joint emergency management plans with the United States and would coordinate Canadian response to, and assistance in, an emergency in that country.[35]

Other government ministers also have obligations under the Act to identify risks within their area of responsibility—including in relation to critical infrastructure—and to prepare emergency management plans, subject to the oversight of the public safety minister. These plans must contain a number of items, including measures to support Canada's defence efforts in the case of war or other armed conflict.[36]

At the same time the *Emergency Management Act* was introduced, amendments were made to the *Access to Information Act* creating a new disclosure exemption for private-sector emergency management plans supplied in confidence to the government, as they relate to critical infrastructure vulnerabilities.[37]

2) *Public Safety Act*

For its part, the omnibus *Public Safety Act, 2002*, enacted in 2004, enhanced the powers of several ministers to respond to emergencies under assorted statutes. For instance, the transportation minister may impose special emergency measures under the *Aeronautics Act*[38] in response to threats to aviation security. As noted in chapter 13, this power provides the basis of Canada's "no fly" list. Responsible ministers may also issue "interim orders" of various sorts under the *Canadian Environmental Protection Act*,[39] the *Department of Health Act*,[40] the *Food and Drugs Act*,[41]

---

33   *Ibid.*, s. 3.
34   *Ibid.*, s. 4.
35   *Ibid.*, s. 5.
36   *Ibid.*, s. 6.
37   *Access to Information Act*, R.S.C. 1985, c. A-1, s. 20.
38   R.S.C., 1985, c. A-2.
39   S.C. 1999, c. 33.
40   S.C. 1996, c. 8.
41   R.S.C. 1985, c. F-27.

the *Hazardous Products Act*,[42] the *Navigable Waters Protection Act*,[43] the *Pest Control Products Act*,[44] the *Quarantine Act*,[45] the *Radiation Emitting Devices Act*,[46] and the *Canada Shipping Act*.[47]

While the language in each statute varies, ministers are to issue these orders largely in response to "significant" dangers to the environment or to human life or health.[48]

3) National Defence Act

As discussed in detail in chapter 5, the *National Defence Act* permits the deployment of military units in response to a requisition from a provincial attorney general in aid of the civil power. A "call out" of the Forces may be made in response to an actual or anticipated riot or disturbance of the peace, beyond the powers of the civil authorities to suppress, prevent or deal with.[49]

For its part, the governor-in-council or minister of national defence may also deploy the Canadian Forces to perform "public service" duties. Similarly, the governor-in-council, or the minister of national defence responding to a request from the minister of public safety or any other minister, may authorize military assistance in law enforcement, so long as such assistance is required to deal effectively with the matter at issue and it is in the national interest.[50] All these deployment powers could prove important in a disaster situation.

B. PROVINCIAL EMERGENCY LAWS

Canadian provinces also have their own emergency laws. Most follow a similar structure, anticipating the declaration of an emergency on either a localized or more geographically attenuated basis. Each also anticipates the subsequent application of emergency plans. Indeed, the development of emergency management plans by provincial governments, departments or agencies thereof, and/or municipalities or regions is generally

---

42 R.S.C. 1985, c. H-3.
43 R.S.C. 1985, c. N-22.
44 R.S.C. 1985, c. P-9.
45 S.C. 2005, c. 20.
46 R.S.C. 1985, c. R-1.
47 R.S.C. 1985, c. S-9.
48 See *Public Safety Act, 2002*, S.C. 2004, c.15, Parts 1, 3, 6, 9, 10, 15, 18, 20, 21, & 22.
49 See *ibid.*, ss. 74–81 and *National Defence Act*, R.S.C. 1985, c. N-5, ss. 274–85.
50 *National Defence Act, ibid.*, s. 273.6.

an obligation under the statutes. The advent of an emergency usually allows government to exercise unusual powers of varying sorts. The statutes also make it an offence to disregard emergency instructions and provide for the imposition of differing penalties.

1) Definitions of "Emergency"

Provincial statutes often distinguish between "disasters" and "emergencies." The distinction between the two appears to be one of timing. Disasters are usually an actual calamity requiring a response to remedy a serious harm. The government response is typically directed at disaster recovery, a matter that may not necessitate special powers. Emergencies, on the other hand, are present or imminent events that require a coordinated response to forestall harm. This response may require special governmental authority.

The terms used to describe the harm in question vary between provinces. Most statutes include simply a generic reference to harm of a serious magnitude, while others enumerate specific circumstances that might give rise to such harm. Some statutes provide a generic definition and then list different sorts of harms as illustrative.

2) Declaring a State of Emergency

Provincial emergency declarations are typically issued by the lieutenant governor-in-council — that is, the provincial cabinet — or the relevant minister, when the issuing entity is satisfied an emergency, as defined in the legislation, exists. Generally, in declaring a state of emergency, authorities are to specify the area covered by the declaration and the nature of the emergency. Most such declarations expire after two weeks, although they typically may be renewed.

In some statutes, parallel powers exist for municipal governments and/or provincial ministers responsible for municipalities to issue municipal emergency declarations.

3) Powers during an Emergency

Once an emergency is declared, the lieutenant governor-in-council, a relevant minister, and/or emergency management boards (or other local authorities) have special powers granted to them under the relevant Act. These powers may be quite broad.

Emergency laws typically grant the government the power to do all acts necessary to alleviate the emergency, and often enumerate an

Table 9.1: Definitions of Emergency in Provincial Legislation

Province	Distinction between Crises		Type of Injury
	Disaster	Emergency	
Alberta[1]	×	×	Harm to safety, health or welfare or damage to property
British Columbia[2]	×	×	Harm to health, safety or welfare of people, or damage to property
Manitoba[3]	×	×	Loss or life, harm or damage to safety, health, welfare or people, damage to property or the environment
New Brunswick[4]	×	×	Harm to property, the environment or the health, safety or welfare of the civil population
Newfoundland[5]	×	×[6]	Endangers or is likely to endanger the safety, welfare and well-being of some or all of the civil population of the province
Nova Scotia[7]		×	Harm to property or the health, safety or welfare of people
Ontario[8]		×	Danger of major proportions that could result in serious harm to persons or substantial damage to property and that is caused by the forces of nature, a disease or other health risk, an accident or an act whether intentional or otherwise
Prince Edward Island[9]	×	×	Harm to property, the environment or the health, safety or welfare of the civil population
Quebec[10]	×[11]		Serious harm to persons or substantial damage to property and requiring unusual action on the part of the affected community, such as a flood, earthquake, ground movement, explosion, toxic emission or pandemic
Saskatchewan[12]		×[13]	Loss of life or harm or damage to the safety, health or welfare of people; or damage to property or the environment.

[1] *Disaster Services Act*, R.S.A. 2000, c. D-13.
[2] *Emergency Program Act*, R.S.B.C. 1996, c. 111.
[3] *Emergency Measures Act*, C.C.S.M. c. E80.
[4] *Emergency Measures Act*, L.N.-B. 1978, c. E-7.1.
[5] *Emergency Measures Act*, R.S.N.L. 1990, c. E-8.
[6] Distinguishes between a "civil disaster" and a "war emergency."
[7] *Emergency Management Act*, S.N.S. 1990, c. 8.
[8] *Emergency Management Act and Civil Protection Act*, R.S.O. 1990, c. E.9.
[9] *Emergency Measures Act*, R.S.P.E.I. 1988, c. E.6.1.
[10] *Civil Protection Act*, R.S.Q. c. S-2.3.
[11] Distinguishes between major and minor disasters, with minor disasters affecting only a few people.
[12] *Emergency Planning Act*, S.S. 1989–90, c. E-8.1.
[13] The Saskatchewan definition of emergency includes a list of calamities that in other statutes would be labelled disasters, as well as a reference to a present or imminent situation or condition causing one of the enumerated harms.

Table 9.2: Issuing Declaration of Provincial Emergencies

Province	Issuing entity	Duration	Power of Renewal
Alberta	Lt.Governor-in-Council (LGC)	14 days	May be continued by legislative resolution
British Columbia	LGC	14 days	May be continued by the LGC for additional periods of 14 days
Manitoba	Minister	14 days	May be continued by the LGC for additional periods of 14 days
New Brunswick	Minister	14 days	May be continued by the minister, with approval of the LGC, for additional periods of 14 days
Newfoundland	LCG	Until terminated	
Nova Scotia	Minister	14 days	May be continued by the minister, with approval of the LGC, for additional periods of 14 days
Ontario	LCG or Premier	An order from the premier terminated in 72 hours unless confirmed by the LGC; a declaration from the LGC terminates in 14 days	May be continued by the LGC for one additional period of 14 days, and then again by the legislature for an additional period of up to 28 days
Prince Edward Island	Minister	14 days	May be continued by the minister, with approval of the LGC
Quebec	Government	10 days	May be continued by the government for an additional period of 10 days, or with the consent of the legislature, for a maximum period of up to 30 days
Saskatchewan	LGC	14 days	May be continued by the LGC for additional periods of 14 days

illustrative list of specific powers. Representative powers granted to the government during an emergency include: the power to enter premises without warrants; to order evacuations of livestock and people; to demolish trees, structures or crops where necessary to prevent the spread of the emergency; to implement emergency plans; to utilize personal property including premises for purposes of responding to the emergency; to provide essential services and facilities; and often to require some sort of price control for essential goods.

These statutes also often include a provision limiting liability for actions undertaken pursuant to the fact or one of the emergency plans developed under the Act. Thus, officials and individuals are not liable for damage or injury suffered as a result of the good faith implementation of measures or the exercise of legitimately granted powers under the Act in times of emergency, although the government itself may still be liable for failures and omissions.

Table 9.3:   Illustrative Powers during Emergency

Power	Alberta	BC	Manitoba	NB	Newfoundland	NS	Ontario	PEI	Quebec	Saskatchewan
Trigger emergency plan	×	×	×	×		×	×	×	×	×
Use any real and/or personal property for emergency purposes	×	×	×	×	×[1]	×		×		×
Require any qualified person to render aid of a type the person is qualified to provide	×	×	×	×		×	×[2]	×	×	×
Control or prohibit travel	×	×	×	×	×	×	×	×	×	×
Coordinate provision of essential goods and/or services	×	×	×	×	×	×	×	×	×	×
Order evacuation	×	×	×	×	×	×	×	×	×	×
Authorize the entry into any building or on any land (generally without warrant)	×	×	×		×	×		×	×	×
Closing any place							×	×	×	
Cause a demolition or removal of any trees, structures or crops	×	×	×	×	×	×		×	×	×
Construct works to alleviate effects		×					×			

Power	Alberta	BC	Manitoba	NB	Newfoundland	NS	Ontario	PEI	Quebec	Saskatchewan
Fix prices for food, clothing, fuel, equipment, medical supplies, or other essential supplies or services	×	×		×	×	×	×			×
Disposing of waste							×			
Requiring disclosure of information							×			
Authorize the conscription of persons needed to meet an emergency	×			×	×	×		×		×

[1] Newfoundland law allows the government to regulate "the acquisition by purchase, lease or otherwise of goods, chattels or lands and the sale, lease, allocation or other disposition of those goods, chattels or lands."

[2] Ontario law allows authorization for these people to perform these functions, but not the power to require these services.

PART III: PUBLIC HEALTH LAW

Public health—or as some prefer to call it "health protection and promotion"—includes: "disease surveillance, disease and injury prevention, health protection, health emergency preparedness and response, health promotion, and relevant research undertakings." [51] The public health system is, in other words, the frontline in responding to new or epidemic diseases of natural or human origin. Diseases of this sort may constitute a particularly dramatic (and difficult) form of threat. This section discusses both the international and national laws relating to epidemic diseases.

---

51   Standing Senate Committee on Social Affairs, Science and Technology, *Reforming Health Protection and Promotion in Canada: Time to Act* (November 2003), online: www.parl.gc.ca/37/2/parlbus/commbus/senate/com-e/soci-e/rep-e/rep-finnov03-e.htm.

A. INTERNATIONAL LAW

1) International Human Rights Law

There is relatively little international law in the area of public health.[52] International human rights law does, however, recognize a right to health.[53] The *International Covenant on Economic, Social and Cultural Rights*, for instance, promises to everyone "the enjoyment of the highest attainable standard of physical and mental health" and obliges states to prevent, treat and control "epidemic, endemic, occupational and other diseases."[54]

Public health may also justify constraints on other rights. For instance, under the *International Covenant on Civil and Political Rights*, liberty of movement and the rights of free expression, free association and free assembly may be curbed by law where necessary to protect public health.[55] The latter is not a defined term in the Covenant. However, a group of experts convened by the International Commission of Jurists in 1984 proposed the *Siracusa Principles*.[56] Though of no legal force, the Principles provide a helpful interpretive tool. Under the Principles, "public health" should include only "measures dealing with a serious threat to the health of the population or individual members of the population. These measures must be specifically aimed at preventing disease or injury or providing care for the sick and injured." [57]

2) International Law and Epidemic Diseases

More specific public health-related international treaties have existed for over a century. These instruments have typically been designed to impede the cross-border movement of epidemic diseases, especially cholera and plague. The modern manifestation of these rules exists in the form of the International Health Regulations (IHR), promulgated by the World Health Organization.

---

52   For overviews of this area, see Obijiofor Aginam, *Public Health Governance: International Law and Public Health in a Divided World* (Toronto: University of Toronto Press, 2005); David Fidler, *International Law and Public Health* (Ardsley, NY: Transnational Publishers, 2000).

53   See, for example, *Universal Declaration of Human Rights*, A/RES/217A(III) (1948), Art. 25.

54   ICESCR (1966), 993 U.N.T.S. 3, Art. 12.

55   ICCPR (1966), 999 U.N.T.S. 171, Arts. 12, 19, 21, & 22.

56   *Siracusa Principles on the Limitation and Derogation of Provisions in the International Covenant on Civil and Political Rights*, UNESCOR, 41 Sess., U.N. Doc. E/CN.4/1984/4 (1984).

57   *Ibid.* at para. 25.

a) World Health Organization

The World Health Organization (WHO) is a specialized organ of the United Nations, created by an international treaty—the Constitution of the World Health Organization—in 1948. At the time of this writing, there were 193 parties to the WHO Constitution, giving it an essentially universal coverage.

Tasked with "the attainment by all peoples of the highest possible level of health,"[58] one of the WHO's functions is "to propose conventions, agreements and regulations, and make recommendations with respect to international health matters."[59] Regulations proposed by the WHO may be adopted by the "Health Assembly"[60]—an assembly of the delegates of all the state parties to the WHO.[61] WHO's existing rules concerning epidemic diseases are found in the International Health Regulations (IHR), an instrument dating from 1951 and substantially revised in 2005.[62]

b) International Health Regulations (2005)

Since their inception, the IHR have focused on surveillance, obliging states to inform the WHO of "notifiable" diseases occurring within their territories. The diseases subject to this notification regime originally included cholera, plague, yellow fever, smallpox, relapsing fever and typhus, but this list was shortened with time. The inadequacies of this limited list became acutely obvious by the turn of the century, not least during the 2003 SARS outbreak: unknown to science until then, SARS was not a notifiable disease.

After substantial negotiations, the IHR were re-crafted in 2005. The express purpose of the IHR (2005) is to "prevent, protect against, control and provide a public health response to the international spread of disease in ways that are commensurate with and restricted to public health risks, and which avoid unnecessary interference with international traffic and trade."[63] It includes notification requirements, as well as provisions aimed at pre-emption of epidemics.

---

58 *Constitution of the World Health Organization* (1946), 14 U.N.T.S. 185, Art. 1 [WHO Constitution].

59 *Ibid.*, Art. 2(k).

60 *Ibid.*, Art. 21.

61 *Ibid.*, Art. 10.

62 These amended regulations came into force in June 2007.

63 IHR (Revision of the International Health Regulations, 58th World Health Assembly, WHA58.3, Agenda item 13.1 (23 May 2005), Art. 2 [IHR (2005)].

i)   Notification

Parties must report public health emergencies of international concern arising within their territories, as well as their responses to them.[64] Such an emergency is defined as an "extraordinary event" that constitutes "a public health risk to other States through the international spread of disease" and potentially requires "a coordinated international response."[65]

Like the old regulations, the IHR (2005) lists certain diseases as requiring notification.[66] However, notification obligations may extend beyond this list. Whether a public health event crosses this latter notification threshold is determined according to a matrix, applied by each state in gauging the seriousness of any disease outbreak. Considerations in this decision tool include whether the number of instances or deaths is large, an assessment of the health risk posed by the outbreak, and the prospect of cross-border movement.[67] Where a public health emergency of international concern does occur, the WHO may issue temporary or standing recommendations designed to impede the spread of the disease.[68]

ii)   Pre-emption

More pre-emptively, states are obliged to "develop, strengthen and maintain" their "capacity to detect, assess, notify and report" the required health events[69] and to respond "promptly and effectively" to them.[70] At ports of entry to their territory, states must develop particular medical and diagnostic capacities.[71] Upon arrival or departure, travellers may be required by states to provide destination and itinerary information and to undergo searches of their cargo and also a "non-invasive medical examination" designed to achieve the public health objective in the least intrusive manner possible.[72] Medical examinations, vaccinations, prophylaxis or health measures may be administered only with the travel-

---

64   *Ibid.*, Art. 6.

65   *Ibid.*, Art. 1.

66   These include smallpox, influenza caused by a new subtype, and SARS. Other diseases must automatically be assessed according to the matrix discussed below. These diseases include cholera, plague, yellow fever, and viral hemorrhagic fevers.

67   IHR (2005), above note 63, Annex 2.

68   *Ibid.*, Arts. 15 & 16.

69   *Ibid.*, Art. 5.

70   *Ibid.*, Art. 13.

71   *Ibid.*, Art. 19.

72   *Ibid.*, Art. 23.

ler's consent,[73] but such intervention may be a condition of entry into the state.[74] Further, where there is an imminent public health risk, the state may oblige fuller medical examination, treatment, or quarantine.[75]

In all instances, states are to treat travellers "with respect to their dignity, human rights and fundamental freedoms and minimize any discomfort or distress associated with such measures."[76] Further, health measures undertaken by states must be "initiated and completed without delay, and applied in a transparent and non-discriminatory manner."[77] The IHR (2005) also imposes rules on the disclosure and processing of personal data. Namely, such data must be processed fairly and lawfully, be adequate, relevant, and not excessive in relation to the public health risk, accurate and not kept longer than necessary.[78]

iii) Public Health Infrastructure

The IHR (2005) also includes new requirements that parties collaborate with one another to detect, assess and respond to public health crises and to share resources in order to do so.[79] The regulations call for the "mobilization of financial resources to support developing countries in building, strengthening and maintaining" their public health capacities.[80] Ultimately, the effectiveness of this instrument will depend on the extent to which wealthier state parties are prepared to bolster these capacities.

B. CANADIAN PUBLIC HEALTH LAWS

1) Federal

a) Coordination of Public Health

The 2003 SARS outbreak prompted a serious rethink of Canada's public health infrastructure. That system has been divided between a federal role (exercised by Health Canada) and detailed provincial and territorial public health mechanisms and laws. These levels of government did not always coordinate effectively. As a consequence, both the *ad hoc* National Advisory Committee on SARS and Public Health (Naylor

---

73   *Ibid.*
74   *Ibid.*, Art. 31.
75   *Ibid.*
76   *Ibid.*
77   *Ibid.*, Art. 42.
78   *Ibid.*, Art. 45.
79   *Ibid.*, Art. 44.
80   *Ibid.*

Report)[81] and the Standing Senate Committee on Social Affairs, Science and Technology (Kirby Report)[82] recommended the creation of an arm's-length federal public health agency to coordinate national responses to public health crises and enhance disease surveillance and control in Canada.

In response, the government created the Public Health Agency of Canada in 2004, an entity whose existence was affirmed by legislation that came into force in 2006.[83] That body is charged with aiding the minister of health in fulfilling his or her public health responsibilities. It comprises several branches, one of which is the Infectious Disease and Emergency Preparedness (IDEP) Branch. This entity—tasked with responding to public health emergencies—includes a Centre for Infectious Disease Prevention and Control (CIDPC) as well as a Centre for Emergency Preparedness and Response (CEPR). CIDPC aims to "decrease transmission of infectious diseases and to improve the health status of those infected."[84] CEPR, meanwhile, is Canada's "central coordinating point for public health security issues." It is responsible for:

> developing and maintaining national emergency response plans for the Public Health Agency of Canada; monitoring outbreaks and global disease events; assessing public health risks during emergencies; keeping Canada's health and emergency policies in line with threats to public health security and general security for Canadians in collaboration with other federal and international health and security agencies; laboratory safety and security, quarantine issues and travel health advisories; and being the health authority in the Government of Canada on bioterrorism, emergency health services and emergency response.

b) *Quarantine Act*

A second plank in the modernization of Canada's federal public health system was the promulgation of a new *Quarantine Act*.[85] This statute—which came into force in 2006—updated antiquated nineteenth-

---

81   National Advisory Committee on SARS and Public Health, *Learning from SARS: Renewal of Public Health in Canada* (October 2003), online: www.phac-aspc. gc.ca/publicat/sars-sras/naylor/.

82   Standing Senate Committee on Social Affairs, Science and Technology, *Reforming Health Protection and Promotion in Canada: Time to Act* (2003), online: www. parl.gc.ca/37/2/parlbus/commbus/senate/com-e/soci-e/rep-e/repfinnov03-e.htm.

83   *Public Health Agency of Canada Act*, S.C. 2006, c. 5.

84   Public Health Agency of Canada, *About the Agency* (2006), online: www.phac-aspc.gc.ca/about_apropos/index.html.

85   *Quarantine Act*, above note 45.

century legislation. The *Quarantine Act* applies at Canada's borders, zones over which the federal government has jurisdiction. It is directed at protecting "public health by taking comprehensive measures to prevent the introduction and spread of communicable diseases."[86]

i)   Assessment of Travellers

Travellers arriving in Canada are to present themselves to a government screening officer at the entry point.[87] Travellers departing Canada may also be asked to report to this person, if the minister has adjudged such departure screening necessary to prevent the spread of a communicable disease.[88]

Travellers are obliged to respond to questions posed to them by a screening officer or a quarantine officer (a medical professional appointed to serve this function by the minister). Specifically, they are required to disclose any reasonable grounds they may have to suspect exposure to a communicable disease. They then must comply with reasonable measures ordered by the officer to prevent the introduction or spread of that ailment.[89] These steps may include isolation by a screening officer of the traveller until that person is assessed by a quarantine officer. Indeed, the screening or quarantine officer may request that a peace officer arrest a traveller who the peace officer believes on reasonable grounds has refused to be isolated or comply with the reasonable measures ordered by the screening or quarantine officer.[90]

The quarantine officer may require the traveller to undergo a health assessment if he or she believes that person has been exposed to a communicable disease, or that person has not cooperated with the initial screening undertaken by the screening or quarantine officers.[91] Other persons at the entry or departure point may also be required to undergo a health assessment if they have been exposed.[92] Health assessments amount to nonintrusive medical examinations. A more elaborate medical examination may also be ordered by the quarantine officer.[93] Subsequently, the person may be required to undergo medical

---

86   *Ibid.*, s. 4.
87   *Ibid.*, s. 12.
88   *Ibid.*, ss. 10 and 13.
89   *Ibid.*, s. 15.
90   *Ibid.*, s. 18.
91   *Ibid.*, s. 19.
92   *Ibid.*, s. 20.
93   *Ibid.*, s. 22.

treatment prescribed by the quarantine officer.[94] A failure to do so is a criminal offence.[95]

ii) Detention

Where the traveller fails to follow a treatment regime, a provincial court judge may issue an arrest order. A person arrested in this manner, or one who has not cooperated with the medical exam, or a person who the quarantine officer believes is contagious, may be detained.[96] However, the traveller is not to be detained if the quarantine officer believes reasonably that, among other things, the person does not pose a risk of significant harm to public health or if there are other, reasonable means to prevent or control this harm.[97]

Once detained, the traveller must be given an opportunity to undergo a medical examination at least every seven days, and to have the need for their detention reconsidered. Where a detention is confirmed, the traveller may seek a review by a second health professional, who will then assess the matter within forty-eight hours.[98] The minister may also intervene and assess the detention.[99]

Where a traveller has been detained because he or she has refused to cooperate in medical assessments or examinations or to pursue the treatment mandated by the quarantine officer, the quarantine officer must seek an order from a provincial superior court or the Federal Court ordering the assessment, examination or treatment. The court may make this order if persuaded that "the order is appropriate to prevent or control a risk of significant harm to public health" and "other reasonable means are not available to prevent or control the risk."[100]

Information on travellers who have been detained and/or examined must be conveyed by the quarantine officer to provincial public health authorities of any province concerned.[101]

iii) Other Powers

The Act also gives the government substantial powers to intervene with "conveyances" — forms of transportation — suspected of carrying infect-

---

94 *Ibid.*, s. 26.
95 *Ibid.*, s. 68.
96 *Ibid.*, s. 28.
97 *Ibid.*, s. 32.
98 *Ibid.*, s. 29.
99 *Ibid.*, s. 30.
100 *Ibid.*, s. 31.
101 *Ibid.*, s. 33.1.

ed travellers.[102] These include powers to stop a conveyance at an entry or departure point to Canada, and enter, inspect or divert that vehicle.

Also of note, the governor-in-council may issue an emergency order prohibiting or limiting the entry into Canada of persons who have been in a foreign country where there is an outbreak of communicable disease that would pose an imminent and severe risk to public health in Canada, the entry of these persons would contribute to the spread of this disease and there are no reasonable alternatives.[103]

2) Provincial

Provincial laws contain powers similar to those in the federal *Quarantine Act*, but applicable within Canada and not at its borders. These provisions are generally found in the public health acts of the province,[104] although some are found in provincial emergency laws.

Generally, these statutes (or their regulations) define communicable diseases that trigger patient and/or medical reporting and treatment obligations. Health authorities are then charged with investigating these instances and taking remedial measures. Thus, these authorities — most often the chief medical officer of health — often have the power to enter premises without a warrant to investigate possible cases of illness, to issue disinfecting orders, and to order the closure of businesses and facilities. They may also have the authority to order isolation/quarantine, treatment and related measures, although the degree to which such orders are themselves legally binding varies between provinces. In many cases, these orders are voluntary unless brought before a judge and made into a court order.

The Ontario *Health Protection and Promotion Act* is illustrative of this pattern. Various medical professionals have an obligation to report to the medical officer of health certain reportable diseases.[105] Where a medical officer of health believes, on reasonable and probable grounds, that a communicable disease exists, or may break out, that presents a

---

102 *Ibid.*, s. 34 *et seq.*
103 *Ibid.*, s. 58.
104 *Public Health Act,* R.S.A. 2000, c. P-37 (Alberta); *Health Act,* R.S.B.C. 1996, c. 179 (British Columbia); *Public Health Act,* C.C.S.M. c. P210 (Manitoba); *Health Act,* R.S.N.B. 1973, c. H-2 (New Brunswick); *Communicable Diseases Act,* R.S.N.L. 1990, c. C-26 (Newfoundland & Labrador); *Health Protection Act,* S.N.S. 2004, c. 4 (Nova Scotia); *Health Protection and Promotion Act,* R.S.O. 1990, c. H.7 (Ontario); *Public Health Act,* R.S.P.E.I. 1988, c. P-30 (Prince Edward Island); *Public Health Act,* R.S.Q. c. S-2.2 (Quebec); *Public Health Act,* 1994, S.S. 1994, c. P-37.1 (Saskatchewan).
105 *Health Protection and Promotion Act, ibid.*, s. 25.

risk to public health, he or she may order a person to take or refrain from taking any action in order to minimize the risk presented by the disease. These orders may be directed at specified individuals or a class of individuals, with the latter contacted through the media.[106]

Where in relation to a virulent communicable disease a person has failed to comply with an order by the medical officer of health to isolate themselves, undergo a medical examination or treatment or act in a manner minimizing contact with other people, the officer may apply to the Ontario Superior Court of Justice and receive a court order. That order may result in the person being taken into custody by the police and detained in a medical facility for up to four months, examined and treated. That period may be extended by the court for further periods of four months.[107]

---

106 *Ibid.*, s. 22.
107 *Ibid.*, s. 35. For an assessment of this statute and of quarantine law generally, see Nola Ries, "Quarantine and the Law" (2005) 43 Alta. L. Rev. 529.

PART FOUR

NATIONAL SECURITY TOOLS AND TECHNIQUES

CHAPTER 10

SECRECY

Few credible observers would deny that there are secrets states must keep in safeguarding the security of their citizens. However, as Chapter 1 demonstrates, national security is an imprecise concept. As a consequence, it has been used in the past in many different states "to suppress precisely the kinds of speech that provide protection against government abuse," including damage to the environment, corruption, wasting of public assets and other forms of wrongdoing by government officials.[1]

National security should not be used to cloak governments from criticism or accountability. As David Paciocco has argued:

> while national security typically presents itself as a justification for secrecy, there is an increased need for openness when a government is attempting to deal with a security threat. … [R]esponding to security threats increases the risk of abuse. … This is particularly so where states choose to use the criminal law to achieve security. The power of the state is being used against individuals, and courts are called upon to make profoundly political decisions about the reach of government power.[2]

---

1 Sandra Coliver, "Commentary on *The Johannesburg Principles on National Security, Freedom of Expression and Access to Information*," in Sandra Coliver *et al.*, eds., *Secrecy and Liberty: National Security, Freedom of Expression and Access to Information* (The Hague: Martinus Nijhoff Publishers, 1999) at 12–13.
2 David Paciocco, "When Open Courts Meet Closed Government" (2005) 29 Sup. Ct. L. Rev. (2d) 385 at 396–97.

There is merit, in other words, in openness, even on national security matters.

Indeed, some observers have even argued that transparency *enhances*, rather than prejudices, national security by increasing a flow of information essential in the coordination of national security efforts. Alasdair Roberts has urged that

> an informed public can help policymakers to formulate better policy, monitor the readiness of national security bureaucracies and act independently to preserve security. An information-rich environment is one in which citizens and frontline government employees are better able to make sense of unfolding events and respond appropriately to them. ... In the jargon of the American military, a policy of transparency can be a powerful "force multiplier," which helps to build a state that is resilient as well as respectful of citizen rights.[3]

From this perspective, national security matters should not be excluded, *prima facie*, from transparency laws. Instead, boundaries need to be drawn between information whose disclosure truly prejudices national security, and other, less problematic information. Deciding where to draw this line is tremendously difficult.

In Canada, how government balances disclosure with secrecy is ultimately a legal issue. Several federal statutes limit citizen access to government information on national security grounds. The most notable of these are the *Access to Information Act*,[4] the *Canada Evidence Act*[5] and the *Security of Information Act*.[6] However, a number of other, less information-specialized statutes also include controls on government information.

Speaking generally, Canadian secrecy laws can be divided into three categories: laws limiting open government rules otherwise applicable to the executive branch; laws that constrain the open court concept and disclosure rules typically applied by Canada's courts; and, statutes that criminalize the wrongful disclosure of particularly sensitive information. This chapter examines each of these areas.

---

3   Alasdair Roberts, "National Security and Open Government" (Spring 2004) 9:2 Geo. Pub. Pol'y Rev. 69 at 82.
4   R.S.C. 1985, c. A-1 [Access Act].
5   R.S.C. 1985, c. C-5, s. 38 [CEA].
6   R.S.C. 1985, c. O-5 [SOIA].

PART I: OPEN GOVERNMENT

A. CONCEPT OF OPEN GOVERNMENT

Access to information is an essential attribute of democracy. As one of the founders of the United States, James Madison noted, "a popular government without popular information or the means of acquiring it is but a prologue to a farce or a tragedy, or perhaps both. Knowledge will forever govern ignorance; And the people who mean to be their own Governors, must arm themselves with the power which knowledge gives."[7]

Madison's sentiments were echoed repeatedly in discussions of what would become the United States *Freedom of Information Act* (FOIA),[8] introduced in 1966. There, it was argued that "free people are, of necessity, informed; uninformed people can never be free."[9] In signing the FOIA, President Johnson noted that "this legislation springs from one of our most essential principles: A democracy works best when the people have all the information that the security of the Nation permits. No one should be able to pull curtains of secrecy around decisions which can be revealed without injury to the public interest."[10] In a 1978 decision under the FOIA, the U.S. Supreme Court echoed this comment, noting that "the basic purpose of FOIA is to ensure an informed citizenry, vital to the functioning of a democratic society, needed to check against corruption and to hold the governors accountable to the governed."[11]

Similar views were expressed in Canada during discussions of federal information access laws. Prime minister Pierre Trudeau noted in 1975 that "democratic progress requires the ready availability of true

---

7   Letter from James Madison to W.T. Barry (4 August 1822) in S. Padover, ed., *The Complete Madison* (New York: Harper, 1953) at 337, cited in T. Murray Rankin, *Freedom of Information in Canada: Will the Doors Stay Shut?* (Ottawa: Canadian Bar Association, 1979) at 1 [Rankin, *Freedom of Information in Canada*].

8   *Freedom of Information Act* of 4 July 1966, Pub. L. No. 89-487, 80 Stat. 250 (5 U.S.C. § 552).

9   Freedom of Information: Hearings on S. 1666 and S. 1663. Before the Subcomm. on Admin. Practice and Procedure of the Senate Comm. on the Judiciary, 88th Cong. 3 (1964) (statement of Sen. Edward Long), cited in Charles J. Wichmann III, "Ridding FOIA of those 'Unanticipated Consequences': Repaving a Necessary Road to Freedom" (1998) 47 Duke L.J. 1213 at 1217.

10 Statement by the President Upon Signing Bill Revising Public Information Provisions of the *Administrative Procedure Act*, Weekly Comp. Pres. Doc. 895 (4 July 1966).

11 *NLRB v. Robbins Tire and Rubber Company*, 437 U.S. 214 at 242, 57 L. Ed. 2d 159 at 178 (1978).

and complete information. In this way people can objectively evaluate the government's policies. To act otherwise is to give way to despotic secrecy."[12] President of the Privy Council Walter Baker underscored this point in 1979, urging that "if this Parliament is to function, if groups in society are to function, if the people of the country are to judge in a knowledgeable way what their government is doing, then some of the tools of power must be shared with the people, and that is the purpose of freedom of information legislation."[13]

These views continue to be expressed by the information commissioners appointed pursuant to the federal government's key information law, the *Access to Information Act* (Access Act). Then information commissioner John Grace used colourful language to describe this perspective in his 1998 annual report:

> Any society aspiring to be free, just and civil must depend upon and nurture a wide array of methods for exposing, and imposing sanctions on, ethical failures. ... In one way or another, all the checks and balances designed to limit abuses of government power are dependent upon there being access by outsiders to governments' insider information. ...Yes, webs of intrigue are more easily woven in the dark; greed, misdeeds and honest mistakes are more easily hidden. A public service which holds tight to a culture of secrecy is a public service ripe for abuse.[14]

The courts have also recognized the importance of free access to information in a democracy. In his reasons in *Dagg v. Canada (Minister of Finance)*, La Forest J. urged that "the overarching purpose of access to information legislation ... is to facilitate democracy. It does so in two related ways. It helps to ensure first, that citizens have the information required to participate meaningfully in the democratic process, and secondly, that politicians and bureaucrats remain accountable to the citizenry."[15] While La Forest J. was writing in dissent, his approach to

---

12   Pierre Elliott Trudeau, quoted by G. Baldwin, M.P., in *Minutes of Proceedings and Evidence of the Standing Joint Committee on Regulations and other Statutory Instruments*, 30th Parl., 1st Sess. (1974–75) 22:7, cited in Rankin, *Freedom of Information in Canada*, above note 7.

13   *House of Commons Debates* (29 November 1979) at 1858, cited in Canada, The Standing Committee on Justice and the Solicitor General on the Review of the *Access to Information Act* and the *Privacy Act, Open and Shut: Enhancing the Right to Know and the Right to Privacy* (Ottawa: Queen's Printer, 1987) at 4.

14   Canada, Information Commissioner, *Annual Report 1997–1998* (Ottawa: Minister of Public Works and Government Services Canada, 1998) at 4.

15   [1997] 2 S.C.R. 403 at para. 61 [*Dagg*].

interpreting the Access Act was endorsed by the majority in that case and has since been followed by the lower courts.[16]

More recently, the Supreme Court has noted that the federal *Access to Information Act* makes information "equally available to each member of the public because it is thought that the availability of such information, as a general matter, is necessary to ensure the accountability of the state and to promote the capacity of the citizenry to participate in decision-making processes."[17]

B. OPEN GOVERNMENT AND INTERNATIONAL LAW AND PRACTICE

1) International Law

a) *Universal Declaration of Human Rights*

International human rights law favours a large measure of openness. Article 19 of the *Universal Declaration of Human Rights* (UDHR) provides that "everyone has the right to freedom of opinion and expression; this right includes [the right to] ... *seek... and impart information* and ideas through any media and regardless of frontiers."[18] As the U.N. Special Rapporteur on freedom of expression has noted, this provision creates a right to disclosure of information.[19]

---

16 See, for example, *Canada (Attorney General) v. Canada (Information Commissioner)*, 2004 FC 431 at para. 22; *Yeager v. Canada (Correctional Service)*, [2003] 3 F.C. 107 at para. 39 (C.A.); *Rubin v. Canada (Minister of Transport)*, [1998] 2 F.C. 430 at para. 36 (C.A.).

17 *Canada (Information Commissioner) v. Canada (Commissioner of the Royal Canadian Mounted Police)*, [2003] 1 S.C.R. 66 at para. 32.

18 *Universal Declaration of Human Rights*, A/RES/217 A (III) (1948) [emphasis added].

19 Commission of Human Rights, Civil and Political Rights Including the Question of: Freedom of Expression, U.N. ESC, 56th Sess., U.N. Doc. E/CN.4/2000/63 (18 January 2000) at paras. 42–44 ("the Special Rapporteur wishes to state again that the right to seek, receive and impart information is not merely a corollary of freedom of opinion and expression; it is a right in and of itself. As such, it is one of the rights upon which free and democratic societies depend. It is also a right that gives meaning to the right to participate which has been acknowledged as fundamental to, for example, the realization of the right to development" and noting "[p]ublic bodies have an obligation to disclose information and every member of the public has a corresponding right to receive information; 'information' includes all records held by a public body, regardless of the form in which it is stored"). See Chapter 2 for a discussion of the UDHR's legal status.

b)   *International Covenant on Civil and Political Rights*

Meanwhile, Article 19 of the *International Covenant on Civil and Political Rights*[20] (ICCPR) ratified by (and thus directly binding on) Canada, also provides that "everyone shall have the right to freedom of expression; this right shall include freedom to *seek, receive and impart information and ideas of all kinds*, regardless of frontiers; either orally, in writing or in print, in the form of art, or through any other media of his choice." Pursuant to Article 19(3), this right is subject *only* to such restrictions "as are provided by law and are necessary,

> (a)   For respect of the rights or reputations of others;
> (b)   For the protection of national security or of public order (*ordre public*), or of public health or morals."

None of these exceptions is defined in the covenant itself, a matter of concern.[21]

i)   Siracusa Principles

For this reason, a group of experts convened by the International Commission of Jurists in 1984 proposed the *Siracusa Principles*.[22] Though of no legal force, the Principles provide a helpful interpretive tool, defining passages such as "national security." Taken together, the *Siracusa Principles* impose sensible constraints, designed to guard against governments invoking the Article 19(3) exceptions to stave off legitimate critiques or mask improper motivations.[23]

---

20   *International Covenant on Civil and Political Rights* (1976), 999 U.N.T.S. 171 [ICCPR].

21   Erica-Irene A. Daes, *A Study on the Individual's Duties to the Community and the Limitations on Human Rights and Freedoms under Article 29 of the Universal Declaration of Human Rights* (New York: United Nations, 1990) ("[t]he terms 'public safety' and 'national security' are not sufficiently precise to be used as the basis for limitation or restriction of the exercise of certain rights and freedoms of the individual. On the contrary, they are terms with a very broad meaning and application. Therefore they can be used by certain States to justify unreasonable limitations or restrictions.").

22   *Siracusa Principles on the Limitation and Derogation of Provisions in the International Covenant on Civil and Political Rights*, UNESCOR, 41 Sess., U.N. Doc. E/CN.4/1985/4 (1985) [*Siracusa Principles*].

23   Thus, the *Siracusa Principles* urge that the phrase "rights and reputation" in the Covenant does not mean a limitation "to protect the State and its officials from public opinion or criticism." *Ibid.* at para. 37. "Public order" is defined "as the sum of rules which ensure the functioning of society or the set of fundamental principles on which society is founded. Respect for human rights is part of public order." *Ibid.* at para. 22. "Public health" should include only "measures dealing with a serious threat to the health of the population or individual members of

ii) Johannesburg Principles

In the specific area of national security, the *Siracusa Principles* are amplified by a second soft-law instrument: the 1995 *Johannesburg Principles*.[24] Like the *Siracusa Principles*, this document is not a binding legal instrument, but has attracted endorsements from international organizations.[25]

In their material parts, the *Johannesburg Principles* underscore that "everyone has the right to freedom of expression, which includes the freedom to seek, receive and impart information and ideas of all kinds." They acknowledge that these rights "may be subject to restrictions on specific grounds, as established in international law, including for the protection of national security." However, any restriction must be "prescribed by law and ... necessary in a democratic society to protect a legitimate national security interest." In practice, this requirement obliges a government to show that "the expression or information at issue poses a serious threat to a legitimate national security interest; ... the restriction imposed is the least restrictive means possible for protecting that interest; and ... the restriction is compatible with democratic principles."

As noted in Chapter 2, the *Principles* carefully circumscribe what is meant by a "legitimate" national security interest. Thus, *Principle 2* provides that a restriction justified on the ground of national security "is not legitimate unless its genuine purpose and demonstrable effect is to protect a country's existence or its territorial integrity against the use or threat of force, or its capacity to respond to the use or threat of force, whether from an external source, such as a military threat, or an internal source, such as incitement to violent overthrow of the government." Principle 2 further specifies:

> a restriction sought to be justified on the ground of national security is not legitimate if its genuine purpose or demonstrable effect is

---

the population. These measures must be specifically aimed at preventing disease or injury or providing care for the sick and injured." *Ibid.* at para. 25. "Public morals" may only be invoked to limit rights where the "limitation in question is essential to the maintenance of respect for fundamental values of the community." *Ibid.* at para. 27. "National security" is given the most comprehensive definition. Under the *Siracusa Principles*, "[n]ational security may be invoked to justify measures limiting certain rights only when they are taken to protect the existence of the nation or its territorial integrity or political independence against force or threat of force." *Ibid.* at paras. 29–30. It is not an appropriate response to "merely local or relatively isolated threats to law and order." In relation to national security, the *Siracusa Principles* have now been superseded by the more detailed—and arguably more authoritative—*Johannesburg Principles*, discussed below.

24 The *Johannesburg Principles on National Security, Freedom of Expression and Access to Information*, U.N. Doc. E/CN.4/1996/39 (1996) [*Johannesburg Principles*].

25 See Chapter 2.

to protect interests unrelated to national security, including, for example, to protect a government from embarrassment or exposure of wrongdoing, or to conceal information about the functioning of its public institutions, or to entrench a particular ideology, or to suppress industrial unrest.

In this manner, the *Principles* set a high threshold of national security legitimacy, with a clear focus on actual or threatened use of physical force. National security would not, therefore, apply where the secret related to some question of economic advantage or policy; say, for example, an anticipated Bank of Canada interest rate change. Nor would it attach to simple diplomatic correspondence, or information about Canada's negotiating position in a trade agreement. Other justifications may exist for restraining access to this information, but these justifications must flow from rationales other than national security—perhaps public order.

The *Principles* also contain standards curbing government responses to unauthorized disclosure of secrets. Thus, Principle 15 precludes punishment of a person on national security grounds "for disclosure of information if (1) the disclosure does not actually harm and is not likely to harm a legitimate national security interest, or (2) the public interest in knowing the information outweighs the harm from disclosure." Likewise, Principle 16 condemns subjecting a person "to any detriment on national security grounds for disclosing information that he or she learned by virtue of government service if the public interest in knowing the information outweighs the harm from disclosure."

iii) Human Rights Committee

Additional guidance on the scope of Article 19(3) may be extracted from views enunciated by the U.N. Human Rights Committee in response to individual complaints brought pursuant to the ICCPR. The committee has held that a justification under Article 19(3) "must be provided by law, it must address one of the aims set out in paragraph 3 (a) and (b) (respect of the rights and reputation of others; protection of national security or of public order, or of public health or morals), and it must be necessary to achieve a legitimate purpose."[26] The committee has rejected invocations of national security or public order to justify infringements of Article 19 where governments have failed to explain precisely how exercise of the Article 19 right threatens these interests.[27]

---

26   *Malcolm Ross v. Canada,* UNICCPROR, 70th Sess., U.N. Doc. CCPR/C/70/D/736/1997 (2000) at para. 11.2.

27   See, for example, *Jong-Kyu Sohn v. Republic of Korea,* UNICCPROR, 54th Sess., U.N. Doc. CCPR/C/54/D/518/1992 (1995) (rejecting invocation of national security and

2) Comparative Practice

There is also a body of comparative law influential in understanding information law and policy. As of 2006, more than sixty-eight countries had introduced freedom of information laws.[28] Building on this rich experience, the international free-expression nongovernmental organization "Article 19" proposes nine "best practice" principles that should guide government policies on access to information.[29] These principles "are based on international and regional law and standards, evolving state practice (as reflected, *inter alia,* in national laws and judgments of national courts) and the general principles of law recognised by the community of nations."[30]

Several of these standards are worth flagging in this book. First, access to information law should favour maximum disclosure. This principle obliges the government body refusing disclosure to bear the onus of demonstrating the legitimacy of this course of action.[31]

Further, exemptions from access "should be clearly and narrowly drawn and subject to strict 'harm' and 'public interest' tests."[32] The legitimacy of an exception should be measured via a three-part analysis. First, "the information must relate to a legitimate aim listed in the law." Second, "disclosure must threaten to cause substantial harm to that aim." Third, "the harm to the aim must be greater than the public interest in having the information."[33] Legitimate exceptions include, *inter alia,* the protection of national security, defence and international relations,[34] at least where there is a real prospect of harm to these inter-

---

public order to restrain speech allegedly directed at inciting a national strike). Further, the committee has rejected the national security or public order justification where Article 19 rights are violated "to safeguard an alleged vulnerable state of national unity." *Albert Womah Mukong v. Cameroon,* UNICCPROR, 51st Sess., U.N. Doc. CCPR/C/51/D/458/1991 (1994) (the committee "considers that the legitimate objective of safeguarding and indeed strengthening national unity under difficult political circumstances cannot be achieved by attempting to muzzle advocacy of multi-party democracy, democratic tenets and human rights") at 9.7.

28 David Banisar, *Freedom of Information and Access to Government Record Laws around the World* (2006), online: www.freedominfo.org/documents/global_survey2006.pdf [Banisar, *Freedom of Information*].

29 Toby Mendel, *Freedom of Information: A Comparative Legal Survey* (2003), online: www.article19.org/work/regions/latin-america/FOI/pdf/TMendelComp.Survey.pdf [Mendel, *Freedom of Information*].

30 *Ibid.* at 23.

31 *Ibid.* at 26.

32 *Ibid.* at 28.

33 *Ibid.* at 28–29.

34 *Ibid.* at 29.

ests. Indeed, most freedom of information laws include national security exemptions.[35]

Finally, laws on government secrecy inconsistent with access laws should be subordinated to these access laws, since the latter already include carefully demarcated exceptions capturing any legitimate secrecy objectives governments might have.[36]

C. CANADIAN OPEN GOVERNMENT LAWS

1) *Access to Information Act*

An assessment of whether Canada's information laws reflect these international benchmarks requires close scrutiny of the *Access to Information Act*, the federal open government law.

a) Right to Access

The Access Act creates a broad principle of access in its first dozen or so sections. It then devotes a sizeable portion of its remaining sections to the creation of exceptions and caveats to this principle.

The express purpose of the Act is "to extend the present laws of Canada to provide a right of access to information in records under the control of a government institution in accordance with the principles that government information should be available to the public, that necessary exceptions to the right of access should be limited and specific and that decisions on the disclosure of government information should be reviewed independently of government."[37]

The key provision of the Act, section 4, provides that every Canadian citizen and permanent resident "has a right to and shall, on request, be given access to any record under the control of a government institution," subject to other sections in the Act.

Notably, the Federal Court has referred to this right as "quasi-constitutional" in nature.[38] In part, this status reflects language in subsection 4(1) specifying that the right in section 4 applies notwithstanding any other statute.[39]

---

35   Banisar, *Freedom of Information*, above note 28.
36   Mendel, *Freedom of Information*, above note 29 at 34.
37   Access Act, above note 4, s. 2.
38   *AstraZeneca Canada Inc. v. Canada (Health)*, 2005 FC 1451 at para. 49, aff'd 2006 FCA 241.
39   *Canada Post Corporation v. Canada (Minister of Public Works)*, [1995] 2 F.C. 110 at 129 (C.A.) ("subsection 4(1) contains a 'notwithstanding clause' which gives

Nevertheless, it remains unclear whether the right to access articulated in section 4 also has a truly constitutional counterpart. Lower courts have refused to find a right to information disclosure in subsection 2(b) of the *Canadian Charter of Rights and Freedoms*,[40] the constitutional free expression provision,[41] or in the unwritten principles of the Constitution.[42] Yet, in the context of its open court jurisprudence, the Supreme Court apparently agrees that "freedom of expression in section 2(b) protects both listeners and readers."[43] It is not a tremendous leap to apply similar reasoning to openness of government generally. Whether the courts will eventually do so or not remains to be seen.

b) Exemptions to Access

To temper the potency of section 4, the Act includes a large number of reasonably well-defined exemptions limiting access to information. These exemptions can be classed in two ways: injury-based/class-based and mandatory/discretionary.

i) *Injury-based versus Class-based*

Injury-based exemptions may only be employed where the government concludes that disclosure may produce the harm enumerated by the Act.[44] By comparison, class-based exemptions are triggered as soon as

---

the Act an overriding status with respect to any other Act of Parliament").

40 Part I of the *Constitution Act, 1982*, being Schedule B to the *Canada Act 1982* (U.K.) 1982, c. 11.

41 *Criminal Lawyers' Assn. v. Ontario (Ministry of Public Safety and Security)* (2004), 184 O.A.C. 223 at para. 42 (Div. Ct.) (declining to find s. 2(b) applied where access had been denied under the Ontario law) [*Criminal Lawyers' Assn.*]; *Ontario (Attorney General) v. Fineberg* (1994), 19 O.R. (3d) 197 at 204 (Div. Ct.) ("it is not possible to proclaim that s. 2(b) entails a general constitutional right of access to all information under the control of government"); *Yeager v. Canada (Correctional Service)*, above note 16 at para. 65 (citing *Fineberg* and then stating: "Without endorsing all the reasons for decision given in that case, I am in respectful agreement with the conclusion of the Motions Judge that the respondent's *Charter* right was not contravened here").

42 *Criminal Lawyers' Assn.*, *ibid.* at para. 42 (holding that the unwritten "democratic principle ... is more concerned with matters relating to the proper functioning of responsible government, and with the proper election of legislative representatives and the recognition and protection of minority and cultural identities, than it is with promoting access to information in order to facilitate the expressive rights of individuals").

43 *Ruby v. Canada (Solicitor General)*, 2002 SCC 75 at para. 52 [*Ruby*].

44 See, for example, *Rubin v. Canada (Minister of Transport)*, above note 16 at para. 36, citing *Canada Packers Inc. v. Canada (Minister of Agriculture)*, [1989] 1 F.C. 47 at 60 (C.A.) ("Subsection 2(1) provides a clear statement that the Act should be interpreted in the light of the principle that government information

the requested information is found to fall within a certain class of information, as defined by the Act. There need not be any subsequent assessment of whether injury would result from disclosure, creating a substantial number of exceptions that do not meet the international best practice standards described above.

ii) Mandatory versus Discretionary

With mandatory exemptions, the government is obliged to decline disclosure, subject in a few instances to a public interest override. This override allows disclosure where the public interest in disclosure outweighs the interest in nondisclosure.

In fact, the majority of exceptions in the Act are not mandatory, but rather discretionary. Thus, the government *may* choose to decline disclosure of a document captured by the exemption. While these discretionary exemptions do not include a public interest override, the 2002 government Access to Information Review Task Force concluded that such an override "is not necessary" as discretionary exemptions "already imply a balancing of the public interest in protecting the information, and the public interest in disclosure."[45]

How the Access Act's national security exemptions fit into this classification scheme is discussed later in this chapter and is shown in Table 10.1.

---

should be available to the public and that exceptions to the public's right of access should be 'limited and specific.' With such a mandate, I believe one must interpret the exceptions to access in paragraphs [20(1)] (c) and (d) to require a *reasonable expectation of probable harm*") [emphasis added].

45   Access to Information Review Task Force, *Report: Access to Information: Making it Work for Canadians* (2002) at 43, online: www.atirtf-geai.gc.ca/report/report1-e.html [Access to Information Review Task Force]. Authority supporting this conclusion exists in the caselaw. See, for example, *Rubin v. Canada (Minister of Transport)*, [1995] 105 F.T.R. 81 at para. 30 (T.D.) ("While not every exemption has a subsection 20(6) public interest override clause, each exemption is subject to section 2. Thus, all exemptions must meet an implicit injury test that by its very nature means balancing the harm of release against the injury that comes with non-release. Paragraph 16(1)(c) has a public interest emphasis because it stipulates an explicit injury test"), rev'd, but aff'd on this ground, above note 16 at para. 40 ("As for the third issue, of whether or not to consider the public interest as an independent step under the test for reasonable expectation of probable injury ... [s]uffice it to say that I am in general agreement with the method adopted by the Trial Judge"). See also *Dagg*, above note 15 at para. 16 (discussing para. 8(2)(m)(i) of the *Privacy Act* and commenting "the Minister is not obliged to consider whether it is in the public interest to disclose personal information. However in the face of a demand for disclosure, he is required to exercise that discretion by at least considering the matter. If he refuses or neglects to do so, the Minister is declining jurisdiction which is granted to him alone").

Table 10.1: Access Act National Security Exemptions

	Class Test	Injury Test
Mandatory Exemptions	1. Section 13: Information received in confidence from other governments or an international organization. If the body gives disclosure permission (or this body has itself made public the information), the information may be disclosed. 2. Section 20: Information supplied in confidence by third parties concerning emergency management plans relating to the vulnerability of critical infrastructure, subject to a public interest override. 3. Section 24: Information protected under other, listed statutes.	
Discretionary Exemptions	1. Paragraph 16(1)(a): Information obtained or prepared by listed investigative bodies pertaining to crime prevention, law enforcement or threats to the security of Canada, if less than twenty years old. 2. Paragraph 16(1)(b): Information on techniques or plans for specific lawful investigations.	1. Section 15: Information that could reasonably be expected to be injurious to the conduct of international affairs or to the defence of Canada or an allied state, or the prevention or suppression of subversive or hostile activities. 2. Paragraph 16(1)(c): Information that could reasonably be expected to be injurious to law enforcement or to the conduct of lawful investigations, including information on confidential sources. 3. Paragraph 16(1)(d): Information that could reasonably be expected to be injurious to the security of penal institutions. 4. Subsection 16(2): Information that could reasonably be expected to facilitate the commission of an offence, including information that is technical information relating to weapons or potential weapons; or on the vulnerability of particular buildings or other structures or systems. 5. Section 17: Information the disclosure of which could reasonably be expected to threaten the safety of individuals.

c) Review

The Act creates a mechanism for policing government decisions on disclosure and its use of exemptions. An office of the information commissioner is created, and is charged with investigating access complaints brought by information requesters.[46] The commissioner—an officer of Parliament—has extensive powers to conduct investigations, but has no power to compel the release of the information if he or she feels that such release is warranted. Instead, to compel disclosure, the information commissioner, or any requester dissatisfied with the outcome of the commissioner's investigation, must bring an application in the Federal Court.[47]

d) Exclusions

As well as exemptions, the Access Act also includes three exclusions: classes of information to which the Act does not apply at all. Because this information is excluded entirely from the Act, the information commissioner has no powers to consider whether it should be disclosed. The national security exclusion is discussed further later in this chapter.

2) *Privacy Act*

a) Act's Multiple Purposes

In many respects, the *Privacy Act*[48] is the flipside of the Access Act. While the latter's purpose is the promotion of disclosure, the *Privacy Act* has both a nondisclosure and a disclosure function. First, the Act is designed to "protect the privacy of individuals" in relation to personal information about those individuals held by government. Second, individuals are to be given a right of access to their personal information in the possession of government.[49] In light of these purposes, the Supreme Court of Canada has agreed that the *Privacy Act* has a "special status," potentially of a "quasi-constitutional" nature.[50]

---

46   Access Act, above note 4, s. 30.

47   *Ibid.*, ss. 41 & 42.

48   R.S.C. 1985, c. P-21.

49   *Ibid.*, s. 2.

50   *Lavigne v. Canada (Office of the Commissioner of Official Languages)*, [2002] 2 S.C.R. 773 at para. 24 [*Lavigne*], citing with approval *Canada (Privacy Commissioner) v. Canada (Labour Relations Board)*, [1996] 3 F.C. 609 at 652 (T.D.) ("A purposive approach to the interpretation of the *Privacy Act* is … justified by the statute's quasi-constitutional legislative roots") and at para. 23, indicating that the Court recognizes the "quasi-constitutional" statute of the *Privacy Act*.

How the Act addresses its first purpose of protecting privacy is discussed in Chapter 11. This section addresses the Act's second objective — disclosure of a person's own personal information.

b) Disclosure Purpose

The disclosure provisions of the *Privacy Act* parallel the comparable sections in the Access Act. Indeed, the two Acts are woven together in a "seamless code."[51]

Every Canadian citizen or permanent resident has a right to access personal information contained in a personal information bank and any other personal information held by a government institution which the requester can describe sufficiently to allow retrieval.[52] Coupled with this right of access is a right to request correction of this personal information.[53] "Personal information" means "information about an identifiable individual that is recorded in any form,"[54] a definition that is "deliberately broad" and "is entirely consistent with the great pains that have been taken to safeguard individual identity."[55]

A number of exemptions exist under the Act. Like the Access Act, these exemptions may be classed as mandatory and discretionary, and as class-based and injury-based. National security exemptions are discussed in section D that follows.

The office of the privacy commissioner polices government use of exceptions under the Act, exercising powers of investigation and recommendation similar to those of the information commissioner. Ultimately, a requester (or the commissioner him- or herself) dissatisfied with the government response to efforts to extract personal information has a right to apply to the Federal Court for judicial review and seek a court order compelling disclosure.

Finally, like the Access Act, the *Privacy Act* augments its exemption regime with several exclusions that mimic in large part the exclusions from the Access Act. The national security exclusion is discussed in section D that follows.

---

51   *Dagg,* above note 15 at para. 45, LaForest J., dissenting but not on this point; *Canada (Information Commissioner) v. Canada (Commissioner of the Royal Canadian Mounted Police),* above note 17 at para. 22 ("[t]he *Access Act* and the *Privacy Act* are a seamless code with complementary provisions that can and should be interpreted harmoniously").

52   *Privacy Act,* above note 48, s. 12.

53   *Ibid.*

54   *Ibid.,* s. 3.

55   *Lavigne,* above note 50 at para. 26, citing with approval *Canada (Information Commissioner) v. Canada (Solicitor General),* [1988] 3 F.C. 551 at 557 (T.D.).

D. OPEN GOVERNMENT AND SECRECY LAWS

Despite the presumptions in favour of disclosure found in the Access Act and the *Privacy Act*, open government is substantially limited by government secrecy laws. This section describes how national security may provide a justification for reversing the presumption of disclosure otherwise prevailing under Canada's free information laws.

1) Access Act and *Privacy Act*

a) National Security Exemptions

While principally information disclosure laws, the Access Act and the disclosure rules in the *Privacy Act* include careful limits on disclosure tied to national security.

Section 16 of the Access Act (and its *Privacy Act* equivalent) allow the government to refuse release of requested records less than twenty years old containing information prepared by a government investigative body in the course of lawful investigations of activities suspected of constituting "threats to the security of Canada" within the meaning of the *Canadian Security Intelligence Service Act*.[56] Section 16 contains a number of other potential national security provisions, such as information that could facilitate an offence (including in relation to critical infrastructure), and information the disclosure of which could be injurious to law enforcement.

Meanwhile, under section 15—an exception whose *Privacy Act* equivalent the Supreme Court of Canada has labelled a "national security"[57] exemption—the government may refuse to disclose any record requested under the Act "that contains information the disclosure of which could reasonably be expected to be injurious to the conduct of international affairs, the defence of Canada or any state allied or associated with Canada or the detection, prevention or suppression of subversive or hostile activities."[58]

While "international affairs" is not defined, the expression "defence of Canada or any state allied or associated with Canada" is limited to efforts by Canada and foreign states "toward the detection, prevention or suppression of activities of any foreign state directed toward actual or potential attack or other acts of aggression against Canada or any

---

56   R.S.C. 1985, c. C-23. See also *Privacy Act*, above note 48, s. 22.

57   *Ruby*, above note 43 at para. 5.

58   Access Act, above note 4, s. 15. See also *Privacy Act*, above note 48, s. 21.

state allied or associated with Canada."[59] Meanwhile, the expression "subversive or hostile activities" is also carefully delimited.[60]

Other national security-like exemptions in the Access Act include "information the disclosure of which could reasonably be expected to threaten the safety of individuals."[61] Also notable is the exemption for information obtained in confidence from other countries.[62]

The *Privacy Act* also has an express exemption for information collected in preparing government security clearance assessments, where disclosure would reveal the identity of the person providing the information.[63]

Read together, these provisions provide government with substantial power to shield national security secrets from the effects of the Access Act and disclosure provisions of the *Privacy Act*. It is notable that the security and intelligence community itself apparently has few quibbles with the scope of the Access Act exemptions. In an August 2001 study prepared for the government's Access to Information Review Task Force, security and intelligence specialist Wesley Wark reported that "both the Canadian Security and Intelligence Service and the Communications Security Establishment, the two main collectors of sensitive intelligence in the community, regard the Access Act as offering sufficient protection."[64] Indeed, given the breadth of these exemptions, Wark labels access to contemporary intelligence records under the Act "a fiction" and concludes that "the current Access exemptions provide powerful and sufficient tools" for protecting intelligence information.[65]

59   Access Act, *ibid.*, s. 15(2).

60   *Ibid.* The expression means: "espionage against Canada or any state allied or associated with Canada, … sabotage, … activities directed toward the commission of terrorist acts, including hijacking, in or against Canada or foreign states, … activities directed toward accomplishing government change within Canada or foreign states by the use of or the encouragement of the use of force, violence or any criminal means, … activities directed toward gathering information used for intelligence purposes that relates to Canada or any state allied or associated with Canada, and … activities directed toward threatening the safety of Canadians, employees of the Government of Canada or property of the Government of Canada outside Canada."

61   Access Act, above note 4, s. 17; *Privacy Act*, above note 48, s. 26.

62   Access Act, *ibid.*, s. 13; *Privacy Act*, *ibid.*, s. 19.

63   *Privacy Act*, *ibid.*, s. 23.

64   Wesley Wark, *The Access to Information Act and the Security and Intelligence Community in Canada: Report 20 - Access to Information Review Task Force* (August 2001), online: www.atirtf-geai.gc.ca/paper-intelligence1-e.html.

65   *Ibid.*

b) National Security Exclusion

Notwithstanding the breadth of long-standing Canadian exemptions from Canada's access statutes, the government moved to enhance its power to keep information secret in its 2001 *Anti-terrorism Act* (ATA).[66] Specifically, since 2001, the *Canada Evidence Act*[67] now has a central place in government secrecy law.

i) Attorney General Certificate

As discussed below, the *Canada Evidence Act*'s primary purpose is to set out evidentiary rules for "proceedings."[68] Among its provisions are special rules limiting access to certain sensitive information during these proceedings. For the most part, the decision on whether to disclose this sensitive information is in the hands of the Federal Court. However, section 38.13 of the *Canada Evidence Act* empowers the Attorney General to personally issue a certificate "in connection with a proceeding for the purpose of protecting information obtained in confidence from, or in relation to, a foreign entity as defined in subsection 2(1) of the *Security of Information Act* or for the purpose of protecting national defence or national security."[69]

Notably, the minister may only issue the certificate in response to an order or decision requiring the disclosure of that information under any federal statute. However, issuance of the certificate has the effect of barring any subsequent disclosure of the information in a proceeding. In other words, the certificate may reverse an order from the Federal Court authorizing disclosure under section 38.06 of the Act, discussed below.

ii) Implications for the Access Act

The certificate may also bar disclosure under the *Access to Information Act*. Indeed, amendments introduced to the Access Act by the ATA give certificates clear primacy over the right to access. They do so by creating a new exclusion. Section 69.1 now specifies that the Access Act "does not apply" to information covered by a *Canada Evidence Act* certificate issued before an access complaint is filed with the Information Commissioner and, if issued after a complaint, quashes all proceedings in relation to that complaint.[70] At first blush, this appears to permit the government to stamp information as "top secret" and to use a certifi-

---

66   S.C. 2001, c. 41.
67   CEA, above note 5, s. 38.
68   *Ibid.* A "proceeding ... means a proceeding before a court, person or body with jurisdiction to compel the production of information."
69   *Ibid.*, s. 38.13.
70   Access Act, above note 4, s. 69.1.

cate to remove, *ab initio*, that information from the carefully tailored balance of access and exceptions set out in the Access Act regime.

This drastic result appears to be ruled out, at least in part, by the requirement in section 38.13 of the *Canada Evidence Act* that the certificate only be issued in response to an order or decision requiring disclosure. In defending the ATA, the government argued that since the information commissioner has no power to "order" or make a decision "requiring" disclosure, in theory, a certificate should only issue once a Federal Court has ordered disclosure on judicial review under the Access Act.[71]

However, as correctly noted by the information commissioner, the commissioner does have power under the Access Act to order disclosure to the office of the information commissioner *itself*, in the course of investigating an access complaint.[72] Thus, it is now "open to the Attorney General to issue a secrecy certificate for the purpose of resisting an order made by the Information Commissioner requiring that records be provided to him" or her.[73]

Indeed, this seems to be the exact intent of the ATA amendment to the Access Act. Subsection 69.1(2) indicates that a certificate "discontinues ... all proceedings under this Act in respect of the complaint, including an investigation, appeal or judicial review."[74] Since an "investigation" under the Access Act is undertaken by the information commissioner, this section anticipates a certificate being issued to circumscribe the commissioner's powers precisely in the fashion feared. Notably, the government has tried to bar disclosure to the information commissioner using the *Canada Evidence Act* in the past,[75] even prior to the introduction of this new section.

The breadth of subsection 69.1(2) also exceeds that strictly necessary to bring the Access Act into conformity with the amended *Canada Evidence Act*. While the *Canada Evidence Act* precludes the specific in-

---

71   Information Commissioner, *Annual Report 2001–2002* (Ottawa: Minister of Public Works and Government Services Canada, 2002) at 19 (citing then Minister of Justice McClellan, "the certificate could only be issued after the judicial review of an access or privacy request").

72   Access Act, above note 4, s. 36.

73   Information Commissioner, *Annual Report 2001–2002*, above note 71 at 19.

74   Access Act, above note 4, s. 69.1(2).

75   See, for example, *Canada (Attorney General)* v. *Canada (Information Commissioner)*, [2002] 3 F.C. 606 at para. 9 (T.D.) ("Three of the applications were brought by the Information Commissioner for orders in the nature of *certiorari* quashing certificates issued pursuant to sections 37 and 38 of the *Canada Evidence Act*, pursuant to which certain information and documents ... were not provided to the Information Commissioner").

formation covered in a certificate from being disclosed in a proceeding, the new Access Act provision discontinues all proceedings in respect to the "complaint."

In critiquing this language, the information commissioner has noted that access requests are typically made on a subject-matter, rather than individual government record, basis. Various exemptions on access may apply to assorted records falling within this subject-matter. In response to a complaint concerning nondisclosure, the commissioner reviews the use of each exemption in relation to *each* record. Under new subsection 69.1(2), the application of a certificate to a single record covered in an access complaint discontinues "all proceedings" in respect of the *complaint,* not simply proceedings in relation to that single record. The information commissioner summarizes the impact of this language as follows: "The federal government has given itself the legal tools to stop in its tracks any independent review of denials of access under the *Access to Information Act.* The interference is not even limited to the information covered by the secrecy certificates,"[76] as it also captures all other information raised in the complaint.[77]

The information commissioner also views the new amendments as an unnecessary overreaction: "the *Access to Information Act* posed no risk of possible disclosure of sensitive intelligence information, ... no such information had ever been disclosed under the Act in the 18 years of its life and ... the *Access to Information Act* régime offered as much or more secrecy to intelligence information as do the laws of our allies."[78] As noted above, this conclusion is supported by Professor Wesley Wark's assessment concerning the sufficiency of national security protection under the regular Access Act exemptions.

iii) Appeal Mechanism

In a mild response to criticisms sparked by its changes, the government amended bill C-36 prior to its promulgation as the ATA to create

---

76   Information Commissioner, *Annual Report 2001–2002,* above note 71 at 16.

77   In 2007, a senate committee recommended that the CEA be amended to clarify that a certificate does not halt a complaint being investigated by the information commissioner, but only those aspects of his or her investigation touching on the information covered by the certificate. Special Senate Committee on the *Anti-terrorism Act, Fundamental Justice in Extraordinary Times* (February 2007) at 82, online: www.parl.gc.ca/39/1/parlbus/commbus/senate/Com-e/anti-e/rep-e/rep02feb07-e.htm.

78   Information Commissioner, *Annual Report 2001–2002,* above note 71 at 20. For an academic critique of the amendments, see Patricia McMahon, "Amending the *Access to Information Act*: Does National Security Require the Proposed Amendments of Bill C-36" (2002) 60 U.T. Fac. L. Rev. 89.

an appeal mechanism for certificate determinations under the *Canada Evidence Act*. Thus, the minister's certificate decision may be challenged before a single judge of the Federal Court of Appeal. The role of this judge is simply to determine that the information covered by the certificate relates to the permissible grounds for issuing a certificate, in which case the judge must confirm the certificate.[79]

The information commissioner, in his review of this appeal mechanism, called it "woefully inadequate." In his words:

> The reviewing judge is not permitted by this amendment to conduct any of the usual types of judicial review of an administrative decision (*de novo*, legality, correctness); rather the reviewing judge's sole authority is to review the information covered by the certificate for the purpose of deciding whether or not it "relates to":
>
> 1. information disclosed in confidence from, or in relation to, a foreign entity;
> 2. national defence; or
> 3. security.
>
> One would be hard pressed to imagine any operational information held by any of our investigative, defence, security, intelligence, immigration or foreign affairs institutions, which would not "relate to" one or more of these three broad categories. ... This form of judicial review is significantly less rigorous than the independent review of secrecy certificates available in our major allied countries. This form of review has been aptly termed "window dressing" because it does not subject the Attorney General to any meaningful accountability for the use of certificates.[80]

To this criticism might be added the observation that the expressions "national defence" and "security" are undefined, rendering it very difficult for a judge to second-guess the executive branch.

In 2007, a special senate committee examining anti-terrorism law recommended that the Act be amended to "specify the way in which information must 'relate to' information obtained in confidence from a foreign entity, or to national defence or national security, in order for that aspect of the certificate to be confirmed by a judge"[81] and that the judge be empowered to consider "whether the public interest in disclosure outweighs in importance the public interest in non-disclosure."[82]

---

79   CEA, above note 5, s. 38.131.
80   Information Commissioner, *Annual Report 2001–2002*, above note 71 at 20.
81   Senate, *Fundamental Justice in Extraordinary Times*, above note 77 at 65.
82   *Ibid.* at 67.

iv) Implications for the Privacy Act

The new attorney general's certificate exclusion under the *Privacy Act* tracks very closely the Access Act equivalent. Notably, however, the *Privacy Act* specifies that a attorney general's certificate discontinues "all proceedings" in relation to the certified personal information, not the complaint *per se*.[83] This provision likely bars investigations and court reviews only in relation to the *specific* information covered by the certificate, not investigations and court review of a complaint as a whole that may include both certificate information and other information not captured by the certificate.

2) Secrecy Provisions in Other Statutes

Layered onto the secrecy regime created by the key statutes discussed above is a potpourri of other federal laws restricting access to government information for reasons of national security. Examples of these provisions are set out in Table 10.2.

PART II: OPEN COURTS AND ADJUDICATIVE DISCLOSURE

A. THE OPEN COURT PRINCIPLE

Fair trial rights in international law require a presumptively open court.[84] In Canadian law also, court proceedings are presumptively open. The Supreme Court of Canada has repeatedly underscored this point,[85] pointing to the common law and relying on the *Charter of Rights and Freedoms*. For instance, the Supreme Court has held that "freedom of expression in section 2(b) protects both listeners and readers."[86] It therefore supports "open courts": "openness permits public access to information about the courts, which in turn permits the public to dis-

---

83 *Privacy Act*, above note 48, s. 70.1.

84 See, for example, ICCPR, above note 20, Art. 14, applicable to criminal proceedings and any suit at law determining rights or obligations, and requiring a "public hearing," except in limited circumstances such as when required by national security.

85 See, for example, *Attorney General of Nova Scotia v. MacIntyre*, [1982] 1 S.C.R. 175 at 187; *Canadian Broadcasting Corp. v. New Brunswick (Attorney General)*, [1996] 3 S.C.R. 480 at paras. 21 & 22; *Edmonton Journal v. Alberta (Attorney General)*, [1989] 2 S.C.R. 1326.

86 *Ruby*, above note 43 at para. 52.

Table 10.2: Extraneous National Security Secrecy Provisions

Statute	National Security Provision	Definition of National Security or Its Similes
Corrections and Conditional Release Act, S.C. 1992, c. 20, s. 183	Under the *Act,* a Correctional Investigator, or his or her delegate, may disclose information required for his or her investigation, but may not disclose "information obtained or prepared in the course of lawful investigations pertaining to … activities suspected of constituting threats to the security of Canada … if the information came into existence less than twenty years before the anticipated disclosure."	"Threats to the security of Canada" given the same meaning as the equivalent term in the CSIS Act
Official Languages Act, R.S.C. 1985 (4th Supp.) c. 31, s. 68	The Commissioner of Official Languages is to "avoid disclosing any matter the disclosure of which would or might be prejudicial to the defence or security of Canada or any state allied or associated with Canada" in his or her annual report to Parliament.	None
Expropriation Act, R.S.C. 1985, c. E-21, s. 5	Where land is expropriated for "a purpose related to the safety or security of Canada or a state allied or associated with Canada" and the public interest so demands, the government need not provide specifics on this purpose in its notice of intent to expropriate.	None
Canadian Human Rights Act, R.S.C. 1985, c. H-6, ss. 33, 45, & 46	Members of the Human Rights Commission receiving information in the course of their investigations are to "take every reasonable precaution to avoid disclosing any matter the disclosure of which … might be injurious to international relations, national defence or security or federal-provincial relations."[4] Similarly, they are to guard against disclosing "information obtained or prepared by any investigative body of the Government of Canada … in relation to national security." Moreover, the government may notify the Commission during its investigation of a complaint that the practice impugned by the complaint was based on considerations relating to the security of Canada. In such instances, the Commission must dismiss the complaint or refer it to the Review Committee established by the *Canadian Security Intelligence Service Act* for its own review.	None
Canadian Environmental Protection Act, S.C. 1999, c. 33, s. 320	Information disclosure under the *Act* is constrained by a provision indicating that the Minister of Defence may prevent the release of information, the disclosure of which could reasonably be expected to be injurious to the defence or security of Canada or of a state allied or associated with Canada.	None

cuss and put forward opinions and criticisms of court practices and proceedings."[87]

Further, it is axiomatic in international[88] and Canadian criminal and constitutional law that the accused in criminal matters be given full disclosure of the state's evidence against them. Subject to legitimate exceptions for privileged evidence, the Crown in Canada has a legal duty to disclose its relevant evidence to the defence. As the Supreme Court of Canada noted in the leading authority on this point, "the right to make full answer and defence is one of the pillars of criminal justice on which we heavily depend to ensure that the innocent are not convicted. Recent events have demonstrated that the erosion of this right due to non-disclosure was an important factor in the conviction and incarceration of an innocent person."[89] As a consequence, the

> Crown obligation to disclose all relevant and non-privileged evidence, whether favourable or unfavourable, to the accused requires that the Crown exercise the utmost good faith in determining which information must be disclosed and in providing ongoing disclosure. Failure to comply with this initial and continuing obligation to disclose relevant and non-privileged evidence may result in a stay of proceedings or other redress against the Crown, and may constitute a serious breach of ethical standards.[90]

Read together, these rules create an open and transparent system of judicial adjudication. These principles may, however, be tempered in the interest of national security.

B. NATIONAL SECURITY AND OPEN COURTS

Some jurisdictions have charged special courts—often military in nature—with the adjudication of terrorist matters.[91] Officials in states

---

87   *Ibid.* at para. 53, citing *Canadian Broadcasting Corp. v. New Brunswick (Attorney General)*, above note 85 at para. 23.
88   ICCPR, above note 20, Art. 14(3)(b) specifies that an accused in criminal cases is "[t]o have adequate time and facilities for the preparation of his defence." The U.N. Human Rights Committee interprets "facilities" as including "access to documents and other evidence which the accused requires to prepare his case." U.N. Human Rights Committee, *General Comment 13*, U.N. Doc. HRI/GEN/1/ Rev.6 at 135 (2003) at para. 9.
89   *R. v. Stinchcombe*, [1991] 3 S.C.R. 326 at para. 17.
90   *R. v. Chaplin*, [1995] 1 S.C.R. 727 at para. 21.
91   The U.S. Military Commissions are discussed in Chapter 14.

such as Australia have also called for special criminal procedures in terrorism cases. These proposed rules include trial before judge alone, an approach applied by the United Kingdom during the troubles in Northern Ireland.[92] These measures are motivated, in large part, by efforts to control access to secret intelligence and relax conventional rules of criminal procedure.[93]

By the time of this writing, Canada had not opted for special terrorism courts in criminal matters, although the Air India inquiry in progress in 2007 was charged with examining this issue.[94] Canadian law makers

---

92   Nathalie O'Brien, "Call for Terrorism Court" *The [Sydney] Australian* (30 June 2006).

93   See *ibid*. See also United States, *Manual for Military Commissions* (Washington, DC: Department of Defense, 2007) Rule 505 (Classified information).

94   The Commission of Inquiry into the Investigation of the Bombing of Air India Flight 182 has been charged, among other things, with examining "whether the unique challenges presented by the prosecution of terrorism cases, as revealed by the prosecutions in the Air India matter, are adequately addressed by existing practices or legislation and, if not, the changes in practice or legislation that are required to address these challenges, including whether there is merit in having terrorism cases heard by a panel of three judges." P.C. 2006-293 (1 May 2006). If the government were to pursue such a system, two obvious problems would present themselves. First, the *Canadian Charter of Rights and Freedoms*, above note 40, guarantees trial by jury. Section 11(f) provides that any person charged with an offence has the right, "except in the case of an offence under military law tried before a military tribunal, to the benefit of trial by jury where the maximum punishment for the offence is imprisonment for five years or a more severe punishment." Jury trials have been described by the Supreme Court of Canada as fundamental to Canadian criminal justice. *R. v. Pan*, 2001 SCC 42 at paras. 40 and 42. Second, the creation of special tribunals might present its own difficulties. Canada's court system bifurcates jurisdiction between assorted courts. The most potent of these judicial bodies are the provincial superior — or "section 96" — courts. The provincial superior courts exercise the better part of the judicial jurisdiction inherited from the Royal Courts of the United Kingdom, including in the area of criminal law. Section 96 of the *Constitution Act, 1867* (U.K.), 30 & 31 Vict. C. 3, reprinted in R.S.C. 1985, App. II, No. 5, imposes important limits on the reallocation of judicial powers from provincial superior courts to other tribunals. Thus, section 96 is "a means of protecting the 'core' jurisdiction of the superior courts so as to provide for some uniformity throughout the country in the judicial system .... The jurisdiction which forms this core cannot be removed from the superior courts by either level of government, without amending the Constitution." *MacMillan Bloedel Ltd. v. Simpson*, [1995] 4 S.C.R. 725 at para. 15. Section 96 has been invoked to prevent either level of government to strip away too much provincial superior court jurisdiction, including over criminal matters. For instance, Parliament may tinker with superior court jurisdiction over criminal matters, but it may not seek to enact a "complete obliteration of Superior Court criminal law jurisdiction." *McEvoy v. New Brunswick*, [1983] 1 S.C.R. 704. Whether this standard permits the select-

have instead focused on devising special *in camera* (closed door) and *ex parte* (hearings in the absence of both parties) procedures applicable to national security cases. The sections that follow discuss two forms of adjudicative secrecy practised in Canada and overlapping in a somewhat uncertain manner: secret proceedings and secret evidence.

1) Secret Proceedings and National Security

a) Constitutional Limitation on Secret Proceedings

National security does not negate the open court principle. In *Re Vancouver Sun*, the Supreme Court examined the propriety of holding an *in camera* "investigative hearing" under section 83.28, a provision incorporated into the *Criminal Code* by the 2001 *Anti-terrorism Act*.[95] In its analysis, the Court observed that "the open court principle is a fundamental characteristic of judicial proceedings, and that it should not be presumptively displaced in favour of an *in camera* process." [96] Instead, if proceedings are to be closed, that decision must be made by the judge as an exercise of discretion, relying on the standard rules for ordering publication bans. Thus, a court must be persuaded that

> (a) such an order is necessary in order to prevent a serious risk to the proper administration of justice because reasonably alternative measures will not prevent the risk; and
>
> (b) the salutary effects of the publication ban outweigh the deleterious effects on the rights and interests of the parties and the public, including the effects on the right to free expression, the right of the accused to a fair and public trial, and the efficacy of the administration of justice.[97]

This test applies "to all discretionary actions by a trial judge to limit freedom of expression by the press during judicial proceedings."[98]

In sum, the "open court" principle suggests that statutorily prescribed "secret trials" would sit uncomfortably with the Canadian legal tradition, and could run counter to constitutional guarantees. The question of closed proceedings must be one left in the hands of judge, not mandated *ex ante* by statute. Further, where judges exercise that

---

ive removal of some criminal law jurisdiction (i.e., over terrorism matters) is unclear.

95   "Investigative hearings" are discussed in Chapter 15. This provision automatically sunsetted in February 2007, after Parliament failed to approve its extension.

96   2004 SCC 43 at para. 4.

97   *Ibid.* at para. 29.

98   *Ibid.* at para. 31.

discretion, they must balance the national security impulse against the public interest in openness.

b)   Existing Statutory Limitations on Open Hearings

i) *General* Criminal Code *Rule*

The central provision in the *Criminal Code* curtailing the open court principle for criminal proceedings on national security grounds is section 486. Section 486 now reads, in part:

> Any proceedings against an accused shall be held in open court, but the presiding judge or justice may order the exclusion of all or any members of the public from the court room for all or part of the proceedings if the judge or justice is of the opinion that such an order is … necessary to prevent injury to international relations or national defence or national security.

In *Re Vancouver Sun*, the Supreme Court expressly extended its test for closing courts to section 486.[99] Constitutionally, therefore, an additional element of discretion must be read into section 486: a court must be persuaded that "the salutary effects" of the closed court are proportionate to its deleterious effects on the rights and interests of the parties and the public.[100]

ii)   Canada Evidence Act

Vancouver Sun applies a balancing approach that should also be undertaken in other contexts. For example, as noted, the *Canada Evidence Act* tasks a Federal Court judge with determining the propriety of disclosing information the government wishes not to disclose on national security grounds in a "proceedings." However, this entire Federal Court process is itself ensnared in secrecy: no person shall in connection with a proceeding disclose either the information in question, or even the fact that an application is made to the Federal Court concerning that information's disclosure.[101] Further, the Federal Court is obliged to safeguard the secrecy of the information (and knowledge of the very existence of the proceeding)[102] and hold the hearing in private.[103]

---

99   *Ibid.*, citing *Canadian Broadcasting Corp. v. New Brunswick (Attorney General)*, above note 85 at para. 67 *et seq.*

100 See *Canadian Broadcasting Corp. v. New Brunswick (Attorney General)*, *ibid.* at para. 71.

101 CEA, above note 5, s. 38.02.

102 *Ibid.*, ss. 38.04 and 38.12(2).

103 *Ibid.*, s. 38.11.

Disclosure of the existence of the proceedings may be allowed by the court. The structure of the Act suggests, however, that this disclosure will only be made once the court has decided the fate of the secret information actually at issue in the proceedings.[104] The court is not "opened," in other words, in advance of the merits of the case being decided, and the court apparently has no discretion under the Act to do so. The constitutionality of this *Canada Evidence Act* provision is, therefore, suspect.

Indeed, the Federal Court concluded in 2007 that certain aspects of the Act violated the open court principle. Specifically, those provisions obliging the Federal Court to hold a *Canada Evidence Act* application and records confidential and to hold the hearing in private were read down to apply only where the government requests an *ex parte* hearing.[105] Left open was whether the Act's prohibition on the disclosure of the very existence of an application was a violation of the open court principle, although an earlier Federal Court decision casts doubt of the legitimacy of this section.[106] This is a matter that will likely attract further constitutional scrutiny in the future.[107]

2) Secret Evidence and National Security

While courts should not rush to close their proceedings, the above discussion suggests that the open court principle may be limited to allow the presentation of secret evidence on an *ex parte* basis.[108] Secret evidence, in other words, is permissible in Canadian law, subject to important constitutional constraints. The *Canada Evidence Act* provides the most significant tool available to government to resist disclosure to parties of national security information. Several other, more specific common law rules and statutes also include disclosure-limiting provisions.

---

104 Sections 38.06(1) & (2) appear only to apply to the assessment of the information over which the government is claiming confidentiality. The disclosure of the existence of a proceeding is tied in s. 38.02(2) to the s. 38.06 process, and indeed to the expiry of any appeal or time for appeal following that process. It would seem, therefore, that disclosure of the existence of a proceeding can only follow an assessment of the merits of the government's claims in relation to that information.

105 *Toronto Star Newspapers v. Canada*, 2007 FC 128.

106 *Citizen Group v. Canada (Attorney General of Canada)*, 2004 FC 1052 at paras. 35–40.

107 For a critique of the CEA from the "open courts" perspective, see Jeremy Patrick-Justice, "Section 38 and the Open Courts Principle" (2005) 54 U.N.B.L.J. 218.

108 *Ruby*, above note 43 at para. 54.

a)   Informer Privilege

The most likely secret at issue in a national security proceeding is the identity of informers. For example, information withheld in *Immigration Refugee Protection Act* (IRPA) security-certificate proceedings discussed below may include details "concerning human or technical sources."[109]

Informer identity is already richly protected in the Canadian law of evidence by the "informer privilege":

> The rule gives a peace officer the power to promise his informers secrecy expressly or by implication, with a guarantee sanctioned by the law that this promise will be kept even in court, and to receive in exchange for this promise information without which it would be extremely difficult for him to carry out his duties and ensure that the criminal law is obeyed.[110]

It "prevents not only disclosure of the name of the informant, but of any information which might implicitly reveal his or her identity."[111]

Informer privilege is subject to the "innocence at stake" exception; that is, secrecy will give way where "disclosure of the informer's identity is necessary to demonstrate the innocence of the accused."[112] Where informer privilege yields to the innocence at stake doctrine, "the State then generally provides for the protection of the informer through various safety programs."[113]

b)   *Canada Evidence Act*

Amendments made by the ATA to section 38 of the *Canada Evidence Act* contain special rules limiting access to "potentially injurious information" and "sensitive information" in "proceedings", including criminal trials.[114] The concepts of potentially injurious information and sensitive information are broadly defined: potentially injurious information means "information of a type that, if it were disclosed to the public,

---

109 CSIS, Backgrounder No. 14, *Certificates under The Immigration and Refugee Protection Act (IRPA)* (2005), online: www.csis-scrs.gc.ca/en/newsroom/backgrounders/backgrounder14.asp.

110 *Bisaillon v. Keable*, [1983] 2 S.C.R. 60 at 105.

111 *R. v. Leipert*, [1997] 1 S.C.R. 281 at para. 18.

112 *Ibid.* at para. 21.

113 *R. v. McClure*, 2001 SCC 14 at para. 45.

114 CEA, above note 5, s. 38. A "proceeding ... means a proceeding before a court, person or body with jurisdiction to compel the production of information." For a discussion of the scope of s. 38 in relation to the earlier doctrine of "public interest immunity," see Hamish Stewart, "Public Interest Immunity after Bill C-36" (2003) 47 Crim. L.Q. 249.

could injure international relations or national defence or national security," whereas sensitive information means "information relating to international relations or national defence or national security that is in the possession of the Government of Canada, whether originating from inside or outside Canada, and is of a type that the Government of Canada is taking measures to safeguard."[115]

Participants in a proceeding must notify the federal attorney general when they intend (or believe another participant or person intends) to disclose these classes of information. The attorney general may then authorize disclosure, or alternatively, may deny this authorization, in which case the matter is taken up by the Federal Court.

i) Injury to International Relations, National Defence or National Security

Summarizing the test to be applied by the Federal Court under section 38, the Federal Court has identified three steps: first, an assessment of whether the evidence is relevant to the proceeding in question; second, a determination of whether disclosure would be injurious to international relations, national defence or national security; and, third, a determination of whether the public interest in disclosure outweighs the public interest in nondisclosure.[116] This section and the one that follows discuss the last two steps.

Under section 38.06, a specially designated Federal Court judge authorizes disclosure unless persuaded that it would be injurious to international relations, national defence or national security. The terms "international relations, national defence or national security" in section 38 are undefined, a situation that attracted some negative commentary from a special senate committee in 2007[117] and efforts at definition by the Federal Court.[118]

---

115 CEA, *ibid.*, s. 38. Note that the inclusion of a type of information—sensitive information—that relates to national security, but the disclosure of which would not injure that security has been criticized as too sweeping. See, for example, Peter Rosenthal, "Disclosure to the Defence after September 11: Sections 37 and 38 of the *Canada Evidence Act*," (2003) 48 Crim. L.Q. 186 at 191.

116 *Canada (Attorney General) v. Khawaja*, 2007 FC 490 at para. 62 *et seq.* [*Khawaja*]; *Canada (Attorney General) v. Commission of Inquiry into the Action of Canadian Officials in Relation to Maher Arar*, 2007 FC 766 at paras. 37 *et seq.* [*Arar Commission*].

117 Senate, *Fundamental Justice in Extraordinary Times*, above note 77 at 64 (recommending that the expression "international relations" be defined to specify the sort of injury triggers application of this concept in the Act).

118 *Arar Commission*, above note 116 at para. 68 ("'national security' means at a minimum the preservation of the Canadian way of life, including the safeguard-

In weighing whether disclosure would in fact be injurious, the Federal Court of Appeal has concluded that deference is owed the minister:

> the Attorney General's submissions regarding his assessment of the injury to national security, national defence or international relations, because of his access to special information and expertise, should be given considerable weight by the judge. ... The Attorney General assumes a protective role vis-à-vis the security and safety of the public. If his assessment of the injury is reasonable, the judge should accept it.[119]

Nevertheless, there must still be a "sound evidentiary basis" for the government's claim of injury.[120] The anticipated injury must be probable, and "not simply a possibility or merely speculative".[121] Moreover, the "Attorney General is ... under an obligation to ensure that the information presented to the Court is complete, and that due diligence has been met with respect to ensuring that the privileges are properly claimed."[122]

The Federal Court has underscored that it will not sanction the use of the *Canada Evidence Act* to deny disclosure "when the Government's sole or primordial purpose for seeking the prohibition is to shield itself from criticism or embarrassment."[123]

ii) Public Interest Balancing

Even where disclosure would be injurious, the information may still be released if the public interest in disclosure exceeds the injury.[124] In these circumstances, the judge considers "both the public interest in disclosure and the form of and conditions to disclosure that are most likely to limit any injury to international relations or national defence or national security resulting from disclosure,"[125] and authorizes the

---

ing of the security of persons, institutions and freedoms in Canada"). The court then listed a number of specific sorts of information raising national security concerns, discussed further below.

119 *Canada (Attorney General) v. Ribic*, 2003 FCA 246 at para. 19.

120 *Khawaja*, above note 116 at para. 157.

121 *Arar Commission*, above note 116 at para. 49.

122 *Khawaja*, above note 116 at para. 158. See also *Arar Commission*, *ibid.* at para. 47 (making similar points).

123 *Arar Commission*, *ibid.* at para. 58, citing *Carey v. Ontario*, [1986] 2 S.C.R. 637 at paragraphs 84–85 ("the purpose of secrecy in government is to promote its proper functioning, not to facilitate improper conduct by the government").

124 CEA, above note 5, s. 38.06(2).

125 In weighing the public interest in disclosure, the Federal Court "is free to consider those factors it deems necessary in the circumstances." *Khawaja*, above note 116 at para. 93. A partial, but not exclusive list includes: "(a) the nature

release, if at all, "subject to any conditions that the judge considers appropriate, of all of the information, a part or summary of the information, or a written admission of facts relating to the information."[126] The Supreme Court has referred to this process as reflecting a parliamentary concern for "striking a sensitive balance between the need for protection of confidential information and the rights of the individual."[127] However, the Federal Court has suggested that the government claim of national security confidentiality puts one finger on that balance: the "public interest served by maintaining secrecy in the national security context is weighty. In the balancing of public interests here at play, that interest would only be outweighed in a clear and compelling case for disclosure."[128] More recent decisions have highlighted considerations that should drive the public interest inquiry. These include:

> (a) The extent of the injury; (b) The relevancy of the redacted information to the procedure in which it would be used, or the objectives of the body wanting to disclose the information; (c) Whether the redacted information is already known to the public, and if so, the manner by which the information made its way into the public domain; (d) The importance of the open court principle; (e) The importance of the redacted information in the context of the underlying proceeding; (f) Whether there are higher interests at stake, such as human rights issues, the right to make a full answer and defence in the criminal context, etc; (g) Whether the redacted information relates to the recommendations of a commission, and if so whether the information is important for a comprehensive understanding of the said recommendation.[129]

Courts clearly have the principal role to play under the *Canada Evidence Act* test. As the Federal Court has indicated, "Parliament has required the designated judge to balance competing interests, not sim-

---

of the public interest sought to be protected by confidentiality; (b) whether the evidence in question will 'probably establish a fact crucial to the defence'; (c) the seriousness of the charge or issues involved; (d) the admissibility of the documentation and the usefulness of it; (e) whether the [party seeking disclosure] have established that there are no other reasonable ways of obtaining the information; and (f) whether the disclosures sought amount to general discovery or a fishing expedition." *Khan v. Canada (Minister of Citizenship and Immigration)*, [1996] 2 F.C. 316 (T.D.) at para. 26.

126 CEA, above note 5, s. 38.06.
127 *Charkaoui v. Canada (Citizenship and Immigration)*, 2007 SCC 9 at para. 77.
128 *Singh (J.B.) v. Canada (Attorney General)*, [2000] F.C.J. No. 1007 at para. 32 (T.D.); *Canada (Attorney General) v. Kempo*, 2004 FC 1678 at para. 110 [*Kempo*].
129 *Arar Commission*, above note 116 at para. 98.

ply to protect the important and legitimate interests of the state."[130] The court has also held that under section 38 of the Act, "the designated judge has a very broad discretion to exercise."[131]

iii) Attorney General Certificate

However, the *Canada Evidence Act* allows the government to short-circuit a court disclosure order. As noted earlier in this chapter, section 38.13 of the Act empowers the attorney general to personally issue a certificate "in connection with a proceeding for the purpose of protecting information obtained in confidence from, or in relation to, a foreign entity as defined in subsection 2(1) of the *Security of Information Act* or for the purpose of protecting national defence or national security."[132] Issuance of the certificate has the effect of barring any subsequent disclosure of the information in a proceeding for fifteen years (and for a further period if the certificate is renewed at the end of that fifteen years). In other words, the certificate may reverse an order from the Federal Court authorizing disclosure under section 38.06, subject to a limited appeal before a single judge of the Federal Court of Appeal.[133]

iv) Fair Trial Protections

The system established by the Act would be vulnerable to constitutional attack in those circumstances where a person's innocence in a criminal trial can only be proven by evidence which a Federal Court refuses to disclose, or which is subject to an attorney general's certificate barring that disclosure. To compel trials to proceed even where the only evidence available to establish the accused's innocence is withheld from him or her would be an unquestionable violation of section 7.[134]

---

130 *Canada (Attorney General)* v. *Ribic* (2002), 221 F.T.R. 310 at para. 22 (T.D). See also *Khawaja*, above note 116 at para. 92 ("Parliament has tasked the Federal Court with the responsibility of balancing the competing public interests").

131 *Ribic* v. *Canada,* 2002 FCT 290 at para. 2.

132 CEA, above note 5, s. 38.13.

133 CEA, *ibid.*, s. 38.131. The government urges that the attorney general certificate process is necessary to bar release of information obtained in confidence under international intelligence-sharing arrangements, a matter discussed in chapter 12. Canada, *Government Response: Seventh Report of the Standing Committee on Public Safety and National Security, "Rights, Limits, Security: A Comprehensive Review of the* Anti-terrorism Act *and Related Issues* (Presented to the House on 18 July 2007) at 16, online: http://cmte.parl.gc.ca/CMTE/CommitteePublication. aspx?COM=10804&Lang=1&SourceId=213371.

134 For an assessment of s. 38 of the CEA's overall compliance with s. 7, see Kathy Grant, "The Unjust Impact of Canada's *Anti-terrorism Act* on an Accused's Right to Full Answer and Defence" (2003) 16 Windsor Rev. Legal Soc. Issues 137.

The Act sidesteps this possible clash between legal rights and the state's secrecy preoccupation by providing criminal trial judges with an escape from the dilemma:

> The person presiding at a criminal proceeding may make any order that he or she considers appropriate in the circumstances to protect the right of the accused to a fair trial, [other than ignoring a Federal Court determination on disclosure or a Attorney General's certificate].

Among the permissible orders are:

(a) an order dismissing specified counts of the indictment or information, or permitting the indictment or information to proceed only in respect of a lesser or included offence;

(b) an order effecting a stay of the proceedings; and

(c) an order finding against any party on any issue relating to information the disclosure of which is prohibited.[135]

c)   Secret Evidence in Other Circumstances

i)   *Scope*

Canadian law includes a number of other secret evidence provisions, usually tied to *ex parte* proceedings. Under the Access and *Privacy Acts*, for example, a Federal Court reviewing a government decision not to disclose certain national security information must allow the government to make *ex parte* submissions of confidential information.[136] A similar provision is found in the *Canada Evidence Act*.[137]

In the immigration "security-certificate" process under the *Immigration Refugee Protection Act* (IRPA) (as it existed at the time of this writing), on request of the government, "the judge is to hold closed, *ex parte* hearings if in the opinion of the judge, disclosure of information at issue in the hearings would be injurious to national security or to the safety of any person."[138] Throughout the proceedings, the Federal Court must ensure the confidentiality of the secret information if, in the opinion of the judge, its disclosure would be injurious to national security, among other things. The court is to provide persons subject to the certificate with a summary of the information or evidence that enables them to be reasonably informed of the case against them, but

---

135 CEA, above note 5, s. 38.14.

136 *Privacy Act*, above note 48, s. 51; Access Act, above note 4, s. 52.

137 CEA, above note 5, s. 38.11.

138 *Immigration and Refugee Protection Act*, S.C. 2001, c. 27, s. 78 [IRPA]. Bill C-3, on first reading at the time this book went to print, would change the "would be injurious" standard to "could be".

that does not include anything that in the opinion of the judge would be injurious to national security or pose a danger to the safety of any person if disclosed.[139]

The terrorist listing provisions of the *Criminal Code* contain similar provisions, albeit ones giving the court more discretion to decline *ex parte* hearings.[140] As discussed in chapter 7, in a challenge to a terrorist group listing decision under section 85.05 of the *Criminal Code*, a judge may, at the request of the attorney general, hear all or part of the government's evidence or information in the absence of the applicant and any counsel representing the applicant, "if the judge is of the opinion that the disclosure of the information would injure national security or endanger the safety of any person."[141] The judge is, however, to provide a summary of the confidential information. Analogous language is found in the sections governing the terrorist-financing certificate process in the *Charities Registration (Security Information) Act*[142] and in the terrorism financing regulations under the *United Nations Act* discussed in Chapter 7.[143]

ii) Constitutionality

These provisions raise two issues: first, the *ex parte* nature of the proceedings they allow and, second, the related absence of full disclosure of confidential information by the government.

a. *Ex Parte* Proceedings

In theory, *ex parte* proceedings—that is, hearings in the presence of only one party to the case—might be open. In practice, an *ex parte* proceeding under at least some statutes must also be an *in camera* hearing, resulting in a closed court. In *Ruby v. Canada*,[144] at issue was whether criminal defence lawyer Clayton Ruby was entitled to access information that may or may not have been collected on him by CSIS. The government claimed that any such information was exempted by the national security exemptions contained the *Privacy Act*. Mr. Ruby challenged this decision, in part by bringing a constitutional challenge to the requirement under the Act that the entire procedure be *in camera* and that, on

---

139 *Ibid.*, s. 78.

140 *Criminal Code*, R.S.C. 1985, c. C-46, s. 83.05.

141 *Ibid.*, s. 83.05(6)(a).

142 S.C. 2001, c. 41, s. 113; s. 6. But note that here, the court "shall" allow the *ex parte* proceedings. See discussion in Chapter 7.

143 *Regulations Implementing the United Nations Resolutions on the Suppression of Terrorism*, S.O.R./2001-360, s. 2.2 and *United Nations Al-Qaida and Taliban Regulations*, S.O.R./99-444, s. 5.4.

144 *Ruby*, above note 43.

the request of the government, hearings also be held on an *ex parte* basis. He argued, in particular, that the *ex parte* procedures were contrary to *Charter* section 7 fundamental justice procedural protections.

Without deciding whether section 7 was triggered by a violation of privacy, the Supreme Court of Canada rejected Mr. Ruby's claim on the *ex parte* issue, holding that fundamental justice was not violated. The procedure complained of did not, in the Court's view, "fall below the level of fairness required by s. 7."[145] In supporting its conclusion, the Court noted that even the appellant had agreed that "the state's legitimate interest in protection of information which, if released, would significantly injure national security is a pressing and substantial concern."[146] This consideration clearly led the Court to temper its expectations as to the procedure guaranteed by section 7.

However, in keeping with its developing section 2 open court jurisprudence, the Court held that the sweeping *in camera* requirement applicable to all of the proceeding (and not just the *ex parte* portion) was unconstitutional. It therefore "read down" the *in camera* provision to apply only to circumstances where the government requests an *ex parte* proceeding; it allowed, in other words, mandatory *ex parte, in camera* hearings. It did not then go that extra step and question whether a mandatory *ex parte* provision that also triggered a *mandatory* closed court was consistent with section 2.

In fact, on the authority of *Re Vancouver Sun* there is reason to query whether closing the court indirectly through this sort of mandatory *ex parte* proceedings can be constitutional, absent a full balancing test that weighs the security interests against the public interest. Nevertheless, *Ruby* was followed by the Federal Court in 2007 in *Toronto Star*,[147] a case that limited the reach of mandatory *in camera* features of the *Canada Evidence Act* to only those circumstances in which the government compelled the holding of an *ex parte* hearing. As in *Ruby*, the Federal Court did not question the legitimacy of a closed court process produced automatically by mandatory *ex parte* proceedings.

b. Nondisclosure of Confidential Evidence

Courts have accepted nondisclosure of the actual confidential evidence presented in these *ex parte* sessions as constitutionally appropriate where motivated by national security concerns. In *Chiarelli v. Canada (Minister of Employment and Immigration)*,[148] the respondent was ordered

---

145 *Ibid.* at para. 51.
146 *Ibid.* at para. 43.
147 Above note 105.
148 [1992] 1 S.C.R. 711.

deported from Canada after the government determined that the respondent was likely to engage in organized crime. The respondent was given only limited access to evidence adduced at the relevant hearing. The respondent challenged the constitutionality of this procedure. The Supreme Court of Canada held that while the individual has a strong interest in a fair procedure in the hearings, "the state also has a considerable interest in effectively conducting national security and criminal intelligence investigations and in protecting police sources."[149]

The Court cited with approval a U.K. House of Lords decision, *R. v. Secretary of State for the Home Department, ex parte Hosenball*,[150] in which Lord Denning observed that "the public interest in the security of the realm is so great that the sources of information must not be disclosed, nor should the nature of the information itself be disclosed, if there is any risk that it would lead to the sources being discovered." In the result, the Supreme Court in *Chiarelli* concluded that fundamental justice did not require that the respondent be given access to "criminal intelligence investigation techniques or police sources used to acquire that information."[151]

In *Suresh*, the Supreme Court held that, confronted with the prospect of being deported to torture under the then *Immigration Act*, an individual "must be informed of the case to be met" and that an "opportunity be provided to respond to the case presented to the Minister," including through the presentation of evidence countering the view that he constituted a national security threat.[152] Information provided by the government to inform a person of the case against him or her was, however, legitimately "[s]ubject to privilege or similar valid reasons for reduced disclosure, such as safeguarding confidential public security documents."[153] Further, the Court emphasized that "the Minister must be allowed considerable discretion in evaluating future risk and security concerns. This factor also suggests a degree of deference to the Minister's choice of procedures since Parliament has signaled the difficulty of the decision by leaving to the Minister the choice of how best to make it."[154] National security, in other words, limits the sort of

---

149 *Ibid.* at 716.
150 [1977] 3 All E.R. 452 at 460 (C.A.).
151 Above note 148.
152 *Suresh v. Canada (Minister of Citizenship and Immigration)*, 2002 SCC 1 at paras. 122–23.
153 *Ibid.* at para. 122.
154 *Ibid.* at para. 120.

procedures courts will insist upon as part of constitutional fundamental justice, even outside any section 1 analysis.[155]

In *Charkaoui*, the Court rejected a balancing of section 7 rights outside of a section 1 analysis[156] but did conclude that the section 7 "protection may not be as complete as in a case where national security constraints do not operate."[157] At issue was the IRPA security certificate process discussed in full in Chapter 14. The Court underscored that "before the state can detain people for significant periods of time, it must accord them a fair judicial process."[158] In particular, the "magistrate must make a decision based on the facts and the law"[159] and "the affected person be informed of the case against him or her, and be permitted to respond to that case."[160] As discussed in the next section, the Court invoked a special advocate model as a possible solution in the effort to balance secrecy with due process.

c. Special Advocate Issue

In March 2002, Federal Court Justice Hugessen publicly complained that the IRPA security certificate procedures make judges "a little bit like a fig leaf." He proposed "some sort of system somewhat like the public defender system where some lawyers were mandated to have full access to the CSIS files, the underlying files, and to present whatever case they could against the granting of the relief sought."[161] Systems of this sort are employed by Canada's chief allies, most notably the United Kingdom.[162] In the U.K., the special advocate has a very limited role, in part because of the strict secrecy obligations imposed upon him or her. Not least, once the special advocate has seen the secret evidence, he or she may not have any additional contact with the interested person, except in writing and under the supervision

---

155 For a critique of this approach, see David Mullan, "Deference from *Baker* to *Suresh* and Beyond: Interpreting the Conflicting Signals" in David Dyzenhaus, ed., *The Unity of Public Law* (Oxford: Hart, 2004) at 47.

156 *Charkaoui*, above note 127 at para. 22 *et seq.*

157 *Ibid.* at para. 27.

158 *Ibid.* at para. 28.

159 *Ibid.* at para. 48.

160 *Ibid.* at para. 53.

161 Justice Hugessen, at a March 2002 conference held at the Canadian Institute for the Administration of Justice entitled "Terrorism, Law and Democracy," reproduced in Memorandum of Fact and Law of Mohamed Harkat (18 November 2004), Federal Court File No. DES-4-02.

162 See, for example, the special attorney procedure available for the U.S. Alien Terrorist Removal Court, 8 U.S.C. § 1534 and the special advocate procedure under the U.K. *Special Immigration Appeals Commission Act 1997* (U.K.), 1997, c. 68, s. 6, recently extended to control order proceedings under the *Prevention of Terrorism Act 2005* (U.K.), 2005, c. 2.

of the relevant tribunal. Exculpatory details that might be provided by an interested person questioned by an advocate fully apprised of the government's case generally do not come to light. Further, special advocates have reported difficulties in obtaining full disclosure of the government file on the interested party, including exculpatory information. The system has, therefore, been criticized[163] and without question falls short of conventional fair trial standards. The House of Lords has given a lukewarm blessing to the use of special advocates in at least control order cases.[164]

It should be noted, however, that the presence of the same special advocate in terrorism immigration matters has at least allowed that individual to note contradictions in the intelligence evidence used by the government in different cases.[165] The system also permits a skilled advocate with access to the secret information to challenge confidentiality claims and to press for greater disclosure of that information to the interested person and their nonsecurity cleared counsel.

As this book went to press, Canada was moving to adopt a special advocate, after considerable debate over the last several years. The Federal Court of Appeal, in the *Charkaoui* case, was sympathetic to the difficulties the IRPA *ex parte* process produces, noting "[t]here is no doubt that the system, as it exists, complicates the task of the designated judge who must, in the absence of an applicant and his counsel, concern himself with the latter's interests in order to give equal treatment to the parties before him."[166] Yet, the Court of Appeal held that it was for Parliament to set up such a system, not for the courts to demand it as part of minimal constitutional guarantees.[167] Similar views have been expressed by the Federal Court in other IRPA national security detention cases.[168] Up until 2007, the Federal Court had resolved concerns about the *ex parte* nature of proceedings by adopting a pseudo-inquisitorial style in an effort to probe the government evidence.[169]

---

163 See, in particular, U.K. House of Commons and House of Lords, *Joint Committee On Human Rights — Nineteenth Report* (16 July 2007), online: www.publications.parliament.uk/pa/jt200607/jtselect/jtrights/157/15709.htm.

164 *Secretary of State v. MB*, [2007] UKHL 46 (a challenge to the *ex parte* nature of proceedings in relation to "control orders," a concept discussed in Chapter 14, in which the law lords warned that a special advocate may not always cure the impairment of the fair trial right and concluded that a residual discretion should rest with the judge to determine whether a fair trial had been accorded).

165 Sam Knight, "Secret Terror Courts Questioned after Evidence Bungle" [*London*] *Times* (12 October 2006).

166 2004 FCA 421 at para. 124.

167 *Ibid.* at paras. 121–26.

168 *Harkat (Re)*, 2004 FC 1717 at para. 43 *et seq.*; *Mahjoub v. Canada (Minister of Citizenship and Immigration)*, 2005 FC 156 at para. 62.

169 See *Harkat (Re)*, 2005 FC 393 at para. 93 *et seq.*

The Supreme Court in *Charkaoui* concluded that this effort to re-suscitate something approximating an adversarial system was inad-equate.[170] In a passage worthy of citation in full, the Court noted the deficiencies of the IRPA system:

> The judge, working under the constraints imposed by the *IRPA*, simply cannot fill the vacuum left by the removal of the traditional guarantees of a fair hearing. The judge sees only what the ministers put before him or her. The judge, knowing nothing else about the case, is not in a position to identify errors, find omissions or assess the credibility and truthfulness of the information in the way the named person would be. Although the judge may ask questions of the named person when the hearing is reopened, the judge is prevented from asking questions that might disclose the protected information. Likewise, since the named person does not know what has been put against him or her, he or she does not know what the designated judge needs to hear. If the judge cannot provide the named person with a summary of the information that is sufficient to enable the person to know the case to meet, then the judge cannot be satisfied that the information before him or her is sufficient or reliable. De-spite the judge's best efforts to question the government's witnesses and scrutinize the documentary evidence, he or she is placed in the situation of asking questions and ultimately deciding the issues on the basis of incomplete and potentially unreliable information.[171]

For these reasons, the IRPA confidentiality rules violated section 7. They also violated section 1; the government had shown no reason why it had failed to adopt a special advocate model. While acknowledg-ing its shortcomings, the Court showed evident enthusiasm for such an approach. In October 2007, the government tabled Bill C-3, a law project that proposed amending IRPA to create a system of special ad-vocates.[172]

---

170 *Charkaoui*, above note 127 at para. 51 ("The judge is not afforded the power to independently investigate all relevant facts that true inquisitorial judges enjoy. At the same time, since the named person is not given a full picture of the case to meet, the judge cannot rely on the parties to present missing evidence. The result is that, at the end of the day, one cannot be sure that the judge has been exposed to the whole factual picture").

171 *Ibid.* at para. 63.

172 The Court struck down the offending IRPA provisions, but suspended the effect of its judgment for a year to allow Parliament to enact a constitutionally compli-ant system.

A security-cleared special advocate has been endorsed in other circumstances as well.[173] At least one court has concluded that a special advocate is constitutionally required: the Federal Court concluded in 2007 in *Khawaja* that *ex parte* proceedings under the *Canada Evidence Act* would not violate *Charter* section 7's guarantee of full answer and defence in relation to an underlying criminal proceeding so long as a security-cleared *amicus* was appointed to probe the government position during the *ex parte* sessions.[174]

Meanwhile, in its 2007 report on anti-terrorism law, a special senate committee recommended that the special advocate process be extended to all proceedings where "information is withheld from a party in the interest of national security and he or she is therefore not in a position to make full answer and defence," including under IRPA, the *Criminal Code* terrorist group listing process, the *Charities Registration (Security Information) Act* and the *Canada Evidence Act*.[175] Moreover, the committee urged that the special advocate be empowered to communicate with the affected parties after receiving confidential information, subject to guidelines designed to bar the release of secret information.

---

173   As the Federal Court of Appeal noted in *Charkaoui*, above note 127 at para. 123, in *Canada (Attorney General) v. Ribic*, above note 119 "after an agreement between the parties and with the consent of the Attorney General of Canada, a special counsel was appointed with access to the protected information. He assisted Mr. Ribic's counsel, participated in the private and in camera hearings in his place and asked the witnesses the questions which the latter wished to have clarified." Similarly, when the Security Intelligence Review Committee scrutinizes CSIS activities on an *ex parte* basis in response to a complaint senior SIRC counsel (or sometimes a special counsel) "will cross-examine witnesses on [the complainant's] behalf and may provide [the complainant] with a summary of the information presented in [the complainant's] absence." SIRC, "Complaints," online: www.sirc-csars.gc.ca/cmpplt/index-eng.html. The SIRC lawyer is able to meet with the interested person after seeing the secret information. In the Arar inquiry, the commission counsel discussed lines of cross-examination with Mr. Arar and his counsel and had access to secret information. Commission counsel was able to meet with Mr. Arar after seeing this material. Further, the inquiry also appointed *amici* who reviewed all evidence and offered submissions on what could be released publicly. See discussion in Michael Code & Kent Roach, "The Role of the Independent Lawyer and Security Certificates" (2006) 52 Crim. L.Q. 85 at 102.

174   *Canada (Attorney General) v. Khawaja*, 2007 FC 463.

175   Senate, *Fundamental Justice in Extraordinary Times*, above note 77 at 42. By the time of this writing, the government was continuing to study special advocates and their use, including outside the IRPA context. Canada, *Government Response*, above note 133 at 23.

The counterpart Commons committee also recommended a comprehensive "panel of special counsel" for national security cases.[176]

Exactly how special advocates might operate in Canada was unclear by the time of this writing. A simple importation of the U.K. model—with its strict rules of noncontact during the secret phase of the case between the special advocate and the interested party—would probably invite further court challenges. A U.K.-style model would constitute a departure from the closest analogy to a special advocate in the Canadian context—counsel employed during complaints about CSIS brought before the Security Intelligence Review Committee. The latter system allows access by the SIRC lawyer or outside counsel to the interested person throughout the proceeding.[177] The SIRC lawyer or outside counsel may then question the interested person, albeit subject to a strict obligation not to disclose secret information. Even with that restriction, SIRC outside counsel regard this questioning, done in an oblique manner to avoid involuntary disclosures of secret information, as central in unearthing potentially exculpatory information.[178] Further, SIRC has access to all CSIS information, excepting Cabinet confidences. In these circumstances, concerns that the security service might fail to disclose relevant (and indeed, exculpatory) information are minimized. Given this SIRC precedent, it is difficult to see how the more restrictive U.K. model would satisfy the minimal impairment standard if scrutinized in any future section 1 analysis. As it existed at first reading, Bill C-3 constituted a minimalist proposal, sketching out a role for special advocates but leaving many of the pressing issues raised by the U.K. experience to be resolved by Federal Court judges, if at all.

By the time of this writing, there had also not been much discussion of an alternative process to special advocates, one that has been employed at least once in Canada: access by the individual's own lawyers to security information pursuant to a confidentiality agreement. In the Air India trial,[179] counsel for the defendants were allowed access to information over which the government claimed national security confidentiality. In return, they undertook not to disclose this information to their clients. Subsequently, counsel negotiated with the Crown and CSIS on whether individual documents were of real importance to the defence

---

176 House of Commons Subcommittee on the Review of the *Anti-terrorism Act*, *Rights, Limits, Security: A Comprehensive Review of the Anti-terrorism Act and Related Issues* (March 2007) at 81, online: http://cmte.parl.gc.ca/cmte/CommitteePublication.aspx?COM=10804&Lang=1&SourceId=199086.

177 See discussion in note 173 above. Information obtained by personal communication, SIRC and independent counsel (July and August 2007).

178 Information obtained by personal communication, SIRC and independent counsel (July and August 2007).

179 Decision reported as *R. v. Malik*, 2005 BCSC 350.

and should be disclosed in the public interest. This system of examination and discussion reportedly "allowed counsel for the parties to resolve every disclosure dispute involving potentially privileged documents."[180] Documents that were released in this manner were then available to the defendants, while other documents were returned to CSIS.

3) Secrecy Doctrines

Court jurisprudence relating to the *Canada Evidence Act*, Access Act and *Privacy Act*, and IRPA gives some indication of the secrecy doctrines that animate the government's national security confidentiality claims. Security intelligence services focus in part on the importance of secrecy in protecting sources and methods. CSIS, for example, opposes disclosure of information that may:

a) identify or tend to identify Service employees or internal procedures and administrative methodology of the Service, such as names and file numbers;

b) identify or tend to identify investigative techniques and methods of operation utilized by the Service;

c) identify or tend to identify Service interest in individuals, groups or issues, including the existence or absence of past or present files or investigations, the intensity of investigations, or the degree or lack of success of investigations;

d) identify or tend to identify human sources of information for the Service or the content of information provided by a human source;

e) identify or tend to identify relationships that the Service maintains with foreign security and intelligence agencies and would disclose information received in confidence from such sources; and

f) identify or tend to identify information concerning the telecommunication system utilized by the Service.[181]

In arguing that these or other interests would be impaired by disclosure, the government often invokes the "mosaic effect," a concept that has been raised in several cases.[182] Put simply, the mosaic effect

---

180 Code & Roach, "The Role of the Independent Lawyer and Security Certificates," above note 173 at 107. See *ibid.* at 109 for a discussion of the implications of this approach for the solicitor-client relationship and an argument that this relationship is not unduly impaired.

181 CSIS affiant's testimony, reported in *Khawaja*, above note 116 at para. 132. See also the similar list produced in *Arar Commission*, above note 116 at para. 69.

182 See, for example, *Khawaja, ibid.* at para. 135; *Kempo*, above note 128; *Re Zundel*, 2005 FC 295; *Cemerlic v. Canada (Solicitor General)*, 2003 FCT 133; *Canada (Minister of Citizenship and Immigration) v. Singh*, [1998] F.C.J. No. 978 (T.D.);

posits that the release of even innocuous information can jeopardize national security if that information can be pieced together with other data by a knowledgeable reader. The result is a mosaic of little pieces of benign information that cumulatively discloses matters of true national security significance. As urged by one CSIS official in a public affidavit in Federal Court:

> assessing the damage caused by disclosure of information cannot be done in the abstract or in isolation. It must be assumed that information will reach persons with a knowledge of Service targets and the activities subject to this investigation. In the hands of an informed reader, seemingly unrelated pieces of information, which may not in themselves be particularly sensitive, can be used to develop a more comprehensive picture when compared with information already known by the recipient or available from another source.[183]

The mosaic effect has been accepted by Canadian courts, and has guided decisions on disclosure. At core, the doctrine is sensible. As noted by the Federal Court in one of the first cases to apply the doctrine,

> in security matters, there is a requirement to not only protect the identity of human sources of information but to recognize that the following types of information might require to be protected: ... information pertaining to the identity of targets of the surveillance whether they be individuals or groups, the technical means and sources of surveillance, the methods of operation of the service, the identity of certain members of the service itself, the telecommunications and cypher systems and, at times, the very fact that a surveillance is being or is not being carried out. This means for instance that evidence, which of itself might not be of any particular use in actually identifying the threat, might nevertheless require to be protected if the mere divulging of the fact that CSIS is in possession of it would alert the targeted organization to the fact that it is in fact subject to electronic surveillance or to a wiretap or to a leak from some human source within the organization.[184]

The use of the mosaic effect outside of the context of security investigations involving confidential informers and techniques might,

---

Ternette v. Canada (Solicitor General), [1992] 2 F.C. 75 (T.D.); Henrie v. Canada (Security Intelligence Review Committee), [1989] 2 F.C. 229 (T.D.), aff'd [1992] F.C.J. No. 100 (C.A.) [Henrie]; Re Jaballah, [2003] 4 F.C. 345 (T.D.); Ruby v. Canada (Solicitor General), [1998] 2 F.C. 351 (T.D.).

183 Reproduced in Kempo, ibid. at para. 62.
184 Henrie, above note 182 at para. 29 (T.D.).

however, greatly erode open government and open courts. Since the doctrine applies to innocuous information, the future use of which can never be predicted, it could be deployed to stave off disclosure of virtually *any* piece of information.

There must therefore be an outer limit where even information related to an investigation is disclosable. Some information is so innocuous that it strains plausibility to urge that it be kept secret. In *O'Neill v. Canada*, for example, the RCMP resisted disclosure on national security grounds of the location of an RCMP building "even though it has an exterior sign indicating that it is an RCMP building."[185] Moreover, the location of the building had already been disclosed in the Arar inquiry. Not surprisingly, the Ontario Superior Court of Justice ordered the release of the information in the *O'Neill* proceedings.

The Federal Court also appears attuned to the difficulties in applying the mosaic effect theory. It has held that "by itself the mosaic effect will usually not provide sufficient reason to prevent the disclosure of what would otherwise appear to be an innocuous piece of information. Something further must be asserted as to why that particular piece of information should not be disclosed."[186]

PART III: INFORMATION OFFENCES

This chapter has described laws that permit the government to maintain the secrecy of information that would otherwise be subject to disclosure under open government or open court rules. A final issue in this area is how the government may react in circumstances where sensitive, national-security information is obtained in an illicit or unauthorized manner. To grapple with this prospect, Canadian law includes a number of information disclosure offences. First, it criminalizes unauthorized disclosure of sensitive information. Second, it proscribes physical spying—that is, the physical infiltration of sensitive locations. The *Security of Information Act* (SOIA) is the key statute creating both of these types of offences.

---

185 *Canada (Attorney General) v. O'Neill*, [2004] O.J. No. 4649 at para. 69 (S.C.J.).
186 *Khawaja*, above note 116 at para. 136; *Arar Commission*, above note 116 at para. 84 (making similar observations).

A. BACKGROUND TO THE *SECURITY OF INFORMATION ACT*

Originally enacted in 1939 as the *Official Secrets Act*,[187] the SOIA was amended substantially and renamed in December 2001, as part of the *Anti-terrorism Act*. The 1939 Act, for its part, was a variant on the 1889 U.K. *Official Secrets Act*, and had two main foci. First, it created an offence of espionage or spying and second, in section 4, it criminalized wrongful dissemination of information, sometimes called "leakage."[188]

This wartime statute was roundly condemned, beginning at least in the 1960s, for its breadth and ambiguity. Thus, the Royal Commission on Security (the Mackenzie Commission) called the 1939 law "an unwieldy statute, couched in very broad and ambiguous language."[189] In 1986, the Law Reform Commission condemned the statute "as one of the poorest examples of legislative drafting in the statute books."[190] It called the Act and other laws criminalizing "crimes against the state" as "out of date, complex, repetitive, vague, inconsistent, lacking in principle and over-inclusive," as well as potentially unconstitutional under the *Charter of Rights and Freedoms*.[191]

In particular, the commission took issue with then section 3 of the Act, relating to spying, which could be interpreted as imposing an onus of proving innocence on the accused. This reverse onus, the commission speculated, was inconsistent with subsection 11(d) of the *Charter*, which guarantees the presumption of innocence until proven guilty.[192] Criticism of the statute was voiced by the government itself in 1998, when the then solicitor general called the Act "badly outdated and overbroad."[193]

Perhaps for these reasons, the Act has rarely been invoked. The Canadian Security Intelligence Service reports that since 1939 there have been two dozen prosecutions under the Act, but only six in the

---

187 R.S.C. 1970, c. O-3. This Act, in turn, is an "adoption of the English statutes as enacted in Great Britain (1911 (U.K.) c. 28, and 1920 (U.K.), c. 75)." *R. v. Toronto Sun Publishing Limited*, (1979) 24 O.R. (2d) 621 at 623 (Prov. Ct.) [*Toronto Sun*].

188 See Canada, Canadian Security Intelligence Service [CSIS], *Security of Information Act* (2 April 2004), online: www.csis-scrs.gc.ca/en/newsroom/backgrounders/backgrounder12.asp.

189 Canada, Mackenzie Commission, *Report of the Royal Commission on Security* (Ottawa: The Queen's Printer, 1969) at para. 204.

190 Canada, Law Reform Commission, *Crimes against the State* (Ottawa: Law Reform Commission, 1986) at 30.

191 *Ibid.* at 38–39.

192 *Ibid.* at 39.

193 *House of Commons Debates*, No. 096 (30 April 1998) at 1010 (Hon. Andy Scott).

past forty years.[194] In one of these cases, Stephen Ratkai pleaded guilty in 1989 to charges under the espionage provisions of the statute for spying for the U.S.S.R. In sentencing Ratkai to two concurrent terms of nine years, the court commented that the object of the *Official Secrets Act* "is to protect the safety and interests of the state. Every country has an obligation to protect its citizens and its territory and countries must depend and rely upon its citizens to ensure [their] safety and security. What is disturbing and despicable about offences of this nature is that a citizen betrays his country which he has a duty to protect and defend."[195]

However, in *R. v. Toronto Sun*—probably the leading case on the *Official Secrets Act*—the court was moved much less by the Act's objectives than by its awkward structure. At issue in this pre-*Charter* case was whether a newspaper and its editors had violated the Act by printing excerpts of a top secret document concerning Soviet intelligence activities in Canada. The court concluded that they had not, as the allegedly secret information had been previously invoked in the public domain. However, the court was also critical of the Act itself. In the court's words,

> since the *Official Secrets Act* is a *restricting* statute, and seeks to curb basic freedoms, such as freedom of speech and the press, it should be given strict interpretation. … The statute must, in clear and unambiguous language, articulate the restriction it intends to impose upon a citizen. A reading of ss. 3 and 4 of the *Official Secrets Act* amply demonstrates its failure to do so; the provisions are ambiguous and unwieldy. … A complete redrafting of the Canadian *Official Secrets Act* seems appropriate and necessary.[196]

B. UNAUTHORIZED DISCLOSURE

1) Security Information

a) Special Operational Information and Persons Permanently Bound to Secrecy

The ATA repealed and replaced the much criticized 1939 espionage provision. The current *Security of Information Act* now includes a series of offences listed under the heading "Special Operational Information

---

194 Canada, Canadian Security Intelligence Service, *Security of Information Act*, above note 188.

195 *R. v. Ratkai*, [1989] N.J. No. 334 at para. 8 (S.C.T.D.).

196 *Toronto Sun*, above note 187 at 632.

and Persons Permanently Bound to Secrecy." Most notably, persons employed at a number of security and intelligence government agencies are deemed (or are named by the government) permanently bound to secrecy.[197] As Table 10.3 suggests, these persons are criminally liable for the communication of "special operational information" under sections 13 and 14. "Special operational information" is a defined term and basically means military and intelligence-related information that the government seeks to "safeguard."[198]

These provisions supplement sections of the *Canadian Security Intelligence Service Act* which criminalize unauthorized disclosure of information from which the identity of any CSIS informant or operative may be discerned.[199]

b) Public Interest Override

"Special operational information" is exempted from the whistleblower disclosure provisions found in the *Public Servants Disclosure Protection Act*.[200] However, the offences in sections 13 and 14 of the SOIA are subject to a carefully defined "public interest defence." Thus, "no person is guilty of an offence under section 13 or 14 if the person establishes that he or she acted in the public interest." A person "acts in the public interest" if his or her purpose is to disclose illegal actions performed in the course of some other person's official functions in circumstances where "the public interest in the disclosure outweighs the public interest in non-disclosure."[201]

i) *Public Interest Balancing*

In weighing the relative public interests of disclosure versus nondisclosure, the Act instructs a court to consider whether the disclosure is narrowly confined to that required to forestall the alleged offence, the seriousness of this alleged offence, whether the whistleblower resorted to other reasonable alternatives prior to disclosure, whether the whistleblower had reasonable grounds to believe that disclosure was in the pub-

---

197 SOIA, above note 6, s. 8 and accompanying schedule. Further, under s. 10, other persons may be designated "a person permanently bound to secrecy" if certain senior government officials believe that "by reason of the person's office, position, duties, contract or arrangement ... the person had, has or will have authorized access to special operational information; and ... it is in the interest of national security to designate the person."

198 *Ibid*, s. 8.

199 *Canadian Security Intelligence Service Act*, R.S.C. 1985, c. C-23, s. 18 [CSIS Act].

200 S.C. 2005, c. 46, s. 17.

201 SOIA, above note 6, s. 15.

Table 10.3: Information Offences

Type of Information	Person to Whom Prohibition Applies	Prohibition in the Offence
"Special operational information"	Persons permanently bound by secrecy	Intentionally and without authority, communicates or confirms information that, if it were true, would be special operational information[1]
	Every person	Intentionally and without authority, communicates or confirms special operational information[2]
	Every person	Intentionally and without lawful authority, communicates special operational information to a foreign entity or to a terrorist group if the person believes, or is reckless as to whether, the information is special operational information[3]
Information the government is "taking measures to safeguard"	Every person with a security clearance given by the Government of Canada	Intentionally and without lawful authority, communicates, or agrees to communicate, to a foreign entity or terrorist group any information that is of a type that the Government of Canada is taking measures to safeguard[4]
	Every person	Without lawful authority, communicates to a foreign entity or terrorist group information while believing (or reckless as to whether) that information is safeguarded and in order to increase the capacity of that foreign entity or terrorist group to do harm to Canadians[5]
	Every person	Without lawful authority, communicates to a foreign entity or to a terrorist group information while believing (or reckless as to whether) that information is safeguarded and harm to Canadian interests results[6]
Any information obtained or accessed in the course of the performance of duties and functions under the CSIS Act or participation in the administration or enforcement of the Act	Every person	Discloses this information and from it the identity of "(a) any other person who is or was a confidential source of information or assistance to the Service," or "(b) any person who is or was an employee engaged in covert operational activities of the Service" can be inferred[7]

Type of Information	Person to Whom Prohibition Applies	Prohibition in the Offence
Trade secret	Every person	At the direction of, for the benefit of or in association with a foreign economic entity, fraudulently and without colour of right, communicates a trade secret to another person or organization or obtains, retains, alters or destroys a trade secret "to the detriment of" Canada's economic interests, international relations or national defence or national security[8]

7 CSIS Act, s. 13.

8 *Ibid.*, s. 14.

9 *Ibid.*, s. 17.

10 *Ibid.*, s. 18.

11 *Ibid.*, s. 16.

12 *Ibid.*

13 *Ibid.*, s. 18.

14 The economic espionage offence in s. 19 is constrained in s. 19(3) by certain defences protecting independent development of trade secrets or reverse engineering.

lic interest, the nature of that public interest, the harm or risk created by disclosure and any exigent circumstances justifying disclosure.

ii) Procedural Prerequisites

Except where necessary to avoid grievous bodily harm, the public interest defence only exists where two prerequisites are met. First, prior to disclosure, the whistleblower must have provided all relevant information to his or her deputy head or the deputy attorney general of Canada and have received no response within a reasonable time. Subsequently, the whistleblower must have also provided the information to the Security Intelligence Review Committee or, where the alleged offence concerns the Communications Security Establishment, to the Communications Security Establishment commissioner, and not received a response within a reasonable time.

The Act leaves open the question of what would constitute a "reasonable time." Likewise, it does not address whether the public interest defence would apply were the responses received from these review bodies inadequate. Indeed, it does not spell out exactly how the review bodies are to respond to the disclosures, a point made by the special senate committee reviewing anti-terrorism laws in 2007.[202]

2) Criminalized Leakage

The ATA was notable as much for what it did not do as for what it did change in SOIA. The 2001 amendments left intact section 4, criminalizing leakage; that is, the simple unauthorized disclosure (or, in some cases, receipt) of secret (or sometimes merely official) information. This omission provoked substantial controversy soon after.

a)   Criticisms of Leakage Provision

As with its now repealed espionage counterpart, section 3, the precise scope of section 4 of the 1939 *Official Secrets Act* is difficult to discern from the drafting of the section itself. In *Keable v. Canada (Attorney-General)*,[203] the Supreme Court held that "Section 4 of the *Official Secrets Act* makes it clear that it is the duty of every person who has in his possession information entrusted in confidence by a government official and subject to the Act, to refrain from communicating it to any unauthorized person." However, the section is much broader in its scope than this interpretation suggests.

---

202 Senate, *Fundamental Justice in Extraordinary Times*, above note 77 at 94.
203 [1979] 1 S.C.R. 218 at 250–51.

Indeed, communication of information is criminalized in a fashion likely to render most public service "whistleblowing" a crime. As the Law Reform Commission noted in 1986, the then *Official Secrets Act* "always treats the loquacious public servant and the secret agent alike: both may be charged under the same section (section 4), the punishment is the same, and, more importantly, the terrible stigma of prosecution under the [Act] is identical for both, because the public and the news media are unable to discern whether it is a case of calculated espionage or careless retention of documents."[204]

So broadly crafted is section 4 that it was difficult to imagine that the government would, for example, fail to secure convictions for the almost daily "leaks" of written government information that fill newspaper pages. More than that, it seems likely that it could be used to secure the conviction of the journalist and newspaper reporting these leaks.

b) Constitutionality of Leakage Provision

The historical absence of prosecutions brought under section 4 likely reflected a sober appreciation of the political consequences flowing from aggressive uses of secrecy law. However, a law of this breadth could be used to either threaten a prosecution or obtain warrants, both tactics that raise civil liberties issues. Most notoriously, in January 2004, the RCMP raided *Ottawa Citizen* reporter Juliet O'Neill's home and office looking for leaked information pertaining to Maher Arar, the Canadian deported by U.S. officials to Jordan and then incarcerated and tortured in Syria. The warrant alleged a violation by Ms. O'Neill of section 4 of the *Security of Information Act*.[205]

That warrant, and the resulting search of Ms. O'Neill's home and office, sparked a constitutional challenge to section 4.[206] Specifically, Ms. O'Neill and the *Ottawa Citizen* contended that section 4 violated section 2(b) of the *Charter* by infringing on the freedom of the press to gather and disseminate information of public interest and concern, and contravened section 7 of the *Charter* on the basis of vagueness and overbreadth. Those claims were accepted by the Ontario Superior Court of Justice in

---

204 Law Reform Commission, *Crimes against the State*, above note 190 at 37.
205 Gowling LaFleur Henderson LLP, "Juliet O'Neill and CanWest Attack Unconstitutional Search and Seizure" (media advisory, 28 January 2004); Notice of Application and Constitutional Issue, filed on behalf of the applicants Juliet O'Neill and the *Ottawa Citizen* on 11 February 2004, at para. 4, online: www.gowlings.com/resources/pdfs/noticeofapplication4.pdf.
206 *Ibid.*

2006,[207] a decision the government chose not to appeal. Section 4 was also critiqued by the special senate committee on anti-terrorism law in 2007.[208] That body urged much clearer definitions of the information protected by the section and a public interest override where the public interest in disclosure exceeds the public interest in nondisclosure.

c) United Kingdom Model

By the time of this writing, it seemed certain given these developments, that section 4 would be altered in the near future. The actual direction the government will take in modifying the *Security of Information Act* was unknown by the time of this writing.[209] There is reason to believe, however, that the government might look to the U.K. experience. As noted by the court in the *O'Neill* case, section 4 of the *Security of Information Act* compared unfavourably to its closest equivalent, the U.K. *Official Secrets Act 1989*.[210] That Act also figured in the senate committee's discussion of this issue.

In most of its "leakage" provisions, the U.K. Act is much more moderate (and intelligible) than is section 4 of the *Security of Information Act*. Thus the 1989 Act makes it an offence, in section 1, for civil servants to disclose information relating to security or intelligence, but only if this disclosure is damaging. This damage is measured by any actual harm it causes to "the work of, or of any part of, the security and intelligence services." Alternatively, that civil servant is liable if the information is of the sort that disclosure is "likely to cause such

---

207 *O'Neill v. Canada (Attorney General)*, [2006] O.J. No. 4189 at para. 62 and 71 (holding, *inter alia*, that s. 4 failed "to define in any way the scope of what it protects and then, using the most extreme form of government control, criminalizes the conduct of those who communicate and receive government information that falls within its unlimited scope including the conduct of government officials and members of the public and of the press" and that "the lack of delineation of a zone of risk by these sections gives no guidance to law enforcement officials to be able to determine whether a crime has been committed under them, with the result that there are no controls on the exercise of their discretion and there is the danger of arbitrary and ad hoc law enforcement").

208 Senate, *Fundamental Justice in Extraordinary Times*, above note 77 at 94 *et seq.*

209 In its July 2007 response to a Commons review of the anti-terrorism law, the government indicated that it was considering "legislative options to reform section 4" and underscored that an anti-leakage provision was desirable. Canada, *Government Response*, above note 133 at 20.

210 (U.K.), 1989 c. 6 [U.K. *Official Secrets Act*]. For a full discussion of the U.K. Act, see John Wadham & Kavita Modi, "National Security and Open Government in the United Kingdom" in Campbell Public Affairs Institute, *National Security and Open Government: Striking the Right Balance* (Syracuse, NY: Campbell Public Affairs Institute, 2003).

damage."[211] Ignorance of the security and intelligence nature of the information is a defence, as is the reasonable absence of belief that disclosure would be damaging.

Parallel provisions regulating disclosure of information relating to "defence" and to "international relations" are contained in sections 2 and 3 of the Act. The concepts of "defence" and "international relations" are both defined. Further, in both sections the disclosure is only an offence if it causes damage, a concept spelled out in detail in each instance. A lack of knowledge of (or reasonable belief as to) the subject-matter nature of the information is again a defence.

The Act also creates other offences for secondary leaking of secrets by recipients of wrongfully leaked documents. A person who receives a document relating to defence or international relations commits an offence under section 5 if they subsequently disclose it, knowing or having reasonable cause to believe, that the information is protected by section 2 or 3. However, this subsequent disclosure must itself be damaging and the person must know, or have reasonable cause to believe, the disclosure to be damaging.

Thus, unlike the unconstitutionally overbroad and vague section 4 of the *Security of Information Act*, the U.K. *Official Secrets Act* carefully defines the sorts of information captured by the criminalization of disclosure. Again, unlike the Canadian law, it also layers on a requirement that disclosure of even this sensitive information be "damaging" (within the meaning of the Act) before criminal culpability will attach.

3) Economic Information

SOIA does more than protect government information. CSIS reported in 2005 that "Canada's national and economic security continue to be threatened by espionage and foreign-influenced activity." Increased global competition has prompted states to "shift the focus of their intelligence collection from traditional political and military matters to the illicit acquisition of economic and technological information." Economic espionage — "illegal, clandestine, or coercive activity by foreign governments in order to gain unauthorized access to economic intelligence, such as proprietary information or technology, for economic advantage" — is costly to the Canadian economy, resulting in "lost contracts, jobs and markets, and a diminished competitive advantage."[212]

---

211 U.K. *Official Secrets Act*, ibid., s. 1(4).
212 CSIS, *Espionage and Foreign-Influence Activity*, online: www.csis-scrs.gc.ca/en/priorities/espionage.asp. See also Jim Judd, Director of CSIS, Standing Senate Committee on National Security and Defence, Evidence (30 April 2007).

To grapple with this challenge, the SOIA now includes an economic espionage provision. It is a crime for any person acting at the behest of a foreign economic entity to disclose a trade secret or obtain, retain, alter or destroy a trade secret. The person must be acting fraudulently and unlawfully and to the detriment of Canada's economic interests, international relations or national defence or national security. Notably, disclosure of a reverse engineered trade secret is not an offence.[213]

C. SPYING OFFENCES

On top of penalizing unauthorized information disclosure, the SOIA also criminalizes physical infiltration and spying. To do so, it begins by enumerating a number of acts identified by the statute as "prejudicial to the safety or interests of the State." These are set out in Table 10.4. Certain actions taken to facilitate these prejudicial events are criminalized.[214] For instance, for a purpose prejudicial to the safety or interests of the state, it is an offence to use or wear "without lawful authority, any military, police or other official uniform or any uniform so nearly resembling such a uniform as to be calculated to deceive, or falsely represents himself to be a person who is or has been entitled to use or wear any such uniform," to tamper with a passport or other official documents or to impersonate the proper holder of that document or of a public office.[215] The *Criminal Code* also criminalizes passport forgery.[216]

In addition, the SOIA makes it an offence to conduct reconnaissance for a foreign government. Thus, a person commits a crime if he or she "for any purpose prejudicial to the safety or interests of the State, approaches, inspects, passes over, is in the neighbourhood of or enters a prohibited place at the direction of, for the benefit of or in association with a foreign entity."[217] A "foreign entity" includes the government of a foreign state or a political faction seeking to assume that role.[218] As

213 SOIA, above note 6, s. 19.
214 SOIA, above note 6, s. 5.
215 *Ibid.* Under the Act, "prohibited place" means "any work of defence" owned or occupied by the government, including such things as arsenals, ships, factories, dockyards, and the like. Further, a "prohibited place" may also include a privately owned establishment used to store, manufacture or repair any "munitions of war." Finally, the government may itself designate prohibited places where information relating to such a place "would be useful to a foreign power." SOIA, *ibid.*, s. 2.
216 *Criminal Code*, above note 140, s. 57.
217 SOIA, above note 6, s. 6.
218 *Ibid.*, s. 2.

discussed in Chapter 7, the same reconnaissance done for a terrorist group is also criminalized.[219]

Table 10.4: Acts Prejudicial to the Safety or Interests of the State and That Harm Canadian Interests

Category of Harm	Description in the SOIA
Military	• impairs or threatens the military capability of the Canadian Forces, or any part of the Canadian Forces; • interferes with the design, development or production of any weapon or defence equipment of, or intended for, the Canadian Forces, including any hardware, software or system that is part of or associated with any such weapon or defence equipment.
Criminal	• commits, in Canada, an offence against the laws of Canada or a province that is punishable by a maximum term of imprisonment of two years or more in order to advance a political, religious or ideological purpose, objective or cause or to benefit a foreign entity or terrorist group;[1] • commits, inside or outside Canada, a terrorist activity.
Economic	• damages property outside Canada because a person or entity with an interest in the property or occupying the property has a relationship with Canada or a province or is doing business with or on behalf of the Government of Canada or of a province; • adversely affects the stability of the Canadian economy, the financial system or any financial market in Canada without reasonable economic or financial justification.
Public Safety	• causes or aggravates an urgent and critical situation in Canada that endangers the lives, health or safety of Canadians; • interferes with a service, facility, system or computer program, whether public or private, or its operation, in a manner that has significant adverse impact on the health, safety, security or economic or financial well-being of the people of Canada or the functioning of any government in Canada; • endangers, outside Canada, any person by reason of that person's relationship with Canada or a province or the fact that the person is doing business with or on behalf of the Government of Canada or of a province; • contrary to a treaty to which Canada is a party, develops or uses anything that is intended or has the capability to cause death or serious bodily injury to a significant number of people by means of (i) toxic or poisonous chemicals or their precursors, (ii) a microbial or other biological agent, or a toxin, including a disease organism, (iii) radiation or radioactivity, or (iv) an explosion.

---

219 *Ibid.*, s. 6.

Category of Harm	Description in the SOIA
Political	• causes or aggravates an urgent and critical situation in Canada that threatens the ability of the Government of Canada to preserve the sovereignty, security or territorial integrity of Canada; • impairs or threatens the capability of the Government of Canada to conduct diplomatic or consular relations, or conduct and manage international negotiations.
Security and Intelligence	• impairs or threatens the capabilities of the Government of Canada in relation to security and intelligence.

[1]   In 2007, the special senate committee recommended the elimination of this reference to "political, religious or ideological purposes, objective or cause." Senate, *Fundamental Justice in Extraordinary Times*, above note 77 at 99.

SURVEILLANCE

The ability to forestall threats to national security often hinges on the timely availability of information. The Government of Canada's 2004 national security strategy urges,

> [i]ntelligence is the foundation of our ability to take effective measures to provide for the security of Canada and Canadians. To manage risk effectively, we need the best possible information about threats we face and about the intentions, capabilities and activities of those who would do us harm. The best decisions regarding the scope and design of security programs, the allocation of resources and the deployment of assets cannot be made unless decision makers are as informed as possible.[1]

As this passage suggests, national security investigations tend to be prospective, aimed at anticipating and pre-empting threats. In this environment, surveillance and monitoring of anticipated threats, and timely distribution of relevant information between security and intelligence agencies is essential.[2] That was the lesson—and the great failure—of 9/11.

---

1   Canada, *Securing an Open Society: Canada's National Security Policy* (2004) at 15, online: www.army.dnd.ca/lf/Downloads/natsecurnat_e.pdf [Securing an Open Society].
2   See also on this point, Stanley A. Cohen, *Privacy, Crime and Terror: Legal Rights and Security in a Time of Peril* (Markham, ON: LexisNexis Butterworths, 2005) at 57.

Surveillance and information sharing necessarily trench, however, on individual privacy. Excessive surveillance and information sharing raise the spectre of an omniscient state. Information collected initially for a public interest purpose might be deployed more cynically in the future. As Alan Dershowitz writes, "experience teaches us that information secured for the limited purpose of preventing only terrorism will often be used by the government to prosecute other less serious crimes, such as drugs, pornography and fraud."[3] On this same theme, Canada's privacy commissioner warned in 2005 that "the logic of anti-terrorism could permeate all spheres of law enforcement and public safety and this could result in large-scale systems of surveillance that will increasingly erode privacy rights in Canada."[4]

Democracies tend, therefore, to be suspicious of the surveillance state. In Dershowitz's words, the "history of creeping expansion and misuse of power creates an understandable sense of mistrust that animates much of the opposition to changes that might increase the effectiveness of measures to prevent terrorism, ranging from surveillance, to profiling, to interrogation methods designed to gather preventive intelligence rather than evidence for use at trials." In fact, a 2006 survey reported that "more than half of Canadians don't trust the government to protect their personal information, while nearly 50 per cent believe anti-terrorism laws drafted to guard national security violate their privacy."[5]

As in other areas of national security, the challenge lies in balancing competing interests. This chapter begins with an overview of privacy law protections, before examining specific "lawful access" laws—that is, legal regimes permitting electronic surveillance for law enforcement or national security reasons.[6] Chapter 12 then examines national security information sharing within and between governments.

---

3   Alan Dershowitz, "Can't Live with Big Brother" *National Post* (7 September 2006) A23.

4   Opening Statement by Jennifer Stoddart, Privacy Commissioner of Canada, *Independent Review Mechanism for the National Security Activities of the RCMP*, Commission of Inquiry into the Actions of Canadian Officials in Relation to Maher Arar (16 November 2005), online: www.privcom.gc.ca/speech/2005/sp-d_051116_e.asp.

5   Carly Weeks, "Canadians Leery of Anti-terror Laws, Poll Shows" *Ottawa Citizen* (14 November 2006) A5.

6   For an extremely detailed, magisterial study of many of the same issues discussed in this chapter, see Cohen, *Privacy, Crime and Terror*, above note 2.

PART I: PRIVACY PROTECTIONS

A. INTERNATIONAL PRIVACY LAW

Privacy rights are entrenched in international human rights law. Article 12 of the *Universal Declaration of Human Rights*[7] provides that "no one should be subjected to arbitrary interference with his privacy, family, home or correspondence, nor to attacks on his honour or reputation. Everyone has the right to the protection of the law against such interferences or attacks." The *International Covenant on Civil and Political Rights* contains identical language.[8]

International "soft-law" standards also exist. Notable among these are the Organization for Economic Cooperation and Development's *Guidelines Governing the Protection of Privacy and Transborder Data Flows of Personal Data*.[9] These guidelines provide that "there should be limits to the collection of personal data and any such data should be obtained by lawful and fair means and, where appropriate, with the knowledge and consent of the data subject."[10] This person should be notified of the use to which this information will be put, and any subsequent disclosure of this information should be consistent with this use.[11] The United Nations General Assembly has also proposed guidelines with similar provisions.[12]

B. CONSTITUTIONAL PRIVACY PROTECTIONS

1) Reasonable Expectation of Privacy

In Canada, privacy has been given constitutional protection in the *Canadian Charter of Rights and Freedoms*.[13] Section 8 of the *Charter* guarantees

---

7   A/RES/217 A (III) (1948). As discussed in Chapter 2, the UDHR is viewed in whole or in part an expression of customary international law, and therefore binding on all states.

8   (1976), 999 U.N.T.S. 172, Art. 17 [ICCPR].

9   Paris, 1981, online: www.oecd.org/document/18/0,2340,en_2649_34255_1815186_1_1_1_1,00.html.

10   *Ibid.*, Principle 7.

11   *Ibid.*, Principles 9 & 10.

12   United Nations General Assembly, *Guidelines Concerning Computerized Personal Data Files*, 14 December 1990, online: www.unhchr.ch/html/menu3/b/71.htm.

13   Part I of the *Constitution Act, 1982*, being Schedule B to the *Canada Act 1982* (U.K.) 1982, c. 11.

the privacy right to be free from unreasonable searches and seizures.[14] Supreme Court jurisprudence makes clear that this section hinges on a "reasonable expectation of privacy."[15] This reasonable expectation of privacy requires an assessment "as to whether in a particular situation the public's interest in being left alone by government must give way to the government's interest in intruding on the individual's privacy in order to advance its goals, notably those of law enforcement."[16]

a)   Zones of Privacy

In defining the scope of this "reasonable expectation," Canadian courts have spoken of three "zones" of privacy: "The territorial zone refers to places such as one's home. Personal or corporeal privacy is concerned with the human body (body, images such as photographs, voice or name). Finally, a person can make a claim to informational privacy that shelters intimate details concerning matters such as health, sexual orientation, employment, social views, friendships and associations."[17] Justice La Forest, in R. v. Dyment, wrote of this third, informational form of privacy as follows: "In modern society, especially, retention of information about oneself is extremely important. We may, for one reason or another, wish or be compelled to reveal such information, but situations abound where the reasonable expectations of the individual that the information shall remain confidential to the persons to whom, and restricted to the purposes for which it is divulged, must be protected."[18]

b)   Electronic Surveillance

The Supreme Court of Canada has been emphatic that electronic surveillance may transgress a reasonable expectation of privacy and constitute a search and seizure regulated by section 8 of the *Charter*.[19] For this reason, "the statutory provisions authorizing them [electronic sur-

---

14   See *Lavigne v. Canada (Office of the Commissioner of Official Languages)*, [2002] 2 S.C.R. 773 at para. 25 (labelling this a privacy right) [*Lavigne*].

15   *R. v. B. (S. A.)*, 2003 SCC 60 at para. 38.

16   *Ibid.*, citing *Hunter v. Southam Inc.*, [1984] 2 S.C.R. 145 at 159–60.

17   *Ruby v. Canada (Solicitor General)*, [2000] 3 F.C. 589 at para. 166 (C.A.), var'd [2002] 4 S.C.R. 3 [*Ruby*]. In *Ruby*, the Federal Court of Appeal was following *R. v. Dyment*, [1988] 2 S.C.R. 417 at 428, La Forest J., concurring (speaking of three zones: "those involving territorial or spatial aspects, those related to the person, and those that arise in the information context") [*Dyment*].

18   *Dyment, ibid.* at 429–30, La Forest J., concurring.

19   *R. v. Duarte*, [1990] 1 S.C.R. 30 at paras. 18 & 19 ("as a general proposition, surreptitious electronic surveillance of the individual by an agency of the state constitutes an unreasonable search or seizure under s. 8 of the *Charter* … [O]ne can scarcely imagine a state activity more dangerous to individual privacy than

veillance] must conform to the minimum constitutional requirements demanded by s. 8."[20] In this last regard, protecting individuals from "unjustified state intrusions upon their privacy" requires "a means of preventing unjustified searches before they happen, not simply of determining, after the fact, whether they ought to have occurred in the first place."[21] In *Hunter*, the Court suggested that this objective "can only be accomplished by a system of prior authorization, not one of subsequent validation."[22]

For this reason, electronic surveillance is rendered constitutional by "subjecting the power of the state to record our private communications to external restraint and requiring it to be justified by application of an objective criterion."[23] This external restraint is supplied by a "detached judicial officer."[24] Indeed, authorization from this official is required even if one party to the private communication consents to the surveillance.[25]

In terms of "objective" criteria justifying the intercept, the judicial officer must be persuaded that an "offence has been or is being committed and that interception of private communications stands to afford evidence of the offence."[26] However, the Federal Court of Appeal has concluded that a slightly different standard may legitimately apply to warrants obtained by CSIS: a judge must be persuaded that the intercept is necessary for a legitimate national security purpose, and not necessarily to investigate an offence *per se*.[27]

---

electronic surveillance and to which, in consequence, the protection accorded by s. 8 should be more directly aimed") [*Duarte*].

20　*R. v. Pires*, 2005 SCC 66 at para. 8.
21　*Hunter v. Southam Inc.*, above note 16 at 160.
22　*Ibid.*
23　*Duarte*, above note 19 at para. 25.
24　*Ibid.* (noting that "[i]f privacy may be defined as the right of the individual to determine for himself when, how, and to what extent he will release personal information about himself, a reasonable expectation of privacy would seem to demand that an individual may proceed on the assumption that the state may only violate this right by recording private communications on a clandestine basis when it has established to the satisfaction of a *detached judicial officer* that an offence has been or is being committed and that interception of private communications stands to afford evidence of the offence") [emphasis added].
25　*Ibid.* at para. 50.
26　*Ibid.* at para. 25.
27　See *Atwal v. Canada*, [1988] 1 F.C. 107 at para. 36 (C.A.).

2) Other Constitutional Privacy Protections

The *Charter*'s section 7—protecting against deprivation of life, liberty or security of the person—may also incorporate privacy protections.[28] Summarizing Supreme Court jurisprudence on section 7, the Federal Court of Appeal has held that it "includes the right to privacy of information in regard to intimate questions as well as the use of personal information."[29]

In another case considering the constitutionality of certain provisions of the *Privacy Act*,[30] the Federal Court of Appeal held that the fact that "the Act provides for the acquisition and accumulation of personal information and its dissemination, in circumstances where the person affected may be unable to test the truth of the information so acquired, may bring into issue the right of privacy … and the potential application of section 7 of the *Charter*."[31] While the Supreme Court has yet to definitively announce that section 7 protects privacy rights, such a conclusion seems plausible in light of its jurisprudence to date.[32]

C. STATUTORY PROTECTIONS

1) *Privacy Act*

The principal restrictions on government use of personal information are set out in the *Privacy Act*. This Act, in the words of the Supreme Court of Canada, is "a reminder of the extent to which the protection of privacy is necessary to the preservation of a free and democratic society."[33] The following section outlines the Act's key attributes.

28 *Lavigne*, above note 14 at para. 25.
29 *Zarzour v. Canada* (2000), 268 N.R. 235 at para. 68 (C.A.) [*Zarzour*], citing *B.(R.) v. Children's Aid Society of Metropolitan Toronto*, [1995] 1 S.C.R. 315 at 368; *R. v. Morgentaler*, [1988] 1 S.C.R. 30; *R. v. Mills*, [1999] 3 S.C.R. 668 at paras. 80 & 81 and *Blencoe v. British Columbia (Human Rights Commission)*, 2000 SCC 44.
30 R.S.C., 1985, c. P-21.
31 *Ruby*, above note 17 at paras. 170 (C.A.) and 33 (S.C.C.) ("it is unnecessary to the disposition of this case to decide whether a right to privacy comprising a corollary right of access to personal information triggers the application of s. 7 of the *Charter*").
32 See *M. (A.) v. Ryan*, [1997] 1 S.C.R. 157 at para. 79, L'Heureux-Dubé J., dissenting, concluding that she had spoken for the Court in *R. v. O'Connor*, [1995] 4 S.C.R. 411 on whether privacy protection was available in that case under s. 7. See discussion in Barbara McIsaac, Rick Shields, & Kris Klein, *The Law of Privacy in Canada*, looseleaf (Scarborough, ON: Carswell, 2004) at section 2.2.1.
33 *Lavigne*, above note 14 at para. 25.

a) Collection and Use of Personal Information

The *Privacy Act* admonishes that no personal information is to be collected by a government institution unless it relates directly to an operating program or activity of the institution.[34] "Personal information" means "information about an identifiable individual that is recorded in any form,"[35] a definition that is "deliberately broad" and "is entirely consistent with the great pains that have been taken to safeguard individual identity."[36]

The Act sets out requirements as to how this information must be collected. First, any information that is collected for an administrative purpose — that is, personal information used in a decision-making process directly affecting the individual — should, wherever possible, come directly from the individual concerned.[37] Second, the government institution has a duty to inform the individual as to how the information will be used. Both of these collection-procedure obligations may be ignored if compliance with them would result in the collection of inaccurate information, or if it would defeat the purpose of gathering the information, or prejudice its use.[38]

Personal information controlled by a government institution may only be used for purposes consistent with the authorized justification for which it was collected, except with permission from the individual to whom it relates.[39]

Personal information used by a government institution for an administrative purpose must be retained for a standard period of two years, or until the completion of a privacy access request by the person to whom the information relates.[40] Government records, including those with personal information, may not be destroyed without the permission of the national archivist of Canada.[41]

b) Disclosure of Personal Information

Section 8 of the Act bars nonconsensual disclosure of personal information under the control of a government institution, subject to cer-

---

34 *Privacy Act*, above note 30, s. 4.
35 *Ibid.*, s. 3.
36 *Lavigne*, above note 14 at para. 26, citing with approval *Canada (Information Commissioner) v. Canada (Solicitor General)*, [1988] 3 F.C. 551 at 557 (T.D.).
37 This requirement need not be met when the individual concerned authorizes the government to collect the information from another source, or where information is disclosed to the institution under other provisions of the Act itself. See, specifically, *Privacy Act*, above note 30, s. 8.
38 *Privacy Act*, *ibid.*, s. 5.
39 *Ibid.*, s. 7.
40 *Ibid.*, s. 6; *Privacy Act Regulations*, S.O.R./83-508, s. 4.
41 *Zarzour*, above note 29 at para. 24.

tain enumerated exceptions. These exceptions—set out in subsection 8(2)—are broad.

i)   Consistent Use

The *Privacy Act* provides that personal information may be disclosed, among other things, "for the purpose for which the information was obtained or compiled by the institution or for a use consistent with that purpose."[42] Stanley Cohen has noted that this exception to the Act's nondisclosure provision "provides government institutions with discretionary latitude to operate effectively within their mandates."[43] For instance, information collected for law enforcement purposes is often released to other law enforcement agencies, including those in other jurisdictions, on a "consistent use" justification.[44]

ii)   Law Enforcement

On top of this important "consistent use" exception, the Act enumerates more specific disclosure justifications relevant to national security. For instance, information may be released by government agencies to a specified investigative body for the purpose of law enforcement or a lawful investigation[45] or under a federal–provincial or international agreement, for the purpose of law enforcement or lawful investigation.[46]

iii)   Public Interest

Also notable, information may be released "for any purpose where, in the opinion of the head of the institution, ... the public interest in disclosure clearly outweighs any invasion of privacy that could result from disclosure."[47]

iv)   Other Statutory Authorizations

Privacy Act nondisclosure principles are also subject to other Acts of Parliament that authorize disclosure.[48] As discussed in the next chapter, there are several statutes in the national security area that include

---

42   *Privacy Act*, above note 30, s. 8(2)(a).

43   Cohen, *Privacy, Crime and Terror*, above note 2 at 391.

44   Commission of Inquiry into the Actions of Canadian Officials in Relation to Maher Arar, *A New Review Mechanism for the RCMP's National Security Activities* (2006) at 115, online: www.ararcommission.ca/eng/EnglishReportDec122006. pdf [Arar inquiry, Policy Report]

45   *Privacy Act*, above note 30, s. 8(2)(e).

46   *Ibid.*, s. 8(2)(f).

47   *Ibid.*, s. 8(2)(m).

48   *Ibid.*, s. 8(2)(b).

their own rules on when and why information may be shared between Canadian government agencies.

v) Charter *Implications*

These disclosure principles must, however, be read with an eye to the *Charter* and its privacy protections. Authorized disclosure between government agencies under the *Privacy Act* does not vitiate the *Charter*'s section 8 search and seizure provisions. Information sharing may not be employed by state agencies to circumvent constitutional privacy protections. Law enforcement agencies, for example, may not avoid constitutional search and seizure obligations by receiving otherwise protected information from administrative or other bodies not subject to the same constitutional strictures.[49] Where law enforcement agencies propose obtaining private information from other bodies that is protected by a reasonable expectation of privacy, warrants must be obtained, even in circumstances where disclosure of personal information is permissible under the *Privacy Act*.[50]

This supplemental warrant requirement may not exist, however, where law enforcement agencies share information with other agencies on a "consistent use" basis, assuming that the information was already obtained lawfully under a warrant.[51]

c) Enforcement by the Privacy Commissioner

The government institution must generally keep a record of the use to which personal information is put, as well as any reason for which this information is disclosed. These data are deemed part of the personal information to which they relate.[52]

Where the government uses or discloses personal information in a fashion inconsistent with the Act, an individual may make a complaint to the privacy commissioner, triggering significant investigative powers. The privacy commissioner may also initiate an investigation

---

49 See, for example, *R. v. Colarusso*, [1994] 1 S.C.R. 20 at para. 93 (rejecting an approach where "property is seized by one state agent for a purpose for which the prerequisites for search may not be as demanding, and another state agent, one forming part of the law enforcement apparatus of the state, is permitted to claim the fruits of the search (the resulting information) for use for law enforcement purposes without regard to the rightly stringent prerequisites of searches for those purposes"). See also discussion in Cohen, *Privacy, Crime and Terror*, above note 2 at 98, 120 and 137.

50 Cohen, *Privacy, Crime and Terror, ibid.* at 120.

51 *Ibid.* at 391.

52 *Privacy Act*, above note 30, s. 9.

on his or her own where he or she concludes that there are reasonable grounds.[53]

Where the commissioner concludes that a government institution has failed to comply with privacy protections, he or she provides the head of that institution with a report setting out findings from the investigation and the commissioner's recommendations.[54] This report may subsequently be included in the privacy commissioner's annual report to Parliament.[55]

2) *Personal Information Protection and Electronic Documents Act*

a) Application to Government

In 2001, Parliament enacted the *Personal Information Protection and Electronic Documents Act* (PIPEDA),[56] the long-awaited extension of privacy protections beyond the public sector. Part I of this Act is directed at regulating use of personal information by commercial organizations. This part does not apply to government institutions covered by the *Privacy Act*.[57] Nevertheless, the PIPEDA is relevant in discussing national security. Its provisions may be employed to extract information from private sector entities in the interest of national security.

b) Collection, Use and Disclosure of Personal Information

The purpose of Part I of the PIPEDA "is to establish, in an era in which technology increasingly facilitates the circulation and exchange of information, rules to govern the collection, use and disclosure of personal information in a manner that recognizes the right of privacy of individuals with respect to their personal information and the need of organizations to collect, use or disclose personal information for purposes that a reasonable person would consider appropriate in the circumstances."[58]

To this end, Division 1 of the Act incorporates into Canadian law a model Code for the Protection of Personal Information.[59] Among other things, this code calls on organizations to identify the purposes for which personal information is collected prior to this collection, and to

---

53 *Ibid.*, s. 29.
54 *Ibid.*, s. 37.
55 *Ibid.*, ss. 37, 38, & 39.
56 S.C. 2000, c. 5 [PIPEDA].
57 *Ibid.*, s. 4(2)(a).
58 *Ibid.*, s. 3.
59 *Ibid.*, Sch. I.

disclose this purpose to the individuals from whom the information is obtained.[60] Consent of the individual is required for the collection, use and disclosure of the personal information,[61] particularly where subsequent use and disclosure is for a purpose other than that for which the information was collected.[62]

Information may only be collected,[63] used,[64] or disclosed to third parties[65] without the knowledge or consent of the person to whom it pertains in limited circumstances. These limited circumstances include several justifications relevant to national security matters, as set out in Table 11.1.

c)   Notification of Personal Information

The privacy code also provides that an individual is to be informed "of the existence, use, and disclosure of his or her personal information and shall be given access to that information."[66] An individual makes a request in relation to this information in writing. The organization must then respond with due diligence, and in any event within thirty days (subject to possible extensions).

However, the PIPEDA contains several exceptions limiting disclosure of information to the individual to whom it relates. For instance, the organization may decline access to information where granting access to that individual could reasonably be expected to threaten the life or security of another individual.[67]

Most notably, an individual whose personal information has been disclosed to the government by an organization regulated by the Act may be denied access to the information disclosed, or even knowledge of the disclosure, on national security grounds. Where an organization regulated by the PIPEDA receives a request from an individual for personal information relating to national security, the defence of Canada or the conduct of international affairs, the organization must notify the government. The government must then, within thirty days, communicate to the organization any objection it would have to compliance with the individual's request, on national security grounds. If the government does object, the organization must reject the individual's request,

---

60   *Ibid.*, Sch. I, Principle 2.
61   *Ibid.*, Sch. I, Principle 3.
62   *Ibid.*, Sch. I, Principle 4.
63   *Ibid.*, s. 7(1).
64   *Ibid.*, s. 7(2).
65   *Ibid.*, s. 7(3).
66   *Ibid.*, Sch. I, Principle 9.
67   *Ibid.*, s. 9(3)(c).

Table 11.1: PIPEDA: Collection, Use and Disclosure of Personal Information Without Knowledge or Consent

Grounds	Collected without Knowledge or Consent	Used without Knowledge or Consent	Disclosed without Knowledge or Consent
Law enforcement	Paragraph 7(1)(b) — Collection with the knowledge or consent of the individual could be reasonably expected to compromise the availability or the accuracy of the information and the collection is reasonably related to investigating a contravention of the laws of Canada or a province	Paragraph 7(2)(d) — Original collection with the knowledge or consent of the individual could be reasonably expected to compromise the availability or accuracy of the information and the collection is reasonably related to investigating a contravention of the laws of Canada or a province; or Paragraph 7(2)(a) — Organization has reasonable grounds to believe information could be useful in law enforcement or investigation.	Paragraph 7(3)(c.1) — Disclosure is made to a government institution that has made a request for the information, identified its lawful authority to obtain the information and indicated that: ... (ii) the disclosure is requested for the purpose of enforcing any law of Canada, a province or a foreign jurisdiction, carrying out an investigation relating to the enforcement of any such law or gathering intelligence for the purpose of enforcing any such law, or (iii) the disclosure is requested for the purpose of administering any law of Canada or a province. Paragraph 7(3)(c.2) — Disclosure made to the Financial Transactions and Reports Analysis Centre of Canada, under the *Proceeds of Crime (Money Laundering) and Terrorist Financing Act* (see discussion in Chapter 12). Subparagraph 7(3)(d)(i) — Disclosure made on the initiative of the organization to an investigative body or government institution, and the organization has reasonable grounds to believe that the information relates to a breach of an agreement or a possible contravention of the laws of Canada, a province or a foreign jurisdiction. Paragraph 7(3)(h.2) — Disclosure made by an investigative body and the disclosure is reasonable for law enforcement.

Grounds	Collected without Knowledge or Consent	Used without Knowledge or Consent	Disclosed without Knowledge or Consent
National security	Paragraph 7(1)(e) — Collection is made for the purposes of making a disclosure under sub-paragraphs 7(3)(c.1)(i) or 7(3)(d)(ii) (see far right column)	Paragraph 7(2)(d) — Information was collected pursuant to Paragraph 7(1)(e) (see left column).	Subparagraph 7(3)(c.1)(i) — Disclosure is made to a government institution that has made a request for the information, identified its lawful authority to obtain the information and indicated that it suspects that the information relates to national security, the defence of Canada or the conduct of international affairs. Subparagraph 7(3)(d)(ii) — Disclosure is made on the initiative of the organization to an investigative body or a government institution and the organization suspects that the information relates to national security, the defence of Canada or the conduct of international affairs.
Emergencies		Paragraph 7(2)(b) — Information used for the purpose of acting in respect of an emergency that threatens the life, health or security of an individual.	Paragraph 7(3)(e) — Disclosure made to a person who needs the information because of an emergency that threatens the life, health or security of an individual and, if the individual whom the information is about is alive, the organization informs that individual in writing without delay.
Disclosure required by law	Paragraph 7(1)(e)(ii)	Paragraph 7(2)(d) — Information was collected pursuant to Paragraph 7(1)(e) (see far left column).	Paragraph 7(3)(i)

decline to disclose the information in question to the individual, and notify the privacy commissioner.[68]

d) Enforcement by the Privacy Commissioner and the Federal Court

Under Division 2 of Part 1 of the Act, individuals may file complaints with the privacy commissioner against an organization believed not to be complying with the Act's provisions on collection, use or disclosure of personal information. Complaints may also be filed regarding refusals to grant access to that personal information, or for nonadherence to assorted other "recommendations" contained in the Code for the Protection of Personal Information appended to the Act. The commissioner may then investigate the matter, if he or she is persuaded that there are reasonable grounds to do so.[69] The commissioner's powers to conduct this investigation are analogous to those he or she possesses for an equivalent investigation under the *Privacy Act*.[70]

Unless the complaint is frivolous or it falls under other limited exceptions, the commissioner must prepare a report detailing his or her findings and recommendations and any settlement that was reached by the parties. As with the equivalent determination under the *Privacy Act*, the report must also include, where appropriate, a request that the organization describe any action taken or proposed to be taken to implement the recommendations contained in the report or provide reasons why no such action has been taken or is proposed. The report must also note that recourse is available under the Act in the Federal Court.[71]

In this last respect, the complainant, or the commissioner, may apply to the Federal Court for a binding legal order requiring compliance with the PIPEDA by the organization. The court also has the power to award damages to the complainant, including damages for any humiliation that the complainant has suffered.[72]

As well as investigating complaints, the commissioner also has an auditing function: he or she may audit the personal information management practices of an organization where he or she has reasonable grounds to believe that the organization is contravening the Act or the accom-

---

68 *Ibid.*, ss. 9(2.2)–(2.4).
69 *Ibid.*, s. 11.
70 *Ibid.*, s. 12. See discussion on *Privacy Act*, above note 30.
71 *Ibid.*, s. 13.
72 *Ibid.*, ss. 14–16.

panying privacy code.[73] The commissioner provides the results of this audit to the organization, along with any relevant recommendations.[74]

Beyond that, the commissioner's only enforcement power is to include the audit's findings in his or her annual report to Parliament.

PART II: SURVEILLANCE

The flipside of privacy laws are "lawful access" rules permitting surveillance, most notably in the form of eavesdropping. Lawful access laws govern the "lawful interception of communications and the lawful search and seizure of information, including computer data."[75]

In the United States, lawful access issues have become particularly contentious in the post-9/11 era. The *U.S.A. PATRIOT Act*,[76] for example, relaxed traditional requirements for electronic intercept warrants. More dramatically, since soon after 9/11 the U.S. National Security Agency has intercepted "certain international communications into and out of the United States of people linked to al Qaeda or an affiliated terrorist organization."[77] Indeed, news reports suggest that the amount of information vacuumed up by the NSA under the program appears to be much greater than U.S. government officials have asserted.[78] By the time of the writing, the Bush administration's policy appears to have changed, as discussed in chapter 12. However, for several years, the NSA acted without warrant, pursuant to a presidential executive order issued under the president's constitutional authority as "commander-in-chief." This power, claimed the administration, trumps or

---

73 *Ibid.*, s. 18.

74 *Ibid.*, ss. 19 and 25.

75 Canada, Department of Justice, *Lawful Access: FAQ*, consultation report prepared for the Department of Justice, online: www.canada.justice.gc.ca/en/cons/la_al/summary/faq.html.

76 Public Law 107-56, 107th Congress (2001).

77 U.S. Department of Justice, Letter to Members of Congress (22 December 2005) at 1, online: www.epic.org/privacy/nsa/olc_release1.pdf.

78 Eric Lichtblau & James Risen, "Spy Agency Mined Vast Data Trove, Officials Report" *New York Times* (24 December 2005) at 1 (querying Administration claims that intercepts have only targeted persons linked to al-Qaeda and reporting "[w]hat has not been publicly acknowledged is that NSA technicians, besides actually eavesdropping on specific conversations, have combed through large volumes of phone and Internet traffic in search of patterns that might point to terrorism suspects. Some officials describe the program as a large data-mining operation").

limits competing statutory restrictions that would otherwise require warrants for these electronic intercepts.[79]

By the time of this writing, Canada has not acted as dramatically as the United States. It has, however, made numerous changes to its lawful access laws to respond to contemporary security threats.

A. *CRIMINAL CODE*

1) Existing System

The key lawful access provisions are found in the *Criminal Code*.[80] That statute imposes a warrant regime designed to prevent unauthorized intercept of a "private communication"; that is,

> any oral communication, or any telecommunication, that is made by an originator who is in Canada or is intended by the originator to be received by a person who is in Canada and that is made under circumstances in which it is reasonable for the originator to expect that it will not be intercepted by any person other than the person intended by the originator to receive it.[81]

Unauthorized intercept of a private communication is a crime.[82] This interception is, however, permissible in several circumstances,[83] including by a peace officer in exigent circumstances where one of the communicators is likely to cause serious harm to a person or property and the peace officer believes on reasonable grounds that the intercept is immediately necessary to stop this act.[84]

a) Intercept Authorization
More typically, an authorization permitting the intercept may be issued by a judge. The broadest authorization may be granted by a judge satisfied that the intercept permission would "be in the best interests of the administration of justice" and, except with terrorism offences and a few

---

79 *Ibid.* See also Letter from Attorney General Alberto Gonzales to Senator William Frist (19 January 2006), online: www.epic.org/privacy/nsa/oip_release1. pdf.

80 See, for example, Part VI Invasion of Privacy provisions in the *Criminal Code*, R.S.C. 1985, c. C-46.

81 *Ibid.*, s. 183.

82 *Ibid.*, s. 184.

83 *Ibid.*, s. 184(2).

84 *Ibid.*, s. 184.4.

other crimes, "that other investigative procedures have been tried and have failed, other investigative procedures are unlikely to succeed or the urgency of the matter is such that it would be impractical to carry out the investigation of the offence using only other investigative procedures."[85] As this discussion suggests, the rules for investigations of terrorism offences are more permissive. In particular, there is no need for the judge to be satisfied that the intercept is the last available option.

"Terrorism offences" is a defined concept, discussed in Chapter 7. It is notable, however, that it includes a large number of inchoate offences associated with an actual terrorist activity. Put another way, terrorism offences encompass a whole range of activity that may be fairly remotely connected to actual violence. The relaxation of the intercept authorization requirements for these terrorism offences contributes to what Cohen has described as the post-9/11 state's "enlarged capacity to peer into the individual's private life," including its power to "examine the trappings of simple associations and lifestyle, and ambiguous activities that the jurisprudence has often described as 'mere preparation.'"[86]

b) Mechanics

Application for the intercept authorization is made by the government on an *ex parte* basis, and must include details on the proposed target, scope and duration of the intercept.[87] If granted, the authorization must spell out the nature of the private communication that may be intercepted, as well as the identity, if known, of the persons subject to intercept, and such other terms and conditions as the judge believes warranted in the public interest.[88] Generally, an authorization endures for sixty days, subject to renewals of up to sixty days' duration. However, authorizations and renewed authorizations for intercepts justified by investigations of terrorism offences may last for up to one year.[89]

Generally, the person subject to the intercept must be notified by the government of the intercept within ninety days after the expiry of the authorization.[90] This period may be extended and re-extended in allotments of up to three years by a judge in the interests of justice if an investigation of the offence triggering the original authorization is ongoing. However, with terrorism offences, the rule is less demanding of

---

85   *Ibid.*, s. 186.

86   Cohen, *Privacy, Crime and Terror*, above note 2 at 203.

87   *Criminal Code*, above note 80, s. 185.

88   *Ibid.*, s. 186(4).

89   *Ibid.*, s. 186.1.

90   *Ibid.*, s. 196.

the state: the grant of an extension does not depend on the persistence of an ongoing investigation.[91]

2) Computer Intercepts

The rules governing intercept of computer communication are murky, with some experts taking the view that e-mail communication falls within the special system for intercept of "private communication" discussed above, and others suggesting that written communication stored in computers is subject to regular search warrants.[92]

In 2005, the Martin government tabled in Parliament the *Modernization of Investigative Techniques Act* (MITA).[93] This bill, if enacted as law, would have required telecommunications providers to make their services intercept-capable. Further, they would have been obliged to provide to designated security and intelligence authorities, on request, subscriber information, including subscriber name and address, telephone number, e-mail address, Internet Protocol address and other identifiers. No warrant was required to access this subscriber information.

The MITA bill ultimately died on the order paper in 2006. However, by the time of this writing, further government efforts to modernize electronic intercept law were anticipated.[94]

B. CSIS ACT

The *Canadian Security Intelligence Service Act* (CSIS Act) allows CSIS to engage in intelligence-gathering activities involving authorized invasions of privacy. To this end, the Act creates a judicial warrant system. CSIS may apply for such a warrant if it "believes, on reasonable grounds, that a warrant ... is required to enable the Service to investigate a threat to the security of Canada" or to assist the ministers of national defence

---

91   *Ibid.*

92   See discussion in Cohen, *Privacy, Crime and Terror*, above note 2 at 490 *et seq.*

93   Bill C-74, *An Act regulating telecommunications facilities to facilitate the lawful interception of information transmitted by means of those facilities and respecting the provision of telecommunications subscriber information*, 1st Sess., 38th Parl., 2005.

94   For a discussion of the related issue of computer "data-mining," see Wayne N. Renke, "Who Controls the Past Now Controls the Future: Counter-Terrorism, Data Mining and Privacy" (2006) 43 Alta. L. Rev. 779. For a more general discussion of surveillance technology and law, see Arthur Cockfield, "The State of Privacy Laws and Privacy-Encroaching Technologies after September 11: A Two-Year Report Card on the Canadian Government" (2003–4) 1 U.O.L. & T.J. 325.

or foreign affairs in "the collection of information or intelligence relating to the capabilities, intentions or activities of ... any foreign state or group of foreign states"[95] or foreign nationals (other than permanent residents). The warrant request must first be approved by the minister of public safety. It is then brought before a designated judge of the Federal Court, along with supporting information justifying its necessity.

If persuaded, among other things, that the warrant is necessary for CSIS to perform its duties and other less intrusive investigative techniques have been tried or would be fruitless, the judge may issue the warrant. This warrant authorizes the persons to whom it is directed to

> intercept any communication or obtain any information, record, document or thing and, for that purpose,
> (a) to enter any place or open or obtain access to any thing;
> (b) to search for, remove or return, or examine, take extracts from or make copies of or record in any other manner the information, record, document or thing; or
> (c) to install, maintain or remove any thing.[96]

The warrant also authorizes "any other person to assist a person who that other person believes on reasonable grounds is acting in accordance with such a warrant," notwithstanding "any other law."[97]

Warrants for investigations of subversion—that is, the matters described in paragraph (d) of the definition of "threat to the security of Canada"[98]—endure for up to sixty days, subject to renewal by the judge for up to the same period, to allow CSIS to continue to perform its functions. For other investigations, the warrant may be issued (and renewed) for periods of up to one year. Unlike the *Criminal Code* intercept provisions, there is no obligation that the target of the intercept be eventually apprised of the warrant.

The CSIS warrant provisions have withstood constitutional challenges.[99]

---

95   *Canadian Security Intelligence Service Act*, R.S.C. 1985, c. C-23, s. 21, cross-referenced to s. 16 [CSIS Act].

96   *Ibid.*, s. 21(3).

97   *Ibid.*, s. 24.

98   Section 2(d) of the CSIS Act reads: "activities directed toward undermining by covert unlawful acts, or directed toward or intended ultimately to lead to the destruction or overthrow by violence of, the constitutionally established system of government in Canada."

99   See *Atwal v. Canada*, above note 27 at para. 36.

> Since the [CSIS] Act does not authorize the issuance of warrants to investigate offences in the ordinary criminal context, nor to obtain evidence of such offences, it is entirely to be expected that section 21 [authorizing inter-

C. *NATIONAL DEFENCE ACT*

The Department of National Defence houses both the Canadian Forces' defence intelligence units and the Communications Security Establishment.

1) Defence Intelligence

Defence intelligence entities include military signals intelligence operations, such as the Canadian Forces SIGINT Operations Centre (CF-SOC). These military units do not operate under a unique lawful access regime in terms of intercepting private communications. To make such an intercept lawfully while in Canada, they must, therefore, be acting to assist law enforcement or CSIS. These agencies in turn must be acting pursuant to a lawful access permission obtained under the *Criminal Code* or the CSIS Act.[100]

2) Communications Security Establishment

The Communications Security Establishment (CSE) operates under different rules. Amendments made in 2001 to the *National Defence Act* created a specific statutory mandate for CSE's intercept activity.

a) Assistance to Law Enforcement Intercepts

Under these 2001 rules, CSE may provide assistance to law enforcement and security agencies. These law enforcement assistance practices

---

cepts] does not require the issuing judge to be satisfied that an offence has been committed and that evidence thereof will be found in execution of the warrant. What the Act does authorize is the investigation of threats to the security of Canada and, *inter alia*, the collection of information respecting activities that may, on reasonable grounds, be suspected of constituting such threats. Having regard to the definition of "judge," paragraph 21(2)(a) of the Act fully satisfies, *mutatis mutandis*, the prescription of *Hunter v. Southam Inc.* as to the minimum criteria demanded by section 8 of legislation authorizing a search and seizure. The judge is required to be satisfied, on reasonable and probable grounds established by sworn evidence, that a threat to the security of Canada exists and that a warrant is required to enable its investigation. In my opinion, that is an objective standard.

In *Corp. of the Canadian Civil Liberties Assn. v. Canada (Attorney General)*, (1998) 40 O.R. (3d) 489 (C.A.), the Canadian Civil Liberties Association sought to challenge the CSIS Act provisions on s. 8 grounds. The Ontario Court of Appeal refused them public interest standing to do so, concluding, *inter alia*, that the arguments presented by the CCLA on the s. 8 violation were "weak." *Ibid.* at para. 88.

100 See discussion in Arar inquiry, Policy Report, above note 44 at 149.

"are subject to any limitations imposed by law on federal law enforcement and security agencies in the performance of their duties."[101] As such, they are constrained by the "lawful access" provisions found in the *Criminal Code* and CSIS Acts, discussed above, and by the respective legal mandates of law enforcement and CSIS. Acting in this capacity, therefore, CSE is a technological appendage of the police or other federal agencies such as CSIS, rather than a self-standing entity with its own legal powers to conduct intercepts.[102]

b) Foreign Intelligence Intercepts

CSE also has a more autonomous intelligence-gathering function in relation to another of the Establishment's legislated purposes: "to acquire and use information from the global information infrastructure for the purpose of providing foreign intelligence, in accordance with Government of Canada intelligence priorities."[103] "Foreign intelligence" is "information or intelligence about the capabilities, intentions or activities of a foreign individual, state, organization or terrorist group, as they relate to international affairs, defence or security."[104]

The rules governing foreign intelligence intercepts vary, depending on whether they have a Canadian nexus.

i) Purely Foreign Intercepts

Foreign intelligence intercepts that are truly foreign have no Canadian nexus and thus are not "private communications" as defined by both the *Criminal Code* and the *National Defence Act*. They may, therefore,

---

101 *National Defence Act*, R.S.C 1985, c. N-5, ss. 273.64(1)(c) and 273.64(3) [NDA].

102 See discussion in Canada, Communications Security Establishment Commissioner, *Annual Report 2004–2005* (Ottawa: Minister of Public Works and Government Services Canada, 2005) at 6 (discussing CSE assistance provided to law enforcement, noting that the RCMP is the largest recipient of this assistance and observing that "[w]hen providing assistance to the RCMP, the scope of which is limited and defined in policy, CSE does so as an agent. Before agreeing to act in that capacity, however, CSE must first satisfy itself that the RCMP is authorized to make the request and then be satisfied that it has the authority to provide the assistance the RCMP has requested"). Note, however, that the CSE commissioner observed in 2007 that the CSE also provides the RCMP with intelligence under CSE's foreign intelligence intercept mandate, discussed in the next section. He queried whether this more general mandate "was the appropriate authority in all instances for CSE to provide intelligence support to the RCMP in the pursuit of its domestic criminal investigations." Canada, Communications Security Establishment Commissioner, *Annual Report 2006–2007* (Ottawa: Minister of Public Works and Government Services Canada, 2007) at 13.

103 NDA, above note 101, s. 273.64.

104 *Ibid.*, s. 273.61.

be collected as long as consistent with the CSE mandate. They are not subjected to any statutorily based oversight mechanism.[105]

ii) Intercepts with Canadian Nexus

a. Ministerial Authorizations

The situation is different where there is a Canadian dimension to the intercept. The Act admonishes that CSE's foreign intelligence activities "shall not be directed at Canadians or any person in Canada; and ... shall be subject to measures to protect the privacy of Canadians in the use and retention of intercepted information."[106] To enforce this requirement, the Act sets up a system of ministerial authorizations relating to the intercept of "private communications" in order to obtain "foreign intelligence."

A "private communication" is defined by the *National Defence Act* in keeping with the definition found in the *Criminal Code*. It is, therefore, "any oral communication, or any telecommunication" originating or intended to be received in Canada that reasonably would not be expected by its originator to be intercepted other than by the intended recipient.[107]

CSE intercepts of these private communications may only be authorized by the minister of national defence if he or she is satisfied that:

(a) the interception will be directed at foreign entities located outside Canada;

(b) the information to be obtained could not reasonably be obtained by other means;

---

105 This appears to be the interpretation preferred by Justice Lamer, former Commissioner of the CSE. See Canada, Communications Security Establishment Commissioner, *Annual Report 2003–2004* (Ottawa: Minister of Public Works and Government Services Canada, 2004) at 6 (suggesting that the permission to intercept private communications in addition to a power to intercept other more truly foreign communications as follows: "Today, ... CSE is in a better position to fulfil its foreign intelligence responsibilities because, with the Minister's consent, it can follow targeted foreign communications even if they have a connection with Canada"). See also, Communications Security Establishment Commissioner (then Claude Bisson), *Annual Report 2002–2003* (Ottawa: Minister of Public Works and Government Services Canada, 2003) at 6 ("Whatever else CSE may intercept, it is the interception of private communications [i.e., "communications of Canadians"] that is specifically authorized by the Minister"), online.

106 NDA, above note 101, s. 273.64(2).

107 *Ibid.*, s. 273.61, cross-referencing the *Criminal Code*, above note 80, s. 183.

(c) the expected foreign intelligence value of the information that would be derived from the interception justifies it; and

(d) satisfactory measures are in place to protect the privacy of Canadians and to ensure that private communications will only be used or retained if they are essential to international affairs, defence or security.

These ministerial authorizations persist for up to one year, and may be renewed for supplemental periods of one year.[108] There is no obligation imposed by the statute that targets be apprised ultimately of the existence of the authorization.

As of 2006, four ministerial authorizations for the intercept of private communications for foreign intelligence were in place.[109] CSE reported in 2005 that the ministerial authorization regime had "yielded a wide range of operational benefits in the last three years." Specifically, authorizations had "allowed CSE to improve its understanding of the global communications environment, a vital step in acquiring foreign intelligence and protecting Canada's most sensitive information and infrastructure" and "to develop independent, cutting-edge Canadian collection and protection programs that would have been impossible without the legal shield provided by the Authorizations." These capabilities, reported the agency, "have been welcomed by CSE's clients and partners as crucial to the Government's collective national security efforts, and have led to expanded cooperation and information sharing at home and abroad."[110]

b.   Review

Still, the intercept rules have attracted mild criticism from the CSE commissioner. The commissioner of the Communication Security Establishment is the independent official charged with reviewing CSE's compliance with its mandate and the rules on intercepts established in the *National Defence Act*.[111] In his 2005–6 report, then CSE commissioner (and former chief justice) Antonio Lamer noted a "lack of clarity" in the intercept policies, making "it difficult for my staff to assess

---

108   NDA, *ibid.*, s. 273.68.

109   Arar inquiry, Policy Report, above note 44 at 144. But see Canada, Communications Security Establishment Commissioner, *Annual Report 2006–2007*, above note 102 at 18 ("Certain foreign intelligence collection activities were conducted under three ministerial authorizations that were in effect from March 2004 to December 2006. These ministerial authorizations focused on acquiring communications of foreign intelligence value from the global information infrastructure").

110   CSE, *CSE's Ministerial Authorization*, online: www.cse-cst.gc.ca/media-room/ministerial-authorization-e.html.

111   See discussion in Chapter 3.

compliance with certain of the conditions that the legislation requires to be satisfied before a ministerial authorization is given." Specifically, the commissioner took the view that

> it should be possible to identify a clear linkage between the government intelligence priorities, the foreign entities targeted and the activity or class of activities for which ministerial authorization is needed. However, reviews completed by my office, including the most recent one, have shown that supporting documentation provided by CSE as part of requests for the Minister's authorization address the underlying foreign intelligence requirements only in general terms.[112]

The commissioner complained also of varying legal understandings of the *National Defence Act* intercept authorization rules held by his office and the Department of Justice. Justice Gonthier, the commissioner by the time of this writing, echoed these concerns in his 2006-7 annual report.[113]

The special senate committee on anti-terrorism law recommended in 2007 that the NDA be amended to clarify whether, to receive ministerial authorization, the standard to be met is reasonable belief or reasonable suspicion.[114]

c.   Constitutional Issues

There are also obvious constitutional issues raised by CSE intercept of private communications, not least, the section 8 protections in the *Charter* concerning searches and seizures.

Past CSE commissioners apparently considered the statutory checks and balances on intercept of private communications sufficient to meet *Charter* standards. In his 2002–3 report, then Commissioner Claude Bisson noted "before December 2001, CSE would have been in violation of privacy related provisions of both the *Criminal Code* and the *Canadian Charter of Rights and Freedoms* had it intercepted communications without the certainty that, in doing so, it would not intercept private communications."[115] However, Antonio Lamer, in his 2004–5

---

112 Canada, Communications Security Establishment Commissioner, *Annual Report 2005–2006* (Ottawa: Minister of Public Works and Government Services Canada, 2006) at 10.

113 Canada, Communications Security Establishment Commissioner, *Annual Report 2006–2007*, above note 102 at 3.

114 Special Senate Committee on the *Anti-terrorism Act, Fundamental Justice in Extraordinary Times* (2007) at 78, online: www.parl.gc.ca/39/1/parlbus/commbus/senate/Com-e/anti-e/rep-e/rep02feb07-e.htm.

115 Canada, Communications Security Establishment Commissioner, *Annual Report 2002–2003*, above note 105 at 3, n1.

report, took the view that the modern regime vitiated this concern: "I am of the opinion that [post-2001 system for ministerial authorization of private communication intercepts] is both reasonable and consistent with other legislation that establishes an authority to engage in activities that would, in the absence of adequate justification, be judged an infringement on the rights of individuals as protected by the *Charter of Rights and Freedoms*."[116]

It is certainly the case that the circumstances in which the minister of national defence may authorize an intercept are, broadly speaking, similar to the grounds for warrants listed in other Acts. Most notable among these is the CSIS Act. Nevertheless, the *National Defence Act* differs from other legislation authorizing lawful access in at least one key respect: the person ultimately authorizing the intercept is not a judicial officer, but instead an executive official; in this case, the minister of national defence. That minister's exact statutory duty under the *National Defence Act* is to manage and direct "all matters relating to national defence."[117] As such, he or she is hardly an independent and disinterested reviewer of government search and seizure requests.

Stanley Cohen, in his careful constitutional review of this mechanism, suggests that it might be found constitutional because, among other things, of the national security justification for the intercept.[118] There is some jurisprudential support for this view.[119] There is, however, also room for disagreement. It is not apparent why the national security impulses driving CSE intercepts of private communications oblige ministerial authorizations while the analogous impulses reflected in CSIS warrants are accommodated by judicial authorizations. Put another way, the national security necessity of ministerial authorizations as opposed to scrutiny by designated judges at the Federal Court is unclear.[120]

---

116 Canada, Communications Security Establishment Commissioner, *Annual Report 2004–2005*, above note 102 at 9. The then former commissioner repeated this view before the Senate, *Fundamental Justice in Extraordinary Times*, above note 114 at 77 (seemingly taking the view that because one side of the communication was foreign, a judicial warrant would be inappropriate).

117 NDA, above note 101, s. 4.

118 Cohen, *Privacy, Crime and Terror*, above note 2 at 232.

119 *Hunter v. Southam*, above note 16 at 186 (suggesting, without actually deciding, that the search and seizure standard developed in that case might be different "where state security is involved").

120 In some of his writings, former justice minister Irwin Cotler has, in fact, called for judicial involvement in the CSE intercept authorization process. Irwin Cotler, "Terrorism, Security and Rights: The Dilemma of Democracies" (2002–3) 14 N.J.C.L. 13 at 45.

c) Cyber Security

CSE is also charged with providing "advice, guidance and services to help ensure the protection of electronic information and of information infrastructures of importance to the Government of Canada."[121] As with foreign intelligence intercepts with a Canadian nexus, activities conducted to fulfill this mandate "shall not be directed at Canadians or any person in Canada; and ... shall be subject to measures to protect the privacy of Canadians in the use and retention of intercepted information."[122]

Amendments to the *National Defence Act* enacted in 2004[123] but not in force at the time of this writing embellish the CSE's responsibilities in the area of cyber security and exempt it from the application of the *Criminal Code* lawful access rules. Under the new provisions, the minister of national defence may authorize any DND public servant or agent performing computer-related duties in DND or the Canadian Forces (CF) to "intercept private communications in relation to an activity or class of activities specified in the authorization, if such communications originate from, are directed to or transit through any such [national defence] computer system or network." This authorization must be "for the sole purpose of identifying, isolating or preventing any harmful unauthorized use of, any interference with or any damage to those systems or networks, or any damage to the data that they contain." The minister may also authorize the chief of defence staff to issue a similar directive to CF officers or noncommissioned members.

Before taking either of these steps, the minister must be satisfied, among other things, that the information could not reasonably be obtained by other means, consent by the persons participating in the communication cannot be reasonably obtained, information will be used and retained only to the extent essential to deal with the harmful use, interference or damage to the computer systems and that measures are in place to protect the privacy of Canadians. To this end, the minister may impose conditions protecting privacy.

Table 11.2 summarizes Canada's lawful access rules.

---

121 NDA, above note 101, s. 273.64.
122 *Ibid.*
123 *Public Safety Act, 2002*, S.C. 2004, c. 15, s. 78, introducing ss. 273.8 & 273.9 of the *NDA, ibid.*

Table 11.2: Lawful Access Powers

Agency	Type of Infringement of Privacy	Grounds for Infringement	Pre-requisites to Infringement	Duration	Notification of Target
Law enforcement	*Criminal Code*—Interception of private communication—regular process	Investigating a criminal offence	By authorization, where a judge is satisfied • that it would be in the best interests of the administration of justice to do so; and • that other investigative procedures have been tried and have failed, other investigative procedures are unlikely to succeed or the urgency of the matter is such that it would be impractical to carry out the investigation of the offence using only other investigative procedures.	60 days, subject to subsequent renewals of up to 60-day periods	90 days after intercept, subject to extensions in the interest of justice and where investigation ongoing of up to 3 years
	Criminal Code—Interception of private communication—terrorism offences	Investigating a terrorism offence	By authorization, where a judge is satisfied • that it would be in the best interests of the administration of justice to do so	1 year, subject to subsequent renewals of up to 1 year periods	90 days after intercept, subject to extensions in the interest of justice of up to 3 years
Communications Security Establishment	*National Defence Act*—Interception of communications that are *not* private communications (i.e., that	Acquiring information from the global information infra-	No statutory rules		

Agency	Type of Infringement of Privacy	Grounds for Infringement	Pre-requisites to Infringement	Duration	Notification of Target
Communications Security Establishment (cont'd)	have no nexus to Canada)	structure for the purpose of providing foreign intelligence			
	National Defence Act — Interception of private communications	For the sole purpose of obtaining foreign intelligence	Authorized by the minister of national defence on the basis that: • the interception will be directed at foreign entities located outside Canada; • the information to be obtained could not reasonably be obtained by other means; • the expected foreign intelligence value of the information that would be derived from the interception justifies it; and • satisfactory measures are in place to protect the privacy of Canadians and to ensure that private communications will only be used or retained if they are essential to international affairs, defence or security.	Up to 1 year, subject to renewal for up to one year.	No statutory rules
		For the sole purpose of	Authorized by the minister of national defence on the basis that:	Up to 1 year, subject to renewal for up to	No statutory rules

Agency	Type of Infringement of Privacy	Grounds for Infringement	Pre-requisites to Infringement	Duration	Notification of Target
Communications Security Establishment (cont'd)		protecting the computer systems or networks of the Government of Canada from mischief, unauthorized use or interference	• the interception is necessary to identify, isolate or prevent harm to Government of Canada computer systems or networks; • the information to be obtained could not reasonably be obtained by other means; • the consent of persons whose private communications may be intercepted cannot reasonably be obtained; • satisfactory measures are in place to ensure that only information that is essential to identify, isolate or prevent harm to Government of Canada computer systems or networks will be used or retained; and • satisfactory measures are in place to protect the privacy of Canadians in the use or retention of that information	1 year	
		To provide technical and operational assistance to	Subject to any limitations imposed by law on the assisted federal law enforcement and security agencies in the performance of their duties.		

Agency	Type of Infringement of Privacy	Grounds for Infringement	Pre-requisites to Infringement	Duration	Notification of Target
Communications Security Establishment (cont'd)		federal law enforcement and security agencies in the performance of their lawful duties.			
Canadian Security Intelligence Agency	Interception of any communication or obtaining any information, record, document or thing and, for that purpose: • to enter any place or open or obtain access to any thing; • to search for, remove or return, or examine, take extracts from or make copies of or record the information, record, document or thing; or • to install, maintain or remove any thing	Investigate a threat to the security of Canada or to collect information or intelligence relating to the capabilities, intentions or activities of any foreign state or group of foreign states or foreign person, other than a permanent resident.	By warrant, where a judge is satisfied that the facts justify the belief, on reasonable grounds, that a warrant is required to serve the purpose in the column to the left. The judge must also be satisfied that: • other investigative procedures have been tried and have failed (or why it appears that they are unlikely to succeed); • the urgency of the matter is such that it would be impractical to carry out the investigation using only other investigative procedures; or • without a warrant under the Act it is likely that information respecting the threat to the security of Canada would not be obtained.	Up to 1 year (60 days for investigations of subversion), subject to renewal for these same periods.	No statutory rules

PART III: COMPELLED DISCLOSURE FROM PRIVATE SECTOR ENTITIES

Since 9/11, the new political environment has precipitated the passage of other laws easing government access to private information on national security grounds. These are not lawful access laws, but rather compelled disclosure provisions; that is, these new rules enlist private sector entities as virtual agents of the state, obliging them to release and report information to government agencies in certain circumstances.

The most controversial privacy-restricting statute is the *Public Safety Act*, enacted in 2004. The privacy commissioner objected to this legislation's breadth and its creation of a "general, rather than specific, regime for coopting private sector organizations by pressing them into service in support of law enforcement activities,"[124] and not just anti-terrorism efforts.[125] Of particular concern, in the commissioner's view, were the amendments made by the statute to the *Aeronautics Act*[126] and the PIPEDA.[127] The latter's provisions are discussed above. The complicated new regime under the amended *Aeronautics Act* and related transportation-regulating statutes is discussed in the section that follows, as are financial transaction disclosure rules.

A. COMMERCIAL PASSENGER INFORMATION

Several (apparently duplicative) Canadian statutes and regulations empower the government to compel disclosure of passenger and travel information from commercial carriers before passenger arrival in Canada.[128]

---

124 Jennifer Stoddart, Privacy Commissioner of Canada, "Public Safety and Privacy: An Inevitable Conflict?" (lecture, Reboot Communications Public Safety Conference Strategies for Public Safety Technology and Counter-Terrorism: Prevention, Protection and Pursuit, Ottawa, 27 April 2004), online: www.privcom. gc.ca/speech/2004/sp-d_040427_e.asp.

125 George Radwanski, Privacy Commissioner of Canada (Appearance before the Subcommittee on National Security of the Standing Committee on Justice and Human Rights, Ottawa, 10 February 2003).

126 R.S.C. 1985, c. A-2.

127 Jennifer Stoddart, Privacy Commissioner of Canada (Statement to the Senate Standing Committee on Transport and Communications regarding Bill C-7, 18 March 2004).

128 For a media assessment of how several of these various transportation data systems overlap and interact, see Don Butler, "Canadian Airline Passengers Will Be Kept under Close Scrutiny" *Ottawa Citizen* (23 January 2007).

1) *Aeronautics Act*

The *Aeronautics Act* provisions allow the Department of Transport, the RCMP and CSIS to extract personal information from air carriers and related entities in the interest of transportation security. [129]

The amendments empower the government to require any air carrier or operator of an aviation reservation system to provide information set out in a schedule to the *Public Safety Act* under certain defined circumstances. Information listed in the Act's schedule includes assorted passenger biographical, booking, ticketing, flight, and itinerary information. The circumstances in which provision of this information may be required are set out in Table 11.3, and involve primary disclosure by the air carrier to the government. Secondary and tertiary disclosure of this information by the government is controlled by a series of special rules, again outlined in Table 11.3.

---

129 *Aeronautics Act*, above note 126, ss. 4.81 & 4.82.

Table 11.3: Primary, Secondary and Tertiary Disclosure Rules of Passenger Information under the *Aeronautics Act*

Primary Disclosure	Grounds for Primary Disclosure	Secondary Disclosure	Grounds for Secondary Disclosure	Tertiary Disclosure	Grounds for Tertiary Disclosure
Subsection 4.81(1): To the Minister of Transport or a designated officer of the Department of Transport	Subsection 4.81(1): For the purposes of transportation security, (a) information in the schedule on board persons on board or expected to be on board an aircraft should the Minister or the officer be of the opinion that there is an immediate threat to that flight; (b) information in the schedule on a particular person that comes into the air carrier or aviation reservation systems control within 30-days after the information is requested	Paragraph 4.81(3)(a): To the Minister of Citizenship and Immigration	Subsection 4.81(3): Only for the purposes of transportation security.	Paragraph 4.81(4)(a): Only to persons in the Department of Citizenship and Immigration.	Subsection 4.81(4): Only for the purposes of transportation security.
		Paragraph 4.81(3)(b): To the Minister of National Revenue	Subsection 4.81(3): Only for the purposes of transportation security.	Paragraph 4.81(4)(b): Only to persons in the Department of National Revenue.	Subsection 4.81(4): Only for the purposes of transportation security.
		Paragraph 4.81(3)(c): To the CEO of the Canadian Air Transport Security Authority	Subsection 4.81(3): Only for the purposes of transportation security.	Paragraph 4.81(4)(c): Only to persons in the Canadian Air Transport Security Authority.	Subsection 4.81(4): Only for the purposes of transportation security.
		Paragraph 4.81(3)(d): To a person designated by the Commissioner of the RCMP under subs. 4.82(2) (see below)	Subsection 4.81(3): Only for the purposes of transportation security.	Subsection 4.82(7): Tertiary disclosure apparently governed by the secondary and tertiary disclosure rules for RCMP and CSIS designates noted below.	
		Paragraph 4.81(3)(e): To a person designated by the	Subsection 4.81(3): Only for the purposes of	Subsection 4.82(7): Tertiary disclosure	

Primary Disclosure	Grounds for Primary Disclosure	Secondary Disclosure	Grounds for Secondary Disclosure	Tertiary Disclosure	Grounds for Tertiary Disclosure
Subsection 4.81(1) (cont'd)		Director of CSIS under subs. 4.82(3) (see below)	transportation security.	apparently governed by the secondary and tertiary disclosure rules for RCMP and CSIS designates noted below.	
Subsection 4.82(4): To a person designated by the Commissioner of the RCMP under subs. 4.82(2)	Subsection 4.82(4): For the purposes of transportation security, (a) information in the schedule on the persons on board or expected to be on board; or (b) information in the schedule on a particular person that comes into the air carrier or aviation reservation systems control within 30-days after the information is requested	Subsection 4.82(6): To any other person designated by the Commissioner of the RCMP under subs. 4.82(2) Subsection 4.82(8): To the Minister of Transport, any peace officer, any employee of CSIS, or to the Canadian Air Transport Security Authority or any air carrier or operator of an aviation facility, along with the Minister of Transport Subsection 4.82(9): To an Aircraft Protective Officer (an undefined person under the Act)	Subsection 4.82(8): Designated person has reason to believe that the information is relevant to transportation security[1] Subsection 4.82(9): If the designated person believes that the information may assist this person in performing duties relating to transportation security		

Primary Disclosure	Grounds for Primary Disclosure	Secondary Disclosure	Grounds for Secondary Disclosure	Tertiary Disclosure	Grounds for Tertiary Disclosure
Subsection 4.82(4) (cont'd)		Subsection 4.82(10): To the extent necessary to respond to a threat to transportation security or the life, health or safety of a person, to a person in a position to take measures to respond to the threat who needs the information to respond	Subsection 4.82(10): Designated person has reason to believe that there is an immediate threat to transportation security or the life, health or safety of a person		
		Subsection 4.82(11): To any peace officer	Subsection 4.82(11): If designated person has reason to believe that the information would assist in the execution of a warrant		
		Subsection 4.82(7): As required by the purpose noted to the right	Subsection 4.82(7): For the purpose of complying with a subpoena or document issued or order made by a court, person or body with jurisdiction to compel the production of information, or the purpose of complying with rules of court relating to the production of information		

Primary Disclosure	Grounds for Primary Disclosure	Secondary Disclosure	Grounds for Secondary Disclosure	Tertiary Disclosure	Grounds for Tertiary Disclosure
Subsection 4.82(3): To a person designated by the Director of CSIS under subs. 4.82(3).	Subsection 4.81(5): For the purposes of transportation security or the investigation of activities relating to violence against persons or property for political, religious or ideological objectives within Canada or a foreign state (a) information in the schedule on the persons on board or expected to be on board or (b) information in the schedule on a particular person that comes into the air carrier or aviation reservation systems control within 30-days after the information is requested	Subsection 4.82(6): To any other person designated by the Director of CSIS under subs. 4.82(3). Subsection 4.82(8): To the minister of transport, any peace officer, any employee of CSIS, or to the Canadian Air Transport Security Authority or any air carrier or operator of an aviation facility, along with the minister of transport Subsection 4.82(9): To an aircraft protective officer (an undefined person under the Act) Subsection 4.82(10): To the extent necessary to respond to a threat to transportation security or the life, health or safety of	Subsection 4.82(8): Designated person has reason to believe that the information is relevant to transportation security. Subsection 4.82(9): If the designated person believes the information may assist this person in performing duties relating to transportation security Subsection 4.82(10): If the designated person has reason to believe that there is an immediate threat to transportation		

Primary Disclosure	Grounds for Primary Disclosure	Secondary Disclosure	Grounds for Secondary Disclosure	Tertiary Disclosure	Grounds for Tertiary Disclosure
Subsection 4.82(3) (cont'd)		a person, disclosure may be made to a person in a position to take measures to respond to the threat and who needs the information to respond	security or the life, health or safety of a person		
		Subsection 4.82(11): To any peace officer	Subsection 4.82(11): If the designated person has reason to believe that the information would assist in the execution of a warrant		
		Subsection 4.82(12): To an employee of CSIS	Subsection 4.82(12): If authorized by a senior designated person, for the purpose of an investigation of activities relating to violence against persons or property for political, religious or ideological objectives within Canada or a foreign state		
		Subsection 4.82(7): As required by the purpose noted to the right	Subsection 4.82(7): For the purpose of complying with a subpoena or document		

Primary Disclosure	Grounds for Primary Disclosure	Secondary Disclosure	Grounds for Secondary Disclosure	Tertiary Disclosure	Grounds for Tertiary Disclosure
			issued or order made by a court, person or body with jurisdiction to compel the production of information, or the purpose of complying with rules of court relating to the production of information		
Subsection 4.83(1): To a competent authority in a foreign state	Subsection 4.83(1): Information may be provided in accordance with the laws of the foreign state either where the aircraft is Canadian and flying an international route or where an aircraft is departing from Canada and is scheduled to land in a foreign state	Subsection 4.83(2): Information provided to a foreign state may be collected by a Canadian government institution (as defined under the *Privacy Act*).	Subsection 4.83(2): Information can be collected only for the purpose of protecting national security or public safety or for the purpose of defence or administering or enforcing any federal statute prohibiting, controlling or regulating the importation or exportation of goods or the movement of people in or out of Canada	Subsection 4.83(2): Any further disclosure	Subsection 4.83(2): Only for the purpose of protecting national security or public safety or for the purpose of defence or administering or enforcing any federal statute prohibiting, controlling or regulating the importation or exportation of goods or the movement of people in or out of Canada.

[1] Note that it is not entirely clear from the drafting if this purpose is meant to modify simply disclosure to an air carrier or operator of an aviation facility, or to apply also to the other persons who may receive secondary disclosure.

With respect to information released to the Department of Transport, following primary, secondary or tertiary disclosure, the information must be destroyed within seven days of that disclosure.[130] The information retention regime is slightly different where information is disclosed by the air carrier or reservation system to the RCMP or CSIS. Here, information disclosed directly to these bodies (or presumably obtained as a secondary disclosure from the Department of Transport) need not be destroyed if it is reasonably required for security purposes.[131] Where information is retained, a record setting out the reasons for this retention must be prepared and the RCMP and CSIS must review their retention decisions annually to determine whether the purposes for retaining information persist.[132]

Secondary disclosure by CSIS and the RCMP must also be documented. Secondary disclosure in most instances requires the CSIS or RCMP discloser to keep a record summarizing the information disclosed, the reasons for the disclosure and the name of the person or body to whom the information was disclosed.[133]

2) IRPA and *Customs Act*

Other statutes also require disclosure of passenger information. Thus, the *Immigration and Refugee Protection Act* (IRPA)[134] supplements the disclosure obligations of transportation companies under the *Aeronautics Act*. Under the IRPA, a person who owns or operates a transportation facility must disclose to the government assorted passenger identity and travel information.[135] Regulations under the Act require transporters to provide, on request and before arriving in Canada, passenger biographical and travel information.[136]

For its part, regulations under the *Customs Act*[137] anticipate commercial carriers, travel agents and operators of a reservation system being obliged by the government to provide identification and travel

---

130 *Ibid.*, ss. 4.81(6), (7), & (8). This destruction requirement applies despite any other Act of Parliament, *ibid.*, s. 4.81(9).

131 *Ibid.*, s. 4.82(14).

132 *Ibid.*, s. 4.82(15). The document destruction and retention rules in ss. 4.82(14) & (15) apply despite any other Act of Parliament. *Ibid.*, s. 4.82(17).

133 *Ibid.*, s. 4.82(13).

134 *Immigration and Refugee Protection Act*, S.C. 2001, c. 27 [IRPA].

135 *Ibid.*, ss. 148 & 149.

136 *Immigration and Refugee Protection Regulations*, S.O.R./2002-227, s. 269.

137 R.S.C. 1985 (2d Supp.), c. 1.

information about persons on board a commercial conveyance — that is, a transportation vehicle.[138]

The Canada Border Services Agency has in fact developed an Advance Passenger Information/Passenger Name Record (API/PNR) program requiring commercial carriers (currently limited to airlines) prior to arriving in Canada to provide the Agency with passenger biographical information (Advance Passenger Information) and travel information (Passenger Name Record).[139] This data is used by CBSA to "identify persons who may be involved with, or who are at risk to import goods related to terrorism or terrorism-related crimes, or other serious crimes that are transnational in nature."[140]

Similar advance warning systems for cargo arriving in Canada have been phased in under the Advance Commercial Information project.[141]

B. DISCLOSURE OF FINANCIAL INFORMATION

A key plank of the post-9/11 counterterrorism strategy has been impeding financial flows linked to terrorist entities. Terrorism financing was the key preoccupation of the U.N. Security Council in issuing Resolution 1373, almost immediately after 9/11. It is also the subject of one of the most recent anti-terrorism treaties, the *International Convention for the Suppression of the Financing of Terrorism*. Canada has ratified this latter instrument and is also compelled to respond to Security Council Resolution 1373.

Terrorism is funded both by some terrorist-supporting states and by revenue-generating activities; for instance, drug trafficking or more *bona fide* business or charitable activities. Monies earned in this manner may be laundered in various ways to disguise their origins.[142] In 2005–6, the Canadian government identified approximately $256 million worth of transactions related to suspected terrorist activity financing

---

138 *Passenger Information (Customs) Regulations*, S.O.R./2003-219.

139 See Canada Border Services Agency, Memorandum D2-5-11 (31 May 2006), online: www.cbsa.gc.ca/E/pub/cm/d2-5-11/d2-5-11-e.pdf.

140 *Ibid.*

141 Canada Border Services Agency, *Advance Commercial Information* (2006), online: www.cbsa.gc.ca/import/advance/menu-e.html. See *Reporting of Imported Goods Regulations*, S.O.R./86-873.

142 Financial Transactions and Reports Analysis Centre of Canada [FINTRAC], *Guideline 1: Backgrounder* (March 2003) at 11 *et seq.*, online: www.fintrac.gc.ca/publications/guide/Guide1/1_e.asp.

and other threats to the security of Canada.[143] Several notorious terrorist organizations—including Hezbollah and the Tamil Tigers—reportedly engage in fundraising in Canada,[144] sometimes through extortion and other forms of pressure.[145]

Impeding transactions of this sort depends, in some measure, on timely disclosure of suspicious transactions by financial and other institutions. To enable this disclosure, Parliament enacted the *Proceeds of Crime (Money Laundering) and Terrorist Financing Act* in 2000,[146] amended in 2001 and 2006. The Act creates a Financial Transactions and Reports Analysis Centre (FINTRAC) tasked with reviewing financial data disclosed to it by financial institutions, among other entities, for evidence of money laundering and terrorist financing.

Subject to an express statutory exception for information privileged by the solicitor–client relationship,[147] the Act requires every person or entity—defined for the most part as those involved in financial services[148]—to report certain "prescribed" financial transactions to the centre.[149] The regulations refine the reporting requirement, requir-

---

143 Canada, FINTRAC, *Annual Report 2006*, online: www.fintrac.gc.ca/publications/annualreport/2006/menu_e.asp.

144 See Stewart Bell, "Hezbollah raising Funds Here: Report; Lebanese terrorist Group Also Procuring equipment in Canada" *National Post* (14 December 2006); Stewart Bell & Graeme Hamilton, "Tigers Use Pressure to Raise Funds, Police Say" *National Post* (10 May 2007).

145 See *ibid.* and Human Rights Watch, *Funding the "Final War": LTTE Intimidation and Extortion in the Tamil Diaspora* (March 2006), online: http://hrw.org/reports/2006/ltte0306/.

146 S.C. 2000, c. 17 [Proceeds Act].

147 *Ibid.*, s. 12.

148 *Ibid.*, s. 5. Regulations under the Act once also included lawyers "receiving or paying funds, other than those received or paid in respect of professional fees, disbursements, expenses or bail; … purchasing or selling securities, real property or business assets or entities; and … transferring funds or securities by any means." S.O.R./2001-317, s. 5. A clear challenge to solicitor-client privilege, the constitutionality of this measure was challenged by Canada's law societies in British Columbia court. The B.C. Supreme Court issued an interlocutory injunction barring the application of the provision. *Law Society of British Columbia v. Canada (Attorney General)*, 2001 BCSC 1593. This decision was upheld on appeal. 2002 BCCA 49. Parallel court proceedings arose across the country. The lawyer provision in the regulations was subsequently removed by the government. S.O.R./2003-102. At the time of this writing, the law societies were negotiating professional responsibility rules on, for example, cash transactions, that they urge will grapple with terrorism financing issues without impairing solicitor-client rules. See Standing Senate Committee on Banking, Trade and Commerce, *Issue 5—Evidence*, 39th Parl., 1st Sess. (22 June 2006).

149 Proceeds Act, above note 146, s. 9.

ing financial service companies of various sorts to report transfers in cash or through electronic networks of more than $10,000, along with related information such as the account numbers and personal identifier information of the transacting parties.[150]

In addition, the Act provides that "every [enumerated] person or entity … shall report to the Centre … every financial transaction that occurs or that is attempted in the course of their activities and in respect of which there are reasonable grounds to suspect that … the transaction is related to the commission or the attempted commission of a terrorist activity financing offence."[151] "Terrorism activity financing offences" are discussed in Chapter 7. As with the regular reports, these financial transaction reports are to include account and personal identifier information.[152] The person or entity reporting this suspicious activity is not to reveal that it has made the report, with the intent of impeding a criminal investigation.[153] Failure to comply with these reporting rules is a criminal offence.[154]

Financial disclosure requirements are also found in the *Criminal Code* and in the *Suppression of Terrorism Regulations*, made under the *United Nations Act* in direct response to U.N. Security Council Resolution 1373. Both instruments require financial institutions to ascertain on a continuing basis whether they are in possession or control of property owned or controlled by or on behalf of a listed entity—that is, an organization or person listed by the Security Council's 1267 Committee or unilaterally by the governor-in-council because of terrorist connections. The listing process is described in greater detail in Chapters 6 and 7. Financial institutions must report monthly to their respective regulators that they are either not in possession of property owned by a listed person or, where they are, provide details on that property. Failure to meet these disclosure requirements is a crime.[155]

These and other financial disclosure requirements are summarized in Table 11.4.

150 S.O.R./2002-184, as amended, s. 12.
151 Proceeds Act, above note 146, s. 7.
152 S.O.R./2001-317, as amended.
153 Proceeds Act, above note 146, s. 8.
154 *Ibid.*, s. 75 *et seq.*
155 *Regulations Implementing the United Nations Resolutions on the Suppression of Terrorism*, S.O.R./2001-360, s. 9 [*Suppression of Terrorism Regulations*]; *Criminal Code*, above note 80, s. 83.12.

Table 11.4: Financial Disclosure Requirements

Entity	Disclosure Trigger	Disclosed Information	Agency to Whom Disclosure Is Made
Every person in Canada and every Canadian outside Canada	Existence of property in their possession or control that they know is owned or controlled by or on behalf of a terrorist group.	Notice of the existence of this property and information about a transaction or proposed transaction in respect of it	Commissioner of the RCMP, the Director of CSIS[1] and FINTRAC[2]
Assorted financial services institutions, businesses and practitioners	Monthly reporting requirement	Notice of whether they are in possession or control of property owned or controlled by or on behalf of a "listed entity" and if they are, the number of persons, contracts or accounts involved and the total value of the property	Regulators of the respective financial service bodies[3]
	Transfers in cash or through electronic networks of more than $10,000	Assorted information on the transaction and the transacting entities or persons	FINTRAC[4]
	Where there are reasonable grounds to suspect that a transaction is related to the commission of a terrorist activity financing offence	Assorted information on the transaction and the transacting entities or persons	FINTRAC[5]

[1] *Criminal Code, ibid.,* s. 83.1; *Suppression of Terrorism Regulations, ibid.,* s. 8.
[2] *Proceeds Act,* above note 146, s. 7.1.
[3] *Criminal Code,* above note 80, s. 83.11; *Suppression of Terrorism Regulations,* above note 155, s. 7.
[4] *Proceeds Act,* above note 146, s. 9 and S.O.R./2002-184, as amended, s. 12.
[5] *Proceeds Act, ibid.,* s. 7 and S.O.R./2001-317, as amended.

CHAPTER 12

INTELLIGENCE SHARING

The sharing of information between and within states is among the most sensitive and controversial intelligence issue in the post-9/11 era. It lay at the heart, for example, of the Arar inquiry's key findings. There, the RCMP's ill-considered provision to American authorities of raw information, along with sensationalist commentary on the putative affiliation of Mr. Arar and his wife, Monia Mazigh, with al-Qaeda, was the likely cause of Arar's treatment at the hands of the U.S. authorities, including his ultimate rendition to Syria. Further, as Justice O'Connor underscored repeatedly in his report, "the RCMP provided American authorities with information about Mr. Arar without attaching written caveats, as required by RCMP policy, thereby increasing the risk that the information would be used for purposes of which the RCMP would not approve, such as sending Mr. Arar to Syria."[1]

Although critical of the performance of the RCMP on the specifics of the Arar case, Justice O'Connor nevertheless underscored the importance of international information sharing to national security.[2] Indeed, as a matter of international law, information sharing of some sort is probably mandatory in the area of anti-terrorism.

---

1   Commission of Inquiry into the Actions of Canadian Officials in Relation to Maher Arar, *Report of the Events Relating to Maher Arar: Analysis and Recommendations* (Ottawa: Public Works and Government Services Canada, 2006) at 13 [Arar inquiry, Factual Report].

2   *Ibid.* at 22.

Canadian government information sharing is subject to the *Privacy Act*[3] and its standards discussed in Chapter 11. The exceptions to the limits on disclosure found in this statute are, however, quite extensive and leave ample room for information to migrate within and among governments. This chapter reviews other rules that might govern *Privacy Act*–compliant intelligence sharing at both the international and domestic level. It examines, first, information sharing between states and then information sharing within Canada.

PART I: INFORMATION SHARING AMONG STATES

Intelligence sharing among allied states is a regular practice, one that has accelerated in the post-9/11 environment. This information exchange is influenced by both multilateral and bilateral international instruments. Among other things, these include U.N. Security Council resolutions and intelligence-sharing agreements.

A. U.N. SECURITY COUNCIL RESOLUTIONS

Pre-9/11 U.N. Security Council resolutions, such as Resolution 1269 (1999), "called upon" states to "exchange information in accordance with international and domestic law, and cooperate on administrative and judicial matters in order to prevent the commission of terrorist acts." After 9/11, this hortatory language gave way to binding legal dictates. Thus, in resolution 1373, the council decided that all states must, *inter alia*, "take the necessary steps to prevent the commission of terrorist acts, including by provision of early warning to other States by exchange of information ... [and] afford one another the greatest measure of assistance in connection with criminal investigations or criminal proceedings relating to the financing or support of terrorist acts, including assistance in obtaining evidence in their possession necessary for the proceedings." As a result, information sharing is now a mandatory counterterrorism obligation.

---

3   R.S.C., 1985, c. P-21.

B. INTELLIGENCE-SHARING AGREEMENTS

Similar mutual legal assistance language is found in some anti-terrorism treaties,[4] and in more generic mutual legal assistance treaties.[5] In addition, states have entered into a number of specific intelligence-sharing arrangements.

1) Overview

The "security of information" (SOI) agreements of the North Atlantic Treaty Alliance (NATO) discussed later in this chapter illustrate the latter type of instrument. Canada also has a number of bilateral intelligence-sharing arrangements with key allies, including the United States. For example, the 2002 Canada–U.S. Security Cooperation Agreement established a "binational" defence planning group within NORAD. It specified that in the workings of this body, "both Governments shall exchange and provide access to this classified military information, technology, and material to the maximum extent possible in accordance with national laws, policies and directives, including the 1962 General Security and Information Agreement" (CANUS agreement). This 1962 CANUS agreement was released in 2002 under the *Access to Information Act*[6] and is described further below.

Other bilateral intelligence and/or cooperation agreements between Canadian and foreign intelligence agencies are commonplace. Under the *Proceeds of Crime (Money Laundering) and Terrorist Financing Act*, the minister of public safety and FINTRAC itself may establish agreements with foreign governments or international agencies with mandates similar to that of the centre. These arrangements concern the exchange of information relating to the investigation or prosecution of, among others, terrorist activity–financing offences.[7] These agreements must restrict use of the information to this purpose, and further specify that the shared

---

4   See, for example, *International Convention for the Suppression of the Financing of Terrorism*, U.N. Doc. A/RES/54/109 (2000), Art. 18(3).

5   As of 2001, Canada had twenty-seven bilateral mutual legal assistance treaties that, among other things, "cover legal cooperation on terrorism-related offences." Canada, *Report of the Government of Canada to the Counter-Terrorism Committee of the United Nations Security Council on Measures taken to implement Resolution 1373* (2001), online: www.dfait-maeci.gc.ca/trade/resolution_1373_dec14-en.asp.

6   R.S.C. 1985, c. A-1 [Access Act].

7   *Proceeds of Crime (Money Laundering) and Terrorist Financing Act*, S.C. 2000, c. 17, s. 56 [Proceeds Act].

information is not subject to further disclosure without the consent of the centre.[8] Once an agreement is concluded, the centre may disclose information to the foreign or international agency where the centre has reasonable grounds to suspect the information to be relevant to the investigation or prosecution of a terrorist activity–financing offence.[9]

In a similar fashion, paragraph 17(1)(b) of the CSIS Act[10] empowers CSIS to "enter into an arrangement or otherwise cooperate with the government of a foreign state or an institution thereof or an international organization of states or an institution thereof" for the purpose of performing CSIS's functions.[11] CSIS reported in 2006 that by 2004–5 it had "more than 250 relationships with foreign agencies in approximately 140 countries. ... The agreements give the Service access to intelligence that might not otherwise be available to it, and can lead to cross-training, personnel exchanges and joint operations."[12]

Canada, the United Kingdom, the United States, Australia and New Zealand also collaborate in signals intelligence, pursuant to a confidential agreement dating in its original form to 1947.[13] As described by the Communications Security Establishment, "Canada is a substantial beneficiary of the collaborative effort within [this] partnership to collect and report on foreign communications." This collaboration—well publicized as the so-called ECHELON network—drew scrutiny from the European Parliament in 2001, which described it as a "global system for intercepting communications."[14]

---

8   *Ibid.*, s. 56.
9   *Ibid.*, s. 56.1.
10   *Canadian Security Intelligence Service Act*, R.S.C. 1985, c. C-23 [CSIS Act].
11   A 2003 ministerial direction governing RCMP foreign intelligence and security cooperation practices specifies that CSIS is the lead agency in liaising with these foreign entities. For this reason, the "RCMP will inform CSIS of any and all exchanges between the RCMP and a foreign security or intelligence service, unless the foreign party precludes such notification." Minister of Public Safety and Emergency Preparedness [PSEP], Ministerial Direction, *National Security Related Arrangements and Cooperation* (2003) at para. E.
12   Canada, CSIS, *2004–2005 Annual Public Report* at 14, online: www.csis-scrs. gc.ca/en/publications/annual_report/2004/report2004.asp.
13   Library of Parliament, *The Communications Security Establishment: Canada's Most Secret Intelligence Agency*, BP-343E (1993), online: www.parl.gc.ca/information/library/PRBpubs/bp343-e.htm.
14   European Parliament, *Report on the Existence of a Global System for the Interception of Private and Commercial Communications (ECHELON Interception System)* (2001/2098(INI)), A5-0264/2001 (11 July 2001) at 133, online: www.europarl. europa.eu/sides/getDoc.do?pubRef=-//EP//NONSGML+REPORT+A5-2001-0264+0+DOC+PDF+V0//EN.

Meanwhile Canadian and U.S. customs agencies collaborate to share airline passenger information that raises security concerns, and terrorist-related "lookouts" and "watch lists."[15]

2) Core Principles

Intelligence-sharing agreements are often themselves secret. Alasdair Roberts has, however, reconstructed the attributes of the NATO arrangements.[16] Two main features are a "need to know" approach to information distribution and a policy of "originator control."

a) Need to Know

Under need to know, "individuals should have access to classified information only when they need the information for their work, and access should never be authorized 'merely because a person occupies a particular position, however senior.'"[17]

b) Originator Control

"Originator control," meanwhile, puts control over the use and distribution of the information in the hands of the state from which it comes. A 1950 NATO information policy instrument reads, for instance:

> The parties to the North Atlantic Treaty ... will make every effort to ensure that they will maintain the security classifications established by any party with respect to the information of that party's origin; will safeguard accordingly such information; ... and will not disclose such information to another nation without the consent of the originator.[18]

---

15   Commission of Inquiry into the Actions of Canadian Officials in Relation to Maher Arar, *A New Review Mechanism for the RCMP's National Security Activities* (2006) at 161, online: www.ararcommission.ca/eng/EnglishReportDec122006. pdf [Arar inquiry, Policy Report]. Exactly what sort of watch information is exchanged is somewhat unclear. The Canada Border Services Agency, for example, claims that it does not use the U.S. Automated Targeting System, an expansive traveller and cargo database. Don Butler, "Border Agency Denies Using U.S. Terror Screening Program" *Ottawa Citizen* (21 December 2006) A1.

16   Alasdair Roberts, "Entangling Alliances: NATO's Security Policy and the Entrenchment of State Secrecy" (2003) 36 Cornell Int'l L.J. 329 [Roberts, "Entangling Alliances"].

17   *Ibid.* at 337, citing NATO Security Committee, *A Short Guide to the Handling of Classified Information* (Brussels: NATO Archives, 22 August 1958), document AC/35-WP/14: 4.

18   NATO, Security System for the North Atlantic Treaty Organization (Brussels: NATO Archives, 1 December 1949), document DC 2/1: 4. Reprinted in Roberts, "Entangling Alliances," above note 16 at 338.

Other agreements include similar originator control and so-called third-party provisions. Among other things, the 1962 CANUS instrument provides that the parties will: "not release the information to a third Government without the approval of the release Government"; "undertake to afford the information substantially the same degree of protection afforded it by the release Government"; and "will not use the information for other than the purposes given."

A 1996 Canada–Australia agreement on sharing of "defence-related" information provides that "the receiving Party shall not permit Transmitted Information to be used for any purpose other than that for which it is provided without the prior written consent of the originating Party" and that "the receiving Party shall not disclose, release or provide access to Transmitted Information, or anything incorporating Transmitted Information, to any third party, including any third country government, any national of a third country, or any contractor, organization or other entity other than the Parties, without the prior written consent of the originating Party or unless such disclosure, release or access is otherwise in accordance with the provisions of another agreement or arrangement between the Parties."[19]

Analogous provisions are likely commonplace in other international information-sharing agreements. CSIS told a Federal Court in 1996 that the information it receives is "invariably provided in confidence and on the explicit or implicit understanding that neither the information nor its source will be disclosed without the prior consent of the entity which provided it."[20] This principle is "widely recognized within the policing and security intelligence communities,"[21] an observation confirmed by RCMP, DND and Foreign Affairs submissions in the same case.

Originator control may be exercised through the use of "caveats." As described by the Arar inquiry, caveats are "written restrictions on the use and further dissemination of shared information."[22] For instance, the RCMP's standard caveats for classified information during the period of the Arar inquiry read:

---

19 *Agreement between the Government of Australia and the Government of Canada Concerning the Protection of Defence Related Information Exchanged between Them* (October 1996), A.T.S. 1996 No. 16.

20 Affidavit of Ms. Margaret Ann Purdy (then Director General of the Counter Terrorism Branch) (31 October 1994), cited in *Ruby v. Canada (Solicitor General)*, [1996] 3 F.C. 134 at para. 24 (T.D.) [*Ruby*].

21 *Ibid.* (court summary of affidavit).

22 Arar inquiry, Factual Report, above note 1 at 49, n2.

This document is the property of the RCMP. It is loaned to your agency/department in confidence and it is not to be reclassified or further disseminated without the consent of the originator.

This document is the property of the Government of Canada. It is provided on condition that it is for use solely by the intelligence community of the receiving government and that it not be declassified without the express permission of the Government of Canada.[23]

In the Arar inquiry factual report, Justice O'Connor observed:

There is no guarantee that a recipient of information to which a caveat is attached will honour that caveat. The system is based on trust and caveats are not legally enforceable. However, the ability and willingness of agencies to respect caveats and seek consent before using information will affect the willingness of others to provide information in the future—a significant incentive for agencies to respect caveats.[24]

As a middle power with limited foreign intelligence capacities, Canada is particularly inclined to observe caveats on information supplied by foreign intelligence services. CSIS, for example, told the Federal Court in 1996 that "CSIS receives sensitive information, not just because of the third party rule which requires CSIS to treat the information as confidential, but also because there is confidence on the part of information providers that the Canadian government understands the need for confidentiality and has in place practices and procedures to safeguard information."[25] Without this confidence in Canada's ability to restrict disclosure, some allies "may discontinue the alliance or association. Others may continue their alliance, but with a reluctance to be candid."[26] Similar views were expressed in this and other cases[27] by the RCMP, DND and Foreign Affairs. The RCMP—which reports that it receives seventy-five times more information from partner agencies that it provides—implies caveats even when documents do not contain emphatic language on sharing information with third parties.[28]

---

23   *Ibid.* at 340.
24   *Ibid.* at 105–6.
25   *Ruby*, above note 20 at para. 26.
26   *Ibid.* at para. 27.
27   See, for example, *Ribic v. Canada (Attorney General)*, 2003 FCT 10 at para. 10; *Canada (Attorney General) v. Khawaja*, 2007 FC 490 at para. 122 *et seq.* [Khawaja].
28   *Khawaja, ibid.* at para. 127.

3) Impact on Open Government and Open Courts

The net effect of originator control over information sharing may be to greatly limit open government laws. For instance, the 1996 Canada–Australia defence-related information agreement pledges each party to "take all steps legally available to it to keep Transmitted Information free from disclosure under any legislative provision." As discussed in Chapter 10, this obligation is accomplished in Canada, in part, by exempting from access laws information obtained in confidence from foreign governments.[29] This third government confidences provision is mandatory in the Access Act and *Privacy Act*—that is, there is no discretion on the part of Canada to disclose such information without the foreign government's consent.

It is true, however, that government use of this or other national security exemptions under the Access Act and *Privacy Act* is subject to review by the information or privacy commissioner and potentially the Federal Court. For exactly this reason, the Access Act and *Privacy Act* regimes provide for mandatory *in camera*, *ex parte* proceedings; that is, closed-door proceedings in which only the government side is present. In *Ruby*, the government successfully resisted a challenge to these "closed court" rules.[30] One affiant in that case urged that the "existence and operations of our *Access to Information and Privacy Acts* have given rise to concern on the part of some of our intelligence allies about our ability to ensure the protection of information they give us in confidence."[31]

---

29   See Access Act, above note 6, s. 13 (except where permission is received from the foreign government, "a government institution shall refuse to disclose any record requested under this Act that contains information that was obtained in confidence from … the government of a foreign state or an institution thereof"). See *Privacy Act*, above note 3, s. 19 for the equivalent provision exempting disclosure of personal information to the person to whom it relates on the grounds that it was received in confidence from a foreign government.

30   See Chapter 10.

31   *Ruby*, above note 20 at para. 40, citing John M. Fraser, a former member of the Canadian Foreign Service (16 November 1994). In *Ruby*, the issue was whether criminal defence lawyer Clayton Ruby was entitled to access information that may or may not have been collected on him by CSIS. The government claimed that any such information was exempted by the "national security" exemption contained in s. 21 of the *Privacy Act*, above note 3. Mr. Ruby challenged this decision, in part by bringing a constitutional challenge to the *ex parte* (and *in camera*) features of the judicial review procedure under the Act. The Supreme Court, in [2002] 4 S.C.R. 3, ultimately denied Ruby's constitutional challenge, for reasons outlined in Chapter 10.

To further bolster government control over foreign information, the 2001 *Anti-terrorism Act*[32] grafted new provisions onto the Access Act and *Privacy Act* and the *Canada Evidence Act*[33] allowing the government to exempt entirely from the Access Act and *Privacy Act* infrastructure national security information and information obtained in confidence from a foreign government. This step would preclude review under these Acts by the Federal Court and the information and privacy commissioners.[34]

The need to protect information received in confidence from foreign governments has justified closed-court rules in other contexts. For example, the provisions allowing *in camera* and *ex parte* proceedings and limiting disclosure of information in the *Immigration and Refugee Protection Act* security-certificate process are motivated, in part, by the need to keep foreign-provided intelligence secret.[35] CSIS reports, for example, the reasons for nondisclosure of information in IRPA security-certificate proceedings include the need to protect "methods or information communicated in confidence from a foreign agency."[36]

4) Impact on Human Rights and Civil Liberties

International information sharing as practised in the post-9/11 era has five quite pointed implications for human rights and civil liberties: due process; the use of torture intelligence; the use of Canadian origin information; the impact of global intercept capacity in a world in which privacy is regulated nationally; and, the related issue of the migration of private information across international borders.

a) Due Process
First, as the discussion above suggests, international information-sharing arrangements, operationalized through domestic secrecy rules, preclude full access to information by persons subject to criminal or administrative proceedings.

---

32 S.C. 2001, c. 41.
33 R.S.C. 1985, c. C-5 [CEA].
34 For a discussion of these provisions, see Chapter 10 and Craig Forcese, "Clouding Accountability: Canada's Government Secrecy and National Security Law 'Complex'" (2005) 36 Ottawa L. Rev. 49.
35 See *Almrei v. Canada (Minister of Citizenship and Immigration)*, [2005] 3 F.C.R. 142 at para. 75 (C.A.); *Re Charkaoui*, [2004] 3 F.C.R. 32 at paras. 69 *et seq.* (F.C.).
36 CSIS, Backgrounder No. 14, *Certificates under the Immigration and Refugee Protection Act (IRPA)* (2005), online: www.csis-scrs.gc.ca/en/newsroom/backgrounders/backgrounder14.asp. This issue has also arisen in prosecutions in relation to terrorist offences. See *Khawaja*, above note 27 at para. 123 *et seq.*

National security confidentiality in court proceedings is inevitable and, used appropriately, desirable. However, blanket prohibitions on disclosure because of simple foreign provenance gives secrecy law an extended reach in an intelligence-importing country like Canada. It is likely that not every piece of foreign information truly must be held secret because it would jeopardize the security interests of the providing state. At the very least, the government should be obliged to seek permission to disclose from the foreign source in an effort to separate truly sensitive information from more benign data. This is an obligation that probably already exists in the Access Act and *Privacy Act* contexts[37] and has also been invoked by the Federal Court in relation to the *Canada Evidence Act*.[38] In the latter context, the court examines whether "good faith efforts were made and continue to be made to obtain such consent."[39]

Moreover, the government cannot claim "third-party" confidentiality over information that, although obtained from a foreign partner, it has received also by other means. Refusal to disclose this information must instead be grounded in another justification.[40] Nor can third-party confidentiality be used "to protect the mere existence of a relationship between Canada and a foreign state or agency, absent the exchange of information in a given case."[41]

b)   Torture Intelligence

Second, information provided by foreign government may be suspect on human rights grounds. Security service rules attempt to grapple with this problem. The 2003 ministerial direction governing RCMP foreign intelligence and security cooperation practices specifies that these arrangements "may be established and maintained as long as they remain compatible with Canada's foreign policy," including consideration of the foreign entity's "respect for democratic or human rights."[42]

Likewise, in entering into a paragraph 17(1)(b) cooperation arrangement, CSIS apparently completes a review of the foreign agency's

---

37   See *Cemerlic v. Canada (Solicitor General)*, 2003 FCT 133 at paras. 18 *et seq.* (discussing s. 19 of the *Privacy Act*).

38   *Khawaja*, above note 27 at para. 146 ("it is not open to the Attorney General to merely claim that information cannot be disclosed pursuant to the third party rule, if a request for disclosure in some form has not in fact been made to the original foreign source").

39   *Ibid.* at para. 152.

40   *Ibid.* at para. 147; *Ottawa Citizen Group Inc. v. Canada (Attorney General)*, 2006 FC 1552 at para. 66.

41   *Khawaja, ibid.* at para. 148.

42   Canada, Minister of PSEP, Ministerial Direction, *National Security Related Arrangements and Cooperation*, above note 11 at para. D.

human rights record in assessing potential new foreign arrangements. Further, according to the Service's documents, "if there are allegations of human rights abuses, the Service always ensures to use a cautious approach when liaising with the foreign agency and closely scrutinizes the content of the information provided to, or obtained from, the foreign agency" either "in an effort to *avoid instances* where the security intelligence information exchanged with the latter is used in the commission of acts which would be regarded as human rights violations" or "to *ensure* none of the security intelligence information exchanged with the latter is used in the commission of acts which would be regarded as human rights violations."[43]

However, CSIS's review body, the Security Intelligence Review Committee, reported in its 2004–2005 annual report that at least one of the CSIS foreign arrangements that it audited "did not provide an adequate analysis of potential human rights issues."[44] Further, it objected to CSIS's claim that it "ensures" that information exchanged is not the cause or product of human rights abuses:

> the use of the term "ensure" implies that CSIS will make certain that the information shared does not lead to—or result from—acts that could be regarded as human rights violations. However, the Committee concluded that CSIS was not in a position to provide such an absolute assurance. ... Second, while CSIS is cautious when sharing information with foreign agencies, it cannot determine in all cases how that information is used by the recipient agency. Similarly, the Service is rarely in a position to determine how information received from a foreign agency was obtained. As [former CSIS director] Mr. Elcock stated to the [Arar] Commission, when it comes to information that may have been the product of torture, 'the reality is in most cases we would have no knowledge that it was derived from torture. You may suspect that it was derived from torture, but that is about as far as one will get in most circumstances.'[45]

As discussed at length in Chapter 15, torture is among the gravest of human rights abuses. How information extracted via torture is used must, therefore, be closely regulated. One view is that any reliance — formal or informal — on intelligence produced by torture is tacit complicity in the torturing act. It is probably unrealistic, however, to

43 These documents are found as CNSLArchives Doc. #05-01, online: www.nationalsecuritylaw.ca [emphasis added].
44 Canada, SIRC, *Annual Report 2004–2005* (Ottawa: Public Works and Government Services Canada, 2005).
45 *Ibid.*

expect that a Canadian security and intelligence agency would ignore completely urgent information—for example, warning of an imminent bombing—even if provided by a torturing foreign intelligence service. At the very least, they would be expected to investigate the allegation.

There is, however, an outer limit on the use to which the information should be put. Without question, information produced by torture is inadmissible in a Canadian court proceeding.[46] More generally, governments should not rely on information obtained via torture or cruel, inhuman or degrading (CID) treatment to deprive an individual of their liberty, remove or render a person to a foreign state or designate a person a security threat or person of interest.[47]

These limits are essential for at least two reasons. First, such actions would compound a violation of one right with a limitation on another and thus should be impermissible as a matter of principle. Second, information produced via coercion is notoriously unreliable, a matter discussed in Chapter 15.

The Arar inquiry's findings affirm these observations. Justice O'Connor criticized CSIS, for example, for failing to assess the reliability of information provided by Syrian authorities extracted from Mr. Arar, and for failing to warn other agencies when distributing that information that it could have been produced by torture. CSIS relied on this information at least twice, to Mr. Arar's detriment.[48] Similar criticisms were directed at Foreign Affairs and the RCMP,[49] sparking Justice O'Connor's recommendation that "Canadian agencies should accept information from countries with questionable human rights records only after proper consideration of human rights implications. Information received from countries with questionable human rights records should be identified as such and proper steps should be taken to assess its reliability."[50] Consistent with these views, the Federal Court has concluded in *Immigration and Refugee Protection Act* security-certificate cases that the government makes a reviewable error if it fails to properly weigh evidence to determine whether it was the product of torture.[51]

---

46   See, for example, *Criminal Code*, R.S.C. 1985, c. C-46, s. 269.1(4).

47   This is the position taken in the *Ottawa Principles on Human Rights and Anti-terrorism*, Principle 4.3.2, online: http://aix1.uottawa.ca/~cforcese/hrat/principles.pdf.

48   Arar inquiry, Factual Report, above note 1 at 198.

49   *Ibid.* at 34.

50   *Ibid.* at 348.

51   *Mahjoub v. Canada*, 2006 FC 1503 at para. 36 *et seq.*

c) Constraints on Use of Canadian-origin Information

The Arar inquiry pointed, however, to another troubling aspect of information sharing, as practised in the immediate post-9/11 environment: the inability to control information supplied by the Canadian government once shared with a foreign agency. In the Arar case, the RCMP failed to abide by its own policy by not attaching caveats to the information provided to American authorities. Justice O'Connor underscored the importance of this limitation:

> The RCMP should never share information in a national security investigation without attaching written caveats in accordance with existing policy. The RCMP should review existing caveats to ensure that each precisely states which institutions are entitled to have access to the information subject to the caveat and what use the institution may make of that information. Caveats should also generally set out an efficient procedure for recipients to seek any changes to the permitted distribution and use of the information.[52]

Caveats, however, are effective only where foreign agencies choose to abide by them. As noted above, they may do so out of self-interest, fearing that a failure to honour these conditions will stall future information sharing. It seems unlikely, however, that tacit information sharing in violation of caveats would be detected by a country with limited foreign intelligence capacities, such as Canada. Further, information is inherently fungible, and can seep into decision making in ways that can never be traced. Caveats are not, in other words, a guarantor that information will be used properly.

In these circumstances, Canadian authorities may have to be circumspect in how they share information with problematic foreign agencies. The Arar inquiry addressed this issue in part:

> The RCMP should ensure that, whenever it provides information to other departments and agencies, whether foreign and domestic, it does so in accordance with clearly established policies respecting screening for relevance, reliability and accuracy and with relevant laws [for example, the *Privacy Act*] respecting personal information and human rights.[53]

There may be instances, however, where even reliable information otherwise disclosable under the *Privacy Act* should not be shared. The government, for instance, may have to withhold reliable information concerning the terrorist affiliations of a suspect in foreign custody if

---

52   Arar inquiry, Factual Report, above note 1 at 339.
53   *Ibid.* at 334.

disclosure is likely to induce torture or other human rights abuses. In 2006, the Security and Intelligence Review Committee (SIRC) expressed concern that "even though CSIS was fully compliant in providing certain information to a foreign agency, this could have contributed to that agency's decision to detain a Canadian citizen (who was also a CSIS target) upon arrival in that foreign country."[54] It also expressed concern "that questions submitted by CSIS to this agency via a third party may have been used in interrogating a Canadian citizen in a manner that violated his human rights."[55]

While not identified by SIRC, the person in question was almost certainly Maher Arar. SIRC recommended that CSIS "amend its policy governing the disclosure of information to foreign agencies, to include consideration of the human rights record of the country and possible abuses by its security or intelligence agencies" and that it "review its procedures so that the parameters and methods of exchange—as well as the Service's expectations—are communicated to the foreign agency prior to entering into new foreign arrangements."[56]

In the Arar Inquiry itself, Justice O'Connor called on the RCMP and CSIS to

> review their policies governing the circumstances in which they supply information to foreign governments with questionable human rights records. Information should never be provided to a foreign country where there is a credible risk that it will cause or contribute to the use of torture. Policies should include specific directions aimed at eliminating any possible Canadian complicity in torture, avoiding the risk of other human rights abuses and ensuring accountability.[57]

Put another way, there may be an outer limit on Canada's obligations to cooperate in anti-terrorism investigations tied to human rights principles. In Justice O'Connor's words, "the need to investigate terrorism and the need to comply with international conventions relating to terrorism do not in themselves justify the violation of human rights."[58]

d) Intelligence Sharing, Technology Change and Patchwork Laws

The Arar inquiry reported that Canada's primary signals intelligence entity—the CSE—does not normally share information with its

---

54   Canada, SIRC, *Annual Report, 2005–2006* (Ottawa: Public Works and Government Services Canada, 2006) at 13.
55   *Ibid.*
56   *Ibid.* at 14.
57   Arar inquiry, Factual Report, above note 1 at 345.
58   *Ibid.* at 346.

international partner agencies that relates to the interception of private communications—that is, communications with a Canadian nexus—"although it may provide relevant intercepted information relating to national or alliance security." Even then, "the CSE does not disclose identifying information it may have collected on a Canadian citizen except in response to a formal request, after consultations with relevant Canadian security and intelligence partners, and provided that the request meets CSE criteria."[59] CSE does not, in other words, spy on Canadians for allied services.

However, in 1999, a former CSE employee made well-publicized accusations that ECHELON—the name popularly used to describe the signals intelligence collaboration between Canada, the United Kingdom, the United States, Australia and New Zealand—was being used to circumvent the privacy laws of each country. Since privacy laws tend to restrict states' ability to monitor their own citizens but not those located in other countries, each state's agency allegedly was asked to spy on the other state's citizens[60] and, presumably, share the results.[61]

These accusations have been firmly rejected by the CSE[62] and there is no evidence of which this author is aware that Canadian intelligence agencies actively collaborate to circumvent Canadian privacy laws. Presumably, such behaviour would be detected by CSE or CSIS oversight and review mechanisms.

i)   Information Sharing of Canadian Intercepts

It seems certain, however, that information on Canadians captured by foreign intelligence services in the course of their regular functions is provided to Canada under information-sharing agreements. That is likely one of the very purposes of these agreements. It is also possible that foreign intelligence services draw (and then share) intelligence from communications that occur *entirely* in Canada. Changes in technology and recent policy developments in the United States may increase the likelihood of this situation arising.

---

59   *Ibid.* at 147.

60   See "Ottawa Snoops on Canadians, Says Ex-spy; Bypasses Law by Letting Allies Track Communication" *Toronto Star* (19 June 1999) 1.

61   See allegations made by Canadian Association of University Professors (CAUT), *Submission to the House of Commons, Subcommittee on Public Safety and National Security Regarding the Review of the* Anti-terrorism Act (Feb. 2005), online: www.caut.ca/en/publications/briefs/2005anti_terrorism_brief.pdf.

62   See James Gordon, "Canadians Assured Over Phone Tapping: Spy Agency Denies U.S.-style Domestic Tracking System" *Calgary Herald* (13 May 2006) A.15.

As noted in Chapter 11, since soon after 9/11, the NSA has "intercept[ed] certain international communications into and out of the United States of people linked to al Qaeda or an affiliated terrorist organization."[63] It has done so without warrant, pursuant to a presidential executive order issued under the president's constitutional authority as "commander-in-chief." This power, claims the administration, trumps or limits competing statutory restrictions that would otherwise require warrants for these electronic intercepts.[64]

The Bush Administration has been assailed by critics of this reasoning and opponents of the NSA program, and indeed a U.S. federal court ruled the practice unconstitutional in 2006.[65] At heart, the controversy in the United States stemmed from the fact that at least one participant in these surveilled conversations is in the United States—and potentially a United States citizen. In early 2007, the Bush Administration announced that future intercepts would be authorized under the regular law; that is, by the special Foreign Intelligence Surveillance Court under an amended *Foreign Intelligence Surveillance Act* (FISA).[66]

To date, surveillance of communications between *non*-U.S. locales has not sparked similar unease. Such eavesdropping is, after all, what the NSA does in the regular course of its affairs. Nevertheless, journalistic reports on the domestic intercept program have pointed to the new scope of this "foreign" spying: much communication between non-U.S. locales is now routed *through* the United States,[67] to the point that it is sometimes difficult to distinguish between U.S. and international-based communications.[68] The U.S. government has, in fact, encouraged telecommunications firms to route communications through the United States as a means of facilitating NSA intercepts.[69]

---

63   U.S. Department of Justice, Letter to Members of Congress (22 December 2005) at 1, online: www.epic.org/privacy/nsa/olc_release1.pdf.

64   *Ibid.* See also Letter from Attorney General Alberto Gonzales to Senator William Frist (19 January 2006), online: www.epic.org/privacy/nsa/oip_release1.pdf.

65   See *ACLU v. Nat'l Sec. Agency*, 438 F. Supp. 2d 754 (E.D. Mich. 2006).

66   50 U.S.C 1801 *et seq.* See Associated Press, "Foreign Intelligence Court to Oversee Domestic Spying Program" *U.S.A. Today* (17 January 2007).

67   Philip Bobbitt (former National Security Council senior director), "Why We Listen" *New York Times* (30 January 2006) 23 ("[o]wing to globalization of telecommunications, many telephone calls between parties in foreign countries or with an American at one end are routed through American networks. By analyzing this traffic, the National Security Agency has been gathering clues to possible terrorist activities").

68   James Risen & Eric Lichtblau, "Spying Program Snared U.S. Calls" *New York Times* (21 December 2005) 1.

69   Eric Lichtblau & James Risen, "Spy Agency Mined Vast Data Trove, Officials Report" *New York Times* (24 December 2005) 1 ("[o]ne outside expert on com-

Some American officials have taken the view that under U.S. law, eavesdropping of foreign calls transiting through the United States must be authorized by a FISA warrant.[70] It is not clear if that is the dominant view.[71] There is every reason to presume, therefore, that the NSA has engaged (and possibly will continue to engage) in warrantless surveillance of transiting foreign communications.

Canadian communications may be acutely vulnerable to this intercept. The Canadian–U.S. telecommunications system is integrated. At present, a purely domestic Canadian call may be routed through U.S. systems, depending on traffic loads. Overseas Canadian calls are almost certainly passing through the United States.[72] Internet-based communication—whether written or voice—may be conducted via servers physically located in the United States. While following this path along the switches of cooperative U.S. telecommunications firms or Internet providers, it could be subject to intercept by the NSA.

There is then a possibility that this information is subsequently put into circulation in Canada itself. In preparing this book, access to information requests addressing the question of information sharing of NSA intercepts were filed with the Privy Council Office, the Department of National Defence and with the Canadian Security Intelligence Service. The Department of National Defence replied that it had no such records, as did the Privy Council Office. In a standard response to questions concerning intelligence techniques, CSIS was unwilling to either confirm or deny that such documents existed. However, CSIS did respond to a subsequent letter on this issue via a telephone conversation in April 2006.

CSIS will not discuss the specifics of its intelligence-gathering methods, and the precise nature of its intelligence-sharing arrangements. The April 2006 conversation was therefore phrased in usually hypothetical terms. It is clear from that conversation that it would be inappropriate for CSIS to ask the U.S. agencies to intercept Canadian

---

munications privacy who previously worked at the NSA said that to exploit its technological capabilities, the American government had in the last few years been quietly encouraging the telecommunications industry to increase the amount of international traffic that is routed through American-based switches").

70   Ibid. ("[n]ow that foreign calls were being routed through switches on American soil, some judges and law enforcement officials regarded eavesdropping on those calls as a possible violation of those decades-old restrictions, including the Foreign Intelligence Surveillance Act, which requires court-approved warrants for domestic surveillance").

71   The FISA seems to impose an authorization requirement only on electronic surveillance sent or received in the United States, implicitly excluding transiting communications. See 50 U.S.C § 1801(f).

72   Information drawn from personal conversations with telecommunications experts.

communications; that is, CSIS would act inappropriately were it to ask the U.S. government to intercept a particular Canadian communication as it passed through the United States, in some effort to circumvent Canadian lawful access laws. Such behaviour would draw the attention, and likely ire, of CSIS's review institutions, the inspector-general and the Security Intelligence Review Committee.

However, it is also fair to posit that CSIS *does* or at least *could* receive intelligence from the U.S. government processed from transiting Canadian communications. This would not occur through design, but rather through happenstance; that is, through the ongoing process of exchange of intelligence between allied agencies. This is intelligence the sharing service obtained through means it views as legitimate. It would be surprising if the U.S. government would withhold information material to Canadian security discovered through its surveillance. It would be even more surprising—and indeed troubling—if CSIS were to ignore this information.

ii) Regulating this Practice

Whether and how privacy and lawful access laws might be adjusted to regulate this information sharing is unclear. Changes in technology—not least Internet phone calls—will likely increase the amount of Canadian communication subject to intercept by foreign intelligence agencies. And as result, not of design but of happenstance, the evolution of technology will increase the amount of information CSIS or other agencies receive about Canadian communications that is not subjected to conventional lawful access controls in the CSIS Act or elsewhere. For this reason, if left unregulated, the scope of communications subject to capture and then sharing by a foreign agency may expand to the point that Canadian lawful access and privacy laws become moot.

This is not to say that Canadian law would be indifferent to this practice. Supreme Court jurisprudence, for instance, suggests that information-sharing arrangements between administrative and law enforcement bodies cannot be employed to circumvent constitutional protections that require the police to obtain warrants.[73] By analogy, it seems implausible that international information-sharing agreements involving sharing of communication originating in Canada, but collected by foreign agencies, can be used to vitiate Canadian privacy requirements.

On the other hand, it is difficult to imagine a lawful access regime that could effectively govern these practices. Canadian lawful access law will not apply to regulate the actions of the foreign

---

73   R. v. *Colarusso*, [1994] 1 S.C.R. 20 at para. 93. See discussion in Chapter 11.

agency.[74] Nor in the current environment does it seem likely the United States and other allied states could be persuaded by agreement or otherwise to seek Canadian authorization to intercept transiting communications. Put another way, transiting communications will remain especially vulnerable to foreign intercept.

Once the foreign agency processes its intercepts and discerns in them matters of importance to Canadian national security, imposing a system of judicial approval on Canadian receipt of that information would be a largely meaningless, *pro forma* action. A judge is unlikely to bar a Canadian agency from relying on information with already established, demonstrable relevance to Canadian national security.

The best that might be expected is a statutory amendment expressly prohibiting any active or tacit policy among Canadian agencies encouraging foreign intercepts of intra-Canadian communications. The onus will ultimately lie on Canadian review and oversight bodies to make sure that this standard is honoured.

e)   Intelligence Sharing, Compelled Disclosure and Transnational Businesses

A related issue concerns the transfer by private enterprises of personal information (as opposed to communications) across borders. Much Canadian information, for instance, is in the possession of U.S. companies or their Canadian subsidiaries and thus is amenable to search by U.S. authorities under the *U.S.A. PATRIOT Act*. That statute expanded the capacity of the FBI to compel disclosure of "any tangible things (including books, records, papers, documents, and other items) for an investigation to obtain foreign intelligence information not concerning a United States person or to protect against international terrorism or clandestine intelligence activities."[75]

In 2004, the BC privacy commissioner warned that these powers lowered the threshold for compelling information, and allowed U.S. authorities to extract information in circumstances where Canadian authorities—governed by the typical warrant-obtaining standard of reasonable cause—could not do the same.[76] Information on Canadians in the possession of companies based in the United States—a regu-

---

74   See, by analogy, *R. v. Terry*, [1996] 2 S.C.R. 207 at para. 18 ("The practice of cooperation between police of different countries does not make the law of one country applicable in the other country").

75   50 U.S.C § 1861.

76   Information & Privacy Commissioner for British Columbia, *Privacy and the USA Patriot Act* (2004) at 70, online: www.oipc.bc.ca/sector_public/archives/usa_patriot_act/pdfs/report/privacy-final.pdf [USA Patriot Act].

lar occurrence in the integrated U.S./Canadian economy—would be
amenable to seizure under the *U.S.A. PATRIOT Act* provisions.[77] This
prospect has prompted Canada's privacy commissioner to urge the
government to adopt guidelines minimizing transborder private information flows by federal contractors.[78] The federal government was developing a strategy in this area in 2006.[79]

A secondary issue is whether Canadian-origin information that
is obtained by foreign authorities may then be shared under information-sharing agreements with Canadian officials, independently of any
strictures imposed by Canadian privacy laws. In 2004, the BC privacy
commissioner concluded that there was no legal barrier on CSIS, for
example, receiving information on Canadians provided by U.S. authorities employing U.S. enhanced disclosure powers.[80] As noted, however,
information sharing arrangements between administrative and law
enforcement bodies cannot be employed to circumvent constitutional
protections that require the police to obtain warrants. Likewise, inter-

---

77   See also *British Columbia Government and Services Employees' Union v. British
      Columbia (Minister of Health Services)*, 2005 BCSC 446 at para. 59 *et seq.* (con-
      cluding on the basis of expert evidence that the *U.S.A. PATRIOT Act* could reach
      information held by a U.S. subsidiary in Canada). This issue has also been con-
      troversial in Europe, where a European Union body has criticized the Society
      for Worldwide Interbank Financial Telecommunications, or SWIFT, for sharing
      data on financial transactions with U.S. intelligence and law enforcement
      authorities. See EU, Article 29 Working Party, *Press Release on the SWIFT Case
      following the adoption of the Article 29 Working Party opinion on the processing of
      personal data by the Society for Worldwide Interbank Financial Telecommunication*
      (23 November 2006), online: http://ec.europa.eu/justice_home/fsj/privacy/news/
      docs/PR_Swift_Affair_23_11_06_en.pdf; Dan Bilefsk, "European Union Panel
      Says Banks Broke Law by Giving Data to U.S." *New York Times* (22 November
      2006). By the time of this writing, the Canadian privacy commissioner had also
      launched an investigation into SWIFT. Canada, Privacy Commissioner, *News
      Release: Privacy Commissioner launches investigation of SWIFT* (14 August 2006),
      online: www.privcom.gc.ca/media/nr-c/2006/nr-c_060814_e.asp.
78   Canada, Privacy Commissioner, *Annual Report to Parliament 2005–2006*, online:
      www.privcom.gc.ca/information/ar/200506/200506_pa_e.asp.
79   Treasury Board, *Privacy Matters: The Federal Strategy to Address Concerns About
      the U.S.A PATRIOT Act and Transborder Data Flows* (March 2006), online: www.
      tbs-sct.gc.ca/pubs_pol/gospubs/TBM_128/pm-prp/pm-prp_e.asp. See also
      recommendation of the Special Senate Committee on the *Anti-terrorism Act,
      Fundamental Justice in Extraordinary Times* (February 2007) at 91, online: www.
      parl.gc.ca/39/1/parlbus/commbus/senate/Com-e/anti-e/rep-e/rep02feb07-e.htm
      (calling on the federal government to "protect personal information provided
      under outsourcing contracts to external entities").
80   Information & Privacy Commissioner for British Columbia, *Privacy and the
      USA Patriot Act*, above note 76 at 77.

national information-sharing agreements involving data originating in Canada should not annul Canadian privacy requirements. That said, as with shared communication intercepts, effective regulation of this practice might prove difficult.

PART II: INFORMATION SHARING WITHIN GOVERNMENT

Information sharing failures *between* U.S. government agencies was one of the major preoccupations of the U.S. 9/11 Commission. That body noted the impact of legislative "walls"—as exaggerated by administrative interpretations—sealing off information held by U.S. agencies from one another. It also critiqued the "need-to-know" doctrine that animated national information sharing in the pre-9/11 era. In the commission's words, this approach "assumes that it is possible to know, in advance, who will need to use the information. Such a system implicitly assumes that the risk of inadvertent disclosure outweighs the benefits of wider sharing. Those Cold War assumptions are no longer appropriate."[81] The *U.S.A. PATRIOT Act*[82] dismantled many of these impediments,[83] although efficient information sharing within U.S. governments and agencies reportedly remains a problem.[84]

Information sharing within Canada, between Canadian agencies, is closely regulated by law, but was never as strictly controlled as in the United States.[85] The strictures found in the *Charter* and the *Privacy*

---

81   9/11 Commission, *The 9/11 Commission Report* (New York: W.W. Norton & Co., 2004) at 417.
82   Pub. L. 107-56, 115 Stat. 272, 278-81 (2001).
83   U.S. Department of Justice, *Fact Sheet: Attorney General's Guidelines for Information Sharing* (23 September 2002), online: www.fas.org/irp/agency/doj/fs092302. html.
84   Elizabeth Williamson, "Group Attempting to Simplify Byzantine Terror-Alert System" *Washington Post* (24 January 2007) A21.
85   It is true, however, that some Canadian agencies—such as the Canadian Air Transport Security Authority—complain that they do not have adequate access to the security intelligence required to perform their functions. See Auditor General of Canada, *Canadian Air Transport Security Authority: Special Examination Report* (December 2006) at 13, online: www.catsa-acsta.gc.ca/english/ about_propos/rep_rap/oag_bvg/CATSA%20Spec_Exam_E.pdf; CATSA Advisory Panel, *Flight Plan: Managing the Risks in Aviation Security* (2006), online: www. tc.gc.ca/tcss/CATSA/Final_Report-Rapport_final/chapter1_e.htm. It also seems likely that the Air India inquiry, in progress at the time of this writing, will discuss problems in RCMP and CSIS information-sharing practices.

Act on nonauthorized disclosure of personal information are described in Chapter 11. As noted, those rules, and their exceptions, apply to all government information sharing, international and domestic.

This section discusses briefly more specific rules governing information sharing within the Canadian security and intelligence, law enforcement and defence communities.

A. INFORMATION SHARING BY SECURITY INTELLIGENCE AGENCIES

1) CSIS

CSIS has broad domestic information-sharing powers. First, CSIS is empowered under the CSIS Act to "assist the Minister of National Defence or the Minister of Foreign Affairs, within Canada, in the collection of information or intelligence relating to the capabilities, intentions or activities of" foreign states and persons, "in relation to the defence of Canada or the conduct of the international affairs of Canada."[86] The information-sharing implications of collecting information for another department are obvious.[87]

Second, section 17 of the CSIS Act provides that, for the purpose of performing its duties and functions, CSIS may enter into cooperation agreements with "any department of the Government of Canada or the government of a province ..., or ... any police force in a province, with the approval of the Minister responsible for policing in the province"[88] By early 2006, CSIS had "29 Memoranda of Understanding in place with domestic partners so that information could be exchanged."[89] Seventeen of these agreements were with federal departments or agencies, and ten were with provincial and municipal entities, such as governments, agencies and police forces. For example, the CSIS/RCMP memorandum of understanding obliges CSIS to disclose information to the RCMP that might assist the Force in fulfilling its responsibilities. However, it need not provide information that would betray an informant's identity or which is subject to a caveat attached by the originator of the information.[90]

---

86 CSIS Act, above note 10, s. 16.
87 Arar inquiry, Policy Report, above note 15 at 149 (noting that the "military usually receives finished intelligence products from CSIS").
88 CSIS Act, above note 10, s. 17.
89 Canada, SIRC, *Annual Report, 2005–2006*, above note 54 at 35.
90 Arar inquiry, Policy Report, above note 15 at 139.

Third, under section 19 of the CSIS Act, CSIS may disclose information obtained in the performance of its duties and functions for the purposes of performing these duties and functions, the administration or enforcement of the CSIS Act or as required by any other law. It may also disclose such information,

(a) where the information may be used in the investigation or prosecution of an alleged contravention of any law of Canada or a province, to a peace officer having jurisdiction to investigate the alleged contravention and to the Attorney General of Canada and the Attorney General of the province in which proceedings in respect of the alleged contravention may be taken;

(b) where the information relates to the conduct of the international affairs of Canada, to the Minister of Foreign Affairs or a person designated by the Minister of Foreign Affairs for the purpose;

(c) where the information is relevant to the defence of Canada, to the Minister of National Defence or a person designated by the Minister of National Defence for the purpose; or

(d) where, in the opinion of the Minister, disclosure of the information to any minister of the Crown or person in the federal public administration is essential in the public interest and that interest clearly outweighs any invasion of privacy that could result from the disclosure, to that minister or person.[91]

When it exercises this section 19 disclosure power, CSIS must submit a report with respect to the disclosure to the Security Intelligence Review Committee.[92] That committee reported in 2005–6 that CSIS made 335 disclosures to law enforcement, 1,340 to Foreign Affairs and 2,357 to National Defence during the year.[93]

CSIS information-sharing rules under both sections 17 and 19 include an express reference to CSIS performing its "duties and functions." Stanley Cohen urges that because of this language, CSIS "cannot and should not become a stalking horse or proxy for law enforcement. CSIS must be conducting *bona fide* investigations and/or performing duties that genuinely form part of its own mandate."[94]

Checks on CSIS's disclosure discretion exist in the form of departmental, inspector-general and SIRC oversight and review of CSIS activity. Notably, SIRC has the power to review cooperation agreements

---

91   CSIS Act, above note 10, s. 19.
92   *Ibid.*, s. 19(3).
93   Canada, SIRC, *Annual Report, 2005–2006*, above note 54 at 33.
94   Stanley A. Cohen, *Privacy, Crime and Terror: Legal Rights and Security in a Time of Peril* (Markham, ON: LexisNexis Butterworths, 2005) at 407.

(both foreign and domestic) entered into by CSIS and to "monitor the provision of information and intelligence pursuant to those arrangements."[95]

2) FINTRAC

As noted in Chapter 11, FINTRAC receives financial information disclosable to it under the *Proceeds of Crime (Money Laundering) and Terrorist Financing Act*.[96] It may also collect information relevant to its functions from publicly available sources such as commercial databases or "that is stored in databases maintained by the federal or provincial governments for purposes related to law enforcement or national security"[97] where the centre has entered into an agreement with the sharing government agency specifying the nature of limits on the information that may be collected from these databases.[98]

The centre is generally precluded from disclosing "designated," nonpublicly available information, but where it has reasonable grounds to believe that this information would be "relevant to investigating or prosecuting ... a terrorist activity financing offence," it must do so to an appropriate police force or, in some circumstances, other law enforcement agencies like the CBSA or, where the information raises matters that lie within its mandate, to the CSE.[99] Meanwhile, designated information the centre believes is relevant to threats to the security of Canada is to be disclosed to CSIS.[100] Designated information includes certain data related to the transaction, as well as personal identifying information.

To obtain further, more detailed information, the attorney general and CSIS may also apply for a court order compelling disclosure of information in the centre's possession relevant to investigating a terrorist activity financing offence or a threat to the security of Canada, respectively.[101]

---

95 CSIS Act, above note 10, s. 38(a)(iii).
96 Above note 7.
97 *Ibid.*, s. 54.
98 *Ibid.*, s. 66.
99 *Ibid.*, s. 55.
100 *Ibid.*, s. 55.1.
101 *Ibid.*, s. 60 *et seq.*

B. INFORMATION SHARING BY DEFENCE AGENCIES

1) CSE

In performing its core function under the *National Defence Act* "to acquire and use information from the global information infrastructure for the purpose of providing foreign intelligence, in accordance with Government of Canada intelligence priorities,"[102] CSE's SIGINT program "produces intelligence in response to Government priorities for several hundred clients at numerous federal departments and agencies."[103] A chief customer is the Department of Foreign Affairs and International Trade, the department charged with maintaining Canada's foreign relations.[104] Further, if CSE acquired intelligence by happenstance in its other activities relevant to the functions of the RCMP or CSIS, that information would be provided to these agencies.[105]

CSE also has more formal law enforcement and CSIS information-sharing arrangements. Pursuant to the *National Defence Act*, the CSE is charged, among other things, with providing "technical and operational assistance to federal law enforcement and security agencies in the performance of their lawful duties."[106] As noted in Chapter 11, these law enforcement assistance practices "are subject to any limitations imposed by law on federal law enforcement and security agencies in the performance of their duties."[107] Pursuant to this function, information sharing between CSE and its partner agencies occurs, and indeed CSE is briefed on the intelligence needs of its partners and may request that its counterpart agencies in allied states gather relevant data.[108]

CSE's intelligence reports are generally "minimized";[109] that is, they withhold the names of Canadian citizens or permanent residents or information identifying citizens of Canada, the U.S., U.K., Australia or

---

102 *National Defence Act*, R.S.C 1985, c. N-5, s. 273.64 [NDA].
103 Communications Security Establishment [CSE], *CSE: An Overview*, online: www.cse-cst.gc.ca/media-room/cse-overview-e.html.
104 Arar inquiry, Policy Report, above note 15 at 145. In 2007, CSE indicated that the agency had established listening posts in Afghanistan to supply intercept intelligence on the Taliban to the Canadian Forces, DFAIT and the Canadian International Development Agency. Stewart Bell, "Canada Listening In on Taliban Exchanges" *National Post* (1 May 2007).
105 Arar inquiry, Policy Report, *ibid.* at 144.
106 NDA, above note 102, s. 273.64.
107 *Ibid.*, s. 273.64(3).
108 Arar inquiry, Policy Report, above note 15 at 145.
109 *Ibid.* at 271.

New Zealand. These identifying data will be disclosed to a domestic agency if justified by the government's intelligence priorities and the mandate of the requesting agency.[110]

2) Defence Intelligence

At the time of this writing, policies were being developed for the exchange of information between Defence Intelligence and civilian security and intelligence agencies and other bodies.[111] The Arar inquiry reported in 2006 that the Canadian Forces/DND Defence Intelligence body will "provide information about general security threats to CSIS, and will provide criminal intelligence information and products to the RCMP," on a "need to know" basis.[112]

C. INFORMATION SHARING BY LAW ENFORCEMENT AGENCIES

1) RCMP

The RCMP shares information with other Canadian agencies in a number of circumstances. For example, the military receives raw information from the RCMP concerning criminal activities by DND or Canadian Forces personnel.[113]

More generally, the Force has more than one thousand memoranda of understanding with agencies on issues such as training and sharing of police technologies and services.[114] These agreements typically exclude national security information. However, under a CSIS–RCMP Memorandum of Understanding, the Force provides CSIS with data relevant to the CSIS mandate.[115] More informal information sharing—including of national security information—frequently occurs at the investigative level.[116]

110　*Ibid.* at 147.
111　*Ibid.* at 150.
112　*Ibid.* at 149, n86.
113　*Ibid.* at 149.
114　*Ibid.* at 112.
115　*Ibid.*
116　*Ibid.* at 113.

2) Canada Border Services Agency

With responsibilities under scores of statutes, the Canada Border Services Agency's (CBSA) information-sharing authorization stems from a number of sources, not all of which are detailed here. As noted in Chapter 11, the CBSA collects advance biographical and travel information for persons arriving in Canada on commercial carriers.

The CBSA may be authorized to disclose this "information for the purposes of national security, the defence of Canada or the conduct of international affairs."[117] Specific regulations made under this IRPA provision, for example, provide that passenger and travel information may be shared by the CBSA with any Canadian government department "for the purposes of the Act" if it relates, for instance, to terrorism.[118]

Under the terms of the *Customs Act*, customs data may also be shared in a number of circumstances, including if reasonably related to "national security or defence of Canada"[119] and to a peace officer to facilitate a criminal investigation.[120]

---

117 *Immigration and Refugee Protection Act*, S.C. 2001, c. 27, s. 150.1.

118 *Protection of Passenger Information Regulations*, S.O.R./2005-346, s. 9.

119 *Customs Act*, R.S.C. 1985 (2d Supp.), c. 1, s. 107(4)(h). For a comprehensive list of disclosure responsibilities and roles under the *Customs Act*, see CBSA, D1-16-2-INTERIM, *Interim Administrative Guidelines for the Provision to others, Allowing access to others, and Use of Customs Information* (2003), Annex B, online: www.cbsa.gc.ca/E/pub/cm/d1-16-2-interim/README.html.

120 *Customs Act, ibid.*, s. 107(5)(a).

CHAPTER 13

INTERCEPTION AND INTERDICTION

Surveillance and information sharing are merely means to an end. Maintenance of national security may depend on acting on this information. As discussed in Chapter 14, one response is to detain persons constituting sufficiently grave security risks. A more modest reaction involves intercepting and interdicting persons with hostile or adverse objectives, barring them from entering the country or having access to sensitive information or facilities.

Interception and interdiction is systematized by screening individuals for security risks, thereby identifying, minimizing and ideally forestalling the security threat presented by these people. Broadly speaking, security screening can be divided into several categories: security assessments of government personnel in support of the Government Security Policy; security screening of non-Canadians to prevent security risks from entering or remaining in Canada; and the listing of persons viewed as constituting a security risk for the purpose of controlling their access to sensitive modes of transportation. Other issues include assessments of Canadians on national security grounds prior to the issuance of passports. This chapter examines laws governing these screening processes.

PART I: GOVERNMENT SECURITY

The Canadian Security Intelligence Service (CSIS) reports that "in their quest for political and military intelligence, foreign intelligence services constantly attempt to infiltrate key Canadian government departments."[1] Preventing this infiltration depends on careful vetting of those with access to government information and sensitive facilities. This objective, in turn, depends on security screening and clearances. Canada has a Government Security Policy setting out rules and procedures in this area. International intelligence-sharing agreements may also contain relevant principles.

A. GOVERNMENT SECURITY POLICY

As the Supreme Court has observed, the government's "power to grant or deny security clearances as a condition of appointment remained part of the royal prerogative or more appropriately, in our times, a function of management controlled by the Crown."[2] Any government "must have trust in their employees and officers to preserve that degree of security which a government requires to operate effectively."[3]

The government's current Security Policy is issued by Treasury Board as an exercise of its powers under the *Financial Administration Act*.[4] As discussed fully in Chapter 10, secrecy is a major preoccupation in maintaining national security. For this reason, the policy underscores the need to ensure that "individuals with access to government information and assets are reliable and trustworthy." The government must "ensure the individual's loyalty to Canada in order to protect itself from foreign intelligence gathering and terrorism. Special care must be taken to ensure the continued reliability and loyalty of individuals, and prevent malicious activity and unauthorized disclosure of *classified* and *protected* information by a disaffected individual in a position of trust."[5]

---

1   Canada, CSIS, *Espionage and Foreign Interference* (2005), online: www.csis-scrs.gc.ca/en/priorities/espionage.asp. See also the 2006 comments of the minister of public safety, cited in Stewart Bell, "Alleged Spy in Canadian Agents' Sights for Awhile, Day Hints: Espionage 'Growth Industry' in Canada" *National Post* (28 November 2006).

2   *Thomson v. Canada (Deputy Minister of Agriculture)*, [1992] 1 S.C.R. 385 at 395 [*Thomson*].

3   *Ibid.*

4   R.S.C., 1985, c. F-11, s. 7.

5   Treasury Board Secretariat, *Government Security Policy* (2002) at para. 10.9, online: www.tbs-sct.gc.ca/pubs_pol/gospubs/TBM_12A/gsp-psg_e.asp [emphasis added].

The policy admonishes departments to limit access to this classified and protected information and other assets "to those individuals who have a need to know the information"—that is, must have access to information in order to perform their duties—and "who have the appropriate security screening level."[6]

Security screening is obligatory under some of Canada's information-sharing arrangements with foreign governments. The 1996 Canada–Australia defence information-sharing agreement, for example, limits access to the shared information to government personnel who are "nationals of either of the Parties, unless the originating Party has given its prior written consent otherwise," "require the information for the performance of their official duties," and "have been Security Screened to the appropriate level."[7] In addition, each state may review the security standards, procedures and practices of the other, and is to "inform the other of any changes to its security standards, procedures, and practices which have an effect on the manner in which" exchanged defence information is protected.[8]

1) Information Classification

Under the Government Security Policy, "classified" information is "information related to the national interest that may qualify for an exemption or exclusion under the *Access to Information Act* or *Privacy Act*, and the compromise of which would reasonably be expected to cause injury to the national interest."[9] "Protected" information is "information related to *other than the national interest* that may qualify for an exemption or exclusion under the *Access to Information Act* or *Privacy Act*, and the compromise of which would reasonably be expected to cause injury to a non-national interest."[10] A "national interest" "concerns the defence and maintenance of the social, political and economic stability of Canada."[11]

2) Reliability and Security Assessments

To meet its security obligations, each department must ensure that individuals (other than governor-in-council appointees) requiring access

---

6   *Ibid.* at paras. 10.8 & 10.9.
7   *Agreement between the Government of Australia and the Government of Canada concerning the Protection of Defence Related Information exchanged Between Them* (October 1996), A.T.S. 1996 No. 16, Art. 6 [Canada–Australia Agreement].
8   *Ibid.*, Art. 9.
9   *Government Security Policy*, above note 5 at Appendix B.
10   *Ibid.* [emphasis added].
11   *Ibid.*

to government assets undergo a "reliability check and are granted a reliability status." Reliability status "indicates successful completion of a reliability check; allows regular access to government assets and with a need to know to protected information." Those officials to be given a need-to-know access to classified (as opposed to merely protected) information must also "undergo a security assessment" and be "granted a security clearance at the appropriate level." Further, those with access to "facilities that are critical to the national interest or to restricted areas for major events" must have a "site access clearance."[12]

3) Security Clearances

a) Levels

To regulate access to classified information, the government employs three information security-clearance levels: Confidential (Level I), Secret (Level II) and Top Secret (Level III).[13] Individuals are cleared to these different levels as required by the sorts of information to which they must have access to perform their functions.[14]

b) Legal Considerations

The Supreme Court has ruled that the government must meet common law procedural fairness requirements in making clearance decisions. In its words, "fairness requires that a party must have an adequate opportunity of knowing the case that must be met, of answering it and putting forward the party's own position." [15] In keeping with this jurisprudence, the policy establishes procedural safeguards for the security assessments. For instance, security checks may only be initiated on the consent of the person. These individuals must be treated in a fair and unbiased manner and given an opportunity to explain adverse information prior to a final decision being made.[16] Further, the CSIS Act requires that denied security clearances be communicated to the person within ten days[17] and establishes a complaints mechanism described below.

---

12   *Ibid.* at para. 10.9.
13   *Ibid.* at Appendix B.
14   Canada, CSIS, *Backgrounder No. 9: Security Screening* (2004), online: www.csis-scrs.gc.ca/en/newsroom/backgrounders/backgrounder09.asp.
15   *Thomson*, above note 2 at 402.
16   Treasury Board, *Government Security Policy*, above note 5 at para. 10.9.
17   *Canadian Security Intelligence Service Act*, R.S.C. 1985, c. C-23, s. 42 [CSIS Act].

c) Mechanics

Security screening for all government departments (except the RCMP) is a core CSIS function.[18] The CSIS Act authorizes the Service to provide "security assessments to departments of the Government of Canada," and under arrangements approved by the public safety minister, with provincial entities.[19] CSIS may conduct investigations in support of these assessments.[20]

In practice, CSIS plays an important role in conducting security assessments of persons with access to sensitive facilities, including the secure zone in airports, government buildings and nuclear facilities. It also assesses clearances for information access. Confidential (Level I) and Secret (Level II) information security clearances are obtained following a check against CSIS databanks. If that search pinpoints questionable information, a field investigation may be performed. Such a field investigation must precede any Top Secret (Level III) clearance. A field investigation includes "CSIS records checks, the interview of friends, neighbours and employers, local police checks and possibly an interview of the applicant."[21]

CSIS does not itself make the decision on whether to grant the person the required security clearance. It merely provides advice on that question to the relevant government department. For example, decisions on security clearances for airport employees rest with Transport Canada.[22] Where CSIS finds no adverse information, it simply issues a "notice of assessment." It provides an "information brief" when CSIS discovers information that might affect a department's security clearance or site access decisions. Finally, CSIS may recommend that clearance or site access not be given in the form of a "denial brief."[23] The latter two responses are comparatively rare. In 2005–6 information-related security-clearance assess-

---

18   The RCMP performs its own security assessments for its personnel.

19   CSIS Act, above note 17, s. 13. With approval with the ministers of public safety and of foreign affairs, CSIS may also enter into an arrangement with a foreign state or international organization authorizing the Service to provide security assessments to this entity. As described by CSIS, "foreign screening typically falls within two categories: database checks and enquiries on Canadian residents wishing to take up residence in another country; or field checks and enquiries on former and current Canadian residents who are being considered for classified access in another country." CSIS, *Backgrounder No. 9: Security Screening*, above note 14.

20   CSIS Act, *ibid.*, s. 15.

21   CSIS, *Backgrounder No. 9: Security Screening*, above note 14.

22   *Aeronautics Act*, R.S.C. 1985 A-2, s. 4.8.

23   Canada, SIRC, *Annual Report 2005–2006* (Ottawa: Public Works and Government Services Canada, 2006) at 42–43.

ments, CSIS issued nineteen information briefs and one denial brief, out of a pool of almost 38,000 security assessments. In responses to almost 60,000 site access requests, it issued only four information briefs.[24]

4) Appeals

A department's security-clearance denials are reviewable before the Security Intelligence Review Committee (SIRC), the review body created by the CSIS Act. A person who is dismissed, demoted, transferred or denied a promotion or transfer as a government employee or is denied a contract to provide goods or services to the government may file a complaint with SIRC where this treatment stems from a denied security clearance.[25]

SIRC must respond with a statement "summarizing such information available to the Committee as will enable the complainant to be as fully informed as possible of the circumstances giving rise to the denial of the security clearance."[26] It will then investigate the matter, and upon completion, will provide the minister of public safety, CSIS and the complainant and the complainant's department with "a report containing any recommendations that the Committee considers appropriate, and those findings of the investigation that the Committee considers it fit to report to the complainant."[27] In 2005–6, SIRC responded to two complaints of denied security clearances, in both instances critiquing the quality of CSIS's assessment and recommending that the security clearance be given.[28] The Supreme Court has ruled, however, that SIRC recommendations are just that; recommendations. The government need not abide by them.[29]

5) Other Possible Forms of Review

A government denial of security clearance must comply with standard administrative law rules. As noted above, these requirements would include common law procedural fairness. They would also include errors of discretion—that is, a sufficiently unreasonable decision. An egre-

---

24 *Ibid.*
25 CSIS Act, above note 17, s. 42. See Chapter 3 for a discussion of SIRC's structure and functions.
26 *Ibid.*, s. 46.
27 *Ibid.*, s. 52.
28 Canada, SIRC, *Annual Report 2005–2006*, above note 23 at 22 *et seq.*
29 *Thomson*, above note 2.

gious government denial of security clearance would likely be amenable to judicial review. [30]

Moreover, where a person suffers workplace disadvantage because of a security clearance decision, the question may end up before an employment tribunal.[31] In other instances, security classification issues may be raised in civil litigation concerning wrongful dismissal.[32]

PART II: IMMIGRATION AND CITIZENSHIP SECURITY SCREENING

CSIS is charged with advising "any minister of the Crown on matters relating to the security of Canada" or providing "any minister of the Crown with information relating to security matters or criminal activities" in relation "to the exercise of any power or the performance of any duty or function by that Minister under the *Citizenship Act* or the *Immigration and Refugee Protection Act*."[33] It may conduct investigations in support of these functions.[34] Pursuant to this authority, CSIS advises Citizenship and Immigration Canada (CIC) and the Canada Border Services Agency (CBSA) on the screening of immigration, refugee and citizenship candidates and applicants.

A. BORDER SCREENING

The *Immigration and Refugee Protection Act* (IRPA) lists a number of circumstances justifying inadmissibility of a foreign national or permanent resident to Canada.[35] Included among these are several security

---

30   See, for example, *Thomson, ibid.* (accepting that a government decision could be reviewed for lack of evidence, but disagreeing that there was any such absence of evidence); *DiMartino v. Canada (Minister of Transport)*, 2005 FC 635 (applying procedural fairness in the context of an airport access clearance).

31   See, for example, *Kampman v. Canada (Treasury Board)*, [1996] 2 F.C. 798 (C.A.) (a case in which the Public Service Commission Appeal Board heard a complaint concerning a dismissal caused by a loss of a security clearance).

32   See, for example, *Douglas v. Canada*, [1993] 1 F.C. 264 (T.D.) (concerning a dismissal generated by career limitations imposed by the Canadian Forces, including in the area of security clearance, because of the plaintiff's sexual orientation).

33   CSIS Act, above note 17, s. 14.

34   *Ibid.*, s. 15.

35   *Immigration and Refugee Protection Act*, S.C. 2001, c. 27, s. 33 *et seq.* [IRPA].

grounds. These are: "engaging in an act of espionage or an act of sub-version against a democratic government, institution or process as they are understood in Canada"; "engaging in or instigating the subversion by force of any government"; "engaging in terrorism"; "being a danger to the security of Canada"; "engaging in acts of violence that would or might endanger the lives or safety of persons in Canada"; or "being a member of an organization that there are reasonable grounds to believe engages, has engaged or will engage in" one of these sorts of acts.[36] Further, a person is excluded from refugee status in Canada if they are guilty of an act contrary to the purposes and principles of the United Nations.[37] Terrorism constitutes such an act.[38]

1) Foreigner Screening

To assist immigration authorities in administering these rules, CSIS conducts security screening of foreign visitors, immigrants and refugee applicants seeking permanent residence status.[39] Given delays in the processing of refugee claims and because some refugees may never apply for permanent residency, CSIS and CIC recently introduced a new program to interdict refugee applicants posing security risks much earlier in the refugee adjudication process. To this end, CSIS now completes "front-end screening" of refugee applicants, identifying security issues as early as possible. It also participates in a CBSA port of entry interdiction program designed to identify security risks at the time of entry into the country.[40] In 2006, CSIS found adverse information in 1 out of every 250 immigration applications or refugee claims screened.[41]

2) Lookouts

On the basis of domestic and allied information provided by security and intelligence agencies, the Canada Border Services Agency may also place "lookouts" red-flagging individual travellers or vehicles. These

36   *Ibid.*, s. 34. See also the discussion in Chapter 14.

37   *Ibid.*, s. 96; Sch.

38   *Pushpanathan v. Canada (Minister of Citizenship and Immigration)*, [1998] 1 S.C.R. 982 at paras. 66 and 120.

39   CSIS, *Backgrounder No. 9: Security Screening*, above note 14.

40   Canada CSIS, *Backgrounder No. 15: Screening of Refugee Claimants* (2004), online: www.csis-scrs.gc.ca/en/newsroom/backgrounders/backgrounder15.asp. For an assessment of "front end screening," see Canada, SIRC, *Annual Report 2003–2004* (Ottawa: Public Works and Government Services Canada, 2004) at 5 *et seq.*

41   Canada, SIRC, *Annual Report 2005–2006*, above note 23 at 44.

may include names of persons inadmissible under the IRPA or those produced in national security investigations. They may also list persons known to have smuggled controlled goods out of Canada in violation of export control rules.

Information collected from carriers under the Advance Passenger Information/Passenger Name Record (API/PNR) program discussed in Chapter 11 are matched against the lookout lists, and computer-based risk assessments are generated. Persons generating high-risk scores for possible involvement with terrorism, among other crimes, are subjected to closer scrutiny upon arrival in Canada.[42] Individuals listed in lookouts may be denied entry to Canada and/or questioned and searched to secure information on the possible commission of an offence.[43]

Pursuant to a 2005 memorandum of understanding between Canada and the United States, lookouts triggered by possible terrorism concerns or serious infractions of customs and immigration laws are reportedly shared between the two countries.[44]

3) Advance Screening

Canada also collaborates with the United States in a Free and Secure Trade (FAST) program, expediting cross-border movement of low-risk importers, truck drivers and carriers. FAST is administered by the Canada Border Services Agency, but CSIS conducts security assessments of individual FAST applicants—typically truck drivers.[45]

B. SCREENING UNDER THE *CITIZENSHIP ACT*

The *Citizenship Act* contains rules denying citizenship to security risks. A person may be denied citizenship if subject to an immigration removal order or a declaration from the government that the person constitutes a threat to the security of Canada.[46]

---

42 Commission of Inquiry into the Actions of Canadian Officials in Relation to Maher Arar, *A New Review Mechanism for the RCMP's National Security Activities* (2006) at 160–61, online: www.ararcommission.ca/eng/EnglishReport-Dec122006.pdf [Arar inquiry, Policy Report].

43 *Ibid.* at 157–58.

44 *Ibid.* at 161. See also Don Butler, "Canadians To Face More Pre-flight Scrutiny" *Ottawa Citizen* (23 January 2007) A1.

45 Canada, CSIS, *2003 Public Report*, online: www.csis-scrs.gc.ca/en/publications/annual_report/2003/report2003.asp.

46 *Citizenship Act*, R.S.C. 1985, c. C-29, ss. 5 and 20.

A declaration of this sort follows an investigation by SIRC or a retired judge, sparked by a request for such a review by the governor-in-council.[47] SIRC or the retired judge investigate the matter in the same manner SIRC would follow in assessing a complaint under the CSIS Act.[48] Once it receives the report of the investigating entity, the governor-in-council may bar the bestowal of citizenship where it has reasonable grounds to believe the person would act in a manner threatening national security. A declaration to this effect endures for two years and may be renewed. It is conclusive proof of the matters it describes.[49]

Presumably to determine whether the government should trigger this process, citizenship applicants are screened on security grounds by CSIS. While the *Citizenship Act* itself does not invoke this screening as a prerequisite to citizenship, the Act's regulations preclude vetting of an application by a Citizenship Judge until the citizenship registrar has made "the inquiries necessary to determine whether the person in respect of whom the application is made meets the requirements of the Act and these Regulations with respect to the application."[50] As interpreted by Citizenship and Immigration Canada, these requirements include a security clearance.[51]

As of 2006, CSIS finds adverse information via these security reviews in about one in every 2,500 citizenship applications.[52]

PART III: TRANSPORTATION SECURITY SCREENING

To secure vulnerable means of transportation, Canada employs transportation security-screening measures.

A. PHYSICAL SEARCH

Most obviously, all travellers are subject to physical search and screening before entering a secure zone in an airport and boarding an aircraft.[53]

---

47 *Ibid.*, ss. 19 & 19.1.
48 For a review of this complaints procedure, see Chapter 3.
49 *Citizenship Act*, above note 46, s. 20.
50 *Citizenship Regulations, 1993*, S.O.R./93-246, s. 11.
51 See discussion in *Platonov v. Canada (Minister of Citizenship and Immigration)*, 2005 FC 569 at para. 13.
52 Canada, SIRC, *2005–2006 Annual Report*, above note 23 at 44.
53 *Aeronautics Act*, above note 22, s. 4.85; *Canadian Aviation Security Regulations*, S.O.R./2000-111, s. 5 *et seq.*

This function is performed by the Canadian Air Transport Security Authority (CATSA), a Crown corporation established in 2002.[54] All persons entering the restricted area of an airport must submit to screening, and may not attempt to circumvent this search. The regulations prohibit false claims that a person is carrying a weapon or dangerous item that could jeopardize the security of the airport or aircraft.[55] More detailed screening rules applied by CATSA are confidential.[56]

B. NO FLY LIST

The *Aeronautics Act* also allows the transport minister or his or her designate to direct any person to do anything required to respond to an immediate threat to aviation security,[57] and authorizes the governor-in-council to make broad regulations on aviation security.[58]

In 2006, the government proposed regulations putting in place "Passenger Protect," a system that includes a passenger watch-list. The regulations, in force in June 2007,[59] are used to exclude persons believed to constitute a threat to civil aviation from aircraft.

---

54   The effectiveness of CATSA screening systems sparked controversy in early 2007, with the release of an auditor general report that concluded, among other things, that CATSA's hiring, training, and oversight practices were in need of adjustment. Because of these and other problems, the auditor general concluded that CATSA "does not have reasonable assurance that screening operations are conducted economically, efficiently, effectively, and in the public interest, in accordance with its mandate." Auditor General of Canada, *Canadian Air Transport Security Authority: Special Examination Report* (December 2006) at 3, online: www.catsa-acsta.gc.ca/english/about_propos/rep_rap/oag_bvg/index.shtml.

55   *Canadian Aviation Security Regulations*, above note 53, s. 5 *et seq.*

56   *Aeronautics Act*, above note 22, s. 4.79. The key instrument governing passenger screening is the *Security Screening Order*. This nonpublic instrument "specifies at which aerodromes and on which flights screening must be conducted, how screening [of] passengers and non-passengers must be performed, and how staff is to be deployed to screening points. It prescribes what CATSA must screen for, what equipment to use, and the procedures to be employed. In addition, CATSA must ensure that any person passing beyond a screening point into a restricted area is in possession of a boarding pass, ticket or other document." CATSA Advisory Panel, *Flight Plan: Managing the Risks in Aviation Security* (2006), online: www.tc.gc.ca/tcss/CATSA/Final_Report-Rapport_final/chapter1_e.htm#12www.tc.gc.ca/tcss/CATSA/Final_Report-Rapport_final.

57   *Aeronautics Act*, ibid., ss. 4.76 & 4.77.

58   *Ibid.*, s. 4.71.

59   S.O.R./2007-82 (26 April 2007).

These dangerous persons are identified by a "Passenger Protect Advisory Group" comprising CSIS, RCMP and other government departments. Relying on CSIS and RCMP intelligence, as well as information from foreign intelligence sources, the Advisory Group lists persons believed to pose an immediate threat to aviation security, including those who have been involved with a terrorist group and can reasonably be suspected of endangering aviation.

A list, with names, dates of birth and gender, is supplied to the airlines, who are then obliged to screen passengers by checking listed names against passenger identification when these clients arrive at check-in. Where passenger data matches that on the list, the airline is required to contact a special 24-hour Transport Canada office. The Transport Canada officer then decides whether to issue an emergency order under the *Aeronautics Act* precluding boarding by the passenger, and, where the order is made, the RCMP is notified.[60]

This "no fly" program has elicited stern responses from civil liberties organizations who warn that it will reflect ethnic profiling[61] and is likely to be riddled with errors.[62] Moreover, they fear that listed names will be supplied by Canada to foreign jurisdictions, who may then maltreat listed persons who come within their reach. Weeks after it was introduced in June 2007, Canada's federal and provincial privacy commissioners issued a joint statement deploring the system and calling for its suspension.[63]

The Transport Canada program includes some checks and balances, including a review of listed names at thirty-day intervals for accuracy. In the event of "false positives" — that is, matches of persons with the same name as those on the list but who are not the listed person — "the Department will work with the individual and the air carrier to solve the problem as soon as possible. The nature of the problem will be

---

60 Transport Canada, *Passenger Protect Program* (October 2006), online: www.
tc.gc.ca/vigilance/sep/passenger_protect/menu.htm; Regulatory Impact Analysis Statement, *Identity Screening Regulations*, S.O.R./2007-82 (26 April 2007), online: http://canadagazette.gc.ca/partII/2007/20070516/html/sor82-e.html.

61 See, for example, B.C. Civil Liberties Association, News Release "Government Shielding No-Fly Program from Parliament" (27 October 2006), online: www.
bccla.org/pressreleases/06nofly.pdf.

62 See, for example, B.C. Civil Liberties Association, News Release, "Civil Liberties Group Challenges Leaders to Come Clean on No-Fly Lists" (19 January 2006), online: www.bccla.org/pressreleases/06nofly.htm. See also Don Butler, "Will the No-fly List Fly?" *Ottawa Citizen* (14 January 2007) A1.

63 Resolution of Canada's Privacy Commissioners and Privacy Enforcement Officials Passenger Protect Program — Canada's Aviation No-fly List (28 June 2007), online: www.privcom.gc.ca/nfl/res_20070628_e.asp.

investigated and follow-up action will be taken, including a notation indicating that a false positive exists for a particular name."[64]

There is also an appeal mechanism for those who have been listed. An appeal may be brought to Transport Canada's Office of Reconsideration (OOR), "which would review the application and validate the information through appropriate sources" and then ask an "independent external advisor" to review the listing decision. Transport Canada also expects that persons will have an option of complaining to SIRC, the Commission for Public Complaints against the RCMP (CPC) (or its successor), or the Canadian Human Rights Commission. Judicial review of the listing decision before the Federal Court is a final option.[65]

By the time of this writing, it was not anticipated, however, that persons will be given advance notice of listing decisions, instead being notified of their status only when they arrive at check-in counters (or try to check-in at automated wickets). Transport Canada has asserted that advance notification of persons not already ticketed would be difficult, if not impossible, because these persons may not be easily located.[66] Whether this position will stand up to scrutiny if reviewed in court on grounds of common law procedural fairness remained uncertain by the time of this writing.

PART IV: OTHER SECURITY SCREENING ISSUES

National security preoccupations have contributed to developments in two other areas related to security screening: the development of modern identification and the issuance of Canadian passports.

A. IDENTIFICATION

At the time of this writing, Canada had no national identification card for Canadian citizens, although such a document existed for permanent residents. A "maple leaf" card for Canadians has, however, been discussed and proposed within government. In 2003, the House of Commons immigration and citizenship committee canvassed opinion

---

64 Transport Canada, *Passenger Protect Program*, above note 60.
65 Regulatory Impact Analysis Statement, *Identity Screening Regulations*, above note 60.
66 *Ibid.*

on the issue, summarizing a number of issues raised by this proposal.[67] From a national security perspective, a national identification card with electronically archived biometric identifiers would presumably make document and identity fraud more difficult, reducing the risk of infiltration by persons assuming the identity of others. However, privacy concerns rank first among the objections to such a plan, especially if the cards permit the compilation of a comprehensive electronic profile of the holder. Critics have also complained that use and possession of the card would become compulsory, creating a sort of "internal passport" carried by Canadians to perform everyday functions.

B. PASSPORTS

While debate on the merits of a national identity card continued at the time of this writing, changes to Canada's passport practices were evolving more rapidly. Canada appears to be moving toward a biometric passport, or at least biometric processing (for example, iris scanning to expedite security checks) at international airports.[68] The government has also amended its passport issuance rules to incorporate clear national security criteria into decision making.

The government's power to issue a Canadian passport stems from the royal prerogative. It is not, in other words, a practice governed by legislation. The government's passport rules are found in the Canadian Passport Order.[69] That instrument provides that "any person who is a Canadian citizen under the Act may be issued a passport,"[70] and sets out the requirements to be met prior to the issuance of this document. A passport may be refused or revoked on a number of grounds, not least to prevent a person charged with a criminal offence or subjected

---

67   House of Commons, Standing Committee on Citizenship and Immigration, *A National Identity Card for Canada?* (October 2003), online: http://cmte.parl. gc.ca/cmte/committeepublication.aspx?com=3280&lang=1&sourceid=61198.

68   Passport Canada, *Biometrics in the International Travel Context* (2004), online: www.ppt.gc.ca/newsroom/news.aspx?lang=e&page=/newsroom/20040201.aspx. See United States, White House, *U.S.-Canada Smart Border/30 Point Action Plan Update* (2002), online: www.whitehouse.gov/news/releases/2002/12/20021206-1.html ("The United States and Canada have agreed to develop common standards for the biometrics that we use and have also agreed to adopt interoperable and compatible technology to read these biometrics. In the interest of having cards that could be used across different modes of travel, we have agreed to use cards that are capable of storing multiple biometrics").

69   S.I.-81-86, as amended.

70   *Ibid.*, s. 4.

to a term of imprisonment from fleeing the relevant jurisdiction.[71] In 2004, the government amended the Passport Order to allow refusals or revocations "if the Minister [of foreign affairs] is of the opinion that such action is necessary for the national security of Canada or another country."[72]

This amendment followed a successful challenge of a passport refusal by an applicant whose family members reportedly included prominent supporters of al-Qaeda. In *Khadr v. Canada (Attorney General)*,[73] the government conceded that the refusal—predicated on national security—was not authorized by the Passport Order as it then existed. In a subsequent proceeding, the Federal Court concluded that the Order created a legitimate expectation as to the manner and criteria by which a passport application would be judged. Since those criteria were not followed, the applicant was entitled to a reassessment of his application, according to the criteria existing in the Order at the time the application was filed.[74]

In light of this holding, the court did not reach the issue of whether the government had a constitutional obligation to issue a passport. It did observe, however, that the mobility rights found in section 6 of the *Canadian Charter of Rights and Freedoms*[75] would be hollow if a citizen's international mobility could be *de facto* restricted by a refusal to issue a passport.[76] This reasoning suggests strongly that passport denials and revocations may be sustained only on section 1 grounds. As this book has noted in several places, a significant enough national security concern seems a likely candidate for a section 1 justification, although the government would obviously need to show that rejection of a passport application is sufficiently connected to this preoccupation.

---

71   *Ibid.*, ss. 9 & 10.

72   *Ibid.*, s. 10.1.

73   2004 FC 1719.

74   2006 FC 727 [*Khadr*]. Of course, even if the applicant were issued a passport under the original criteria, that passport could subsequently be *revoked* under the new, national security-oriented amendments. This is exactly what happened to Khadr. Allison Hanes, "Ottawa Revokes Khadr's Passport: 'Black Sheep' of Family Had Pondered Barbados Vacation" *National Post* (31 August 2006) A.4.

75   Part I of the *Constitution Act, 1982*, being Schedule B to the *Canada Act 1982* (U.K.) 1982, c. 11.

76   *Khadr*, above note 74 at para. 62 *et seq.*

CHAPTER 14

DETENTION

Mere security clearance and access control may be insufficient to pre-empt threats to national security. In some instances, those persons who pose the threat may have to be detained, often in circumstances where the evidence justifying their imprisonment would not support a criminal conviction. In such circumstances, the state's dilemma is acute. As Laws L.J. of the English Court of Appeal has noted, discussing terrorism:

> This grave and present threat [of terrorism] cannot be neutralised by the processes of investigation and trial pursuant to the general criminal law. The reach of those processes is marked by what can be proved beyond reasonable doubt.... In these circumstances the state faces a dilemma. If it limits the means by which the citizens are protected against the threat of terrorist outrage to the ordinary meas-ures of the criminal law, it leaves a yawning gap. It exposes its people to the possibility of indiscriminate murder committed by extremists who for want of evidence could not be brought to book in the crim-inal courts. But if it fills the gap by confining them without trial it affronts "the most fundamental and probably the oldest, most hardly won and the most universally recognised of human rights": freedom from executive detention.[1]

---

1 *A and others v. Secretary of State for the Home Department*, [2004] EWCA Civ 1123 at paras. 154–55.

As this passage suggests, detention on the basis of suspected anticipated actions, rather than in response to actual, provable past actions,
is an enormously controversial practice. Reviewing so-called preventive detention in seventeen countries in 1993, Steven Greer concluded
that "preventive detention on the grounds of public or state security is
a flimsy and highly suspect justification for the deprivation of liberty.
Abuse of power is seemingly widespread throughout the jurisdictions
surveyed here.... [M]uch more rigorous criteria than generally apply
ought to be met if the practice is to be convincingly defended."[2]

Since 1993, preventive detention has become more commonplace,
even in those countries generally hostile to the practice. Detentions without criminal trials of foreign nationals suspected of being national security threats have provoked particular controversy in the post-9/11 era. The
long-term detention of suspected terrorists by the U.S. military at various
locations outside of the United States is the most famous example.

In Canada, preventive detention laws were in a state of evolution by
the time of this writing. Criminal law preventive detention provisions
were enhanced as part of Canada's 2001 anti-terrorism law.[3] By 2007,
however, some of these powers had expired and the government had
tabled Bill S-3 in an effort to revive them. Moreover, the government
had relied upon immigration "security certificates" to detain five suspected terrorists after 2001 pending efforts to remove them from the
country.[4] In part because these individuals have resisted deportation
to states that may torture them, the men subject to security certificates
at the time of this writing had been behind bars for long periods: by
the beginning of 2007, the average period of detention for the men still
imprisoned at that time was almost six years.[5] This is a period of deten-

---

2   Steven Greer, "Preventive Detention and Public Security: Towards a General
    Model," in Andre Harding & John Hatchard, eds., *Preventive Detention and Se-
    curity Law: A Comparative Survey* (Dordrecht: M. Nijhoff, 1993) at 36 [*Preventive
    Detention*].

3   See *Criminal Code*, R.S.C. 1985, c. C-46, s. 83.3.

4   *Immigration and Refugee Protection Act*, S.C. 2001, c. 27, s. 77 *et seq.* [IRPA]. For
    representative cases concerning these five men see, for example, *Mahjoub v.
    Canada (Minister of Citizenship and Immigration)*, 2005 FC 156 [*Mahjoub*]; *Almrei
    v. Canada (Minister of Citizenship and Immigration)*, 2004 FC 420; *Jaballah (Re)*,
    2005 FC 399; *Charkaoui (Re)*, 2003 FC 1419, aff'd 2004 FCA 421; *Harkat (Re)*
    2005 FC 393.

5   This figure was calculated in relation to the three men still detained as of
    January 2007. As this book was completed, two men (Mahjoub and Jaballah)
    were released on conditions, pending the resolution of their cases. There were,
    therefore, four men subject to security certificates, but released on conditions,
    and one other still detained. The precise fate of the security certificate process,

tion longer than the average sentence for *convicted* attempted murderers in Canada.[6] In early 2007, the Supreme Court of Canada declared aspects of the security-certificate procedure unconstitutional, without denouncing the concept in principle, and the government subsequently tabled bill C-3 in an effort to amend the process in response to the Court's ruling.[7]

Similar practices in the United Kingdom have also sparked controversy. In December 2004, the United Kingdom's highest court of appeal—the House of Lords—declared indefinite detention of foreign terrorist suspects without trial under immigration law contrary to U.K. human rights obligations.[8] In the words of Lord Nicholls of Birkenhead, "indefinite imprisonment without charge or trial is anathema in any country which observes the rule of law."[9] The Blair government responded by developing a new regime of "control orders" imposing constraints on the liberties of both foreigners and U.K. citizens where security grounds warrant.

Meanwhile, official preventive detentions appear to have been supplemented in some states by a practice of "extraordinary rendition" — the extralegal removal of persons to face prolonged detention (and possibly torture) at the hands of foreign governments.[10] Detention in these cases is coupled with "disappearances."

This chapter reviews international and domestic laws applicable to preventive detention. It begins with a review of pertinent international human rights and humanitarian law principles. It then assesses domestic law, focusing first on conventional criminal law detention powers and then on specialized anti-terrorism detention law, assessed in a comparative context. Next, it examines detentions under immigration law—most notably the security certificate process. Finally, it examines foreign detentions and their implications for Canadian law and practice.

---

at least as applied to these individuals, was uncertain, following the release of *Charkaoui v. Canada (Citizenship and Immigration)*, 2007 SCC 9 [*Charkaoui*].

6   See Statistics Canada, *Sentenced Cases and Outcomes in Adult Criminal Court, by Province and Yukon Territory (Canada)* (2003 data), online: www40.statcan. ca/l01/cst01/legal21a.htm.

7   *Charkaoui*, above note 5.

8   *A and others v. Secretary of State for the Home Department*, [2004] UKHL 56.

9   *Ibid.* at para. 74.

10 For a discussion of this practice, see, for example, Committee on International Human Rights of the Association of the Bar of the City of New York & Center for Human Rights and Global Justice, New York University School of Law, *Torture by Proxy: International and Domestic Law Applicable to "Extraordinary Renditions"* (October 2004), online: www.chrgj.org/docs/TortureByProxy.pdf.

PART I: INTERNATIONAL PRINCIPLES RELEVANT TO DETENTION

A. INTERNATIONAL HUMAN RIGHTS STANDARDS

A right to liberty and the obligation not to interfere with the liberty interest via arbitrary detention are basic principles of international human rights law[11] and of the constitutional traditions of liberal democracies.[12] Where the detention is provoked by criminal charges, the state must subsequently provide the accused with a fair trial before an independent and impartial tribunal.[13] The fair trial obligation includes important procedural guarantees, extending to the accused an ability to mount an effective defence and confront the witnesses against him or her.[14]

On the other hand, where a person is detained in noncriminal proceedings, international law contains fewer, emphatic procedural guarantees. International law simply provides that all detentions must be authorized by law and followed by judicial proceedings assessing the legitimacy of the detention.[15] These rights on detention are the focus of this discussion.

---

11   See, for example, the *Universal Declaration of Human Rights*, G.A. res. 217A (III), U.N. Doc A/810 at 71 (1948), Arts. 3 and 9; the *International Covenant on Civil and Political Rights*, 999 U.N.T.S. 171 [ICCPR], Art. 9; the *American Declaration of the Rights and Duties of Man* (Adopted by the Ninth International Conference of American States, Bogota, Colombia, 1948), Art. 25; the *American Convention on Human Rights*, 1144 U.N.T.S. 123, Art. 7; and the *European Convention for the Protection of Human Rights and Fundamental Freedoms*, 213 U.N.T.S. 222, Art. 5; and the *African Charter on Human and People's Rights*. (1982), 21 I.L.M. 58, Art. 7.

12   See, for example, *Canadian Charter of Rights and Freedoms*, Part I of the *Constitution Act, 1982*, being Schedule B to the *Canada Act 1982* (U.K.) 1982, c. 11, ss. 7, 9, & 10; U.S. Bill of Rights, 4th and 5th Amendments.

13   See, for example, the *Universal Declaration of Human Rights*, above note 11, Art. 10; ICCPR, above note 11, Art. 14; the *American Declaration of the Rights and Duties of Man*, above note 11, Art. 26; the *American Convention on Human Rights*, above note 11, Art. 8; and the *European Convention on Human Rights and Fundamental Freedoms*, above note 11, Art. 6; and the *African Charter on Human and People's Rights*, above note 11, Art. 7.

14   See, for example, the ICCPR, *ibid.*, Art. 14; the *American Convention on Human Rights*, *ibid.*, Art. 8; the *European Convention on Human Rights and Fundamental Freedoms*, *ibid.*, Art. 6.

15   See, for example, the ICCPR, *ibid.*, Art. 9; the *American Declaration of the Rights and Duties of Man*, *ibid.*, Art. 25; the *American Convention on Human Rights*, *ibid.*, Art. 7; the *European Convention on Human Rights and Fundamental Freedoms*, *ibid.*, Art. 5.

1) Limitations on Detention

The *International Covenant on Civil and Political Rights* (ICCPR) provides in Article 9 that "no one shall be deprived of his liberty except on such grounds and in accordance with such procedure as are established by law." Further, "anyone who is arrested shall be informed, at the time of arrest, of the reasons for his arrest and shall be promptly informed of any charges against him." Article 9 invokes a right to *habeas corpus*: "anyone who is deprived of his liberty by arrest or detention shall be entitled to take proceedings before a court, in order that that court may decide without delay on the lawfulness of his detention and order his release if the detention is not lawful."

The standards applied *during* detention are also the subject of international law. Article 10 of the ICCPR provides that "all persons deprived of their liberty shall be treated with humanity and with respect for the inherent dignity of the human person."[16] Meanwhile, Article 7 of the ICCPR and the *Convention against Torture and Other Cruel, Inhuman or Degrading Treatment or Punishment*[17] ban torture and cruel, inhuman and degrading (CID) treatment. These instruments are discussed in detail in Chapter 15.

It should be recalled that all of these detention rights (other than the ban on torture and CID treatment) are subject to derogation under the ICCPR "in time of public emergency which threatens the life of the nation and the existence of which is officially proclaimed."[18]

2) Disappearances

One extremely serious violation of the liberty interest (and in many instances the right to life) is the practice of "disappearances": the secret detention of persons without providing information on their fate.

In its *Declaration on the Protection of All Persons from Enforced Disappearances*,[19] the U.N. General Assembly declared that this practice "constitutes a violation of the rules of international law guaranteeing, *inter alia*, the right to recognition as a person before the law, the right to liberty and security of the person and the right not to be subjected

---

16 See U.N. Human Rights Committee, *General Comment 20*, U.N. Doc. HRI\GEN\1\Rev.1 at 30 (1994) at para. 2 (noting that Art. 10 "complements" the obligations in Art. 7).

17 A/RES/39/46, annex, 39 U.N. GAOR Supp. (No. 51) at 197, U.N. Doc. A/39/51 (1984) (entered into force 26 June 1987) [Torture Convention].

18 ICCPR, above note 11, Art. 4.

19 A/RES/47/133, 47 U.N. GAOR Supp. (No. 49) at 207, U.N. Doc. A/47/49 (1992) [Disappearances Declaration].

to torture and other cruel, inhuman or degrading treatment or punishment. It also violates or constitutes a grave threat to the right to life."

The General Assembly Declaration called on each state to "take effective legislative, administrative, judicial or other measures to prevent and terminate acts of enforced disappearance in any territory under its jurisdiction" and suggested that "all acts of enforced disappearance shall be offences under criminal law punishable by appropriate penalties which shall take into account their extreme seriousness."

A General Assembly resolution is not binding international law in its own right. However, as the General Assembly resolution suggests, disappearances are already recognized as a violation of international law. Recent instruments amplify this fact. An *International Convention for the Protection of All Persons from Enforced Disappearance* was opened for signature in 2007 and will come into force once it attracts a sufficient number of ratifications. The treaty will prohibit enforced disappearances in all circumstances, "whether a state of war or a threat of war, internal political instability or any other public emergency."[20] An "enforced disappearance" is "the arrest, detention, abduction or any other form of deprivation of liberty committed by agents of the State or by persons or groups of persons acting with the authorization, support or acquiescence of the State, followed by a refusal to acknowledge the deprivation of liberty or by concealment of the fate or whereabouts of the disappeared person, which place such a person outside the protection of the law."[21]

The *Rome Statute of the International Criminal Court*, meanwhile, includes "enforced disappearance of persons" as one of the predicate acts of a crime against humanity (that is, the disappearance is part of a widespread or systematic attack directed against any civilian population). Likewise, the Torture Convention may also bar disappearances. In its 2006 report on the United States compliance with the Torture Convention, the treaty body established by that instrument—the Committee Against Torture—concluded that disappearances and the maintenance of secret detention centres constituted a *per se* violation of the treaty.[22]

---

20   E/CN.4/2005/WG.22/WP.1/Rev.4 (2005), Art. 1 [Disappearances Convention].
21   *Ibid.*, Art. 2.
22   CAT/C/USA/CO/2 at para. 22 (18 May 2006).

B. STANDARDS IN INTERNATIONAL HUMANITARIAN LAW

International humanitarian law (IHL)—most notably the Geneva Conventions, their additional protocols and customary international law equivalents—apply in circumstances of "armed conflict," a concept discussed in Chapter 5. The Third and Fourth Geneva Convention and Additional Protocol I contain rules on detentions. Most of these provisions are applicable to armed conflicts arising between two or more state parties to the Conventions; that is, international conflicts. Common Article 3 of these Conventions and Additional Protocol II contains language on detentions in noninternational conflicts; that is, conflicts between a state and a nonstate actor, usually in a civil war context. Where armed conflict exists, the Geneva Conventions and their additional protocols act as *lex specialis*, displacing conflicting international rules to the extent of any inconsistency.

Many of the detailed rules discussed below also exist as customary international law, and are therefore binding on all states.

1) Power to Detain

The state's powers to detain persons during an armed conflict are extensive. As summarized by the U.N. human rights special rapporteurs reviewing the treatment of detainees at the United States' Guantanamo Bay naval base,

> any person having committed a belligerent act in the context of an international armed conflict and having fallen into the hands of one of the parties to the conflict (in this case, the United States) can be held for the duration of hostilities, as long as the detention serves the purpose of preventing combatants from continuing to take up arms against the United States.[23]

Several issues related to detention have, however, become controversial in the campaign against terrorism. These include: the extent to which detainees in this nontraditional struggle are entitled to prisoner of war status; the related issue of how long these persons may be detained; and questions surrounding detainee transfers.

---

23 *Situation of detainees at Guantánamo Bay*, U.N. Doc. E/CN.4/2006/120 (15 February 2006) at para. 19 [Special Rapporteurs Report].

2) Prisoners of War

a) Combatants Entitled to PW Status or Treatment

Once captured in an *international* armed conflict, certain classes of individuals are entitled to "prisoner of war" (PW) status. These persons are summarized in Table 14.1. Speaking generally, "any member of the armed forces of a Party to a conflict is a combatant and any combatant captured by the adverse Party is a prisoner of war."[24] Armed forces "consist of all organized armed forces, groups and units which are under a command responsible to that Party for the conduct of its subordinates, even if that Party is represented by a government or an authority not recognized by an adverse Party. Such armed forces shall be subject to an internal disciplinary system which, *inter alia*, shall enforce compliance with the rules of international law applicable in armed conflict."[25]

Armed forces are typically the key combatants in an international conflict.

---

24 ICRC, *Rules Relating to the Conduct of Combatants and the Protection of Prisoners of War* (1988), online: www.icrc.org/Web/eng/siteeng0.nsf/html/57JMJT. See *also Protocol Additional to the Geneva Conventions of 12 August 1949, and relating to the Protection of Victims of International Armed Conflicts* [AP I], Art. 44.

25 AP I, *ibid.*, Art. 43.

Table 14.1: Status Possibilities in International Conflicts

Status	Description	Standard of Treatment
Persons entitled to PW status	Members of the armed forces of the parties, even if that party is possessed of a government or an authority not recognized by the detaining state.[1] To fall into this definition, the units must under a command responsible to a Party to the conflict for the conduct of its subordinates, and must be subject to an internal disciplinary system which, *inter alia*, shall enforce compliance with the rules of international law applicable in armed conflict.[2] If these conditions are met, armed forces may include regular and also "auxiliary and reserve forces, and even irregular forces and organized resistance movements."[3] Members of other militias and members of other volunteer corps, including those of organized resistance movements, belonging to a party to the conflict and operating in or outside their own territory, even if this territory is occupied, where the following conditions are fulfilled: (a) That of being commanded by a person responsible for his subordinates; (b) That of having a fixed distinctive sign recognizable at a distance; (c) That of carrying arms openly; (d) That of conducting their operations in accordance with the laws and customs of war.[4] Persons who accompany the armed forces without actually being members thereof, such as civilian members of military aircraft crews, war correspondents, supply contractors, members of labour units or of services responsible for the welfare of the armed forces, provided that they have received authorization from the armed forces which they accompany, who shall provide them for that purpose with an identity card.[5] Members of crews, including masters, pilots and apprentices, of the merchant marine and the crews of civil aircraft of the Parties to the conflict, who do not benefit by more favourable treatment under any other provisions of international law.[6]	Substantial and detailed rights set out in Geneva Convention III and Additional Protocol I.

Status	Description	Standard of Treatment
Persons entitled to PW status (cont'd)	Inhabitants of a non-occupied territory, who on the approach of the enemy spontaneously take up arms to resist the invading forces, without having had time to form themselves into regular armed units, provided they carry arms openly and respect the laws and customs of war (so-called *levée en masse*).[7]	
Persons entitled to PW treatment but not status	Persons listed in the boxes above who have been received by neutral or non-belligerent Powers on their territory and whom these Powers are required to intern under international law.[8] Persons belonging, or having belonged, to the armed forces of an occupied country, if the occupying state considers it necessary by reason of such allegiance to intern them, in particular where such persons have made an unsuccessful attempt to rejoin the armed forces to which they belong and which are engaged in combat.[9] Members of armed forces who are medical personnel and chaplains.[10]	
Persons not entitled to PW status or treatment	Combatants who fail to distinguish themselves from the civilian population and who do not carry arms openly in each engagement or while visible to the adversary while they are engaged in a military deployment preceding the launching of an attack in which they are to participate.[11]	"Given protections equivalent in all respects to those accorded to prisoners of war" by Geneva Convention III and by Additional Protocol I.[12]
	Mercenaries[13] Spies[15] Other combatants not listed in the categories above.	At a minimum, humane treatment, including "fundamental guarantees."[14]
	Non-combatant civilians interned by a foreign state because the security of the state "makes it absolutely necessary."	Substantial and detailed rights set out in Geneva Convention IV, including the right to be subjected to a disciplinary regime "consistent with humanitarian principles, and …

Status	Description	Standard of Treatment
Persons not entitled to PW status or treatment (cont'd)		imposing on internees [no] physical exertion dangerous to their health or involving physical or moral victimization."[16] Further, "the laws in force in the territory in which they are detained will continue to apply to internees who commit offences during internment."[17]

[1] Geneva Convention III, above note 26, Art. 4.
[2] Ibid.
[3] U.K. Ministry of Defence, *The Manual of the Law of Armed Conflict* (Oxford: Oxford University Press, 2004) at 143 [U.K. Ministry of Defence, *Manual*].
[4] Geneva Convention III, above note 26, Art. 4.
[5] *Ibid.*
[6] *Ibid.*
[7] *Ibid.*
[8] *Ibid.*
[9] *Ibid.*
[10] *Ibid.*, Art. 33.
[11] AP I, above note 24, Arts. 44(3) & (4). Note, however, that while the person is entitled to PW treatment, that treatment does not preclude prosecution for violating the laws of war. In this case, a combatant who fails to distinguish himself from a civilian would almost certainly be subject to prosecution for perfidy. See AP I, Art. 37 (prohibiting "the feigning of civilian, non-combatant status"). See discussion in U.K. Ministry of Defence, *Manual*, above note 3 at 43–44.
[12] AP I, *ibid.*, Art. 44.
[13] *Ibid.*, Art. 47.
[14] *Ibid.*, Art. 75.
[15] *Ibid.*, Art. 46.
[16] Geneva Convention IV, below note 43, Art. 100.
[17] *Ibid.*, Art. 117.

However, as Table 14.1 portrays, PW status (or at least treatment) is accorded to a substantial number of other classes of combatants, in addition to members of armed forces. For example, combatants may include "members of other militias and members of other volunteer corps, including those of organized resistance movements, belonging to a party to the conflict … where the following conditions are fulfilled: (a) That of being commanded by a person responsible for his subordinates; (b) That of having a fixed distinctive sign recognizable at a distance; (c) That of carrying arms openly; (d) That of conducting their operations in accordance with the laws and customs of war." [26]

b) Unprivileged Belligerents

There is no express concept of "unlawful" or "illegal" combatant in the Geneva Conventions or their Additional Protocols, notwithstanding the use of these terms in the post-9/11 era. However, there is an implicit status of unprivileged belligerent: PW status and treatment are denied to spies, mercenaries and, by default, to any sort of combatant not listed as entitled to them in the Geneva Conventions.

In practice, the determination of those combatants entitled to PW status or treatment and those who are not may be a complicated question of fact — especially for those combatants who are not members of formal armed forces. For this reason, Geneva Convention III[27] and the Additional Protocol I[28] both specify that, where there is doubt, the status of combatants in an international conflict is to be determined by a competent tribunal, and pending that body's ruling, combatants are to be treated as PWs.

This issue arose most controversially in the 2001 war in Afghanistan between the United States and its allies and the Taliban and al-Qaeda. In a now famous legal memorandum, then U.S. deputy assistant attorney general (and professor of law) John Yoo argued that the Geneva Conventions apply only to states, and thus do not attach to al-Qaeda detainees or even to the Taliban, the *de facto* government of a "failed state."[29] His assertion that Afghanistan under the Taliban "was without the attributes of statehood necessary to continue as a party to

---

26 *Geneva Convention relative to the Treatment of Prisoners of War*, Art. 4 [Geneva Convention III].

27 *Ibid.*, Art. 5.

28 AP I, above note 24, Art. 45.

29 Memo 4 (9 January 2002), in Karen Greenberg & Joshua Dratel, eds., *The Torture Papers: The Road to Abu Ghraib* (Cambridge: Cambridge University Press, 2005) at 29–30.

the Geneva Conventions"[30] was presented without reference to authority; not surprising, given the disconnect between this statement and international law's doctrines of state continuity. A state is not relieved of obligations—or disentitled to rights—in international law where governments are illegitimate.[31] President Bush subsequently declared that the Geneva Conventions would apply to the Taliban, but not to al-Qaeda.[32] Nevertheless, during the 2001 conflict, the United States took the firm view that neither the Taliban nor al-Qaeda qualified for PW status, and declined to test this presumption in front of a status-determination tribunal. It has since held many fighters captured during this conflict for prolonged periods at Guantanamo Bay naval base.[33]

Whether the United States has met its obligations under the Third Geneva Convention in relation to at least Taliban fighters captured in 2001–2 is disputable. On the one hand, it seems plausible that the Taliban did not qualify for lawful combatancy status.[34] On the other hand, critics urge that doubt did exist as to the status of Taliban fight-

---

30   *Ibid.* at 30.

31   See, for example, *Anguilar-Amory and Royal Bank of Canada Claims (Great Britain v. Costa Rica)* (1923), 1 R.I.A.A. 375.

32   George W. Bush, *Memorandum: Humane Treatment of Al Qaeda and Taliban Detainees*, para. 2(a) (Feb. 7, 2002), online: www1.umn.edu/humanrts/OathBe-trayed/Bush%202-7-02.pdf.

33   Recent developments in this area are described below. To date, the United States has not conducted Geneva Convention III status-review assessments. The Combatant Status Review Tribunals introduced in 2004 do not assess PW status questions, a point also discussed below.

34   Exactly what standard would apply to measure whether the Taliban were lawful combatants is a matter of contention. See, for example, Joseph Bialke, "Al-Qaeda & Taliban Unlawful Combatant Detainees, Unlawful Belligerency, and the International Laws Of Armed Conflict" (2004) 55 A.F.L. Rev. 1 at 51 *et seq.* ("there is no question, doubt, or ambiguity that they failed en masse to meet any of the four criteria of lawful belligerency and, subsequently then, equally no doubt as to their status as unlawful combatants") and at 20, n24 *et seq.* Note that Bialke urges that the Taliban were required to meet the "four criteria" to be lawful combatants. These criteria are those discussed at note 26, above, and the accompanying text, found in Geneva Convention III. The United States has regularly asserted that these four criteria must be met by combatants to be entitled to lawful belligerent status. This view is not shared, at least in relation to "armed forces," by those who point to the definition of "armed force" in AP I. See discussion in Robert Goldman & Brian Tittemore, "Unprivileged Combatants and the Hostilities in Afghanistan: Their Status and Rights Under International Human Rights and Humanitarian Law," in *American Society of International Law: Task Force Papers* (December 2002), online: www.asil.org/taskforce/goldman.pdf. These authorities urge that a violation of the four criteria by a member of an armed force may constitute a violation of IHL, but that it does not strip them (in most instances) of privileged combatant status *per se.* See Bialke, *ibid.* at 16.

ers.[35] Not least, the fact that members of the Taliban were noncompliant with IHL—a common justification for applying the unlawful belligerent label—should not be taken as automatically disentitling all those fighting for the then *de facto* government of Afghanistan to PW status. If the standard for PW status were the absence of any war crimes committed by members of an armed force, few militaries in a situation of armed conflict would satisfy this requirement.[36] In these circumstances, critics suggested that the most appropriate course in a clear international conflict between two state parties to the Geneva Conventions was to test the status of detainees in front of a competent tribunal, as required by Geneva Convention III, something that has never happened.[37]

It is important to note that the scope of unprivileged belligerent status is much broader in noninternational than in international conflicts. The former are not governed (for the most part) by the Geneva Conventions, and there is no PW concept. The analysis of the PW situation in Afghanistan by the time of this writing is, therefore, very different than was the case in 2001–2, a matter discussed further below.

c) Treatment of Detainees

i) *PW Treatment*
PW status brings with it a number of privileges too numerous to list in a general treatise like this one. One of the most important distinctions between PWs and unprivileged belligerents—that is, those not entitled

---

35   See discussion in George H. Aldrich, "The Taliban, Al Qaeda, and the Determination of Illegal Combatants" (2002) 96 A.J.I.L. 891. See also, for example, Organization of American States, Inter-American Commission on Human Rights, *Detainees in Guantanamo Bay, Cuba; Request for Precautionary Measures*, Inter-Am. C.H.R. (13 March 2002).

36   See discussion in Goldman & Tittemore, "Unprivileged Combatants," above note 34 at 27.

37   More recently, the United States has conducted status reviews (albeit to determine whether individuals should be detained at all and not to decide whether they are PWs). This approach followed *Hamdi v. Rumsfeld*, 542 U.S. 507 (2004). In this case, the U.S. Supreme Court concluded that the detention of U.S. citizens as enemy combatants necessitated some meaningful means of contesting that detention in front of a neutral decision-maker. In *Rasul v. Bush*, 542 U.S. 466 (2004), the Court agreed that detainees at Guantanamo Bay could seek *habeas corpus* remedies in U.S. federal court, pursuant to the statute law governing those courts. Subsequently, the Bush administration established combatant status review tribunals, assessing the detention of detainees at Guantanamo Bay to confirm whether they were being properly held. See Order Establishing Combatant Status Review Tribunal, Deputy Secretary of Defense (7 July 2004), online: www.defenselink.mil/releases/release.aspx?releaseid=7530.

to PW status or treatment—is that the former cannot be prosecuted by the detaining state for bearing arms in the conflict and conducting hostilities, if done in a manner otherwise lawful under IHL.[38] This so-called combatant's privilege, discussed in Chapter 5, does not extend to unprivileged belligerents, who may be prosecuted by the detaining state for their acts of violence during the conflict.

Because PW status and the related combatant's privilege exist only in international conflicts,[39] combatants in noninternational conflicts may be prosecuted more readily for their activities. It should be noted, however, that Additional Protocol II does call upon the authorities in power at the end of the conflict to "endeavour to grant the broadest possible amnesty to persons who have participated in the armed conflict, or those deprived of their liberty for reasons related to the armed conflict, whether they are interned or detained."[40]

ii) Treatment of Unprivileged Belligerents

a. International Armed Conflicts

It is important to note that even unprivileged belligerents are entitled to certain fundamental guarantees while detained.[41] For instance, Additional Protocol I (applicable to international conflicts) specifies that

> any person arrested, detained or interned for actions related to the armed conflict shall be informed promptly, in a language he understands, of the reasons why these measures have been taken. Except

---

38 Geneva Convention III, above note 26, Art. 99, for example, provides that "No prisoner of war may be tried or sentenced for an act which is not forbidden by the law of the Detaining Power or by international law." Combatant's privilege also has customary international law status. For a discussion of combatant's privilege, see Robert Goldman & Brian Tittemore, "Unprivileged Combatants," above note 34; Knutt Dormann, "The Legal Situation of "Unlawful/Unprivileged Combatants" (2003) 849 Int'l Rev. Red Cross 45 at 45 ("[lawful] combatants cannot be prosecuted for lawful acts of war in the course of military operations even if their behaviour would constitute a serious crime in peacetime. They can be prosecuted only for violations of international humanitarian law, in particular for war crimes"); Kenneth Watkin, *Warriors without Rights? Combatants, Unprivileged Belligerents, and Struggle over Legitimacy* (Cambridge, MA: Harvard Program on Humanitarian Policy and Conflict Research, 2005) at 12; Bialke, "Al-Qaeda & Taliban," above note 34 at 9.

39 Dormann, "Legal Situation," *ibid.* at 47 ("The law applicable in non-international armed conflicts does not foresee a combatant's privilege [i.e. the right to participate in hostilities and impunity for lawful acts of hostility"]).

40 *Protocol Additional to the Geneva Conventions of 12 August 1949, and relating to the Protection of Victims of Non-International Armed Conflicts*, Art. 6(5) [AP II].

41 AP I, above note 24, Art. 75 (discussed more fully below).

in cases of arrest or detention for penal offences, such persons shall be released with the minimum delay possible and in any event as soon as the circumstances justifying the arrest, detention or internment have ceased to exist.[42]

Even civilians who take up arms in a manner not authorized by IHL may still be subject to the Geneva Conventions' supplemental rules on civilian internment.[43] Geneva Convention IV governs the conduct of an occupying power in relation to civilians, or more correctly those "who, at a given moment and in any manner whatsoever, find themselves, in case of a conflict or occupation, in the hands of a Party to the conflict or Occupying Power of which they are not nationals"[44] who are not otherwise protected by Geneva Conventions I through III (for example, prisoners of war). Geneva Convention IV allows internment of these people, but only if the security of the detaining state "makes it absolutely necessary."[45]

Moreover, "any protected person who has been interned or placed in assigned residence shall be entitled to have such action reconsidered as soon as possible by an appropriate court or administrative board designated by the Detaining Power for that purpose." Subsequent reconsideration must be done at least twice yearly "with a view to the favourable amendment of the initial decision, if circumstances permit."[46]

---

42   *Ibid.*

43   For a comprehensive analysis of the applicability of *Convention relative to the Protection of Civilian Persons in Time of War* [Geneva Convention IV] to illegal combatants, see Dormann, "Legal Situation," above note 39 at 73 ("The fact that a person has unlawfully participated in hostilities is not a criterion for excluding the application of GC IV, though it may be a reason for derogating from certain rights in accordance with Article 5 thereof").

44   Geneva Convention IV, *ibid.*, Art. 4. Note, however, that Article 4 also provides that "nationals of a neutral State who find themselves in the territory of a belligerent State, and nationals of a co-belligerent State, shall not be regarded as protected persons while the State of which they are nationals has normal diplomatic representation in the State in whose hands they are." For example, belligerents fighting with the Taliban in 2001, who came from states allied with the United States, would not be protected by the Convention.

45   *Ibid.*, Art. 42.

46   *Ibid.*, Art. 43.

b.   Noninternational Conflicts

In noninternational conflicts, Common Article 3 guarantees humane treatment of all detainees.[47] Likewise, Additional Protocol II includes its own, detailed rules on treatment of persons interned by reason of the conflict or prosecuted for conduct in it.[48] Commenting on these internee protections, the Canadian Forces IHL manual notes: "Since noninternational armed conflicts often reflect ideological and emotional conflict even more than is the case in international conflicts, the need to protect those detained or in any way restricted for reasons connected with the conflict is very important."[49]

3) Duration of Detention

Prisoners of war are to be released and repatriated without delay upon cessation of hostilities.[50] Civilians interned in an international conflict per Geneva Convention IV are also to be released as soon as the circumstances justifying internment expire, and in any event after the end of hostilities. However, internees being prosecuted for indictable crimes may be detained pending the outcome of that prosecution and any subsequent period of incarceration on conviction.[51] This Geneva Convention IV provision applies presumptively to civilian unprivil-

---

47   Common Art. 3 of *Convention for the Amelioration of the Condition of the Wounded and Sick in Armed Forces in the Field*, *Convention for the Amelioration of the Condition of Wounded, Sick and Shipwrecked Members of Armed Forces at Sea*, *Convention relative to the Treatment of Prisoners of War*, and *Convention relative to the Protection of Civilian Persons in Time of War*. Article 3 bars, *inter alia*, "The passing of sentences and the carrying out of executions without previous judgment pronounced by a regularly constituted court affording all the judicial guarantees which are recognized as indispensable by civilized peoples."

48   AP II, Arts. 4–6. Note also that pursuant to Common Art. 3 of the Geneva Conventions, applicable in noninternational conflicts, the following is prohibited in relation to persons not actively participating in the conflict: "The passing of sentences and the carrying out of executions without previous judgment pronounced by a regularly constituted court affording all the judicial guarantees which are recognized as indispensable by civilized peoples."

49   Canada, Department of National Defence (JAG), *Law of Armed Conflict at the Operational and Tactical Level* (2001) at 17-4, online: www.dnd.ca/jag/training/publications/law_of_armed_conflict/loac_2004_e.pdf.

50   Geneva Convention III, above note 26, Art. 118.

51   Geneva Convention IV, above note 43, Art. 133. See also AP I, above note 24, Art. 75(3), also applicable to international conflicts, specifying that "Any person arrested, detained or interned for actions related to the armed conflict ... shall be released with the minimum delay possible and in any event as soon as the circumstances justifying the arrest, detention or internment have ceased to exist" ("except in cases of arrest or detention for penal offences").

eged belligerents, requiring that these persons be released at the end of an international armed conflict unless prosecuted for their crimes.[52] Put another way, detention under the Geneva Conventions may persist only for the duration of an international armed conflict, except if extended as part of a criminal prosecution for indictable offences.

The post-9/11 era has produced several controversies concerning these provisions.

a)   Indefinite Detention

i)   International Conflict
First, a key preoccupation in the campaign against terrorism is the ambiguous nature of the conflict. If the "war on terror" is viewed as a *bona fide* "armed conflict" as that term is understood in IHL, its inherent ambiguity may result in prolonged, indeterminate detentions. As discussed below, this is a matter raised—but not yet resolved—in U.S. courts.

The most plausible view is that the "war on terror" has never constituted an armed conflict outside of the Afghan (and Iraq) theatres, a matter discussed in Chapter 6. For exactly this reason, the U.N. human rights special rapporteurs applied the human rights law described above—and not the *lex specialis* of IHL—in assessing the validity of Guantanamo Bay detentions of persons captured in places like Bosnia.[53]

ii)   Noninternational Conflict
It is also notable that the conflict in Afghanistan (and Iraq) is no longer between two state parties to the Geneva Conventions, instead amounting to a counterinsurgency campaign by a domestic government supported by foreign forces. In these circumstances, there is almost certainly no longer an international conflict.[54] Some Canadian officials

---

52   See Special Rapporteurs Report, above note 23 at 22.

53   *Ibid.* at 14.

54   See *ibid.* at 9 (taking this view). See also International Committee of the Red Cross, *International Humanitarian Law and Terrorism: Questions and Answers* (May 2004) (describing the conflict in Afghanistan since the establishment of the new government in June 2002 as noninternational), online: www.icrc. org/Web/Eng/siteeng0.nsf/html/5YNLEV. There is, however, a view expressed among legal scholars that the participation of an international military in an otherwise noninternational, civil conflict "internationalizes" that armed conflict, and attracts the application of the full Geneva Conventions. See discussion in Helen Duffy, *The "War on Terror" and the Framework of International Law* (Cambridge: Cambridge University Press, 2005) at 220 [*War on Terror*] and also the debate recorded in International Committee of the Red Cross, *XXVIIth Round Table on Current Problems of International Humanitarian Law: "International Humanitarian Law and Other Legal Regimes: Interplay in Situa-*

apparently take the view that the noninternational nature of the current Afghan conflict means that the Geneva Conventions "do not apply as a matter of treaty law."[55] This statement is true, to a point. The better part of the Geneva Conventions does not apply. For instance, Taliban prisoners in the current Afghan conflict are not entitled to PW status under Geneva Convention III. As noted, the PW concept in the latter instrument applies only in international conflicts. However, detainees in a noninternational conflict are certainly entitled to minimum standards of humane treatment, under Common Article 3, as amplified by Additional Protocol II and/or customary international law.[56]

Unlike Geneva Convention III and IV, Common Article 3 and Additional Protocol II contain no clear rule on how long detentions may endure. Nevertheless, Protocol II does imply that such detentions may endure for the period of the conflict,[57] and calls on the authorities in power at the end of hostilities to "grant the broadest possible amnesty

---

tions of Violence" (2003) at 3 and n7, online: www.icrc.org/Web/eng/siteeng0.nsf/htmlall/5UBCVX/$File/Interplay_other_regimes_Nov_2003.pdf. Some support for this view may be found in *Prosecutor v. Tadic* (Appeal on Jurisdiction), Case IT-94-1-AR72 (ICTY Appeals Chamber 1995). In that case, the Appeals Chamber of the International Criminal Tribunal for the former Yugoslavia concluded that the participation of the Serbian military in the civil conflict between the Bosnian government and the Bosnian Serb militias created a situation of "international" armed conflict, within the meaning of Common Article 2 of the Geneva Conventions. That judgment concerned an intervention where one state used a nonstate proxy to engage in armed conflict against another state. It is not, therefore, analogous to a situation where a state intervenes *in alliance* with a state government to combat a nonstate actor. It is difficult to see how the latter situation meets the requirements of Common Article 2 for international conflict: that is, a situation in which two state parties are in a situation of armed conflict. For a discussion of "internationalized armed conflicts," see James Stewart, "Towards a Single Definition of Armed Conflict in International Humanitarian Law: A Critique of Internationalized Armed Conflict" (2003) 850 Int'l Rev. Red Cross 313.

55   Then Minister of Foreign Affairs Peter MacKay, Standing Committee on National Defence, 30th Parl., 1st Sess., Evidence (6 June 2006). See also Paul Koring, "Troops Told Geneva Rules Don't Apply to Taliban" *Globe and Mail* (31 May 2006) A1 (quoting Canadian Forces officer as observing that the prisoner of war provisions do not apply in noninternational conflicts).

56   AP II, above note 40, Arts. 4–6. It should be noted that Afghanistan is not a party to AP II. At least portions of AP II are, however, customary international law. See, for example, the discussion of detention provisions in Jean-Marie Henckaerts & Louise Doswald-Beck, *Customary International Humanitarian Law* (Cambridge; New York: Cambridge University Press, 2005) at 451 *et seq.*

57   AP II, *ibid.*, Art. 2 suggests that detentions may last up to and beyond the end of an armed conflict, so long as they comport with the standards of treatment set out in Arts. 5–6.

to persons ... deprived of their liberty for reasons related to the armed conflict, whether they are interned or detained."[58] The latter is an implicit postconflict release provision.[59]

b) Criminal Prosecution of Detainees

i) Applicable Principles
A second controversy concerns the nature of the criminal proceedings that may be brought against detainees, potentially producing extended criminal detention or even more severe penalties. As indicated, unprivileged belligerents do not enjoy combatant's privilege and are liable to criminal prosecution for their acts of violence. IHL, however, constrains the nature of these trials.

a. International Conflicts
As noted above, Additional Protocol I, applicable to international conflicts, specifies that "any person arrested, detained or interned for actions related to the armed conflict shall be informed promptly, in a language he understands, of the reasons why these measures have been taken."[60] Where the person is tried for penal offences, a number of fair trial guarantees echoing those found in international human rights laws exist. Not least, "no sentence may be passed and no penalty may be executed on a person found guilty of a penal offence related to the armed conflict except pursuant to a conviction pronounced by an impartial and regularly constituted court respecting the generally recognized principles of regular judicial procedure."[61]

---

58   *Ibid.*, Art. 6.
59   To be sure, the matter of whether AP II permits prolonged detentions during the conflict is not clear-cut. It might be argued, therefore, that regular human rights law persists in full form in any examination of the process surrounding the period of detention. If one accepts the (sometimes disputed) view that a state's forces deployed abroad must meet that state's human rights obligations, the duration of any detention made by Canada in Afghanistan is to be measured against Canada's obligations under the ICCPR. As noted above, the latter instrument anticipates in Art. 9 court proceedings to justify a detention occurring soon after a person is detained. Long-term detention in a prison camp might violate these requirements. This assumes, of course, that the state in question does not make a derogation under Art. 4 of the ICCPR owing to a "public emergency which threatens the life of the nation" as it is entitled to with respect to Art. 9.
60   AP I, above note 24, Art. 75(3).
61   *Ibid.*, Art. 75(4).

b.   Noninternational Conflicts

Similar rules exist for noninternational conflicts. Common Article 3 of the Geneva Conventions bars "the passing of sentences and the carrying out of executions without previous judgment pronounced by a regularly constituted court affording all the judicial guarantees which are recognized as indispensable by civilized peoples." Additional Protocol II amplifies these rights and, among other things, obliges trials before "a court offering the essential guarantees of independence and impartiality."[62]

ii)   United States Practice

In the United States, the Bush administration has not embraced these rules on prosecutions enthusiastically in the "war on terror."[63] In November 2001, President Bush issued an order on the trial of "non-citizens in the war against terrorism."[64] Directed at persons believed to be members of al-Qaeda, the order authorized the defense secretary to establish "military commissions" for the trial of these individuals, when declared "enemy combatants."

These commissions were widely derided as failing to meet basic due process standards.[65] They were challenged successfully on constitutional grounds before the U.S. Supreme Court in *Hamdan v. Rumsfeld*.[66] Among other things, the Court invoked Common Article 3 of the Geneva Conventions (concluding it applied to what it characterized as the noninternational conflict between the United States and al-Qaeda). The Court held that whatever else this provision signifies, it usually requires a trial according to an ordinary courts-martial process.[67]

In response, Congress passed the *Military Commissions Act of 2006*,[68] creating new military court adjudicative arrangements for non-U.S. citizens labelled "unlawful enemy combatants" and stripping U.S. federal courts of jurisdiction over these individuals. Human rights groups immediately voiced concern about the due process standards in the new

---

62   AP II, above note 40, Art. 6(2).
63   It should be noted that the United States is not a party to Additional Protocols I and II, having signed but not ratified these instruments.
64   "Detention, Treatment, and Trial of Certain Non-Citizens in the War against Terrorism," 66 Fed. Reg. 57833 (13 November 2001).
65   See, for example, Human Rights Watch, *Briefing Paper on U.S. Military Commissions* (23 June 2006), online: http://hrw.org/backgrounder/usa/gitmo0705/.
66   126 S. Ct. 2749 (2006).
67   *Ibid.* at 2797.
68   Pub. L. No. 109-366, 120 Stat. 2600 (17 October 2006).

mechanism,[69] and by the time of this writing, new constitutional challenges were making their way through the U.S. courts.[70]

One key issue that remained outstanding at the time of this writing was the potential extension of the new military commissions to persons detained by the United States in circumstances other than the armed conflict in Afghanistan (or Iraq). The U.S. rules do not appear to distinguish between persons captured in the latter conflicts and detentions arising in other circumstances. However, as already noted, detentions outside of an armed conflict are governed by international human rights, including the fair trial rights found in the ICCPR. The U.N. Human Rights Commission has observed that these human rights guarantees are often not met by military or specialized tribunals and has urged that "the trying of civilians by such courts should be very exceptional and take place under conditions which genuinely afford the full guarantees stipulated in article 14" of the ICCPR.[71] Further, detainees are guaranteed a right to *habeas corpus* by Article 9 of the ICCPR, a right clearly denied by the 2006 Act.

By the time of this writing, the U.N. Expert on Human Rights and Counter-terrorism had expressed concern about compatibility of the new *Military Commissions Act* with U.S. obligations under both international humanitarian and human rights law.[72]

---

69   See, for example, Human Rights Watch, *Q & A: Military Commissions Act of 2006* (October 2006), online: http://hrw.org/backgrounder/usa/qna1006/. For a discussion of use of evidence produced by coercion in these commissions, see Chapter 15.

70   See, for example, *Hamdan v. Rumsfeld*, 464 F. Supp.2d 9 (D.D.C. 2006); *Boumediene v. Bush* 2007 U.S. App. LEXIS 3682 (D.C. Cir. 2007). In both cases, the constitutional objections to the removal of federal court *habeas corpus* jurisdiction were rejected. The matter is currently before the Supreme Court.

71   Human Rights Committee, *General Comment No. 13* (1984) at para. 4, online: www.unhchr.ch/tbs/doc.nsf/(Symbol)/bb722416a295f264c12563ed0049dfbd?O pendocument. See also Inter-American Commission on Human Rights, *Report on Terrorism and Human Rights*, OEA/Ser.L/V/II.116 Doc. 5 rev. 1 corr. (22 Oct. 2002) at para. 231 ("It has been widely concluded in this regard that military tribunals by their very nature do not satisfy the requirements of independent and impartial courts applicable to the trial of civilians, because they are not a part of the independent civilian judiciary but rather are a part of the Executive branch, and because their fundamental purpose is to maintain order and discipline by punishing military offenses committed by members of the military establishment").

72   U.N., Press Release, UN Expert On Human Rights And Counter Terrorism Concerned That Military Commissions Act Is Now Law In United States (27 October 2006).

c) Detainee Transfers

Detainee questions become especially complicated when individuals are transferred between two detaining powers. Transfers of detainees captured by the Canadian Forces to the U.S. military and, more recently, to Afghan authorities have fuelled substantial controversy. In both instances, critics have suggested that these detainees may be abused in the hands of their new captors, imposing on Canada an obligation either to decline the transfer and/or to supervise the detainee's subsequent treatment.

i) Applicable Principles

Geneva Convention III, governing transfer of prisoners of war in an international conflict, is clear. PWs may only be transferred by a party to the Convention to another party to the Convention, and only after the detaining party "has satisfied itself of the willingness and ability of such transferee Power to apply the Convention." Moreover, "if that [transferee] Power fails to carry out the provisions of the Convention in any important respect" and is notified of this by the "protecting power" (typically, the International Committee of the Red Cross), the original detaining state must "take effective measures to correct the situation or shall request the return of the prisoners of war. Such requests must be complied with."[73] Geneva Convention IV—relating to the treatment of civilians in occupied states—contains identical guarantees applicable to civilian detainees.[74]

ii) Canadian Practice

a. Transfer to U.S. Forces

In the initial phase of operations in Afghanistan against the Taliban and al-Qaeda, Canadian Forces personnel transferred detained fighters to U.S. forces. As noted, the United States' fixed presumption that these fighters were "unlawful combatants" not entitled to PW status and its failure to test this supposition in front of a tribunal may have ran counter to U.S. obligations under the Geneva Convention.[75] If so, then once apprised of this fact, further Canadian Forces transfers to U.S. custody might be inconsistent with Canadian transfer obligations

---

73 Geneva Convention III, above note 26, Art. 12.
74 Geneva Convention IV, above note 43, Art. 45.
75 See discussion above. This was, in fact, the conclusion of the Organization of American States, Inter-American Commission on Human Rights, *Detainees in Guantanamo Bay, Cuba; Request for Precautionary Measures*, above note 35.

under the Geneva Conventions.[76] This question generated controversy in Canada in 2002.[77]

b.   Transfer to the Afghan Government

The situation by the time of this writing was more complex. As noted, the conflict in Afghanistan is almost certainly no longer an international conflict governed by the Geneva Conventions, other than Common Article 3. The Geneva Convention PW and detainee transfer provisions no longer apply. Additional Protocol II, applicable to such conflicts,[78] contains rules on the appropriate treatment of detainees, but is silent on the transfer issue.[79]

However, in any conflict — international or noninternational — IHL does not entirely displace human rights law. This is acutely the case in relation to the prohibition on torture, a ban that is nonderogable even in the most extreme circumstances under the ICCPR and that almost certainly extends to the extraterritorial actions of a state's military.[80] Transfer of persons where there are grounds to believe they would face

---

76   If the United States nevertheless accorded the detainees PW treatment, there would be no real noncompliance with the Convention and Canada would likely remain compliant with its transfer obligations. A United States failure, however, to apply the PW treatment standards in Geneva Convention III would mean that the associated failure to undergo a status determination justifying this position could constitute a significant breach of U.S. obligations, raising concerns about Canada's own compliance with its obligations if it were to transfer detainees.

77   See summary in Janet Bagnall, "Prisoners Put Canada on Spot" [Montreal] Gazette (19 January 2002) B.2.

78   As noted, Afghanistan is not a party to AP II. The relevant detention principles contained in AP II may, however, apply as a matter of customary international law. See Henckaerts & Doswald-Beck, Customary International Humanitarian Law, above note 56 at 306 et seq. and 428 et seq.

79   Although, of course, a transfer that amounts to aiding and abetting a violation of certain prohibitions in IHL — such as the bar on torture and inhuman treatment — would obviously be prohibited as a matter of international criminal law. Rome Statute of the International Criminal Court, U.N. Doc. A/CONF.183/9, Arts. 8 and 25 [Rome Statute]. Aiding and abetting requires more than the absence of due care. Summarizing the international jurisprudence on this issue, a U.S. federal court recently described the elements of this inchoate offence as follows: "1) that the principal violated international law; 2) that the defendant knew of the specific violation; 3) that the defendant acted with the intent to assist that violation, that is, the defendant specifically directed his acts to assist in the specific violation; 4) that the defendant's acts had a substantial effect upon the success of the criminal venture; and 5) that the defendant was aware that the acts assisted the specific violation." Presbyterian Church of Sudan v. Talisman Energy, Inc., 2006 U.S. Dist. LEXIS 64579 at *86 (S.D.N.Y.).

80   See Chapter 2.

torture would be a violation of these human rights standards.[81] This may be true even if the transfer takes place outside a state's territory.[82]

This issue has played out recently in public debates concerning transfers of Taliban fighters captured by the Canadian Forces to Afghan authorities. Human rights groups and others worried in 2006 and 2007 about Afghanistan's record on torture of prisoners and what that record might bode for transferees.[83] This concern is warranted: given Afghanistan's unsatisfactory track record on torture, Canada and other NATO countries run a serious risk that that country's prisons will produce an Abu Ghraib-like scandal, one that tarnishes the reputation of NATO armies transferring detainees to Afghan authorities. Indeed, at the time of this writing in 2007, allegations of maltreatment of detainees transferred from Canadian custody to Afghan authorities were front-page news.[84] To guard against an unwitting transfer to problematic Afghan prisons, some analysts have suggested that NATO sponsor development of a modern prison facility run by Afghans, but closely monitored by NATO.[85]

By the time of this writing, however, the response to these concerns was confined to a (now amplified) detainee transfer "arrangement."[86] That 2005 instrument specifies that both Canada and Afghanistan will "treat detainees in accordance with the standards set out in the Third Geneva Convention." The agreement also indicates that transferees may not be subject to the death penalty and that the International Commit-

---

81   See discussion below at note 229. See also the conclusions of Human Rights Committee, *General Comment 20*, Art. 7 (44th sess., 1992)

82   There does not appear to be any clear ICCPR jurisprudence on this question. However, the United States has defended its practice of extraordinary rendition from criticism under Art. 3 of the Torture Convention, above note 17, by arguing that that provision's bar on removal to torture applies only to removals from the territory of the United States. The U.N. Committee Against Torture has rejected this interpretation. U.N. Doc. CAT/C/U.S.A/CO/2 at para. 20 (18 May 2006).

83   David Pugliese, "Soldiers Risk War Crimes Charges" *Ottawa Citizen* (10 April 2006) A1.

84   See, for example, Graeme Smith, "From Canadian Custody into Cruel Hands" *Globe and Mail* (23 April 2007) A1.

85   For discussion, see, for example, David Bosco, "A Duty NATO is Dodging in Afghanistan" *Washington Post* (5 November 2006) B.7.

86   See *Arrangement for the Transfer of Detainees Between the Canadian Forces and the Ministry of Defence of the Islamic Republic of Afghanistan* (version dated 18 September 2005), online: www.forces.gc.ca/site/operations/archer/Afghanistan_Detainee_Arrangement_e.pdf and supplemental arrangement (version dated 3 May 2007), online: http://geo.international.gc.ca/cip-pic/afghanistan/pdf/agreement_detainees_030507.pdf.

tee of the Red Cross (ICRC) is to "have a right to visit detainees at any time while they are in custody." The arrangement also alludes to a role to be played by the Afghanistan Independent Human Rights Commission on the question of detainees.

In its initial iteration in 2005, this arrangement was condemned as inadequate under international law.[87] Some of this criticism of Canada's noncompliance with international law was likely exaggerated, assuming the arrangement operated as intended. As a factual matter, the ICRC reportedly expressed satisfaction in 2006 with the way that detainee transfers had occurred.[88] There was, however, ambiguity in one of the key promises in the arrangement: to "treat detainees in accordance with the standards set out in the Third Geneva Convention."[89] Moreover,

---

87   See, for example, Michael Byers, *Legal Opinion on the December 18, 2005 Arrangement for the Transfer of Detainees between the Canadian Forces and the Ministry of Defence of the Islamic Republic of Afghanistan* (7 April 2006), online: www.ceasefire.ca/atf/cf/%7B0A14BA6C-BE4F-445B-8C13-51BED95A5CF3%7D/ Michael%20Byers%20Opinion%20Canada-Afghanistan%20Arrangement%207% 20April%202006.pdf.

88   John Ward, "Prisoner Rules Respected: Red Cross" *The [Montreal] Gazette* (2 October 2006) A.10. At the time this writing, exactly what information the ICRC could provide on transferees was a matter of considerable confusion and political debate in Parliament.

89   Much hinges on how the word "standards" is interpreted. Does this word mean that detainees are entitled to *actual* PW status or treatment, or instead does it mean that they are entitled to be processed according to the procedure anticipated in Geneva Convention III; that is, they receive PW status or treatment *so long as* they meet the requirements for PW treatment under Geneva Convention III? The agreement seems to anticipate at least some detainees *not being* PWs. Article 8 specifies that "should any doubt exist whether a detainee may be a Prisoner of War, the detainee will be treated humanely, at all times and under all circumstances, in a manner consistent with the rights and protections of the Third Geneva Convention." This passage creates its own ambiguities. What if there is *no* doubt that the detainee is *not* a PW? Most (and probably all) of the detainees in the Afghan theatre are not entitled to this PW status, as they do not fall into classes of combatants recognized by the Convention. If the intent of the agreement is to accord all detainees, no matter what their status, PW treatment, why does the agreement not simply say that PW treatment is to be accorded to all detainees, plain and simple? The government seems to take the view that PW treatment is accorded to all detainees under the agreement. See Ms. Colleen Swords (Assistant Deputy Minister, International Security Branch and Political Director, Department of Foreign Affairs and International Trade), Standing Committee on National Defence, 30th Parl., 1st Sess. (11 December 2006) ("the arrangement includes a commitment to treat detainees humanely and in accordance with the standards set out for prisoners of war in the Third Geneva Convention, which affords detainees with the highest treatment standard regardless of their status *and obviates the need for status determination*") [emphasis added].

unlike the agreements struck between Afghanistan and other NATO countries, the Canadian arrangement included no follow-up monitoring of transferred detainees by Canadian officials themselves.

In early 2007, a legal challenge to the Canadian Forces prisoner exchange practices was brought by human rights groups in Federal Court.[90] With allegations of detainee abuse in the hands of Afghan authorities a recurring press story, and faced with an application in the Federal Court case for an interlocutory injunction on further prisoner transfers, the government concluded a revised transfer arrangement with Afghanistan in May 2007.[91]

Under the amendments, the prohibition on torture and cruel, inhuman or degrading treatment is emphatic and the precise role of the Afghan Independent Human Rights Commission in monitoring detainees is clearer. Further, Canadian officials are to have "full and unrestricted access to any persons transferred by the Canadian Forces to Afghan authorities while such persons are in custody." The Canadian government is to be notified before transferred prisoners are tried, released, transferred to another state or undergo any "material change of circumstances ... including any instance of alleged improper treatment." The Afghan government also agrees to record-keeping obligations, to limiting the number of detention facilities in which detainees will be held and to an investigative procedure should allegations of mistreatment come to the attention of the Canadian government.

By the time of this writing, the revised arrangement compared quite favourably with similar agreements concluded between Afghanistan and other NATO states.

Still, the ambiguity on the reach of Geneva Convention III is unfortunate. That ambiguity appears to have been in part corrected by the more emphatic treatment promises made in the amended 2007 agreement.

90 This application for judicial review urged extraterritorial application of the *Charter of Rights and Freedoms* to the actions of the Canadian Forces in Afghanistan. The matter had not been decided by the time of this writing.

91 *Arrangement for the Transfer of Detainees Between the Government of Canada and the Government of the Islamic Republic of Afghanistan* (Amendment dated 3 May 2006), online: http://geo.international.gc.ca/cip-pic/afghanistan/pdf/agreement_detainees_030507.pdf.

PART II: DOMESTIC STANDARDS

Like international law, the *Canadian Charter of Rights and Freedoms*[92] includes protections against arbitrary detentions. Section 7 guarantees everyone the right to liberty, and the right not be deprived of it without "fundamental justice." Section 9 codifies the right not to be arbitrarily detained or imprisoned, and guards against detentions made at the sole discretion of law enforcement.[93] Section 10 guarantees that upon arrest or detention, everyone has the right to "(a) be informed promptly of the reasons therefor; (b) to retain and instruct counsel without delay and to be informed of that right; and (c) to have the validity of the detention determined by way of *habeas corpus* and to be released if the detention is not lawful."

The content of these constitutional guarantees is best fleshed out with reference to specific detention powers in Canadian law. Section A of Part II begins by examining standard criminal law detention powers under the *Criminal Code*. These powers apply to all offences, including in the national security area. Section B focuses on the special detention rules now available in relation to terrorist activities, an area of some uncertainty in Canadian law by the time of this writing.

A. STANDARD CRIMINAL LAW

1) *Criminal Code* Arrest Powers

Under the *Criminal Code*, peace officers may make arrests pursuant to a warrant or, in limited circumstances, without a warrant. Warrants are typically issued by a justice in response to an information—a complaint of criminal conduct about a person.[94] They are, in other words, retrospective, concerning a completed crime and designed generally to forestall a failure to appear before a court by the accused in that crime.

Warrantless arrest is also possible in limited circumstances. For instance, under the *Criminal Code*, peace officers who witness a breach of the peace may arrest persons they find "committing" a breach of the peace or who, on reasonable grounds, "the peace officer believes

---

92 Above note 12.
93 See, for example, *R. v. Ladouceur*, [1990] 1 S.C.R. 1257 at para. 36.
94 *Criminal Code*, above note 3, s. 504 *et seq.*

is about to join in or renew the breach of the peace."[95] Because, on the express terms of this section, there must be a breach of the peace before the arrest power arises, the arrest here is only modestly pre-emptive.

A peace officer may also arrest without warrant a person he or she finds committing a crime. There is a pre-emptive aspect to this power: he or she may arrest a person who has committed an indictable crime or who, on reasonable grounds, the peace officer believes *is about to commit* an indictable offence.[96] The Supreme Court's constitutional jurisprudence grafts on an objective test to this subjective belief by the peace officer: "objectively there must exist reasonable and probable grounds for the warrantless arrest to be legal."[97] An arrest probably constitutes an arbitrary detention in violation of the *Charter of Rights and Freedoms* where there is an entire absence of reasonable and probable grounds.[98] Further, the power of warrantless arrest is more limited if the arrestee is in their dwelling house.[99]

There is no clear authority on how proximate a prospective indictable crime must be to permit this form of warrantless arrest. However, at least one provincial court of appeal has suggested that warrantless arrest under the *Criminal Code* is available to prevent harm likely to occur in the "immediate future." Warrantless arrest is not meant "as a mechanism whereby the police can control and monitor on an ongoing basis the comings and goings of those they regard as dangerous and prone to criminal activity."[100]

---

95 *Ibid.*, s. 31.

96 *Ibid.*, s. 495 [emphasis added].

97 *R. v. Feeney*, [1997] 2 S.C.R. 13 at para. 24.

98 See, for example, *R. v. Duguay* (1985), 18 C.C.C. (3d) 289 at 296 (Ont. C.A.) ("It cannot be that every unlawful arrest necessarily falls within the words 'arbitrarily detained.' The grounds upon which an arrest was made may fall 'just short' of constituting reasonable and probable cause. The person making the arrest may honestly, though mistakenly, believe that reasonable and probable grounds for the arrest exist and there may be some basis for that belief. In those circumstances the arrest, though subsequently found to be unlawful, could not be said to be capricious or arbitrary. On the other hand, the entire absence of reasonable and probable grounds for the arrest could support an inference that no reasonable person could have genuinely believed that such grounds existed. In such cases the conclusion would be that the person arrested was arbitrarily detained").

99 *Ibid.*

100 *Brown v. Regional Municipality of Durham* (1998), 167 D.L.R. (4th) 672 at paras. 74 & 75 (Ont. C.A.) [*Brown*] (discussing common law arrest powers but applying similar strictures to *Criminal Code* warrantless arrest rules).

2) Common Law Arrest Powers

The persistence of a supplemental, common law pre-emptive, "ancillary" arrest power in response to breaches of the peace is contested.[101] Some courts have held, however, that a pre-emptive common law arrest power persists in parallel to the *Criminal Code* to prevent breaches of the peace.[102] In *Brown v. Regional Municipality of Durham*, the Ontario Court of Appeal compared this ancillary common law arrest power to the *Criminal Code* warrantless arrest provisions, urging that the common law power endured and was available where the apprehended breach was "imminent and the risk that the breach will occur" was "substantial." For this reason "the mere possibility of some unspecified breach at some unknown point in time will not suffice."[103]

3) Postarrest Procedure

A person detained by a peace officer must be brought before a justice, usually within twenty-four hours.[104] However, where a justice is not available in that period, the *Criminal Code* specifies that the "person shall be taken before a justice as soon as possible."[105] Once before the justice, control over the accused shifts to the courts, and the regular criminal law arraignment and bail provisions apply. An accused denied bail is detained pending the outcome of the criminal proceedings. In practice, this may be a lengthy incarceration, but its duration is linked to a judicial process adjudicating the guilt of the individual in question.

If a conviction is entered, the offender is sentenced, often to a period of imprisonment. Because the sentence is time-limited, detention is not indefinite. Indeterminate detention may, however, be imposed via a special process of declaring the offender a "dangerous offender." This designation—which then justifies an indefinite sentence—is reserved

---

101 See discussion in Tim Quigley, *Procedure in Canadian Criminal Law* (Scarborough, ON: Carswell, 1997) at 84, n17.

102 *Brown*, above note 100.

103 *Brown*, *ibid*. at paras. 74 & 75 (discussing common law arrest powers but applying similar strictures to *Criminal Code* warrantless arrest rules). See also *R. v. Clayton*, 2007 SCC 32 at para. 29, citing *R. v. Mann*, 2004 SCC 52 at para. 40 (discussing common law powers to search incident to arrest and noting that "[t]he officer's decision to search must also be reasonably necessary in light of the totality of the circumstances. It cannot be justified on the basis of a vague or non-existent concern for safety, nor can the search be premised upon hunches or mere intuition").

104 *Criminal Code*, above note 3, s. 503 *et seq*.

105 *Ibid*., s. 503(1).

for particularly brutal criminals or repetitive criminal activity of a particularly harmful sort.[106] It is relatively uncommon: between 1978 and 2004, it was applied to 384 offenders. As of April 2005, the 335 dangerous offenders then incarcerated represented 2.5 percent of the total federal inmate population.[107]

In *R. v. Lyons*, the Supreme Court considered the constitutionality of dangerous offender status. Its reasoning strongly suggests that indeterminate detention under this regime was consistent with section 7 of the *Charter* only because it was part and parcel of the sentence handed down upon conviction for a criminal offence.[108]

B. ANTI-TERRORISM PREVENTIVE DETENTION

Special, anticipatory detention of feared terrorists has become a fixture in the post-9/11 environment. Some of these practices build on existing criminal law procedures. Others create an entirely parallel system. Among the most notorious of the latter practices are those associated with U.S. military custody of terrorism suspects at Guantanamo Bay and the CIA use of secret overseas detention facilities. Also controversial has been the United Kingdom system of "control orders." This section will briefly outline these two comparative practices, as well as the new system in Australia, before focusing on Canadian law.

1) Comparative Context

a) U.S. Anti-terrorism Preventive Detention
United States laws on preventive detention are paradoxical. On the one hand, that state has pursued an aggressive and controversial approach to the detention of terrorism suspects in offshore locations by the military and the Central Intelligence Agency. On the other, its civilian domestic laws generally reject preventive detention *per se*.

i) *Conventional Instruments*
U.S. Assistant Attorney General Viet Dinh urged in 2003 that "we do not engage in preventive detention. In this respect, our detention

---

106 *Ibid.*, Part XXIV.

107 Canada, PSEPC, *Statistics on Special Applications of Criminal Justice* (2006) at 103, online: www.securitepublique.gc.ca/res/em/_fl/section_e.pdf.

108 *R. v. Lyons*, [1987] 2 S.C.R. 309, 37 C.C.C. (3d) 1 at 21–22 (considering what was then Part XXI and what is now Part XXIV of the *Criminal Code*).

differs significantly from that of other countries, even our European partners.... What we do here is perhaps best described as preventative prosecution."[109] By "preventative prosecution," Viet Dinh meant a policy of aggressively enforcing even minor criminal and regulatory laws against those feared to pose a terrorist threat.

a.   Immigration Law

It is not entirely true that U.S. law does not include special terrorism-related preventive detention provisions. The *U.S.A. PATRIOT Act*, for example, amended U.S. immigration law to allow for mandatory detention of aliens certified a terrorist risk, pending removal, or for successive six-month periods "if the release of the alien will threaten the national security of the United States or the safety of the community or any person."[110] As Viet Dinh's statement suggests, however, the U.S. government has preferred to use stringent enforcement of more conventional immigration laws rather than resorting to this special anti-terrorism provision.[111] These conventional infractions include remaining past the expiration of visas, entering the United States without inspection or entering the country on invalid papers.

This policy—also called "preventive charging"[112]—is benign in principle but its application has produced controversy in the United States. Almost eight hundred persons with suspected terrorism connections were detained on conventional immigration law grounds in the immediate wake of 9/11. A 2003 U.S. Department of Justice report re-

---

109 Assistant Attorney General for the Office of Legal Policy Viet Dinh, "Life After 9/11: Issues Affecting the Courts and the Nation, Panel Discussion at U. of Kan. L. Sch.," reprinted in (2003) 51 U. Kan. L. Rev. 219 at 223. U.S. Department of Justice, *The* U.S.A. PATRIOT Act: *Myth vs. Reality* ("As of February 2004, the Attorney General had not used section 412. Numerous aliens who could have been considered have been detained since the enactment of the *U.S.A. PATRIOT Act*. But it has not proven necessary to use section 412 in these particular cases because traditional administrative bond proceedings have been sufficient to detain these individuals without bond"), online: www.lifeandliberty.gov/subs/add_myths.htm.

110 8 U.S.C § 1226a.

111 U.S. Department of Justice, *Questions Submitted by the House Judiciary Committee to the Attorney General on* U.S.A. PATRIOT Act *Implementation*, Ques. 36 at 17 (2002), online: www.epic.org/privacy/terrorism/usapatriot/foia/doj_submission1.pdf. It is not clear that U.S. policy will continue to eschew formal preventive detention. U.S. officials are reportedly interested in emulating the U.K. preventive detention laws, discussed further below. See Eric Lichtblau, "In Wake of Plot, Justice Dept. Will Study British Terror Laws" *New York Times* (15 August 2006) A15.

112 Robert Chesney, "The Sleeper Scenario: Terrorism-Support Laws and the Demands of Prevention" (2005) 42 Harv. J. on Legis. 1 at 31.

viewing this record concluded that administrative practices associated with these detentions produced unduly lengthy periods of incarceration, and in some instances unsatisfactory conditions of detention.[113] The median length of detention between arrest and release or removal from the United States was in the range of 100 days.[114]

b.   Material Witness Provisions

The United States has also employed so-called material witness laws to detain suspected terrorists. U.S. federal law allows a judge to order the arrest of a person if the testimony of that person "is material in a criminal proceeding, and if it is shown that it may become impracticable to secure the presence of the person by subpoena." A person is to be released "if the testimony of such witness can adequately be secured by deposition, and if further detention is not necessary to prevent a failure of justice." However, "release of a material witness may be delayed for a reasonable period of time until the deposition of the witness can be taken."[115] Like preventive charging, this practice too has been criticized as a form of *de facto* preventive detention.[116]

The post-9/11 U.S. practice of stretching existing legal instruments to allow preventive detention without developing a frank preventive detention law has attracted criticism. As Alan Dershowitz has argued, laws are contorted to serve the end of preventive detention but without the accountability a true preventive detention law should have.[117] Not least, there is no careful jurisprudence carefully parsing the propriety and limits of this *de facto* preventive detention.

ii)   *Extraordinary Instruments*

a.   Scope

The United States has also opted for extraordinary military or CIA detentions in foreign locations, potentially beyond the reach of effective judicial oversight by U.S. courts. The scope of these detentions is now well documented. By November 2006, 430 detainees remained at Guantanamo naval base, in Cuba, while 345 had been released since

---

113 Office of the Inspector General, United States Department Of Justice, *The September 11 Detainees: A Review Of The Treatment Of Aliens Held On Immigration Charges In Connection With The Investigation Of The September 11 Attacks* (2003) at 195 *et seq*, online: www.usdoj.gov/oig/special/0306/chapter10.htm.

114 *Ibid.*, estimated from fig. 9 at 105.

115 18 U.S.C. § 3144.

116 See, for example, Laurie L. Levenson, "Detention, Material Witnesses & the War on Terrorism" (2002) 35 Loy. L.A. L. Rev. 1217.

117 Alan Dershowitz, *Preemption* (New York: W.W. Norton, 2006) at 118.

2002.[118] The precise number of persons that have been in secret detention in overseas locations by the CIA is uncertain. In September 2006, the Bush administration admitted to the existence of these facilities and stated that they had served their interrogation purposes.[119] Fourteen CIA detainees were transferred to Guantanamo. According to the administration's background brief:

> [A] small number of suspected terrorist leaders and operatives captured during the war have been held and questioned outside the U.S., in a separate program operated by the CIA. The [fourteen] detainees recently transferred to the U.S. Naval Base at Guantanamo Bay were previously held and questioned by the CIA. The CIA program focused on a number of suspected terrorist leaders and operatives—dangerous men with unparalleled knowledge about terrorist networks and plans for new attacks.[120]

b.   AUMF Resolution

Relative to the more constrained instruments discussed above, or those employed by other states, the legal authority for these military and paramilitary detentions is amorphous. The Bush administration has used the U.S. Congress' *Authorization for Use of Military Force Joint Resolution* (AUMF) to detain even U.S. citizens. Issued immediately after the 9/11 attacks, the AUMF authorizes the president to

> use all necessary and appropriate force against those nations, organizations, or persons he determines planned, authorized, committed, or aided the terrorist attacks that occurred on September 11, 2001, or harbored such organizations or persons, in order to prevent any future acts of international terrorism against the United States by such nations, organizations or persons.[121]

---

118   U.S. Department of Defense, News Release, No. 1177-06 (17 November 2006). For an assessment of the fate of 245 of those thus far released, see Andrew Selsky, "Some Gitmo Detainees Freed Elsewhere" *Associated Press* (15 December 2006) (reporting that "205 of the 245 were either freed without being charged or were cleared of charges related to their detention at Guantanamo. Forty either stand charged with crimes or continue to be detained").

119   The White House, *President Discusses Creation of Military Commissions to Try Suspected Terrorists* (September 2006), online: www.whitehouse.gov/news/releases/2006/09/20060906-3.html.

120   The White House, *Fact Sheet: Bringing Terrorists to Justice* (September 2006), online: www.whitehouse.gov/news/releases/2006/09/20060906-2.html. For the background to this decision, see Dafna Linzer & Glenn Kessler, "Decision to Move Detainees Resolved Two-Year Debate among Bush Advisors" *Washington Post* (8 September 2006) A.1.

121   Pub. L. No. 107-40, § 2(a), 115 Stat. 224 (18 September 2001).

In *Hamdi v. Rumsfeld*,[122] the U.S. Supreme Court held that the AUMF permitted the military detention of an American citizen captured fighting alongside Taliban forces in Afghanistan, and then detained in the United States by the military. A plurality of the Court considered the individual's detention "necessary and appropriate," as this term was used in the AUMF, because "the capture and detention of lawful combatants and the capture, detention, and trial of unlawful combatants, by 'universal agreement and practice,' are 'important incidents of war.'"[123] Specifically, detention necessary "to prevent a combatant's return to the battlefield is a fundamental incident of waging war." More recently, the U.S. Fourth Circuit has held that the military may also detain U.S. citizens who have taken up arms against the United States captured *within* the United States.[124]

c.   Commander-in-Chief Powers

The legal basis for detention of noncitizens stems from both the AUMF and, the administration has urged, from the president's constitutional commander-in-chief power. A presidential military order issued in November 2001 pursuant to these powers authorizes military detention of "any individual who is not a United States citizen" where there is "reason to believe that such individual,"

> (i) is or was a member of the organization known as al Qaida; (ii) has engaged in, aided or abetted, or conspired to commit, acts of international terrorism, or acts in preparation therefor, that have caused, threaten to cause, or have as their aim to cause, injury to or adverse effects on the United States, its citizens, national security, foreign policy, or economy; or (iii) has knowingly harbored one or more individuals described in subparagraphs (i) or (ii) …; and (2) it is in the interest of the United States that such individual be subject to this order.[125]

The president's commander-in-chief power, exercised directly or through the vehicle of this order, has served as the basis for detentions by U.S. personnel of foreign terrorist suspects in Afghanistan and at Guantanamo[126] and, presumably, those at CIA overseas "black sites."

---

122 Above note 37.

123 *Ibid.* at 518, citing *Ex parte Quirin*, 317 U.S. 1 at 28 (1942).

124 *Padilla v. Hanft*, 423 F.3d 386 (4th Cir. 2005).

125 *Military Order—Detention, Treatment, and Trial of Certain Non-Citizens in the War against Terrorism*, 66 Fed. Reg. 57833 (13 November 2001).

126 *United States Written Response to Questions Asked by the [U.N.] Committee Against Torture* (May 2006) at 17, online: www.state.gov/g/drl/rls/68554.htm.

d. Implications

Detention under any of these presidential powers is indeterminate and possibly prolonged. The president's powers to detain are indexed to a shadowy "war" on terror. As one U.S. lower court has noted,

> The [U.S.] government ... has been unable to inform the Court how long it believes the war on terrorism will last. ... Indeed, the government cannot even articulate at this moment how it will determine when the war on terrorism has ended. ... At a minimum, the government has conceded that the war could last several generations, thereby making it possible, if not likely, that "enemy combatants" will be subject to terms of life imprisonment at Guantanamo Bay. ... Short of the death penalty, life imprisonment is the ultimate deprivation of liberty, and the uncertainty of whether the war on terror—and thus the period of incarceration—will last a lifetime may be even worse than if the detainees had been tried, convicted, and definitively sentenced to a fixed term.[127]

In *Hamdi*, the U.S. Supreme Court's plurality acknowledged that the malleable nature of an indefinite "war on terror" might precipitate something akin to indeterminate detention. It was unprepared, however, to address this possibility while more or less conventional combat operations were ongoing in Afghanistan.[128] Nevertheless, the Court also concluded that the detention of U.S. citizens as enemy combatants necessitated some meaningful means of contesting that detention in front of a neutral decision-maker.

In 2004, the Bush administration established combatant-status review tribunals, assessing the detention of detainees at Guantanamo Bay to confirm whether they were being properly held as "enemy combatants."[129]

---

127 *In re Guantanamo Detainee Cases*, 355 F. Supp. 2d 443 at 465 (D.D.C. 2005).

128 Pointing to this reasoning, some legal scholars urge that prolonged detention of terrorist suspects under the law of wars, with some checks and balances, is preferable to criminal prosecutions. See Jack Goldsmith & Eric Posner, "A Better Way on Detainees" *Washington Post* (4 August 2006) A17.

129 See *Order Establishing Combatant Status Review Tribunal, Deputy Secretary of Defense* (7 July 2004), online: www.defenselink.mil/news/Jul2004/d20040707review.pdf. "Enemy combatants" means, essentially, a member of al-Qaeda or Taliban engaged in hostilities against the United States. The tribunal does not seem empowered to determine whether individuals are entitled to PW status or not. This is not, in other words, a status adjudication under Geneva Convention III. See discussion in Robert M. Chesney, "Judicial Review, Combatant Status Determinations, and the Possible Consequences of Boumediene" (2007) 48 Harv. Int'l L.J. Online 62 at n7. See also the documents in *Begg v.*

That process was given legislative imprimatur by the *Detainee Treatment Act of 2005.*[130]

b) U.K. Anti-terrorism Preventive Detention

i) *Criminal Law*

The primary United Kingdom anti-terrorism statute is the *Terrorism Act 2000,*[131] as amended by several more recent Acts. The 2000 Act allows a constable to arrest without a warrant a person whom he or she reasonably suspects to be a terrorist[132] — that is, a person suspected of having been "concerned in the commission, preparation or instigation of acts of terrorism" or having committed any of several enumerated offences.[133] The reference to preparation or instigation gives these arrest powers a strong pre-emptive bent.

A detention under the Act is subject to periodic review by a "review officer" — a police official who has not been directly involved in the investigation in connection with which the person is detained. The first review occurs as soon as practicable after the detention, and is repeated at twelve-hour intervals.[134] The review officer may renew the detention during these reviews on several grounds, including to permit questioning and to allow the government to decide whether to charge or deport the individual.[135] This initial period of detention is to endure for no more than forty-eighty hours.[136]

A longer period of detention requires a judicial warrant. The latter instrument is available where a judicial authority is persuaded there

> (a) are reasonable grounds for believing that the further detention of the person to whom the application relates is necessary to obtain relevant evidence whether by questioning him or otherwise or to preserve relevant evidence, and (b) the investigation in connection with which the person is detained is being conducted diligently and expeditiously.[137]

Bush, Civil Action No. 04-CV-1137 (RMC) (D.D.C.), online: www.cageprisoners.com/downloads/moazzambegg.pdf.

130 Pub. L. No. 109-148, Tit. X, 119 Stat. 2739.

131 *Terrorism Act 2000* (U.K.), 2000, c. 11.

132 *Ibid.*, s. 41.

133 *Ibid.*, s. 40.

134 *Ibid.*, Sch. 8, para. 21.

135 *Ibid.*, Sch. 8, para. 23.

136 *Ibid.*, s. 41.

137 *Ibid.*, Sch. 8, para. 32.

The 2000 Act permitted a maximum detention under a judicial warrant of seven days,[138] later extended to fourteen days in 2003.[139] In a highly controversial amendment passed as part of the *Terrorism Act 2006*, detentions may now be renewed for supplemental periods of seven days, up to a maximum of twenty-eight days.[140] This lengthy period is actually much shorter than the ninety-day period originally sought by the Blair government, but resisted by Parliament.

In the 2006 Act, the grounds for the extended detention were also modified. Detention may be renewed not simply to allow questioning, but also "pending the result of an examination or analysis of any relevant evidence or of anything the examination or analysis of which is to be or is being carried out with a view to obtaining relevant evidence."[141]

In sum, the U.K. authorities now have sweeping power to detain persons for up to four weeks in order to question that person or to pursue investigative leads. U.K. Home Office statistics indicate that between 11 September 2001 and 30 September 2005, 895 people were arrested under the 2000 Act, with 496 ultimately released without charge.[142]

ii) Immigration Law

After the 9/11 attacks, the United Kingdom amended its immigration law to allow for the indefinite detention of terrorism suspects where those persons could not be deported because, for instance, they would be tortured in the country to which they were removed.[143] Indefinite detention of this sort offends Article 5 of the *European Convention on Human Rights*, guaranteeing a right to liberty except in certain circumstances. That Convention permits, however, derogations from the liberty right "in time of war or other public emergency threatening the life of the nation ... to the extent strictly required by the exigencies of the situation, provided that such measures are not inconsistent with [the state's] other obligations under international law."

For this reason, at the same time as it amended its immigration law, the United Kingdom claimed a derogation from the Convention (and also the ICCPR) because

> there exists a terrorist threat to the United Kingdom from persons suspected of involvement in international terrorism. In particular,

---

138 *Ibid.*, Sch. 8, paras. 29 and 36.

139 *Criminal Justice Act 2003* (U.K.), 2003, c. 44, s. 306.

140 *Terrorism Act 2006* (U.K.), 2006, c. 11, s. 23.

141 *Ibid.*, s. 24.

142 U.K. Home Office, *Terrorism Act 2000*, online: www.homeoffice.gov.uk/security/ terrorism-and-the-law/terrorism-act/.

143 *Anti-terrorism, Crime and Security Act 2001* (U.K.), 2001, c. 24, s. 23.

there are foreign nationals present in the United Kingdom who are suspected of being concerned in the commission, preparation or instigation of acts of international terrorism, of being members of organisations or groups which are so concerned or of having links with members of such organisations or groups, and who are a threat to the national security of the United Kingdom.

The legality of the U.K. measures was adjudicated by the House of Lords in *A and others v. Secretary of State for the Home Department*.[144] In that case, the law lords rejected the U.K. approach. As noted above, the law lords firmly declared indefinite detention contrary to the European Convention. Addressing the U.K. derogation from that instrument, most of the judges were unprepared to second-guess the government on the question of whether the campaign against terrorism constituted a "war or other public emergency threatening the life of the nation." They concluded, however, that there was no reason to presume that foreign nationals (as opposed to U.K. nationals) presented the greatest threat. There was, therefore, no rational link between the law and addressing the security concern, and thus the measure was not "strictly required by the exigencies of the situation."

iii) Control Orders

In response to *A and others*, the U.K. Parliament enacted the *Prevention of Terrorism Act 2005* permitting the imposition of "control orders" directed at the activities of both foreign and U.K. nationals suspected of terrorist activity.[145]

a. Types of Control Orders

A control order is an instrument imposing obligations on a person "for purposes connected with protecting members of the public from a risk of terrorism."[146] They come in two species: nonderogating control orders—those that do not constitute a violation of the *European Convention on Human Rights*—and derogating control orders—those that would amount to a violation of the European treaty, unless a proper derogation was entered.

Nonderogating orders may be made by the Home Secretary, subject to limited judicial supervision, and endure for up to twelve months and longer with extensions. Derogating measures require a more substantial judicial review and blessing and last for up to six months and

---

144 Above note 8.
145 *Prevention of Terrorism Act 2005* (U.K.), 2005, c. 2.
146 *Ibid.*, s. 1.

longer with extensions. Control orders may, in other words, be renewed indefinitely.

Moreover, significant penalties are attached to disregard of these provisions: persons who violate control orders are subject to up to five years' imprisonment on conviction on indictment.[147]

b. Availability

These measures are imposed where "necessary for purposes connected with preventing or restricting involvement by that individual in terrorism-related activity." Thus, for nonderogating orders there must be reasonable grounds for suspecting that the individual is or has been involved in terrorism-related activity and that the order is necessary, for purposes connected with protecting members of the public from a risk of terrorism.[148] Derogating orders, by comparison, require a higher degree of certainty concerning the person's involvement in terrorism-related activity.[149]

Terrorism-related activity is a broadly defined term that captures actual involvement in the commission, preparation or instigation of acts of terrorism, as well as "conduct which gives encouragement to the commission, preparation or instigation of such acts." Indeed, it reaches as far as conduct that supports or assists persons believed to be involved in terrorist-related activity, including those who encourage the instigation of such acts.[150]

c. Content of Control Orders

The constraints that may be imposed by control orders are extensive. The list enumerated in the Act includes limits on possession of articles or use of services or facilities and the carrying on of specified activities. Restrictions may be imposed on the nature of employment, membership in associations or communications with other persons. Control orders may also regulate a person's place of residence and those who can have access to it and place limitations on presence in certain places or movement within or from the United Kingdom. The person may be required to allow searches of him- or herself or residence, to wear electronic monitoring equipment and to report to the authorities.[151] In their strictest form, these control orders could confine the suspect to a particular place, amounting to *de facto* detention. Presumably this

---

147 *Ibid.*, s. 9.
148 *Ibid.*, s. 2.
149 *Ibid.*, s. 4.
150 *Ibid.*, s. 1.
151 *Ibid.*

latter sort of constraint could only be achieved through a derogating control order.

d.   Recent Developments

To date, the U.K. government has not employed "derogating control orders." However, as of late 2006, sixteen "nonderogating" control orders were in place in the United Kingdom.[152] Some of these measures have been challenged successfully in U.K. courts as incompatible with the *European Convention on Human Rights*.[153] In the meantime, several persons subject to control orders are unaccounted for,[154] sparking renewed debate in the United Kingdom on the merits of measures short of outright detention.[155]

c)   **Australia**

i)   *Criminal Law*

In 2005, Australia introduced its own system of preventive detention and control orders.[156] This statute is notable for its comprehensive detail, far in excess of what exists under Canadian law.

Under the Australian law, a person may be preventively detained if the police have reasonable grounds to suspect that he or she "will engage in a terrorist act" that is imminent (or at least expected to occur within fourteen days) or "possesses a thing that is connected with the preparation for, or the engagement of a person in, a terrorist act" or "has done an act in preparation for, or planning, a terrorist act." The

---

152 Written Ministerial Statement from the Home Secretary, Dr. John Reid, *Control Order Powers—11 September–10 December 2006*, online: http://security.homeoffice.gov.uk/news-publications/news-speeches/home-sec-statement.

153 See, for example, *Secretary of State for the Home Department v. JJ and others*, [2006] EWHC 1623 (Admin) at para. 99 (Q.B.) (holding that "six control orders [essentially confining persons to their apartments for eighteen hours a day] impose obligations that are incompatible with the Respondents' right to liberty under art 5. It follows that the Secretary of State had no power to make the orders and they must therefore all be quashed"), aff'd [2006] EWCA Civ 1141 (C.A.). These rulings provoked animated criticism of the British courts by current and former government officials. See Ben Russell, "Law Lords Are Undermining 'War on Terror,' Says Clarke" [*London*] *Independent* (18 January 2007); Ben Leapman, "Reid Says Human Rights Laws Soft on Terrorists" *Sunday Telegraph* (12 May 2007).

154 Devika Bhat, "Terror Suspect on Run Despite Control Order, Home Office Admits" [*London*] *Times* (17 January 2007).

155 BBC, "Blair Hits Back on Control Orders" (17 October 2006), online: http://news.bbc.co.uk/2/hi/uk_news/politics/6057814.stm.

156 *Anti-Terrorism Act (No. 2), 2005*, No. 144, 2005, Sch. 4.

preventive detention must substantially assist "in preventing a terrorist act occurring" and must be reasonably necessary for this purpose.[157]

Preventive detention may be authorized by an issuing authority (typically a judicial official) for an initial period of up to twenty-four hours,[158] and renewed for up to an additional twenty-four hours.[159] Notably, however, Australian state law may be used to increase the period of detention to a period of up to fourteen days. The Australian provisions also include potent penalties for disclosing the existence of the preventive detention by the detainee and his or her lawyer, among others, in all but limited circumstances.[160]

It should be noted that Australian law also allows detention for the purposes of investigative questioning in terrorism matters. This procedure is discussed in Chapter 15.

ii)   Control Orders

The Australian control order regime allows a court, on application by the government, to impose obligations on a person where satisfied, on a balance of probabilities, that "making the order would substantially assist in preventing a terrorist act" or that "the person has provided training to, or received training from, a listed terrorist organisation." Further, the court must be persuaded on a balance of probabilities that "each of the obligations, prohibitions and restrictions to be imposed on the person by the order is reasonably necessary, and reasonably appropriate and adapted, for the purpose of protecting the public from a terrorist act."[161]

The Act enumerates the restraints that may be imposed by control orders. These include such things as prohibitions or restrictions on the person being at (or away from) specified areas or places, communicating or associating with specific individuals, accessing certain telecommunications or technology, possessing specific substances or engaging in specified activities. A control order may also include requirements that the person wear a tracking device, report to specified persons at specified times and places or participate in specified counselling or education. A control order may endure for up to twelve months for adults, and for a briefer period of time for persons aged sixteen to seventeen.[162]

---

157 *Ibid.*, Sch. 4, s. 105.4.
158 *Ibid.*, Sch. 4, s. 105.8.
159 *Ibid.*, Sch. 4, s. 105.14.
160 *Ibid.*, Sch. 4, s. 105.41.
161 *Ibid.*, Sch. 4, s. 104.4.
162 *Ibid.*, Sch. 4, s. 104.5. Control orders are not available for those younger than sixteen.

2) Canadian Criminal Law

Canadian anti-terrorism preventive detention under the *Criminal Code* is mild when contrasted against the detention powers available in the United Kingdom and the United States. In Canada, there is no true anti-terrorism preventive detention. Rather, there may be detention pending imposition of a peace bond, the Canadian equivalent of a control order. While the peace bond concept was enhanced by the 2001 *Anti-terrorism Act*, it predates that statute. At the time of this writing, Canadian anti-terrorism preventive detention was in a state of flux, largely because of the termination of section 83.3 recognizance with conditions followed by the government's effort in Bill S-3 to reenact almost identical provisions.

a)   Section 83.3 Recognizance with Conditions

i)   *Background*
Section 83.3 of the *Criminal Code* represented the best-publicized form of "preventive detention" prior to its expiry in 2007. Formally entitled "recognizance with conditions," these provisions were clearly designed to foil terrorist plots on the cusp of execution. Stanley Cohen describes their purpose this way:

> The whole scheme is designed to disrupt nascent suspected terrorist activity by bringing a person before a judge who would then evaluate the situation and decide whether it would be useful … to impose conditions on the person. The purpose … is not to effectuate an arrest but merely to provide a means of bringing a person before a court for the purposes of judicial supervision.[163]

With the consent of the federal attorney general, a peace officer was authorized to lay an information before a provincial court judge if that peace officer *believed* on reasonable grounds that a "terrorist activity" would be carried out and *suspected* on reasonable grounds that the imposition of recognizance with conditions or arrest on the person was needed to prevent that terrorist activity.[164] Terrorist activity is a carefully (but broadly) defined term, discussed in detail in Chapter 7. The judge could then require that the person named in the information appear in court.

Under exigent circumstances, where the grounds for laying an information existed (or that information had in fact been laid) and a peace

---

163   Stanley Cohen, *Privacy, Crime and Terror* (Markham, ON: LexisNexis Butterworths, 2005) at 218.
164   *Criminal Code*, above note 3, s. 83.3.

officer suspected on reasonable grounds that a person must be detained to prevent a terrorist activity, a person could be arrested without warrant. Subsequently, an information was to be laid, and then the person was to be brought before a provincial judge without delay and within twenty-four hours, unless a judge was unavailable. In the latter instance, the person was to be brought before a judge "as soon as possible."

Whether arrested with or without warrant, when the person ultimately appeared before the judge, the latter was to order the person's release unless the peace officer showed cause for the detention, including the likelihood that a terrorist activity would be carried out if the person was released.

Alternatively, where the judge declined to order release, he could adjourn further proceedings for no longer than forty-eight hours pending a full hearing on the peace bond issue. The effect of these provisions was theoretically to enable a preventive detention on suspicions of terrorist activity for an initial period of up to twenty-four hours (and perhaps longer if a judge was not available within that period) following the arrest and then, where the judge agreed to an adjournment but did not release the detainee, detention for another forty-eight hours. Preventive arrest could endure, in other words, for some seventy-two hours.

When a full hearing was held, the judge was to consider whether the peace officer had reasonable grounds for his or her suspicion. If he or she did, the judge could order the person to enter into a recognizance of up to twelve months' duration, a limitation on liberty equivalent to the still existing peace bond power discussed below.

ii) Criticisms

By 2007, section 83.3 had never been used. Nevertheless, it remained amongst the most controversial of the provisions introduced by the 2001 *Anti-terrorism Act*. In particular, the prospect of detention prior to a full hearing before a judge for up to seventy-two hours on suspicions of terrorist activity generated disquiet.

To ease concerns, Parliament inserted requirements that the attorney general and minister of public safety report annually on the provision's use.[165] The section was also equipped with an automatic sunsetting provision, with the effect of terminating the provision in early 2007 unless overridden by vote in Parliament.[166] Both the Commons national security committee[167] and the senate special committee

165 *Ibid.*, s. 83.31.
166 *Ibid.*, s. 83.32.
167 House of Commons Subcommittee on the Review of the *Anti-terrorism Act*, *Review of the* Anti-Terrorism Act *Investigative Hearings and Recognizance with*

on anti-terrorism law[168] recommended that this provision be extended in 2006 and 2007 respectively. However, a motion to renew the provision was defeated by the opposition parties in February 2007. In October 2007, the government tabled Bill S-3, a law project that proposed restoring section 83.3 and subjecting it to renewable five year sunsetting periods to be preceded by a parliamentary review.

b)   Regular Recognizance with Conditions

i)   Mechanics

The expiry of section 83.3 likely had an incidental effect on police abilities to disrupt terrorist plots. As discussed in Chapter 7, Canada's anti-terrorism criminal law casts a wide net, largely because of its expansive approach to so-called inchoate crimes associated with terrorist activity — facilitating, harbouring, instructing and the like. Since these expansive new crimes reach so far, it is likely that a formative player in a terrorist activity would have committed a criminal offence along the way to generating whatever suspicions attract police to him or her.[169] Police could, in other words, commence regular criminal proceedings against the individual.

Moreover, for some time, the standard *Criminal Code* has permitted courts to impose recognizance with conditions — so-called peace bonds — on individuals, where there are reasonable grounds to fear these persons might engage in various criminal acts. For example, a person labouring under a fear (based on reasonable grounds) that an individual may commit certain personal injury offences,[170] sexual offences,[171] certain offences relating to intimidation of the justice system or a journalist, or a criminal organization offence[172] may bring the matter to a provincial court judge (although in some instances only with permission of the attorney general).

Conditions (October 2006), online: http://cmte.parl.gc.ca/cmte/CommitteePublication.aspx?COM=10804&Lang=1&SourceId=193467.

168 Special Senate Committee on the *Anti-terrorism Act, Fundamental Justice in Extraordinary Times* (February 2007), online: www.parl.gc.ca/39/1/parlbus/commbus/senate/Com-e/anti-e/rep-e/rep02feb07-e.htm.

169 See discussion in David Paciocco, "Constitutional Casualties of September 11: Limiting the Legacy of the *Anti-terrorism Act*" (2002) 16 Sup. Ct. Law Rev. (2d) 185 at 200 [Paciocco, "Constitutional Casualties"].

170 *Criminal Code*, above note 3, ss. 810 and 810.2.

171 *Ibid.*, s. 810.1.

172 *Ibid.*, s. 810.01.

After 2001, this list was expanded to include a terrorism offence.[173] Under section 810.01, a person "who fears on reasonable grounds that another person will commit ... a terrorism offence may, with the consent of the Attorney General, lay an information before a provincial court judge." If the provincial court judge is persuaded that these reasonable grounds for the fear exist, he or she may order the defendant to "enter into a recognizance to keep the peace and be of good behaviour" for up to twelve months, and may impose other reasonable conditions. A refusal by the accused to enter into the recognizance is punishable by imprisonment for up to twelve months. A breach of a recognizance is a criminal offence, punishable by up to two years imprisonment if a conviction is secured on indictment.[174]

These peace bond powers are obviously pre-emptive in nature, available against a person who has committed no offence. On its face, the imposition of a peace bond on a potential terrorist seems a modest, even farcical, reaction to the threat of terrorist activity, especially in an era of suicide bombers. A peace bond is, however, intended to "out" potential threats and disrupt the "preparatory phase of incipient terrorist activity."[175] Further, a peace bond may be associated with detention. Unlike section 83.3, the regular peace bond process does not authorize arrest without warrant. However, there may still be detention in the lead up to the peace bond: once an information has been laid, a warrant may be issued for the person resulting in their arrest pending imposition of the peace bond by the judge.[176]

Under regular criminal procedure, a person detained by a peace officer must be brought before a justice within twenty-four hours,[177] or where a justice is not available in that period, "as soon as possible."[178] Once taken before the judge, the regular bail rules would apply, permitting (but not obliging) release pending adjudication of the peace bond issue.[179]

ii) Criticisms

In sum, like section 83.3, the regular peace bond process could produce detention, albeit presumably for only a brief period of time. Just as in section 83.3, the peace bond itself could impose important restrictions

---

173   *Ibid.*

174   *Ibid.*, s. 811.

175   Cohen, *Privacy, Crime and Terror*, above note 163 at 218–19 (discussing s. 83.3).

176   The possibility is allowed by cross-referencing in the *Criminal Code*, above note 3: ss. 810.01(7), 810(5), 788, 795, and 503.

177   *Criminal Code, ibid.*, s. 503 *et seq.*

178   *Ibid.*, s. 503(1).

179   *Ibid.*, s. 515. See also *R. v. Cachine* (2001), 154 C.C.C. (3d) 376 (B.C.C.A.).

on liberty. But unlike section 83.3, the regular peace bond provision is not subject to any sunsetting. Nor are there reporting obligations on the government obliging disclosure of how often it has been used. Moreover, section 83.3 allows the government to react to feared "terrorist activity." The section 810.01 process permits the government to respond to feared "terrorism offences." As discussed in Chapter 7, the two concepts are closely linked. However, "terrorist offences" is a much broader concept than "terrorist activity." In the result, more behaviour can be subjected to the peace bond procedure under the regular process than is the case under section 83.3.

The potentially formidable reach of the peace bond should not be underestimated. A peace bond is a government-crafted, judicially imposed set of behavioural standards tailored to individual persons. Onerous conditions imposed as a part of the recognizance may be easily breached, permitting the subsequent incarceration of a feared security risk for behaviour that is benign in its own right. Put another way, a peace bond with a hair-trigger allows a state to use retrospective punishment for easily proved and potentially banal peace bond violations as a means of achieving robust anti-terrorism preventive detention.[180] In comments on section 83.3 that apply equally to section 810.01, David Paciocco regards the peace bond process as "intuitively offensive." It is a way to "extend the reach of criminal consequences where the requirements of full proof cannot be met."[181]

To the best of this author's knowledge, like section 83.3, the section 810.01 anti-terrorism recognizance provision had not been employed by the time of this writing. Some sense of the scope of a peace bond might, however, be drawn from the conditions placed on release pending the outcome of immigration security certificate adjudications, a topic discussed below. These release agreements highlight the sort of the measures government is likely to view as necessary to hobble feared terrorist risks. For example, the conditions under which Mohammed Harkat was released in 2006 run to five pages. Among other things, any computer with Internet connectivity must be kept in a locked portion of his residence to which he has no access.[182] If a similar condition were imposed as part of a recognizance, Harkat could be incarcerated

---

180 See, for example, discussion in Paciocco, "Constitutional Casualties," above note 169 at 203–4 ("Anyone who is placed under section 83.3 recognizance will invariably be subjected to intense surveillance, and, if a breach is detected, arrest will occur and efforts will be made to obtain interim as well as punitive detention").

181 *Ibid.* at 200.

182 The release order is reproduced in *Harkat v. Canada (Minister of Immigration and Citizenship)*, 2006 FCA 215.

for two years were he to enter into a room with an Internet-equipped computer.

iii) Constitutionality

The constitutionality of anti-terrorism peace bonds has never been tested. One species of peace bond—that guarding against sex offences directed at minors—was upheld on constitutional grounds by the Ontario Court of Appeal in *R. v. Budreo*.[183] There, the defendant urged that the peace bond amounted to a "status offence"; that is, "an offence based on a person's status alone, ... based on a person's medical diagnosis or even on a person's past criminal record but without any current offending conduct."[184] For this reason, and because of its overbreadth, the defendant argued the provision violated the fundamental justice promised by section 7 of the *Charter*.

The court agreed that the peace bond amounted to a restraint on liberty, and thus triggered the application of section 7 of the *Charter*. It concluded, however, that fundamental justice was not offended where the provision was largely geared to *bona fide* prevention and was not truly penal in nature. Part of that reasoning appears to rest on the fact that the peace bond was reasonably narrowly tailored, restricting the defendant's liberty in respect to a large, but reasonably discrete group of persons (minors).[185] In rejecting the defendant's supplemental argument that the constraints imposed by peace bond were overbroad, the court noted the reasonably narrow scope of the restrictions, underscoring that their limited focus permitted "a defendant to lead a reasonably normal life."[186]

Some analysts point to this decision in discussing the propriety of anti-terrorism peace bonds.[187] The scope of the peace bond at issue in *Budreo* was, however, much more limited than those likely to employed under the anti-terrorism provisions. In *Budreo,* the instrument restricted liberty in respect to minors. If the Harkat measure is any indication, an anti-terrorism peace bond would have a much broader and more intrusive reach, potentially constraining liberty in every dimension of life.

It is difficult, in these circumstances, to draw a straight line between the holding in *Budreo* and a conclusion on the constitutionality of anti-terrorism peace bonds. It is also notable that *Budreo* court suggested a definite outer limit on the scope of a peace bond: "detention or

---

183 (2000), 46 O.R. (3d) 481 (C.A.) [*Budreo*].
184 *Ibid.* at para. 24.
185 *Ibid.* at para. 32.
186 *Ibid.* at para. 39.
187 See, for example, Cohen, *Privacy, Crime and Terror*, above note 163 at 221.

imprisonment under a provision that does not charge an offence would be an unacceptable restriction on a defendant's liberty and would be contrary to the principles of fundamental justice."[188]

At the very least, greater certainty as to the precise content of peace bonds might usefully be incorporated into the *Criminal Code*.[189] Both the United Kingdom and Australian control order provisions enumerate the potential content of those orders. In both instances, the legislature has turned its mind to this issue. The Canadian approach leaves content to be determined by what the executive government can persuade a judge to impose on a case-by-case basis. It is, in other words, a much less transparent process, less amenable to careful deliberation by policy makers.

Legislating the scope of peace bonds would also enable close constitutional scrutiny on a wholesale basis by both legislators and potentially by the courts. At present, the constitutionality of peace bond use will fall to be determined on a case-by-case basis, where individual defendants choose to pursue challenges.

3) Canadian Immigration Law

Even more potent detention powers are found in Canada's immigration law, the *Immigration and Refugee Protection Act*.[190] Notably, detention powers under this statute exist presumptively to facilitate the removal of non-Canadians, including those who present a risk to national security. These powers are not intended to produce detention for a definite or indefinite period outside of immigration removal proceedings. In practice, however, the immigration law could generate exactly this sort of indefinite detention, a matter discussed below.

Detention powers associated with two IRPA proceedings are of particular interest from a national security perspective: inadmissibility proceedings and security certificates.

a) Inadmissibility Proceedings
First, an immigration officer may detain a foreign national or permanent resident on entry to Canada where there are reasonable grounds for suspecting that the person is inadmissible to Canada "on grounds of security or for violating human or international rights."[191] The Act

---

188 *Budreo*, above note 183 at para. 39.
189 See Kent Roach, "Ten Ways to Improve Anti-terrorism Law" (2006) 51 Crim. L.Q. 102 at 111–12 (discussing this issue).
190 Above note 4.
191 *Ibid.*, s. 55.

lists a number of circumstances that justify inadmissibility on security grounds:

(a) engaging in an act of espionage or an act of subversion against a democratic government, institution or process as they are understood in Canada;

(b) engaging in or instigating the subversion by force of any government;

(c) engaging in terrorism;

(d) being a danger to the security of Canada;

(e) engaging in acts of violence that would or might endanger the lives or safety of persons in Canada; or

(f) being a member of an organization that there are reasonable grounds to believe engages, has engaged or will engage in acts referred to in paragraph (a), (b) or (c).[192]

More generally, an officer may also detain the foreign national or permanent resident (and issue a warrant for their detention) on, among others things, a reasonable grounds for suspecting that the person is inadmissible and is a danger to the public.[193]

A detained person's status is reviewed by the Immigration Division of the Immigration and Refugee Board within forty-eight hours, and then at an initial seven- and subsequently thirty-day interval. The division must release the individual, unless it concludes that the person is, *inter alia*, a danger to the public or the minister is "taking necessary steps to inquire into a reasonable suspicion that they are inadmissible on grounds of security."[194] The division may continue the detention if

satisfied that the permanent resident or the foreign national is the subject of an examination or an admissibility hearing or is subject to a removal order and that the permanent resident or the foreign national is a danger to the public or is unlikely to appear for examination, an admissibility hearing or removal from Canada.[195]

This inadmissibility hearing and removal process is triggered by a report by the immigration officer to the minister expressing the former's opinion on inadmissibility. If the minister agrees with this assessment, the matter is referred to the Immigration Division, which issues a removal order if persuaded that the person is inadmissible.[196]

---

192 *Ibid.*, s. 34.
193 *Ibid.*, s. 55.
194 *Ibid.*, s. 58.
195 *Ibid.*
196 *Ibid.*, ss. 44–45.

b) Security Certificates

Although probably used less frequently than inadmissibility proceedings,[197] a second form of IRPA detention—the security-certificate process—has generated more controversy. There may be good reason for this. While the regular detention provisions described above appear linked to an ongoing (and presumably valid) inadmissibility hearing and removal process, the connection between detention under a security certificate and removal are more tenuous, opening the door to immigration detention even if the detainee is no longer subject to a valid removal order. By the time of this writing, the Supreme Court of Canada had declared unconstitutional significant portions of the security certificate process. [198] The Court suspended the effect of its decision until February 2008, allowing Parliament time to correct the Act's deficiencies. In October 2007, the government tabled bill C-3, proposing amendments reacting to the Court's ruling.

i) Mechanics

In the security-certificate process, the minister of immigration and the minister of public safety together sign a certificate declaring a foreign national or permanent resident inadmissible to Canada on, *inter alia*, grounds of security.[199]

Typically, this certificate is issued in response to a security intelligence report generated by CSIS or, less commonly, the RCMP. CSIS issues such a report where it judges a person a significant threat to the security of Canada. In the past, certificates have been directed at persons suspected of involvement in Islamic, Sikh, Tamil or secular Arab terrorism, right-wing extremism and Russian espionage.[200] CSIS urges that it acts only on reliable, multiple-sourced information. Moreover, it triggers the IRPA provisions where there is sufficient open-source

---

197 Security certificates had been used twenty-seven times between 1991 and March 2006. Commission of Inquiry into the Actions of Canadian Officials in Relation to Maher Arar, *A New Review Mechanism for the RCMP's National Security Activities* (2006) at 138, online: www.ararcommission.ca/eng/EnglishReport-Dec122006.pdf [Arar inquiry, Policy Report].

198 *Charkaoui*, above note 5.

199 IRPA, above note 4, s. 77. A "foreign national" is defined as a person who is not a Canadian citizen or permanent resident. IRPA, *ibid.*, s. 2.

200 Arar inquiry, Policy Report, above note 197 at 138. For a discussion of the removal of a Russian agent in 2006, see Stewart Bell & Adrian Humphreys, "Alleged Spy Says He's Russian" *National Post* (5 December 2006). See also a second case involving an alleged (former) Russian agent, *Miller v. Canada (Solicitor General)*, 2006 FC 912.

information to support release of a public summary document supporting the certificate, as required by the Act.

The CSIS report is usually then considered by the Canada Border Services Agency which advises the minister of immigration on the issuance
of a certificate. CSIS itself, or on occasion the RCMP, communicate their
own recommendation to the minister of public safety, who is also advised
by the department of public safety and emergency preparedness.[201]

Once the ministers issue the certificate, a permanent resident may be
held in detention on national security grounds pursuant to a warrant.[202]
The ministers may issue this warrant where, among other things, they
have reasonable grounds to believe that the person is a danger to national security.[203] This detention is reviewed by a special designated judge of
the Federal Court within forty-eight hours. In this review, the court will
order that the detention be continued if the judge is "satisfied" that the
person continues, among other things, to be a danger to national security.[204] If the judge is so satisfied, the matter is revisited every six months.
The reference to "satisfied" could be construed as obliging fairly searching judicial consideration of the detention order. However, because the
original ministerial detention warrant is based on "reasonable grounds
to believe" the Supreme Court has concluded that court reviews of the
detention should also be based on this standard; that is, a judge is to consider whether "there is an objective basis [that the person is a danger] …
which is based on compelling and credible information."[205]

In the Act as it existed at this writing, foreign nationals, meanwhile,
must be detained once a certificate is issued,[206] and that detention is only
reviewed at a much later point.[207] In *Charkaoui*, the Supreme Court declared the differential detention review between permanent residents
and foreign nationals unconstitutional and read down the act so that the
permanent resident process applied to both categories of individual.[208]

---

201 Arar inquiry, Policy Report, *ibid.* at 136–37.

202 IRPA, above note 4, s. 82. Note that IRPA section numbers cited in this book
will change if and when bill C-3 comes into force.

203 *Ibid.*, s. 82(1).

204 *Ibid.*, s. 83. Bill C-3 would change this provision slightly, requiring the judge
to continue the detention if satisfied that the person's release under conditions
would be injurious, inter alia, to national security.

205 *Charkaoui*, above note 5 at para. 39. Federal Court jurisprudence has described
this standard as "a serious possibility that the facts exist based on reliable, credible evidence." *Charkaoui (Re)*, above note 4 at para.128 (F.C.).

206 IRPA, above note 4, s. 82(2).

207 *Ibid.*

208 *Charkaoui*, above note 5 at para. 91 ("The lack of review for foreign nationals
until 120 days after the reasonableness of the certificate has been judicially

Bill C-3 proposes eliminating the distinction between these two classes of non-nationals in favour of the process described above.

A Federal Court judge assesses the reasonableness of the original security certificate signed by the ministers.[209] A judge may quash the certificate if he or she views it as unreasonable.[210] While the Act is silent on this point, presumably any detention of the person under the Act would also be quashed, if only because its lawful justification has been extinguished.

As discussed in Chapter 10, this assessment is conducted in part on an *ex parte* and *in camera* basis, and the person subject to the certificate is entitled to only limited information of the case to be met. This procedure was declared unconstitutional by the Supreme Court in *Charkaoui*,[211] and Bill C-3 proposes instead the system of special advocates discussed in Chapter 10.

ii) *Possible Indefinite Detention after a Balancing of Risks under the* IRPA
Where the judge views the certificate as reasonable,[212] the judge's decision constitutes a removal order.[213] However, this process may be stayed (for nonrefugees) to allow the government to conduct a "pre-removal risk assessment process" prior to the reasonableness decision by a federal judge. Specifically, the Act provides that nonrefugees subject to a security certificate may be protected from removal if the risk of torture or cruel and unusual treatment is more significant, in the eyes of the government, than the danger that person presents to the security of Canada.[214]

A similar protection is available to refugees subject to security certificates. Pursuant to section 115 of the Act, a refugee may be removed even where they are at risk of torture where the person constitutes a danger to the security of Canada. However, the security risk must be properly balanced against the risk of maltreatment. In *Mahjoub*, Madam Justice Dawson held that, in conducting this section 115 determination,

---

determined violates the guarantee against arbitrary detention in s. 9 of the *Charter*, a guarantee which encompasses the right to prompt review of detention under s. 10(*c*) of the *Charter*").

209 IRPA, above note 4, s. 80. This assessment may be suspended where the minister or the person subject to the certificate seeks protection from removal pursuant to a "pre-removal risk assessment" under the IRPA, described below. Once this process, if undertaken, is completed, the reasonableness review re-commences.

210 *Ibid.*, s. 80(2).

211 See Chapter 10.

212 In addition, any pre-removal risk assessment must be regarded by the judge as lawful.

213 IRPA, above note 4, s. 81(b). However, if the person is successful in the pre-removal risk assessment process, that removal order is stayed. IRPA, *ibid.*, s. 114(1)(b).

214 *Ibid.*, s. 112 *et seq.*, particularly s. 113(d).

the decision-maker must have before him or her cogent evidence upon which to assess and then articulate the danger the person concerned poses to the security of Canada. Once such danger has been determined it must be weighed and balanced against the possible injustice to the person concerned if deported.[215]

If successful on the pre-removal risk or section 115 assessment, there is no longer any prospect that a person will be deported. Relief from the detention is not, however, automatic. In the detention review process, the Federal Court judge contemplates only the national security threat, defined as "an objectively reasonable suspicion of substantial threatened harm."[216] Detainees, in the course of the regular six-month review of their detention, could continue to be detained (or at least subject to the, in practice, stringent conditions on release described below) if the judge is "satisfied" that the permanent resident continues to be a danger to national security.[217]

An obvious quandary emerges if a person is protected from removal under the "pre-removal risk assessment process" or in the section 115 balancing, and yet the court continues to view him or her as a threat to national security. It is in this circumstance that the Act may produce an indefinite detention, albeit interrupted by six month court reviews..

iii) Possible Indefinite Detention after Charter Challenge to Removal
A related quandary could arise where the government concludes that the person *should* be deported, even to torture.

Such a decision is vulnerable to constitutional challenge; namely, is it ever constitutional to deport an individual to face likely torture? This is a question left open by the Supreme Court of Canada in *Suresh*. In that case, the Supreme Court applied section 7 of the *Charter of Rights and Freedoms* and held that "insofar as the *Immigration Act* leaves open the possibility of deportation to torture, the Minister should generally decline to deport refugees where on the evidence there is a substantial risk of torture."[218] However, the Court qualified its holding by refusing

---

215 Above note 4 at para. 56.

216 *Almrei v. Canada (Minister of Citizenship and Immigration)*, above note 4 at para. 101.

217 This procedure applies to permanent residents. Under IRPA, above note 4, s. 84, a judge, meanwhile, may order a foreign national's released only if "satisfied that … the release will not pose a danger to national security or to the safety of any person." However, given the Supreme Court's conclusion in *Charkaoui*, above note 5, that the differential treatment between foreign nationals as opposed to permanent residents was impermissible, it seems likely the permanent resident standards applies to both groups.

218 *Suresh v. Canada (Minister of Citizenship and Immigration)*, [2002] 1 S.C.R. 3 at para. 77 [*Suresh*].

to "exclude the possibility that in exceptional circumstances, deportation to face torture might be justified, either as a consequence of the balancing process mandated by s. 7 of the *Charter* or under s. 1" in exceptional conditions "such as natural disasters, the outbreak of war, epidemics and the like."[219]

Exactly what constitutes these exceptional circumstances remained unclear at the time of this writing. Lower courts, however, have moved to limit the reach of this *Suresh* language. In *Jaballah (Re)*,[220] the Federal Court considered whether the security-certificate detainee in that case could be removed to face substantial risk of torture overseas. While accepting that Jaballah constituted a risk to national security, as claimed by the government, the court did not view his case as the "exceptional" circumstance contemplated by *Suresh*, pointing to the fact that he had not been "personally involved in violence."[221]

The court did not outright bar deportation. Jaballah could still be removed to some third country where he would not be tortured. A willing host of this sort may, however, be uncommon in cases where the person constitutes a *bona fide* security risk. All told, therefore, the constitutional ruling in *Jaballah*, if upheld on appeal, may effectively bar a detainee's removal.

Nevertheless, that person may still persist as a national security risk and will therefore continue to be subject to a valid detention under a security certificate. With no removal possible, and unless the security risk somehow abates, the Act creates a possibility that detention may again be indefinite.

iv) Alternatives to Indefinite Detention

At the time of this writing, there was, however, an emerging Federal Court unease (expressed in practice, and sometimes in prose) with indefinite security-certificate detention. For instance, in *Charkaoui*, the Federal Court judge acknowledged that factual circumstances change with the passage of time, influencing how the court would assess the need for continued detention. In that case, the prolonged period of detention, coupled with the notoriety of the case, "neutralized" the security threat, prompting the judge to order Charkaoui's release on conditions, pending the outcome of the removal proceedings.[222]

Similarly, a second detainee, Mohamed Harkat, was released by the Federal Court, on strict conditions in 2006. In rejecting an expedited

---

219 *Ibid.* at para. 78.
220 2006 FC 1230.
221 *Ibid.* at para. 82.
222 *Charkaoui (Re)*, 2005 FC 248.

government appeal of that decision, the Federal Court of Appeal observed:

> The possible release, albeit under very onerous terms and conditions and for a temporary period, of a foreign national who is being detained without criminal conviction on the basis of a security certificate found by a judge to be reasonable, is an important part of the legislative scheme put in place to deal with terrorism in a non-criminal context. It is the remedy chosen by Parliament to prevent indeterminate or indefinite detention, a concept which is simply not in harmony with our democratic values even when applied to persons who have been found on reasonable grounds to have engaged in terrorist activities.[223]

Two other men, Mohammad Mahjoub and Mahmoud Jaballah, were released in similar circumstances in early 2007.[224]

This practice of judicial release on strict conditions was endorsed by the Supreme Court in *Charkaoui*, and indeed was the feature of the security certificate system that preserved it from being declared cruel and unusual treatment in violation of the *Charter*.[225] The Court concluded that "extended periods of detention under the certificate provisions of the *IRPA* do not violate ss. 7 and 12 of the *Charter* if accompanied by a process that provides regular opportunities for review of detention, taking into account all relevant factors" including: reasons for the detention; length of the detention; reasons for the delay of deportation; anticipated future length of detention; and the availability of alternatives to detention.[226] Bill C-3 proposes codifying the Federal Court's conditional release practice, giving it a statutory imprimatur.

It must be recognized, however, that the conditions imposed to secure release are very aggressive. As noted above, for example, Harkat must not have access to a room with an Internet-equipped computer. Violation of this or any other condition is, according to the release agreement, "an offence within the meaning of section 127 of the *Criminal Code* and shall constitute an offence pursuant to paragraph 124(1)(a)

---

223 *Harkat v. Canada (Minister of Citizenship and Immigration)*, above note 182 at para. 20.

224 *Mahjoub v. Canada (Minister of Citizenship and Immigration)*, 2007 FC 171; *Jaballah v. Canada (Minister of Public Safety and Emergency Preparedness)*, 2007 FC 379.

225 *Charkaoui*, above note 5 at paras. 98 ("I conclude that the *IRPA* does not impose cruel and unusual treatment within the meaning of s. 12 of the *Charter* because, although detentions may be lengthy, the *IRPA*, properly interpreted, provides a process for reviewing detention and obtaining release and for reviewing and amending conditions of release, where appropriate") and 107.

226 *Ibid.* at para. 110 *et seq.*

of the *Immigration and Refugee Protection Act*."[227] Bill C-3 would expressly authorize an arrest where conditions are (or appear about to be) breached and empower the judge to order the person re-detained.

As with peace bonds, strict release conditions allow the state to impose a different code of conduct on suspected security risks than exists under the regular law. Where these closely monitored persons violate the terms of release, the latter may amount to a hair-trigger converting immigration detention into incarceration for criminal offences.

At the time of this writing, it seemed certain that IRPA security certificates would undergo a renovation in the foreseeable future. Whether Canada would abandon this mechanism as a means to deal with feared terrorist threats and resort instead to its equivalent peace bond powers (or actual prosecutions) under the *Criminal Code* remained to be seen.

C. FOREIGN DETENTIONS

Post-9/11 practices raise questions concerning a final sort of detention: detention undertaken by a foreign state. This foreign detention may be tied to Canada in a number of ways. First, the detained person may have been removed from Canada under its immigration laws and subsequently incarcerated by the foreign state. Second, the person may be removed by a third country (most notoriously through a process of "extraordinary rendition") but transit through Canada en route to foreign detention. Third, the foreign detainee may be a Canadian national.

1) Deported Detainees

As discussed above, Canada's immigration law includes several mechanisms for deporting national security threats. In some instances, this removal should be uncontroversial; the removal, for instance, of a Russian sleeper agent to Russia. More problematic are efforts to remove persons to states where they are vulnerable to ill treatment. Terrorist suspects, for example, removed to Middle Eastern states whose governments they oppose might expect detention and subsequent maltreatment at the hands of those governments. In these circumstances, removal from Canada could amount to detention (and torture) by proxy.

---

227 Section 127 of the *Criminal Code*, above note 3, creates an indictable offence liable to imprisonment for up to two years for disobeying an order of a court. Section 124 of the IRPA, above note 4, creates an offence (punishable in s. 125 on indictment with up to two years' imprisonment) for failing to comply with a condition or obligation imposed under the IRPA.

a)   International Standards

The international law in this area is clear. A terrorist is not entitled to refugee status under international refugee law.[228] Like every other person, however, such an individual may not be expelled, returned ("refouler") or extradited "to another State where there are substantial grounds for believing that he would be in danger of being subjected to torture."[229] In assessing these substantial grounds, governments are to "take into account all relevant considerations including, where applicable, the existence in the State concerned of a consistent pattern of gross, flagrant or mass violations of human rights."

These obligations — contained in the U.N. Torture Convention — exist also by virtue of the ICCPR. As noted, that instrument bars torture and cruel, inhuman and degrading treatment and punishment.[230] The U.N. Human Rights Committee — the treaty body established by the ICCPR — has interpreted this prohibition to apply to deportation proceedings: "States parties must not expose individuals to the danger of torture or cruel, inhuman or degrading treatment or punishment upon return to another country by way of their extradition, expulsion or refoulement."[231]

Where substantial grounds to believe torture will occur exist, the bar on removal to torture is absolute and is subject to no derogation. However, states — including Canada — have sometimes sought to justify removals to countries with notorious torture records on the grounds that the prospect of torture is vitiated by "diplomatic assurances"; that is, pledges provided by states that they will not torture the individual. These assurances — intended to guard against an eventuality that is almost always illegal in these states, and yet occurs on a sometimes vast scale — have been roundly condemned by human rights organizations

---

228 *United Nations Convention Relating to the Status of Refugees*, 189 U.N.T.S. 150 (1951), Art. 1(F) (the refugee convention does not apply to a person who there is serious reason to consider has "been guilty of acts contrary to the purposes and principles of the United Nations"). See IRPA, *ibid.*, s. 96; Sch., incorporating this rule. The Supreme Court of Canada has concluded (reasonably) that terrorism constitutes such an act. *Pushpanathan v. Canada (Minister of Immigration and Citizenship)*, [1998] 1 S.C.R. 982 at paras. 66 and 120.

229 Torture Convention, above note 17, Art. 3.

230 ICCPR, above note 11, Art. 7.

231 Human Rights Committee, *General Comment 20*, above note 81, Art. 7.

as ineffective.[232] The Supreme Court of Canada has also queried their utility.[233]

b)   Canadian Law

Canada is a party to the Torture Convention but has not implemented its ban on removals to torture. Indeed, Canada appears to be unique among Western states in anticipating in its statute books removal to torture if the security threats are significant enough. Canada's preparedness to remove persons to torture has generated negative international commentary.[234]

The operations of the pre-removal risk assessment and section 115 processes of the IRPA are discussed above. As noted there, this Canadian approach exploits an uncertainty on the constitutional propriety of such an action left open by the Supreme Court of Canada in *Suresh*. The "exceptional circumstances" language employed by the Supreme Court in *Suresh* is a fragile basis on which to build Canada's national security deportation law. Deportation to torture will also certainly be revisited by the Supreme Court in the foreseeable future. Indeed, recent jurisprudence from the Supreme Court has stressed that, in interpreting the *Charter*, "courts should seek to ensure compliance with Canada's bind-

---

232 See, for example, Human Rights Watch, *Still at Risk: Diplomatic Assurances No Safeguard Against Torture* (April 2005), online: http://hrw.org/reports/2005/eca0405/; Human Rights Watch, *Empty Promises: Diplomatic Assurances No Safeguard Against Torture* (April 2004), online: http://hrw.org/reports/2004/un0404/.

233 *Suresh*, above note 218 at para. 124 ("We would signal the difficulty in relying too heavily on assurances by a state that it will refrain from torture in the future when it has engaged in illegal torture or allowed others to do so on its territory in the past. This difficulty becomes acute in cases where torture is inflicted not only with the collusion but through the impotence of the state in controlling the behaviour of its officials"). The use of assurances in the United Kingdom has also been controversial. There, the government has had mixed success in using assurances to justify removal to torturing regimes. See discussion in Duncan Hooper, "Court Deals Major Blow to Anti-terror Strategy" [*London*] *Daily Telegraph* (28 April 2007).

234 In its 2005 assessment of Canada's compliance with the Torture Convention, the U.N. Committee Against Torture expressed concern at the "failure of the Supreme Court of Canada, in *Suresh v. Minister of Citizenship and Immigration*, to recognize at the level of domestic law the absolute nature of the protection of article 3 of the Convention, which is not subject to any exception whatsoever" and recommended that Canada "unconditionally undertake to respect the absolute nature of article 3 in all circumstances and fully to incorporate the provision of article 3 into the State party's domestic law." *Conclusions and Recommendations of the Committee against Torture: Canada* (07/07/2005) CAT/C/CR/34/CAN, online: www.unhchr.ch/tbs/doc.nsf/(Symbol)/CAT.C.CR.34.CAN.En?Opendocument.

ing obligations under international law where the express words are capable of supporting such a construction."[235] Since the words of the *Charter* are more than capable of being read consistently with Article 3 of the Torture Convention, it seems unlikely the *Suresh* exception can survive close application of this interpretive rule.

By the time of this writing, the government's efforts to deport suspected terrorists to possible torture had been rejected when challenged in court, either because the government failed to weigh evidence of the torture risk properly[236] or, in one case, because the Federal Court was unpersuaded that the risk posed by a particular terrorist suspect constituted the exceptional circumstances allowing a constitutional removal to torture.[237] The senate special committee on anti-terrorism law recommended in 2007 that IRPA be amended to bar emphatically removal where there are "reasonable grounds to believe the individual will be subject to torture in the country to which he or she will be removed."[238]

2) Transiting Detainees

a) Background

The U.S. practice of extraordinary rendition, described in more detail in Chapter 15, is the most notorious means by which a third country engineers a foreign detention. In 2005, controversy over this practice mounted, sparked by reports that detainees were transiting between rendering and accepting states via the airspace of another country. In fall 2005, Canadian media reported that CIA detainee flights were transiting through Canada on the way to secret detention facilities in Eastern Europe. By late 2005, Canada Border Services Agency reported that twenty planes "alleged in the media to have ties to the CIA [had] made 74 flights to Canada" since 9/11.[239]

---

235 *R. v. Hape*, 2007 SCC 26 at para. 56. See also *Health Services and Support — Facilities Subsector Bargaining Assn. v. British Columbia*, 2007 SCC 27 at para. 79.

236 See, for example, *Almrei v. Canada (Minister of Citizenship and Immigration)*, 2005 FC 355 at para. 32; *Mahjoub*, above note 4 at paras. 31–34; *Sogi v. Canada (Minister of Citizenship and Immigration)*, 2004 FC 853.

237 *Jaballah (Re)*, 2006 FC 1230. The Supreme Court noted this case in *Charkaoui*, above note 5 at para. 15, but declined to rule on the legality of removal to torture.

238 Senate, *Fundamental Justice in Extraordinary Times*, above note 168 at 110.

239 "Allegations That CIA Airplanes are Transporting Suspected Terrorists through Canada," undated memo obtained from Privy Council Office under the *Access to Information Act* on 27 February 2006, online: http://aix1.uottawa.ca/~cforcese/ nsarchive/documents/0601.pdf. See also material obtained from Transport Canada on 16 March 2006. These documents include a roster of suspected CIA

Similar U.S. transit flights through the nations of the Council of Europe to other member nations sparked an investigation by that body in 2006 and a review of member states' legal obligations. That assessment[240] canvassed applicable rules of international law, some of which are described here.

b) International Law

A state has sovereign jurisdiction over its airspace.[241] The *Chicago Convention on International Civil Aviation*[242] provides that "every State has complete and exclusive sovereignty over the airspace above its territory."

That same treaty provides that no state aircraft—including aircraft used in military, customs and police services— "shall fly over the territory of another State or land thereon without authorization by special agreement or otherwise, and in accordance with the terms thereof."[243] The regime for civil aircraft is more generous, permitting these vehicles "to make flights into or in transit non-stop across its territory and to make stops for non-traffic purposes without the necessity of obtaining prior permission, and subject to the right of the State flown over to require landing"[244]

The Council of Europe's legal opinion took the view that if "state aircraft" enter the foreign sovereign air space "without a proper authorisation, they may be: intercepted for purposes of identification; directed to leave the violated air space; directed to land for the purpose of further

---

flights and, in the text of some intragovernmental e-mail messages, some plane registration information. Online: http://aix1.uottawa.ca/~cforcese/nsarchive/documents/0602.pdf.

240 Opinion on the International Legal Obligations of Council of Europe Member States in Respect of Secret Detention Facilities and Inter-State Transport of Prisoners, adopted by the Venice Commission at its 66th Plenary Session (Venice, 17–18 March 2006) on the basis of comments by Mssrs. Iain Cameron (Substitute Member, Sweden), Pieter van Dijk (Member, the Netherlands), Olivier Dutheillet de Lamothe (Member, France), Jan Helgesen (Member, Norway), Giorgio Malinverni (Member, Switzerland), and Georg Nolte (Substitute Member, Germany)—opinion no. 363/2005, CDL-AD(2006)009, online: www.coe.int/t/e/human_rights/cddh/3._committees/06.%20terrorism%20(dh-s-ter)/working%20documents/2006/DH-S-TER(2006)006.asp#TopOfPage [Venice Commission].

241 Malcolm Shaw, *International Law*, 5th ed. (Cambridge: Cambridge University Press, 2003) at 463–64.

242 15 U.N.T.S. 295, Art. 1 [Chicago Convention].

243 *Ibid.*, Art. 3.

244 *Ibid.*, Art. 5.

investigation/prosecution; or forced to land for further investigation/prosecution."[245]

It also reasoned that the traditional immunity of state aircraft to search and inspection is conditioned on receiving a preauthorization to enter foreign airspace.[246] However, "state aircraft can only claim immunity inasmuch as they make their state function known to the territorial State through the appropriate channels. If the public purpose was not declared in order to circumvent the requirement of obtaining the necessary permission(s), then the State will be estopped from claiming State aircraft status."[247] Because it has failed to declare itself as a state aircraft and sought the requisite authorization, this vehicle would be in breach of the *Chicago Convention*.[248] In the council's view, the "territorial State could request the airplane to land and could proceed to search and inspection and take the necessary measures to put an end to possible [human rights] violations it might identify."[249]

Human rights obligations make these steps obligatory: "If a Council of Europe member State has serious reasons to believe that an airplane crossing its airspace carries prisoners with the intention of transferring them to countries where they would face ill-treatment in violation of Article 3 of the *European Convention on Human Rights*, it must take all the necessary measures in order to prevent this from taking place."[250]

Article 3 provides that "no one shall be subjected to torture or to inhuman or degrading treatment or punishment." It is identical, on its face, to the obligation found in Article 7 of the ICCPR, a treaty binding on Canada. No doubt for this reason, Amnesty International and other human rights groups have called on all states, including Canada, to "board the plane or require it to land for inspection" if there are grounds to believe that an aircraft is involved in "renditions or other human rights violations."[251]

---

245 Venice Commission, above note 240 at para. 94.

246 *Ibid.* at para. 95.

247 *Ibid.* at para. 103.

248 *Ibid.* at para. 149.

249 *Ibid.* at para. 103.

250 *Ibid.* at para. 159.

251 Amnesty International, *Canada: CIA flights—Canada's Role Needs Greater Scrutiny* (20 January 2006), online: www.amnesty.ca/take_action/actions/canada_CIA_flights.php. The Council of Europe issued a resolution in 2006 calling on member states to "ensure that unlawful inter-state transfers of detainees will not be permitted and take effective measures to prevent renditions and rendition flights through member states' territory and airspace." Council of Europe, Resolution 1507 (2006), para. 19.

3) Consular Protection of Nationals in Foreign Detention

a) Background

In most of the extraordinary rendition cases documented to date, the rendered individuals appear usually to have been nationals of the state to which they have been removed.[252] However, in at least the Maher Arar matter, the rendered individual was also a dual national, domiciled in his second country of nationality—Canada—at the time he was removed to Syria. If renditions of persons living in North America or Europe continue, the Arar situation may turn out to be the norm.[253]

Although outside the context of renditions, other Canadians have also been detained and tortured in foreign states on terrorism suspicions—Abdullah Almalki, Ahmad Abou-El Maati and Muayyed Nureddin. These individuals were detained by foreign governments while within the territory of the foreign state. At the time of this writing it was unclear to what extent, if at all, these detentions followed tip-offs from Canadian officials and whether Canadian officials offered earnest consular protection. An inquiry into these questions was launched in late 2006.

b) Consular Protection and International Law

For the state whose nationals are detained, important issues arise under the law of consular protection. Article 3 of the *Vienna Convention on Diplomatic Relations* lists, as one of the functions of a diplomatic mis-

---

252 See discussion in Committee on International Human Rights *et al.*, *Torture by Proxy*, above note 10 at 9 *et seq.*

253 Indeed, in September 2005 the new U.S. ambassador to Canada reportedly refused to apologize for Mr. Arar's treatment and warned that other dual nationals might suffer the same fate: "Will there be other deportations in the future? I'd be surprised if there's not.... The United States made that decision (to deport Arar) based on the facts it had, in the best interests of the people of the United States, and we stand behind it." Jim Brown, "New U.S. Ambassador Offers No Apologies for Arar's Treatment" *Ottawa Citizen* (19 September 2005) A2. Amnesty International has reported the rendition of a least one other dual national: German-Syrian Muhammad Hayder Zammar, rendered from Morocco to Syria in November 2001. See Amnesty International, *Syrian-born German Held Three Years without Charge in Rat-infested Syrian "Tomb,"* online: http://web.amnesty. org/library/pdf/MDE240662004ENGLISH/$File/MDE2406604.pdf. Dual nationality creates complexities in the area of consular protection. This matter is not discussed in this book. For an analysis, see Craig Forcese, "The Capacity to Protect: Diplomatic Protection of Dual Nationals in the 'War on Terror,'" (2006) 17 E.J.I.L. 369 and Craig Forcese, "Shelter from the Storm: Rethinking Diplomatic Protection of Dual Nationals in Modern International Law" (2005) 37 Geo. Wash. Int'l Law Rev. 469.

sion, "protecting in the receiving state the interests of the sending state and its nationals, within the limits permitted by international law."[254] The *Vienna Convention on Consular Relations* (VCCR) asserts a similar role for consular officials,[255] and some authorities describe the protection of nationals as a consul's central task.[256]

The VCCR also sets out specific responsibilities of "receiving" states in facilitating consular assistance of detained, "sending" state nationals. Thus, Article 36 provides that consular officials are "free to communicate with nationals of the sending State and to have access to them." Nationals of the sending state have a reciprocal freedom to communicate with, and have access to, consular officers of the sending State. Moreover, upon request of that national, the receiving state must inform consular officials that a national is detained. In a provision at issue in two recent International Court of Justice cases,[257] the receiving state must inform "without delay" the detained alien of his or her right to contact consular officials. In *Avena*, the International Court of Justice concluded that this obligation arises immediately upon receiving state officials learning (or suspecting) that the detained individual is a foreign national.[258]

Once notified of the detention, consular officials then have a right to visit and converse with their national and arrange for his or her legal representation, unless refused by the national.[259] Note, however, that international law imposes no obligation on states to provide consular or diplomatic protection.[260]

c)   Consular Protection and Canadian Law and Practice

i)   Recent Controversies
Like other states, Canada extends consular assistance to its nationals abroad. Konrad Sigurdson, then Director General, Consular Affairs Bureau, Department of Foreign Affairs and International Trade (DFAIT), told a parliamentary committee in 2003 that "Canada has one

---

254 500 U.N.T.S. 95 [VCDR].
255 596 U.N.T.S. 261, Art. 5 [VCCR].
256 See discussion in Luke Lee, *Consular Law and Practice*, 2d ed. (Oxford: Clarendon Press, 1991) at 124 *et seq.*
257 See *Avena and Other Mexican Nationals (Mexico v. United States of America)* (2004), ICJ General List No. 128 and *LaGrand (Germany v. United States of America)* (2001), ICJ General List No. 104.
258 *Avena, ibid.* at para. 63.
259 VCCR, above note 255, Art. 36(1)(c).
260 See *Kaunda v. President of the Republic of South Africa*, [2004] 10 B. Const. L.R. 1009 (S. Afr. Const. Ct.) for a discussion of this issue.

of the best consular assistance programs in the world." In 2002, his of-fice "handled close to 170,000 formal cases, involving but not limited to arrest and detention cases, death abroad, medical assistance, repatria-tion, well-being and whereabouts investigations, assistance with loss or theft of property and passports, and the processing of citizenship applications." One percent of these cases concerned arrests or deten-tions, three-quarters of which occurred in the United States, usually on drug-related charges.[261]

Most of these consular cases are apparently resolved without con-troversy. However, several high-profile detentions of Canadian citizens by foreign states have prompted criticism that Canada does not do enough to extend consular assistance to its nationals.[262] The accusa-tions levelled against Canadian officials vary. As noted, in cases such as those of Messieurs Arar, Almalki, El Maati and Nureddin, accusations have been made that Canadian officials were (at best) willfully blind to torture in Syria and inept in their handling of these men's cases.

The findings of the public inquiry into the Arar matter, released in fall 2006, are instructive.[263] Thus, "on receiving a summary of a state-ment made by Mr. Arar while in Syrian custody in early November 2002, DFAIT distributed it to the RCMP and CSIS without informing them that the statement was likely a product of torture. That statement became the basis for heightened suspicion in some minds about Mr. Arar's involvement in terrorism." Further, "CSIS received information about Mr. Arar from the Syrian Military Intelligence (SMI) and did not do an adequate reliability assessment as to whether the information was likely the product of torture. Indeed, its assessment was that it probably was not." Subsequently,

> the RCMP, acting through the Canadian Ambassador, sent the SMI questions for Abdullah Almalki, the subject of the relevant investiga-tion and also in Syrian custody. This action very likely sent a signal to Syrian authorities that the RCMP approved of the imprisonment and interrogation of Mr. Almalki and created a risk that the SMI would conclude that Mr. Arar, a person who had some association with Mr. Almalki, was considered a serious terrorist threat by the RCMP.

261 House of Commons Standing Committee on Foreign Affairs and International Trade, Evidence, 37th Parl., 2d Sess. (25 September 2003).
262 In many of these cases, the citizen in question was a dual national, also pos-sessing the nationality of the injuring state.
263 All quotations in this paragraph drawn from Commission of Inquiry into the Actions of Canadian Officials in Relation to Maher Arar, *Report on the Events Relating to Maher Arar* (2006) at 14–15, online: www.ararcommission.ca/eng/26. htm [Arar inquiry, Factual Report].

Later, "DFAIT failed to take steps to address the statement by Syrian officials that CSIS did not want Mr. Arar returned to Canada." Overall, "on several occasions, there was a lack of communication among the Canadian agencies involved in Mr. Arar's case. There was also a lack of a single, coherent approach to efforts to obtain his release." Government agencies clearly had different agendas, some preoccupied with securing Mr. Arar's release and others apparently viewing his detention as an intelligence-gathering opportunity.

These themes recur in other complaints about Canadian consular and diplomatic practices. Omar Khadr, currently on trial before a U.S. military tribunal for the shooting death of a U.S. solider in the Afghan war, has alleged in proceeding before the Federal Court that Canadian consular officials have not interceded properly with U.S. officials in his case, and indeed that they have collaborated with American intelligence agencies in interrogating him.[264] It should be noted that the Khadr accusations remained unproven.

ii)   Legal and Policy Issues

Arguably, Foreign Affairs Canada's legal power to extend consular protection flows from section 10 of the *Department of Foreign Affairs and International Trade Act* (DFAIT Act):[265] "in exercising his powers and carrying out his duties and functions under this Act, the Minister shall ... (a) conduct all diplomatic and consular relations on behalf of Canada." Alternatively, the diplomatic protection power reflects an unextinguished royal prerogative power over foreign affairs exercised by the federal government.[266] Yet, neither the DFAIT Act nor the royal prerogative specify the manner in which diplomatic and consular functions are to be conducted, nor do they impose a clear affirmative obligation on Canada to provide these services.

More instructive on this point are many readily available information documents on consular services for Canadians published by Foreign Affairs. For example, the government indicates in its pamphlet *Travelling Abroad? Assistance for Canadians* that "the consular services of the Department of Foreign Affairs and International Trade provide assistance to Canadian travellers. We are committed to helping Can-

---

264   *Khadr v. Canada (Minister of Foreign Affairs)*, 2004 FC 1145 [*Khadr*].
265   R.S.C. 1985, c. E-22 [DFAIT Act].
266   See *Black v. Canada (Prime Minister)* (2001), 54 O.R. (3d) 215 (C.A.) [*Black*] for a brief discussion of prerogative powers in the context of foreign affairs. In internal documents, the government characterizes consular services as a prerogative function. See *Manual* I-3, cited in Lee, *Consular Law and Practice*, above note 256 at 127.

adians prepare for foreign travel and to providing you with a variety of services once you're abroad." The document continues: "Canada's offices abroad are there to help you in case of an emergency. Consular staff, both in our foreign offices and in Ottawa, can: ... provide assistance in dealing with the criminal justice system; ... see that you are treated fairly under the country's laws if you are arrested; [and] ... help in the location of missing persons ...," among other things.[267]

In a more specific brochure, tellingly entitled *Canadian Consular Services: Providing Assistance to Canadians Abroad*, Foreign Affairs notes that its consular officials "seek to ensure that you are treated fairly under the country's laws if you are arrested or detained."[268] The department's long-standing brochure "*Bon Voyage, But ...*" repeats this passage,[269] and admonishes "if you do find yourself in legal trouble, contact the nearest Canadian government office at once."[270] Notably, "*Bon Voyage, But ...*" is a document the department notes should be taken by Canadians on every foreign trip.[271]

Meanwhile, in its publication, *A Guide to Canadians Imprisoned Abroad*, the Department specifies that "the Government of Canada *will make every effort* to ensure that you receive equitable treatment under the local criminal justice system. It will ensure that you are not penalized for being a foreigner, and that you are neither discriminated against nor denied justice because you are Canadian."[272]

Foreign Affairs' Consular Service also publishes written "Service Standards." These standards commit the government to "provide to all Canadians effective and efficient service throughout the world. Our commitment is for service characterized at all times by sensitivity, empathy, courtesy, speed, accuracy and fairness. ... Every effort will be made to obtain solutions for specific problems and to provide the required service." Under its schedule of services, the government lists

267 Department of Foreign Affairs and International Trade, *Travelling Abroad? Assistance for Canadians*, online: www.voyage.gc.ca/main/pubs/PDF/travelling_abroad-en.pdf.

268 Foreign Affairs Canada, *Canadian Consular Services: Providing Assistance to Canadians Abroad* (Ottawa: Foreign Affairs Canada, 2005) at 2.

269 Foreign Affairs Canada, *Bon Voyage, But ...* (2006) at 3, online: www.voyage. gc.ca/main/pubs/bon_voyage_but-en.asp www.voyage.gc.ca/main/pubs/bon_voyage_but-en.asp.

270 *Ibid.* at 24.

271 Foreign Affairs Canada, *Traveller's Checklist*, online: www.voyage.gc.ca/main/before/checklist-en.asp.

272 Foreign Affairs Canada, *A Guide to Canadians for Imprisoned Abroad* (2005) at 6 [emphasis added], online: www.voyage.gc.ca/main/pubs/imprisoned_abroad-en.asp.

"Contact with Arrested or Detained Persons" as something done within twenty-four hours, subject to factors "beyond its control."[273]

In sum, in these documents, the government of Canada warns that its capacity to engineer the appropriate treatment of Canadians abroad may be limited, but that it (quite emphatically) undertakes to do what it can. Under these circumstances, Canadians act quite reasonably if they expect the Canadian government to take an interest in their troubles with foreign states.

d) Obligation to Provide Consular Protection

i)   U.K. Experience
In the United Kingdom, an equivalent reasonable belief grounds a domestic legal obligation to provide consular protection. The most notable case is *R. (on the application of Abbasi and another) v. Secretary of State for Foreign and Commonwealth Affairs*, a 2002 decision of the English Court of Appeal.[274] At issue in *Abbasi* was the potentially indefinite detention at Guantanamo Bay of a British national captured by American forces in Afghanistan. Abbasi sought judicial review to compel the United Kingdom to intervene diplomatically with the United States. In concluding that the United Kingdom was under some obligation, the Court of Appeal pointed to the administrative law doctrine of "legitimate expectation":

> [T]he doctrine of "legitimate expectation" provides a well-established and flexible means for giving legal effect to a settled policy or practice for the exercise of an administrative discretion. The expectation may arise from an express promise or "from the existence of a regular practice which the claimant can reasonably expect to continue." ... The expectation is not that the policy or practice will necessarily remain unchanged, or, if unchanged, that it will not be overridden by other policy considerations. However, so long as it remains unchanged, the subject is entitled to have it properly taken into account in considering his individual case.[275]

Canvassing British government public policy assertions on circumstances where it would extend diplomatic protection, the court concluded that "these statements indicate a clear acceptance by the government

---

273 Department of Foreign Affairs, Consular Services, *Service Standards*, online: www.voyage.gc.ca/main/about/service_standards-en.asp.

274 [2002] All E.R. (D) 70.

275 *Ibid.* at para. 82 [citations omitted].

of a role in relation to protecting the rights of British citizens abroad, where there is evidence of miscarriage or denial of justice."[276]

The Court noted the considerable deference owed to the government in the exercise of foreign policy. Nevertheless, "there is no reason why [the government's] decision or inaction should not be reviewable if it can be shown that the same were irrational or contrary to legitimate expectation."[277] Surely, "the court cannot enter the forbidden areas, including decisions affecting foreign policy," but "an obligation to consider the position of a particular British citizen and consider the extent to which some action might be taken on his behalf, would seem unlikely itself to impinge on any forbidden area."[278]

Abbasi succeeded, therefore, in persuading the court of the justiciability of his claim. However, on the facts in *Abbasi*, the Court of Appeal concluded that the government had complied with its duty: "the Foreign and Commonwealth Office have considered Mr Abbasi's request for assistance. … [T]he British detainees are the subject of discussions between this country and the United States both at Secretary of State and lower official levels. We do not consider that Mr Abbasi could reasonably expect more than this."[279] The expectation of diplomatic protection accorded Abbasi was, in other words, quite limited.

ii)   Canadian Experience

a.   *Khadr* Case

This comparative legal experience suggests a potential source for a Canadian legal obligation to provide consular protection. In *Khadr*,[280] a Canadian citizen captured by U.S. forces in Afghanistan and detained at Guantanamo Bay sought a court order compelling the government to extend to him the consular services described in the Foreign Affairs publication, *A Guide to Canadians Imprisoned Abroad*.[281] Mr. Khadr invoked both administrative law and *Charter* section 7. The government moved to strike Mr. Khadr's Notice of Application on the basis that it disclosed no cause of action.

While the Federal Court rejected Khadr's constitutional argument, it accepted his administrative law position. Specifically, Khadr urged that section 10 of the DFAIT Act imposed an affirmative duty on For-

---

276   *Ibid.* at para. 92.
277   *Ibid.* at para. 106.
278   *Ibid.*
279   *Ibid.* at para. 107.
280   *Khadr*, above note 264.
281   This document is described above.

eign Affairs to intercede on his behalf with American authorities. The
Federal Court relied on section 10 and several of the statements made
in Foreign Affairs Canada documents cited above to conclude that

> there is a persuasive case that both the DFAITA [DFAIT Act] and the
> Guide [to Canadians Imprisoned Abroad] create a legitimate and rea-
> sonable expectation that a Canadian citizen detained abroad will re-
> ceive many of the services which Omar Khadr has requested. Indeed,
> Canadians abroad would be surprised, if not shocked, to learn that
> the provision of consular services in an individual case is left to the
> complete and unreviewable discretion of the Minister.[282]

In the result, the court held that Khadr's application "displays a possible
cause of action that the decision of the Minister not to provide the appropriate services (required under the circumstances) set out in the Guide
may constitute a breach of his duties under section 10 of the DFAITA,"
and declined to strike the notice of application in full.[283] At the time of
this writing, the application had not been heard on its merits.

b.   Discussion

The Federal Court's decision in *Khadr* is disputable. Specifically, a main
controversy in Canadian law is whether legitimate expectation extends
not just to the procedural conduct of officials, but also to substantive
outcomes. The conventional view is that it does not.[284] Binnie J. did acknowledge in his concurring reasons in *Mount Sinai Hospital Center v.
Quebec (Minister of Health and Social Services)*,[285] that "in some cases it
is difficult to distinguish the procedural from the substantive."[286] Partially on the strength of this observation, the Federal Court in *Khadr*
asserted that "the expectation in this case is arguably composed of
both procedural and substantive elements."[287] However, it is difficult
to see an expectation that the government will provide consular services as anything other than substantive. The provision of diplomatic
protection is an outcome, not a procedure governing how a particular
outcome is arrived at.[288]

---

282   *Khadr*, above note 264 at para. 22.
283   *Ibid.* at para. 29.
284   See, for example, *Baker v. Canada (Minister of Citizenship and Immigration)*,
      [1999] 2 S.C.R 817 at para. 26 ("the doctrine of legitimate expectations cannot
      lead to substantive rights outside the procedural domain") [*Baker*].
285   [2001] 2 S.C.R. 281 [*Mount Sinai*].
286   *Ibid.* at para. 35.
287   *Khadr*, above note 264 at para. 23.
288   An alternative argument—grounded in public law estoppel—might be invoked
      to capture substantive promises, where there has been actual detrimental reliance

For this reason, it is not clear that the key administrative law holding in the *Khadr* case will be replicated in future cases. Nevertheless, while not discussed in *Khadr*, Canadian administrative law does create duties for consular officials. First, while Foreign Affairs Canada's various documents describing consular services offered Canadians may not create a legitimate expectation that those services—a substantive entitlement—will actually be provided, they certainly create a legitimate procedural expectation that Canadians can *request* those services and have that request *considered*.

Second, in considering this request, consular officers—like any other government official—must properly deploy their discretion to exercise (or not) diplomatic protection.[289] This exercise of discretion is itself amenable to judicial scrutiny, albeit inevitably on a gentle standard of review.[290] Often, such decisions must be patently unreasonable. A patently unreasonable decision has been described as one that is clearly irrational.[291] In the Court's post-*Baker v. Canada* error of discretion cases, a patently unreasonable discretionary decision has repeatedly been conflated with one made in bad faith or in reliance on improper considerations.[292] Whether this standard was violated would

---

on undertakings made by the government. This doctrine remains, however, ill-formed in Canadian law, and in any event, may be defeated where the power exercised by the government official is highly discretionary, involving considerations of high policy. See Binnie J., concurring in *Mount Sinai*, above note 285 at para. 39 *et seq.* Arguably, the conduct of Canada's diplomatic and consular relations is a policy-driven exercise of the sort that might be excluded from public estoppel.

289 This would be true even if diplomatic protection is part of the royal prerogative, rather than a function covered by s. 10 of the DFAIT Act, above note 265. The exercise of prerogative powers is justiciable where it affects the rights of individuals. See *Black*, above note 266 at para. 51 ("the exercise of the prerogative will be justiciable, or amenable to the judicial process, if its subject matter affects the rights or legitimate expectations of an individual. Where the rights or legitimate expectations of an individual are affected, the court is both competent and qualified to judicially review the exercise of the prerogative").

290 See, for example, *Baker*, above note 284 at para. 56 ("[i]ncorporating judicial review of decisions that involve considerable discretion into the pragmatic and functional analysis for errors of law should not be seen as reducing the level of deference given to decisions of a highly discretionary nature"); *Mount Sinai*, above note 285 at para. 58, Binnie, concurring in the result ("[d]ecisions of Ministers of the Crown in the exercise of discretionary powers in the administrative context should generally receive the highest standard of deference, namely patent unreasonableness").

291 *Canada (Attorney General) v. Public Service Alliance of Canada*, [1993] 1 S.C.R. 941 at 963–64, Cory J.

292 *Suresh*, above note 218 at para. 29 ("the reviewing court should adopt a deferential approach to this question and should set aside the Minister's discretionary

turn on the facts. It seems plausible, however, that a refusal to extend consular protection premised on, for instance, a desire to facilitate the extraction by foreign officials of intelligence from the detainee could transgress the improper considerations concept.[293]

In sum, while it is not entirely clear that Canada is legally obliged to extend consular protection, Canada's consular practices are amenable to legal scrutiny for their fairness and reasonableness.

---

decision if it is patently unreasonable in the sense that it was made arbitrarily or in bad faith, it cannot be supported on the evidence, or the Minister failed to consider the appropriate factors"); *Ahani v. Canada (Minister of Citizenship and Immigration)*, [2002] 1 S.C.R. 72 at para. 16 [*Ahani*] (same); *Canadian Union of Public Employees (C.U.P.E.) v. Ontario (Minister of Labour)*, [2003] 1 S.C.R. 539 at para. 176 [*CUPE*] ("In applying the *patent* unreasonableness test, we are not to reweigh the factors. But we are entitled to have regard to the importance of the factors that have been excluded altogether from consideration. Not every relevant factor excluded by the Minister from his consideration will be fatal under the patent unreasonableness standard. The problem here, as stated, is that the Minister expressly excluded factors that were not only relevant but went straight to the heart of the ... legislative scheme"). For a comprehensive discussion of *Suresh* and *Baker* and their impact on administrative law doctrines, see David Elliot, "*Suresh* and the Common Borders of Administrative Law: Time for the Tailor?" (2002) 65 Sask. L. Rev. 469. For a comprehensive discussion of the implications of *Baker*, see David Dyzenhaus, ed., *The Unity of Public Law* (Oxford: Hart Publishing, 2004).

293 There is no precedent on this question. However, in a Federal Court case involving a second Khadr brother, at issue was whether the government acted properly in denying Abdurahman Khadr a passport on national security grounds. At the time the decision was made, issuance of passports was governed by an Order-in-Council, promulgated under the government's royal prerogative, that did not list national security considerations as a ground for denying a passport. In *Khadr v. Canada (Attorney General)*, 2004 FC 1719 at para. 13, the government conceded that the "refusal of a passport application on grounds of national security is not within the authority vested in the Passport Office by the Canadian Passport Order." By analogy, a refusal to extend diplomatic protection on national security grounds—a concept not raised in the DFAIT Act—could be conceived as, at minimum, an improper purpose.

INTERROGATIONS

One of the purposes of detention may be interrogation of the detainee. The 2006 U.S. army interrogation manual defines interrogation as "the systematic effort to procure information to answer specific collection requirements by direct and indirect questioning techniques of a person who is in the custody of the forces conducting the questioning."[1] This chapter discusses the role and utility of interrogation, legal limitations on interrogation techniques and several controversies surrounding interrogation in the post-9/11 era: extreme interrogation techniques; the use in courts of interrogation information produced under potentially problematic circumstances; and judicially assisted interrogation.

PART I: INTERROGATION AND NATIONAL SECURITY

In the criminal justice system, interrogation is generally geared toward gleaning the truth concerning past events and, ideally, in eliciting a confession to a crime. Since the information produced through this questioning is generally useful only to the extent it is admissible in court, police interrogation is constrained by strict rules discouraging

---

1   U.S. Department of the Army, FM 2-22.3 (FM 34-52) Human Intelligence Collector Operations (September 2006) at para. 1.20, online: www.fas.org/irp/dod-dir/army/fm2-22-3.pdf.

oppressive tactics by police investigators. These rules preserve the fundamental rights of the accused while at the same time enhancing the reliability of the evidence produced by interrogation.

The same reasons for constraining interrogation techniques—the need to preserve fundamental rights and enhance reliability—exist in national security investigations. However, the mechanism by which constraints on interrogation are enforced must differ from those relied on in the criminal law context. In national security investigations, criminal prosecution may be an afterthought, and the prospect that interrogation techniques will ever be reviewed by a court in a prosecution produced by the interrogation may be remote. This context compounds the need for careful review and oversight of security and intelligence interrogation functions.

Interrogation in a national security context is also more prospective; that is, it extracts information concerning anticipated events, ideally in sufficient quantity and quality to help prevent those events. Faced with the prospect of an imminent terrorist attack or some other security crisis, the pressure on interrogators to force information from their subjects is enormous.

Persuading uncooperative individuals to divulge information is not, however, a simple task. Interrogation techniques have been honed to persuade the uncooperative. As psychologist (and former U.K. army interrogator) Ian Robbins describes, interrogation of any sort is designed to "assert complete control over the victim and break down any will they might have to resist the interrogator's demands."[2]

For this reason, interrogation is "inherently controversial." Techniques ranging "from trickery and mind games to sleep deprivation, intimidation and humiliation, have been honed over the years, often by drawing on findings from experimental psychology. ... [These techniques] can trigger long-term depression and post-traumatic stress disorder, which without treatment can persist for decades."[3] In Robbins' words:

> When someone is physically tired, unsettled after days or weeks alone in a bare cell, and ignorant of where they are, a sense of powerlessness and anxiety sets in that can quickly turn to disorientation and make them more inclined to talk, confess to something they didn't do, or even turn informer. The more organised forms of interrogation and torture, such as those used by the KGB or the British in Northern

---

2   Ian Robbins [Head of the Traumatic Stress Service at St. George's Hospital, London], "We Have Ways" *New Scientist* (20 November 2004 Issue 2474) at 44.

3   *Ibid.*

Ireland, can result in complete psychological breakdown and total submission. The state of mind associated with this was described by Hinkle as a "brain syndrome," a physiological condition involving impairment of brain function. In such a state, a person is capable of only simple activities, and as it progresses they may become restless, talkative and delirious. Ultimately they become totally confused and can even lapse into unconsciousness.

The ongoing effects on the victim are often profound. They can suffer depression, excessive anxiety and post-traumatic stress disorder, and sometimes full-blown psychosis—even if the interrogation was relatively mild, and even if it didn't involve physical torture.[4]

Torture is the most severe form of interrogation. As described in the psychological literature, torture is a form of psychological abuse producing "suicidal ideation, fearfulness, depression, helplessness, severe anxiety, confusion and anger." The severe psychological effect of torture stems from its "extreme purpose" and its typical association with solitary confinement. Specifically, torture is "directed at crippling the mind of identity of the person." It "systematically attacks victims' personalities in a way that spreads terror and produces humiliation, desperation, and powerlessness." It is aimed at "destroying mental health." Solitary confinement, meanwhile, "may have substantial psychopathological effects such as perceptual changes (generalized hyperresponsivity to external stimuli, hallucinations), affective disturbances (especially anxiety), difficulties with thinking, concentration and memory, and problems with impulse control."[5]

There is substantial doubt that torture or other harsh interrogation methods produce useful information. Reviewing the clinical evidence, the psychological literature on false confessions identifies three different categories of untruthful disclosures:

- Voluntary: a false, "self-incriminating statement that is offered without external pressure from the police."[6]
- Coerced-compliant: a false confession that occurs when "a suspect confesses in order to escape or avoid an aversive interrogation or to gain a promised reward. In these cases, the confession is merely an

---

4   *Ibid.*
5   Shaun Whittaker, "Counseling Torture Victims" (1988) 16 The Counseling Psychologist 272 at 272–73.
6   Saul Kassin, "The Psychology of Confession Evidence" (1997) 52 American Psychologist 221 at 225.

act of compliance, and the suspect privately knows that he or she is truly innocent."[7]

- Coerced-internalized: a false confession that arises when "an innocent person—anxious, tired, confused, and subjected to highly suggestive methods of interrogation—actually comes to believe that he or she committed the crime. This type of false confession is particularly frightening because the suspect's memory of his or her own actions may be altered, rendering the original contents potentially irretrievable."[8]

Coerced-compliant and coerced-internalized confessions are a ready product of torture. As one British psychologist and expert in interrogation observes, "almost anyone, given the right circumstances, can be persuaded to confess to a crime they did not commit. The 'right circumstances' can be anything from long periods of questioning or days of confinement to severe psychological pressure and intimidation. Intelligence officers in search of information can easily make detention and questioning so intolerable that their subjects will say anything for a way out."[9] In fact, clinical studies suggest that interrogator use of false evidence to impugn a detainee's answers[10] and interrogation of sleep-deprived individuals[11] compound the likelihood of false confessions.

These views are affirmed by a 2006 study published by the U.S. National Defense Intelligence College:

> The potential mechanisms and effects of using coercive techniques or torture for gaining accurate, useful information from an uncooperative source are much more complex than is commonly assumed. There is little or no research to indicate whether such techniques succeed in the manner and contexts in which they are applied. Anecdotal accounts and opinions based on personal experiences are mixed, but the preponderance of reports seems to weigh against their effectiveness. ... The accuracy of educed information can be compromised by the manner in which it is obtained. The effects of many common stress and duress techniques are known to impair various aspects of

---

7   *Ibid.*

8   *Ibid.* at 226.

9   Gisli Gudjonsson [Professor of Forensic Psychology at the Institute of Psychiatry, King's College London], "Being Made To Confess to Something, Anything" *New Scientist* (20 November 2004 Issue 2474) at 52.

10   Kassin, "The Psychology of Confession Evidence," above note 6 at 227–28.

11   Mark Blagrove, "Effects of Length of Sleep Deprivation on Interrogative Suggestibility" (1996) 2 Journal of Experimental Psychology: Applied 48.

a person's cognitive functioning, including those functions necessary to retrieve and produce accurate, useful information.[12]

False confessions produce "false positives"—misleading information that diverts resources along investigatory and intelligence *cul de sacs*. Certainly, this seems to have happened in the Maher Arar case. The Arar inquiry reported an uncritical willingness of Canadian security and intelligence agencies to accept as true a false confession provided by a notorious torturing state.[13]

More fundamentally, torture and cruel, inhuman and degrading treatment are evident abuses of the most fundamental rights of human beings. As discussed later in this chapter, the prohibition on torture is among the most robust doctrines in international law.

PART II: LIMITS ON TECHNIQUES OF INTERROGATION

Because interrogation may do such violence to the body and psyche of human beings, its practice is carefully regulated by law.

A. INTERNATIONAL HUMAN RIGHTS STANDARDS

International law guards against extreme forms of interrogation. Two broadly ratified international treaties include a prohibition on both torture and cruel, inhuman and degrading treatment and punishment ("CID treatment"). The *International Covenant on Civil and Political Rights* (ICCPR)[14] provides in Article 7 that "no one shall be subjected to torture or to cruel, inhuman or degrading treatment or punishment." The *Convention against Torture and Other Cruel, Inhuman or Degrading*

---

12   Randy Borum, "Approaching Truth: Behavioral Science Lessons on Educing Information from Human Sources" in Intelligence Science Board, *Educing Information: Interrogation: Science and Art* (Washington, DC: Center for Strategic Intelligence Research, National Defense Intelligence College, 2006) at 35.

13   Commission of Inquiry into the Actions of Canadian Officials in Relation to Maher Arar, *Report of the Events Relating to Maher Arar: Analysis and Recommendations* (2006) at 198, online: www.ararcommission.ca/eng/26.htm [Arar inquiry, Factual Report].

14   999 U.N.T.S. 171 (entered into force 1976) [ICCPR].

Treatment or Punishment ("Torture Convention")[15] includes more detailed prohibitions.

1) Torture

"Torture" is defined in the Torture Convention as:

> any act by which severe pain or suffering, whether physical or mental, is intentionally inflicted on a person for such purposes as obtaining from him or a third person information or a confession, punishing him for an act he or a third person has committed or is suspected of having committed, or intimidating or coercing him or a third person, or for any reason based on discrimination of any kind, when such pain or suffering is inflicted by or at the instigation of or with the consent or acquiescence of a public official or other person acting in an official capacity. It does not include pain or suffering arising only from, inherent in or incidental to lawful sanctions.[16]

The Convention is unequivocal in outlawing torture:

> each State Party shall take effective legislative, administrative, judicial or other measures to prevent acts of torture in any territory under its jurisdiction. ... No exceptional circumstances whatsoever, whether a state of war or a threat of war, internal political instability or any other public emergency, may be invoked as a justification of torture. ... An order from a superior officer or a public authority may not be invoked as a justification of torture.[17]

Moreover, "each State Party shall ensure that all acts of torture are offences under its criminal law. The same shall apply to an attempt to commit torture and to an act by any person which constitutes complicity or participation in torture."[18]

The U.N. Committee Against Torture—the treaty-body established by the Torture Convention—has rejected efforts to justify torture in the name of counterterrorism.[19] Meanwhile, under the ICCPR, torture and

---

15 A/RES/39/46, annex, 39 U.N. GAOR Supp. (No. 51) at 197, U.N. Doc. A/39/51 (1984) (entered into force 26 June 1987) [Torture Convention].

16 *Ibid.*, Art. 1.

17 *Ibid.*, Art. 2.

18 *Ibid.*, Art. 4.

19 See, for example, U.N. Committee Against Torture, *Conclusions and Recommendations of the Committee against Torture : Egypt*. CAT/C/CR/29/4 (2002) at para. 4 ("The Committee is aware of the difficulties that the State party faces in its

CID treatment are among the rights for which no derogation is permitted, even in times of emergency that threaten the life of the nation.[20]

2) Cruel, Inhuman and Degrading Treatment

As noted, the ICCPR bars CID treatment. The Torture Convention also specifies that

> each State Party shall undertake to prevent in any territory under its jurisdiction other acts of cruel, inhuman or degrading treatment or punishment which do not amount to torture as defined in article 1, when such acts are committed by or at the instigation of or with the consent or acquiescence of a public official or other person acting in an official capacity.

CID treatment is not defined in either the Torture Convention or the ICCPR. It is commonly viewed as egregious treatment that falls short of outright torture.[21] No clear standard determines, however, how outrageous this conduct must be to constitute CID treatment. The U.N. General Assembly has urged that the term be "interpreted so as to extend the widest possible protection against abuses, whether physical or mental."[22] However, the U.N. Human Rights Committee—the treaty body established by the ICCPR—has declined to "draw up a list of prohibited acts or to establish sharp distinctions between the different kinds of punishment or treatment [barred by Article 7 of the ICCPR]; the distinctions depend on the nature, purpose and severity of

---

prolonged fight against terrorism, but recalls that no exceptional circumstances whatsoever can be invoked as a justification for torture").

20   ICCPR, above note 14, Art. 4.

21   See, for example, *Declaration on the Protection of All Persons from Being Subjected to Torture and Other Cruel, Inhuman or Degrading Treatment or Punishment*, A/RES/3452, 30 U.N. GAOR, Supp. No. 34, at 91, Art. 1, U.N. Doc. A/10034 (1975) ("Torture constitutes an aggravated and deliberate form of cruel, inhuman or degrading treatment or punishment"); *Restatement (Third) of Foreign Relations Law of the United States* (St. Paul, MN: American Law Institute Publishers, 1987) § 702, Reporters' Note 5 (citing *Ireland v. United Kingdom*, [1978] E.C.H.R. 1 at para. 167 for the proposition that "[t]he difference between torture and cruel, inhuman, or degrading treatment or punishment 'derives principally from a difference in the intensity of the suffering inflicted'"). See also *Mehinovic v. Vuckovic*, 198 F. Supp.2d 1322 at 1348 (N.D. Ga. 2002) ("Generally, cruel, inhuman, or degrading treatment includes acts which inflict mental or physical suffering, anguish, humiliation, fear and debasement, which do not rise to the level of 'torture' or do not have the same purposes as 'torture'").

22   United Nations, *Code of Conduct for Law Enforcement Officials*, adopted by A/RES/34/169 of 17 Dec. 1979, Art. 5, Commentary (c).

the treatment applied."[23] It has further observed that "what constitutes inhuman or degrading treatment falling within the meaning of Article 7 depends on all the circumstances of the case, such as the duration and manner of the treatment, its physical or mental effects as well as the sex, age and state of health of the victim."[24]

In at least one instance, the committee has accepted that the rationale for the treatment may be relevant in determining its legal character. In a case against Australia, it held that a state's legitimate fear of the flight risk posed by prisoners warranted the shackling of those individuals and rendered this act something other than CID treatment.[25] The committee has been reluctant, however, to take this line of reasoning too far. It appears, therefore, to reject state justifications for certain forms of treatment, including corporal punishment,[26] a state action the committee readily declares to be CID treatment.[27] It has also indicated that where an act does, in fact, constitute CID treatment, no justification exonerates the injuring state. As noted, there is no derogation from Article 7 even in times of national emergencies, presumably the most potent public interest motivation imaginable.[28]

Despite an unwillingness to define *ex ante* the exact contours of the CID treatment standard, both the Human Rights Committee and its counterpart under the Torture Convention—the U.N. Committee

---

23   U.N. Human Rights Committee, *General Comment 20*, Art. 7, U.N. Doc. HRI\GEN\1\Rev.1 (1994) at para. 4.

24   *Vuolanne v. Finland*, U.N. Human Rights Committee File 265/87.

25   *Bertran v. Australia*, U.N. Human Rights Committee File 1020/01 at para. 8.2.

26   *Osbourne v. Jamaica*, U.N. Human Rights Committee File 759/97 at para. 9.1 ("Irrespective of the nature of the crime that is to be punished, however brutal it may be, it is the firm opinion of the Committee that corporal punishment constitutes cruel, inhuman and degrading treatment or punishment contrary to article 7 of the Covenant").

27   U.N. Human Rights Committee, *General Comment 20*, above note 23 at para. 5.

28   *Ibid.* at para. 3 ("The text of article 7 allows no limitation. The Committee reaffirms that, even in situations of public emergency such as those referred to in article 4 of the Covenant, no derogation from the provision of article 7 is allowed and its provision must remain in force. The Committee likewise observes that no justification or extenuating circumstances may be invoked to excuse a violation of article 7 for any reasons, including those based on an order from a superior officer or public authority"). See also J. Herman Burgers & Hans Danelius, *The United Nations Convention Against Torture* (Boston: M. Nijhoff, 1988) at 150 ("Unlike in the definition of torture . . . the purpose of the act is irrelevant in determining whether or not the act should be considered to constitute cruel, inhuman or degrading treatment"); Sarah Joseph, Jenny Schultz, & Melissa Castan, *The International Covenant on Civil and Political Rights: Cases, Materials and Commentary* (Oxford: Oxford University Press, 2004) at 212 *et seq.*

Against Torture—have identified specific state practices they view as constituting CID treatment. For instance, the particular acts declared CID treatment by the Committee Against Torture include:

- substandard detention facilities lacking basic amenities such as water, electricity and heating in cold temperatures;[29]
- long periods of pre-trial detention and delays in judicial procedure coupled with incarceration in facilities ill equipped for prolonged detention;[30]
- beating prisoners who are also denied medical treatment and are deprived of food and proper places of detention;[31]
- virtual isolation of detainees for a period of a year;[32]
- use of electro-shock belts and restraint chairs as means of constraint;[33]
- acts of police brutality that may lead to serious injury or death;[34] and,
- deliberate torching of houses.[35]

Commenting specifically on interrogation techniques, the committee has also identified the following as CID treatment: "(1) restraining in very painful conditions, (2) hooding under special conditions, (3) sounding of loud music for prolonged periods, (4) sleep deprivation for prolonged periods, (5) threats, including death threats, (6) violent shaking, and (7) using cold air to chill."[36] The committee's list is roughly analogous to similar lists of techniques found to be inhuman and degrading by the European Court of Human Rights under the *European Convention on Human Rights*[37] and improper by the Israeli Supreme Court.[38]

---

29   Report of the Committee against Torture, U.N. Doc. A/56/44 (2001) at para. 183.
30   *Ibid.* at para. 119.
31   Report of the Committee Against Torture, U.N. Doc. A/53/44 (1998) at para. 175.
32   Report of the Committee Against Torture, U.N. Doc. A/55/44 (2001) at paras. 58 and 61.
33   *Ibid.* at paras. 179 & 180.
34   Report of the Committee Against Torture, U.N. Doc. A/53/44 (1998) at para. 64.
35   *Dzemajl v. Yugoslavia*, U.N. Committee Against Torture File 161/00.
36   Report of the Committee Against Torture, U.N. Doc. A/52/44 (1997) at para. 257.
37   *Ireland v. United Kingdom*, above note 21 at paras. 96 and 246 (discussing protracted standing on the tip of the toes; covering of the head for the duration of the detention; exposure to loud noise for a prolonged period and deprivation of sleep, food and water).
38   *Public Committee against Torture in Israel v. The Government of Israel*, HCJ 5100/94 at para. 29 (Israeli Supreme Court, 1999) (declaring improper the "Shabach" method, composed of several components: the cuffing of the suspect, seating him on a low chair, covering his head with a sack, and playing loud music in the area).

Specific acts identified by the Human Rights Committee as constituting CID treatment do not differ greatly from those invoked by the Committee Against Torture. They include abduction of an individual and then detention without contact with family members;[39] denial of food and water;[40] denial of medical assistance after ill-treatment;[41] death threats;[42] mock executions;[43] whipping and corporal punishment;[44] failure to notify a family of the fate of an executed prisoner;[45] prolonged detention on death row when coupled with "further compelling circumstances relating to the detention";[46] and detention in substandard facilities[47] or conditions.[48] Examples of CID treatment stemming from the conditions of detention include:

- incarceration for fifty hours in an overcrowded facility, resulting in prisoners being soiled with excrement, coupled with denial of food and water for a day;[49]
- incarceration in circumstances falling below the standards set in the U.N. Standard Minimum Rules for the Treatment of Prisoners, coupled with detention *incommunicado*, death and torture threats, deprivation of food and water and denial of recreational relief;[50]
- solitary incarceration for ten years in a tiny cell, with minimal recreational opportunities;[51]

---

39 *N'Goya v. Zaire*, U.N. Human Rights Committee File 542/1993 at para. 5.6; *Basilio Laureano Atachahua v. Peru*, U.N. Human Rights Committee File 540/1993 at para. 8.5.

40 *Miha v. Equatorial Guinea*, U.N. Human Rights Committee File 414/1990 at para. 6.4.

41 *Ibid.* See also *Bailey v. Jamaica*, U.N. Human Rights Committee File 334/1988 at para. 9.3.

42 *Hylton v. Jamaica*, U.N. Human Rights Committee File 407/1990 at para. 9.3.

43 *Linton v. Jamaica*, U.N. Human Rights Committee File 255/1987 at para. 8.5.

44 *Higginson v. Jamaica*, U.N. Human Rights Committee File 792/1998 at para. 4.6; *Sooklal v. Trinidad and Tobago*, U.N. Human Rights Committee File 928/2000 at para. 4.6.

45 *Schedko v. Belarus*, U.N. Human Rights Committee File 886/1999 at para. 10.2.

46 *Bickaroo v. Trinidad and Tobago*, U.N. Human Rights Committee File 555/1993 at para. 5.6.

47 *Adams v. Jamaica*, U.N. Human Rights Committee File 607/1994 (views of 30 October 1996).

48 *Deidrick v. Jamaica*, U.N. Human Rights Committee File 619/1995 at para. 9.3.

49 *Portorreal v. Dominican Republic*, U.N. Human Rights Committee File 188/1984 at paras. 9.2 and 11.

50 *Mukong v. Cameroon*, U.N. Human Rights Committee File 458/1991 at paras. 9.3 & 9.4.

51 *Edwards v. Jamaica*, U.N. Human Rights Committee File 529/1993 at para. 8.3.

- solitary incarceration *incommunicado* for various periods;[52] and
- incarceration with limited recreational opportunities, no mattress or bedding, no adequate sanitation, ventilation or electric lighting, and denial of exercise, medical treatment, nutrition and clean drinking water.[53]

3) Humane Treatment of Detainees

Detention in the circumstances described above may also run afoul of Article 10 of the ICCPR, guaranteeing that states treat persons deprived of their liberty with humanity and dignity. The U.N. Human Rights Committee has concluded that Article 10 rights attach to "anyone deprived of liberty under the laws and authority of the States," including those who are held in prisons or "detention camps."[54]

Article 10 has been interpreted as prohibiting acts less severe than outright CID treatment, particularly where a person has been detained in generally poor conditions but has not been singled out for particularly egregious treatment.[55] The committee has also found violations of Article 10 when detainees are held *incommunicado* for periods of time shorter than those declared CID in other cases.[56]

Compliance with the U.N. Standard Minimum Rules for the Treatment of Prisoners[57] may also be relevant in determining whether a state complies with Article 10.[58] These rules establish detailed standards in such areas as hygiene, food, clothing and bedding, exercise and sport,

---

52 *Campos v. Peru*, U.N. Human Rights Committee File 577/1994 at para. 8.7 (detention incommunicado for one year); *Shaw v. Jamaica*, U.N. Human Rights Committee File 704/1996 at para. 7.1 (detention incommunicado for eight months in overcrowded and damp conditions).
53 *Brown v. Jamaica*, U.N. Human Rights Committee File 775/1997 at para. 6.13.
54 Human Rights Committee, *General Comment 21* Article 10 (44th sess., 1992), Compilation of General Comments and General Recommendations Adopted by Human Rights Treaty Bodies, U.N. Doc. HRI/GEN/1/Rev.6 at 153 (2003) at para. 2.
55 *Griffin v. Spain*, U.N. Human Rights Committee File 493/1992 at para. 6.3 (concluding that Art. 10 applied in relation to generally poor conditions of incarceration, even where Art. 7 CID treatment was not established). See also discussion in Joseph, Schultz, & Castan, *The International Covenant on Civil and Political Rights*, above note 28 at 277, para. 9.139 *et seq.*
56 *Gilboa v. Uruguay*, U.N. Human Rights Committee File 147/1983 at para. 14 (incommunicado detention for fifteen days a violation of Art. 10).
57 Adopted by the First United Nations Congress on the Prevention of Crime and the Treatment of Offenders, held at Geneva in 1955, and approved by the Economic and Social Council by its resolution 663 C (XXIV) of 31 July 1957 and 2076 (LXII) of 13 May 1977.
58 See U.N. Human Rights Committee, *General Comment 21*, above note 54 at para. 5.

medical services, discipline and punishment and contact with the outside world.

B. STANDARDS IN INTERNATIONAL HUMANITARIAN LAW

International humanitarian law contains its own firm prohibitions on abusive forms of interrogation. Common Article 3 of the Geneva Conventions, the provision applicable to noninternational armed conflicts, specifies that persons taking no active part in the conflict—including members of armed forces who have laid down their arms—are not to be subjected to "cruel treatment and torture." Additional Protocol II, amplifying obligations in noninternational conflicts, repeats this requirement.[59]

For international conflicts, Geneva Convention III relative to the prisoners of war specifies that "every prisoner of war, when questioned on the subject, is bound to give only his surname, first names and rank, date of birth, and army, regimental, personal or serial number, or failing this, equivalent information."[60] In other words, prisoners of war are obliged to provide this information.

Interrogators are also free to ask whatever other questions they wish to pose. Prisoners of war are not, however, required to answer these further questions. Nor can they be compelled to do so: "no physical or mental torture, nor any other form of coercion, may be inflicted on prisoners of war to secure from them information of any kind whatever. Prisoners of war who refuse to answer may not be threatened, insulted, or exposed to unpleasant or disadvantageous treatment of any kind."[61] More generally, "prisoners of war must at all times be humanely treated. ... [P]risoners of war must at all times be protected, particularly against acts of violence or intimidation and against insults and public curiosity. Measures of reprisal against prisoners of war are prohibited."[62]

Geneva Convention IV, governing the conduct of an occupying power in relation to civilians, provides that "no physical or moral coercion

---

59 *Protocol Additional to the Geneva Conventions of 12 August 1949, and relating to the Protection of Victims of Non-International Armed Conflicts*, Art. 4 [AP II].

60 *Convention relative to the Treatment of Prisoners of War*, Art. 17 [Geneva Convention III].

61 *Ibid.* See *Convention for the Amelioration of the Condition of the Wounded and Sick in Armed Forces in the Field* [Geneva Convention I] and *Convention for the Amelioration of the Condition of Wounded, Sick and Shipwrecked Members of Armed Forces at Sea* [Geneva Convention II] on wounded and sick soldiers, Art. 12;

62 Geneva Convention III, above note 60, Art. 12.

shall be exercised against" civilians, "in particular to obtain information from them or from third parties."[63] It also expressly outlaws, *inter alia*, torture, corporal punishment and any other measure of brutality.[64]

Under all of the Geneva Conventions, "torture or inhuman treatment" is considered a "grave breach."[65] It is, therefore, a war crime prosecutable before the International Criminal Court,[66] and state parties to the Geneva Conventions are themselves obliged to investigate and prosecute such breaches.[67]

C. CANADIAN STANDARDS

1) Criminal Prohibition

Canadian legal standards for interrogation clearly outlaw torture and inhuman treatment. The *Canadian Charter of Rights and Freedoms*, for instance, prohibits in section 12 "any cruel and unusual treatment or punishment."[68] Section 12 bars behaviour "so excessive as to outrage standards of decency"[69]—a category within which torture and what international law identifies as CID treatment would fall. The *Charter* also guarantees in section 7 the "right to life, liberty and security of the person and the right not to be deprived thereof except in accordance with the principles of fundamental justice."[70] Torture and CID treatment would violate section 7.[71]

---

63 *Convention relative to the Protection of Civilian Persons in Time of War* [Geneva Convention IV] on the duties of occupying powers, Art. 31. See also *Protocol Additional to the Geneva Conventions of 12 August 1949, and relating to the Protection of Victims of International Armed Conflicts*, Art. 75 [AP I].

64 Geneva Convention IV, *ibid.*, Art. 32.

65 Geneva Convention I and II, above note 61, Art. 50; Geneva Convention III, above note 60, Art. 130; Geneva Convention IV, above note 63, Art. 147.

66 *Rome Statute of the International Criminal Court*, U.N. Doc. A/CONF.183/9, 2187 U.N.T.S. 90 (entered into force 1 July 2002), Art. 8 [*Rome Statute*].

67 Geneva Convention I, above note 61, Art. 49; Geneva Convention II, above note 61, Art. 50; Geneva Convention III, above note 60, Art. 129; Geneva Convention IV, above note 63, Art. 146.

68 Part I of the *Constitution Act, 1982*, being Schedule B to the *Canada Act 1982* (U.K.) 1982, c. 11, s. 12 [*Charter*].

69 *R. v. Smith*, [1987] 1 S.C.R. 1045 at 1072; *R. v. Goltz*, [1991] 3 S.C.R. 485 at 499; *R. v. Luxton*, [1990] 2 S.C.R. 711 at 724; *R. v. Wiles*, 2005 SCC 84 at para. 4; *R. v. Morrisey*, 2000 SCC 39 at para. 26 *et seq.*

70 *Charter*, above note 68, s. 7.

71 See, for example, *Suresh v. Canada (Minister of Citizenship and Immigration)*, [2002] 1 S.C.R. 3 at para. 129 (holding that generally to "deport a refugee,

In addition, torture is explicitly criminalized in Canada. To implement Canadian obligations under the Torture Convention, section 269.1 of the *Criminal Code* provides that: "every official, or every person acting at the instigation of or with the consent or acquiescence of an official, who inflicts torture on any other person is guilty of an indictable offence and liable to imprisonment for a term not exceeding fourteen years."[72] This provision applies extraterritorially — that is, it extends to acts committed outside Canada where, for instance, the victim or the accused is Canadian or simply where the accused is within Canada subsequent to the act of torture.[73] The term "officials" in the section means public and peace officers, members of the Canadian Forces and foreign officials exercising similar functions.[74]

For its part, the *Geneva Conventions Act* provides that "every person who, whether within or outside Canada, commits a grave breach" of the Geneva Conventions commits an indictable offence, and is liable to imprisonment for life, where that breach causes death, and otherwise to fourteen years' imprisonment.[75] As noted above, "grave breaches" under the Geneva Conventions include acts of torture or inhuman treatment committed in situations of armed conflict.

2) Civil Liability

In civil law, an act of physical abuse or torture or CID treatment could be actionable for damages as a tort — most likely battery or false imprisonment. Mental torture, producing a fear of imminent physical torture could constitute an assault. A number of civil lawsuits have been

---

where there are grounds to believe that this would subject the refugee to a substantial risk of torture would unconstitutionally violate the *Charter*'s s. 7 guarantee of life, liberty and security of the person"). It follows that the actual infliction of torture must be a violation of s. 7.

72   *Criminal Code*, R.S.C. 1985, c. C-46, s. 269.1.

73   *Ibid.*, s. 7(3.7).

74   *Ibid.*, s. 269.1. As with other *Criminal Code* offences, a conviction may be entered where an accused aids and abets another in an act of torture. See *R. v. Brocklebank* (1996), 106 C.C.C. (3d) 234 (C.M.A.C.) (a torture case in which the court described the test of aiding and abetting as where the accused did or omitted to do something for the purpose of aiding the torturer in the commission of the offence of torture). For one of the few cases in which a conviction was entered in Canada, see *R. v. Rainville*, [2001] J.Q. no 947 (C.Q.) (involving a Canadian Forces training exercise that went too far).

75   *Geneva Conventions Act*, R.S.C. 1985, c. G-3, s. 3.

brought against foreign torturers in Canadian courts, although to date all have failed on state immunity grounds.[76]

PART III: POST-9/11 INTERROGATION CONTROVERSIES

A. EXTREME INTERROGATION TECHNIQUES

In the post-9/11 period, the interrogation techniques employed by states in the questioning of terrorism suspects has fuelled enormous controversy. Much of this debate has focused on whether the so-called stress or alternative interrogation techniques employed by the U.S. military or CIA cross the line of CID treatment or even torture.

Various U.S. government memos describe interrogation "stress" techniques approved for use in overseas military interrogations.[77] News stories, meanwhile, have reported on CIA interrogation strategies. The latter reportedly include: forceful shaking, an open-handed slap "aimed at causing pain and triggering fear," a "hard open-handed slap to the stomach" designed "to cause pain, but not internal injury"; forcing detainees "to stand, handcuffed and with their feet shackled to an eye bolt in the floor for more than 40 hours," producing "exhaustion and sleep deprivation"; chilling the detainee by leaving them to "stand naked in a cell kept near 50 degrees" and dousing them with cold water; and, water-boarding, a process by which a detainee is "bound to an inclined board, feet raised and head slightly below the feet. Cellophane is wrapped over the prisoner's face and water is poured over him," triggering powerful gag reflexes.[78]

---

76 See, for example, *Bouzari v. Iran*, [2002] O.J. No. 1624 at para. 72 (S.C.J.), aff'd (2004), 71 O.R. (3d) 675 (C.A.); *Arar v. Syrian Arab Republic* (2005), 127 C.R.R. (2d) 252 (Ont. S.C.J.).

77 See Karen Greenberg & Joshua Dratel, eds., *The Torture Papers: The Road to Abu Ghraib* (Cambridge: Cambridge University Press, 2005).

78 Brian Ross & Richard Esposito, "CIA's Harsh Interrogation Techniques Described" *ABC News* (18 November 2005). See also Walter Pincus, "Waterboarding Historically Controversial" *Washington Post* (5 October 2006) A.17. For a discussion of the background to CIA interrogations in the "war on terror," see David Johnston, "At a Secret Interrogation, Dispute Flared over Tactics" *New York Times* (9 September 2006). The CIA director denied in 2007 that any of the stress techniques employed at "black sites" constituted torture. See Walter Pincus, "CIA Chief Complains About Agency's Critics in Europe" *Washington Post* (17 April 2007) A.12.

Reports on happenings at Abu Ghraib prison in Iraq disclose even more extreme measures. At Abu Ghraib, concludes a U.S. military report, unauthorized, but intentional violent and sexual abuses included "acts causing bodily harm using unlawful force as well as sexual offenses including, but not limited to rape, sodomy and indecent assault."[79] Media reports have pointed to the use of extreme (and occasionally deadly) interrogation techniques at places like Bagram, Afghanistan and Guantanamo Bay, Cuba.[80]

Summarizing the U.S. record extracted from one hundred thousand government documents disclosed under U.S. information laws, the American Civil Liberties Association reported in 2006

> a systemic pattern of torture and abuse of detainees in U.S. custody in Afghanistan, the U.S. Naval Base Station at Guantánamo Bay, Cuba, Iraq, and other locations outside the United States. In many instances the harsh treatment was ordered as part of an approved list of interrogation methods to "soften up" detainees. ... Reported methods of torture and abuse used against detainees include prolonged incommunicado detention; disappearances; beatings; death threats; painful stress positions; sexual humiliation; forced nudity; exposure to extreme heat and cold; denial of food and water; sensory deprivation such as hooding and blindfolding; sleep deprivation; water-boarding; use of dogs to inspire fear; and racial and religious insults. In addition, around one hundred detainees in U.S. custody in Afghanistan and Iraq have died. The government has acknowledged that 27 deaths in U.S. custody were homicide, some caused due to "strangulation," "hypothermia," "asphyxiation," and "blunt force injuries."[81]

Interrogation techniques employed by allied states in the campaign against terrorism have also generated controversy, especially where detainees are placed in the custody of these nations via "extraordinary rendition" by the United States or another nation. Rendition — covert removals without formal extradition or deportation — is not a new prac-

---

79   Fay-Jones Report (August 2004) in Greenberg & Dratel, *Torture Papers*, above note 77 at 993.

80   See, for example, Tim Golden, "In U.S. Report, Brutal Details of 2 Afghan Inmates' Deaths" *New York Times* (20 May 2005) A.1; David Johnston, "More of F.B.I. Memo Criticizing Guantánamo Methods Is Released" *New York Times* (22 March 2005) A.17. See also Seymour Hersh, *Chain of Command: The Road from 9/11 to Abu Ghraib* (New York: HarperCollins, 2004).

81   ACLU, *Enduring Abuse: Torture and Cruel Treatment by the United States at Home and Abroad* (27 April 2006) at 4, online: www.aclu.org/safefree/torture/25354pub20060427.html.

tice in the United States. The procedure was employed by U.S. officials pre-9/11 to remove expeditiously persons wanted abroad for suspected involvement in terrorism.[82] It is now conducted on a much vaster scale, and its focus has shifted from rendition to "justice" to rendition to interrogation (often in circumstances where torture is likely).[83] Estimates made in 2005 suggested that 150 people had been rendered by the United States since September 11, 2001.[84] News reports name several states — all of whom have been accused by the U.S. State Department of employing torture[85] — as the countries to which individuals have been rendered. These nations include Egypt, Jordan, Morocco and Syria.[86] These actions have fuelled particular controversy in Europe[87] and, after the Arar matter, in Canada.

U.S. actions have been supported by a well-publicized rethink of the laws governing torture, proffered by Bush administration lawyers. In a 1 August 2002 memorandum (since repudiated by the U.S. government), then U.S. assistant attorney general Jay Bybee confined the definition of torture to only the most egregious of acts, producing lasting psychological damage such as post-traumatic stress syndrome or physical pain of an "intensity akin to that which accompanies serious physical injury such as death or organ failure."[88] "Because the acts in-

---

82   Human Rights Watch, *Still at Risk: Diplomatic Assurances No Safeguard Against Torture* (April 2005), online: http://hrw.org/reports/2005/eca0405/; Committee on International Human Rights of the Association of the Bar of the City of New York & Center for Human Rights and Global Justice, New York University School of Law, *Torture by Proxy: International and Domestic Law Applicable to "Extraordinary Renditions"* (October 2004), online: www.chrgj.org/docs/TortureByProxy.pdf.

83   *Ibid.* at 5.

84   Jane Mayer, "Outsourcing Torture" *The New Yorker* (14 February 2005), online: www.newyorker.com/archive/2005/02/14/050214fa_fact6. In 2007, CIA director Michael Haydon claimed that the number of rendered persons is closer to one hundred. See Walter Pincus, "CIA Chief Complains About Agency's Critics in Europe," above note 78.

85   U.S. State Department, *Human Rights Country Reports* (2005) (under the headings "Morocco," "Egypt," "Jordan," and "Syria"), online: www.state.gov/g/drl/rls/hrrpt/2005/c17095.htm.

86   Mayer, "Outsourcing Torture," above note 84.

87   Indeed, it would appear that European intelligence services at least tacitly assisted in some renditions. See, for example, Holger Stark, "Berlin 'Helped CIA' With Rendition of German Citizen" *Der Spiegel* (11 January 2007); Craig Whitlock, "German Lawmakers Fault Abduction Probe" *Washington Post* (4 October 2006) A.18; Tracy Wilkinson, "Details Emerge in Italian Abduction" *Los Angeles Times* (10 January 2007) A.4.

88   Memo 15 (1 August 2002) in Greenberg & Dratel, *Torture Papers*, above note 77 at 214–15. The U.S. government has since distanced itself from this inter-

flicting torture are extreme," wrote Bybee, "there is a significant range of acts that though they might constitute cruel, inhuman, or degrading treatment or punishment fail to rise to the level of torture."[89] The Bush administration further urged that international CID standards did not extend to the treatment by U.S. personnel of foreign nationals overseas.[90] This position has also been repudiated, this time by Congress in the *Detainee Protection Act of 2005*.[91]

B. USE OF INTERROGATION INFORMATION

A second post-9/11 controversy is whether evidence obtained via ill-treatment is admissible in court in terrorist prosecutions or administrative proceedings related to suspected terrorists.[92] As a matter of international law, the answer should be an unequivocal no. The Torture Convention itself provides in Article 15 that "each State Party shall ensure that any statement which is established to have been made as a result of torture shall not be invoked as evidence in any proceedings, except against a person accused of torture as evidence that the statement was made."

---

pretation. See Daniel Levin, *Memorandum for James B. Coney, Deputy Attorney General* (30 December 2005), online: http://news.findlaw.com/hdocs/docs/terrorism/dojtorture123004mem.pdf.

89 Memo 14 (1 August 2002) in Greenberg & Dratel, *Torture Papers, ibid.* at 214.

90 Statement of Senator Dianne Feinstein, "*Nomination of Alberto Gonzales to be Attorney General of the United States*," 151 Cong. Rec. 8 (1 February 2005), online: http://feinstein.senate.gov/05speeches/cr-gonzales.htm, reading a letter from U.S. attorney general Alberto Gonzeles in the follow-up of his senate confirmation hearings in which Gonzales asserted squarely that "[t]here is no legal prohibition under the Convention Against Torture on cruel, inhuman or degrading treatment with respect to aliens overseas."

91 Pub. L. No. 109-148, Tit. X, 119 Stat. 2739.

92 Debate on this issue has been animated in the United States, where evidence obtained by coercion may be admissible before the Military Commissions charged with trying alien unlawful enemy combatants so long as it is not produced by torture. Information obtained by harsh methods short of torture may be admissible, if adjudged reliable and of sufficient probative value and its admission would be in the interest of justice. For the period prior to the enactment of the *Detainee Treatment Act of 2005, ibid.* (30 December 2005), this potentially admissible information includes that obtained through cruel, inhuman, and degrading treatment. See 10 U.S.C § 948r. In practice, U.S. government lawyers have reportedly concluded that statements obtained by the CIA via the "stress" methods described above do not amount to torture. See David Johnston & Neil Lewis, "U.S. Preparing for Trials of Top Qaeda Detainees" *New York Times* (12 January 2007) A.1.

This is a sweeping prohibition. As the United Kingdom House of Lords ruled in *A v. Secretary of State*, discussed further below, the Article "cannot possibly be read ... as intended to apply only in criminal proceedings. Nor can it be understood to differentiate between confessions and accusatory statements, or to apply only where the state in whose jurisdiction the proceedings are held has inflicted or been complicit in the torture."[93]

In Canadian criminal cases, admissibility of coerced evidence has been richly condemned by the common and constitutional law. It seems unlikely, therefore, that evidence obtained by torture or CID treatment would be admitted. Canadian courts in the immigration context have, however, apparently been confronted with intelligence information in circumstances where there is serious uncertainty as to whether it was produced by torture.

1) Statutory Prohibitions

Use of evidence obtained by torture is expressly prohibited under Canada's criminal law. As noted above, section 269.1 of the *Criminal Code* implements Canada's obligations under the Torture Convention. It makes torture a crime and also prohibits the use of torture evidence in Canada:

> In any proceedings over which Parliament has jurisdiction, any statement obtained as a result of the commission of an offence under this section [that is, torture] is inadmissible in evidence, except as evidence that the statement was so obtained.[94]

This bar should apply regardless of whether the torture evidence was obtained in Canada or overseas, an approach adopted in *India v. Singh*, a decision of the BC Supreme Court applying section 269.1's evidentiary rule.[95]

Singh concerned an extradition proceeding in which evidence produced by India in support of the fugitive's removal was allegedly produced by torture. The court concluded that the burden of proof to prove torture on a balance of probabilities standard rested on the fugitive; that is, the person seeking to reject the evidence.

---

93 *A and others v. Secretary of State for the Home Department*, [2005] UKHL 71 at para. 35, Lord Nicholls of Birkenhead.
94 *Criminal Code*, above note 72, s. 269.1(4).
95 (1996), 108 C.C.C. (3d) 274 (B.C.S.C.) [*Singh*].

Meeting this burden in relation to past acts of foreign torture presented obvious difficulties to the fugitive. The court therefore dismissed most of the torture allegations, observing that

> where serious and persuasive allegations of torture are made and are met with affidavits of the police officials allegedly present denying that torture, and where the Court has not had the opportunity of hearing either party's *viva voce* evidence, though strong suspicions remain, there is not enough evidence to convince me on a balance of probabilities that these ... individuals were tortured.[96]

Still, in the one case where no official denial of torture was tendered, the court concluded that evidence was likely extracted under torture, and ruled it inadmissible under section 269.1. This question of burden of proof is discussed further below.

In *Singh*, the fugitive also raised a *Charter of Rights and Freedoms* objection to evidence obtained under torture, pointing to section 7. Section 7 guarantees fundamental justice where life, liberty or security of the person are put in jeopardy. Since acceptance of the torture evidence could result in the fugitive's extradition to India, section 7 interests were clearly engaged.[97] The court reasoned, however, that where the fugitive had not proved the allegation of torture on a balance of probabilities, reliance on that evidence would not amount to a *Charter* violation.

2) Common Law

On top of statutory rules, there are other, strict prohibitions against admitting confessions extracted from the accused themselves by abusive tactics. At common law, for instance, the courts have developed a "confessions rule" designed to minimize the prospect of false confessions by seeking to ensure that a confession is voluntary.[98] Interroga-

---

96   *Ibid.* at 283.

97   See *United States of America v. Ferras*, 2006 SCC 33 at para. 11 (establishing that extradition triggers a s. 7 interest).

98   See discussion in *R. v. Oickle*, [2000] 2 S.C.R. 3 at para. 47 [*Oickle*] ("The common law confessions rule is well-suited to protect against false confessions. While its overriding concern is with voluntariness, this concept overlaps with reliability. A confession that is not voluntary will often (though not always) be unreliable"). The issue of voluntary confessions has arisen in the terrorism context in Australia. See, for example, *R. v. Thomas*, 2006 VSCA 165 (dismissing a terrorism case on the basis of the inadmissibility of evidence obtained by interrogators while the suspect was incarcerated in Pakistan and where Australian officials suggested that the assistance of Australia could only be procured by cooperation).

tion tactics violating this rule will render a confession inadmissible. Such techniques include "outright violence"[99] and "imminent threats of torture,"[100] the suggestion of leniency from the authorities and courts in exchange for an admission,[101] or other threats or inducements of a sort that "raise a reasonable doubt about whether the will of the subject has been overborne."[102]

Oppressive conduct may also violate the common law standard, including "depriving the suspect of food, clothing, water, sleep, or medical attention; denying access to counsel; ... excessively aggressive, intimidating questioning for a prolonged period of time" and possibly use by the police of false evidence to induce a confession.[103] Likewise, police trickery substantial enough to "shock the conscience of the community" may trigger application of the confessions rule.[104]

On top of the confessions rule, evidence extracted via abusive tactics would likely be rejected as unreliable. Generally speaking, out of court statements are inadmissible as hearsay, unless they fall within narrow exceptions. However, these narrow exceptions may be overridden, and indeed hearsay evidence not falling into these categories may be admitted, pursuant to the "principled approach" to hearsay evidence. Thus,

> in "rare cases," evidence falling within an existing exception may be excluded because the indicia of necessity and reliability are lacking in the particular circumstances of the case.... [Conversely, i]f hearsay evidence does not fall under a hearsay exception, it may still be admitted if indicia of reliability and necessity are established on a *voir dire*.[105]

It is difficult to imagine that statements extracted under torture would be regarded as "reliable" by any court. Indeed, in a case involving evidence admissible before an administrative body—the Parole Board—a majority of the Supreme Court of Canada observed that "information extracted by torture could not be considered reliable by the Board. It would be manifestly unfair for the Board to act on this kind of information. As a result, the Board would be under a duty to exclude

---

99 *Oickle, ibid.* at para. 53.

100 *Ibid.* at para. 48.

101 *Ibid.* at para. 49.

102 *Ibid.* at para. 57.

103 *Ibid.* at para. 60.

104 *Ibid.* at paras. 65–66.

105 D.M. Paciocco & L. Stuesser, *The Law of Evidence*, 3d ed. (Toronto: Irwin Law, 2002) at 95–96, cited with approval in *R. v. Mapara*, 2005 SCC 23 at para. 15.

such information, whether or not the information was relevant to the decision."[106]

The admissibility of third-party evidence extracted by torture at common law was a matter addressed even more squarely in *A. v. Secretary of State*, a 2005 decision of the House of Lords. At issue was evidence employed in immigration proceedings concerning suspected terrorists. In a forceful judgment, the law lords rejected the use of evidence obtained by torture. In declaring such evidence anathema to English justice, Lord Nicholls of Birkenhead wrote:

> If an official or agent of the United Kingdom were to use torture, or connive at its use, in order to obtain information this information would not be admissible in court proceedings in this country. That is not in doubt. It would be an abuse of the process of the United Kingdom court for the United Kingdom government to seek to adduce in evidence information so obtained. The court would not for one moment countenance such conduct by the state.[107]

Likewise, there is no room to admit evidence in a judicial proceeding produced by a foreign state via torture. Lord Hope of Craighead put the point strongly, observing:

> Once torture has become acclimatised in a legal system it spreads like an infectious disease, hardening and brutalising those who have become accustomed to its use. ... [O]nce judicial approval is given to such conduct, it lies about like a loaded weapon ready for the hand of any authority that can bring forward a plausible claim of an urgent need. A single instance, if approved to meet the threat of international terrorism, would establish a principle with the power to grow and expand so that everything that falls within it would be regarded as acceptable. Without hesitation I would hold that, subject to the single exception referred to in article 15 [of the *European Convention of Human Rights*, concerning evidence proving an act of torture], the admission of any statements obtained by this means against third parties is absolutely precluded in any proceedings as evidence. I

---

106 *Mooring v. Canada (National Parole Board)*, [1996] 1 S.C.R. 75 at para. 36. See also *Lai v. Canada (Minister of Citizenship and Immigration)*, 2005 FCA 125 at para. 95 [*Lai*] ("Statements obtained by torture or other cruel, inhumane or degrading treatment or punishment are neither credible or trustworthy"); *Harkat (Re)*, 2005 FC 393 at para. 115 *et seq.*; *Mahjoub v. Canada (Minister of Citizenship and Immigration)*, 2006 FC 1503 at para. 26 [*Mahjoub*] ("reliance on evidence likely to have been obtained by torture is an error in law").

107 *A and others v. Secretary of State for the Home Department*, above note 93 at para. 66.

would apply this rule irrespective of where, or by whom, the torture was administered.[108]

Notably, on burden of proof, the law lords took a different approach than did the B.C. Supreme Court in *India v. Singh*, discussed above. Since in the immigration proceedings at issue in *A v. Secretary of State*, the government was relying on secret evidence, the House of Lords reasoned it was implausible to demand that the applicant bear the burden of proof on the torture question. In a view echoed by other law lords, Lord Bingham of Cornwall doubted:

> a conventional approach to the burden of proof is appropriate in a proceeding where the appellant may not know the name or identity of the author of an adverse statement relied on against him, may not see the statement or know what the statement says, may not be able to discuss the adverse evidence with the special advocate appointed (without responsibility) to represent his interests, and may have no means of knowing what witness he should call to rebut assertions of which he is unaware.[109]

Instead, once credible allegations of torture have been presented, it was for the administrative tribunal to probe the torture question and, according to a majority of law lords, exclude evidence it was persuaded on a balance of probabilities was produced by torture. A minority of the House of Lords would have gone further, and required the exclusion of evidence where it was *not* proven on a balance of probabilities that it was *not* produced by torture.

3) *Charter of Rights and Freedoms*

The *Charter* supplements statutory and common law constraints on the use of evidence produced by torture. Section 7 of the *Charter* protects against deprivation of life, liberty and security of the person in violation of "fundamental justice". Section 11(d), meanwhile, guarantees those accused of an offence a "fair" trial. In *Hape*, the Supreme Court signaled clearly that torture evidence would violate these constitutional standards:

> The circumstances in which the evidence was gathered must be considered in their entirety to determine whether admission of the evidence would render a Canadian trial unfair. The way in which the evidence was obtained may make it unreliable, as would be true

---

108 *Ibid.* at para. 113.
109 *Ibid.* at para. 55.

of conscriptive evidence, for example. The evidence may have been gathered through means, such as torture, that are contrary to fundamental *Charter* values. Such abusive conduct would taint the fairness of any trial in which the evidence was admitted.[110]

4) Use of Intelligence Information in Terrorism Cases

Torture intelligence flowing from foreign intelligence services could and may, in fact, be finding its ways into Canada's courtrooms. For one thing, as noted in Chapter 7, Federal Courts reviewing terrorist group listings under, *inter alia*, the *Criminal Code* "may receive into evidence anything that, in the opinion of the judge, is reliable and appropriate, even if it would not otherwise be admissible under Canadian law, and may base his or her decision on that evidence."[111] This language may vitiate statutory and common law bars on use of evidence gathered via torture or cruel, inhuman or degrading treatment,[112] although as discussed below this evidence would likely be rejected on reliability (and constitutional) grounds.

Second, as discussed in Chapter 12, paragraph 17(1)(b) of the *CSIS Act*[113] empowers CSIS, for the purpose of performing its functions, to "enter into an arrangement or otherwise cooperate with the government of a foreign state or an institution thereof or an international organization of states or an institution thereof."

CSIS apparently completes a review of the foreign agency's human rights record in assessing potential new foreign arrangements. However, CSIS's review body, the Security Intelligence Review Committee reported in its 2004–5 annual report, that at least one of the CSIS foreign arrangements that it audited "did not provide an adequate analysis of potential human rights issues."[114] Further, it objected to CSIS's claim

---

110 *R. v. Hape*, 2007 SCC 26 at para. 109.
111 *Criminal Code*, above note 72, s. 83.05(6.1). See also *Charities Registration (Security Information) Act*, S.C. 2001, c. 41, s. 113, s. 6; *Regulations Implementing the United Nations Resolutions on the Suppression of Terrorism*, S.O.R./2001-360, s. 2.2 and *United Nations Al-Qaida and Taliban Regulations*, S.O.R./99-444, s. 5.4.
112 The special senate committee reviewing anti-terrorism law raised a similar concern in 2007, and proposed that this language be amended to clarify that the information received into evidence be "reliable and appropriate." Special Senate Committee on the *Anti-terrorism Act, Fundamental Justice in Extraordinary Times* (February 2007) at 107, online: www.parl.gc.ca/39/1/parlbus/commbus/senate/Com-e/anti-e/rep-e/rep02feb07-e.htm.
113 *Canadian Security Intelligence Service Act*, R.S.C. 1985, c. C-23 [CSIS Act].
114 Canada, Security Intelligence Review Committee, *Annual Report 2004–2005*, online: www.sirc-csars.gc.ca/pdfs/ar_2004-2005-eng.pdf.

that it "ensures" that information exchanged is not the cause or product of human rights abuses: "the Service is rarely in a position to determine how information received from a foreign agency was obtained."[115]

According to testimony in Federal Court, CSIS analysts supplying intelligence used to support security certificates under Canada's immigration laws—the process for detaining and removing foreigners viewed as security risks—have not asked even suspect foreign agencies producing this information if it is the product of torture.[116] A suspicion in IRPA proceedings that intelligence is generated by torture should trigger consideration of section 269.1[117] or at least an assessment of reliability. Federal Courts seem to have adopted the latter approach, declining to give weight to evidence obtained via torture.[118] Moreover, in the highly secretive environment in which IRPA security certificates are adjudicated, they have followed the *A v. Secretary of State* view on burden of proof: "where the issue [of torture] is raised by an applicant offering a plausible explanation why evidence is likely to have been obtained by torture, the decision-maker should then consider this issue in light of the public and classified information. Where the decision-maker finds there are reasonable grounds to suspect that evidence was

---

115 *Ibid.*

116 *Harkat v. Canada*, Court File DES-4-02, Extract of Proceedings, vol. 2, Evidence of P.G. (3 November 2005). See also description in Andrew Duffy, "CSIS Agent Didn't Ask If Informants Were Tortured" *Ottawa Citizen* (4 November 2005) F.1.

117 *Immigration and Refugee Protection Act*, S.C. 2001, c. 27, s. 78(j) [IRPA] provides that "the judge may receive into evidence anything that, in the opinion of the judge, is appropriate, even if it is inadmissible in a court of law, and may base the decision on that evidence." This language is, however, less sweeping that that found in the *Criminal Code* terrorist listing process, above note 72, s. 83.05(6.1), which speaks of allowing evidence that would "not otherwise be admissible under *Canadian law*" [emphasis added]. While the latter language may trump statutory bars on admissibility of evidence—like that in s. 269.1—the IRPA language does not purport to usurp the rest of "Canadian law," and probably should be given a narrower reading. In fact, the government takes the view that s. 269.1 does apply to security certificate cases. It also proposes that the reference to "appropriate" in IRPA, s. 78(j) be supplemented with "reliable" as a further guarantee against the use of torture evidence. Canada, *Government Response: Seventh Report of the Standing Committee on Public Safety and National Security, "Rights, Limits, Security: A Comprehensive Review of the Anti-terrorism Act and Related Issues"* (Presented to the House on 18 July 2007) at 22, online: http://cmte.parl.gc.ca/cmte/CommitteePublication.aspx?COM=10804&Lang=1& SourceId=213371. The approach has now been adopted in Bill C-3. In any event, the use of intelligence extracted under torture and then deployed to justify deportation or detention would undoubtedly trigger s. 7 of the *Charter*. By analogy see, *Singh*, above note 95.

118 *Lai*, above note 106; *Harkat (Re)*, above note 106; *Mahjoub*, above note 106.

likely obtained by torture, it should not be relied upon in making a determination."[119]

C. LEGALLY COMPELLED INTERROGATIONS

In Canada, investigative interrogation has traditionally been the purview of law enforcement, prior to any formal involvement by the judicial system. In this pre-trial questioning, there is no legal compulsion to answer questions posed to those being questioned.

1) Comparative Experience

a)   Civil Law Jurisdictions

This approach varies from that existing in civil law systems, where investigating magistrates perform an important inquisitorial role in deciding whether evidence justifies the bringing of full criminal proceedings. In the French system, for instance, a *juge d'instruction* manages the investigation of crimes after a prosecutor decides in a preliminary inquiry that a crime has been committed. This judicial official supervises a judicial police force and authorizes such things as search warrants and intercepts. The assembled evidence obtained by this investigation is assessed by the *juge*, who decides whether that material supports an indictment and referral to a full trial.[120]

b)   United States

The practice in the United States also differs from that in Canada. In that country, formalized, compulsory pre-trial interrogation takes place as part of the grand jury process. Constitutionally obligatory for federal indictments, the grand jury is a body of laypeople asked to consider the prosecutor's evidence to determine whether probable cause exists supporting an indictment. In the course of that process, the prosecutor questions witnesses *in camera*. These individuals may be summoned by court-issued subpoena and compelled to appear and respond to questions in the absence of their lawyers. A failure to appear or respond to questioning may attract contempt penalties. Grand juries

---

119 *Mahjoub, ibid.* at para. 34.

120 For a summary of several judicial investigations in several civil jurisdictions, see U.K. Joint Committee On Human Rights, *Twenty-Fourth Report: Counter-Terrorism Policy and Human Rights: Prosecution and Pre-Charge Detention* (2006), online: www.publications.parliament.uk/pa/jt200506/jtselect/jtrights/240/240.pdf.

may also subpoena documents and records, and indeed need not meet the conventional standards of probable cause applicable where law enforcement officials seek equivalent search powers. To preserve the right against self-incrimination, derivative use immunity may be extended to the testimony of witnesses; that is, their testimony (and those leads produced by it) may not itself be subsequently used against them in criminal proceedings.[121]

Witnesses may report publicly on their own testimony. However, traditionally, U.S. law imposed strict limits on disclosure of information obtained in grand jury proceedings, subject to a number of exceptions. That secrecy was tempered in national security cases by the *U.S.A. PATRIOT Act*.[122] Now, the government attorney may disclose any grand jury matter involving "foreign intelligence or counterintelligence … or foreign intelligence information … to any Federal law enforcement, intelligence, protective, immigration, national defense, or national security official in order to assist the official receiving that information in the performance of his official duties." Likewise, the government attorney may disclose grand jury matters

> involving, within the United States or elsewhere, a threat of attack or other grave hostile acts of a foreign power or its agent, a threat of domestic or international sabotage or terrorism, or clandestine intelligence gathering activities by an intelligence service or network of a foreign power or by its agent, to any appropriate federal, state, state subdivision, Indian tribal, or foreign government official, for the purpose of preventing or responding to such threat or activities.[123]

No judicial authorization for this disclosure is required.

Because of the breadth of this foreign intelligence or counterintelligence exception, some U.S. jurists have expressed concern that the vast powers of grand juries will be deployed as a true counterterrorism investigative tool, rather than a precursor to criminal proceedings, a tendency that could not be policed by the public and media because of the secrecy surrounding grand jury proceedings.[124]

---

121 For a summary of these grand jury powers, see Sara Beale & James Felman, "The Consequences of Enlisting Federal Grand Juries in the War on Terrorism: Assessing the Patriot Act's Changes in Grand Jury Secrecy" (2002) 25 Harv. J.L. & Pub. Pol'y 699 at 701 *et seq.* [Beale & Felman, "The Consequences of Enlisting Federal Grand Juries"].

122 Pub. L. No. 107-56, § 203(a)(1).

123 USCS Fed. R. Crim. P. 6.

124 See, for example, Beale & Felman, "Consequences of Enlisting Federal Grand Juries," above note 121 at 715 *et seq.*

More than that, the powers of the grand jury might be manipulated for ends unconnected to the criminal process. For example, in 2006, the American Civil Liberties Union contested the legality of a grand jury summons compelling production of "all copies" of a leaked U.S. government document relating to the "war on terror." It urged that the unprecedented grand jury subpoena in this case served no investigative purpose and was intended, instead, to protect the government from embarrassment by removing all copies of the document from the ACLU and suppressing speech.[125] By the time of this writing, the U.S. government had retracted its subpoena.

c) Australia

In 2003, Australia amended the *Australian Security Intelligence Organisation Act*[126] to enhance the anti-terrorism investigation powers of the Australian Security Intelligence Organization (ASIO).[127] The ASIO is Australia's equivalent to CSIS and is charged with a security intelligence collection and analysis function.[128] Under the new provisions, the ASIO, with the authorization of the relevant minister,[129] may seek a warrant from an "issuing authority"—a magistrate or judge—for the questioning of a person in relation to a terrorism offence. If the issuing authority is persuaded that reasonable grounds exist for believing that the warrant will substantially assist the collection of intelligence in relation to a terrorism offence, he or she may issue a warrant valid for a period of no longer than twenty-eight days,[130] subject to renewal.

The person named in the warrant may then be questioned or asked to produce records or things in front of a more senior judge regarding information "that is or may be relevant to intelligence that is important in relation to a terrorism offence."[131]

A person may be questioned for up to a total of twenty-four hours (forty-eight hours if they use an interpreter)[132] and must provide the information requested, if it is in their possession, even if it would incriminate them. Those statements are not admissible in criminal

---

125 See ACLU Memorandum of Law, supporting a motion to quash the subpoena (11 December 2006), online: www.aclu.org/images/asset_upload_file251_27648.pdf.

126 No. 113 of 1979, as amended [ASIO Act].

127 *Australian Security Intelligence Organisation Legislation Amendment (Terrorism) Act 2003*, No. 77, 2003.

128 ASIO Act, above note 126, s. 17.

129 *Ibid.*, s. 34D.

130 *Ibid.*, s. 34E(5).

131 *Ibid.*, s. 34E(4).

132 *Ibid.*, s. 34R.

proceedings against the person,[133] although there does not appear to be a bar on evidence discovered as a result of these statements being so used.

The warrant may also authorize the detention of the person for up to 168 hours[134] if there are reasonable grounds to believe that, absent this detention, the person may fail to appear for questioning, may "alert a person involved in a terrorism offence that the offence is being investigated" or "may destroy, damage or alter a record or thing the person may be requested in accordance with the warrant to produce."[135]

The existence of the warrant is secret while it is in force and disclosure of the warrant or any fact relating to its existence or content or to the questioning or detention of the person subject to the warrant during this period is prohibited, under pain of criminal sanction.[136]

An Australian parliamentary committee reviewing the operation of the warrant system in 2005 reported that some fourteen warrants had been issued in the period 2003–5.[137]

2) Investigative Hearings

a) Background

Canada's answer to these foreign processes has been the "investigative hearing." A mechanism similar to that employed in Australia, investigative hearings were a tool grafted onto the *Criminal Code* by the 2001 *Anti-terrorism Act* to assist in the investigation of actual or anticipated terrorism offences. A peace officer investigating a terrorism offence may apply, with consent of the federal attorney general, for an order from a provincial or superior court judge on the "gathering of information." A judge may then order the person to attend a hearing and be examined, as well as require that individual to bring any thing within his or her possession or control to the proceedings.[138]

Subsequently, a person named in such an order is obliged to "answer questions put to the person by the Attorney General or the Attorney General's agent, and shall produce to the presiding judge things

---

133 *Ibid.*, s. 34L(9).

134 *Ibid.*, s. 34S.

135 *Ibid.*, s. 34F(4).

136 *Ibid.*, s. 34ZS.

137 Parliamentary Joint Committee on ASIO, ASIS and DSD, *ASIO's Questioning and Detention Powers, Review of the operation, effectiveness and implications of Division 3 of Part III in the Australian Security Intelligence Organisation Act 1979* (November 2005), online: www.aph.gov.au/house/committee/pjcaad/asio_ques_detention/report.htm.

138 *Criminal Code*, above note 72, s. 83.28(5).

that the person was ordered to bring, but may refuse if answering a question or producing a thing would disclose information that is protected by any law relating to non-disclosure of information or to privilege."[139]

Fear of self-incrimination is not a ground for refusing to answer a question, but the provision includes derivative use protections; that is, no answer made and no thing provided by a person pursuant to the order and no evidence derived from it, could be employed in a prosecution against that person, except for perjury.[140]

Witnesses may be arrested under warrant where they are about to abscond, fail to appear or are attempting to evade service of the hearing order. These grounds for arrest are, however, more limited than those in Australia.

In 2004, the Supreme Court of Canada upheld the investigative hearing provisions as constitutional under the *Charter*. In *Application under s. 83.28 of the Criminal Code (Re)*,[141] a majority of the Court rejected arguments that investigative hearings violated judicial independence by enlisting judges in a law enforcement investigation. However, the Court also interpreted the protections against self-incrimination liberally, extending derivative use immunity beyond criminal proceedings to administrative matters such as immigration and extradition hearings.[142]

b) Criticisms

Canadian law generally does not enlist judges to play a supporting role in criminal investigations. For this reason, investigative hearings have been a controversial feature of the *Anti-terrorism Act*.[143]

Concern about the reach of investigative hearings prompted Parliament to impose a reporting obligation on the government, obliging annual disclosure of the number of times the power had been used.[144] Parliament also inserted an automatic sunsetting provision, with the

---

139 *Ibid.*, s. 83.28(8).
140 *Ibid.*, s. 83.28(10).
141 2004 SCC 42.
142 For a thorough assessment of this case, see Hamish Stewart, "Investigative Hearings into Terrorist Offences: A Challenge to the Rule of Law" (2005) 50 Crim. L.Q. 376.
143 See, for example, critique by Canadian Association of University Professors (CAUT), *Submission To The House Of Commons, Subcommittee On Public Safety And National Security Regarding The Review Of The* Anti-Terrorism Act (February 2005), online: www.caut.ca/en/publications/briefs/2005anti_terrorism_brief.pdf.
144 *Criminal Code*, above note 72, s. 83.31. By 2007, an investigative hearing had never been used. Efforts to use the power in the Air India investigation were

effect of terminating the investigative hearing power in early 2007 unless overridden by vote in Parliament.[145] The Commons national security committee and special senate committee on anti-terrorism law recommended in 2006 and 2007 respectively that this provision be extended. However, a motion to renew the provision was defeated by the opposition parties in February 2007. As this book went to press, the government tabled Bill S-3, a law project designed to revive the investigative hearings provision.

---

delayed by the constitutional challenge addressed by the Supreme Court in *Application under s. 83.28 of the Criminal Code*, above note 141.

145 *Criminal Code, ibid.*, s. 83.32.

TABLE OF CASES

INDEX

ABOUT THE AUTHOR

Craig Forcese is an associate professor in the Faculty of Law, Common Law Section, University of Ottawa, where he teaches national security law, public international law, administrative law, and public law and legislation and runs the annual foreign policy practicum. Much of his present research and writing relates to international law, national security, and democratic accountability. Prior to joining the law school faculty, he practised law with the Washington D.C. office of Hughes Hubbard & Reed LLP, specializing in international trade law. Craig has law degrees from the University of Ottawa and Yale University, a B.A. from McGill, and an M.A. in international affairs from the Norman Paterson School of International Affairs, Carleton University. He is a member of the bars of Ontario, New York, and the District of Columbia.